Foundation
Zoho

Ali Shabdar

friendsof

DESIGNER TO DESIGNER™

an Apress® company

FOUNDATION ZOHO

ISBN-13 (pbk): 978-1-4302-1991-0

ISBN-13 (electronic): 978-1-4302-1992-7

Printed and bound in the United States of America 9 8 7 6 5 4 3 2 1

Distributed to the book trade worldwide by Springer-Verlag New York, Inc., 233 Spring Street, 6th Floor, New York, NY 10013. Phone 1-800-SPRINGER, fax 201-348-4505, e-mail orders-ny@springer-sbm.com, or visit http://www.springeronline.com.

For information on translations, please e-mail info@apress.com, or visit http://www.apress.com.

Apress and friends of ED books may be purchased in bulk for academic, corporate, or promotional use. eBook versions and licenses are also available for most titles. For more information, reference our Special Bulk Sales–eBook Licensing web page at http://www.apress.com/info/bulksales.

Credits

Lead Editor:
Ben Renow-Clarke

Technical Reviewer:
Ian Piper

Editorial Board:
Clay Andres, Steve Anglin, Mark Beckner, Ewan Buckingham, Tony Campbell, Gary Cornell, Jonathan Gennick, Michelle Lowman, Matthew Moodie, Jeffrey Pepper, Frank Pohlmann, Ben Renow-Clarke, Dominic Shakeshaft, Matt Wade, Tom Welsh

Coordinating Editor:
Kelly Moritz

Copy Editor:
Kim Wimpsett

Compositor:
Kimberly Burton

Indexer:
Brenda Miller

Cover Image Designer:
Corné van Dooren

To Maryam, for being my best friend, my love, and my wife, and to my parents, for their unconditional love and care.

Contents at a Glance

Contents

About the Author

In the past ten years, Ali has worked in almost every field of IT. And from programming and system analysis to training and consulting about Web 2.0 technologies, he has never been able to get enough. He wished he could live for 1,000 more years just to try new technologies.

He admires usable and beautiful websites, develops web applications occasionally, loves anything related to cloud, and is a shameless Apple fan.

He guest blogs occasionally for different websites and is currently working in Dubai as a new media manager.

You can always find him on Twitter (@shabdar) checking and sharing geeky stuff.

About the Technical Reviewer

Ahmed Hussain is a small cog in the soon-to-be giant wheel called Zoho. In the long list of online Zoho Services, he is a member of Zoho Writer—an online word processor and one of the flagship products that was rolled out from Zoho's stable about four years ago. Since then, Zoho has come a long way. It currently has 20 different services lined up for its growing user base and many more in the pipeline. The aim of Zoho in the long run is to be the IT department of small and medium-sized businesses.

Having been part of Zoho since its inception, Ahmed Hussain is a veteran who has gotten a good grasp of the intricacies of various Zoho services. Currently, Ahmed is entrusted with spreading the Zoho message and doubles up as a marketer and a tech writer.

Acknowledgments

I have been reading and enjoying Apress books for many years. It always was a dream to see my name on the cover of an Apress title. Here I am living that dream and checking off another "I want to…" on my bucket list. I know it wouldn't have been possible without the great support I received from Apress.

I'd like to thank everybody at Apress for making this book possible, especially Steve Anglin and Ben Renow-Clarke for their valuable advice.

Thanks to Kelly Moritz and Beth Christmas for being such good friends during the writing process and to Caroline Rose and Kim Wimpsett for coping with my English.

Last but not least, thanks to Zoho Corp. for making the cloud a better place. Kudos to Ahmed Hussain for reviewing the book patiently.

Introduction

Science seems to compete with the universe itself in fascinating us every day, and computer science is no doubt one of science's most fascinating disciplines. I remember saying good-bye to the last mainframe in town back in 1997 (yes, I had the chance to actually see a dinosaur); back then, no one would have imagined in their wildest dreams that we would be able to access the resources of super-fast data centers from our mobile devices anywhere in the world, especially a mere 12 years later.

Today, it sounds rather normal if I tell you that you can run a virtual office completely online. Thanks to great technologies made by great people, Zoho has come up with a suite of applications that allows you to do most of the things you do every day using expensive hardware and software. And they provide it online and for a price of a morning latte.

In this book, you will learn how to start taking your work online, and you will see a handful of good reasons why you should do this. No matter what your business or the size of your organization, you will find at least a few applications useful for solving some of your problems.

In this journey, more than knowledge and ambition, you will need a slight change in mind-set in order to welcome the new era, and I hope this book can play a role in that process, no matter how small.

Who should read this book?

This book is for everybody who uses the Internet. I highly recommend that everybody read at least the first part of the book and use the tools and techniques discussed. It is better to be ready for the next wave of technology now.

Specifically, this book focuses on the following:

- **Small to medium businesses and startups**: You will learn how to virtually run your entire business on the cloud with lots of added features at no cost or just a minimal monthly fee.

- **Students and scholars**: From primary to PhD level, you will be able to improve your productivity dramatically. Using free online tools, you will perform better research, do your homework faster, and work in teams more efficiently.

- **All Internet users**: Moving to the cloud (using SaaS applications) will be the next big thing in the coming years, so you should learn about it now. It is so much fun!

Even if you are not in the previously mentioned groups (I doubt it!), you can still find a lot to learn and use in your daily life.

What you need to know

Before getting ready for this book, all you need is to be a typical Internet user. This means you should have prior experience using the Web and e-mail. That's it!

Being familiar with any productivity software (Sun OpenOffice.org, Microsoft Office, Apple iWork, and so on) is also beneficial, although not required.

You can use any kind of computer that supports modern web browsers (Firefox 3+, Safari 3+, Google Chrome, Internet Explorer 7+, Opera 9+, and so on).

How this book is structured

To make it easier to learn and more fun to read, this book features many visuals. There are also plenty walk-throughs to help you learn the subject more easily.

The first eight chapters of the book focus on daily stuff that every computer user, no matter what level, performs regularly. Processing documents, working with numbers and spreadsheets, preparing presentations, managing documents, planning daily tasks, and checking e-mails are some of the tasks covered.

To get the most from this book, make sure you read Chapter 1 and Chapter 2. Both contain essential information on getting started with Zoho. You can then read the book as you prefer, jumping back and forth between chapters.

In Chapter 9, you'll step into the more advanced areas used in business environments. Databases, invoicing, human resource management, customer relationship management, and project management are among the most important activities every business relies on, and you will learn how to harness the power of Zoho Suite to do it all in no time.

> *Disclaimer: Since all Zoho applications are SaaS based and constantly evolving, you might find some of the detailed steps in this book different slightly from the version you are using. Despite this, the main objectives will remain same. This book helps you get started with Zoho as quickly as possible and stay comfortable with the updates too.*

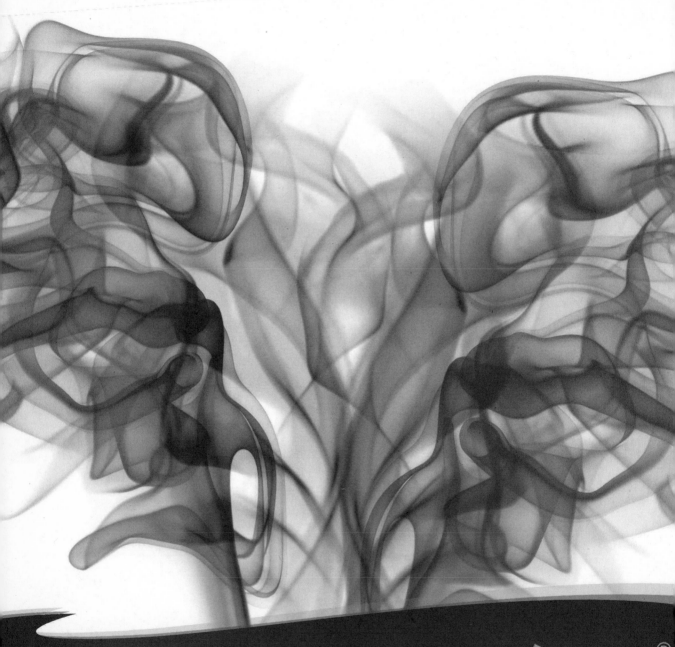

ZOHO®

Work. Online

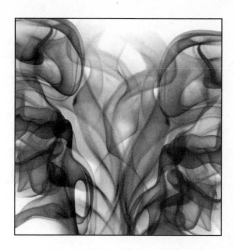

Chapter 1

Getting Up and Running with Zoho

Before you create your Zoho account, let's take a minute to examine what Zoho is. The invention of the Internet is no doubt one of the biggest achievements of the century. Our life today, although we usually take it for granted, looks like sci-fi movies, thanks to living in a cyberworld where every piece of information is just one click away. Any information you need is available in your pocket via mobile devices. You can do your shopping, read e-mails, check the markets, run your company, and play 3D games while commuting to work or yawning in a boring meeting! The Internet has gone through a dramatic change in regard to speed and also its underlying technologies in the last 20 years. It was not long ago that we were sending 20KB files using 8Kbps modems; now we take it for granted that you can check your friends' profiles on your iPhone over a 3G connection (300+ Kbps).

We are in a new era. Another evolution in the computer world is changing the way we look at the Internet. What is this change, and how is it going to impact our lives? That is the question this book tries to answer by showing you how to use one of the most exciting innovations on the Internet, made by Zoho.

Let's start with some relatively new terms and definitions.

What is Web 2.0?

The concept of **Web 2.0** began with a conference-brainstorming session between Tim O'Reilly and the folks at MediaLive International, says O'Reilly in "What Is Web 2.0." According to O'Reilly, "Web 2.0 is the business revolution in the computer industry caused by the move to the Internet as a platform and an attempt to understand the rules for success on that new platform."

Surprisingly, after all these years, the definition of Web 2.0 is still vague, and nobody seems to agree on a single term so far. Just Google `define Web 2.0`, and you get 10s of different (yet similar) results.

My favorite definition, however, is Richard MacManus's. He succinctly wrote in a 2005 article that Web 2.0 is "the Web as a platform."

So, what does the Web as a platform mean?

Let me give you a simple example. Not long ago, everybody kept their photos on their computers. The resources of your local computer, specifically the disk space, were consumed to maintain the data. With the emergence of services such as Flickr (`www.flickr.com`) and Picasa (`www.picasaweb.com`), many people now upload their photo albums to these websites. Although you might still keep a backup of your photos on your hard drive, the slide show or the photo gallery you have on Flickr runs on an Internet platform and not your local computer. You can share photos with friends and fans and have some peace of mind that Flickr will take care of the photos on powerful servers.

This is a very small example of the Web as a platform. It is now expanding to most of the things we do with our computers. Photos, video clips, document, presentations, databases, and almost all sorts of information we deal with either reside on the Web or are portable to the Web.

Of course, such a major change in the technology of the Web deserves to be distinguished as version 2.0.

More advanced examples are social networks and online business applications where our daily lives, personal or business, use the Web as the sole platform.

On the other hand, you might have heard of Web 3.0, which is an even vaguer story! Well, I still don't know if it is just marketing hype or whether there is really something serious going on. Whatever it is, it must be cooler and even more futuristic than Web 2.0. It will exist in "the cloud" (more on that in a minute), it will utilize the power of mobile devices more than ever, and it will go toward the Semantic Web where the Internet is more humanly accessible.

> *The Semantic Web is one of the hottest topics on the future of the Internet, where humans and computers work seamlessly and understand each other better. You can read more on this subject at* `www.semanticweb.org` *and* `www.w3.org/2001/sw/`.

The cloud

So, just what is the cloud? The computer world is full of jargon and weird abbreviations, and **cloud** is one of them. Despite the mysterious cool name, it just means "Internet" in the geek dictionary.

Cloud computing, on the other hand, is using the Internet as the main platform for software and leveraging its resources, such as powerful servers and huge storage facilities, making the software accessible and economically feasible for everyone (Figure 1-1).

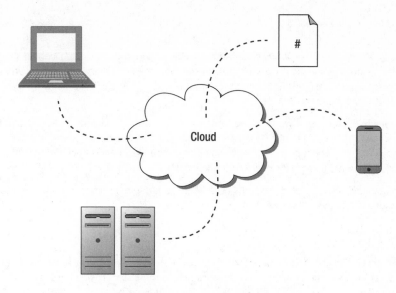

Figure 1-1. Cloud computing

This might not interest you as an end user, but it definitely impacts your life.

The following are some of the services you probably use every day (and probably can't live without!) that are available to you for free and that are updated constantly to give you a better experience:

- YouTube (www.youtube.com)
- Flickr (www.flickr.com)
- Facebook (www.facebook.com)
- Twitter (www.twitter.com)
- Tumblr (www.tumblr.com)
- Last.fm (www.last.fm)
- Hulu (www.hulu.com)

This is just a small list, and I'm sure you can come up with at least ten more services most of us are proudly addicted to!

Have you ever wondered how all these services work and where they reside? They all work and live on the cloud. This means that instead of the companies behind these services having to buy their own servers and hire teams of administrators and system programmers to perform everything in-house, which would be hugely expensive, they use the common platforms available on the cloud to save time and money and provide you with more reliable services.

Let's skip the technical details and see what else cloud computing can do that is important for us.

Office 2.0

Now that you know what Web 2.0 brings you and what cloud computing is doing behind the scenes, the idea of using business software as an online service becomes more viable. Office and productivity packages, customer relationship management systems (CRMs), and all those software systems that no business can live without can run fully on the cloud.

If you are not sold yet, imagine a world where you can use almost any kind of computer device (desktop, laptop, smart phone, and so on) to access online business applications from anywhere in the world without sitting in your office or even using your own computer. You can share documents and contribute to projects anywhere and at any time for free (or for a low cost).

This dream can come true only on the cloud where software and platform are offered to you as a service. Read on, because it gets even more exciting.

SaaS and PaaS

Software as a service (SaaS; pronounced "sass") is a model in which software applications are hosted on an Internet server as a service provided to customers across the Internet. This means there is no need to install any application on the user's computer, which eliminates the burden of software maintenance and local support.

SaaS applications can run on almost any kind of computer that can open web pages. This means you don't need a fancy, superfast computer because they actually run on Internet-based servers and not on your side.

Such services are usually free (with limited or unlimited features) or require the user to pay a low monthly fee. There is no up-front software purchases or installation. Updates and patches are done by the provider as part of the service. This means you always have your hands on the latest version of the software and should not be worried about downloading and installing fat updates and service packs. SaaS providers usually guarantee a 99+ percent uptime and full data security as well.

The emergence of netbooks (low-end, small notebooks) that rely on the processing and storage power of the cloud is strong proof that SaaS is going to be the next big thing. Netbooks have low capacity and processing power compared to notebooks because they don't need to process or store as much data locally. A netbook user needs only a browser and an Internet connection to use the software platforms on the cloud where all the processing and data storage is being performed on powerful servers elsewhere.

These off-site facilities, including powerful servers, security, availability, administration, and so on, form a state-of-the-art platform known as **platform as a service** (PaaS). This platform provides software makers (developers) with tools to speed up the development process and create better solutions that are robust and well priced.

Providing end users with such powerful platforms is usually out of the league of small and even medium-sized companies. PaaS, however, plays this important role and gives everybody the opportunity to enjoy this diabolic power with minimal fees!

I am sure you're wondering why this is important and why anybody should put their precious data on the cloud. How can you even think of dumping your favorite office applications or photo album software and rely on something on the Internet?

Well, that's why you are holding this book in your hands and why you should seriously consider adopting this new way of working.

> You may also pay a visit to the Web 2.0 summit page at en.oreilly.com/web2008/public/content/home and the Go2Web20 page at www.go2web20.net to become familiar with thousands of companies involved in the process.

SaaS advantages

In short, these are some of the advantages SaaS can bring to you, no matter what industry you are in:

- Software is often free or much cheaper to purchase and much cheaper to maintain.
- Believe it or not, your data is safer there just like your money is safer in the bank than under your mattress!
- You can save money by using lower-end hardware. Your salespeople don't need 4GB of memory and 320GB of hard disk space! A $500 netbook will be more than enough.
- There are no software updates, patches, or service packs for SaaS applications. This means fewer IT guys wandering around the office for time-consuming updates and maintenance issues.
- Data is highly portable and highly available since it resides on the cloud, and you can have access to it at any time anywhere.
- Collaboration and teamwork are available out of the box.

It is the future, so you better be ready!

What about Zoho?

As you might have guessed by now, Zoho embraces the features of Web 2.0 and SaaS and provides you with a suite of web applications that fulfills your personal and business needs.

Almost everybody uses office and productivity software at some point. We use word processors to write letters, reports, and essays. We do basic and advanced number calculations in spreadsheets and create eye-catching presentation to sell our ideas in corporate meetings.

With Zoho, you can take productivity and collaboration to the next level. Working on documents, sharing business thoughts, and working in teams all have never been easier.

Zoho gives you all the necessary tools plus a collection of other applications all in one place—on the cloud. Not only can you do almost anything you used to do with traditional packages, but you also have a host of extra services, all (or mostly all) for free!

Business users enjoy a set of applications that solve everyday critical issues for free, or at a nominal charge. With cloud-based applications like CRM, invoicing, project management, human resources (HR) management, databases, reports, and more, Zoho gives you the best of both worlds all in one place.

When you are on the go, Zoho Mobile will make sure you are still connected to your online business center. Supporting the biggest mobile platforms (iPhone, Android, Blackberry, and Windows Mobile), you will be able to work anywhere all the time.

The bottom line is that you can run your life with the Zoho online suite. You can see this for yourself, because I will cover every application and tool in the upcoming chapters.

Getting started

To start using Zoho, you need to first create a Zoho account. Zoho membership is free, and you can use all the applications without paying for anything! However, if you are a business user, some services have paid membership plans that provide more features than the free versions.

> *I'll talk about the paid services as we reach them.*

The good news is that to complete this book, you need only the free services. Surprisingly enough, as you will see, free plans will be enough even for small businesses with one to five employees.

So, let's get started with creating your very first key to the SaaS world.

Creating a Zoho account

Simply log in to www.zoho.com to open the Zoho homepage (Figure 1-2). It might seem crowded at first because all the Zoho applications are listed on the homepage. Believe it or not, I cover all the applications you see on the homepage in this book!

Figure 1-2. Zoho homepage

On the right side, you can see the `Sign In` box. You don't yet have an account, so you should click the `Sign Up` link.

> Zoho accepts OpenID, which means you don't need to actually create an extra account dedicated to Zoho. It allows you to log in with your Google or Yahoo! account. OpenID helps you eliminate the need of creating new accounts for every new service you use online. To get more information on OpenID, check out `http://openid.net/what/`.

To create an account in Zoho, follow these steps:

1. Click **Sign Up** to continue.
2. In the sign-up form (Figure 1-3), enter a username. It should be alphanumeric and between 6 to 30 characters. Dots and underscores are allowed too.

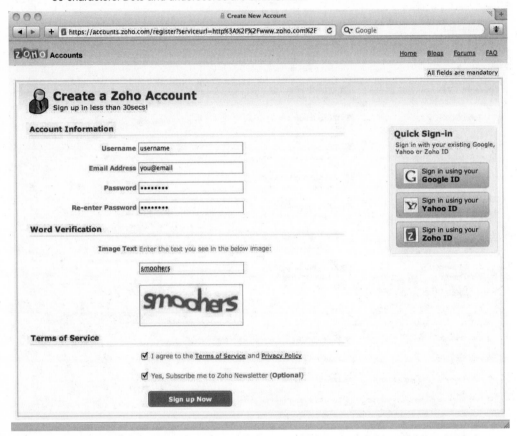

Figure 1-3. Creating a new Zoho account

> *You should choose a suitable username for your account because it might be your online business identity later. IDs such as* **suzy2008** *or* **hell_master** *do not look professional! If you don't have a business name, simply try to your own name.*

3. Enter a password that's 3 to 60 characters in length. Use a complex phrase, with a mix of letters and numbers, and never use your username or any similar combination of it for a password.
4. Enter the verification text, and agree to the terms of service and privacy policy after you've read them.
5. Click **Sign Up** to proceed.

If everything is OK, you will be redirected to the next page where a message notifies you to check your e-mail box for the activation message (Figure 1-4). Just remember to confirm the sign-up process by clicking the confirmation link in less than seven days; otherwise, your account will be disabled, and your username will be blocked. Click `Continue Signing In` to log in to your Zoho account.

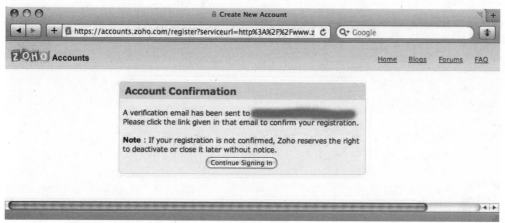

Figure 1-4. Successful account creation

Using Zoho Personal

Once you are logged in, you can select the service you need from the application list, or you can log on to Zoho Personal (`http://personal.zoho.com`) from the link in the welcome box on the home page (Figure 1-5). According to the official documentation, "Zoho Personal is a suite of web-based applications for personal use, academic purposes and even small enterprises. It includes the tools necessary in setting up and assisting you with your business, studies and other related collaborative work."

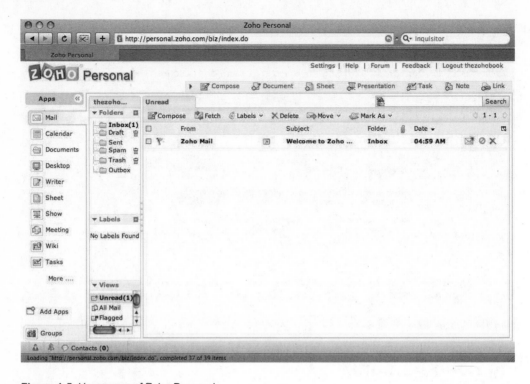

Figure 1-5. Homepage of Zoho Personal

The good thing about Zoho Personal is that it is like a desktop that collects all the productivity applications in one place to make them easier to use. You can still open each application separately from their links on the Zoho homepage if you want. It is just a matter of personal preference.

Once Zoho Personal opens, you might see a dialog box warning you that "The website below wants to store information on your computer using Gears." Make sure you select `I trust this site. Allow it to use Gears`, and click `Allow`. This is because you have installed Google Gears on your system. If you don't have it installed, don't worry. You are going to see how you can use this feature later in this chapter.

As you can see in Figure 1-5, there are two menu bars on top of the page with items common for all applications.

Through the first menu, you can change the settings (of Zoho Personal), get help, check the forums, leave feedback, or just log out of Zoho. There is also an `Upgrade to Business Edition` link, but I will not talk about the business package until Chapter 9.

On the second menu, you can see buttons to create e-mails, documents, spreadsheets, and presentations as well as add new tasks, notes, and links. You can skip these menu bars for now.

On the left side, there is the **Apps** (applications) pane. It holds all application shortcuts in Zoho Personal. When you select an application, the working environment changes to that particular app, and you can start working immediately.

These applications include the following:

- An e-mail client and instant messenger
- A contacts manager, task manager, and calendar
- A word processor, spreadsheet, and presentation applications
- And many more useful tools

I will discuss these applications in detail in the upcoming chapters. But before that, let's take a quick tour around the Zoho Personal environment and perform some basic tasks so you can be better prepared for the rest of your journey.

Customizing Zoho Personal

It is a good idea to check the settings before you start working in order to customize the environment and to know how to perform occasional administrative tasks.

> *You should be careful with the settings, since some options might change the behavior of certain applications.*

For now I will walk you through some basic settings. Later you can customize them as per your requirements.

Whenever you log in to Zoho Personal, it opens Mail by default. This is good when you have your e-mails managed by Zoho. Zoho Mail is a brilliant tool, and I will be covering it in Chapter 6.

To use the default page in Zoho Personal more effectively, you can set what application you want to open. Zoho Personal is your online desktop, so it might be a good idea to open the Desktop page (your **DashBoard**) by default. Desktop lists your recent e-mails, documents as well as tasks, links, and so on (Figure 1-6). I'll discuss all these in detail, but for now let's focus on Desktop and make it your center point when you work on Zoho.

Figure 1-6. The Desktop page

First you need to tell Zoho Personal which items you want to appear in Desktop:

1. Open Desktop by clicking its icon on the sidebar.
2. Click `Manage Content` on the upper-right. The `Manage DashBoard Content` dialog box appears (Figure 1-7).

Figure 1-7. Desktop settings

3. Set all gadgets to **Enabled**. We want all items to be visible on the desktop for now. Later you can remove the unnecessary gadgets from here.

4. Click **Save** to apply the changes.

To make Desktop your default application, follow these steps:

1. With the **Settings** page open, click **Applications** in the **Settings** pane. You can see a list of applications on the right side of the page.

2. Find **Desktop** in the list, and hover your mouse pointer on its icon.

3. Drag the icon, and drop it on top of the list like in Figure 1-8. Desktop is now your default application.

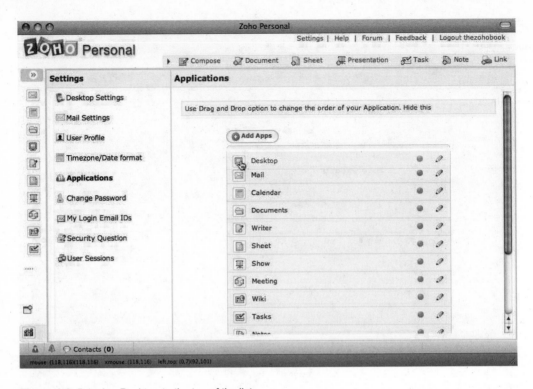

Figure 1-8. Bringing Desktop to the top of the list

Now whenever you log in to Zoho Personal, it opens Desktop with all your recent documents listed. Neat!

Next, you should update your user profile. This profile is useful when you work in teams or share documents publicly.

To change your profile, follow these steps:

1. On the `Settings` page, click `User Profile` (Figure 1-9).

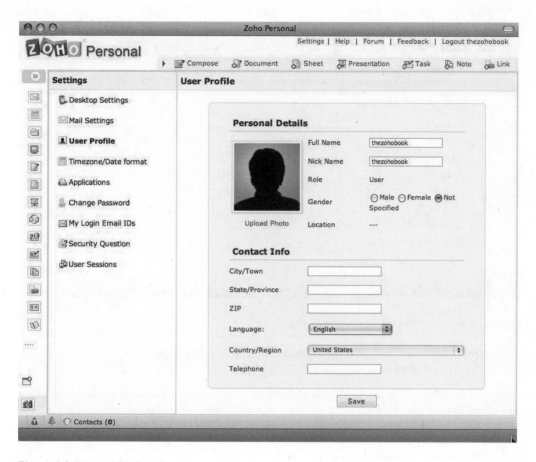

Figure 1-9. User profile settings

2. Fill in the boxes as they apply to you. Giving the proper contact information will help you communicate better with peers, as you will see in the upcoming chapters.

3. Click `Upload Photo` to change the default avatar to your snapshot or your logo. A secondary window will open to guide you through uploading the image file.

4. Click `Close` in the secondary window when you are done uploading the photo.

5. Click `Save` to store your new profile information.

It is good to change the time zone and date settings to your local format, so follow these steps:

1. On the `Settings` page, click `Timezone/Date format` (Figure 1-10).

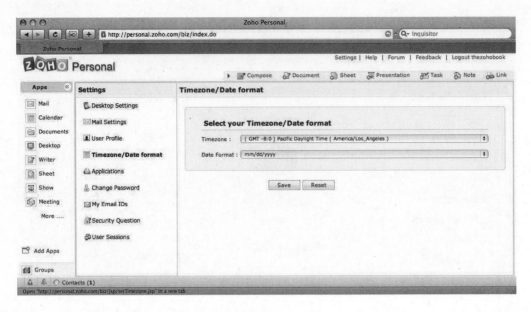

Figure 1-10. Setting the time zone and date format

2. Change the `Timezone` and `Date Format` fields to your local settings.
3. Click `Save` for the changes to take place.

Security is a very important issue, and it is even more important when you are working online. Two of the pillars of data security are to choose good, hard-to-guess passwords and to change them regularly.

To control security measures in Zoho Personal, follow these steps:

1. Click `Change Password` on the `Settings` page (Figure 1-11).

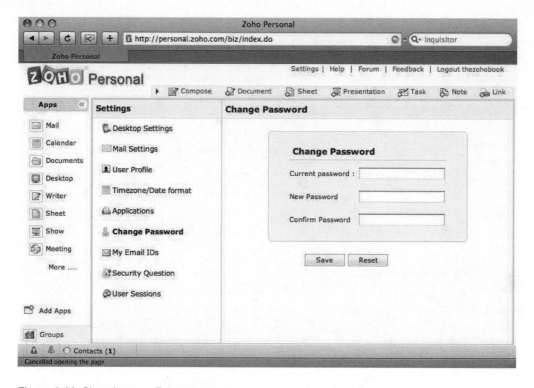

Figure 1-11. Changing your Zoho password

2. Enter the current password in **Current Password**.
3. Enter the new one in **New Password**, and repeat it in the **Confirm Password** box.
4. Click **Save** to apply the new password.
5. Click **Security Question** on the **Settings** page to change the security question too (Figure 1-12). If you forget your password at some point, Zoho will ask this question to let you log in.

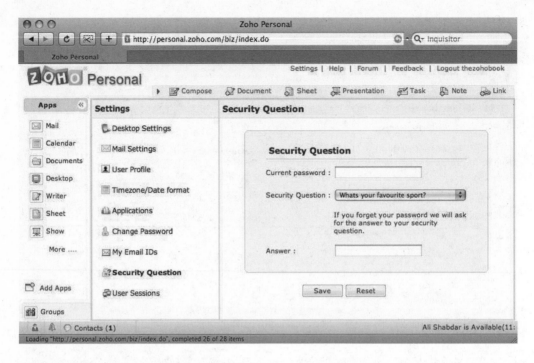

Figure 1-12. Changing the security question

6. In the **Security Question** page, enter your password in **Current password**.
7. Select a security question from the drop-down list.
8. Type in the answer in **Answer**. This answer should be related to the question you selected in step 7.
9. Click **Save** to apply the changes.

Making Zoho easier to reach

The aim of this book is to get you ready to move on to the cloud. To encourage you to start using Zoho as a part of your daily life, you need to make your life a little easier!

Instead of loading Zoho Personal or any other Zoho service in a web browser every time, it is a good idea to have a stand-alone application that runs Zoho just like any other application on your computer.

This way, not only can you run Zoho outside the browser, but also you will not lose your precious data when another tab in your browser crashes the entire thing! Creating stand-alone web applications is possible by using applications like Prism and Fluid.

> *There is good news for Chrome users—you can use such features out of the box. If you click the tiny button called* **Control the current page** *next to address bar, a context menu will appear. Select* **Create application shortcuts**, *and you can actually create an application out of Zoho Personal. Just make sure you have Zoho Personal loaded in the current tab before you do this.*

Prism

Prism is a product of Mozilla Labs created in 2007 and recently updated to version beta 1.0. Prism makes it possible to create applications from the websites you regularly use. They call it Site Specific Browsers (SSB), and in our case we are going to create a Prism application out of Zoho.

> *If you have Firefox installed on your system, you can simply install the Prism add-on and skip the walk-through. Log on to https://addons.mozilla.org/en-US/firefox/addon/6665. Alternatively, search for Prism in the Firefox add-ons, and install Prism for Firefox. After restarting the browser, you can select* **Tools ▸ Convert Website to Application** *to create a Prism application.*

1. Log on to the Mozilla wiki at `http://prism.mozilla.com/started/`, and download the suitable Prism edition for your operating system—Mac OS, Linux, or Windows. Although it is a very straightforward process, you can get help on how to install Prism from the Mozilla website at `http://prism.mozilla.com/`.

2. Install and run Prism. This example demonstrates the use of Prism in Mac OS. A similar approach applies to Linux and Windows.

3. Enter the address of Zoho Personal (`http://personal.zoho.com`) in the **URL** box and enter `Zoho Personal` in the **Name** box (Figure 1-13).

Figure 1-13. Creating a Prism application for Zoho Personal

4. Set the other options as appropriate for your own use, and click OK.

5. Now you have a new application called Zoho Personal that you can run separately from the browser just by double-clicking its icon. Congratulations!

The good thing about Prism is that it is based on Mozilla. This means it works like Firefox and runs Zoho applications better (based on my personal experience). You can also install your favorite Firefox-compliant plug-ins on Prism.

Fluid

If you are a Mac user and you prefer Safari over other browsers, Fluid is for you! Fluid is another free SSB application that is specifically developed for Mac OS X Leopard (version 10.5+) and is based on WebKit (Safari is based on WebKit too). Since it is especially developed for Mac, it brings true and native interaction with the operating system.

To install Fluid, follow these steps:

1. Make sure you have Mac OS 10.5 (Leopard) or newer installed. You can check this by clicking the Apple icon on the menu bar and selecting **About this Mac**; the version number will be visible in the About window.

2. Log on to www.fluidapp.com, and click the download link in the upper right in the **Free Download** section.

3. After downloading, double-click the .zip file to extract the application.

4. You can either drag Fluid to your **Applications** folder (the Mac way) or just run it where it is.

5. Run Fluid to start creating SSB for Zoho Personal.

6. Fill in the boxes as in Figure 1-14, and then click **Create**.

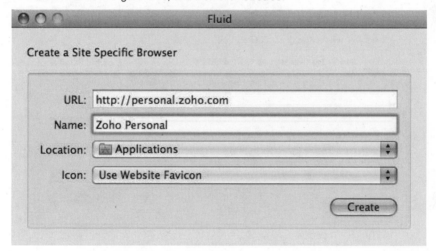

Figure 1-14. Creating a Fluid application for Zoho Personal

7. When the **Success** dialog box is displayed, click **Launch Now** to open the application.

Google Gears

Google Gears is a browser plug-in that provides web applications with some powerful new features. It works on Firefox, Safari, and Internet Explorer. It is also a built-in feature in Google Chrome, so you don't need to install it if you are a Chrome user. It is compatible with Prism and Fluid too.

Throughout this book you'll see features in the Zoho suite that are made possible with Google Gears (or just Gears to make it shorter), so you need to install it in order for those features to work properly.

To install Gears, follow these steps:

1. Log on to the Gears website at gears.google.com
2. If you already have it installed, it will show that Gears is installed; otherwise, click **Install**.
3. For Firefox, a pop-up will appear asking you to install the plug-in. Click **Install Now** to proceed (Figure 1-15). Now skip to step 6.

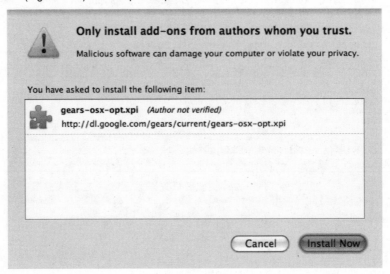

Figure 1-15. Installing Gears on Firefox

4. For Safari (Mac only; Windows is not supported as of this writing), it will download a DMG file (gears-osx-opt.dmg), which you need to mount first and run the installer (Google Gears.mpkg) in the package. Now skip to step 6.
5. For Internet Explorer, it will download an application (GearsSetup.exe). Run the application after download, and proceed with installing it in order to install Gears.
6. After installing Gears, restart your browser for the changes to take effect.

How secure is your data?

An important question that might have already come to mind is, "How safe and how secure is my data on the Zoho servers?"

The short answer is that it is both very safe and very secure. In fact, your data is probably safer with Zoho than it is on your personal computer, which is prone to theft, virus infection, crashes, and so on.

The people who run Zoho invested a lot to provide you with a highly available and secure platform where your data is backed up and checked against viruses 24/7.

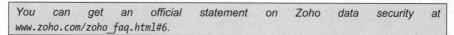

You can get an official statement on Zoho data security at www.zoho.com/zoho_faq.html#6.

Zoho applications are all hosted on highly secure state-of-the-art servers owned by Zoho and located in multiple locations across the United States. It is, however, totally up to you to trust Zoho or any other cloud-based company to keep your data for you.

For the backup obsessed, it is still recommended to keep a local copy of your content (documents, data, etc.) in case of alien invasion or something similar.

Getting help

Apart from this book being your portable reference for the Zoho suite, there are few more ways to get help when you have questions. You can always click **Help** in the top menu bar to get quick help about the application you are using at the moment.

There are also forums where Zoho users from all over the world discuss issues, share their knowledge, and ask for new features. I highly recommend using these forums, since you will get good answers to your questions most of the time. The Zoho support team regularly monitors the forums. You can reach the forums by clicking **Forum** on the top menu bar or by logging onto `http://forums.zoho.com` and choosing the forum related to your application.

Summary

From Web 2.0 to SaaS, this chapter gave you a short overview of what is happening around you and what lies beneath some of online services you use every day.

You also created your very first Zoho account and entered the SaaS realm. Zoho Personal is a good start point to work with this powerful productivity suite. You customized it a bit and familiarized yourself with its intuitive interface. Finally, by installing Prism, Fluid, and Gears, you set up the necessary ground for using Zoho applications on daily basis.

In the next chapter, you'll start working with Writer, the best online word processor available today. You will learn a lot of exciting features that might actually change the way you work completely.

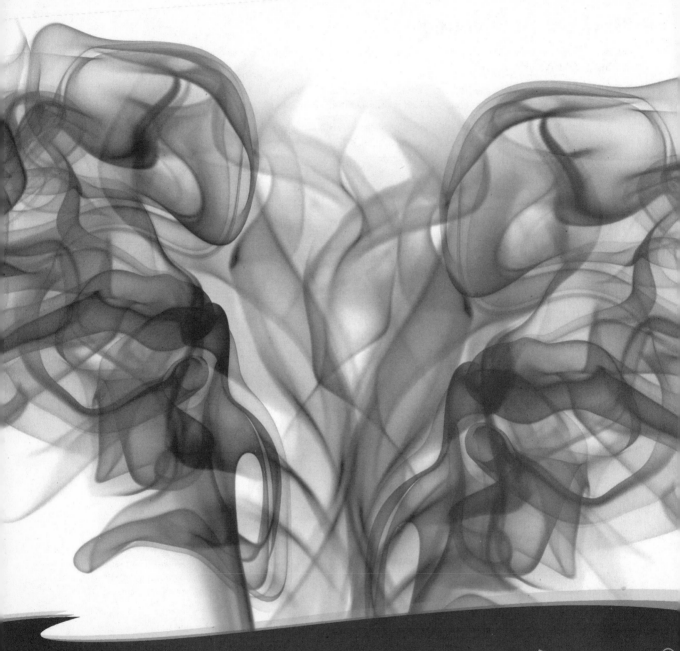

ZOHO ®
Work. Online

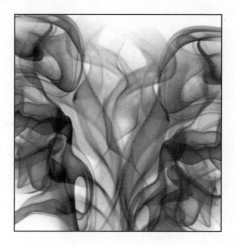

Chapter 2

Processing Your Words

Word processing goes back to the Middle Ages when printing and movable types were first invented. Then, in 1867, Christopher Latham Sholes and his colleagues invented the first manual typewriter. It was a long journey from that point in the history until now, when we have sophisticated word processor software available on the shelf for as low as $30.

> *To read more about the history of modern word processing, see the interesting article by Brian Kunde at* www.stanford.edu/~bkunde/fb-press/articles/wdprhist.html.

Now it is time to make yet another breakthrough in the history of word processing—taking it fully on the cloud.

You are no doubt already familiar with traditional solutions like Sun OpenOffice.org Writer, Microsoft Word, and Apple Pages (part of the iWork package) where you create documents on your local machine (for example, your laptop).

What I'm going to discuss here is a 100 percent Internet-based word processor that is similar to the traditional ones but doesn't need you to install any software on your computer. It works on all systems from anywhere, and amazingly it is completely free!

It is Zoho Writer, and it is part of the Zoho productivity suite.

Getting started

Writer is a powerful word processor that allows you to do the following:

- Create and modify documents
- Format text and apply different styles using a powerful what-you-see-is-what-you-get (WYSYWIG) editor
- Insert images and other content
- Import major document formats (HTML, DOC, DOCX, SXW, ODT, RTF, JPG, GIF, PNG, and TXT files) uploaded from your computer or from the Internet

> *Refer to Table 2-1 to see the supported file formats.*

- Export your documents to major file formats (DOC, DOCX, ODF, ODT, PDF, LaTeX, SXW, RTF, TXT, and HTML) to share with other platforms
- Do revision history, version compare, and version rollback
- Add comments and highlights for collaboration
- And much more

The cloud-based nature of Writer allows you to do the following:

- Access, edit, and share documents with friends/colleagues from anywhere and at any time
- Publish your document for public viewing and commenting

Table 2-1. Document formats supported by Writer

Extension	Format
.doc	Microsoft Word document
.docx	Microsoft Word 2007 document
.sxw	OpenOffice.org text document
.odt	OpenOffice.org text document
.odf	OpenDocument format
.rtf	Rich-text format
.txt	Text file
.html	Hypertext Markup Language (HTML) document
.pdf	Portable Document Format (PDF) document

> *Writer (like other Zoho applications) works well on major browsers (such as Firefox, Safari, and Internet Explorer). But you need to enable JavaScript before you can use it properly. It is usually enabled by default by most browsers, but if you need to enable it and don't know how, please refer to your browser's documentation.*

To see what every feature mentioned in the previous list means and how it can help you live a better life, let's start with a brief look at the Writer environment.

The environment

To open Writer, click its icon in Zoho Personal, or simply log on to `writer.zoho.com`. The user interface should look familiar if you have ever used other word processors (Figures 2-1 and 2-2). It is even more accessible and friendly than some cluttered rivals. This makes the learning curve pretty short.

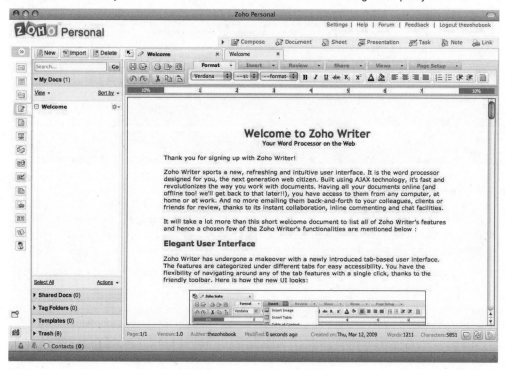

Figure 2-1. Writer's window in Zoho Personal

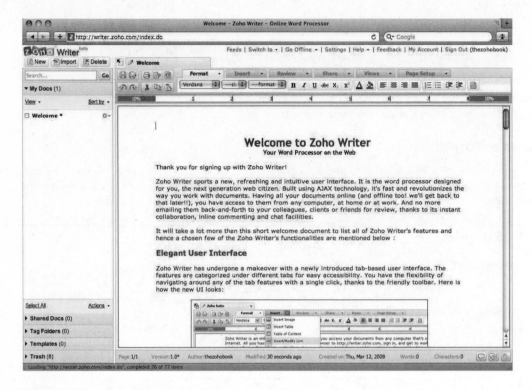

Figure 2-2. Writer's stand-alone window

The screen is divided into two panes (three in Zoho Personal because of the application pane) by default. The sidebar (on the left side of the screen) contains a list of documents you have created or imported as well as shared documents, tags, templates, and the trash can.

The three big buttons on the top of the documents pane allow you to create new documents, import existing documents, and delete documents.

The editor is where you create your documents, and it takes much of the space available on-screen. You can stretch it even more by clicking the `Maximize Editor` icon next to the big `Delete` button.

There are ten shortcut buttons on the upper left of the editor for you to get quick access to the commonly used commands; `Save`, `Save As`, `Print`, `Undo`, `Redo`, `Cut`, `Copy`, and `Paste` are amongst the most common buttons you will use (Figure 2-3).

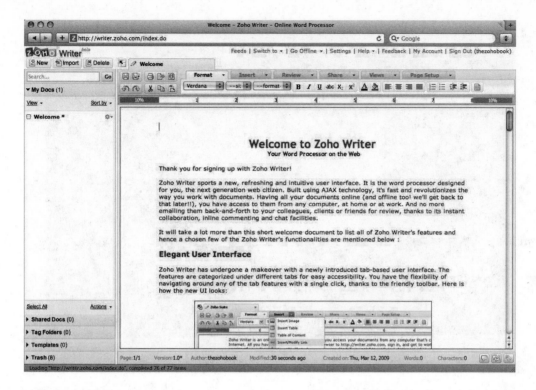

Figure 2-3. Quick shortcuts

The tenth button is `Document Properties` (with an *i*-shaped icon) that opens the `Document Information` dialog box that gives some basic information about the document (Figure 2-4).

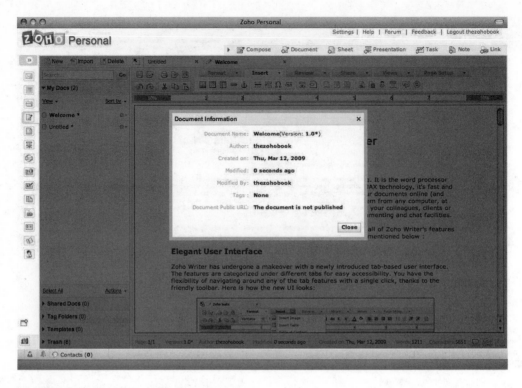

Figure 2-4. `Document Information` dialog box

As of Writer 2.0, Zoho introduced the **MenuTab**, which mixes the menu bar and the toolbar commands in a categorized way. You can do almost everything that is possible in Writer through the **MenuTab**.

It is a good idea to take a quick look at the main sections before proceeding. You'll use most of the features in the next sections.

Going through the MenuTab

When you open Writer, the **Format** tab loads by default. The good thing about the **MenuTab** is that in addition to featuring a toolbar for every tab, it features a related menu too.

Click the tiny arrow on the title of each tab, and a menu with all the commands will appear.

There are six different tabs packed in the **MenuTab**: **Format**, **Insert**, **Review**, **Share**, **Views**, and **Page Setup**. First I'll cover each tab, and later in this chapter I'll show how to use the features they provide in your documents. The **Format** tab (and menu)—as the name suggests—contains all the formatting commands to help your document look better. This is perhaps the most used tab in the **MenuTab** (Figures 2-5 and 2-6).

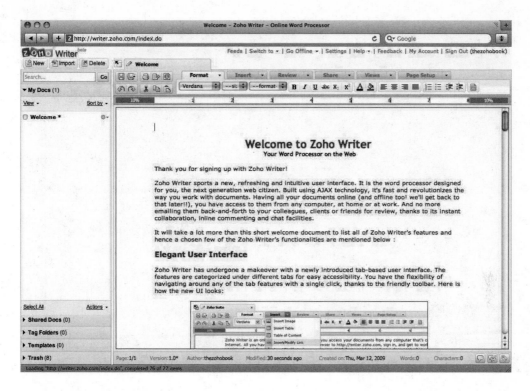

Figure 2-5. The `Format` tab

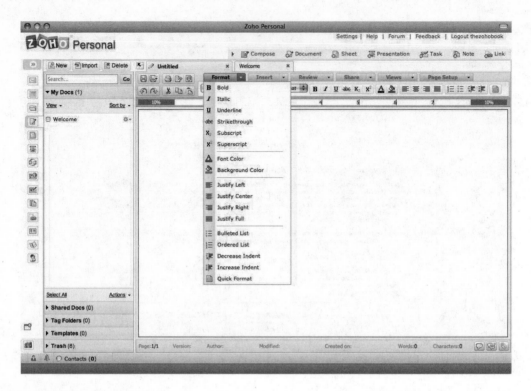

Figure 2-6. The `Format` menu

Next is the `Insert` tab that takes care of adding extra features to your document. You can insert tables, images, and equations, as well as some other advanced document elements (Figures 2-7 and 2-8).

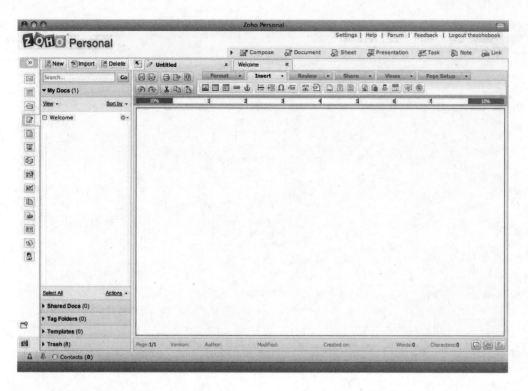

Figure 2-7. The `Insert` tab

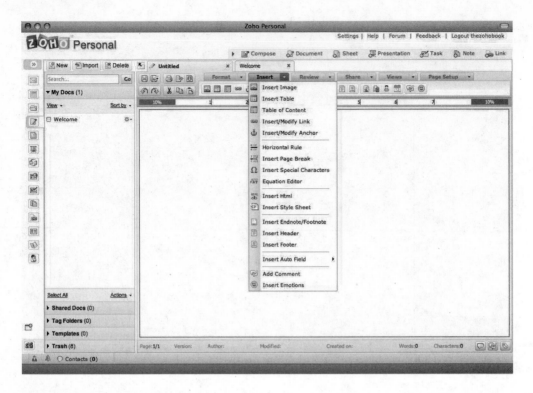

Figure 2-8. The `Insert` menu

The `Review` tab features essential commands to proofread your document as well as taking care of different versions (Figures 2-9 and 2-10).

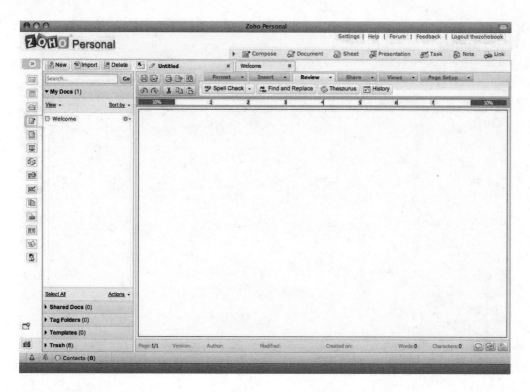

Figure 2-9. The `Review` tab

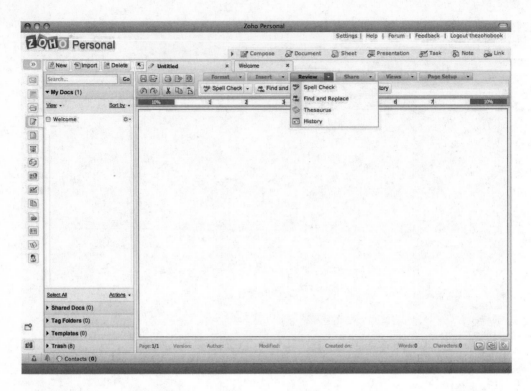

Figure 2-10. The **Review** menu

The **Share** tab is where you unleash the power of Writer. All sharing and collaboration activities are done from here (Figures 2-11 and 2-12).

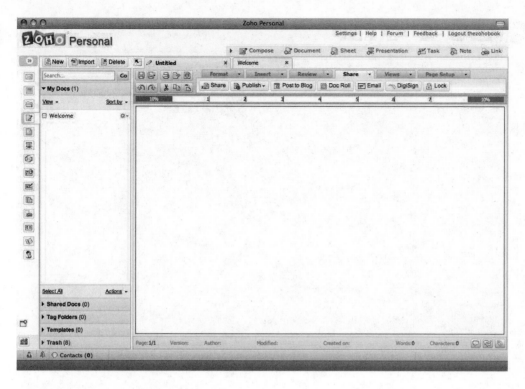

Figure 2-11. The Share tab

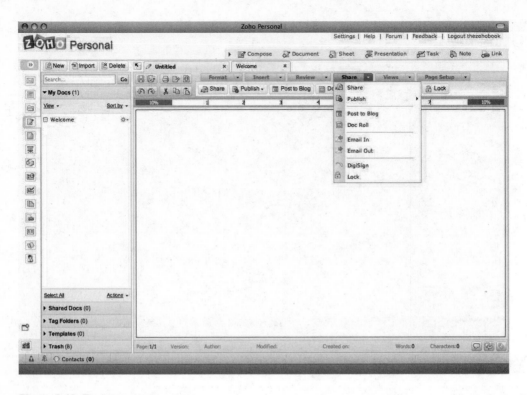

Figure 2-12. The `Share` menu

You can use the `Views` tab to see your documents in different views for different purposes when you are editing, previewing, or making them ready for print. There is even the option to see the document source in HTML too (Figures 2-13 and 2-14).

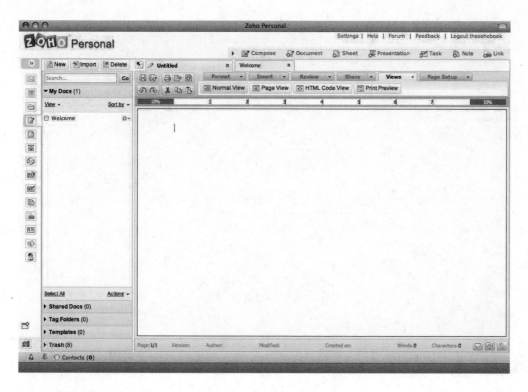

Figure 2-13. The Views tab

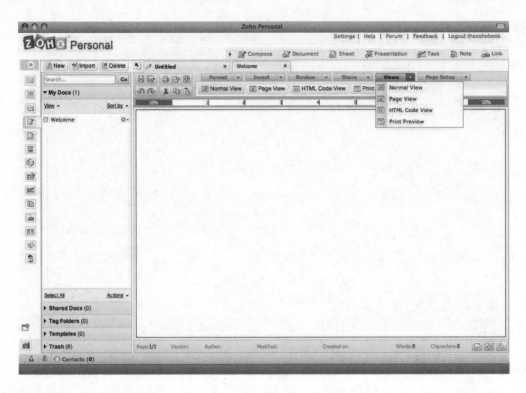

Figure 2-14. The **Views** menu

> *Writer is an online application, so it is quite normal to use HTML as the source language. If you usually won't deal with this feature, then you can totally skip it. However, advanced users can take a sneak peek at this later.*

Finally, the **Page Setup** tab holds the commands responsible for setting up every page of your document, be it adding headers and footers, changing the line height, or setting the page format and layout (Figures 2-15 and 2-16).

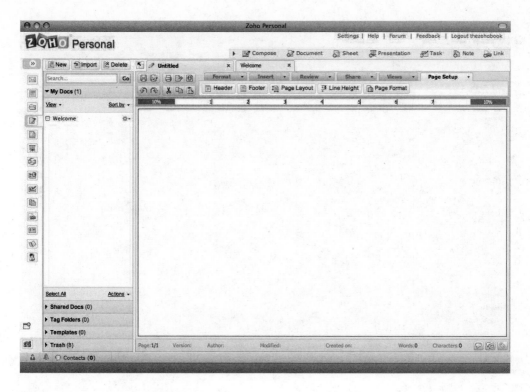

Figure 2-15. The `Page Setup` tab

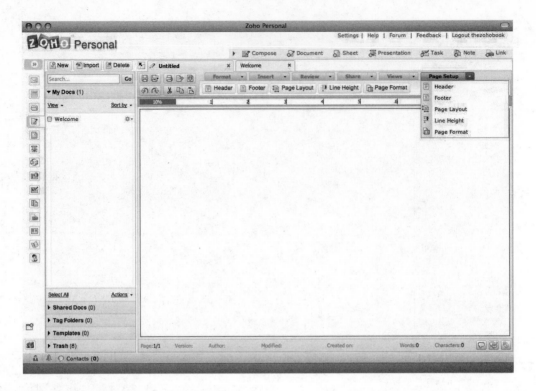

Figure 2-16. The `Page Setup` menu

Now that you are familiar with the basics of the environment, you'll create your very first document in Writer, and you will learn the rest in practice.

Working with documents

Writer is all about processing words and creating documents. In this section, you'll create a new document and use the different tools available to make it look professional.

To make it easier to follow, let's suppose you are working on a short report for your company, a client, or a school. It features formatted text, headings, figures, and a few more elements.

Creating your first document

When you first open Writer, there is only one document put there by the Zoho team, named `Welcome`, for you to get a glimpse of its features. Let's let it be and start creating your own document.

To create a new document, follow these steps:

1. Click `New` on the top of the sidebar. A blank document opens named `Untitled`.

2. Although Writer will save **Untitled** automatically (to keep the information if anything goes wrong), it is a good idea to save the document right now. Click **Save** (to the right of the **MenuTab**).

3. In the **Save** dialog box, enter **Test 1**, and click **Save** (Figure 2-17).

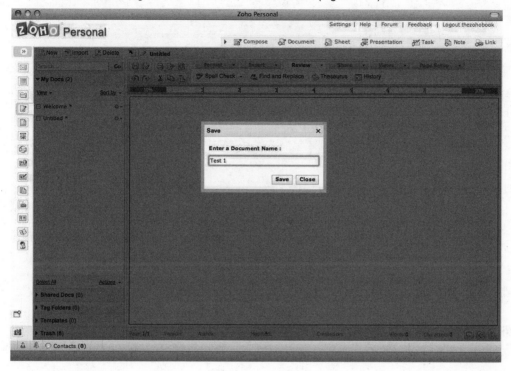

Figure 2-17. Saving your document

4. Start typing a few paragraphs (Figure 2-18). You can insert some dummy text from anywhere. A good place to get dummy text is www.lipsum.org.

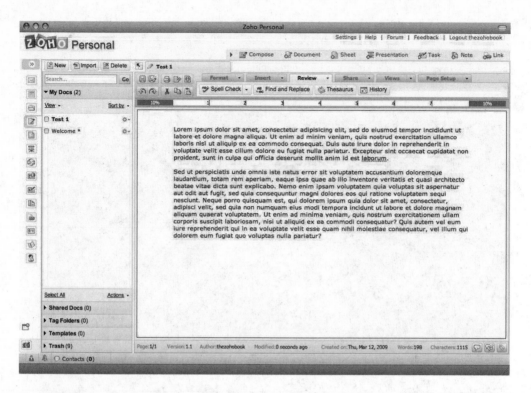

Figure 2-18. A simple document

5. Save the document occasionally while you type.

You'll notice that when you change the document content (even by adding a single character), a star appears in front of the document name. It shows that the document has been autosaved to protect you from data loss in case you forget to save the changed document manually.

Looking at the results, it is not as impressive as we want them to be. You need to format the document. But before that, let's take a closer look at the editor.

There is a ruler on top of the editor to help you when you are working with the document.

There is also a status bar below the editor reporting important information about the document. Now that you have entered some text, you can see the number of words and characters of the document so far. It also shows when the document was created and how long ago (in minutes) it was modified.

You might notice the version number too. Writer starts a document at version 1.0 and adds to the version number (by 0.1) each time you save the document. So, if you save it six times, the version will be 1.6. Versioning is an important part of Writer, and you will be using it more in this chapter.

On the right side of the status bar there are three buttons: `Collaborators`, `Contextual Comments`, and `Tags`. Keep them in mind for now until you see some of them in action later.

Formatting the document

Let's get back to your document; you need to make it look good and easier to read:

1. With the document (`Test 1`) open, add a heading to the document by inserting a line in the first paragraph, `Test Report`.
2. With the cursor on the first line, select `Format` ▸ —format— ▸ `Heading 1` in the `MenuTab`. This changes the style of the first line to `Heading 1`.
3. Below the heading, insert another row, and type `Introduction`.
4. Format it as `Heading 2` by selecting `Format` ▸ —format— ▸ `Heading 2` in the `MenuTab` (Figure 2-19).

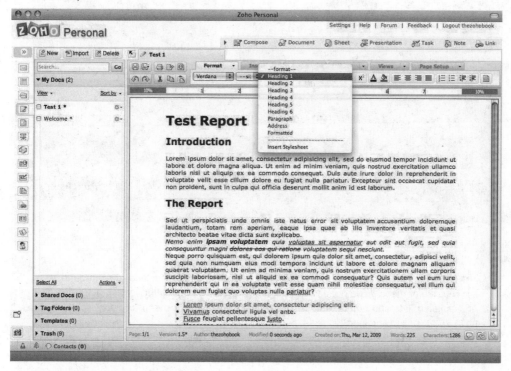

Figure 2-19. Formatting the main heading

5. Create one more heading after one or two paragraphs, and type `The Report`. Then format it as `Heading 2`.
6. Align all of the paragraphs by selecting them all and selecting `Format` ▸ `Justify Full` in the `MenuTab`.

7. The paragraph lines feel compressed. To fix this, adjust the line height by selecting a paragraph. Then select `Page Setup` ▶ `Line Height` (in the `MenuTab`) to open the `Line Spacing` dialog box.

8. Select `Single` in `Line Spacing`, and click `Close` (Figure 2-20).

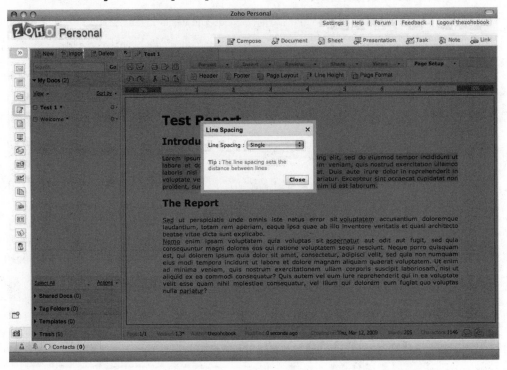

Figure 2-20. Changing the line spacing

9. Try changing the format of a few words to bold, italic, underline, and strikethrough using the `Format` tab or menu. (You need to select the text before changing the format of it.)

10. Add bulleted lists and numbered lists from the `Format` tab or menu too. Just select `Format` ▶ `Bulleted List`, and start typing in the list.

11. Change the text color of the first item in the bulleted list to red. Click `Format` ▶ `Font Color` to open the color mixer, and select red (Figure 2-21).

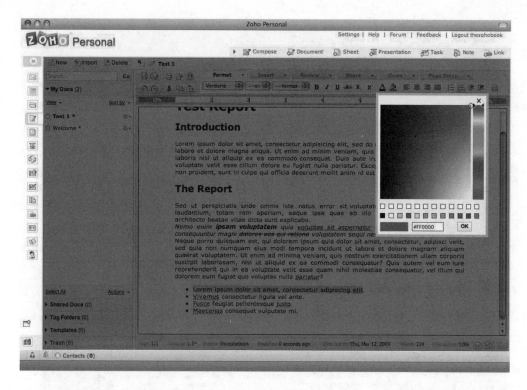

Figure 2-21. Changing the font color

    12. Click OK to proceed and then save the document.

Adding more document elements

Text documents are very common. Most letters, essays, novels, and other types of documents are just pages of formatted text. However, your report needs some eye candy to sell your idea to the audience (well, the imaginary audience for now!).

Adding an image

Visual elements such as images play an important role in transferring the right message to the reader (audience) and creating a professional outcome. You can insert as many images as you need in a word processing document. All major formats (PNG, JPG, GIF, and so on) are supported, but be careful not to insert big files (I recommend a maximum of 1MB) because it makes the documents slower to work with.

Now let's add an image to the document:

    1. In the `MenuTab`, select `Insert ▶ Insert Image`.

    2. In the `Insert Image` dialog box, browse for a file from your computer, or type in a web URL to import the image. It might take a few seconds for the image to load.

You can get the image used in this example from
www.thezohobook.com/files/morocco.jpg.

3. Set the other options as displayed in Figure 2-22.

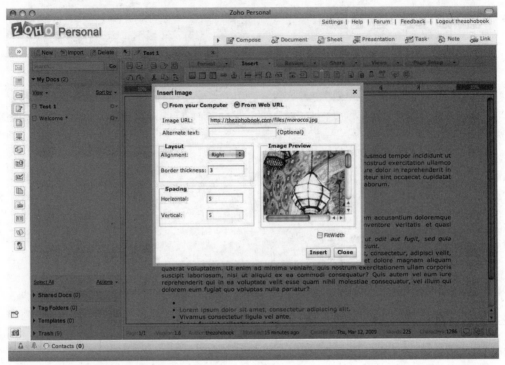

Figure 2-22. Inserting the image

4. Click **Insert** to proceed.
5. Move the image, by dragging and dropping it between text, so it is placed correctly in the document (Figure 2-23). You can also resize the image using the images handles (which appear when you click the image).

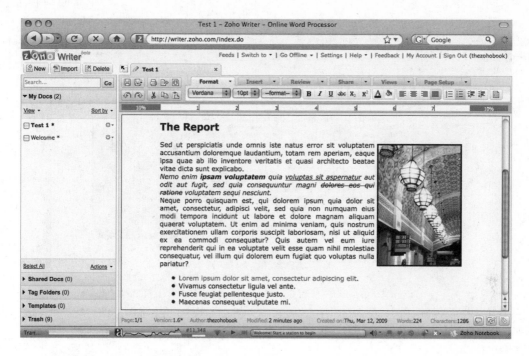

Figure 2-23. Placing the inserted image

Adding a table

I often add information in tabular format. Dates, numbers, or similar groups of information can be formatted in tables to make the document easier to read and more professional. That's where Writer tables come in handy.

To insert a table, follow these steps:

1. In the `MenuTab`, select `Insert ▶ Insert Table`.
2. Select two rows and four columns for the table by moving the mouse pointer on the cells. Then click to insert the table (Figure 2-24).

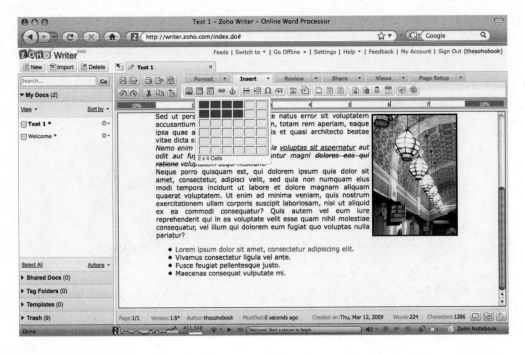

Figure 2-24. Inserting a table

3. In the table, type in the values for each cell. You can navigate through the cells with the keyboard arrow keys. Make it look like Figure 2-25.

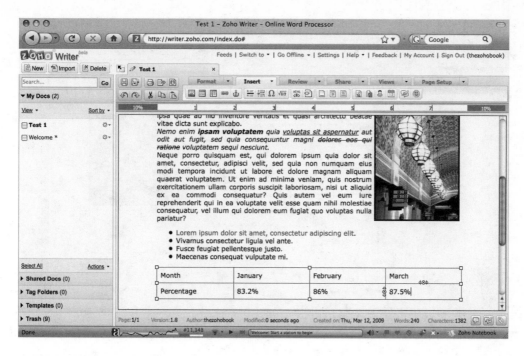

Figure 2-25. Filling in the cells

4. With the cursor on any cell in the first row, right-click to open the context menu.
5. Select **Table Operations ▶ Row Properties** (Figure 2-26).

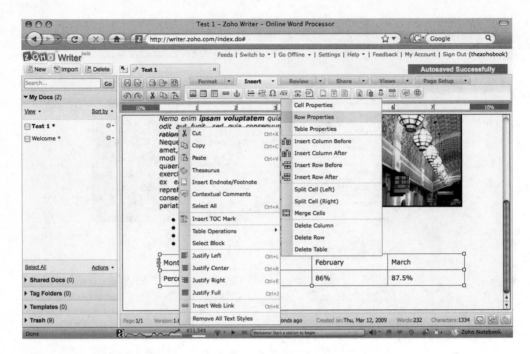

Figure 2-26. Editor context menu

6. In the **Row Properties** dialog box, click the **Background Color** box to open the color mixer.

7. Select a color (**#A9D4F2** here), and click **OK** (Figure 2-27). Then click **OK** in the **Row Properties** dialog box to apply the changes.

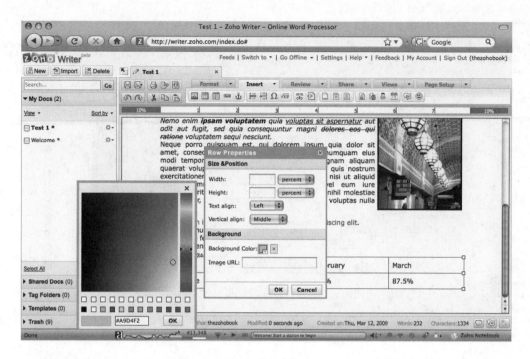

Figure 2-27. Changing the row color

8. Set the same color for the first cell of the second row too this time by selecting `Table Operations ▶ Cell Properties`.

9. Again right-click the table, and select `Table Operations ▶ Table Properties`.

10. In the `Table Properties` dialog box, select the `Table Border Theme` tab, and then select a new border style (Figure 2-28). Click `OK` to proceed.

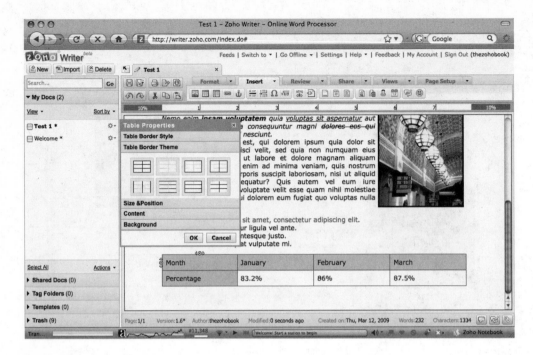

Figure 2-28. Drawing tables

11. To change the text formatting of the cells, select the text in the table (by dragging the mouse pointer or the arrow keys while holding the Shift key), and then change the font name, size, and color just like you do in the body text.

The final table should look like Figure 2-29.

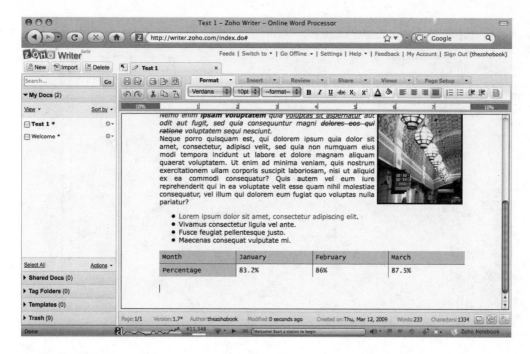

Figure 2-29. The finished table

Adding an equation

If you deal with science and technical writing, Writer allows you to add complex equations. It supports the standard LaTeX equations through an easy-to-use editor.

> *LaTeX is a document preparation system for high-quality typesetting. It is most often used for medium-to-large technical or scientific documents, but it can be used for almost any form of publishing. To learn more about LaTeX, check out* `www.latex-project.org/intro.html`.

To add an equation to the document, follow these steps:

1. Below the table, insert an equation by clicking selecting **Insert ▸ Equation Editor** in the **MenuTab**.

2. In **LaTeX Equation Editor**, select a sample by clicking **Sample Syntax** and copying the syntax of a sample equation (Figure 2-30).

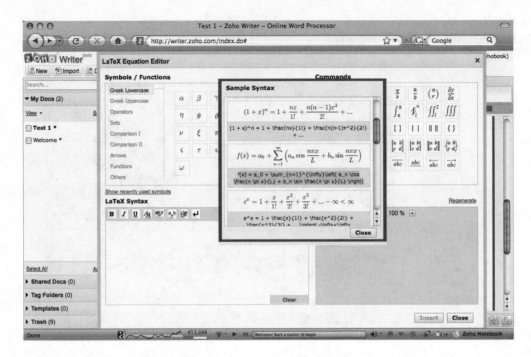

Figure 2-30. LaTeX equation editor

3. Paste the syntax into the **LaTeX Syntax** box to display the equation in the **Preview** pane (Figure 2-31). You can still change the formula by updating the contents of the **LaTeX Syntax** box.

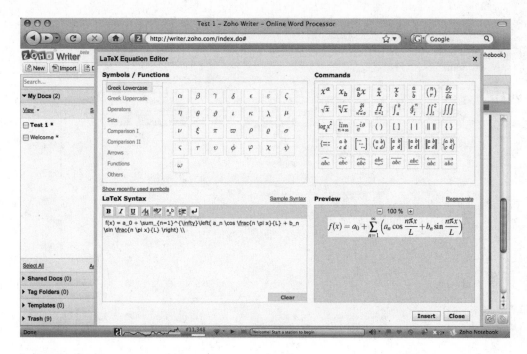

Figure 2-31. Previewing the equation

4. Click **Insert** to place the equation in the document.
5. Select **Format ▶ Justify Center** in the **MenuTab** to align it to the center (Figure 2-32).

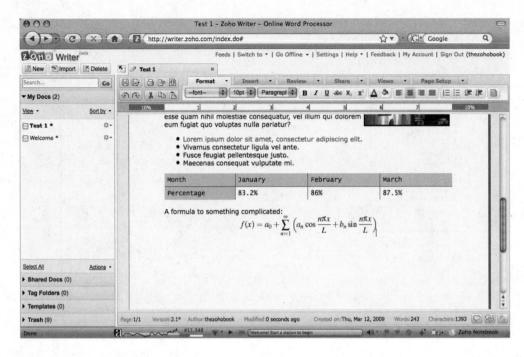

Figure 2-32. The equation in place

Adding endnotes and footnotes

When a document gets long enough, footnotes and endnotes come in handy; they provide the reader with extra, yet nondistracting, content. Footnotes are text appearing in the footer section of a page giving extra explanation, comments, or a reference for the text you created the footnote for. Endnotes do the same but appear at the end of the document.

Remember that after inserting them, footnotes and endnotes will not be visible in edit mode (while you edit the document). You will need to switch to the preview mode (**View ▶ Print Preview**) to check footnotes and endnotes.

To add a footnote to the document, follow these steps:

1. Add a new line right before the equation **A formula to something complicated:** (Figure 2-32).
2. Select the **formula** portion, and select **Insert ▶ Insert Endnote/Footnote** in the **MenuTab**.
3. Select **Footnote** in the **Insert Footnote** dialog box, and type in the **Note** area, as you see in Figure 2-33. Then click **Insert** to proceed.

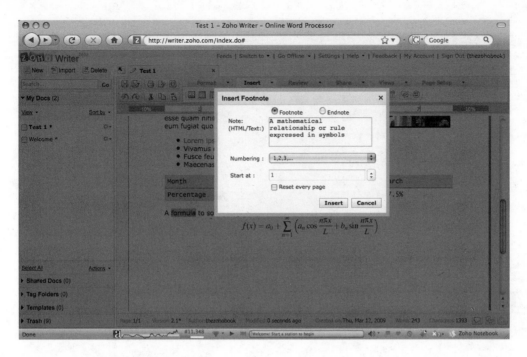

Figure 2-33. Adding a footnote

4. Check the footnote by selecting **Views ▶ Print Preview** in the **MenuTab** (Figure 2-34). Then click **Go back to Editor** to return to editing mode.

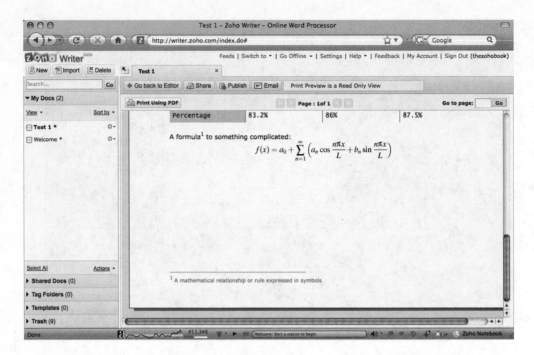

Figure 2-34. Previewing the footnote in print view

Adding a hyperlink

It is worth noting that you can add hyperlinks to documents. Once a reader clicks a link in your document, the destination URL will open in a new browser window (or tab).

To add a link to your report, follow these steps:

1. Add a new line, and type **References:**. Then in the next line, increase the indent (by selecting **Format ▸ Increase Indent** in the **MenuTab**), and type www.lipsum.org.

2. Select the URL (www.lipsum.org), and select **Insert ▸ Insert/Modify Link** in the **MenuTab** to add a hyperlink to the selected text.

3. In the **Insert Link** dialog box, enter the **URL** (http://www.lipsum.org), and then click **Insert** to create the link (Figure 2-35).

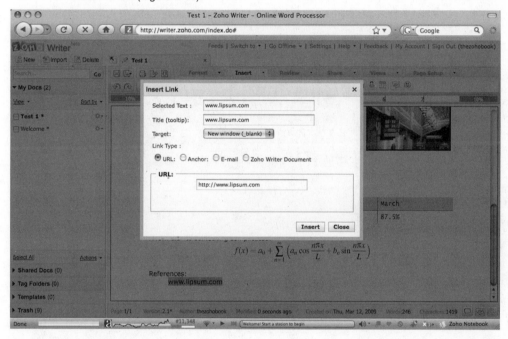

Figure 2-35. Adding a link

4. Save the document.

Printing

I'm not a printing advocate, and I always try not to print unless it is really (I mean really) necessary! But there are times you can't skip printing a document on paper.

Writer, like any other advanced word processor, offers printing facilities. However, since it is a cloud-based application and actually runs through your web browser, it uses the standard printing interface of the browser. This might cause unexpected content to appear on the printout, such as the headers and footers of the browser.

The best way to print in Writer is to print the document to PDF (a simple export) and then print the PDF on actual paper. You can also send the PDF via e-mail from within Writer.

Formatting the page

Before we go through the print process, it is good to check the page settings and add a footer to every page. Headers and footers are useful sections that appear on every page, in which you can add text and images such as your company logo or your address.

1. Select **Insert ▶ Footer** (or **Page Setup ▶ Footer**) in the **MenuTab**.
2. In the **Insert Footer** dialog box, **select Blank-Two Column**, and then click **Insert** (Figure 2-36).

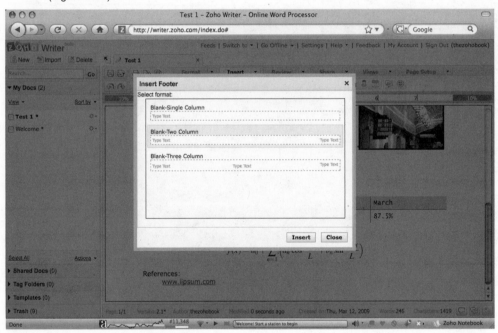

Figure 2-36. Choosing the footer type

3. In the **Footer** box in the bottom of the page, type in Testing Zoho Writer in the left column.
4. Click the right column in the footer, and select **Insert ▶ Insert Auto Field ▶ Insert Page Number** in the **MenuTab** (Figure 2-37).

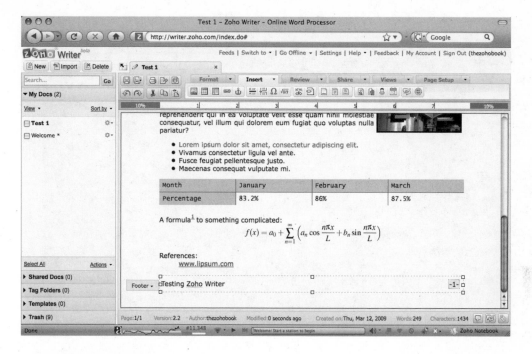

Figure 2-37. Adding a link

5. Select **Page Setup ▸ Page Layout** in the **MenuTab** to set the proper layout for your document. You can choose from different paper sizes and set the page orientation too (Figure 2-38). When you are done, click **Apply** to proceed.

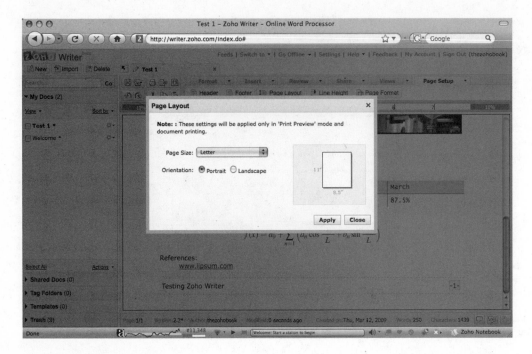

Figure 2-38. Setting the page layout

Printing via PDF

Your document is now ready to be printed, but as I mentioned before, via PDF export. Simply select **Views ▸ Print Preview ▸ Print Using PDF** in the **MenuTab** (Figure 2-39).

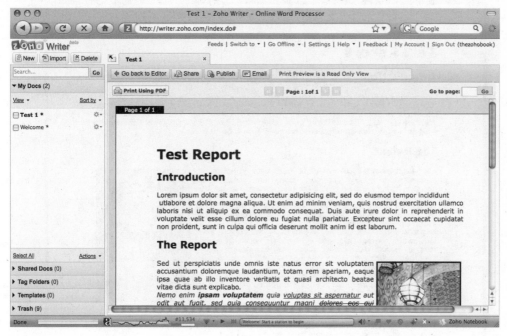

Figure 2-39. Print preview

Based on your browser settings, it might open the PDF file right away or ask you to confirm a download first. After opening the downloaded PDF, you can easily print it and be sure that the output is as you want it to be (Figure 2-40).

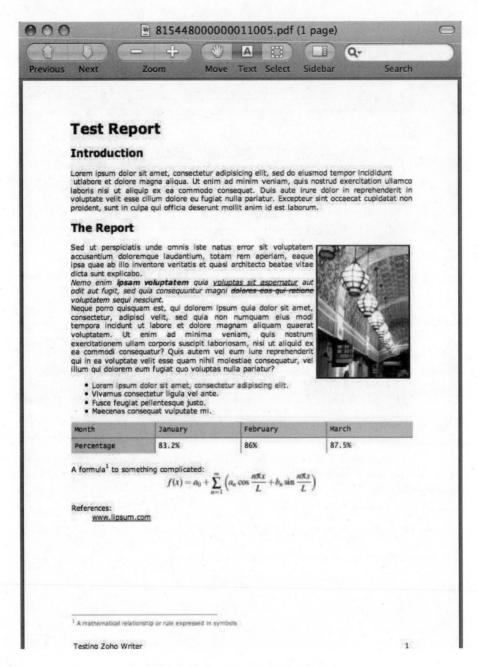

Figure 2-40. Downloaded PDF document

To use PDF files, your computer has to be able to open them. Mac and most Linux users have it already installed. But for Windows users, if you can't open the downloaded PDF document, you need to download and install Adobe Acrobat Reader from `http://get.adobe.com/reader/`.

Sharing and collaborating

One of the greatest aspects of working on the cloud is the ability to share your work with friends and colleagues in a snap and to collaborate "live." You might say, well, what's wrong with the old way? Let me tell you!

In the traditional way, you have to create a document in a word processor on your computer (Word, Pages, and so on) and then send it (for example, by e-mail) to your co-workers to comment on or amend the contents.

These are three of the most important disadvantages of doing it the traditional way:

- It is by nature a slow process to send and receive the files even on the fastest connections. You need to send it first and then wait for the update to be sent back to you. It is not happening in real time (live).
- Keeping track of the different versions of the documents is a hard and error-prone process. Collaborators usually end up having different versions of every document on their local systems. Using tools like CSV or Subversion for this purpose is, in the other hand, simply overkill!
- There is almost no control over read/write permissions of the documents you send and receive unless you password-protect them or just export them as PDF.

Once you see there is a better way to overcome these issues, you will never look back!

Giving public access to documents

Writer allows you to share documents with the world in a breeze.

Suppose you have done some research that you would like to share with everybody so people can read it and give their feedback. The only thing you need to do is to make the document public:

1. Open the document you want to make public, and select **Share ▶ Publish ▶ Make Public** in the `MenuTab`.
2. In the `Public Share` dialog box, read the message, and click **Publish** to proceed (Figure 2-41).

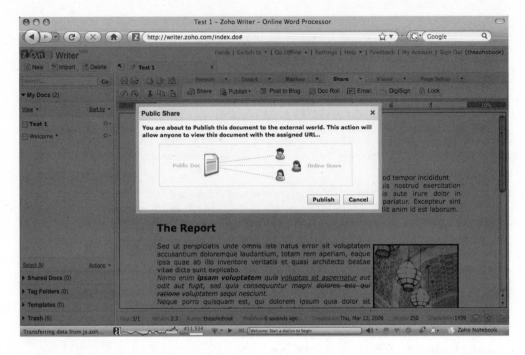

Figure 2-41. Making the document public

3. On the next screen (Figure 2-42), click the link to the public document (`Test-1` here leads to `http://writer.zoho.com/public/thezohobook/Test-1`) to see how it looks like for others. You can also tell **Writer** to **Allow others to give comments** or not.

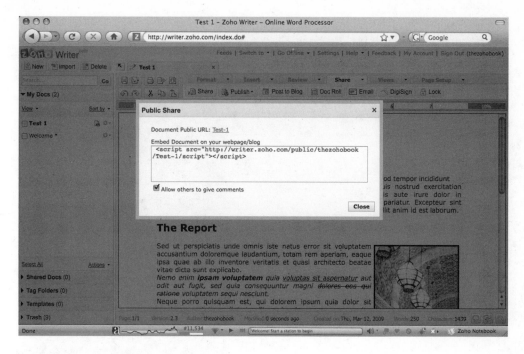

Figure 2-42. Links to the shared document

4. Click **Close** when you are done.

As mentioned, you can just publish the link (URL) of the shared document or embed it in a web page, using the code snippet provided, for the viewers to read the document and leave comments. They can also read others' comments, download the document in different formats (DOC, SXW, PDF, ODF, RTF, TXT, HTML), send it by e-mail, and check the latest version by subscribing to the available RSS feed.

You can cancel the public status of the document by selecting **Share ▶ Publish ▶ Cancel Public Sharing** in the **MenuTab** at any time.

Sharing documents

When working as a team, be it with your colleagues, classmates, or friends, Writer offers you easy-to-use tools to share your documents within the team in a manageable fashion. Collaboration will be a seamless process where you can give others permission to read the document or to be able to update it too. All updates are being registered, and you can easily take control of different versions.

The share process starts with inviting the people. Here's how:

1. Open the document you want to share, and select **Share ▶ Share** in the **MenuTab**.

2. In the **Share This Document** dialog box, there are two boxes on the **Invite** tab: **Read Only Members** and **Read/Write Members**. Choose **Read/Write Members** to specify the people who are allowed to update your document (Figure 2-43).

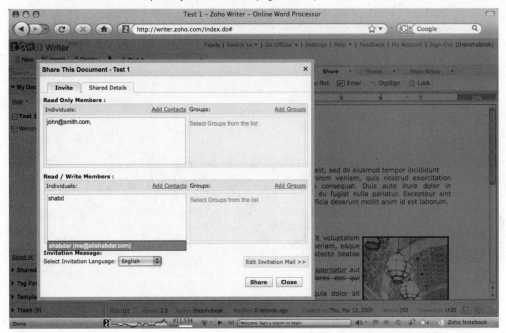

Figure 2-43. Sharing a document with specific people

> *This is where you set access levels for different people. For example, if you want two of your marketing colleagues to contribute to the content but only one of the salespeople to be able to read the document, you need to put the marketers in* **Read/Write Members** *and the salesperson in the* **Read Only Members**.

3. Enter the e-mail address or the Zoho username of the individuals you want to invite. You should separate multiple invitees with comma. You can also invite from the people in your Zoho Contacts (will be covered later in this book) by clicking **Add Contact**, right above the box.

> *If the people you invite don't have Zoho account, they will be directed to the sign-up page in order to create an account before accessing the content.*

4. Customize the invitation e-mail by clicking **Edit Invitation Email >>** so the invitees get a clearer picture of what the message is about (Figure 2-44).

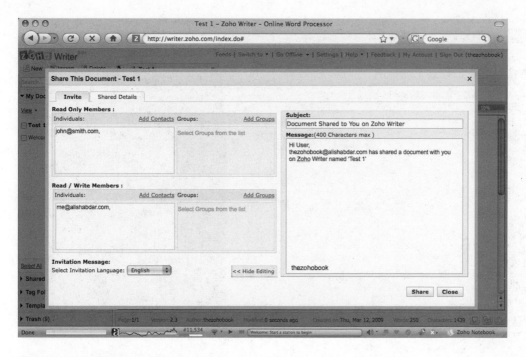

Figure 2-44. Editing the invitation e-mail

5. Click **Share** to dispatch the invitations. Your document is officially shared! The **Shared Details** tab will open automatically for you to check the status of the members as well as being able to change their membership status. You can also remove them from the list (Figure 2-45).

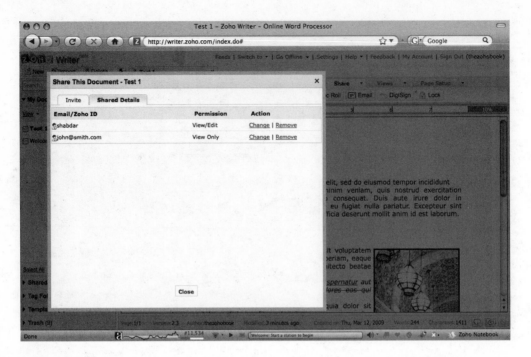

Figure 2-45. Shared details

    6.   Close the dialog box when you are finished checking the list.

Now, every invitee is going to receive an invitation e-mail (similar to Figure 2-46) that contains a link back to the document you just shared in step 5.

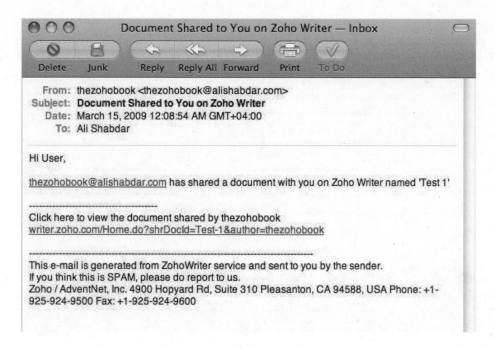

From: thezohobook <thezohobook@alishabdar.com>
Subject: **Document Shared to You on Zoho Writer**
Date: March 15, 2009 12:08:54 AM GMT+04:00
To: Ali Shabdar

Hi User,

thezohobook@alishabdar.com has shared a document with you on Zoho Writer named 'Test 1'

Click here to view the document shared by thezohobook
writer.zoho.com/Home.do?shrDocId=Test-1&author=thezohobook

This e-mail is generated from ZohoWriter service and sent to you by the sender.
If you think this is SPAM, please do report to us.
Zoho / AdventNet, Inc. 4900 Hopyard Rd, Suite 310 Pleasanton, CA 94588, USA Phone: +1-925-924-9500 Fax: +1-925-924-9600

Figure 2-46. The invitation e-mail

Collaborating in action

The aim of sharing documents is to be able to collaborate and work on the content as a team. Collaborators can view (read) the document and post comments, or they can add to or modify the content if they have write permission. Working in such manner needs a paradigm shift from the way you used to work with word processors to what Writer offers you now.

When you share a document, collaborators will have your document listed in their `Shared Docs` list (on the sidebar), making it easier for them to get access to it any time.

Keep the following important points in mind when working on shared documents:

- When you open a shared document, either yours or one shared to you, if a message appears for a moment saying `'USERNAME' is currently editing this document 'DOCUMENT'. Entering shared edit mode...` (where `USERNAME` is the user who currently has the document open and `DOCUMENT` is the document name), it means you are entering collaborating mode (Figure 2-47).

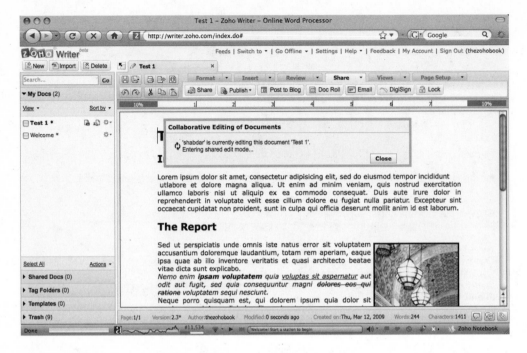

Figure 2-47. Entering collaborating mode

- In collaborating mode, you (or any other collaborator) can lock/unlock a shared document to make sure others do not edit it while you are working on it. To lock a shared document while editing, just select **Share ▸ Lock** in the **MenuTab**. Click it again to unlock the document.

- When multiple users are collaborating on the same document, to avoid possible issues, only one user at a time can update a block (for example, a paragraph), making it read-only for the others. The background color of that particular block also changes (turns light yellow by default) to show other collaborators that it is being modified at the moment (Figure 2-48).

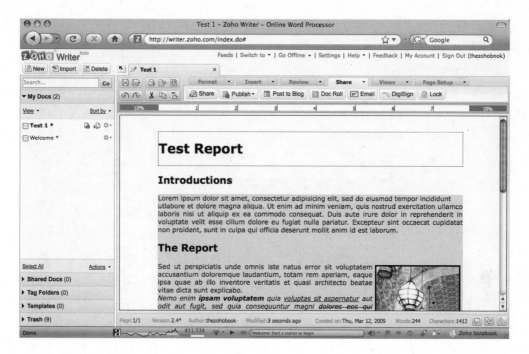

Figure 2-48. Uneditable block

- You can still work on the other parts of the document that are not made read-only.
- When each of the collaborators saves their modifications, Writer increases the document version (for example, from 1.6 to 1.7). This is very good to track the changes. You can revert to an older version or compare two different versions to see what changes were applied to the document from one version to another. This is made possible by selecting **Review ▶ History** in the **MenuTab** (Figure 2-49).

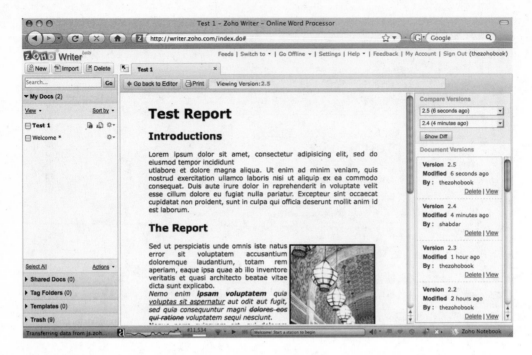

Figure 2-49. Checking the different versions of the document

Doing more with Writer

Writer makes it easy and fun to work with documents and stay productive. But that's not all—there are other features to be discussed.

The rest of this chapter will show you some other features of Writer that will come in handy in day-to-day work.

Dumping your trash

Just like any other trash can, `Trash` on the sidebar holds your dumped documents. To empty the trash can, just open `Trash` on the left pane, and click `Empty Trash`. Those documents are gone forever! So, be careful using it.

On the other hand, if you trashed a document by accident or you just happened to need it again, simply click the document in the `Trash`, and click `Restore` on the top of the document (Figure 2-50).

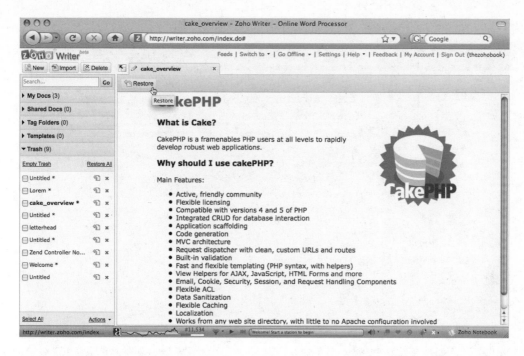

Figure 2-50. Trash can with restore option

Alternatively, you can click **Restore** (the green arrow) or **Delete From Trash** (the red **x**) right next to each item in the trash can. Also, you can select multiple files to remove or restore in one batch.

Using templates

We often use specific formats of documents multiple times. Letters, invoices, meeting agendas, and letterheads are among those documents. Templates define a general format for specific documents and let you use it many times. It is like having scaffolding for a quick start.

For example, you can create a letterhead template and use it for all your official documents without going through adding the logo, address, and other basics every single time. Also, it avoids possible mistakes such as having wrong phone numbers on an invoice header. Using templates is a step forward toward productivity in work and is highly recommended.

Creating new templates

Writer allows you to create new templates as well as import from a collection of online templates made by the Writer community.

To create a new template, follow these steps:

1. Create a new document, and enter the content you want to appear in the template.

2. Click **Save As**, and save it as template, as shown in Figure 2-51.

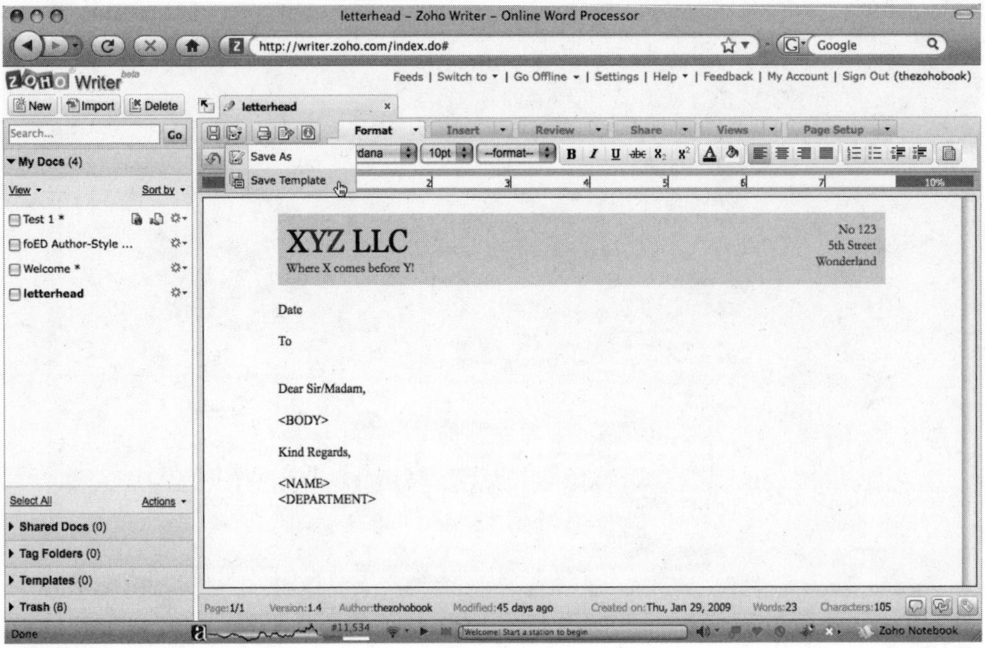

Figure 2-51. Saving the document as a template

3. In the **Save As Template** dialog box, enter a meaningful name for the template for a better reference. Click **OK** to continue (Figure 2-52).

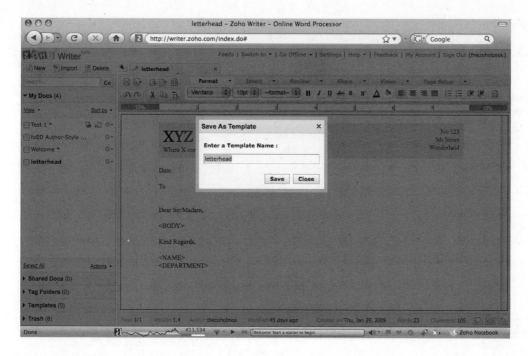

Figure 2-52. Saving the template

As you can see in Figure 2-53, Writer lists the newly made template in the `Templates` list (on the left pane).

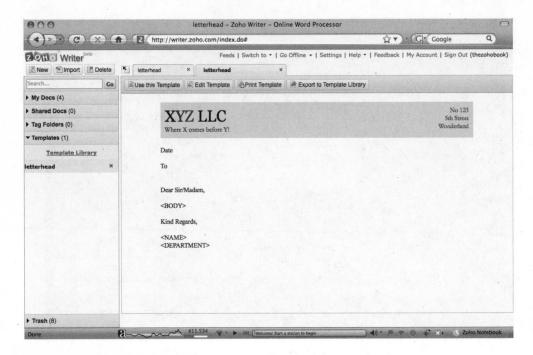

Figure 2-53. Previewing the template

> *If you wonder what <BODY> or <NAME> stands for in the text demonstrated in Figure 2-53, it is just simple text, not some mysterious code! It is a placeholder I made up for the people who use the template to know where to place specific content.*

To use the template, open it, and then click `Use this Template` in the menu bar. Writer will create a new document based on the template.

Using the Zoho Template Library

You can also submit your templates to the `Template Library` to share it with the world. Apart from spreading useful contents with others, there are many good reasons for making your templates available in the library.

Suppose you are a teacher and you want your students to submit their essays in a specific format. Just create a template based on your preferred format and submit it to the library. Then inform your students to download and use it. They can later share their essays with you as a collaborator, and you can comment on their content. No need for endless e-mails back and forth. This is the new age of productivity!

To add a template to the `Template Library`, follow these steps:

1. Open the template you want to share, and click `Export to Temple Library`.
2. Fill in the `Template Name`, `Template Type`, and `Description` fields (Figure 2-54).

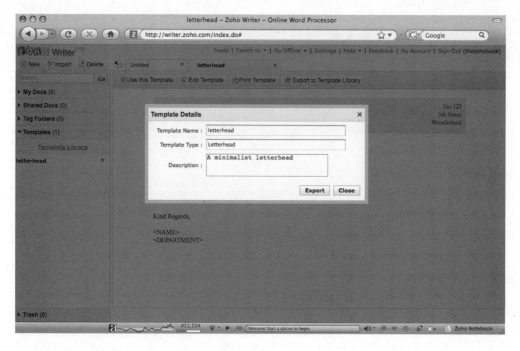

Figure 2-54. Exporting to the `Temple Library`

3. Click **Export** to proceed. Your template is loaded in the library for everybody to use.
4. Close the dialog box to finish the task.

Now let's see how you can import others' templates into Writer so you can save even more time by using ready-made templates.

To import a template from `Template Library`, follow these steps:

1. Click `Temple Library` in the `Templates` pane in the sidebar. The library opens (Figure 2-55).

Figure 2-55. `Template Library` home

2. Find a template you like, and click **Add to my templates** next to the template (Figure 2-56).

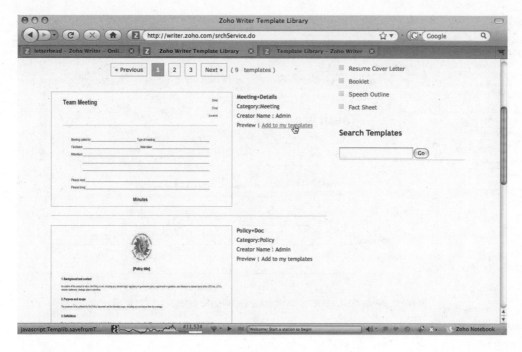

Figure 2-56. Adding a template to Writer from the `Template Library`

3. Go back to the templates list in Writer, and click the title (`Templates`) to refresh the list (Figure 2-57). You can now start using the template.

Figure 2-57. Imported template, ready to use

Working off the cloud

One of the letdowns of working online could be that you need to be online all the time to be able to work. This is generally not an issue these days with Wi-Fi and 3G networks available almost everywhere. But still there are times that you are not connected, like when your plane (your private jet, let's say!) is about to take off or there is no Internet connection during the flight (if you fly economy like me!).

This might mean that you won't be able to use other online applications, but not with Writer! There is a nice feature that you can take Writer offline and work on your documents when there is no Internet connection. You can even have offline access to the documents shared with you.

> *As you might remember from Chapter 1, you installed Google Gears in order to enable Zoho offline facilities. If you didn't do this, please go to Chapter 1, and follow the instructions to install it first.*

To enable the offline mode, follow these steps:

1. In Writer (not available in Zoho Personal), click `Go Offline` in the link bar.
2. If `Offline Download Settings` appears, set how many documents and shared documents you need to have available offline, and click OK to proceed (Figure 2-58).

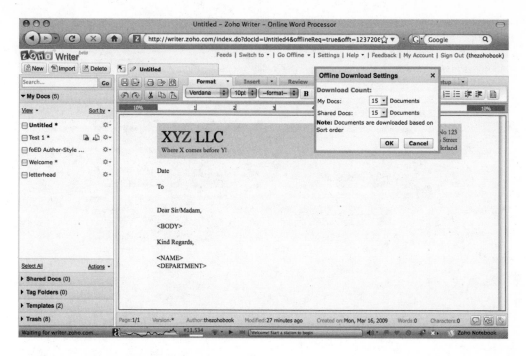

Figure 2-58. Offline download settings

3. If the `Gears` confirmation window appears, check `I trust this site`. Click `Allow` to go to the next step (Figure 2-59).

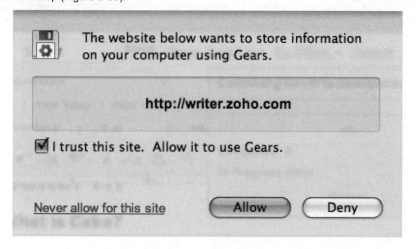

Figure 2-59. Gears confirmation dialog box

> *Figure 2-59 might look different on your computer, but the concept is same. You need to give permission to Gears and Zoho to work with each other.*

4. Wait until it downloads all documents for offline access (Figure 2-60). Then it goes to offline mode.

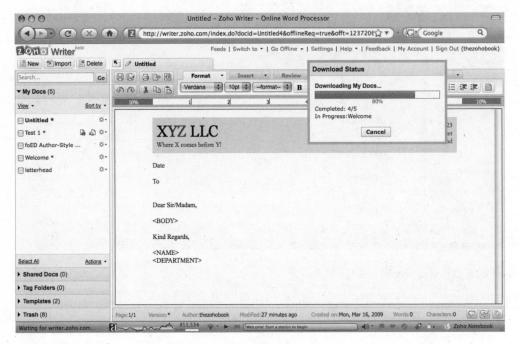

Figure 2-60. Downloading documents for the offline mode

Once offline, you'll notice a box on top of the screen saying `You are Offline`. Pay attention to the URL, which changes to `http://writer.zoho.com/offline` (Figure 2-61).

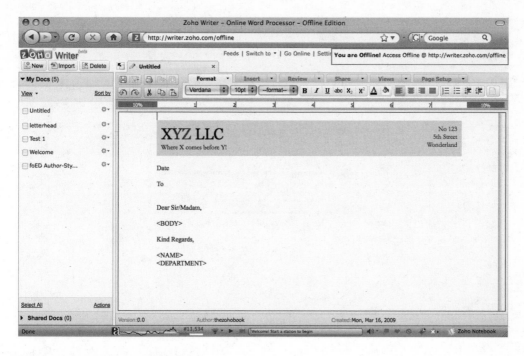

Figure 2-61. Working in offline mode

You can now disconnect from the Internet and keep on working on your documents. You can also save changes you make in the documents. Later when you go online, Zoho will automatically synchronize the documents with the online versions.

To take Writer online, all you need to do is click `Go Online` on the link bar. If there is unsaved content, you need to click `Save and Proceed` when asked (Figure 2-62).

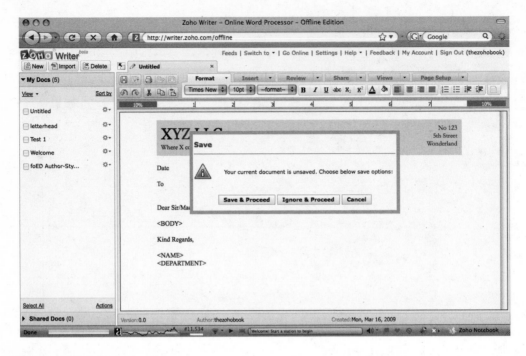

Figure 2-62. Going back online

Setting up feeds

Feeds show a brief but useful set of information about what has been shared with you and with whom you are collaborating. It is a history of your major collaborative actions. Note that these entries will not appear for the documents you own and will show only the ones shared with you (Figure 2-63).

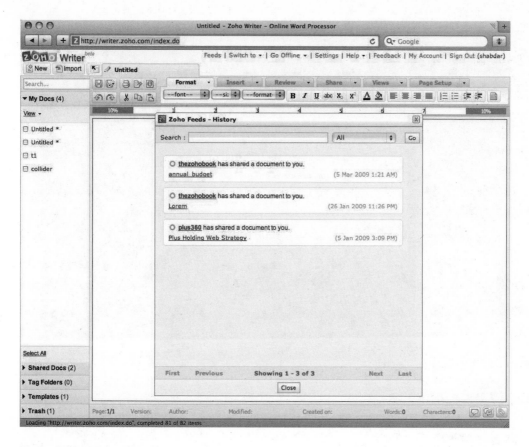

Figure 2-63. Feeds history

Changing some settings

You may do some general customizations by clicking `Settings` on the link bar.

You can change the default spell checker language as well as the default document view. There is also an option for opening each document on a new page and allowing comments for the public documents (Figure 2-64).

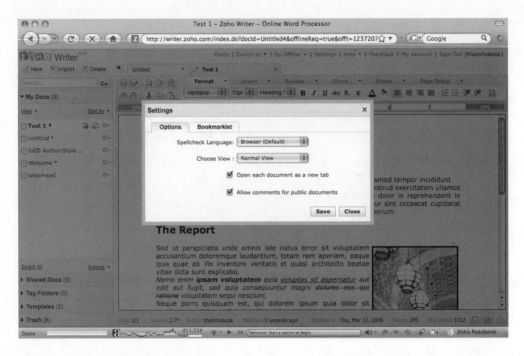

Figure 2-64. `Settings` dialog box

Note that you can still change all of these settings per each document. This is just to set the defaults.

> *Options feeds and offline access are not accessible via Zoho Personal, and you need to directly log on to Writer at* writer.zoho.com. *The Zoho people say that Zoho Personal provides a lighter version of Writer and other applications for now, but they are going to bring these minor missing features into Zoho Personal very soon.*

Using keyboard shortcuts

Keyboard shortcuts are always time-savers. Using the keyboard instead of the mouse helps reduce the risk of repetitive wrist syndromes that are common with people who excessively use computers.

Here is the list of essential keyboard shortcuts you can use in Writer:

- *Ctrl+A*: Select All
- *Ctrl+S*: Save
- Ctrl+X: Cut
- *Ctrl+C*: Copy
- *Ctrl+V*: Paste
- *Ctrl+F*: Find
- *Ctrl+B*: Bold Text

- *Ctrl+I*: Italicize Text
- *Ctrl+U*: Underline Text
- *Ctrl+L*: Justify Left
- *Ctrl+E*: Justify Center
- *Ctrl+R*: Justify Right
- *Ctrl+J*: Justify Full
- *Ctrl+Z*: Undo
- *Ctrl+Y*: Redo
- *Ctrl+K*: Add/Modify Link
- *Ctrl+Home*: Top of the Document
- *Ctrl+End*: End of the Document
- *Shift+arrow keys*: Selects content in a document

Getting help

Writer is very easy to use, but there are times that you won't find the quickest answer by yourself, and using some help will come in handy.

The first stop, as mentioned in Chapter 1, is the Zoho Forums. Writer has a dedicated forum at `http://forums.zoho.com/Zoho-Writer` where you can search for answers and ask your questions.

On the other hand, now that you are a Writer expert, you can help others with their questions too!

The other option is to check Writer-related posts in the Zoho blog at `blogs.zoho.com/category/writer`. I highly recommend checking blogs occasionally or even subscribing to the RSS feed since there are interesting tips and tricks discussed there.

Summary

In this chapter, you learned how to use Writer as your primary word processor application. By practicing more, soon you will appreciate the qualities Writer provides you with, such as the following:

- You have 100 percent freedom with the many formats available to import from and export to.
- Using sharing and collaboration tools you can increase your (and your co-workers') productivity dramatically. Templates are such time-savers too.
- Offline features, on the other hand, will allow you to work with no interruption.

I don't have time here to discuss every single feature of Writer in this chapter, but now that you know all the basics and many of the advanced features, you are ready to start your journey.

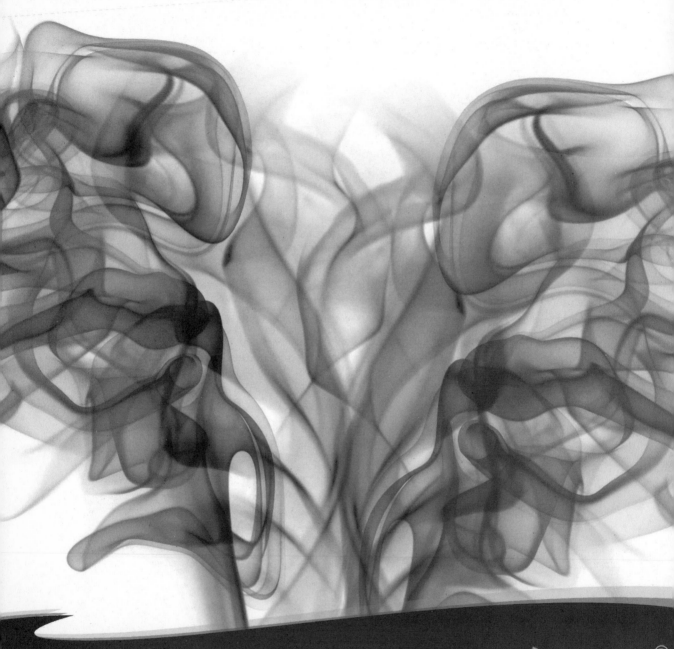

ZOHO®

Work. Online

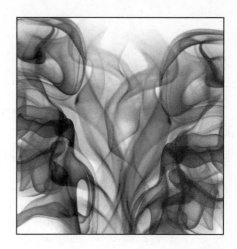

Chapter 3

Of Numbers and Sheets

Not long time ago, people used to struggle with ledger books to keep their accounts in order. It was a big hassle to hand-write all those numbers and make manual calculations at the end of each page and each book, not to mention that human mistakes led to even more headaches fixing and recalculating the values.

Spreadsheets saved us from the dark ages by resembling the very same tables of ledger books in computer-based files with many more features and 100 percent calculation accuracy.

Businesspeople, accountants, scientists, scholars, students, and anybody who deals with some sort of tabular data needs to use spreadsheets at some point, if not regularly.

> *Check Wikipedia at en.wikipedia.org/wiki/Spreadsheet to read about the history of computer-based spreadsheets.*

All said, you are here to see how Zoho helps you take this essential application to the next level. It is a cloud-based solution, similar to Writer, called Zoho Sheet, and it provides you with what you'd expect from a professional spreadsheet application, and even more.

Getting started

Sheet is a spreadsheet application that offers most of the features you expect from a professional package. In addition, Sheet allows you to do the following:

- Access data from anywhere, since it is hosted in the cloud.
- Create, edit, and access your spreadsheets from anywhere. No installation is required.
- Share data instead of attaching it to your e-mails.
- Collaborate with friends, colleagues, and so on.
- Allow multiple users to work on a spreadsheet simultaneously.
- Import data from existing files, and export it to many different formats in a breeze.
- Employ VBA macros and pivot tables to maximize flexibility.
- Sync with remote data on the Web or use the available APIs to build mashups.

> A **mashup** is a web application (often presented in a web page) that consists of two or more pieces of other web applications. These pieces usually integrate with each other to give a unified user experience. For instance, placing Google Maps and a Sheet document on a single web page to help users find the address of the places listed in the map is actually a mashup.

If some of these points look strange to you, don't worry. Just keep reading to see what Sheet has for you under the hood.

The environment

Open Sheet by visiting `http://sheet.zoho.com`, or run it from within Zoho Personal.

If you have ever used spreadsheet software such as Microsoft Excel or Apple Numbers before, you pretty much know how to get started with Sheet. Figure 3-1 shows Sheet running in Zoho Personal, and Figure 3-2 shows it running as a stand-alone application.

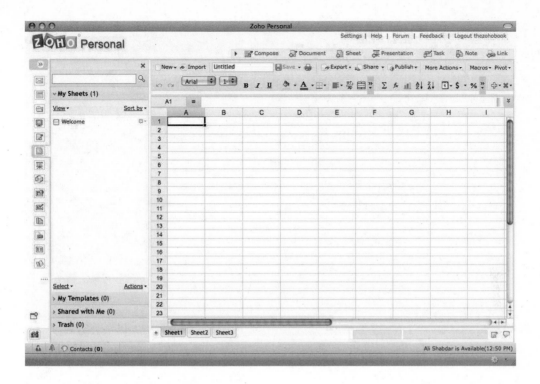

Figure 3-1. Sheet's window in Zoho Personal

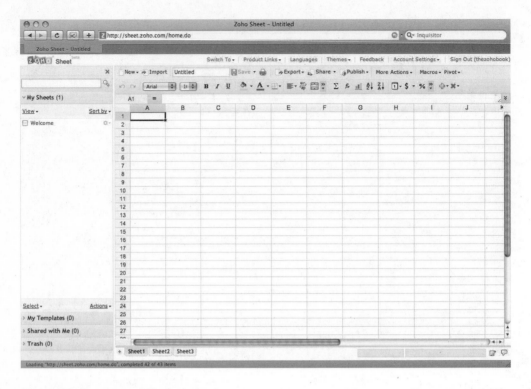

Figure 3-2. Sheet's stand-alone window

The overall environment is similar to Writer, which you saw in Chapter 2, and since you run it from within Zoho Personal, you'll see some common features between the two.

Sheets

Basically, you insert information into **sheets** (shown in Figure 3-3) in which every data entity (a **value**, a piece of information) occupies one cell. If you think about the structure of information you deal with every day, it is usually in tabular structure. Spreadsheets are actually tables with extra features.

For example, invoices, yearly statistics, customer histories, inventory lists, fitness programs, grocery lists, and so on, are all tabular collections of data.

Humans tend to store information in structured ways for easier data access and data management.

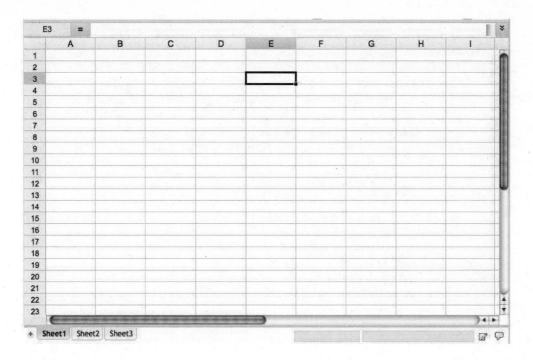

Figure 3-3. A typical sheet

As you are about to see, it is easy to manipulate the data in sheets.

> *I discussed the other elements of the working environment in Chapter 2; therefore, I'll fast-forward here so you can get started using spreadsheets right away.*

Menu bar

The menu bar contains the main features of Sheet (Figure 3-4). It is nicely categorized and very accessible. The following list is a brief on every item on the menu bar. You are going to use them in detail in the next sections, so don't worry if you are not familiar with some concepts.

Figure 3-4. The menu bar

- **New**: Creates a blank document from scratch or based on a template (I'll discuss templates later in this chapter).
- **Import**: Opens the **Import** dialog box allowing you to import data in different formats such as XLS, ODS, SXC, CSV, and TSV. Check Table 4-1 to learn more about the supported formats.
- **Save**: Stores the current spreadsheet. This also opens a drop-down menu offering more options for saving the spreadsheet to a new file, creating a template, or increasing the version number manually (see "Versioning" later in this chapter).
- **Print**: Prints the current spreadsheet using the system's default printing interface.
- **Export**: Saves the current spreadsheet in the following formats: XLS, ODS, SXC, GUMERIC, CSV, TSV, XML, XHTML, HTML, and PDF.
- **Share**: Manages sharing current spreadsheet with others.
- **Publish**: Publishes the content of the current spreadsheet (completely or partially) by embedding it in a website or making it public.
- **More Actions**: Allows you to perform some additional tasks such as managing external data connections, naming ranges/cell, and tagging.
- **Macros**: Manages macro creation as well as access to the VBA Editor.
- **Pivot**: Allows you to create and manage pivot tables and charts.

Table 3-1. Supported File Formats by Sheet

Extension	Format
XLS	Microsoft Excel workbook
ODS	OpenDocument spreadsheet
SXC	OpenOffice spreadsheet
GUMERIC	GNU Gnumeric spreadsheet
CSV	Comma-separated values
TSV	Tab-separated values
XML	XML document
XHTML	XHTML document
HTML	HTML document
PDF	PDF document

Toolbar

The toolbar provides you with extensive formatting features (Figure 3-5). After all, good data needs good presentation to make it clear and easy to read. It also holds a few essential features of Sheet that you can't live without.

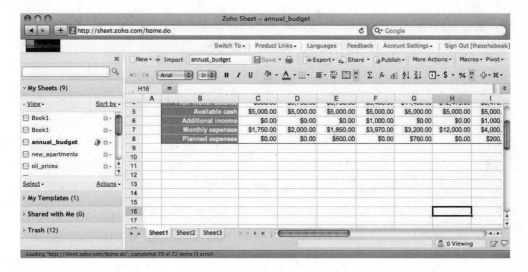

Figure 3-5. The toolbar

As usual, I'll go through every one of the buttons on the toolbar briefly.

If you divide the toolbar into three sections, the first section has the formatting buttons. The second section takes care of calculation and number formatting. The third section manages adding and removing rows and columns.

These are the text-formatting buttons:

- **Undo**: This undoes the last action performed by the user.
- **Redo**: This redoes the last undone action.
- **Font**: This changes the font of the selected range (selected cells). You have a list of 20 fonts to choose from.
- **Font Size**: This changes the font size of the selection.
- **Bold**: This makes the selection text bold.
- **Italic**: This makes the selection text italic.
- **Underline**: This underlines the selection text.

- **Fill Color**: This changes the background color of the selected range. You can either choose from the color picker or enter the hexadecimal code of the color (for example, **#FFFFFF** for white) you want to use.
- **Font Color**: This is the same as **Fill Color**, but it changes the text color of the selected range.
- **Borders**: This changes the border style of the selected cells.
- **More Format Options**: This aligns the text in the selected range to right, left, or center.
- **Wrap Text**: By default, if the text you enter in a cell is longer than the cell width, it doesn't show the extra text. By turning wrapping on, it shows the entire text by breaking it into multiple lines within the same cell.
- **Merge Cells Across**: This merges the cells in the selected range into one single cell.
- **Align Top, Align Middle, Align Bottom**: These three buttons align the text in the selected range horizontally (Figure 3-6).
- **Split Cells Across**: This divides an already merged cell to its original state, making multiple single cells.

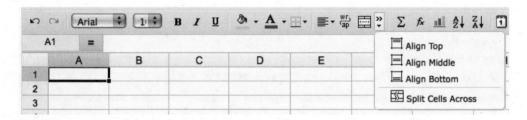

Figure 3-6. More format options (**>>**) buttons

These are the numbers and calculation buttons:

- **Sum**: This calculates the total (numeric) value of a vertical range (numbers in one column) and places the result below the last number.
- **Insert Function**: This opens the **Insert Function** dialog box where you have a long list of mathematical, statistical, engineering, and so on, functions to use in complex calculations. Check http://sheet.zoho.com/functions.do to learn more about these functions.
- **Add Chart**: This shows the **Add Chart** dialog box so you can design complex charts.
- **Sort Ascending**: This sorts the selected range in ascending order.
- **Sort Descending**: This sorts the selected range in descending order.
- **Date/Time**: This formats the selected range based on the selected date format.
- **Currency**: This formats the selected range based on the selected currency format.
- **Percent**: This formats the numbers in the selected range as percentages.
- **Comma**: This separates thousands with a comma in the selected range.

- **Set As Text**: This formats the selected range as text so the numbers won't be treated like ordinary numbers but as text.
- **Increase Decimal**: This increases the decimal point of the numeric values in the selected range by one point. For example, **159.9** will become **159.90**.
- **Decrease Decimal**: This decreases the decimal point of the numeric values in the selected range by one point. For example, **159.90** will become **159.9**.
- **Recalculate (F9)**: This refreshes all values in the sheet by recalculating the applied formulas.

These are the cell management buttons:

- **Insert**: This adds a new row below or above the current row or a column before or after the current column. There is also a link for you to insert images in the sheet as well.
- **Delete**: This removes the current row or column. You can select multiple rows or columns to remove too.

Working with sheets

Each spreadsheet document can have multiple sheets. When Sheet creates a new document, it automatically adds three empty sheets to it. You can add more sheets or remove the redundant sheets easily. Simply click the small **+** button (see Figure 3-7), called **Add Sheet**, that's right before the sheet selector buttons (**Sheet1**, **Sheet 2**, **Sheet3**) to add more sheets.

> **Sheet selectors** are buttons located below the sheet indicated with **Sheet1**, **Sheet2**, and so on. Clicking any of them will open the corresponding sheet.

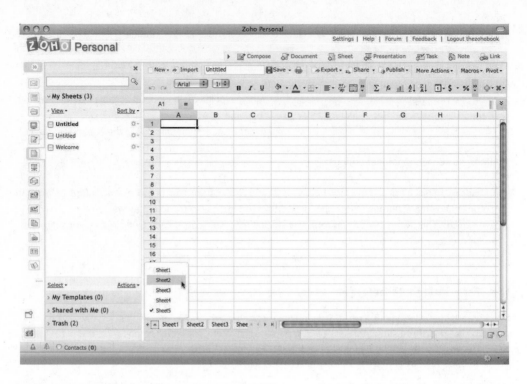

Figure 3-7. Sheet selectors and other buttons

If you right-click any sheet selector (such as **Sheet 2**), you can click **Delete** to remove that particular sheet. A confirmation dialog box will make sure you actually intend to remove it since the action can't be undone.

There is also a tiny arrow button (between **Add Sheet** and the sheet selectors) that opens up a context menu listing all the sheets you can select. This is particularly useful when you have many sheets and there is not enough space to show all sheet selectors, although in such cases a set of sheet navigator buttons will appear next to the sheet selectors.

You can see the numbers (ranging from 1 to 40 by default) before each row and the letters (ranging from *A* to *R* by default) above every column. These identify every single cell on the sheet. For instance, the cell located on the fifth column and third row is named **E3**. Every cell has a unique name throughout the sheet, which means you can't have two **C12** cells on the same sheet, but it is possible to have multiple **C12** cells on a single spreadsheet document simply because it can have multiple sheets.

You can select cells by clicking them or navigating through cells using the keyboard arrow keys.

Start typing, and the text will appear on the current cell (indicated with bold borders) immediately.

Pay close attention to the formula bar between the toolbar and the sheet, as shown in Figure 3-8. You can see the content of the current cell is showing in the **value box**, and the name of the cell (`B2` in this example) shows in the **name box**. As you can see in this figure, the formula bar reads `B2 = Testing Sheet`. Keep this thought in mind because you'll use this feature more in upcoming sections.

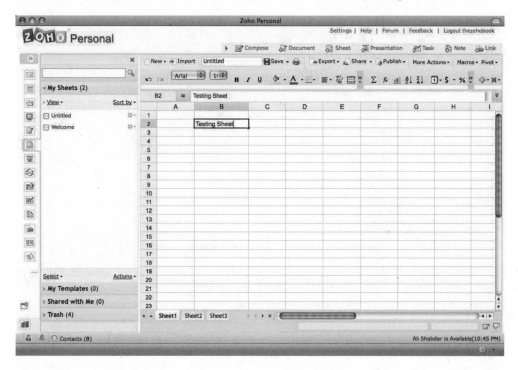

Figure 3-8. Typing in the cells

To select multiple cells, just drag the mouse pointer over cells, and release the mouse button when done. You can also hold down the `Shift` key and use the arrow keys to include more cells in the selection (Figure 3-9).

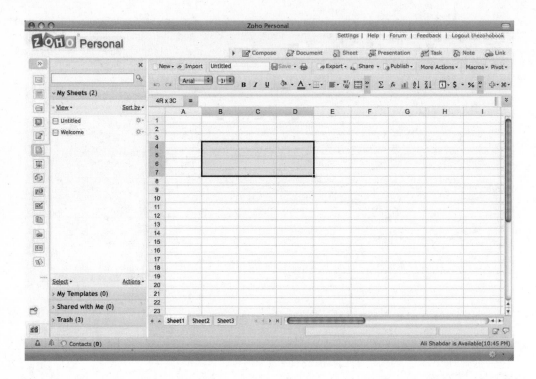

Figure 3-9. Multiselecting cells

You can also resize rows (making it taller or shorter) and columns (making it wider or narrower). Hover the mouse pointer on the row titles (the numbers) or the column titles (the letters). The pointer shape changes to a resize arrow (see Figure 3-10 between **B** and **C**). Drag the row/column you want to resize to the right/left or up/down, and release the mouse button when you reached the desired size.

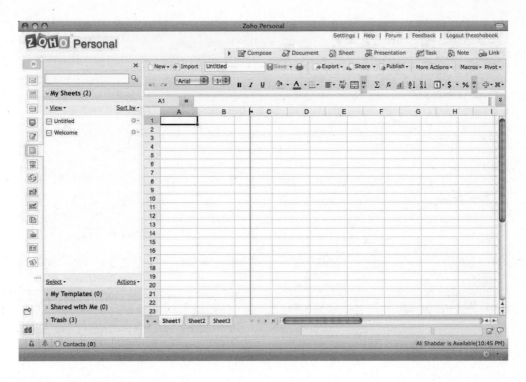

Figure 3-10. Resizing column **B**

Creating your first spreadsheet

Now that you know the very basics of Sheet, let's create a real document. In this walk-through, you'll learn how to create a monthly expense sheet that lists all your monthly expenditures and calculates a summary for every month as well as the amount of the monthly savings or debt based on the monthly income.

1. By default, when you run Sheet, it opens a blank document. However, you can always create a new spreadsheet by selecting **New ▶ Blank Spreadsheet** on the menu bar.
2. Open **Sheet2**. You'll save **Sheet1** for later when you make it the dashboard of your spreadsheet.
3. Right-click the **Sheet2** tab, and click **Rename**. Enter **January** when asked for the sheet name (Figure 3-11).

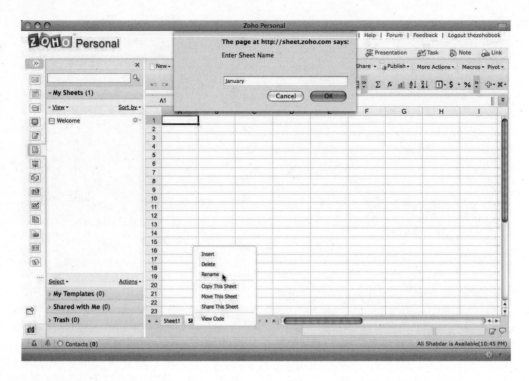

Figure 3-11. Renaming the sheet

4. In cell **B2**, enter **Monthly Expenses – January**. You notice that the text is too big for the cell.

5. Select **B2:D2** (from **B2** to **D2**), and click **Merge Cells Across** in the toolbar.

6. Enter **Date**, **Amount**, and **Details** in **B4**, **C4**, and **D4**, respectively.

7. Save the document as **Expenses** by entering the name right before the **Save** button on the toolbar and clicking **Save**.

8. Widen column **D** (see Figure 3-10) because it might contain longer text. This is only to make it look better and is totally up to you how wide you make a column. The result should look like Figure 3-12.

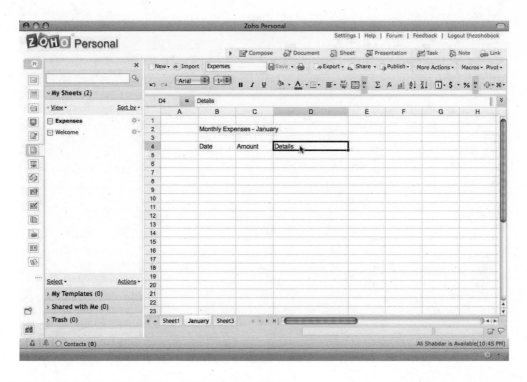

Figure 3-12. Your first spreadsheet: basic headers added

Basic formatting

Nothing is uglier than an ugly spreadsheet except, well, uglier things! You have plenty of tools to format your spreadsheets to be more presentable and more readable. For now, you'll just add some basic touches:

1. Select **B2**, and change the font color to any color you like.
2. Select **B4:D4**, and select **Bottom Borders** from the **Borders** toolbar to draw a thin line below these three cells (Figure 3-13).

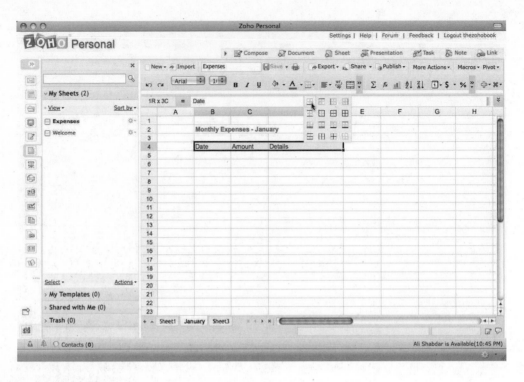

Figure 3-13. Adding a separator line

3. Select the entire column C by clicking the column title (C), and choose $ – US Dollar from the Popular Currencies list on the toolbar. This way, you can make sure any number entered in the Amount column will be properly formatted (Figure 3-14).

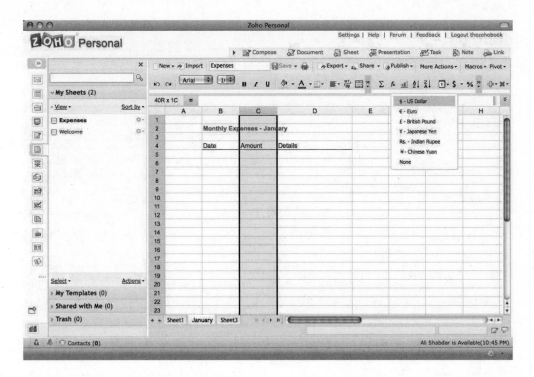

Figure 3-14. Formatting the `Amount` column

Entering data

Well, this beauty needs data. Enter some values similar to Figure 3-15. Keep it between 10 to 15 items for now.

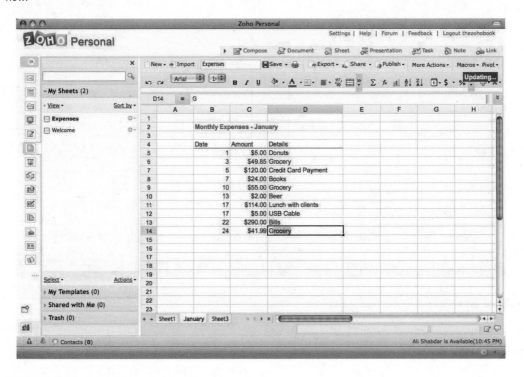

Figure 3-15. Entering data

As you can see in Figure 3-15, when you enter a value in a column that is similar to data you entered before, Sheet tries to autocomplete that cell for you. In this example, `Grocery` is automatically generated by Sheet to save you a few keystrokes.

Does the spreadsheet look familiar so far? The tabular structure of the expense list is similar to many other datasets you use every day. Invoices, telephone bills, and credit reports are all data tables. Columns (such as the date, amount, and so on) are data fields, and every row is a data record. You shouldn't worry about the naming conventions, and you can feel free to call them anything you like. The important point is to learn how to use this simple yet powerful format.

The formula magic

So far, you've made an expense list that you could do on paper too! To add some computer magic to it, you'll now automate your list:

1. To make it more readable, draw a separator line using the border tool (**Top Borders** on the toolbar) on **B20:D20**.

2. Enter **Total** in **D20**.

3. Here goes the real magic: select **C5:C19**, and click **Sum** (the sigma sign) on the toolbar. *Voila*! The total expense amount is calculated and placed in **C20** (Figure 3-16).

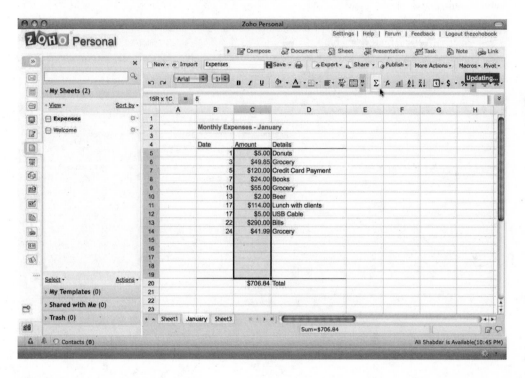

Figure 3-16. Calculating the total expense

You may ask why you selected **C5:C19** and not, for example, **C5:C14**, which contains the data. This is to make sure that if you entered a few more items in the future, it includes in the calculation automatically and doesn't need the range to be changed.

> Note that if you click the cell containing the sum, the formula box (above the sheet) contains =SUM(C5:C19). This is the actual formula applied to *C20* that simply translates to "put the total amount of *C5* to *C19* into *C20*." You'll use more of these formulas later in this chapter as well as in your daily work.

Try changing the values in the formula bar (for example, =SUM(C6:C9)) to get different results before you continue. You can also change the amounts to see that the total updates as the amounts change.

Now you'll add a bit more juice to the sheet and have it calculate the monthly savings based on the monthly income. To perform this calculation, you just need to deduct the total expense amount from your monthly income and display it below **Total**.

1. Insert **4000** in **C21**. Note that it is automatically formatted in currency.
2. Enter **Income** in **D21** as a label.
3. Enter **=c21-c20** in **C22**. The = tells Sheet that the value entered is actually a formula and should be calculated. Press Enter to see the actual result appear in the cell.
4. Enter Savings in **D22** as a label (Figure 3-17).

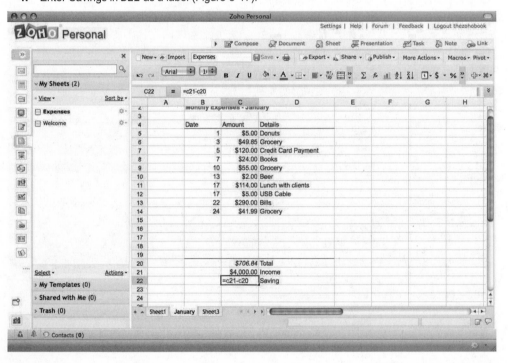

Figure 3-17. Calculating savings

5. Set the font color for **C22:D22** to light gray to just make it more (or less!) distinguishable. You can see the final look in Figure 3-18.

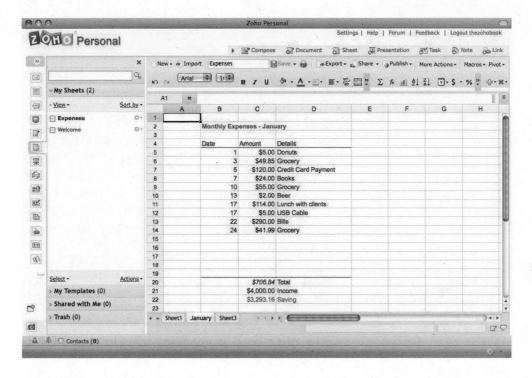

Figure 3-18. Savings changed to light gray

The whole point of this spreadsheet is to keep your monthly expenses, so you still have 11 more months to go. The good news is that I will not bore you with the repetitive task of creating all the remaining months using the same steps you've already completed. There is actually a useful trick to make things easier.

1. Right-click `January` (the sheet button). A context menu appears.
2. Click `Copy This Sheet` (Figure 3-19) to take a snapshot of `January`.

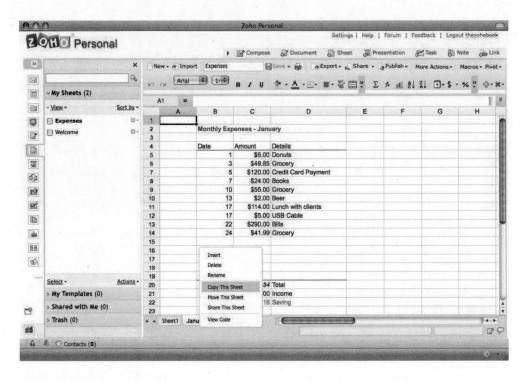

Figure 3-19. Copying `January`

3. In the `Copy This Sheet` dialog box, enter **February** in `Sheet Name`, and select `After the Current Sheet` from the `Place it` drop-down list. Click `OK` to continue (Figure 3-20).

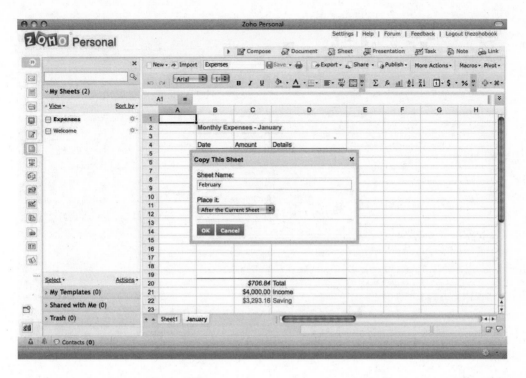

Figure 3-20. `Copy This Sheet` dialog box

Sheet creates a new sheet based on **January** (identical) and names it **February**. This is a custom copy that creates all content and formulas based on the original sheet in a new one.

This feature saved you a ton of time reformatting and reapplying the formulas. If you wonder why it is so exciting, try using the normal copy feature, and then you will see what I mean.

After creating **February**, you can replace the expense items with the ones belonging to the month of February (Figure 3-21).

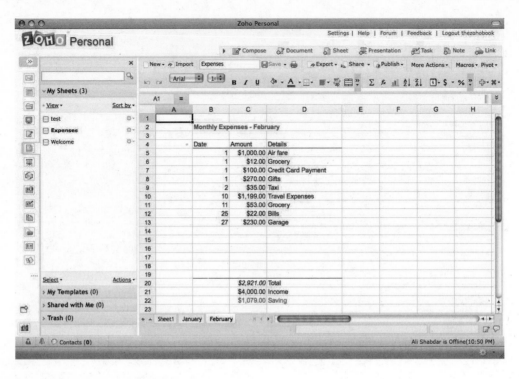

Figure 3-21. Finalizing **February**

To finish this semilong section, you'll now add a yearly calculation to your sheet so you can see how healthy your spending and savings are:

1. Open **Sheet1**, and rename it to **Dashboard**.
2. In **B2**, enter **Yearly Expense Calculator**.
3. Change the font name, size, and color as you like. Draw a bottom border (**Borders ▸ Bottom Borders**) as a separator too.
4. In **C7** and **C9**, enter **Total Spending** and **Total Saving**, respectively.
5. Format **C7:D9** by making the font bold.
6. Set the **D7** and **D9** backgrounds to a light color, and set their currency format to **$ – US Dollar** as before.
7. Draw a separator line using the border tool (**Border Top** on the toolbar) line through **B10:E10**. It should look like Figure 3-22 so far.

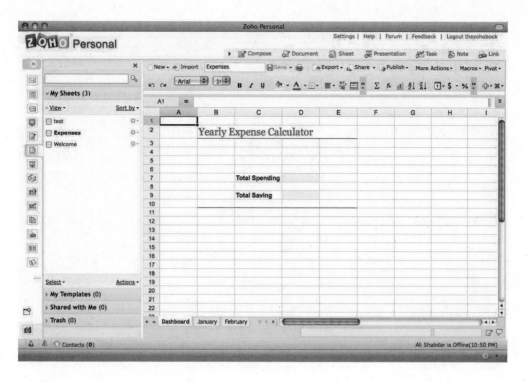

Figure 3-22. Formatting the dashboard

8. Now go back to `January`, and select `C20` (the cell keeping the total expense value).

9. In the formula bar, before the = sign where it reads `C20`, type `jan_spn` (as in "January spending"), and press Enter (Figure 3-23).

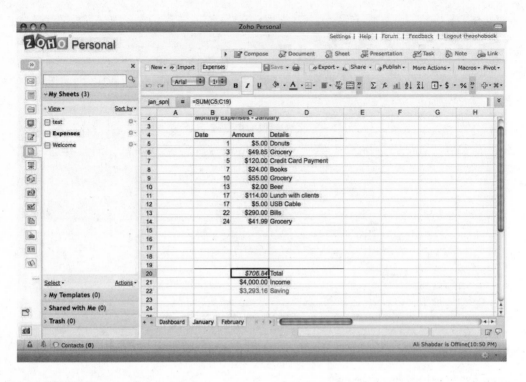

Figure 3-23. Renaming C20 to `jan_spn`

> *By renaming cells, you label them with human-readable titles, which makes it easier to find them and refer to them in other sheets or in the code. It is easier to remember* `jan_spn` *instead of* `C20`, *and it makes complex formulas more readable.*

10. Similarly for `C22`, enter `jan_sav` (as in "January savings"), and press Enter (Figure 3-24).

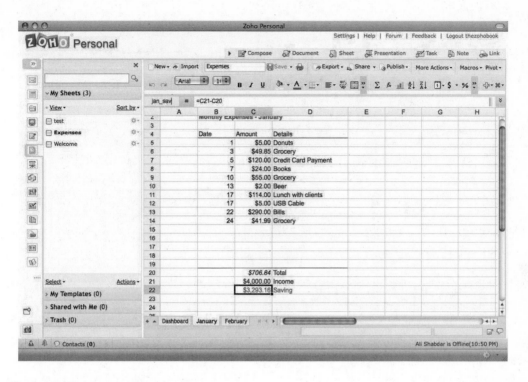

Figure 3-24. Renaming C22 to `jan_sav`

11. Repeat steps 8 and 9 for the **February** sheet. You need to place **feb_spn** for C20 and **feb_sav** for C22.

12. Open **Dashboard** again.

13. Enter =jan_spn+feb_spn in D7.

14. Enter =jan_sav+feb_sav in D9.

15. If everything is OK, you should see that the values are automatically calculated (Figure 3-25).

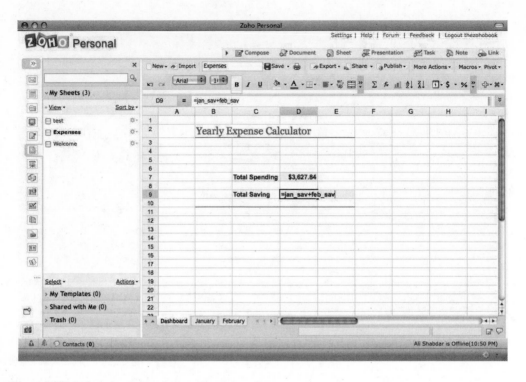

Figure 3-25. Cell names (instead of numbers) in action

As practice, continue creating other months, and update the formulas in the dashboard accordingly.

Adding a chart

The major features of Zoho Sheet are the main focus of this chapter. Although you are not going to see much about advanced techniques and best practices of using spreadsheets here, let's add an exciting feature to the expense calculator: a chart.

Charts are one of the important pillars of information presentation. You can make boring lists of numbers and statistical values shine in the document, formed in easy-to-understand charts and graphs.

In this example, you'll add a chart on the dashboard of the expense calculator to show the yearly expense trend.

1. In G4, enter `Monthly Expenses`, and make it bold by clicking `Bold`.
2. In G5 to G7, enter `Jan`, `Feb`, and `Mar`, respectively.
3. Select G5 to G7. Then move (without clicking) the mouse pointer slowly to the bottom-right corner of the selection range. It changes to a cross (Figure 3-26).

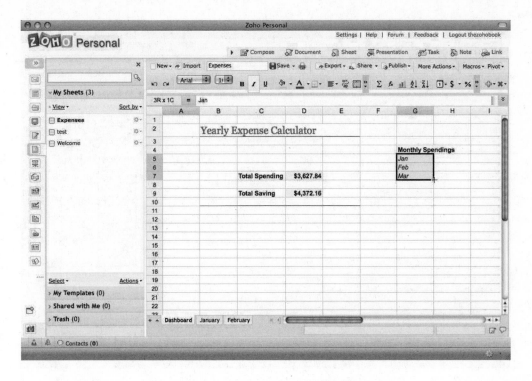

Figure 3-26. The pointer turns to a little cross on the bottom right of the selection.

4. Press and hold the mouse button, and drag it down until you select 12 cells. Then release the button. Sheet does a little magic and fills in the empty cells with the remaining months (Figure 3-27).

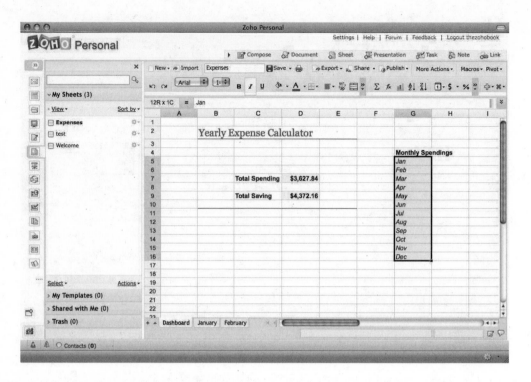

Figure 3-27. Sheet fills in the months automatically.

Autofill is a common feature in all spreadsheet packages. You can use it for numbers and other ordered lists.

5. Enter values for each month. Use the previously created identifiers (**jan_spn**, **feb_spn**), and enter **0** for the rest since you still don't have them (Figure 3-28). Later when you complete the other months, you can come back and enter the respective identifiers.

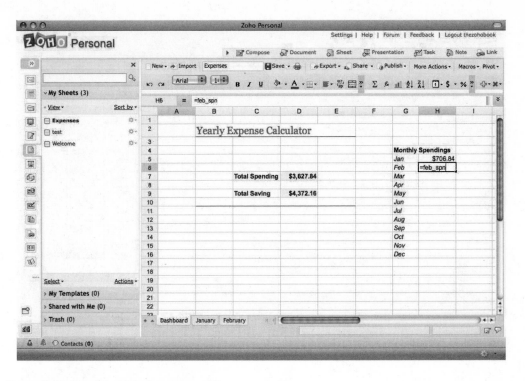

Figure 3-28. Entering values for each month

6. Make sure you have all 12 months' values selected; then click **Add Chart** (the chart button on the toolbar) to open the **Add Chart** dialog box.
7. Select **Line Chart** in the **Chart Type** list, and click **Next** (Figure 3-29).

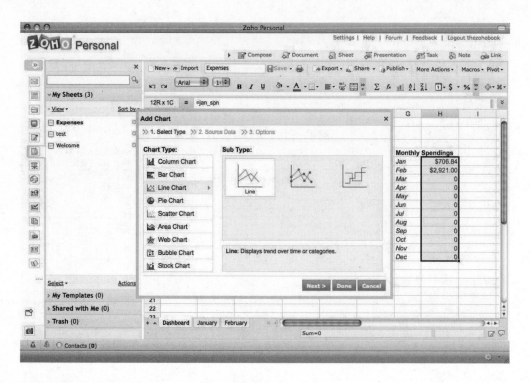

Figure 3-29. `Add Chart` dialog box with line chart selected

8. In `Data Range`, `H5:H16` should be already entered, but if it's not, enter it, and select `Cols` in `Series In`. Then click `Next` to continue (Figure 3-30).

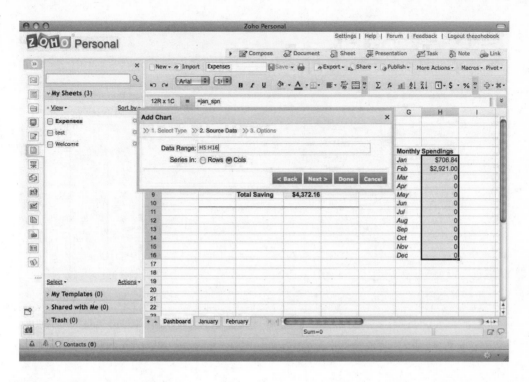

Figure 3-30. Entering source data

9. Enter `Yearly Expense Trend` for `Chart Title`, `Month` for `X-Axis Title`, and `$ Amount` for `Y-Axis Title`. Select `None` for `Data Labels`, and deselect `Show Legend`. Click `Done` to generate the chart (Figure 3-31).

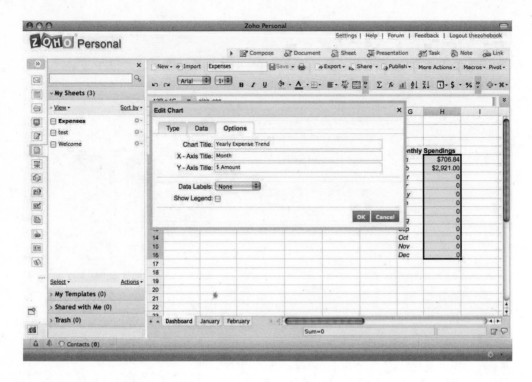

Figure 3-31. Entering options

10. Resize the chart, and place it in a proper way below the other content. Your chart is ready and should look similar to Figure 3-32.

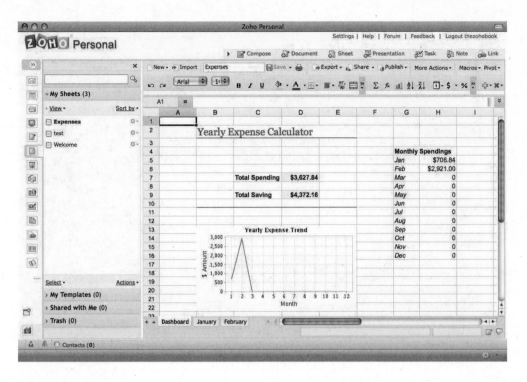

Figure 3-32. Ready chart

If you hover the pointer on the chart, two buttons appear on the upper left, **Edit** and **Publish**. As the label suggests, **Edit** will open the **Edit Chart** dialog box, and you can change everything in the chart.

If you click **Publish**, however, the **Publish Chart** dialog box will appear, providing you with the necessary HTML script to place the chart in any web page (Figure 3-33).

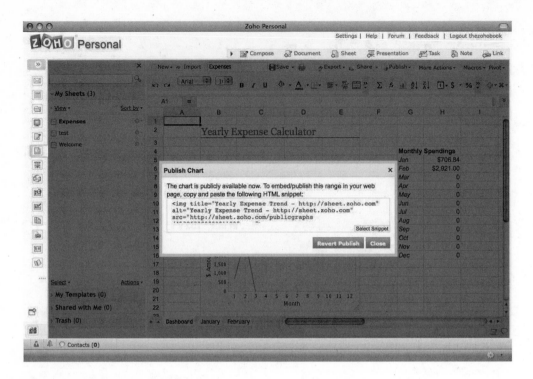

Figure 3-33. `Publish Chart` dialog box

This is a great way to present data. It is readable and **live**, meaning that when the values in the chart change, the chart will update too, and your visitors will always see the latest update.

To unpublish the chart at any time (when this dialog box is closed), move the mouse pointer on the chart, and click `Revert Publish`.

Sharing and collaboration

As you might remember from Chapter 2, one of the most exciting features of Zoho applications, like any other cloud-based suite, is the ability to share the documents easily and collaborate seamlessly with colleagues, teammates, friends, and anyone else.

It is great to be able to work on the annual budget information with the headquarters of your organization overseas without needing to send Excel files back and forth via e-mail.

It might also seem like a dream to have access to the latest version of the statistics of the scientific project of your team, and be able to change it on the fly too, by just sharing an ordinary spreadsheet online.

Before I get in more details of collaborative sharing, I'll quickly mention that you can also share spreadsheets with the world by making them public.

Suppose you have an alarming report on global warming trends in the past two years and you want to share it globally and even receive comments on it.

Here is how to do it:

1. Open the spreadsheet you want to make public, and select **Publish ▸ Make Public** in the menu bar (Figure 3-34). You need to make one or import an existing document (discussed later in this chapter) in case there aren't any available in Sheet.

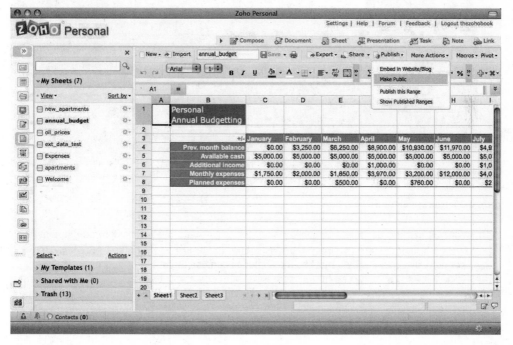

Figure 3-34. The **Publish** menu

2. Leave the check boxes in the **Make Public** dialog box as is, and click **OK** to continue (Figure 3-35).

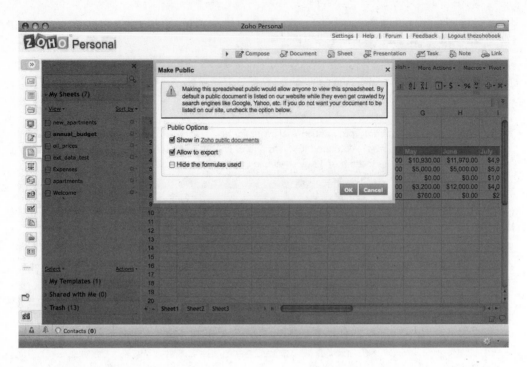

Figure 3-35. `Make Public` dialog box

3. You will see the document is publicly shared and is made available via three different links to access different versions: **Normal**, **HTML**, and **Printable**. Publish any of these links (for example, by sending it by e-mail) so the audience can use them.

4. Click **Embed in Website/Blog**, and an HTML code snippet will appear; copy and paste this HTML into the source code of any web page (Figure 3-36). This is quite useful when you want to create mashups, but you need to have basic knowledge of HTML prior to performing this step.

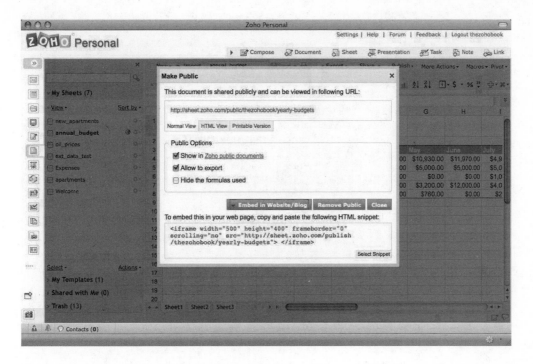

Figure 3-36. Links to the publicly available spreadsheet

You can revert public spreadsheets to private by selecting **Publish ▶ Remove Public** in the menu bar.

> It is important to always remember that making a document public makes it available to everyone. It is not a good idea to make private information public; instead, you should use the sharing options.

Now it's time for more serious talk. In the following walk-through, you'll learn how to share a spreadsheet you have been working on with two of your colleagues for them to check and contribute to the content.

1. With your spreadsheet open, select **Share ▶ Invite** in the menu bar (Figure 3-37).

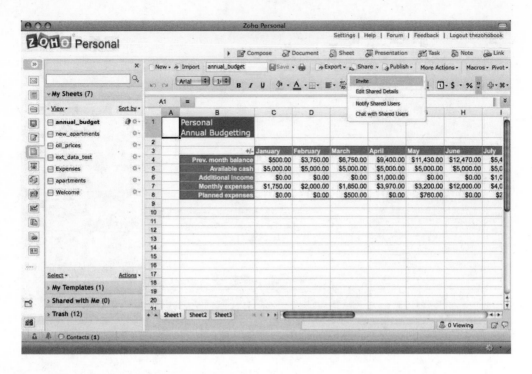

Figure 3-37. Inviting users to share a document

2. In the **Share This Document** dialog box, there are two groups in the left side: **Read Only Members** and **Read/Write Members**. Enter the collaborators' Zoho names (if they have Zoho accounts) or e-mail addresses according to the permissions you want to give them.

3. Click **Edit Invitation Email**, and modify the e-mail as you want.

4. Leave the other options as is, and click **Share** to proceed (Figure 3-38). You are done.

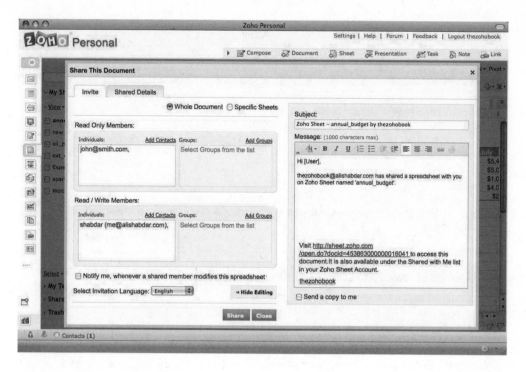

Figure 3-38. Setting the share options

The members will receive an e-mail (similar to Figure 3-39) notifying them about the recent share.

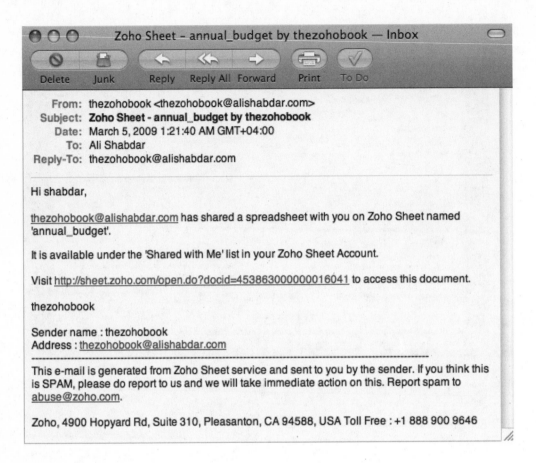

Figure 3-39. Notification e-mail

You can check the share status of the document and change it according to new requirements at any time by selecting **Share ▶ Edit Shared Details** (Figure 3-40).

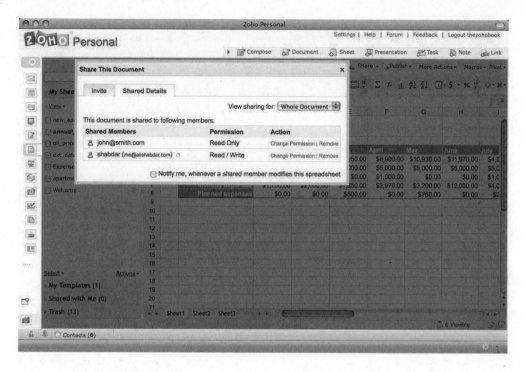

Figure 3-40. Editing shared details

After a successful share, once the members have logged in to their Zoho accounts, they will see the shared spreadsheet listed in `Shared with Me` pane in the left side of the working area (Figure 3-41).

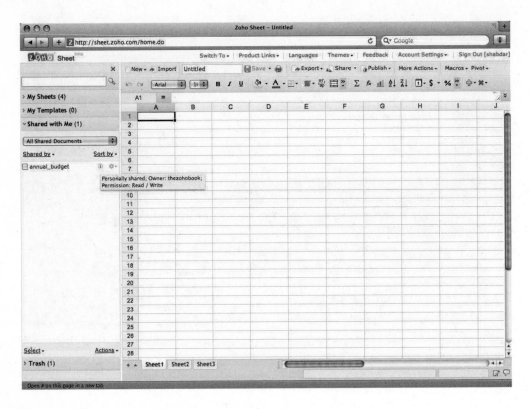

Figure 3-41. Shared documents are listed for members.

There is a good way of checking what is happening to the shared spreadsheet, and it is through the version history. Select **More Options ▶ View Version History** to see what modifications other members have made to the document so far (Figure 3-42).

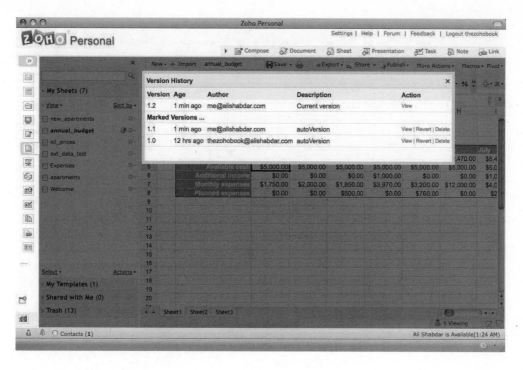

Figure 3-42. `Version History` dialog box

More sheet features

Sheet provides you with many other facilities in order to make working easier and more productive. In this section, I'll go through the most important features that makes Sheet even more competent for the job.

Versioning

As you may remember from Chapter 2, where you could perform versioning on your Writer documents, Sheet too keeps track of the different versions of spreadsheets for you, in case you need to review the changes or maybe revert to an older version.

Let's take a look at this feature:

1. Open **Expenses** (the expense calculator you made before).
2. In the menu bar, select **More Actions ▶ View Version History** (Figure 3-43).

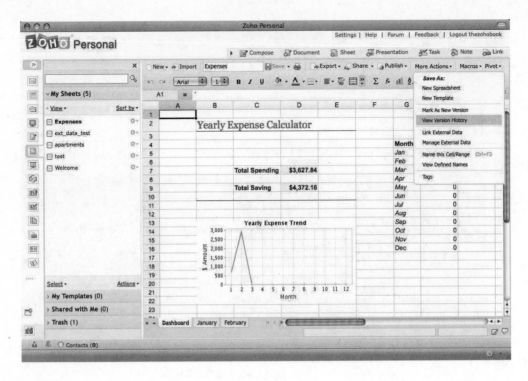

Figure 3-43. `View Version History` menu

You can see a list of all the different versions of the current spreadsheet in the `Version History` dialog box (Figure 3-44).

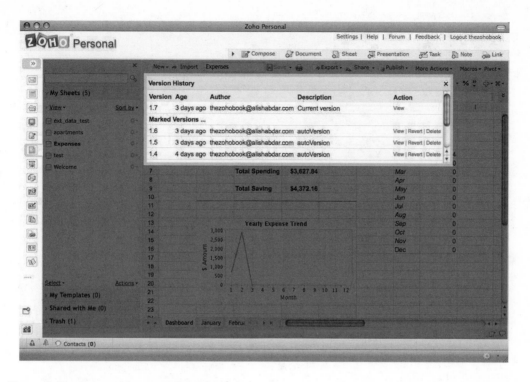

Figure 3-44. `Version History` dialog box

3. Find version 1.2 in the list, and click `View`.
4. The actual version 1.2 loads, and you can see the old content as it was back then (Figure 3-45). Navigate through other versions using the versions drop-down list (`Version` in the toolbar), or perform more actions.

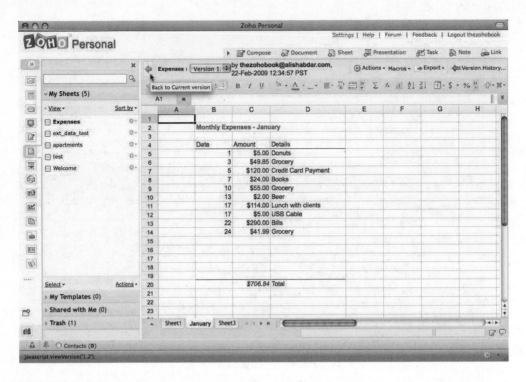

Figure 3-45. Version 1.2 of the document is loaded.

As you can see in Figure 3-45 and Figure 3-46, the menu bar offers new options. You can revert to this version (**More Actions ▶ Revert to this Version**), delete this particular version (**More Actions ▶ Delete this Version**), or export it (**Export**) in case you need a copy of an older version of your document.

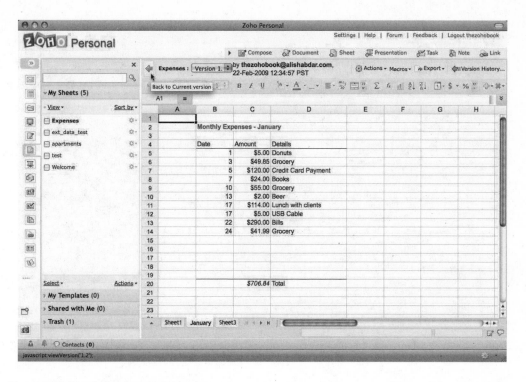

Figure 3-46. Versioning-specific menu bar

5. If you don't want to do anything, just click `Back to Current Version` (the backward green
    arrow on the menu bar) to return to the current version of the document.

One last thing you should know about versioning is that you can manually increase the version of the
document. This might come in handy when you want to set milestones while creating the document to
make it easier for you and the collaborators to recall the exact life cycle of each document.

To do so, select `More Actions ▶ Make As New Version` in the menu bar. You will be asked to enter a
description for the new version in the `Version description` dialog box. Then click `Submit` to proceed
(Figure 3-47).

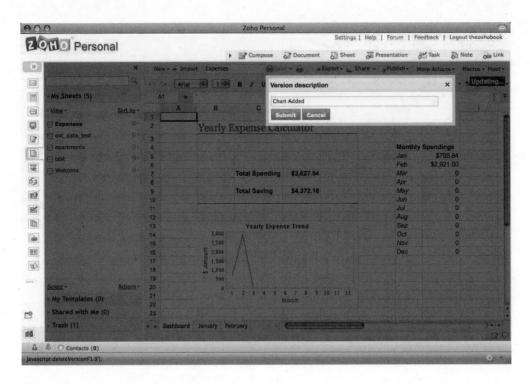

Figure 3-47. Version description dialog box

Later when you refer to the versions list, you can easily find the manually made version in the history (Figure 3-48).

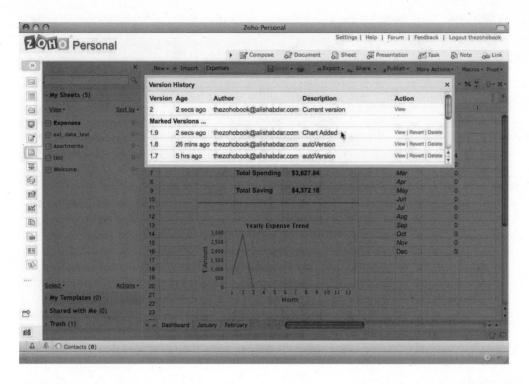

Figure 3-48. Distinguishable versioning

Naming cells

As you saw before with the formula, it is possible to name cells (or a range of cells, with a similar approach) for easier reference.

Earlier you just entered the name in the formula bar right before the = sign. There is, however, an alternative way to do this through **More Actions ▶ Name this Cell/Range** in the menu bar.

You can also manage the names throughout the spreadsheet by selecting **More Actions ▶ View Defined Names**. This opens the **Names List** dialog box. There you can define new names, edit the current ones, or remove them (Figure 3-49).

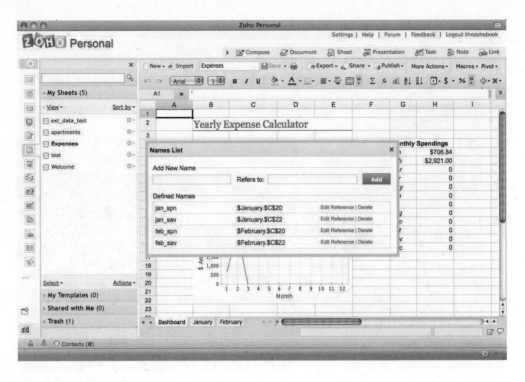

Figure 3-49. `Names List` dialog box

Import and export

Sheet, like any other professional applications, offers a host of file formats that you can import from or export to.

You might import documents to have them available online and to collaborate with colleagues. It is such a joy to not have to worry in a meeting that you forgot your USB stick at home. After all, you are moving your files up on the cloud.

To import data into Sheet, follow these steps:

1. Click **Import** on the menu bar. The **Import** dialog box appears.
2. Browse for the file if you are uploading data from your local computer. You can also import a file hosted on the Internet by selecting **URL** and entering the web address of the file (Figure 3-50).

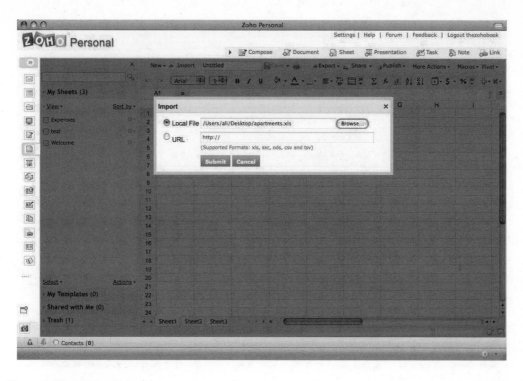

Figure 3-50. `Import` dialog box

3. Click `Submit` to proceed.
4. Wait until Sheet creates a new document (named after the imported filename) and displays it (Figure 3-51). This might take few seconds based on the file size and the connection speed.

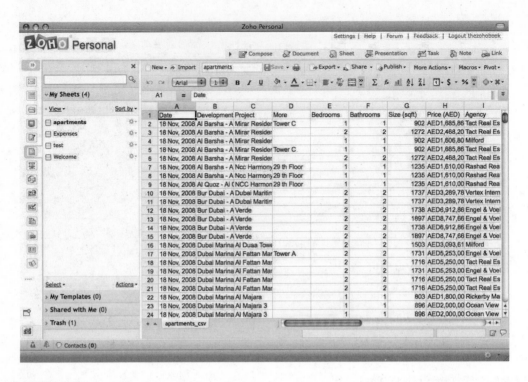

Figure 3-51. File imported successfully

> *You can download the dummy Excel file in this example from the book page on www.friendsofed.com or from http://thezohobook.com/files/apartments.xls.*

To export the spreadsheets to common formats, all you need to do is select the target format from **Export** in the menu bar. You can find the list of supported formats in Table 4-1.

External data sources

Sometimes you'll need to import raw data (not in spreadsheet format) into Sheet. It is often the case that such data gets updated frequently, so you need the latest version every time.

For instance, the latest product price list of your company could be stored in a database on an Internet server, and you can have regular access to it in order to perform some calculations and show the results to your customers in a chart.

Such a scenario would be a painful process with traditional spreadsheet applications, but with Sheet you can actually automate the entire process in a way that almost no further human interference is necessary.

To link a spreadsheet to an external data source, follow these steps:

1. Create a new spreadsheet by selecting **New ▸ Blank Spreadsheet** from the menu bar.
2. Also in the menu bar, select **More Actions ▸ Link External Data** (Figure 3-52).

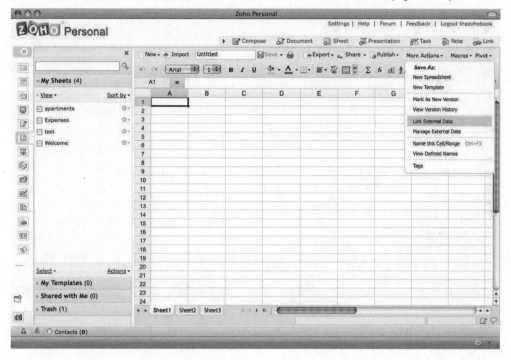

Figure 3-52. Click **Link External Data**.

3. In **External Data Dialog**, select **CSV Data** as the URL type.
4. Enter the URL (web address) of the CSV data source file, and click **Next**. You can use the sample file shown in Figure 3-53, http://thezohobook.com/files/avg_price_dev.csv.

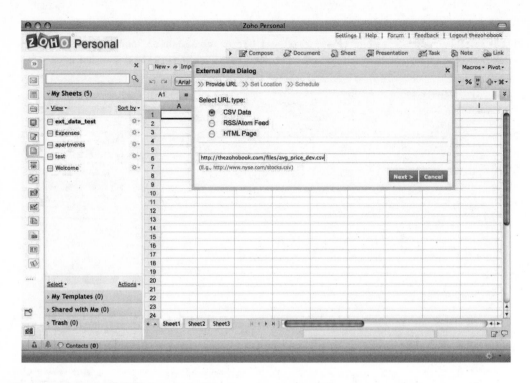

Figure 3-53. Select the URL type.

> **CSV files** *are text files structured to represent data tables consisting rows and columns, just like normal spreadsheets. Different values are separated by commas in each row (representing the cells of a spreadsheet). They are very useful to transfer data between different platforms and applications (such as between a remote database and Sheet). You can get more information about the CSV format at* http://en.wikipedia.org/wiki/Comma-separated_values.

5. Leave the `Sheet name` and `Start cell` settings at the defaults, and click `Next` (Figure 3-54).

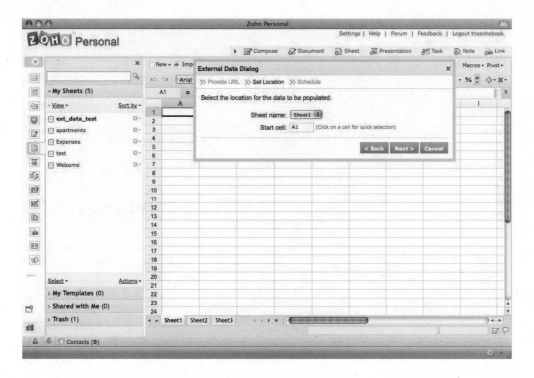

Figure 3-54. Select the location for the data to be populated.

6. Select **Now and schedule periodically** to make Sheet fetch up-to-date data regularly. Then select **Weekly Once** for **Repeat** and **Friday** for **Perform every**. Leave **Time** as it is. Finally, click **Done** to start the process (Figure 3-55).

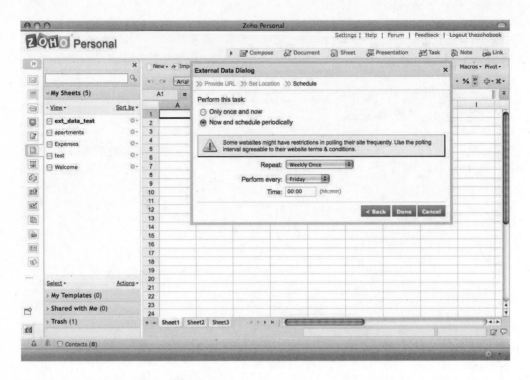

Figure 3-55. Scheduling regular data import

7. If you entered the file address correctly, data will be populated immediately, and you can start working on the sheet right away.

8. Navigate through the data, and check whether everything is OK (Figure 3-56).

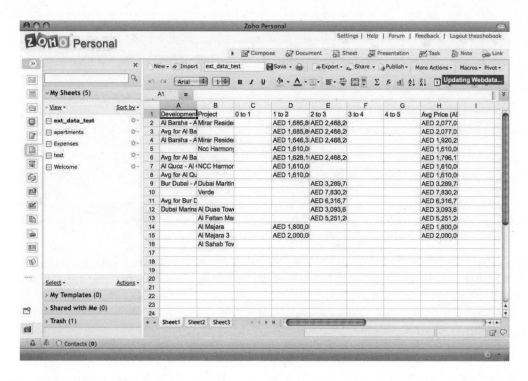

Figure 3-56. Importing web data

> *If you received error messages during the import process, it is probably because the file address is wrong or the server that the CSV file resides on is not allowing Sheet to perform well. In this case, you should contact the administrator of the file server.*

Using macros

If you are a seasoned spreadsheet user who spends days working on complex data structure, you know that one of the most important features that differentiates Microsoft Excel from all other spreadsheet applications is the ability of creating and running macros.

Macros record a sequence of actions used in applications repeatedly. Like templates that provide you with the basic structure of a document, a macro runs like a procedure to perform certain tasks on a document. The macro language of choice in Excel is Visual Basic for Applications (VBA).

> *Visual Basic for Applications (VBA) is a programming language included in Microsoft Office and some other applications. Other vendors (like Zoho) use VBA for their own macro building purposes as well. You can learn more about the VBA used in Sheet from http://vbmacros.wiki.zoho.com/.*

Well, macros are no longer exclusive to Excel because just like Excel, Sheet offers this great feature. That's not all; Sheet uses VBA as the macro language, so you bring your knowledge and potentially the macros you made before directly into Sheet.

If you are not familiar with macros at all, fear not! You'll be amazed how useful macros are. It is also very easy to create your own macros with Sheet and boost your productivity while working on spreadsheets.

Although VBA is a powerful language, you might know that it depends on Microsoft Windows's internal services and won't run on other systems like Mac OS or Linux. Also, it is prone to macro viruses, making it vulnerable to security attacks.

The good news is that with Sheet you have only the positive side! Because Sheet runs on the cloud and not on your computer, it doesn't need Windows to run VBA code, and it won't ruin your day with macro viruses.

Your first macro

You can automate your life in Sheet using macros in two ways: you can record macros, and you can code macros from scratch. I won't go through the VBA coding at all since it is a whole new subject and you can find plenty of valuable resources covering it. However, you will record a simple macro here to get to know this feature. The rest is up to you.

As I just discussed, macros are great doing sequential tasks. In this walk-through, you'll learn how to format data in a sheet and perform basic calculations.

For this purpose, I pasted the monthly oil prices of 2008 (from www.inflationdata.com/inflation/inflation_Rate/Historical_Oil_Prices_Table.asp) into a new document and saved it as **oil_prices** (Figure 3-57). You can insert any kind of data you want or just stick to this example.

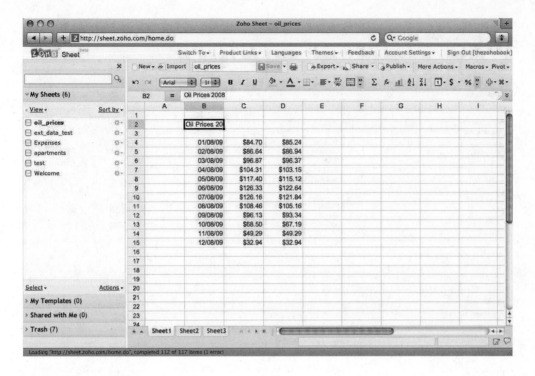

Figure 3-57. Sample data

To record the macro, follow these steps:

1. Select **B2** (as you see in the Figure 3-57) to set the reference cell.
2. In the menu bar, select **Macros ▶ Record Macro** (Figure 3-58).

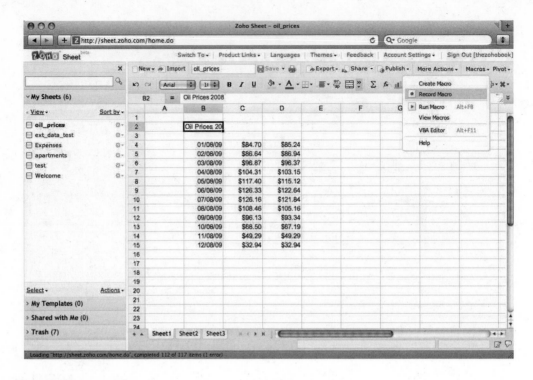

Figure 3-58. `Macros` menu

3. In the `Create Macro` dialog box, make sure `Record` is selected.
4. Fill in `Macro Name` and some description, similar to Figure 3-59.
5. Select `Use Relative Reference` so the macro is created independent of the real cell names. That's why in step 1 you set `B2` as the reference cell.
6. Click `Start Recording` to proceed (Figure 3-59).

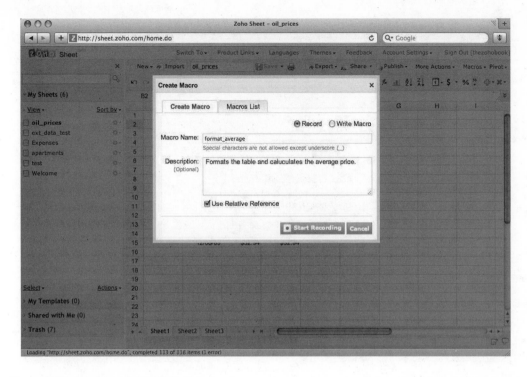

Figure 3-59. `Create Macro` dialog box

7. You can see a new bar appearing above the toolbar indicating **Macro Recording in progress**…. You can click **Stop Recording** or **Cancel** the operation at any time (Figure 3-60).

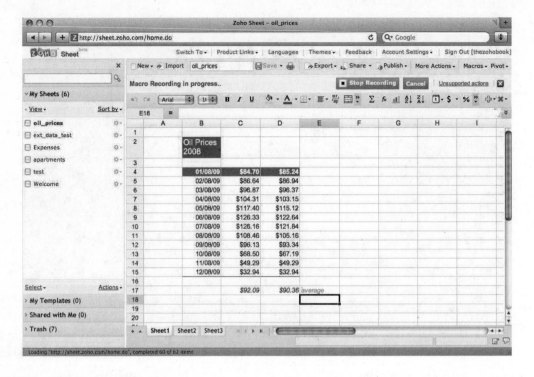

Figure 3-60. Macro recording bar

8. While macro recording is on, format the sheet in a way that the final result looks like Figure 3-61. Note that every single action you do is being recorded.

9. For the average calculations, use the **AVERAGE** function. Enter **=average(c5:c15)** in **C17** and **=average(d5:d15)** in **D17** (Figure 3-61).

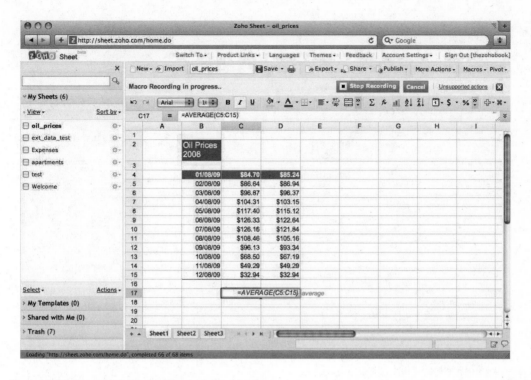

Figure 3-61. Formatted sheet with calculations in place

10. Click `Stop Recording` on the macro bar. It will display a success message (Figure 3-62).

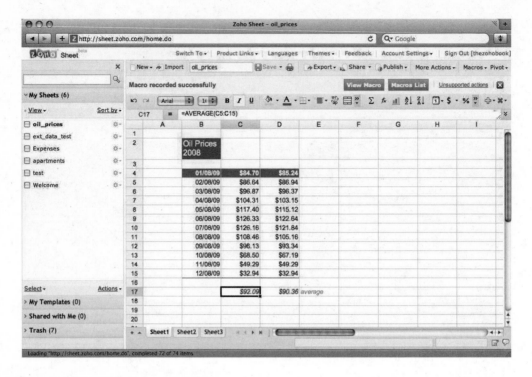

Figure 3-62. Macros recorded successfully

11. Click **View Macro** to review the automatically generated code (Figure 3-63). As you can see, it is fairly easy to read, but do not get tempted to change anything if you are not familiar with VBA. Close the **VBA Editor** dialog box.

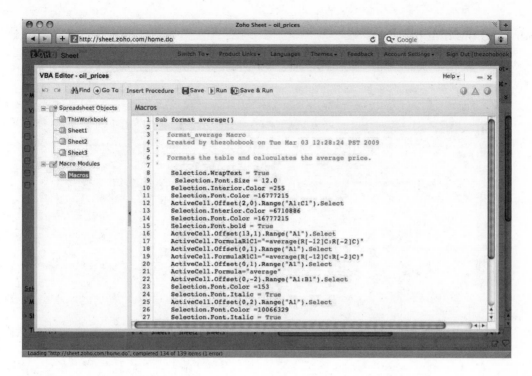

Figure 3-63. Generated VBA code

Running the macro

Now that you have created the macro, let's test it on some sample data:

1. Paste same data (oil prices in this example) into **Sheet2**, and select **B2** as the reference cell (Figure 3-64).

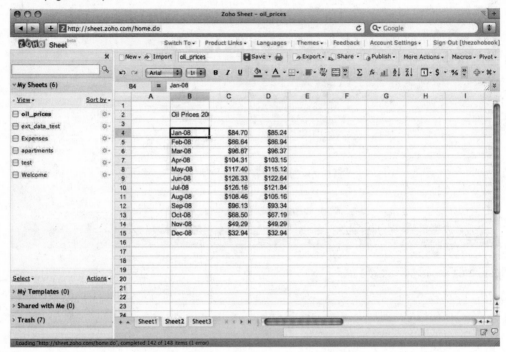

Figure 3-64. Sample data in **Sheet2**

2. In the menu bar, select **Macros ▶ Run Macro**, and click **format_average** (the one that you just created) in the **Click a Macro to run** dialog box (Figure 3-65).

Figure 3-65. Run the macro.

3. In a moment you will see that the sheet has changed to what you wanted. Is that magic or what? The table is formatted, and the average values are calculated with just one click (Figure 3-66).
4. Review the changes to see whether everything went as planned.

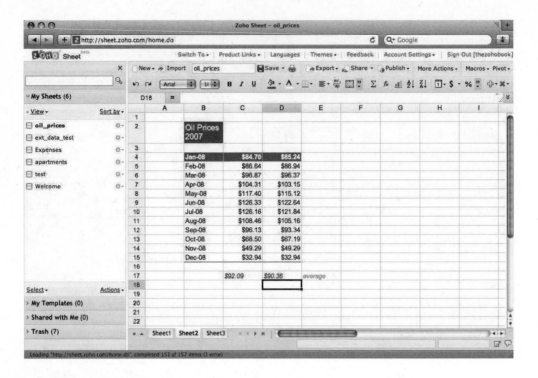

Figure 3-66. Macro applied

In the previous example, whenever you import oil prices (for example, for other years), you just need to run a macro to prepare it. It saves you at least five minutes of work in such a simple example, and you make sure you avoid any human mistakes.

Since macros are stored inside the spreadsheet documents, once you share them with others, they can enjoy the macro automation as well.

This also means if you have Excel spreadsheets with macros, you can import the macros along with the data.

> *For those of you who just fell in love with VBA, there are plenty of good resources to learn VBA. But be careful that they all apply to Microsoft Excel, and you might need to tweak the code while porting it to Sheet.*
>
> *Check out www.xlpert.com/toc.htm to learn VBA online, or log on to the official home page at http://msdn.microsoft.com/en-us/isv/bb190538.aspx.*

Unsupported actions in macros

While recording or creating macros, keep in mind that at the time of this writing, the following actions are not supported:

- New spreadsheet/template creation
- Spreadsheet/template deletion
- Save As options
- Importing and exporting
- Share and publish options
- Collaborative editing
- Versioning
- Tagging
- Document comments
- Pivot tables and pivot charts

Pivot tables and charts

Pivot tables and charts are very useful visual data presentation tools with features such as summarizing, grouping, and calculating data in tabular datasets.

> Zoho added this great feature to Sheet as part of its updates in 2008. If you are interested in learning more about the history of pivot tables, check Wikipedia at http://en.wikipedia.org/wiki/Pivot_table.

Working with pivot tables and charts is very easy. However, you need to import data into Sheet in a certain way to be pivot compliant.

Creating a pivot table

In this section, you'll create a report using a pivot table to show the average price of one- to four-bedroom apartments available through a specific real estate agency:

1. Import data from a locally stored CSV file. You can download the sample file from www.thezohobook.com/files/new_apartment.csv and then import it into Sheet (Figure 3-67).

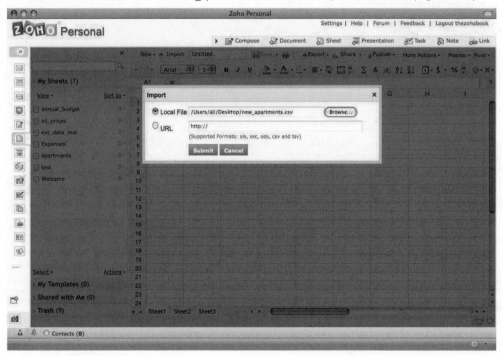

Figure 3-67. Importing a local CSV file

2. When you import local CSV files, Sheet asks you how to import it, **Tabular** or **Normal Spreadsheet**. Select **Tabular**, and click **OK** (Figure 3-68).

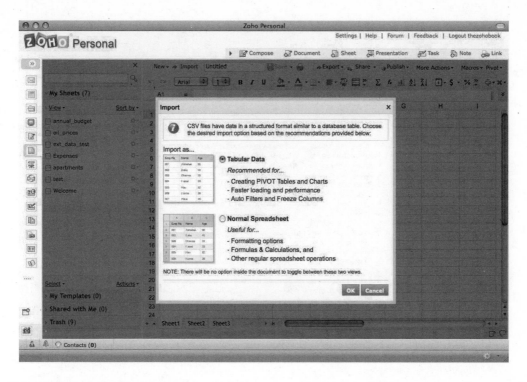

Figure 3-68. Importing tabular data

3. Once the data is loaded, you will immediately notice the difference in the toolbar. This is because the data is loaded in a special format, allowing `Sheet` to treat it similarly to a database table (Figure 3-69). I'll cover databases later in the book, so for now just select `Pivot ▶ Create Pivot Table` on the menu bar to proceed.

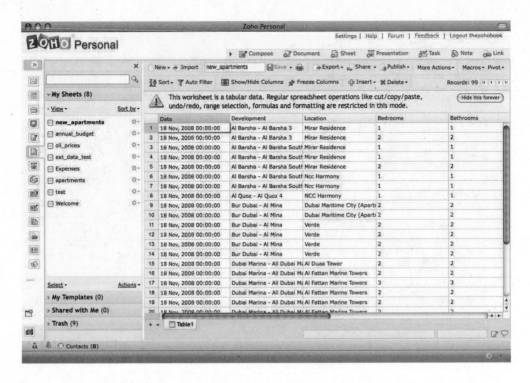

Figure 3-69. Imported data and the extra buttons on the toolbar

4. In the `Create Pivot Report` dialog box, make sure `Pivot Table` is selected. Enter a title and description. Leave the `Data Range` and `Location` fields as is, and click `Design Pivot` (Figure 3-70).

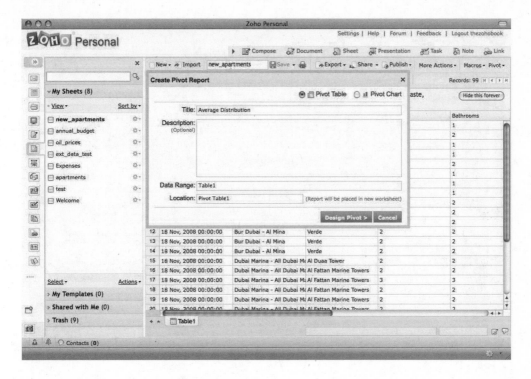

Figure 3-70. `Create Pivot Report` dialog box

5. In the `Design Pivot` dialog box, you'll find all the tools necessary to create sophisticated reports (pivot tables). On the left side, you can see that all data columns are populated automatically in `Fields List`. On the right side, there are sections to define the structure of the pivot table, and there's a `Preview` area at the bottom (Figure 3-71).

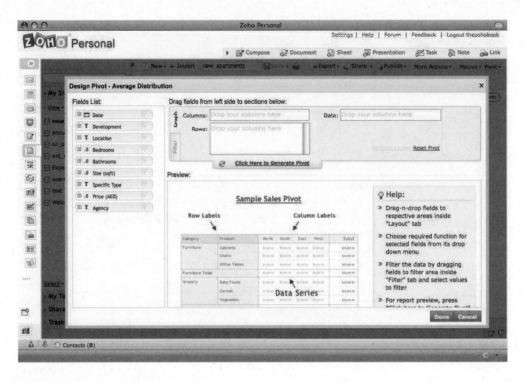

Figure 3-71. The pivot designer

6. Drag **Bedrooms** from the **Fields List** area, and drop it on the **Columns** field in the **Graph** tab. Then drag **Development**, and drop it on **Rows**. Finally, drag **Price (AED)**, and drop it on **Data** (Figure 3-72).

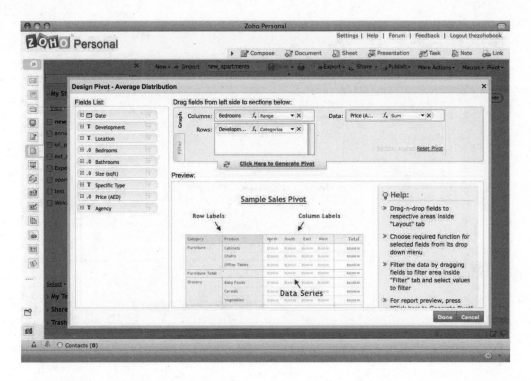

Figure 3-72. Creating the structure of the report

7. Click `Click Here to Generate Pivot` to see a preview of the table. Note that the values in the table are sums, but you need to see the average price of each development. Click the `fx` drop-down list of `Price (AED)` field in `Data`, and select `Average` (Figure 3-73). Then preview it again.

171

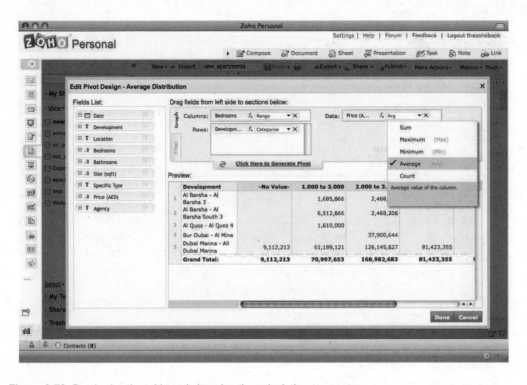

Figure 3-73. Previewing the table and changing the calculation parameters

8. Now click the `Filter` tab, and drag `Agency` to the `Filter` box. Sheet automatically lists different agencies in the table. Select an agency, and preview the table again (Figure 3-74). If it looks satisfactory, click `Done`.

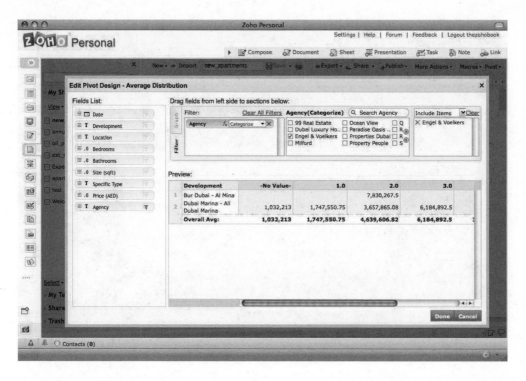

Figure 3-74. Filtering data

9. I also changed the title and description of the table to match my purposes more. Just click **Edit Properties** on the toolbar, and change **Title** and **Description**. Click **Update** to continue (Figure 3-75).

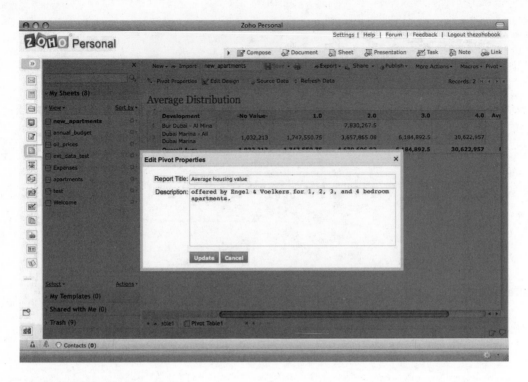

Figure 3-75. Editing pivot properties

10. You can see the final result in the Figure 3-76.

Figure 3-76. Final table

You can change the settings of the pivot table by clicking `Edit Design` on the toolbar. Try moving fields and changing formulas to get different results. You can create complex reports using pivot tables.

Before moving on to the next section, you should know that for ordinary documents where the data is not necessarily tabular, you can still create pivot tables. Select a cell range, and click `Create Pivot Table`. Then follow the instruction to create a pivot tale just like you did in the previous walk-through.

Creating a pivot chart

Similar to pivot tables, pivot charts are quite easy to create. In the following example, you'll add a chart to the `new_apartments` spreadsheet that shows the average prices of different developments:

1. Open `Table1`. You'll notice that since it is not an ordinary sheet (it is a table), it is named `Table1`. In the menu bar, select `Pivot ▶ Create Pivot Chart`.
2. In the `Create Pivot Report` dialog box, enter a title and description, and leave the `Data Range` and `Location` settings as they are. Click `Design Pivot` to continue (Figure 3-77).

Figure 3-77. `Create Pivot Report` dialog box.

3. In the `Design Pivot` dialog box, make sure the `Graph` tab is active (selected). Drag `Development` from `Fields List`, and drop it on `X-Axis`.
4. Drag and drop `Price (AED)` on `Y-Axis`. Change `fx` to `Avg` to display the average price.
5. Once again, drag `Development`, and drop it on `Color`. This will make sure you have a matching chart legend.
6. Finally, drag `Price (AED)`, and drop it on `Text`. Set the `fx` value to `Max` so you can have the highest price shown on the top of each bar (Figure 3-78). This helps show two different values in one chart.

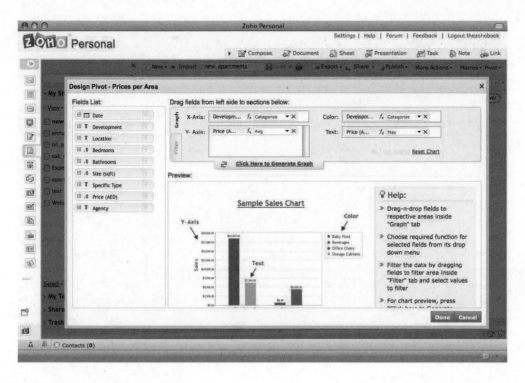

Figure 3-78. Setting up the chart

7. Preview the chart by clicking `Click Here to Generate Graph` (Figure 3-79). If everything is satisfactory, click `Done` to proceed.

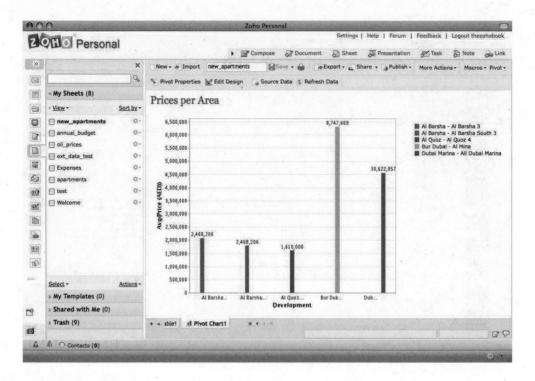

Figure 3-79. Final result

Working with templates

As you'll see throughout this book, the Zoho suite promises you more productivity. Templates are one of the essential tools toward a more productive life. You were introduced to document templates in Chapter 2. Now it is time to use them in Sheet. The concept of templates in Sheet is quite similar to Writer's concept of them. You create templates for the common documents you use the most where they share the same (or fairly similar) format and structure, such as invoices and expense bills.

Here you'll create a simple template based on a monthly expense note and use it to create new documents to save time by not repeating the basic formatting every time:

1. Create a simple sheet like the one shown in Figure 3-80. This is a very simple template, and you can add more stuff to it if you want.

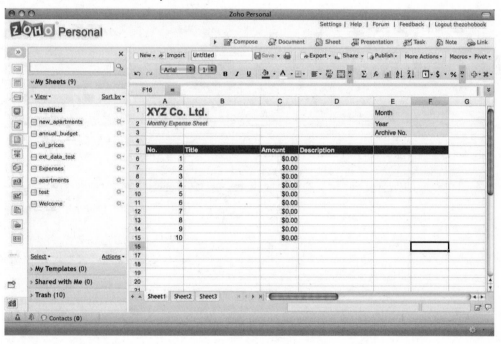

Figure 3-80. A simple expense note

2. In the menu bar, select **Save ▶ New Template** to save it as template (Figure 3-81).

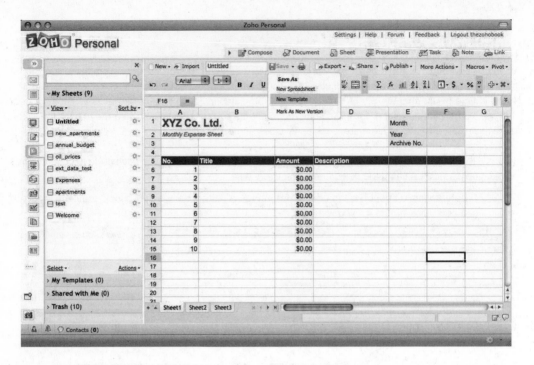

Figure 3-81. Saving as a template

3.   Enter `monthly_expenses` in **Template Name**, and click **OK** to proceed (Figure 3-82).

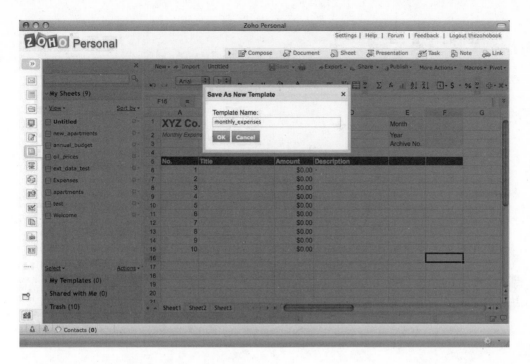

Figure 3-82. `Save As New Template` dialog box

4. The template is created, and you can find it in the left pane in `My Templates`. To create a new spreadsheet based on this template, click the gear button in front of `monthly_expenses`, and click `Create As New Spreadsheet` (Figure 3-83). You can also select `New ▶ From Template List` in the menu bar to create a new spreadsheet based on a template.

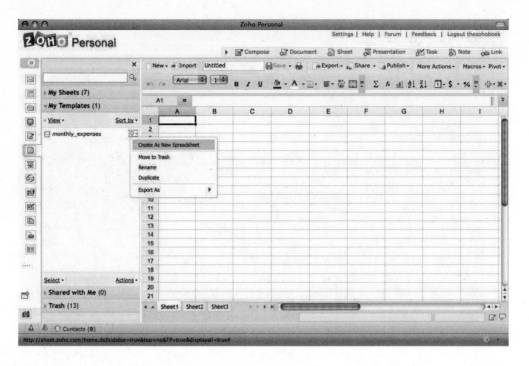

Figure 3-83. `Create As New Spreadsheet` menu item

5. Enter `monthly_expenses_jan` when you are asked for the spreadsheet name (Figure 3-84).

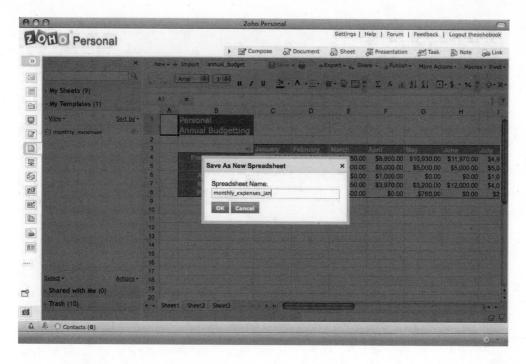

Figure 3-84. `Save As New Spreadsheet` dialog box

6. You can see a new spreadsheet created with all the formatting and settings copied from the base template (Figure 3-85). Continue editing the new document like you normally would.

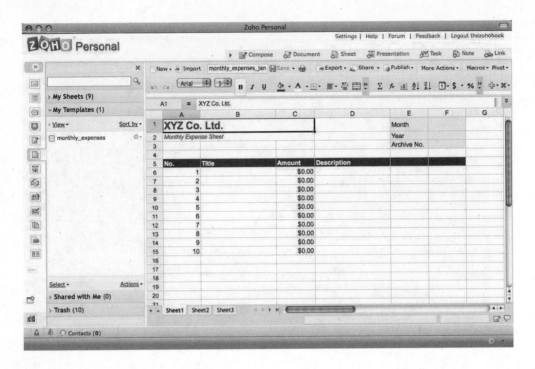

Figure 3-85. A new document is created.

Getting help

After reading this chapter, you should be pretty comfortable working with spreadsheets and manipulating data online.

However, a great source to get answers to your questions is the Zoho community. You can reach out to the experts and ask your questions or leave feedback in the Zoho forum at `http://forums.zoho.com/Zoho-Sheet`.

You can also check out the sample sheets from `http://sheet.zoho.com/samples` or the public sheets made by the community at `http://public.sheet.zoho.com/public` to get some ideas. Your own public sheets will appear here too for the other people to check your talent.

Finally, to make your life easier, make sure you learn the essential shortcuts. You can list them by clicking **Product Links ▶ Keyboard Shortcuts** in the top menu bar, or you can enter the address at `http://sheet.zoho.com/keyboard-shortcuts` directly.

Remember, your best teacher is yourself. The more you practice and use the application, the better you become. So, start using Sheet every day, and you will be amazed how helpful it can be.

Summary

Using spreadsheets helps you store (almost) unlimited amounts of data in an organized and manageable way. You can solve everyday problems like complicated calculations using only spreadsheets.

Many small companies still rely on spreadsheets as their main information storage medium.

Sheet takes this important tool to the cloud and adds some unique features to it. Sharing and collaboration in addition to the online nature of Sheet are all features that allow you to take spreadsheets to the next level, increasing your productivity and boosting teamwork performance.

In the next chapter, you'll see how to take your presentations to the cloud using another SaaS application by Zoho.

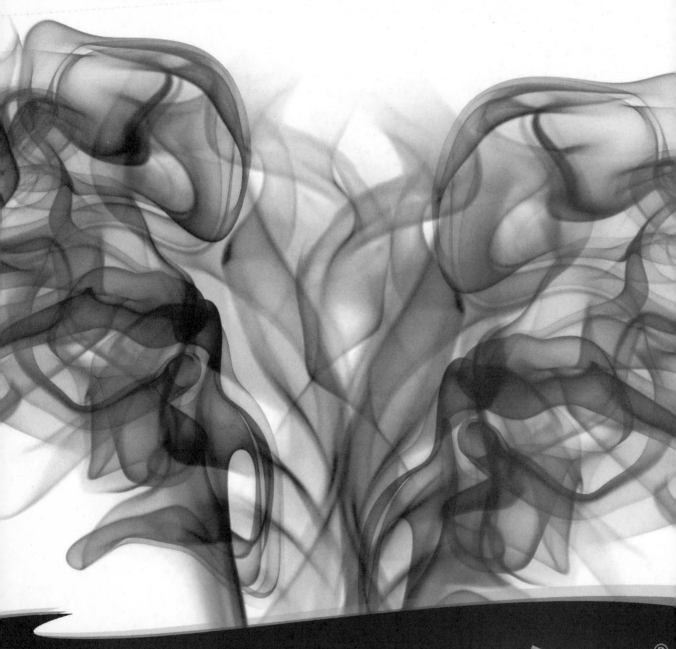

ZOHO®
Work. Online

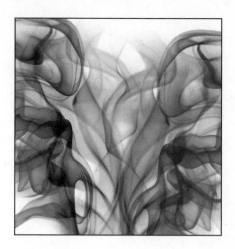

Chapter 4

Present Yourself

Some say it is essential and others say it is a boring corporate routine, but presenting different subjects in a meeting or a conference is inevitable in today's digitized life. Despite the different opinions, you should make sure your presentations are as exciting and engaging as possible.

One of the pillars of an engaging presentation is to use presentation software. You're probably familiar with tools such as OpenOffice.org Impress, Microsoft PowerPoint, or Apple Keynote. These tools help you display information (text, image, and so on) in the form of slide shows and give you the ability to add eye candy to your content.

They all share similar features. You can create the presentation, add extra features, and show it to the audience in a suitable manner.

> *You can get more information about presentation applications on Wikipedia at http://en.wikipedia.org/wiki/Presentation_program.*

In this chapter, you will learn how to use Zoho's weapon in the presentation battle. It is called Show and has everything you need to create eye-catching presentations and more.

Basic features

Zoho Show allows you to create professional presentations. You can do the following with it:

- Create, modify, and showcase slide shows with a user-friendly interface
- Choose from a collection of nice templates to give your presentations a good look and feel

- Use different tools (text, images, shapes, clip art, and so on) to create complex and content-rich material
- Import presentations from popular formats such as PPT and PPS (Microsoft PowerPoint) or ODP and SXI (OpenOffice.org)
- Export presentations to HTML, PPT, PPS, ODP, and PDF
- Share content online and collaborate with the content
- Present online (remote presentations) and run web sessions, without geographical boundaries
- And more

As you might expect, Show is (and will be) completely free of charge for personal use. However, Zoho might introduce nominal monthly charges in the future for business users.

It supports the current versions of almost all major browsers (Internet Explorer, Firefox, Safari, and so on), but because of some technical reasons, Safari and Chrome support is limited to *viewing only* for now.

The environment

To start Show, click its icon on the application bar of Zoho Personal or log on to `http://show.zoho.com`.

When you open Show for the first time (Figure 4-1), it will display two links in the home page, `Create a New Presentation` and `Import a local or online Presentation`.

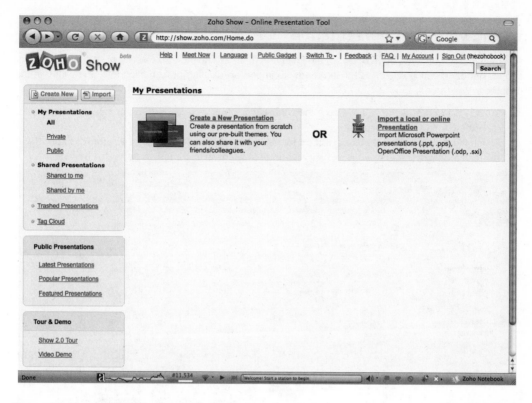

Figure 4-1. Running Show for the first time

On the left side, you can see three panes aligned vertically. The first pane is your control panel and starts with two buttons, **Create New** and **Import**, followed by links to your own presentations or the ones shared to you. You can also access other parts of Show from here. The two other panes contain links to the public presentations as well as the demos and product tours.

The home page is pretty simple because, as you are about to see, the real engine is under the hood. Almost everything else happens in the editor, where the real power of Show is hidden.

Working with presentations

You haven't seen much about Show yet, because almost everything is wrapped in the editing environment where you create, modify, and run your presentations.

In this section, you will create a short presentation about Zoho Show itself. You will add more features to this presentation as you continue with other sections.

Creating your first presentation

As I mentioned, when you open Show for the first time, there are actually no existing presentations, so you should start by creating one. You will learn how to import an existing presentation into Show later in this chapter.

1. On the home page of Show, click the `Create a New Presentation` or `Create New` button on the top of the left pane.
2. In the `Create New Presentation` form (Figure 4-2), enter a name in `Presentation Name`, add a description in `Description`, and enter few tags in `Tags` (separated with comma).

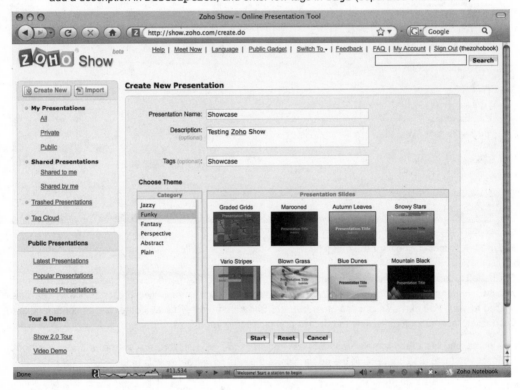

Figure 4-2. Creating a new presentation

> Although not necessary, tags are useful for categorizing documents so you can find them easier later. `Office`, `Important`, `Classified`, `Draft`, and so on, are some examples of the tags you could use for your presentations.

3. Select a presentation theme from `Choose Theme`. I chose `Funky` ▶ `Blue Dunes` for this example.
4. Click `Start` to begin working on the presentation in the editor environment.

Touring the editor

Once you have created a presentation, it opens in the editor environment (Figure 4-3). This is where you will create your masterpiece. It might look intimidating first, but it is extremely easy to use.

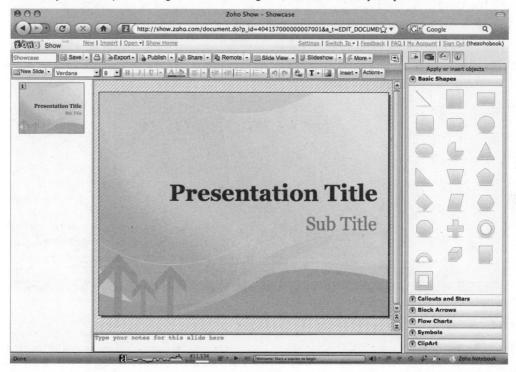

Figure 4-3. The editor environment

Let's take a quick look at the editor before we continue.

On top of the screen there is a link bar (Figure 4-4). On the left, it contains links to popular tasks such as creating new presentations, importing existing files, and opening other presentations. There is also a link to take you back home. On the right side of the link bar, there are links to change the application settings, modify your account, and more.

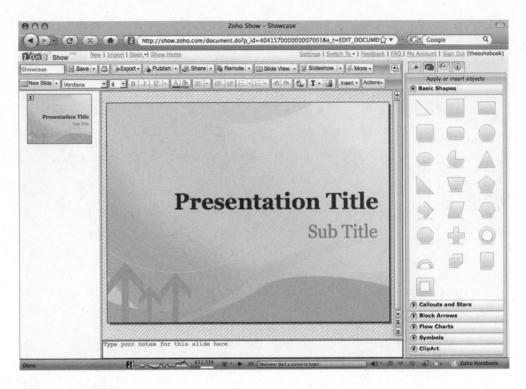

Figure 4-4. The link bar

Below the link bar, there is a menu bar followed by a toolbar holding all commands necessary for the work (Figure 4-5). You can work on your presentation, modify the contents, perform slide shows, share the documents, and collaborate with friends/colleague through the toolbar.

> *Unlike previous chapters where we went through almost every command in the menu bar and toolbar, from now on, since you have a fair idea of the environment of Zoho applications, I will discuss only the commands used in the walk-throughs. You are now ready to find your way through the user interface with minimal effort.*

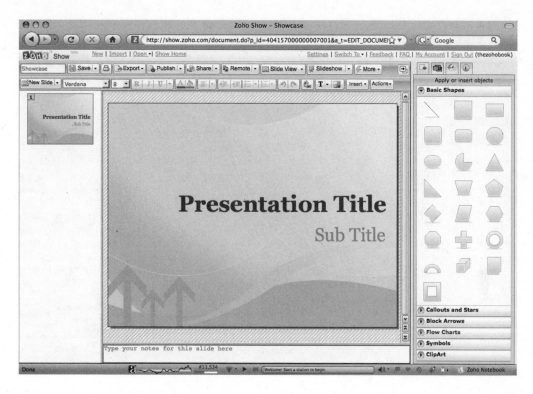

Figure 4-5. The menu bar and toolbar

On the left side of the editor, all slides get listed (Figure 4-6), but you will see only one at the beginning. Every presentation consists of a number of slides created and sorted to tell a story. You can easily scroll through the slide list and find the one you need.

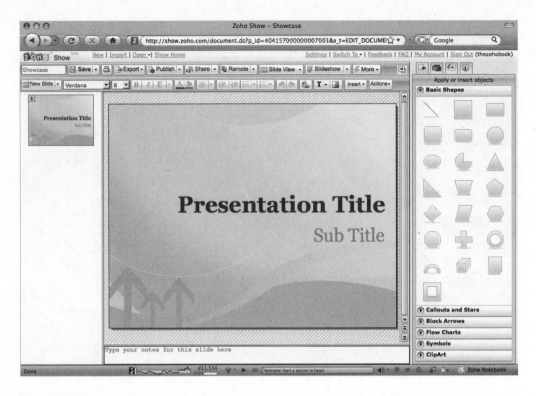

Figure 4-6. The slide list

On the right side, there are four tabs (labeled with icons): `Shapes`, `Themes`, `Version Details`, and `Presentation Info` (Figure 4-7). Every tab contains valuable tools and features that you need to use while working on presentations.

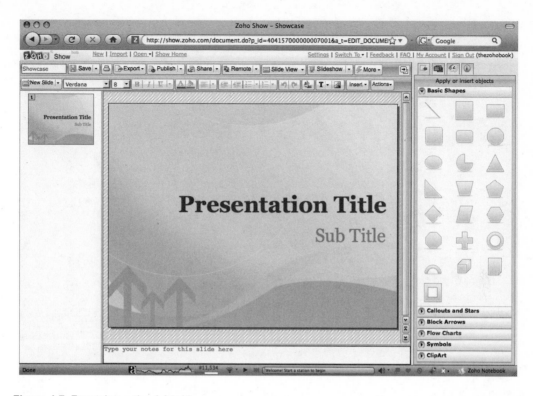

Figure 4-7. Four tabs on the right side

Finally, in the middle, there is the working area where you create one slide of the presentation at a time (Figure 4-8).

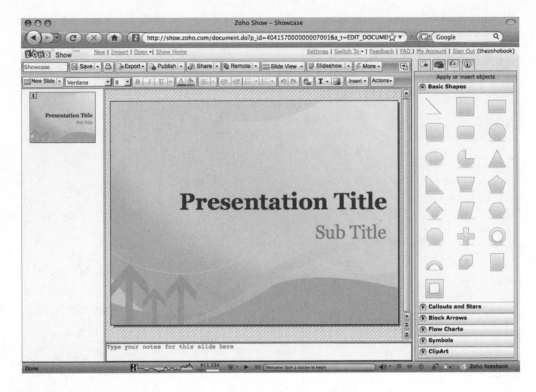

Figure 4-8. The working area

Now, we should finish what we started.

Adding new slides

With the presentation you created earlier open, follow the steps of this walk-through to continue creating your presentation. If you, however, closed the document for any reason, click **Open** on the link bar.

1. In the slide 1 in the working area, click the big title (**Presentation Title**). You can see that a box containing the text appears, and the cursor is placed at the end of the line waiting for your input (Figure 4-9).

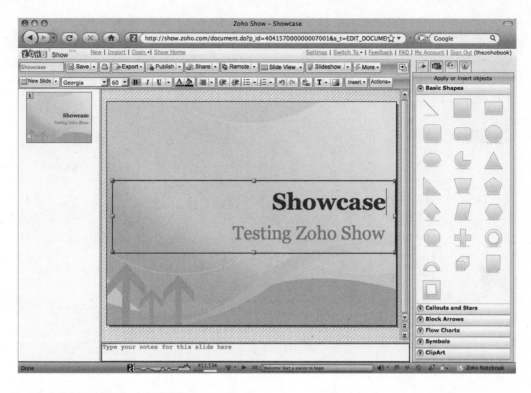

Figure 4-9. Changing the text of titles

2. Change the text to `Showcase`, and then click outside the box for the change to take place.
3. Do the same with the second line (`Sub Title`), and change it to `Testing Zoho Show`. The result should look like Figure 4-10.

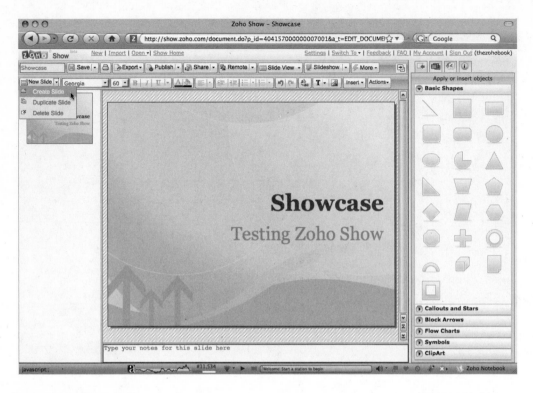

Figure 4-10. First slide done

4. Click `Save` on the menu bar to save your changes.
5. Add a new slide by clicking the `New Slide` button on the toolbar.

> *If you click the small arrow on the `New Slide` button, you will see three items: `Create Slide`, which does the same as `New Slide`; `Duplicate Slide`, which creates a new slide identical to the current slide, and `Delete Slide`, which removes the current slide.*

6. In the `Slide Type` dialog box, select `Title with Points`, and click `Create Slide` (Figure 4-11).

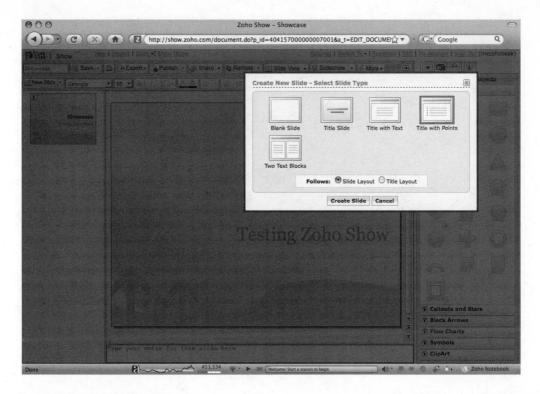

Figure 4-11. Choosing the slide type

7. Replace the contents of the title and the list according to Figure 4-12 just like you did in step 2.

> *To change the bullet style, right-click the container box, and select* **Bullets and Numbering** *from the context menu. The* **Format Bullets and Numbering** *dialog box will appear, and you can change the shape and the color of the bullets there.*

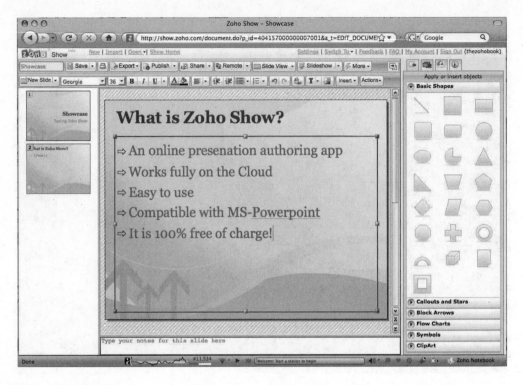

Figure 4-12. Editing slide 2

8. Add another slide, and select **Title with Text** as the slide type (Figure 4-13).

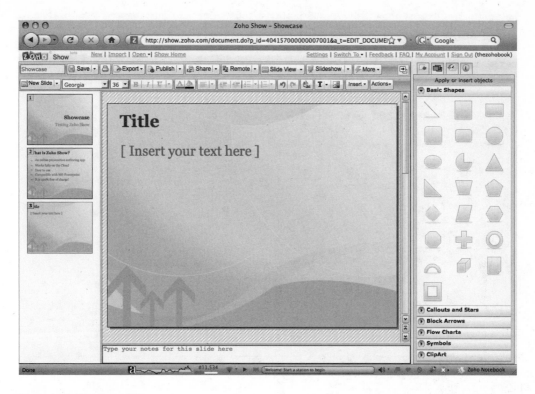

Figure 4-13. The third slide

9. Change the title to `What does it look like?`, and then right-click the text box (where `[Insert your text here]` is), and click `Delete Object` in the context menu to remove it (Figure 4-14).

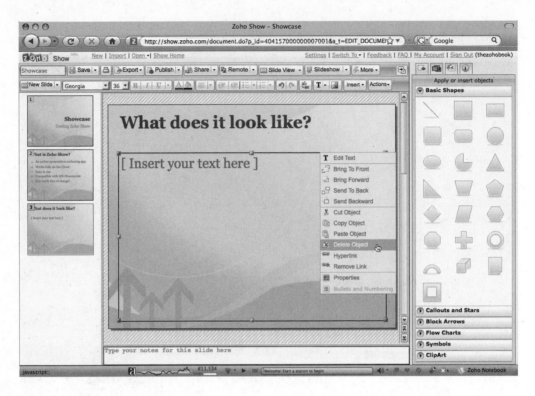

Figure 4-14. Removing the text box

10. Click `Insert Image` icon on the toolbar (or click `Insert ▸ Image`). You can insert images from your local computer as well add online images (Figure 4-15). It is also possible to import pictures from Flickr and Picasa. For now, click `Browse`, and upload a picture file from your local computer. You can also directly add this online image: `http://www.thezohobook.com/files/show_scr.jpg` by clicking `From Url` and entering the link in the text box.

> *Flickr (www.flickr.com) and Picasa (www.picasa.com) are both image-sharing websites and will not be covered in this book. They provide you with tools to upload and share pictures with your friends, family, and the world. You can configure Show to use the pictures you have already uploaded in your online albums in the presentations. But Show can see only the public pictures. You may ignore this step if you are using neither of the services.*

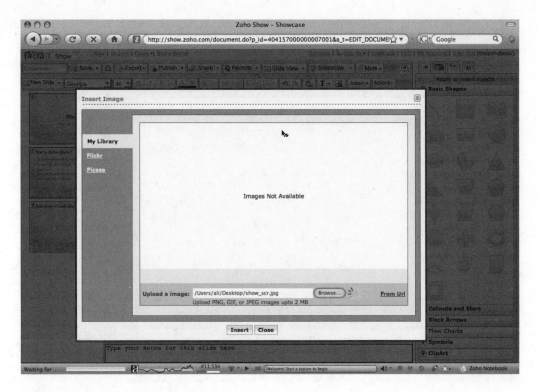

Figure 4-15. Inserting an image to the slide

11. Show will automatically upload the file and list it in **My Library**. Select the image, and click **Insert** to continue (Figure 4-16).

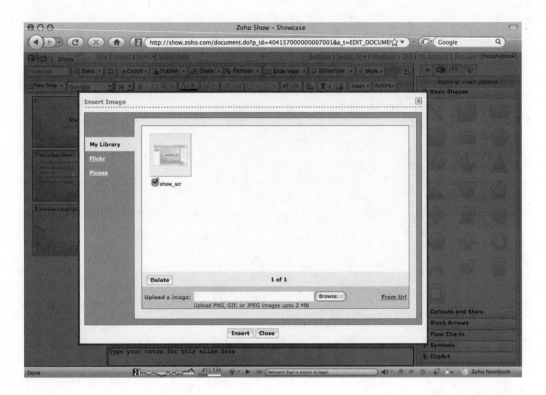

Figure 4-16. Uploaded file listed in `My Library`

12. Right-click the inserted image, and click `Properties` in the context menu (Figure 4-17).

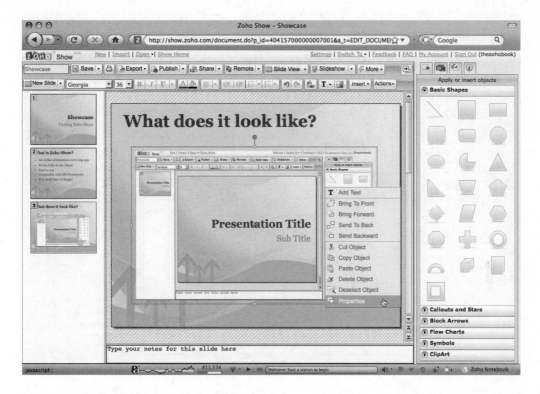

Figure 4-17. The inserted Image and its context menu

13. To have an optimal look for the slide, resize and reposition the image by changing values in the **Properties** dialog box (Figures 4-18 and 4-19). Alternatively, you can use keyboard arrow keys to change the position, and you can use Shift+arrow keys to resize the image. You can also perform this using the image box handles that are visible around the image while selected.

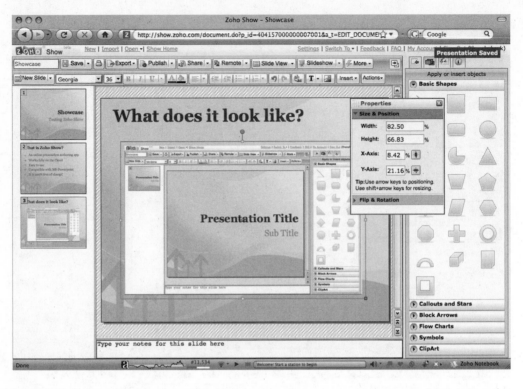

Figure 4-18. Setting the image size and position

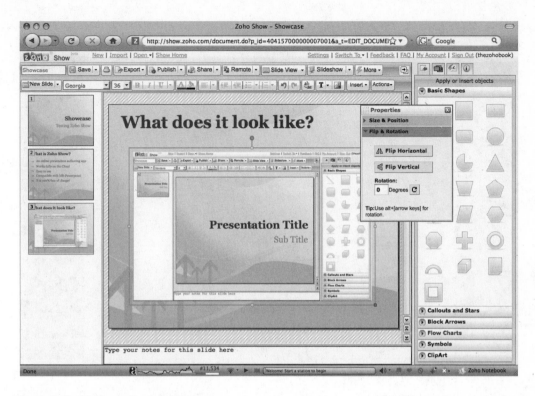

Figure 4-19. Flipping and rotating the image

14. To test the presentation so far, save the presentation, and click the `Slideshow` button on the toolbar to see your first presentation in the real life (Figure 4-20). You can navigate back and forth between the slides to check whether everything is in place. There is a `Fit to Screen` button on the lower right of the slide show window too that stretches the slides to fill the gap (the black surrounding area) on the right and left.

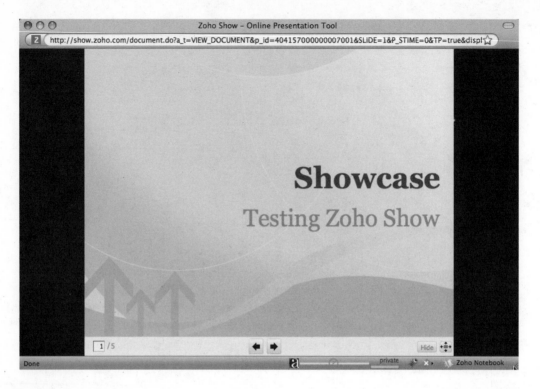

Figure 4-20. The slide show view

Adding objects

Although text and pictures are the forming pillars of presentations, there are more visuals you can add to create a richer experience for the audience (viewers).

To see how to add shapes and other objects to make your points clearer, open slide 3 (and the `Showcase` presentation, if you closed it for any reason), and follow these steps:

1. Open the `Shapes` tab (the first tab on the sidebar), and select `Block Arrows` in the `Shapes tab` (Figure 4-21). Then drag a `Notched Right Arrow`, and drop it anywhere on slide 3.

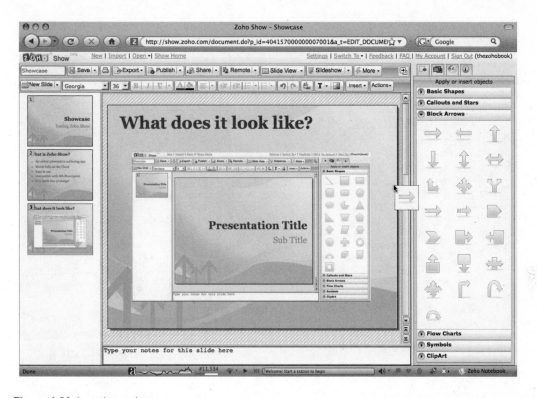

Figure 4-21. Inserting a shape

2. Right-click the shape, and click **Properties** on the context menu. Then select **Solid Fill**, change **Fill Color** to red (#ff0000), and change **Alpha** (transparency) to **0.5** (Figure 4-22).

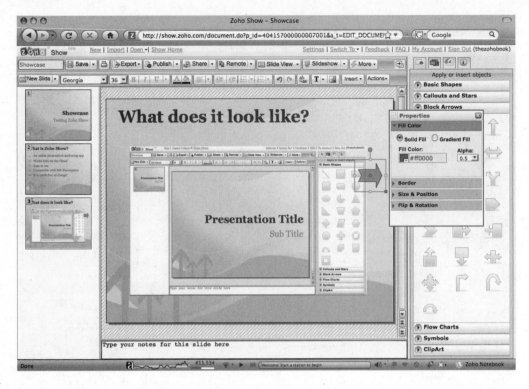

Figure 4-22. Changing the fill style of the shape

    3. Click `Border`, and change the `Border Color` to red (Figure 4-23). Then close the dialog box.

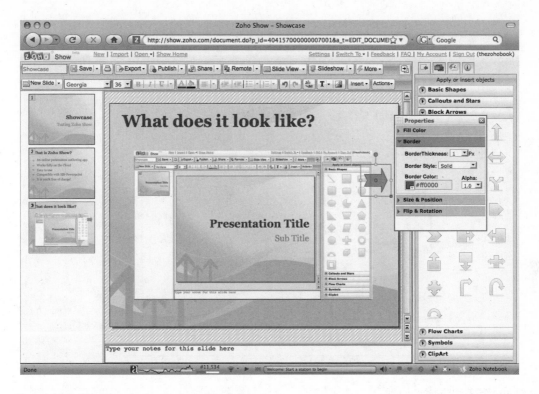

Figure 4-23. Changing the border style of the shape

4.   Grab (select) the arrow shape by using the *rotate handle* (the gold tiny circle attached to the arrow container box), and move the mouse pointer to rotate it so that it is pointing at the image (Figure 4-24).

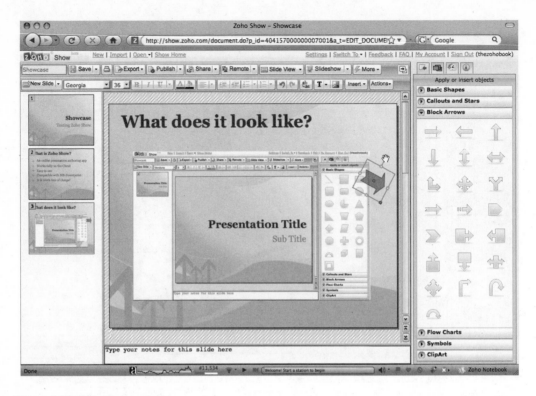

Figure 4-24. Rotating the shape

5. Position the shape as in Figure 4-25, and resize it (with the handles) until you are happy with it.

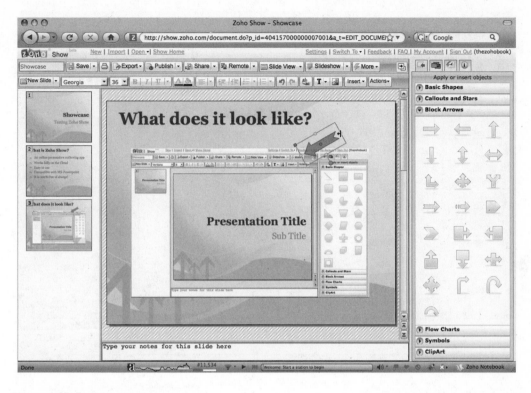

Figure 4-25. Resizing the shape

6. Now, add a text box by clicking the `Text Box` button on the toolbar or clicking `Insert ▶ Text Box ▶ Text Box`.
7. Format the text box by changing the font to `Georgia` and the size to `14`. Then make the container (the surrounding rectangle) smaller using the handlers. It should look like the text box in Figure 4-26.

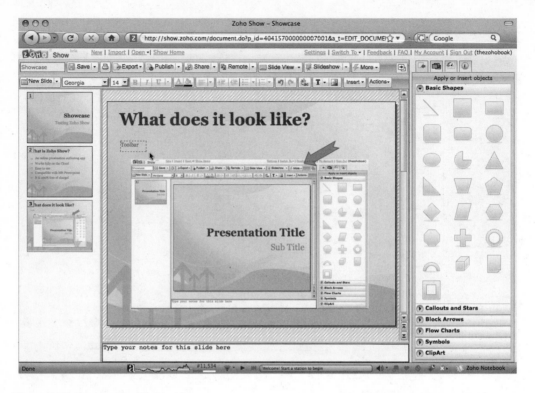

Figure 4-26. The newly added text box

8. Move the text box to the top right of the red arrow you just created (Figure 4-27).

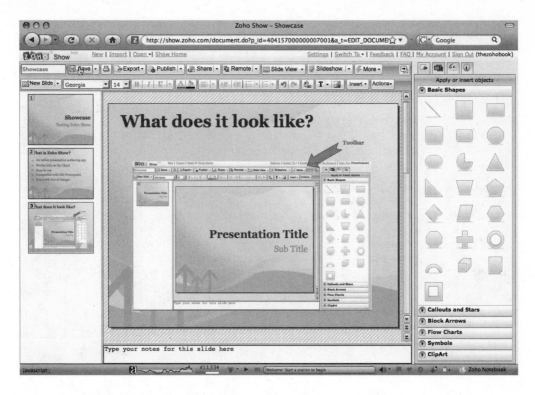

Figure 4-27. Focusing your audience's attention

The arrows and the text box will draw your audience's focus to the subject (the toolbar here) while you're presenting this slide.

Adding embedded objects

It is time to add a chart and a spreadsheet to your presentation to make it more sophisticated. You can insert different objects from other Zoho applications (such as Writer or Sheet) into your slides as well.

1. Add a new slide, with `Two Text Blocks` as the `Slide Type` setting.
2. Change the main heading as well as the left text box, as you see in Figure 4-28. Then remove the text box in the right side.

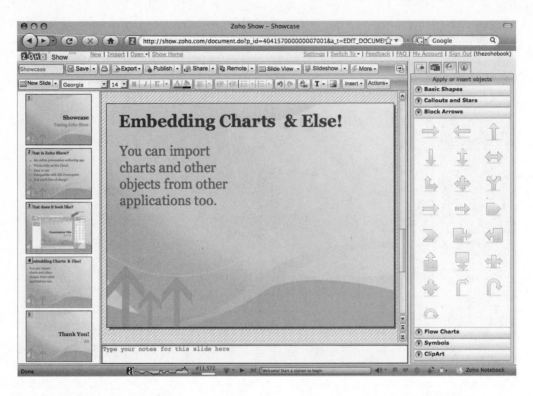

Figure 4-28. The fourth slide so far

3. To see how smoothly Zoho applications work together, you will use a spreadsheet that you created in Sheet in the previous chapter. Open Sheet (in a new window/tab). Load the expense calculator, and open the Dashboard sheet.

4. Move the mouse pointer on the chart, and click the `Publish` link above it.

5. Copy the code snippet in the `Publish Chart` dialog box to the clipboard (Figure 4-29).

> *As you might have noticed, Sheet charts publish as images. This means they are not live (connected to Sheet) and should be imported again manually every time the data is changed in the respective spreadsheet.*

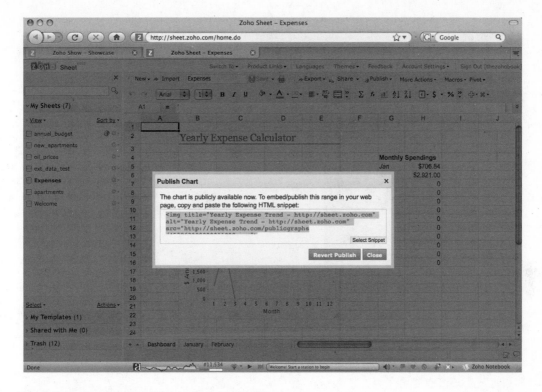

Figure 4-29. Copying the publish code snippet in Sheet

6. Switch back to Show (or open it again if you have closed it), and make sure you are on the same slide you created in step 1. Then click **Insert ▶ HTML Code**, paste the code you just copied, and click **Insert** (Figure 4-30).

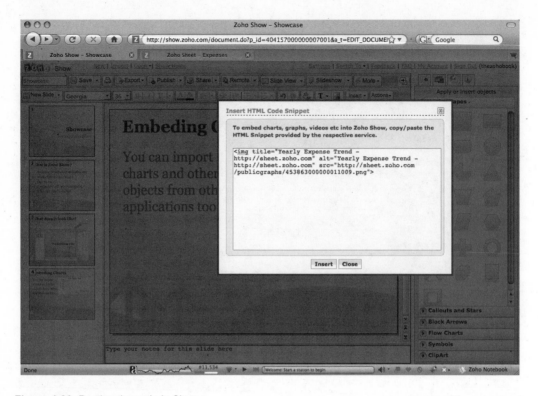

Figure 4-30. Pasting the code in Show

7. You will see the image of the chart is inserted in the slide. Resize and reposition it as you want.

8. Now switch back to Sheet again, and publish the spreadsheet via **Publish ▶ Embed in Website/Blog**. Copy the embed script (see Figure 4-31), and go back to Show.

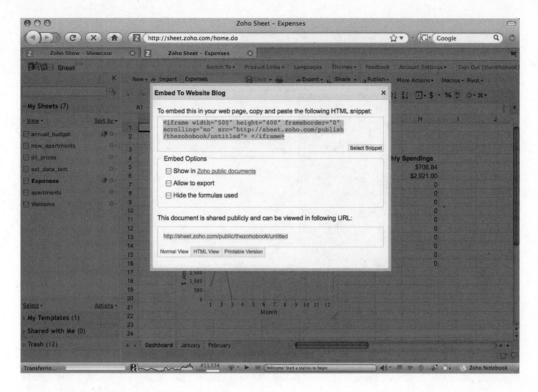

Figure 4-31. Copying the embed code snippet in Sheet

9. In Show, click **Insert ▸ HTML Code**. Paste the code you just copied right in the code box, and click **Insert** (Figure 4-32).

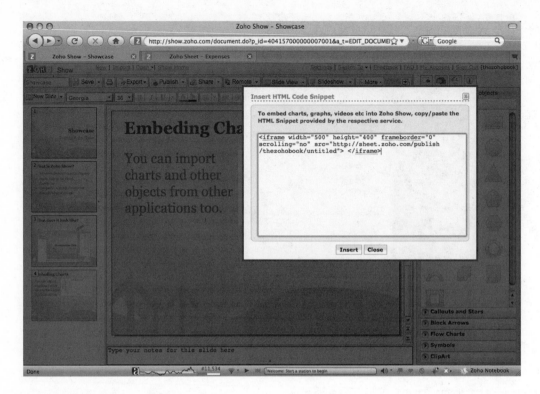

Figure 4-32. Pasting the embed code in Show

10. Save the presentation, and take a look at the impressive slide you just made (Figure 4-33). The spreadsheet (and not the chart since it is just an image) is connected to Sheet, so whenever the original document is updated, it updates the one in your presentation too.

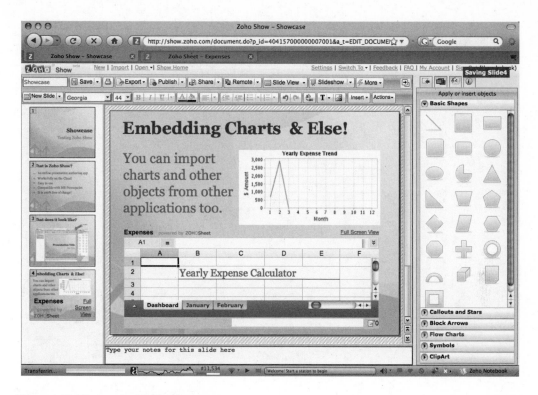

Figure 4-33. The result of embedded content

Embedding objects in presentations from other Zoho applications or third-party services can make your work look more professional. You can demo many mediums from within a single presentation, something that was not possible before with any other software (as far as I know).

Basically, you can add any embeddable web object like YouTube (www.youtube.com) video clips in your slides and create great mashups. The procedure is almost identical to what you did in steps 8 and 9, meaning you should first extract the embed code from the provider (for example, YouTube) and then insert it into Show. Don't worry if you have no idea what all those codes mean. You just need to do a copy and paste to place many objects in your presentations.

Finishing the presentation

To finish our simple presentation, we need to add a final touch: a thank you slide at the end of the presentation. Using the tools you learned in the previous sections, add a new slide containing a proper message (like in Figure 4-34), and save it.

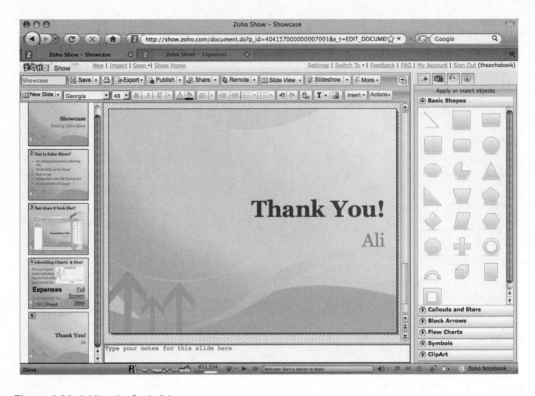

Figure 4-34. Adding the final slide

Congratulations! You have just created a nice presentation in Show. Click the `Slideshow` button on the toolbar to review your work (Figure 4-35).

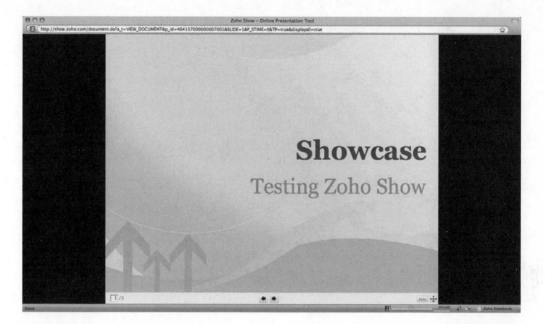

Figure 4-35. Running the slide show

It opens in a new window filling the entire screen. Navigate back and forth using the right and left arrow buttons in the lower middle of the window. Keyboard arrow keys (right/left and up/down) work for navigation too.

You can hide the toolbar during the show by clicking `Hide`. Click the `Fit to Screen` button (the first button on the bottom right) for the slides to fill the black surroundings. This might make the slides too look weird, so test it before using it in a real presentation session.

There is also a context menu (Figure 4-36) that has all the commands you need during the slide show. You can right-click anywhere on the slides to open it.

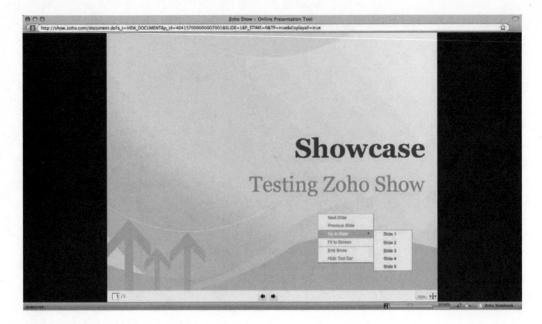

Figure 4-36. The slide show context menu

Sharing and collaborating

Sharing content and collaborating with peers are some of the most exciting features of cloud-based applications. As you saw in the previous chapters, Zoho provides you with state-of-the-art tools to stay productive in a shared environment.

Show also provides you with the same set of tools and features to publish and share your presentations so you can collaborate with friends, colleagues, and so on.

Publishing your presentations

A quick way of sharing your presentations with the world is to publish them. When you publish a presentation, it becomes public, meaning it is accessible globally by everyone and it is listed in Zoho Show's **Public Presentations**. This is great when you have turned an idea into a slide show and you would like everybody to benefit from your wisdom.

Suppose you want to publish a motivational presentation about life and personal development. All you need is to create it in Show (or import it into Show if you have created it elsewhere) and publish it. Then you can embed it in your website or just share the link to your presentation with the world.

Scholars can publish educational content, and businesses can publish presentations, company profiles, and product tours with just using Show as the platform.

> A rule of thumb for sharing any kind of material online, be it presentations, spreadsheets, and so on, is to be careful about what you publish. Check for copyrighted, potentially harmful, or classified information in your work before exposing it to the world.

To publish a presentation, follow these steps:

1. In edit mode (the design environment), open the presentation you want to publish, and then click `Publish ▶ Make Public`.

2. In the `Make Public` dialog box, read through the on-screen note, and make sure you keep `Automatically re-publish when document is modified` selected so the published slide show is always the latest version. Then click `Make Public & Continue` (Figure 4-37).

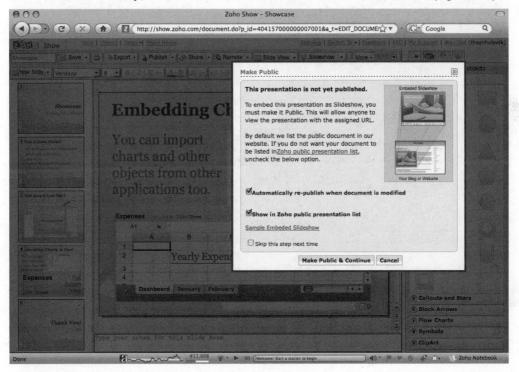

Figure 4-37. Making a presentation publicly accessible

3. After publishing the presentation, you need to let people know about it. Choose any or both of the following:

    a. Copy the HTML code snippet (see Figure 4-38), and paste it into the source code of any web page (for example, a page in your blog) for the people to watch the slide show directly in your website.

b. Publish the direct link (below the HTML code box) to the slide show (for example, via e-mail) so people can just open the link and watch the presentation on their web browsers.

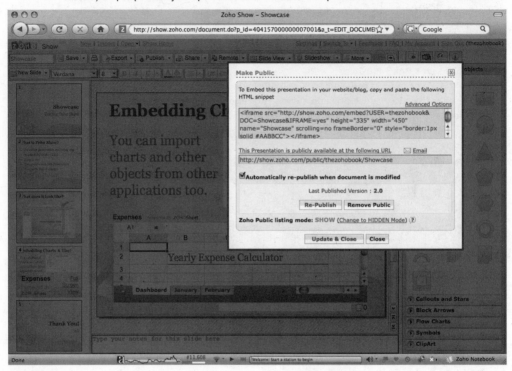

Figure 4-38. Various means to publicize the publicly accessible slide show

4. Before copying the code snippet, click **Advanced Options** to set a few more options for the published slide show (Figure 4-39). You can show/hide the toolbar, make it fit to the screen by default, enable/disable the right-click menu, and so on. Close the window once you're done tweaking.

Figure 4-39. Advanced publishing options

5. Click `Update & Close` in the `Make Public` dialog box.

Remember that you can unpublish the presentation at any time by clicking `Publish ▶ Remove Public`.

> *Whenever you make a presentation public, it gets listed in the Zoho public presentations. You can check this at http://show.zoho.com/latest and see your presentations, the number of views for each one, and the related comments and tags (Figure 4-40).*

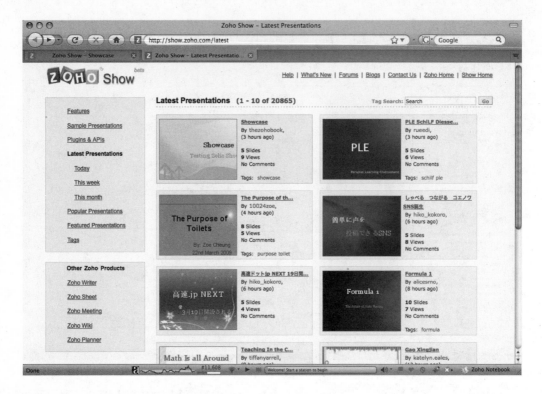

Figure 4-40. Public presentations

Sharing and collaborating

As you may remember from the previous chapters, you can share documents with friends and colleagues so everybody can work on the content as a team. If you want to control who has read or read/write access to your document, sharing is the right way to do it.

To share a document, follow these steps:

1. With your presentation open, click `Share ▶ Invite` in the toolbar.

2. In the `Share This Document` dialog box, enter the e-mail address (or the Zoho ID) of the `Read Only Members` as well the `Read/Write Members` (Figure 4-41).

3. Select the `Notify me, whenever a shared user modifies this presentation` check box to stay tuned to the changes. Any change happening in the document will be reported to you by e-mail.

4. Add a line or two to the invitation message to personalize it a bit more by clicking `Edit Invitation Email`.

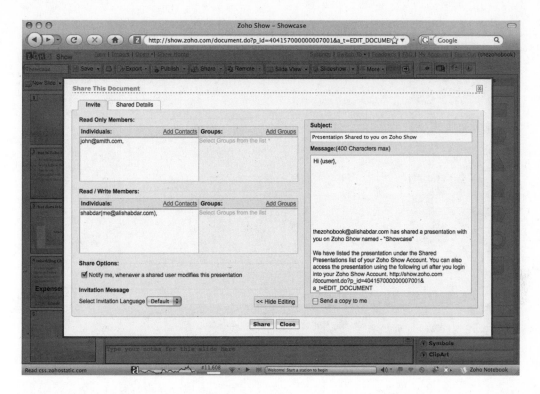

Figure 4-41. Inviting people to share the presentation

5. Click **Share**. The presentation is successfully shared, and the **Shared Details** tab opens automatically for you to review the performed job. You can change the permissions or remove an unwanted share quickly (Figure 4-42).

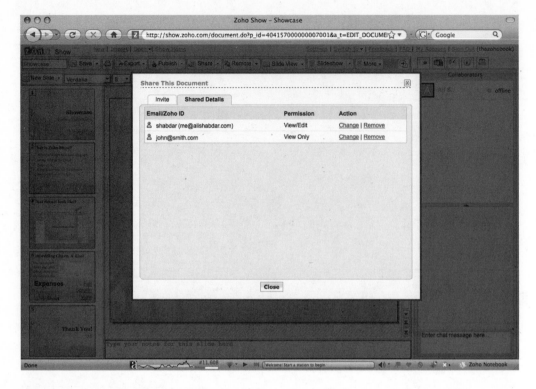

Figure 4-42. Reviewing the member list

Once a presentation is shared, all invitees receive an e-mail message announcing the share along with a link to the shared document. They will also have it listed in their **Shared to Me** presentations.

Collaborating in action

The collaboration process is seamless and happens in real time, which makes it exciting and boosts your (and you team's) productivity. Every change in the document is registered and is easy to track. The collaborators (read/write members you invited previously) are in close contact via e-mail and built-in chat to be able to work in a better way.

When a collaborator opens the presentation—while you have it open too—you (as the owner or just another collaborator) are going to be alerted that somebody has opened the presentation for viewing (Figure 4-43). Once collaborators start editing the contents, their status becomes **Editing** instead of **Viewing**.

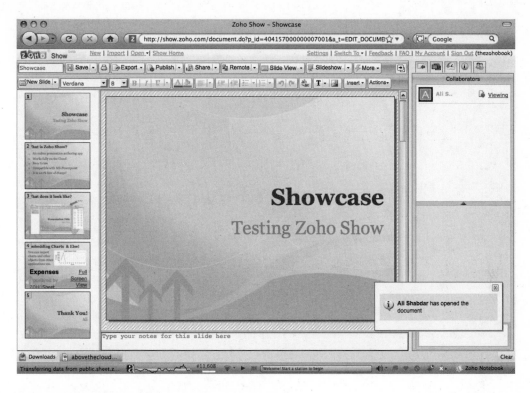

Figure 4-43. Notifying a collaborator's action as it happens

Collaborators can chat during the process by clicking the names (avatars) on the **Collaborators** tab. This is a great help to work together (Figure 4-44).

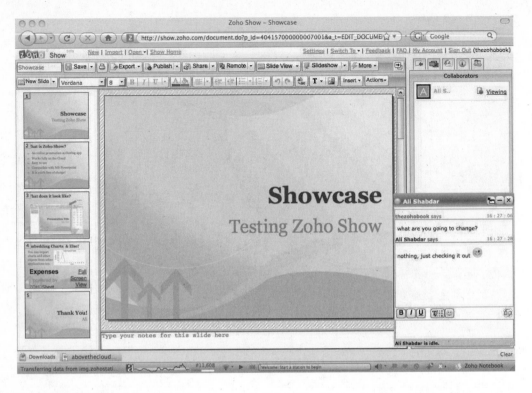

Figure 4-44. Chatting while working

To check the latest activities and the modifications, open the `Version Details` tab. You can see who made the modifications as well as view that particular version.

Revert to or delete a specific version if you need to do so by using the corresponding links below each version in the list (Figure 4-45).

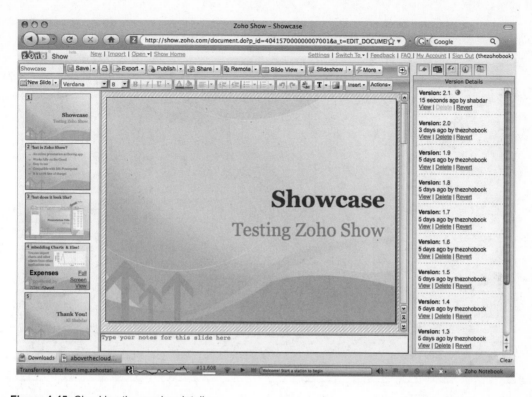

Figure 4-45. Checking the version details

There is a nifty tool, `Notify shared Users`, to send messages to the owner of the document or to all other members from within Show (Figure 4-46). Click `Share ▶ Notify Shared Users` to drop a message to the collaborators. It will be sent to the same e-mail addresses by which they subscribed to Zoho.

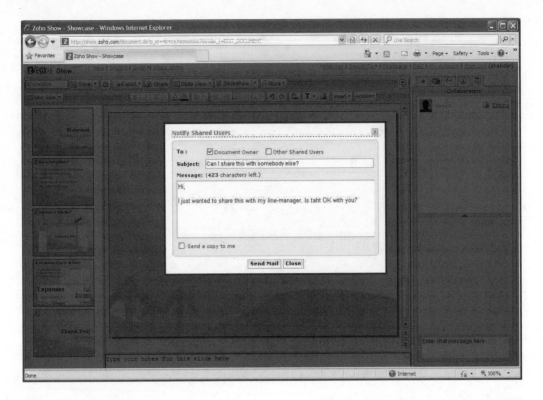

Figure 4-46. Notifying the collaborators

More Show

You have learned all the essential features of Zoho Show, but there are still a few other tools that will make your life easier.

How to use the master layout

You probably often create presentations with common objects throughout the entire presentation. Take your company logo, for example. You usually need to put it in the header or footer of every slide.

> Headers and footers (as you saw in Chapter 2) are optional sections on the top and bottom of each page of a document that usually contain information such as the page title, a logo, the page number, and so on. You can add/edit footers to the slides in Show by clicking **More ▶ Add Footer** in the menu bar, but our focus here is on master layouts.

The hard way to do this is to paste the header or footer into every page and change them all when there is a modification needed. But the easy way, and the way that Show recommends, is to use the master layout.

There are two master documents for every presentation, **Title Master** and **Slide Master**. As the names suggest, they are the templates for the title page and for the other slides, respectively. So, if you apply some changes to the slide master, they will show up in all slides of that particular presentation.

As simple as it sounds, it is doable in few steps:

1. Create a new presentation. You can also use the presentation you made in the previous sections.
2. Click **Slide View ▸ Master View** on the toolbar. You can see the master documents listed in the slide list (Figure 4-47).

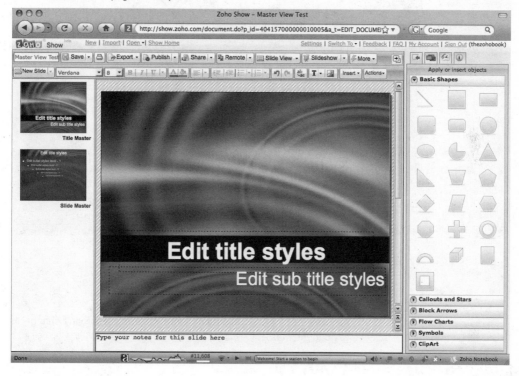

Figure 4-47. The master view

3. Open the **Slide Master**, and place a logo (or anything that should repeat throughout the presentation) in the master document. You can also change the **Title Master** (the first page of the presentation) if you want (Figure 4-48).

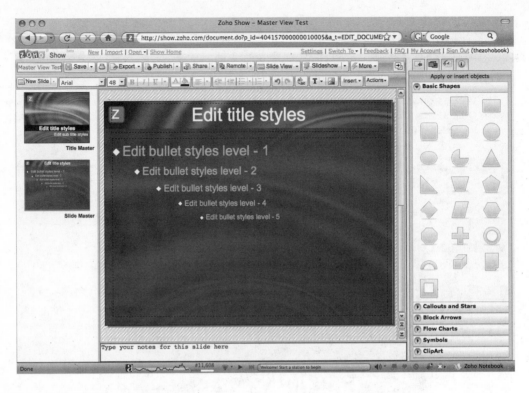

Figure 4-48. Modifying the slide master

4. Save the document for the changes to apply.
5. Go back to the normal view (**Slide View ▶ Normal View**) to see the changes.
6. Add new slides, and you can see that the logo is already there. Note that you can't change the logo from here. You need to go to the master view if you need to modify it.

Taking your cheat sheet with you

You can add a few lines for every slide, reminding you about the details you want to share with your audience during the presentation session. This is especially useful in remote presentations, an exciting subject that you will learn about in the next section.

To add notes, add the text in the box after every slide in the presentation. Try to keep it short because you won't have time to go through a long note during the real presentation (Figure 4-49).

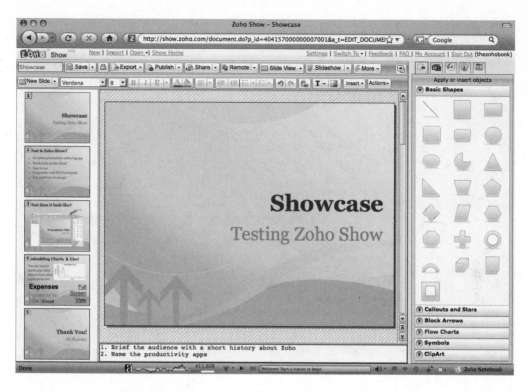

Figure 4-49. Adding a presenter note

Presenting it to the world

One of the great features of Show is the ability to run remote presentations. No matter where your audience is, you can do a live presentation with an unlimited number of participants without them having to install any additional software or plug-in.

Let's see how it works in action:

7. Open the `Showcase` presentation you created earlier in this chapter, and then click `Remote ▶ Start Remote`.

8. If the presentation is not remote yet, first you will be asked to make it so. Click `Make Remote & Continue` (Figure 4-50).

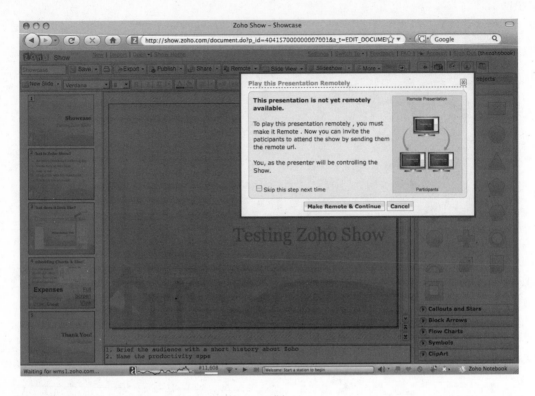

Figure 4-50. Making the presentation remotely accessible

9. On the next screen, you can see the link to the remote presentation. Either send this link manually to the participants or just enter their e-mail addresses in the `Remote Users` box (Figure 4-51). There is also an option to customize the invitation message.

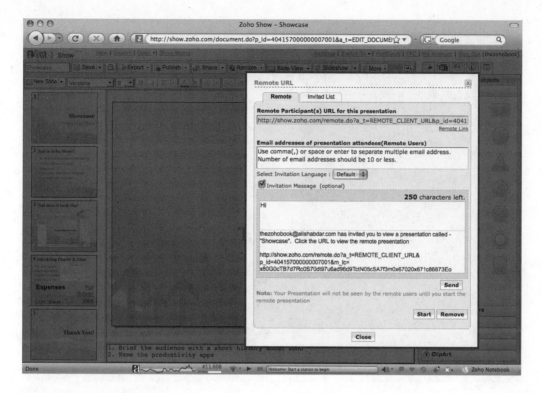

Figure 4-51. Inviting the attendees

10. Click **Send** to dispatch the invitations. You can see a list of invitees on the **Invited List** tab (Figure 4-52).

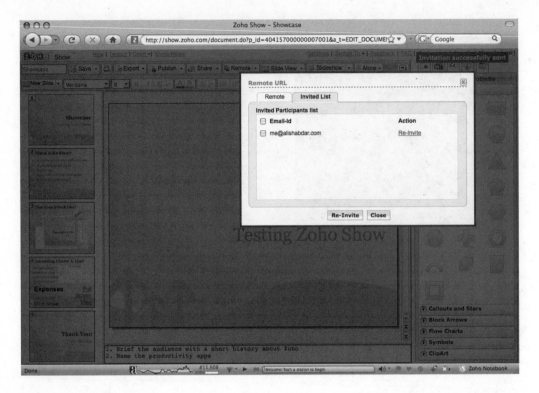

Figure 4-52. Invited people

11. Before the invitees can see your presentation, you need to start it. You can do it either by opening the **Remote** tab and clicking **Start** or by clicking **Remote ▶ Start Remote** on the toolbar after closing the **Remote URL** dialog box.

12. Once the remote presentation screen opens, it fills the entire screen. Click **Start Remote** for the presentation to start; otherwise, the participants who already logged in won't be able to see it (Figure 4-53).

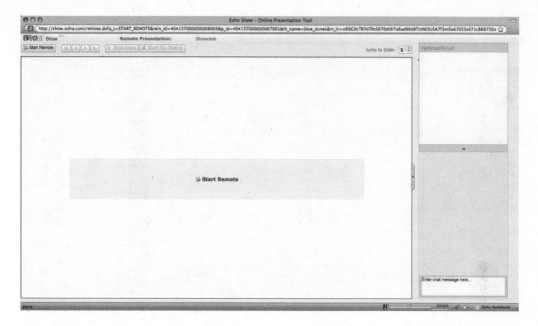

Figure 4-53. The remote presentation window

When you start the presentation, you can show the presenter's notes you entered in the previous section (visible to you only) for your reference. The list of the online participants is also visible on the **Participants List** pane on the right side (Figure 4-54).

If you click a participant's name, a chat window will open so you can chat directly with that person. You can also type public chat messages directly in a text box in the lower right of the pane. Public messages will be visible to everybody.

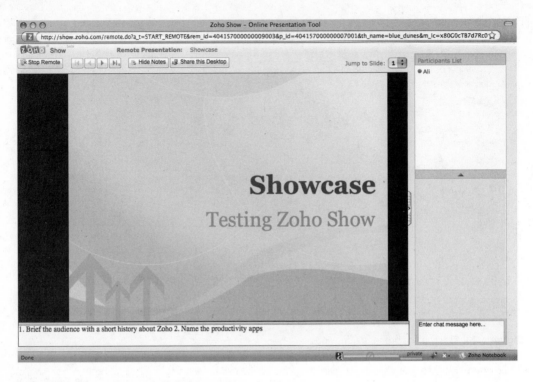

Figure 4-54. The remote presentation is running.

Click `Stop Remote` at any time to immediately end the presentation.

On the other hand, when the participant clicks the link sent to them earlier, they will be redirected to a welcome page where they should enter their screen name (nickname) and then select `Click to attend Remote Show` (Figure 4-55).

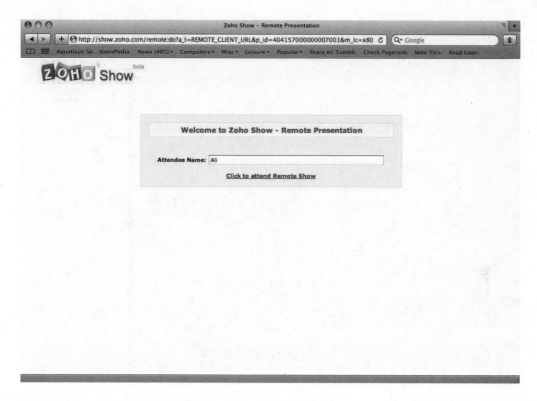

Figure 4-55. The remote presentation page for the participants

After logging in, participants can sit back and enjoy the presentation.

They have the option to ask for permission to run the show themselves by clicking **Request Control** below the presenter's name (in this case, you). This is useful when the actual presenter and the owner of the presentation are not the same person. Also, if the presentation contains different sections that need to be presented by people with different skills, this option will come in handy.

Note that the presenter's mouse pointer is visible to all other participants (Figure 4-56). With the pointer visible and moving in (almost) real time, everybody can see the trace of actions taken while presenting.

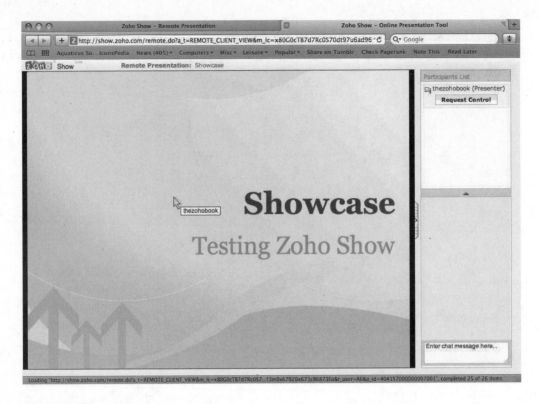

Figure 4-56. The participants' view

Printing your presentations

Although presentations are usually not for printing, sometimes you need to have them on paper for some reason. As you might remember from the previous chapters, the best way to print is to export your document to PDF first. Then you can print it on any printer device.

Click the `Print` button on the toolbar to open the `Print` dialog box. Then you can choose how many slides you want printed on each page and whether you want to print the presenter's notes (Figure 4-57).

Clicking both the `Print` and `Save as PDF` buttons will result in downloading a PDF file containing the presentation. However, clicking `Print` will open the PDF file once it is downloaded and show the `Print` dialog box of your PDF viewer (for example, Adobe Acrobat) too.

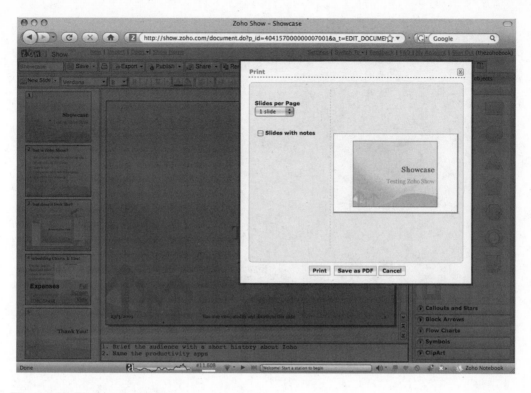

Figure 4-57. Printing presentations

Running a slide show automatically

Sometimes you want a slide show to go through the slides automatically without human interference. You can set how many seconds each slide should be displayed until it is replaced by the next one.

Click **More ▶ Slide Show** Time, and enter the number of seconds in **Time**. Then click **OK** to apply the change (Figure 4-58).

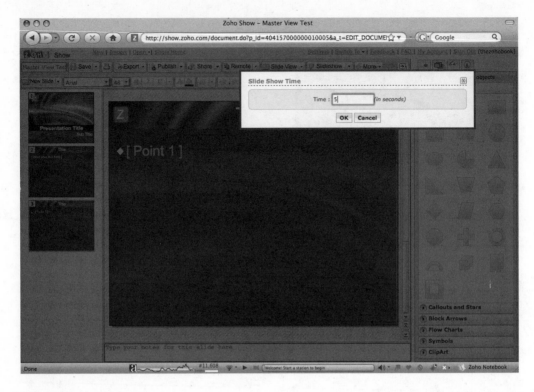

Figure 4-58. Slide show time

Now whenever you run the slide show, it runs automatically. You can see a few more buttons appearing on the toolbar, allowing you to pause the show or to increase/decrease the delays between slides (Figure 4-59).

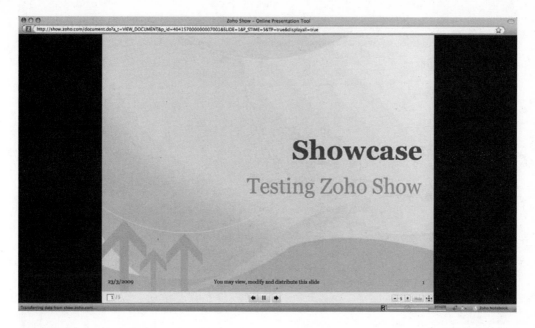

Figure 4-59. Automatic slide show

To set it back to normal, you need to set the delay (`Time`) for **Slide Show Time** back to **0**.

Making it interoperable

Finally, you probably need to import the presentations you have already created with desktop applications like PowerPoint or Impress into Show. Follow these steps:

1. Click the `Import` button on the home page of **Show** or `Import` in the link bar in the editor.
2. Select a presentation file from you local computer or online (Figure 4-60). Files should be smaller than 10MB in size.

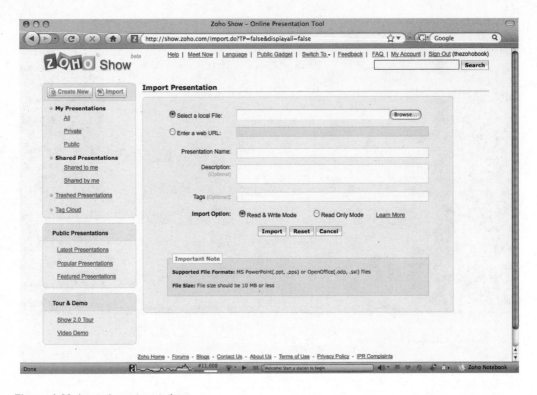

Figure 4-60. Importing presentations

3. Set **Import Option** to **Read & Write Mode**. When you import a presentation for reading and writing, all objects (text boxes, shapes, and so on) will be imported as editable objects, allowing you to make modifications.

4. Click **Import** to proceed with the task.

There are times that some presentations might not import properly and the objects might not be in place. In such cases, you can import them as read-only so the slides will import as images, which means they will look just like the original slide.

You might wonder why you should import presentations as images. Suppose you have a presentation with features that Show doesn't support, but you need to run a remote slide show anyway. You can quickly import it as read-only and run the show.

> *This trick is common in other applications too. For example, when you export a document made in Microsoft Office 2007 to an older format, it converts some objects (that are not supported) to images.*

On the other hand, if you want to open the presentation made in Show in other presentation applications, you can export them as PowerPoint (PPT and PPS) and Impress (ODP) formats by clicking `Export` either on the home page or on the toolbar in the editor.

It is also possible to export the presentations to PDF and HTML for offline viewing. This way, you don't need any presentation software to be installed on the target system.

Getting help

Using Show is very easy, and you can learn it quickly by practicing with the features on the home page and the editor. However, if you need more help, you can always log on to the Zoho forums at `http://forums.zoho.com/Zoho-Show` to find specific answers, or you can check the blogs at `http://blogs.zoho.com/category/show` for a more general perspective.

Checking the public presentations can also give you ideas and help you improve your presentation skills.

Summary

You learned a lot about Show and its features. You created a full-fledged presentation using easy-to-use and powerful tools such as text boxes, images, and shapes. You then went on to make it public for the world to see and shared it with collaborators to work on the contents, opening new doors to the old world of presentations.

Embedding rich content such as spreadsheets, video clips, and so on, was another wonder you made possible with Show.

You now can also run remote presentations easily. Your clients, classmates, and colleagues will be amazed to see what you can do with this free application.

Now you are limited only by your imagination. No specific computer knowledge is actually required to create eye-catching presentations, and practice will be your friend in this journey.

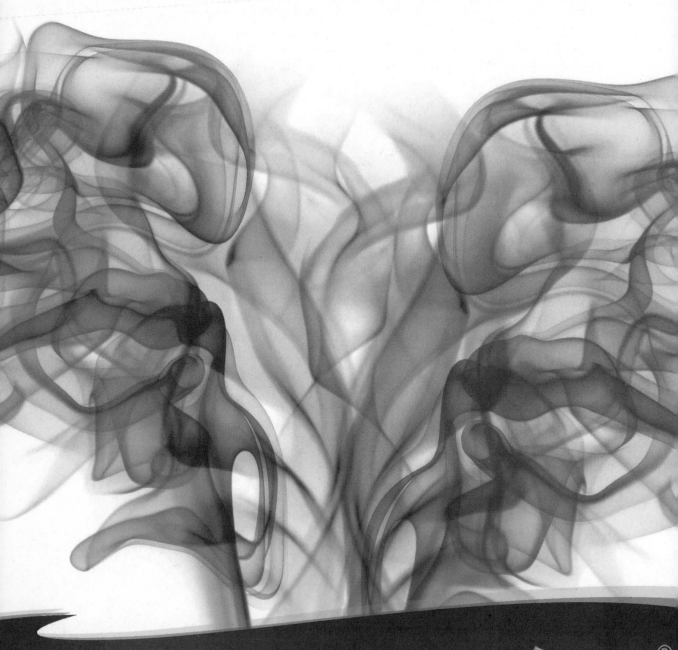

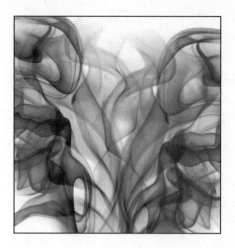

Chapter 5

All in One Box

By now, I am sure you are as excited as I was (and I still am!) when I discovered what SaaS and especially Zoho can do for me. So far, you learned how to use three applications in the Zoho productivity suite. Writer, Sheet, and Show are competent alternatives to their desktop competitors and offer you extra features to help you stay more productive and collaborate easier.

You can now easily create and modify documents (word processing documents, spreadsheets, and presentations), import existing documents, and export them to different formats. You can also publish and share documents to give you maximum flexibility in your daily work.

There is, however, a missing link between these applications—a document manager. The good news is that the Zoho family has another member, Zoho Docs, that is designed exactly for this purpose. Look at it as your online file manager just like Explorer (Windows), Finder (Mac OS), or Nautilus and Konquerer (Linux). With Docs, it is easy to fully take care of your online documents collection.

Although using Docs is pretty straightforward, to make it even easier, you will learn the basics and some of the advanced tricks in this chapter.

Getting started

Docs, essentially, is more than just an online file manager. Not only does it have features that complement the productivity applications, but it also adds a few more features that you will commonly find in a computer-based file manager like Finder or Windows Explorer.

Docs allows you to do the following:

- Store files online, meaning that in addition to storing and managing (administering and searching) your Writer, Sheet, and Show documents, you can import other files too
- Access your important files anywhere at any time because of its cloud-based nature
- Launch online chats and collaboration sessions from within the environment to help you work better in teams

By default, you have 1GB of fee space to store your documents, which is shared between Docs and the other Zoho productivity applications. You can upgrade to paid plans for a negligible monthly fee and get more space if needed.

The environment

To start Docs, log on to http://docs.zoho.com, or select **Docs** in Zoho Personal. Figures 5-1 and 5-2 shows what Docs looks like. As you can see, there is almost no difference between the two environments, so you can choose either of them.

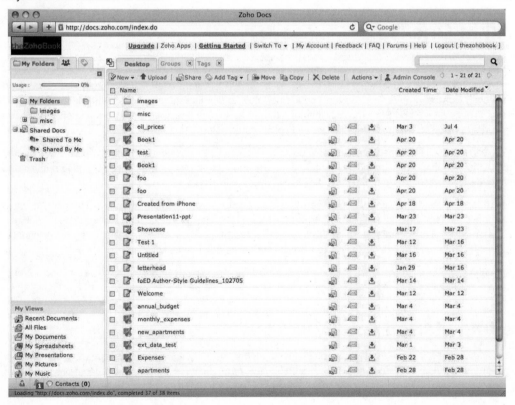

Figure 5-1. Docs as a stand-alone window

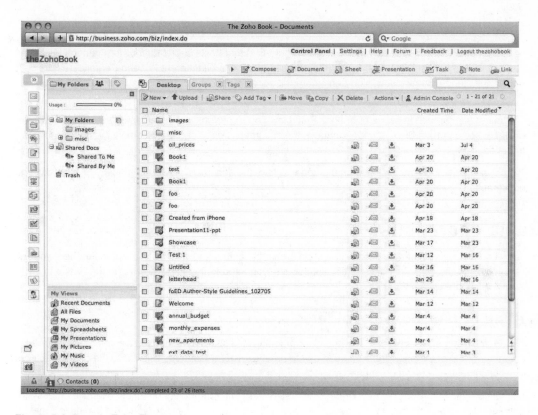

Figure 5-2. Docs in Zoho Personal

The interface of Docs is well organized. It is divided into two sections: the sidebar (on the left side) and the document viewer (covering the biggest portion of the environment).

The sidebar

The sidebar is divided into two panes. The upper pane contains three tabs—**My Folders**, **My Groups**, and **My Tags**—which show (in order) the online folder hierarchy, collaboration groups, and tags to categorize the files.

The lower pane holds **My Views**, which contains shortcuts to list the files (documents) in the viewer based on their types (for example, pictures). I'll discuss the sidebar elements in greater detail in the upcoming sections.

The document viewer by default displays the **Desktop** tab, which lists all the files you have stored in your Zoho account. You will find the documents you created in the previous chapters listed here. Basically, all the documents you create in Zoho's productivity applications (Writer, Sheet, and Show) as well as the files you import (upload) into Zoho appear here.

Other bars

At the top of the screen there is a link bar (see Figure 5-1) that hosts shortcuts for more general tasks that don't specifically affect Docs. You might have noticed that it is a bit different in Zoho Personal (Figure 5-2) than in the stand-alone window. You can ignore this for now because you will use the important links later in the chapter.

The menu bar contains a series of buttons that allow you to perform essential tasks (such as **New**, **Move**, **Delete**, and so on) in Docs. It appears above the document viewer and enables only the buttons relevant to the open tab.

A small search box is also available on the upper right of the document viewer to enable you to quickly find documents.

Basic operations

Just like the days you learned how to create and manage folders and files on your computer, here you will see how to do the same in Docs. As trivial it sounds, you need to first know how to do the basics in order to step into more advanced topics.

Getting organized with folders

A long and cluttered list of files is the enemy of productivity, especially if the files are not named carefully. Folders are one of the basic tools you can use to organize your documents. Similar to the ordinary folders on your computer, you can create and manage folders in Docs to categorize and organize your files.

It is totally up to you how to form your directory tree, where different folders and files resemble an easy-to-manage structure. You can create separate folders for different document types (for example, one for spreadsheets) or for different tasks (for example, a specific project).

> *You don't actually need to put different document types in separate folders (such as spreadsheet files in a Sheets folder) because Docs has a built-in feature called* **My Views** *on the sidebar that allows you to list the files by type.*

To create a new folder, follow these steps:

1. Select **New ▸ Folder** in the menu bar.
2. In the dialog box (Figure 5-3), enter **misc** as the name of the new folder, and click **Add Folder**.

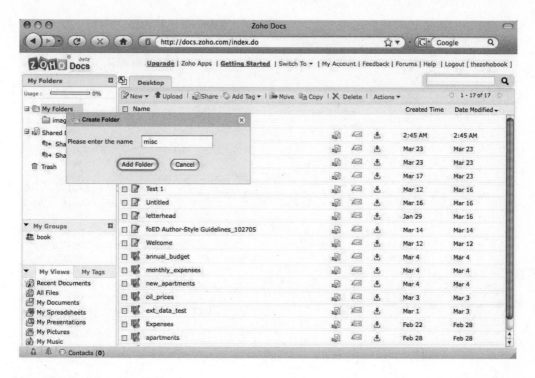

Figure 5-3. Creating a new folder

3. The new folder will be listed in the **Desktop** tab as well as in **My Folders** (in the sidebar). Click the folder name to open it. Obviously, it is empty.

4. Now go back to the root folder (where you created the **misc** folder) by clicking **My Folders** (on the **My Folders** tab). The root folder is listed on the **Desktop** tab again.

5. Drag a document from the list, and drop it on the **misc** folder under **My Folders** (Figure 5-4). This is how you move files to different folders.

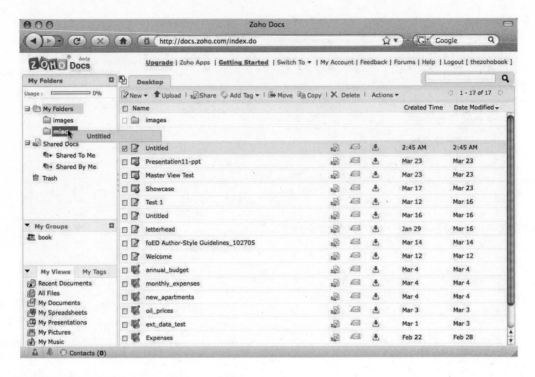

Figure 5-4. Dragging documents between folders

6. Similarly, select two (or more) documents by clicking them, and then perform the drag-and-drop action. All selected files move in one go.

> There is another way to move multiple files from one folder to another. You need to click **Move** on the toolbar after selecting them and then choose the destination folder in the **Move** dialog box (Figure 5-5) and click **Submit**. But dragging and dropping is easier.

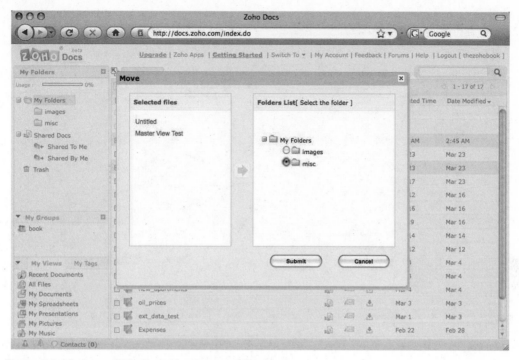

Figure 5-5. Moving multiple files using the `Move` dialog box

Dealing with files

The main objective of Docs is to manage your files, be it the documents you made with Zoho applications or the ones you imported (uploaded from your local computer). You will be able to do basic operations such as creating new documents, viewing and modifying existing documents, and importing and exporting documents created in other applications.

Creating documents

To create a new document, click `New` on the menu bar, and select `Document`, `Spreadsheet`, or `Presentation` (Figure 5-6). This will run Writer, Sheet, or Show, based on your selection, and open an empty document for you to start your work. Based on your browser settings, the new document opens either in a new window or in a new tab in your browser.

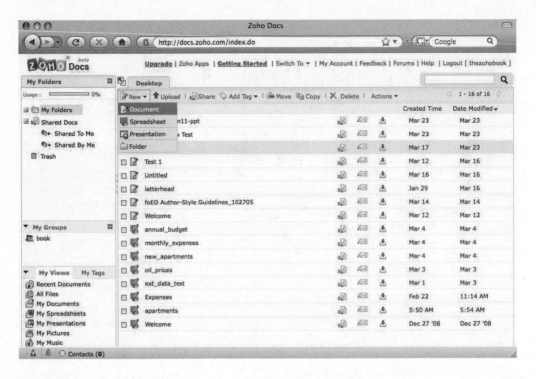

Figure 5-6. Creating new documents

Once you save the document you have been working on, it will be displayed in your documents list in Docs.

> *You might need to refresh the list by clicking its containing folder to see the newly made files.*

Opening and editing documents

One of the nice aspects of Docs is that you can open a number of document types online for viewing and possibly editing, without needing to download them beforehand. These files are word processing documents, spreadsheets, and presentation files that you either created in the Zoho tools (Writer, Sheet, or Show) or imported into Docs. Images, too, can be viewed inside Docs. JPEG, GIF, and PNG are the supported image types for internal viewing. PDF files are also among those files that you can open and view.

For any other document that is not supported, meaning it can't be opened in Docs or in other Zoho tools, it will need to be downloaded, If you, for example, try to open an uploaded MP3 music file (see "Uploading documents" later in this chapter), Docs opens a dialog box with a download link for that file by which you can get the file and open it in your computer.

Now let's open a document for internal viewing:

1. On the **Desktop** tab, find **Showcase** (the presentation you made in Chapter 4), and open it by clicking its name.
2. Since it is a supported document, it will open in a new tab as a slide show (Figure 5-7). Close the tab by clicking the little **x** next to its name above the tab after you have finished interacting with the document.

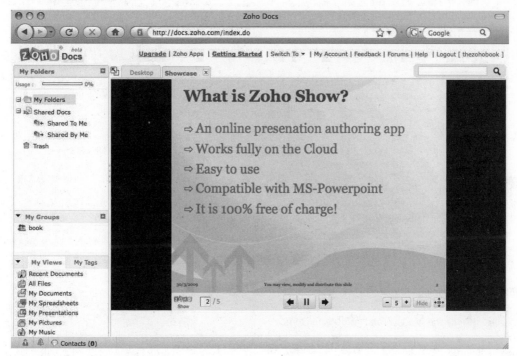

Figure 5-7. Opening a presentation

3. This time open **Showcase** by clicking its icon (Figure 5-8). Show will open the document in a new window in edit mode.

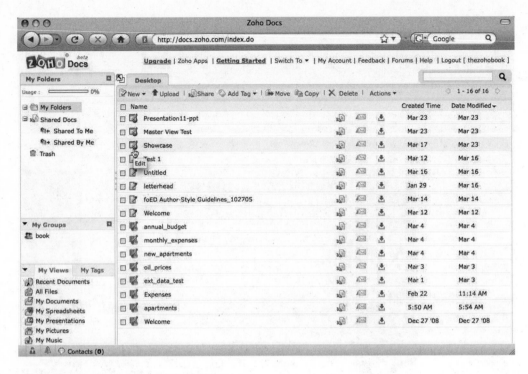

Figure 5-8. Opening a document for editing

4. Close the window, and go back to Docs.

> *If you click the name of a (supported) document, Docs will open it in a new tab for viewing. But if you click the icon of the document (right before name), Docs will open it in a new window running the respective application (Writer, Sheet, Show) in edit mode for you to modify the content.*

Uploading files

When using Docs along with your computer, you are dealing with two different file storage spaces. You have the hard disk of your computer, with all the files stored on it, and you have the online storage space of Zoho accessible by Docs. It's not important how these storage spaces work, but it is important to differentiate them because it might get confusing to work between these two spaces.

Perhaps the most evident difference between the two storage spaces is that the one provided by Zoho is online and accessible from everywhere by just logging into your account through almost any kind of computer that can run a modern browser.

Apart from creating files online, which ends up storing documents online in your Zoho account, you probably have many documents created and stored on your computer. For many reasons, some of which you have already learned throughout this book (such as working online, sharing, and collaboration), you might need to import these files into Docs.

You can do this simply by uploading the files into Docs. Although you can pretty much upload all kinds of files, you are limited to the maximum file size (50MB each) as well as the available quota (the remaining disk space in your account).

Uploading files has another benefit that allows you to have access to your important documents from anywhere at any time, because they are stored in the cloud. You don't need to drag your laptop around just for the sake of having some documents handy. Just log in to your Zoho account from any computer, and get your hands on the precious data.

> *Don't get tempted to upload many files or big ones to waste your web space if you are planning to stick to the free plan. You need that 1GB for Zoho-friendly documents! You can use Mozy (http://mozy.com/) for hassle-free backup or Dropbox (http://www.getdropbox.com/) for file synchronization.*

To upload a file (or more), follow these steps:

1. Click **Upload** on the toolbar.
2. In the **Upload** dialog box (Figure 5-9), add one or more files to the upload queue by clicking **Browse** and selecting them from your computer. Each file gets listed on the right side, and you can remove them by clicking the red **x** in front of them.

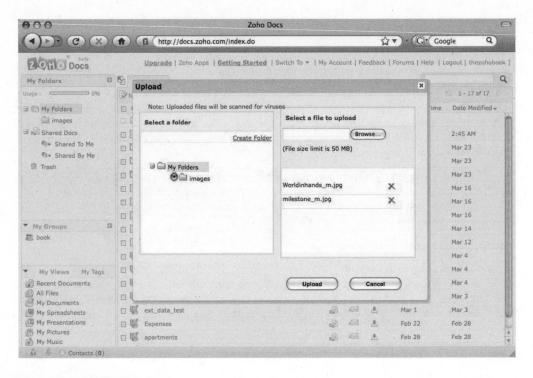

Figure 5-9. Uploading files

3. On the left side, select a destination folder where the files will be uploaded. You can create a new folder during the process (on the fly) too.

4. Once the list is final, click **Upload** to actually start the upload process. This might take a while based on the file's size and the Internet connection speed.

After a successful upload, the file will be listed in the destination folder.

> *A very important point you might have noticed while uploading documents to Docs is that every file gets scanned for viruses before being stored. This makes sure that you and your colleagues work in a clean and (as much as possible) virus-free environment.*

Downloading files

Well, in real life, it is not always the case that you're working 100 percent on the cloud. Sometimes you might have to work on some documents locally because of special software needs or the lack of an Internet connection. In those cases, you will need to download them from Docs to a local computer. After you make the necessary modifications, you can upload them back to Docs to have the latest version in the cloud as well.

To download documents from Docs to your local computer, follow these steps:

1. Click the `Download` button (the third icon in front of the documents). Instead of downloading the document immediately, Docs first shows a dialog box similar to Figure 5-10 with some information about the file. For example, a presentation will have options to download it in different formats, such as PPT, PPS, ODP, and PDF, resembling the export functionality. But for other files (like MP3s), it will just show a single download link.

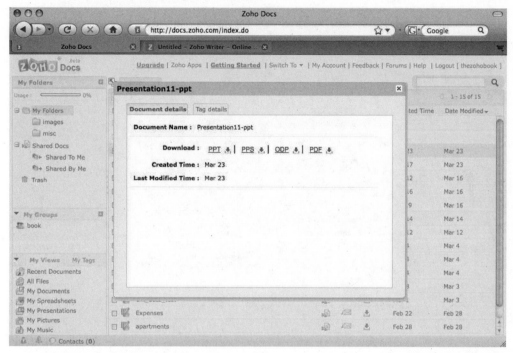

Figure 5-10. Downloading a presentation file

2. Click any of the links to download the document in the respective format.
3. Close the dialog box when you are done.

> *You can export documents to different formats through `Actions` on the toolbar as well. Just select one from the list, and select `Actions` ▶ `Export as XXX` (where `XXX` is the document format).*

Tagging documents

To categorize documents to help you locate them easier in Docs and have a more sensible way of grouping, you can use tags.

Suppose you have two folders, sales and orders, with a few spreadsheets in each one. To categorize them more, tag them with labels such as **important**, **classified**, **draft**, and so on. So, when you search for **drafts**, no matter which folder they are in, they will be listed for you in one place.

To create and use tags, follow these steps:

1. On the **Desktop** tab, select one or more documents.
2. Select **Add Tag ▶ Add Tags**. The **Add Tag** dialog box will appear.
3. Enter the tag(s) separated by comma, and click **Submit** to tag the documents listed under **Selected Files** (Figure 5-11).

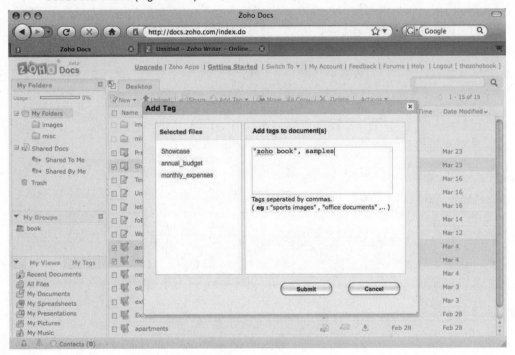

Figure 5-11. Tagging documents with new tags

4. Check the **Add Tag** menu to see that the recently defined tags are listed as menu items for repetitive use. This means that if there are already tags defined, you can just select **Add Tag ▶ <TAG>** to label the document with **<TAG>** straightaway.
5. To use tags to locate documents, click a tag on the **My Tags** tab in the sidebar, and then select a view (**Uploaded files**, **Docs**, **Spreadsheets**, **Presentations**) to find the files (Figure 5-12). So, you can see that there are two steps to find the tagged documents—clicking the corresponding tag and then selecting the proper document type.

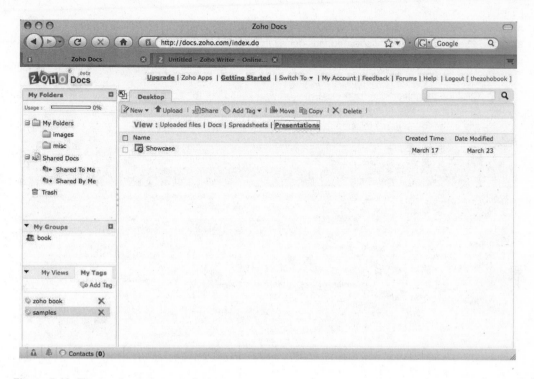

Figure 5-12. Filtering the documents list by tag

More Docs

Apart from full-featured folder and file management facilities, Docs has few more features to help you work online better. Here are some of the features you will be seeing in action:

- The ability to search for documents throughout the system
- Handling compressed (zipped) files
- Managing different versions of a document
- Sending documents to others using e-mail
- Working with colleagues in different groups
- Sharing documents with people

Searching for files

After some time, you will have more and more documents stored in Docs. Although storing them in different folders or tagging them will help you find what you are looking for, it might still take multiple clicks and scrolls to find a document.

A simple solution to this issue is searching for documents. You can search for files by their names (for example, `Showcase`) or their associated tags (for example, `important`).

6. Type in the search phrase, which can be the document name, a portion of it, or a specific tag, in the search box on the upper right of the screen.
7. Click the magnifier icon (or press Enter on your keyboard) to perform the search.
8. Check the results (if there are any) in the newly opened tab, similar to Figure 5-13. You can click any of the found items to open them normally.

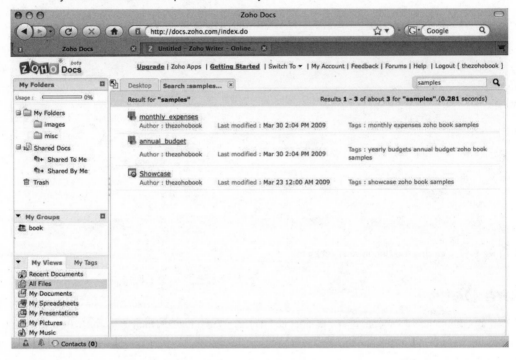

Figure 5-13. Searching for documents

9. Close the tab when you are done.

Because results open in new tabs, you can retain different search results and perform multiple searches without losing the old results.

Using zipped files

Docs also handles compressed files with ease. It can unzip them online, extract their contents, and copy them in the folders. You can use this as a trick when uploading multiple files as follows:

1. On your computer, zip the documents you want to upload.
2. Import the resulting `.zip` file into a folder in Docs by uploading it as you normally do.

3. Select the `.zip` file (in Docs), and then select **Actions ▶ Unzip** to uncompress the archive (Figure 5-14). It places the uncompressed files in the current folder.

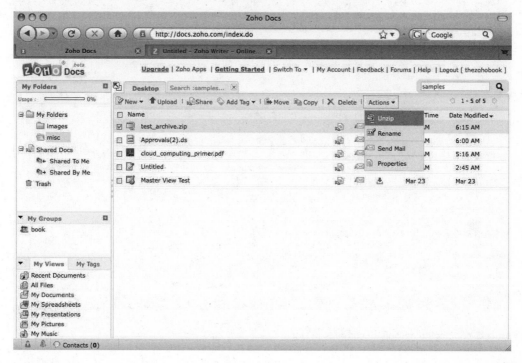

Figure 5-14. Unzipping an uploaded `.zip` file inside Docs

This is a great way to save time when uploading multiple files by both uploading one (`.zip`) file only and compressing the files, especially word processing, spreadsheet, and presentation files.

On the other hand, you can select multiple files in Docs and zip them into one file by selecting **Actions ▶ Zip**. Enter a file name for the `.zip` file, and click **Save** (Figure 5-15).

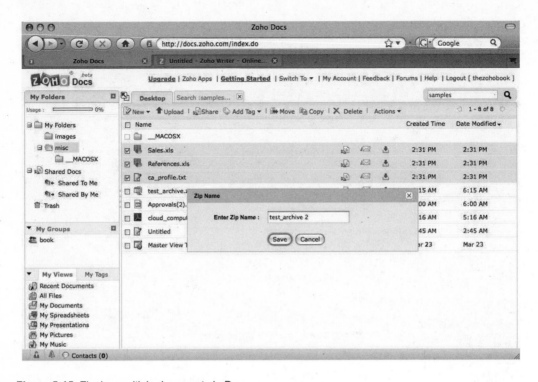

Figure 5-15. Zipping multiple documents in Docs

This helps you save some space if you want to archive files in Docs, and it makes downloading files easier and possibly faster.

> .zip files are archives of multiple files compressed into a single file. All major operating systems have built-in support for .zip files. You can check Wikipedia to get more information.

Managing document versions

There are times that you will upload certain files multiple times. For example, suppose you have a picture document (for example, a product image) that you have changed multiple times. You also keep an online version of the file, which needs to be updated (uploaded again) every time you modify the document.

If you want to retain the older versions of the picture for your reference, you need to find a way to keep them all in one place. They can't have the same name if you just want to store them in the same folder, and saving them in different folders for this reason only is a really bad practice. A lousy, yet effective, way is to give them different names, such as img_01.jpg, img_02.jpg, img_03, and so on.

In Docs, however, there is a much better approach. Upload the new file in the same folder of the old file, and Docs will automatically replace the file with the latest version, but it keeps the old versions in the background as well, in case you need them at some point.

1. Upload a document (such as a text file) to Docs like you normally do.
2. Make some changes in the document on your computer (locally), and upload it again to the very same folder. Docs replaces the older one with the new one, no questions asked.
3. Click the `Download` button to open the document details (Figure 5-16). Then check for the different versions of the document (1.0, 1.1, and so on), and note the `Uploaded Time` setting.

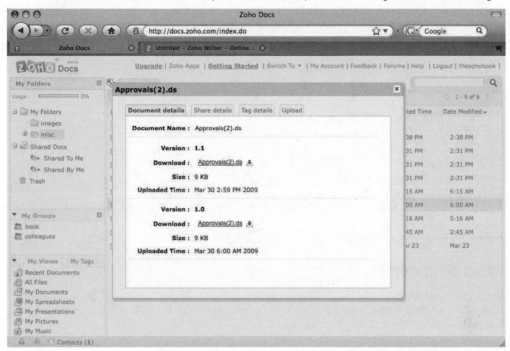

Figure 5-16. Different versions of a file

4. Download an older version by clicking the respective link, and compare it locally with the latest version on your computer.

The versioning facility is a great tool to keep track of the changes made on your online documents. You can revert to any older version for any reason because you have an online version saved for you in a safe place.

The document detail dialog box (that is used for downloading) has an `Upload` tab that allows you to directly upload a newer version of the document into Docs (Figure 5-17). Browse for the latest file on your computer, and click `Upload`. This will upload the file and list all the available versions for your reference.

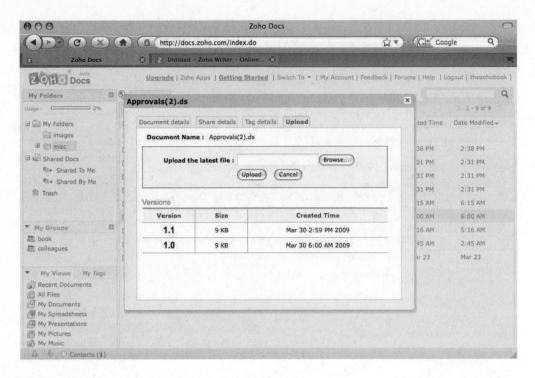

Figure 5-17. Note the current versions of a file while uploading.

Sending documents

A quick way of sending documents to people (for example, friends, clients, and so on) is to use the internal e-mail facility of Docs. It incorporates Zoho Mail (which I'll discuss in detail in Chapter 6) to dispatch documents via e-mail.

To send a single file, follow these steps:

1. For each document, click the `Send Mail` button (the envelope icon). You can also select multiple documents and select `Actions` ▶ `Send Mail` to send them all in a single message.

2. In the `Mail` window (Figure 5-18), enter the recipient(s), the subject, and the message text. There is a formatting toolbar you can use to format the message to make it look more professional.

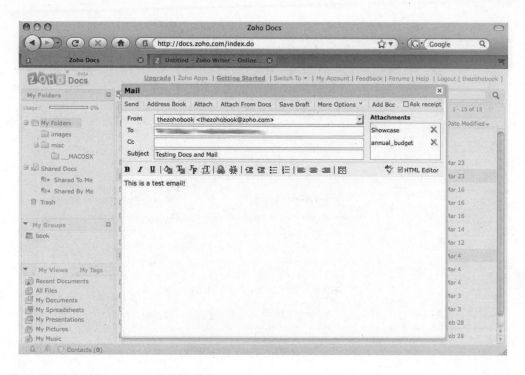

Figure 5-18. Sending documents with Mail

3. Once you are done creating the message, click **Send** to dispatch it immediately.

Working in groups

When you work, you often divide people into smaller groups. **Marketing**, **R&D**, and **Classmates** are all examples of groups in which you team up with different people to perform common purposes.

To make tasks such as sharing documents (covered in the next section) easier, you can create groups and assign people to them. This will allow you to perform bulk actions to the group and affect all members at once.

Docs features two types of groups: personal and organization. For now, we will just stick to personal groups. You can find the available groups on the **My Groups** tab in the sidebar or on the **Groups** tab (if open) in the viewer.

To create a new group, follow these steps:

1. Open the **My Groups** tab in the sidebar (Figure 5-19). The **Groups** tab will open with no groups defined.

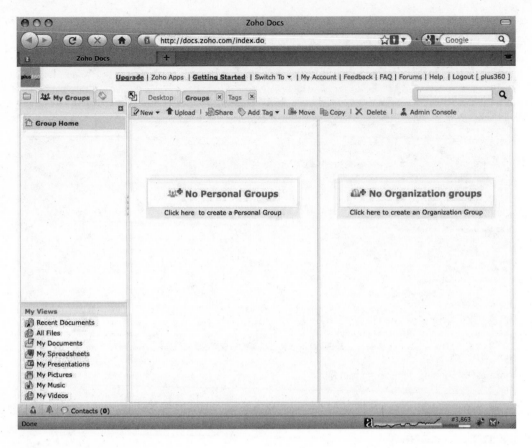

Figure 5-19. The `Groups` tab

2. Click the green + icon on the sidebar (or the link `Click here` in the `Personal Groups` pane) to proceed with creating a new personal group.

3. In the `Create Group` window (Figure 5-20), enter the required information. You need to enter something for `Group Name` and `Members Mail IDs`. You can also enter a short invitation message.

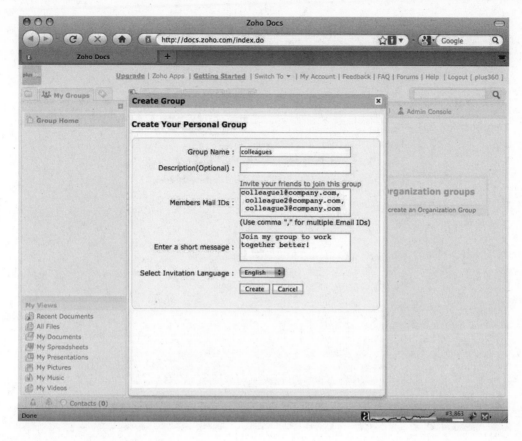

Figure 5-20. Creating a new group

4. Click **Create** to finish the job.

Once the group is created, it will be listed in the **Create Group** window (Figure 5-21). Before closing this window, you can create still more groups by clicking **Create New Group**.

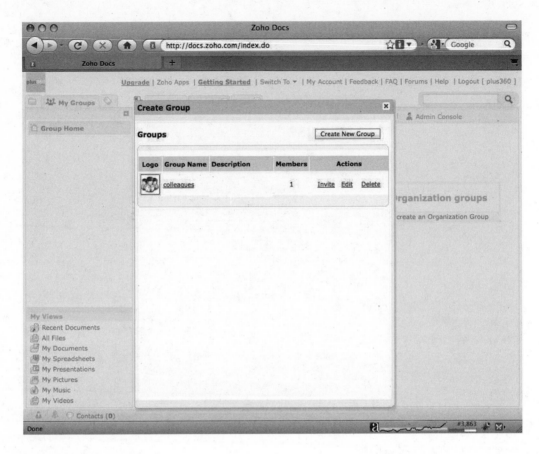

Figure 5-21. Group details

Clicking the group name will open the members' list as well as the pending invitees (Figure 5-22). The invitees won't be able to join the group unless they click the confirmation link in the invitation e-mail sent to them earlier.

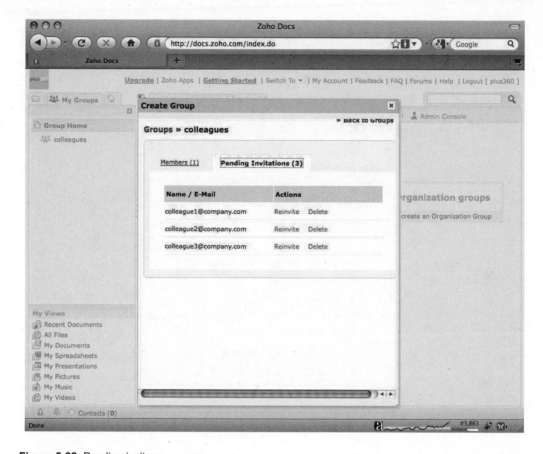

Figure 5-22. Pending invitees

When the invitees receive the invitation message, they can click the link that will take them to Zoho to proceed with the group membership.

> *Don't worry if you are not sure whether some of the recipients have Zoho accounts. They will be directed to open an account before joining your group.*

To customize the look of the group, you can upload a logo and make it distinguishable in the list. You can add members to the group at any time too. You can also remove the members or the invitations if necessary (Figure 5-23). To change the group logo, click `Edit` for a group, and then click `Upload Logo`. A new window will open for you to browse for a picture file (JPEG, GIF, or PNG) smaller than 1MB in size. It will automatically upload the logo and set it to the group.

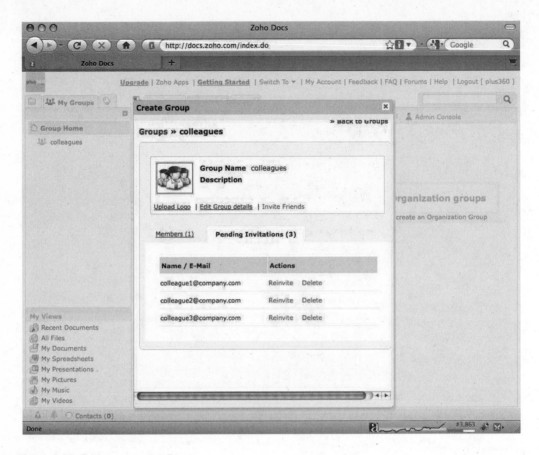

Figure 5-23. Editing group details

Once you close the `Create Group` window, you will see the newly created group is listed under `Personal groups` as well as in the sidebar. For every group there three buttons: `Members Details`, `Group Chat`, and `Send mail to Group`. The first one will open the list of members as well as the pending invitees (Figure 5-24). Click `Group Chat` if you want to open a chat window in which you can chat with the online members immediately.

Figure 5-24. Groups listed with a chat window in the foreground

Finally, click **Send mail to Group** if you want to send a message to all the members. A window will open for you to enter the message information (Figure 5-25). You can also attach documents using **Attach** (which uploads a document from your computer) and **Attach from Docs** (which chooses from the documents available in Docs).

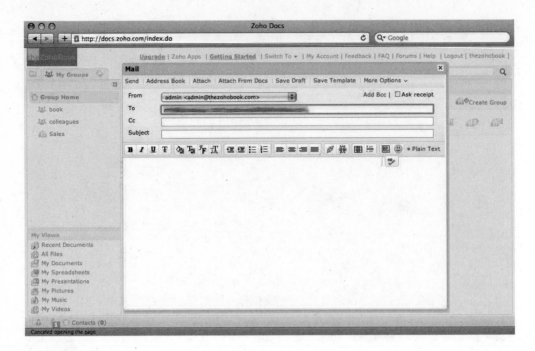

Figure 5-25. Group details

Sharing documents

You have already seen how to share documents with others in the past three chapters. Docs too provides you with the ability to share files quickly and easily. You can share all kinds of files with people for them to read (view) or write (collaborate) contents in a minute.

Although sending documents to individuals or groups by e-mail, as you just saw, is a good way of sharing information, our aim here is to recommend and focus on using the collaboration tools of Zoho whenever possible.

To share files in Docs, follow these steps:

1. On the **Desktop** tab, select two documents, and then click the **Share** button next to it.
2. The **Share Document** dialog box opens with the select file listed in the left pane. Continue with one of the following:

   a. If you are sharing files with individuals, enter the Zoho ID (or e-mail addresses) of the invitees on the **Private Share** tab, and select the proper permission (**Read only**, **Read/Write**) for them (Figure 5-26).

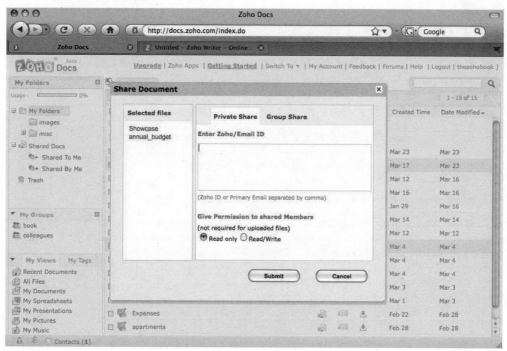

Figure 5-26. Sharing with individuals

b.   If you want to share the documents with a predefined group of people, select the corresponding group(s) on the **Group Share** tab, and set the permissions as well (Figure 5-27).

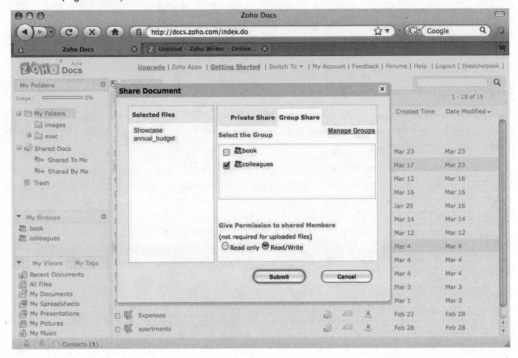

Figure 5-27. Sharing with groups

3.   Click **Submit** to proceed.

Now that you have shared the documents with individuals or groups, they can log in using their Zoho accounts and access the contents. The shared documents are listed under **Shared Docs ▶ Shared To Me** on the **My Folders** tab (Figure 5-28).

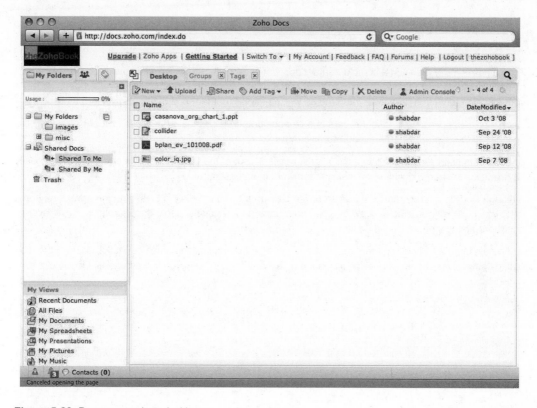

Figure 5-28. Documents shared with you

Group members too can see a list of the documents shared with them by clicking the group name on the **My Groups** tab.

Getting help

After reading this chapter, I don't think you need more help about Docs because you should be able to easily find your way around it.

However, you can check `http://www.zoho.com/online-document-management/zoho-docs-overview.html` if you need any additional help.

I also urge you to share your experience, issues, and suggestions using Zoho applications (and Docs in particular) with the Zoho community at `http://forums.zoho.com/Zoho-Docs`.

Summary

Zoho Docs is more than just a complementary application to Writer, Sheet, and Show. It provides you with a host of easy-to-use features to manage your files in the cloud. It allows you to create, open, and edit various documents from the same interface as well as import (upload) and export (download) them.

Docs also helps you keep different versions of your documents, making it a useful tool in tracking the changes of the content you (and your team) work with.

Sharing data is, like in other Zoho applications, available out of the box. Individuals and groups can easily have access to shared documents, making teamwork even easier.

Although Docs is not recommended as an online backup system for all your files, you can always rely on it to store a globally available copy of your important and regularly used documents to have access anywhere at any time.

In the next chapter, I'll go into more detail about some of the applications (such as Mail and Chat) that you already saw in this chapter as well as introduce a new one that will help you live a better life in the cloud.

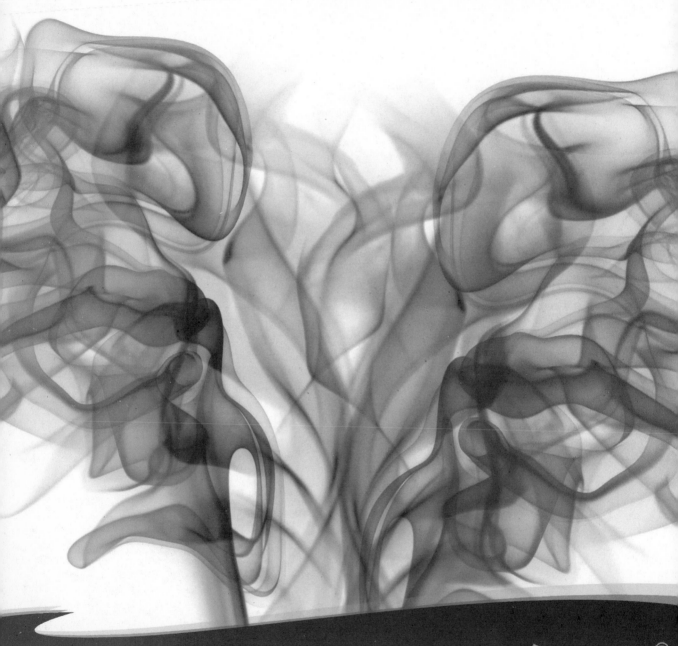

ZOHO®

Work. Online

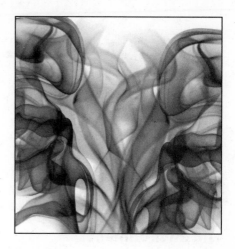

Chapter 6

Live in the Cloud

So far, you have learned how to manipulate and manage your documents in the cloud. However, there are still a few applications to be used to officially claim that you live in the cloud.

As an Internet user, you probably have an e-mail address (such as from Gmail), and you communicate with your friends using your favorite instant messaging (chat) service (such as using Google Talk). You might be also using personal information manager (PIM) software or devices to organize your personal or business life. These are the tools you probably use every day; in fact, many people depend on them. If you are already familiar with the general features of such services, it is much easier to get started with the Zoho offerings.

In this chapter, you'll learn about what Zoho has to offer in this department—that is, Zoho Mail, Zoho Chat, and Zoho Planner. Although it might look like these are yet more tools in a jungle of many, you will see that sometimes it is worth reinventing the wheel. For example, having these tools in the Zoho suite maximizes the interoperability between all Zoho applications to provide you with better performance and improved productivity.

Now you'll see what each one of these applications can do for you.

Zoho Mail

Mail is an e-mail client and is part of the Zoho suite. Although it addresses the old "checking and managing e-mails" issue, it has a few innovations that makes it a serious candidate for the job.

Unlike other e-mail services that oblige you to use an e-mail address of their own (for example, an @gmail.com or @yahoo.com address), you can use your own e-mail address (for example,

@yourcompany.com) or just opt for a Zoho e-mail address (@zoho.com). You will get the @zoho.com address for free anyway, but the great thing is that you have the option of having your other e-mail address hosted and managed by Zoho too.

Mail also features threaded e-mail reading, meaning the messages that are sent back and forth between you and a particular recipient are formed in a conversational tree for a better means of reviewing the full e-mail thread. Clicking the `View Related Mails` icon (if available) in front of every message will open the tree for you to navigate through the conversation.

Spam protection, no ads (although it is totally free of charge), offline support (discussed later), mobile support (iPhone, Blackberry, Android, Windows Mobile, and Nokia smart phones), and an integrated chatting facility are other features of Mail, giving it enough power to be called a professional cloud-based e-mail client.

The environment

Mail is accessible at `http://mail.zoho.com` or from within Zoho Personal. If you are not logged into Zoho, it will ask you to sign in. Use your credentials, and don't mind the `Don't have a Zoho mail account?` message, since you can use the same general Zoho account you use for its other services.

The user interface is similar to other e-mail clients, making it easier for you to master it (Figure 6-1).

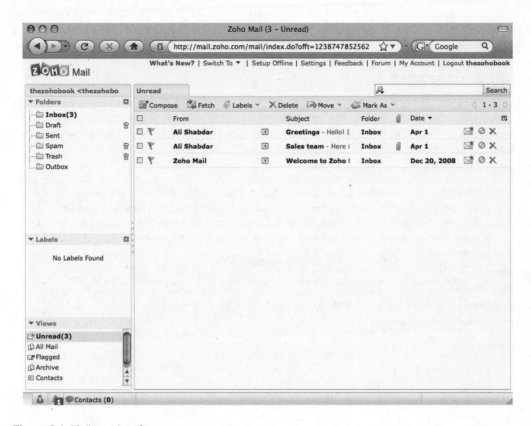

Figure 6-1. Mail user interface

The sidebar (on the left) contains mail folders, labels, and views:

- The `Folders` area lists the folders in your Mail account. You will see how to work with them later in this chapter.
- The `Labels` area shows colored tags used to categorize the messages more flexibly.
- The `Views` area filters the e-mail list for you to find different groups (`Unread`, `Flagged`, and so on) easier.

You can click different folders to see the contents, and you can try different views to filter the message list and find the messages easier.

The biggest portion of the screen is occupied by the message list. When you open Mail, by default the `Unread` tab opens and shows you only the messages that you haven't read yet. Mail opens different objects (as you are about to see) in different views. Each new view opens in a new tab to give you enough space to see and work seamlessly between the different parts.

Above each view (tab) there is a menu bar that contains commands related to the current view.

The search box on the top of the message list allows you to quickly search in the e-mail messages for a specific phrase.

Reading messages

The first thing you should know about reading messages is how to check for new e-mails. Since you won't probably have any e-mails (except the Zoho welcome message) in your **Inbox**, send a couple of test messages to your Zoho address from another e-mail service in order to be able to follow the instruction easier.

To read messages, follow these steps:

1. Click **Fetch** on the menu bar, and Mail lists the new incoming messages if there is any. You will also get a notification box appearing on the bottom right of the screen for a few seconds.

2. Find a message in the list, and click the **Popout** icon, right before the message subject. A new window similar to the one in Figure 6-2 will open containing the message.

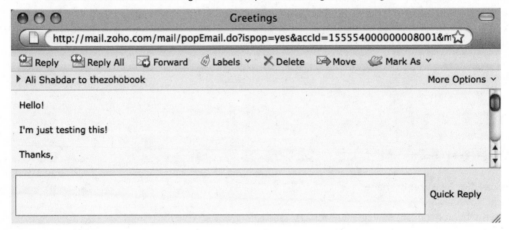

Figure 6-2. Message opened in a new window

3. Close the pop-up window to try another alternative.

4. In the message list, click the subject line (listed in the **Subject** column) to open the message in a pane below the message list, called the **quick-view** (Figure 6-3). The quick-view allows you to see everything in the same page without opening additional windows.

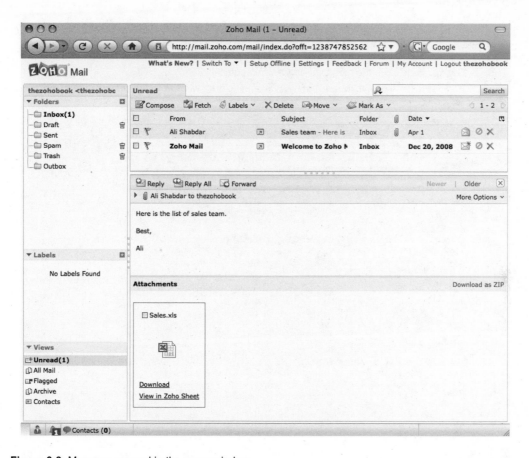

Figure 6-3. Message opened in the same window

It opens the message body followed by the attachments (if there are any), allowing you to quickly download them one by one (**Download**), download them all in a single `.zip` file (**Download as ZIP**), or view the supported documents in the corresponding Zoho applications.

> *Some files such as JPEG (.jpg) or MPEG (.mp3, .mp4) are already compressed, but you can still pack them all in a single .zip file for an easier download.*

For example, in Figure 6-3, the attachment is a spreadsheet document, which is supported by Sheet. Clicking `View in Zoho Sheet` will open it online for your viewing, so you don't have to go through the hassle of downloading the attachments just to check their contents.

There are still a few more tips when you read messages in Mail:

1. In the message list, click a sender's name. A new tab containing all mails received from that particular sender will open, making it easier to manage the flow of messages.

2. Click **More Options** in the quick-view pane or in the pop-up message window. A small menu will open.

- Click **Save** to store the message on your computer.
- Click **Print view** to open the message in a new window ready to be printed on paper (Figure 6-4).

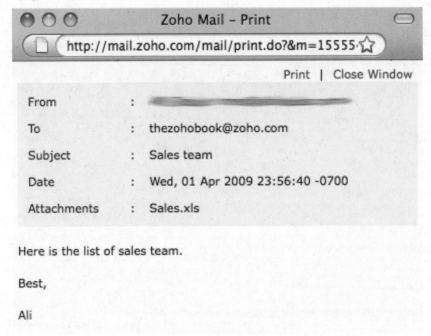

Figure 6-4. Message in print view

Composing messages

In Mail, you can create messages in different ways:

- Composing a new message from scratch (**Compose**)
- Replying to a message (**Reply** and **Reply All**)
- Quick replying (when you open a message in a pop-up window)
- Forwarding an existing message to a new recipient (**Forward**)
- Editing a received message as a new message and sending it to new recipients (**Edit As New**)

In addition, you can save a message as a draft while editing (except for when quick replying) in case you want to finish or send it at a later time.

To compose a message from scratch, follow these steps:

1. Click **Compose** on the toolbar. A new tab will open waiting for you to compose the message.
2. Enter recipients' e-mail addresses in the **To** field, and enter a topic in the **Subject** field for your message.
3. Enter the message body, and use the available tools in the toolbar to format the text if needed (Figure 6-5).

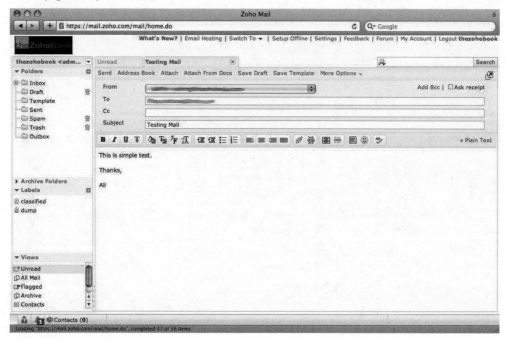

Figure 6-5. Composing a new e-mail

4. Click **Attach From Docs** to attach a document from the ones hosted on Docs. This is an easy way to send your online files.
5. Select from the documents available (Figure 6-6), and then click **OK** to proceed.

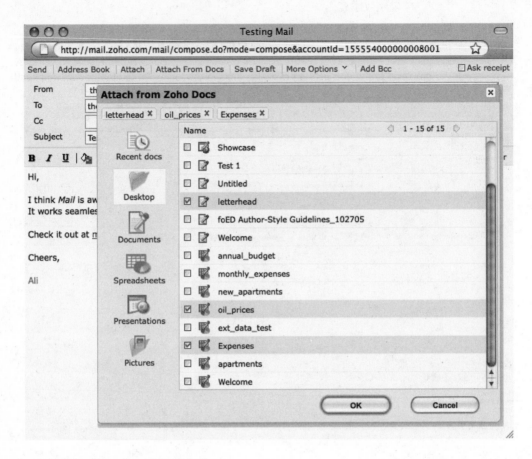

Figure 6-6. Attaching documents from Docs

> You can also attach documents from your local computer by clicking `Attach`. This will open a system dialog box to select and upload files from your computer.

6. Click `Add Image` on the toolbar, and browse for an image (PNG, JPEG, GIF) on your local computer. Then click `OK` to insert the image in the message. Note that this is not an attachment, and it will be placed at the cursor in the message body.

7. Click `Spell Check` on the toolbar to check the spelling of the text you entered (English).

8. Click `Send` to dispatch the message. If successful, a copy of the message will be stored in the `Sent` folder for your reference.

Using more features while composing

You just sent a simple message with an attachment. The message had an image embedded in the body too. There is still more you can do when composing new messages, such as using the Address Book and tweaking the advanced options.

When composing a message, clicking **Address Book** will open a list of contacts you have stored on Zoho. They are accessible through Zoho (where applicable, like in Mail), and you can manage these contacts through Contacts.

1. If you are using Mail stand-alone, do the following:

   a. Click **My Accounts** on the top menu bar.

   b. On the **Accounts** page, click **Contacts** on the sidebar.

   c. If you are using Mail from with Zoho Business, or Zoho Personal, open Contacts from the application bar (on the left).

2. Add new contacts by clicking **Add Contact** on the menu bar.

3. Compose a new message, and click **Address Book** on the menu.

4. Select a contact (or more), and click **To**. Then select another one, and click **CC**. Using **BCC** is similar (Figure 6-7).

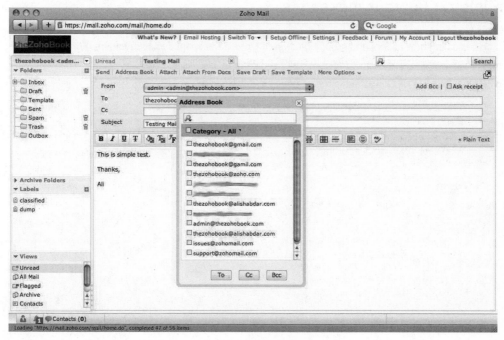

Figure 6-7. Adding recipients from the Address Book

5. Click **More Options** ▸ **Medium** ▸ **High**. This makes your message to appear as high priority in the recipient's inbox.

6. Check **Ask receipt** (upper-right) to receive a notification when the recipient opens the message.

> *Not all e-mail clients support receipts, so you might never receive a notification from some people, even if they have received your message successfully.*

7. Click **Send** to dispatch the message.

Replying to and forwarding messages

Replying to messages and forwarding messages are similar to composing e-mails.

To reply to an e-mail, open it in the preview or pop-up window, and then click **Reply** or **Reply All**. Then compose the reply in the reply tab (or window) as you do for a new message.

Clicking **Forward** will have the same effect, but with a message body containing the message you want to forward to new recipient(s). **Edit As New**, on the other hand, is actually a forward but without forwarding indicators (for example, no **Fwd:** in the subject line).

Administrating your messages

Your **Inbox** can get crowded sometimes. Mail has useful tools to help you manage your e-mails, one of which is creating new folders and grouping different types of messages in such folders. For example, all e-mails from a newsletter you subscribed to could be stored in a dedicated folder called **newsletters**.

To create a folder in **Mail** and move messages to it, follow these steps:

1. Click the plus sign icon on the upper right of the **Folders** tree (on the sidebar). The **New Folder** dialog box opens.

2. Type **work** in the **Folder name**, and select **Inbox** as the parent folder (the containing folder). Then click **OK** to proceed (Figure 6-8).

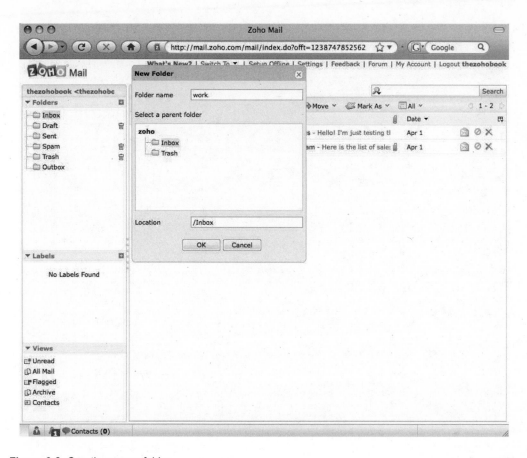

Figure 6-8. Creating a new folder

3. In the message list, select a message or two, and click **Move** on the toolbar.
4. In the **Move Mail** dialog box (Figure 6-9), select **work** as the destination folder, and click OK.

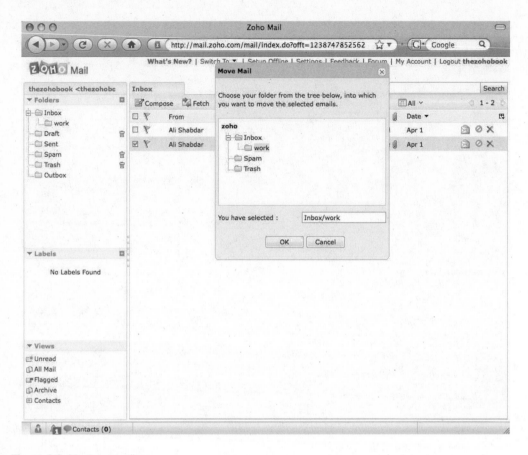

Figure 6-9. Moving e-mails

5. Open the `work` folder (from the `Folders` tree). Drag a message that you moved in the step 4, and drop it on the `Inbox` folder. You can select multiple messages and drag and drop them from folder to folder as well.

> *You can also move messages quickly by clicking the arrow next to the* ***Move*** *button on the toolbar and selecting the destination folder from the drop-down menu.*

Another good way of organizing messages is by using labels. You can define as many labels as you need and assign them nice colors. Then you can tag e-mails with different labels to have them categorized.

1. Click `Labels` ▸ `New Label` on the toolbar.
2. In the `New Label` dialog box, enter `classified` as `Name`, and choose `Yellow` as the color (Figure 6-10).

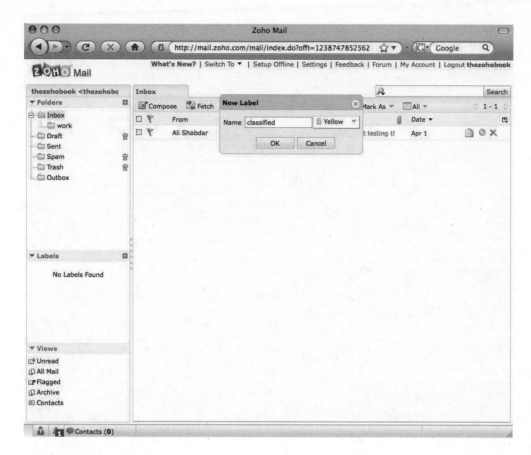

Figure 6-10. Adding new labels

3. Click **OK** to add the label.

4. In the message list in the **Inbox**, select a message (or many messages), and then select **Labels ▶ classified**. A yellow label will appear before the subject line of the selected messages.

> You can tag a message with multiple labels. For example, an e-mail can be tagged as **classified** and **work** at the same time.

5. Click the label of one of the labeled messages. The **Remove Label** dialog box will open (Figure 6-11).

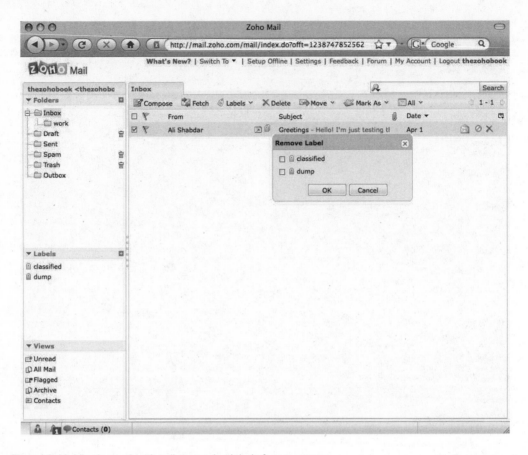

Figure 6-11. Viewing and optionally removing labels for messages

   6.   Select `classified`, and click `OK` to remove the `classified` label from the selected message.

One more way to categorize your e-mails is by using the `Mark As` menu, where you can mark e-mails as `Info`, `Important`, and `Follow-up`. Doing so will highlight their respective flags (located before the `From` column) in different colors. You can remove the flags either by clicking them or by selecting `Mark As` ▶ `Clear Flag`.

Finally, use the archiving facilities to remove the old (or unimportant) messages from the `Inbox` in order to clean it up. Archived messages are still accessible from `Archive` in the `Views` pane (in the sidebar). This is good when you have unimportant e-mails that you don't want in your `Inbox`, but you don't want to delete them either.

Select achievable messages, and click `Mark As` ▶ `Archive` (Figure 6-12).

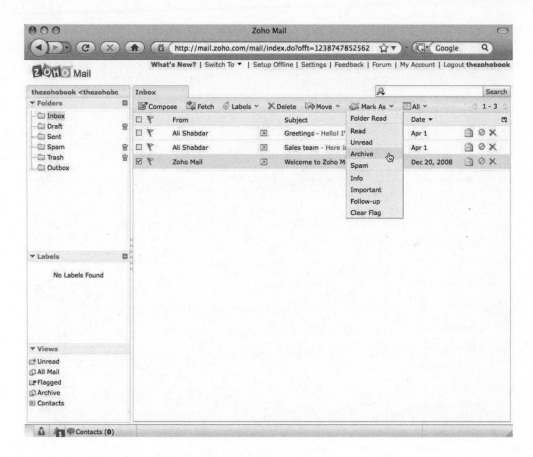

Figure 6-12. `Mark As` menu with a few essential options

To bring messages back to your `Inbox`, open `Views ▶ Archive`, select the messages, and click `Unarchive` in the toolbar. They will be moved back to `Inbox`.

Customizing Mail

It is rather important to know how to customize Mail according to your requirements. You can enable many settings that might make you switch to Mail instantly.

The `Settings` page is divided into two tabs: `Common Settings` and `Personalize`. Each of these tabs contains a few pages that group similar actions together.

My Preferences

The `My Preferences` page has all the basic settings to customize Mail for optimum use:

6. Click **Settings** on the top menu bar. The **Common Settings** tab appears with the **My Preferences** page open (Figure 6-13).

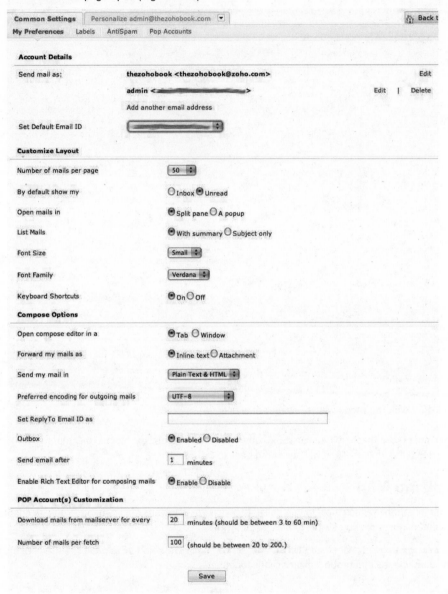

Figure 6-13. My Preferences page in Common Settings

7. Click `Add another email address`, and enter a display name (for example, your name) and the secondary e-mail address (for example, your Gmail address) followed by clicking `Send Verification`. A verification message will be sent to the secondary address, which you need to verify. Then that e-mail address will be added to the list (needs a page refresh), and you will be able to send e-mails (compose) from within Mail with the secondary e-mail address as the sender (appears in the `From` field).

8. Under `Customize Layout`, set the UI behavior as you prefer. For example, change `By default show my` to `Inbox` if you don't like to idea of showing unread messages by default.

9. Under `Compose Options`, set `Outbox` to `Enabled`, and leave the `Send email after` setting to be 1 minute. This is a great feature because there's a pause between the time you click `Send` for a message and the time it is actually being sent; therefore, you have enough time to open the `Outbox` folder and remove it from the send queue if you sent it by mistake.

10. Under `POP Account(s) Customization`, change `Download mails from mailserver for every` to 20 minutes.

11. Click `Save` to apply the changes.

Labels

As you remember from previous sections, labels are used to categorize messages. You could define them from the `Inbox`, but it is also possible to manage labels on the `Settings` page.

12. Open the `Labels` page in `Common Settings`, and add a new label by clicking `Add Label`.

13. Enter `dump` for `Name`, and choose `Grey` for color. Click `OK` to proceed.

Antispam

Spam (junk e-mail) is one of the most common side effects of the Internet. Mail provides you with powerful antispam facilities out of the box, but even the best spam control systems can make mistakes. How many times have you lost an important e-mail because it went to the spam folder and was removed after a while? Or what about spam messages that show up in your `Inbox` when they shouldn't just because the antispam filter didn't recognize them properly?

To overcome this issue, you can specify good and bad messages (that you know for sure) so Mail knows how to treat them successfully:

1. Open the `AntiSpam` page on the `Common Settings` tab.

2. Enter foo@foo.com in the `Black List Domain/ID`, and click the yellow + icon next to it (Figure 6-14). It will be added to the **black list**, meaning all messages sent to you from that specific e-mail address will directly go to the spam folder without appearing in the `Inbox`.

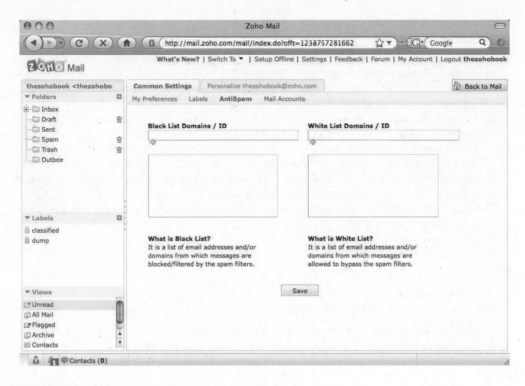

Figure 6-14. `AntiSpam` page on the `Common Settings` tab

3. Enter **zoho.com** in `White List Domains /ID`, and click the yellow + icon next to it. It will be added to the **white list**, meaning any e-mail coming from zoho.com will be considered as not spam and will definitely appear in your `Inbox`.

POP accounts

When you create a Zoho account, you get a zoho.com e-mail for free that is set up by Mail by default. So, all Zoho users have a Zoho e-mail. But what if you already have one or two other e-mails (for example, from Gmail or Yahoo) that you just won't give up simply because you send and receive all your e-mails from Zoho Mail?

Mail has a great feature that allows you to define as many other e-mail accounts as you want, so you can check them all in one front end, Mail. This means that instead of logging into Gmail, Yahoo, and Zoho one by one, you can log into just Mail and receive all the e-mails sent to those other accounts.

This saves the hassle of multiple logins, and you also get to use the exclusive features of Mail, such as an outbox folder with its dispatch delay feature, that are not available in other services. Also, you will be able to integrate with other Zoho applications, as you've been learning about in this book.

Before you start adding accounts, you should know that Mail retrieves the e-mails using the Post Office Protocol (POP). Although you don't need to know any technical details about this, you should know that your e-mail service provider might not support POP. Gmail, for example, gives you free access to POP, but Yahoo charges to enable POP access.

This has nothing to do with Zoho, but you need to check the service availability and required settings before you start adding accounts to Mail. Zoho has made a quick reference available for the common server settings at http://zohomailhelp.wiki.zoho.com/Configuring-Mail-Accounts.html.

To add a Google account (a gmail.com e-mail address) to Mail, follow these steps:

1. On the Common Settings tab, open POP Accounts, and click Add Mail Account to proceed.
2. Fill in the form shown in Figure 6-15. Note that you need to enter your display name and e-mail ID, but the rest should be entered as displayed.

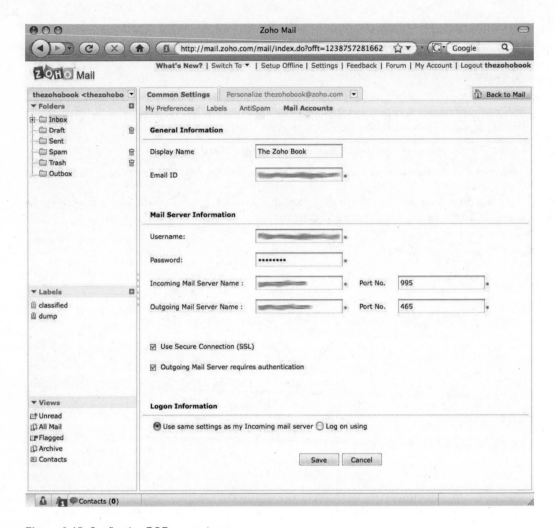

Figure 6-15. Configuring POP account access

> **3.** Click `Save` to store the account.

Similarly, you can add more accounts to Mail. Back in the accounts list, you can see your new e-mails accounts listed after the default Zoho account. You can even set any of them to be the default account (on the `POP Accounts` page) so it opens by default and so it's the default address for composing e-mails.

You can see in Figure 6-16 (on the left side) that you can change the view to any of the accounts. This means if you change it to another account, it will open the `Inbox` of that particular account.

Figure 6-16. Switching between accounts

Personalize

After finishing with the essential settings, let's work on more personal settings such as filters, signatures, and so on. The next stop is the `Settings` page on the `Personalize` tab where you can further customize Mail according to your requirements.

> *A very important point to remember is that any personalization settings you change are applied to the current account only. It means if you have multiple accounts configured in Mail, only the current account will be affected.*

Filters

Filters are a handy way to automate the management of incoming messages. Once defined, each filter evaluates every incoming message against criteria that have been defined in it and then performs the suitable action designated. For example, suppose you receive regular e-mails from a newsletter subscription you have. If you remember from the previous sections, you created a folder for those e-mails to move them there manually. A better scenario is to have them moved to that folder automatically. This is what filters can do for you, saving you a considerable amount of time and effort.

In another example, you might want all e-mails coming from your company (for example, @yourcompany.com) to be examined, and if they are about a particular project, they should be flagged as `Important` and labeled `Classified`. Again, you can make this possible with filters. It is like having a personal assistant inside Mail.

To add a new filter, you should set the criteria (for example, that the sender is yourcompany.com), which, if met, means that certain actions (for example, flag it as `Important`) should be performed:

1. Open the `Filters` subtab, and click `Add Filter`.
2. Enter `work inquiries` in `Filter Name`.
3. In `For incoming messages that`, select `Match all of the following`. Selecting `Match all of the following` will act like a logical AND, performing the actions only if all criteria are met. But selecting `Match any of the following` indicates a logical OR, performing the actions if *any* of the criteria are met.
4. Add the first criterion as `Sender | Ends with | yourcompany.com` (Figure 6-17). Then add another criterion by clicking the + button next to the first criterion, and enter `Subject | Contains | inquiry`. This simply means that this filter will catch all e-mails that are sent from yourcompany.com and that contain the word *inquiry* in their subjects.

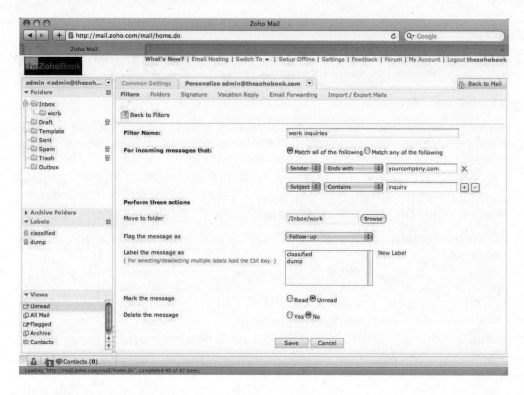

Figure 6-17. Adding a new filter

5. To define actions, click **Browse**, and select the destination folder that the e-mails matching the criteria should be moved to.

6. Choose **Follow-up** in **Flag As**, and leave the rest.

7. Click **Save** to create the filter.

From now on, any e-mail meeting the criteria defined in the filter(s) will be affected by the respective actions. Note that all filters are listed in the **Filters** page and have a green icon before them. Clicking this green icon will turn it gray, meaning the filter is deactivated. Clicking it again will make it green and active again. While deactivated, filters actually don't work, although they still exist in the system, so you can turn them on and off whenever needed.

Filters are huge time-savers. However, you should be careful when you create them not to set criteria or actions that make mistakes such as deleting important e-mails before seeing them.

Before we finish with filters, let me add that Mail allows you to import the filters you already made in your mail clients like Mozilla Thunderbird, so you don't need to create them from scratch. Make sure you read the instructions under **Import Filters** first.

Folders

Back to the other settings, the **Folders** page contains the folder information and allows you to manage your folders. You saw how folders work in the preceding sections, so I'll leave this to you.

Signatures

Professional e-mail messages often end with a signature. It could be just your name or a formatted business card–style signature with your contact information and logo included. Mail allows you to design a professional signature and place it below your outgoing messages:

1. On the **Personalize** tab, open the **Signature** page, and select **Add customized signature in all my outgoing e-mails**. The signature box appears (Figure 6-18).

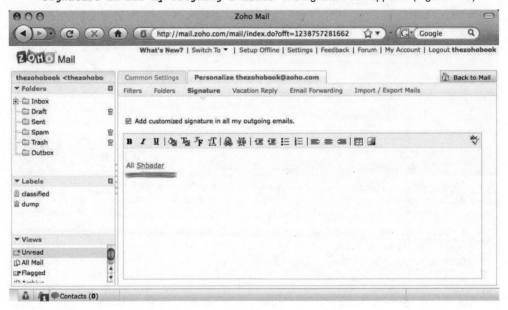

Figure 6-18. Creating a signature

2. Enter your name (or your company name), and change the font and style of the text. Don't make it too big or flashy; it should look professional.
3. Insert a link to your home page and a logo if you have any. The logo image must be small, for example, 150 x 50 pixels. You have plenty of tools to make a nice signature.
4. Click **Save** once you're done.

Vacation reply

Whenever you are away and you won't be able to check your e-mails for some time, it is a good idea to set a vacation reply. Then people who send you messages will be automatically replied to with a message informing them that you will be late replying.

1. On the `Personalize` tab, click `Vacation Reply` (Figure 6-19).

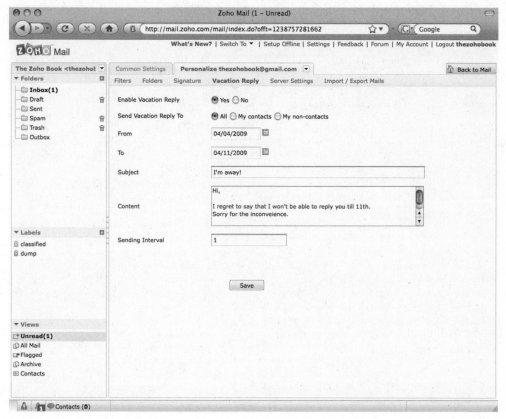

Figure 6-19. Setting a vacation reply

2. Set `Enable Vacation Reply` to `Yes`. Then set `Send Vacation Reply To` to `All`.
3. Assign a date for `From` and `To` to set for what period of time this vacation reply will be functional.
4. Enter something for `Subject` and `Content`, and leave the `Sending Interval` setting to `1`.
5. Click `Save`.

Although it will work only for the period of time you set, make sure to disable it once you come back.

E-mail forwarding

If for any reason you need a copy of your incoming messages to be sent to another e-mail address, e-mail forwarding is the way to go.

1. On the **Personalize** tab of the **Settings** page, open the **Email Forwarding** page (Figure 6-20).

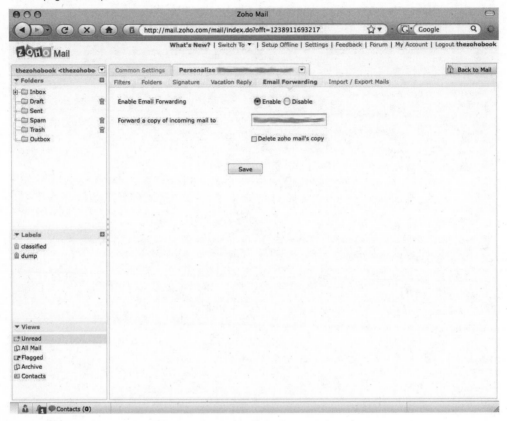

Figure 6-20. Enabling e-mail forwarding

2. For **Enable Email Forwarding**, select **Enable**.
3. Enter the destination e-mail address in **Forward a copy of incoming mail to**.
4. Select **Delete zoho mail's copy** if you don't want to retain a copy in Mail.
5. Click **Save** to apply the changes.

Importing and exporting

When you make Mail your one and only e-mail client, you probably have plenty of e-mails in your old mail client (for example, Outlook, Thunderbird, and so on). You can bring your old messages into Mail to have them accessible all the time on the cloud.

On the other hand, it is possible to export your messages hosted on Mail to a file in your computer for backing up or importing into another application. Zoho supports `.eml` (e-mail) files for both import and export.

1. Export an e-mail in the EML format from a third-party e-mail application that you use (such as Outlook).
6. On the `Personalize` tab, open `Import/Export Mails`. The import form will open by default (Figure 6-21).

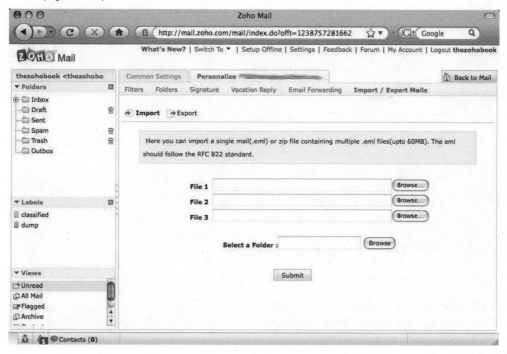

Figure 6-21. Importing message files

7. Click `Browse for File 1`, and select the EML file.
8. Click `Browse` for `Select a Folder`, and set the destination folder to which the important message will be moved.
9. Click `Submit` to start the import process.

> You can import .eml (e-mail) files one by one or compress multiple files in a single .zip file (less than 60MB in size) and upload it to Mail.

10. To export a message from Mail, click `Export` on the `Import/Export Mails` page (Figure 6-22).

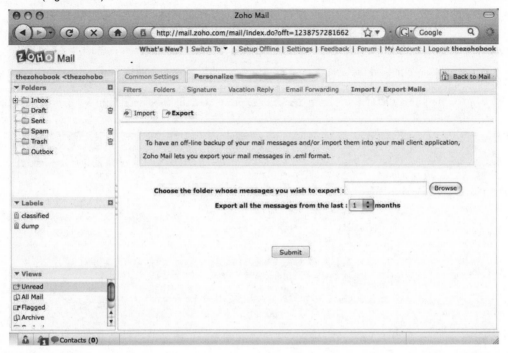

Figure 6-22. Exporting e-mails

11. Click `Browse` to select which Mail folder should be exported, and then select the age of messages.

12. Click `Submit` to proceed. A message will pop up indicating that the export operation is scheduled, and you will be notified about the download link (of the exported file) by an e-mail.

Using Mail off the cloud

One of the downsides of Internet-based e-mail services is that you can't open your `Inbox` when you are not connected to the Internet. A unique feature of `Mail` is that you can have offline access to your `Inbox`. This means you don't need to have an Internet connection all the time to open your inbox.

This feature was first introduced by Mail and takes cloud-based e-mailing to the next level. In the offline mode, you can still open your e-mails and compose messages to be sent when you are back online. However, a few features such as attaching files (locally and from Docs) are disabled, because there is no (presumably) Internet access.

> *Mail offline features uses Google Gears, meaning you need to have it installed on your browser prior to activating this feature. Check Chapter 1 for detailed instructions if you don't have it installed.*

To take Mail offline for the first time, you need to do some basic setup. After that, you can just switch between online and offline mode with one click.

1. Click `Setup Offline`. The `Offline Settings` dialog box opens (Figure 6-23).

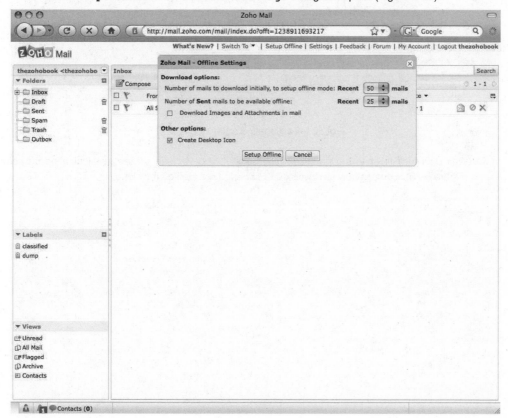

Figure 6-23. Taking Mail offline

2. Leave both of the drop-down boxes as they are. There will be 50 e-mails from your inbox downloaded and available for offline access as well as 25 sent messages.
3. Select `Download Images and Attachments in mail`. It is good to have them in handy, but note that it will take more time to download messages with big attachments.
4. Google Gears will ask you for permission to create a desktop icon (Figure 6-24). Click `OK` to continue.

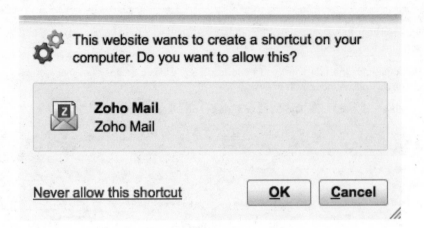

Figure 6-24. Creating a desktop icon

5. Wait until Mail finishes the process. If successful, you will see a message indicating success (Figure 6-25). You can now click **Work Offline** to take Mail off the cloud.

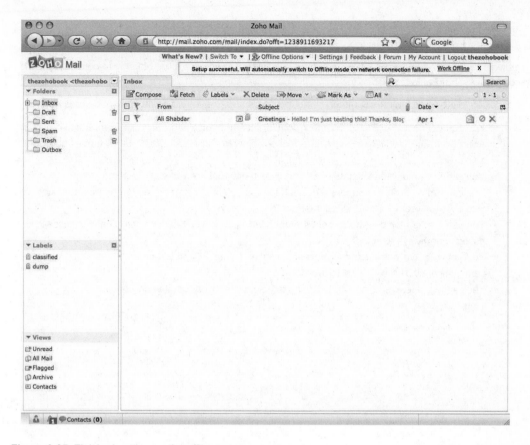

Figure 6-25. Finished setting up the offline access

In the offline mode, you can still check your e-mails (50 of them, as you set) and compose messages, although some features are not available. To go back to normal, click `Try connecting online`. Everything will be same as before.

From now on, you can take Mail offline by selecting `Offline Options ▶ Go Offline` in the top menu bar.

Zoho Chat

Instant messaging is perhaps one of the most used technologies on the Internet. There are many different instant messaging services, such as AOL Instant Messenger (AIM), Yahoo Messenger, Google Chat, and Microsoft Live Messenger, that are available for everybody to join and use.

These services offer a similar set of features and have their own huge fan bases. Zoho tries to address more requirements and provide users with a better experience by introducing Chat. Zoho Chat is not just a chat (instant messaging) client. With its recent major update, Zoho tries to take Chat to the next level, making it a full-fledged business tool.

Individuals, small and medium businesses, and entrepreneurs can use Chat not only to connect to friends, colleagues, and clients but also to maximize the customer service with a state-of-the-art tool—for free!

In addition to the basic features common in other chat clients, Chat offers some unique features:

- You can connect to some of the most popular instant messaging networks from a single platform. Apart from Zoho, you can connect to Yahoo, Google, MSN, Aim, ICQ, and Jabber all from the same window.
- You can have multiple accounts open and chat in different networks at the same time.
- You can run multiple live support sessions for your clients or colleagues to communicate with your sales/support team via embedded interfaces.
- You can create multiple **shout boxes** embedded in your web site for your clients or colleagues to publicly chat with each other.
- You can run live chat sessions between you and your customers or colleagues so you can all communicate via embedded interfaces.
- You can manage events and notifications to help you stay on top of your business.

Getting started with Chat

Run **Chat** by logging into http://chat.zoho.com. You can also open it from within Zoho Personal. The UI looks different from traditional chat applications since you can do a lot more with Chat (Figure 6-26).

Figure 6-26. The user interface of Chat

A quick look at the UI will reveal these elements:

- A link bar on the top of the screen contains general shortcuts to pages like the settings page and your account.
- On the left side there is the accounts pane containing different IM services.
- There is a pane for the advanced features of Chat on the right side of the screen.
- On the event management bar in the bottom right, there are necessary tools to take care of events and appointments.

Since you are logged in to your Zoho account, you can start to chat with other Zoho account holders immediately. Your status is **Available** by default, and everybody (in your contacts) can see you. Change your status by clicking **Select user status** (the tiny arrow on upper right of the accounts pane, next to **Available**).

Let's start with creating more accounts to centralize your chatting in one place. In this example, you'll add a Google account to be able to chat with your Google friends.

1. Click the **Sign in to IM Network** button on the middle of the screen.
6. In the **Instant Sign In** dialog box, select **Google** as **IM Network**. Then enter a proper Google e-mail address and password in **Email Id** and **Password**, respectively (Figure 6-27).

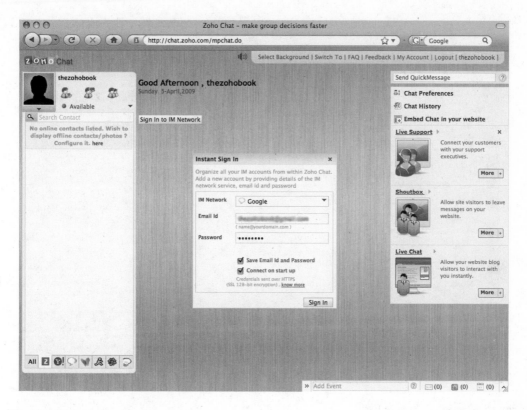

Figure 6-27. Adding a new IM account

> **7.** Click `Sign In` to proceed.

If the login is successful, you can see your Google contacts listed on the left pane (click the `Google` tab if it is not visible).

One of the powerful features of Chat is that you can add as many accounts as you want, and you can chat with multiple people from different networks at the same time. As you can see in Figure 6-28, there are a few accounts added, and it is possible to chat with multiple people from different networks at once.

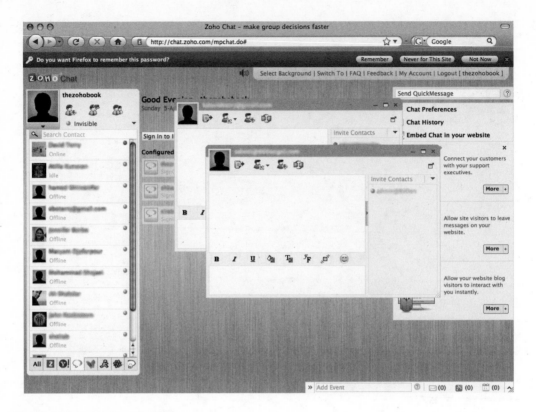

Figure 6-28. Getting busy in Chat

You can always refer to **Chat History,** accessible in the right pane, to get a log of what has been communicated with people (Figure 6-29).

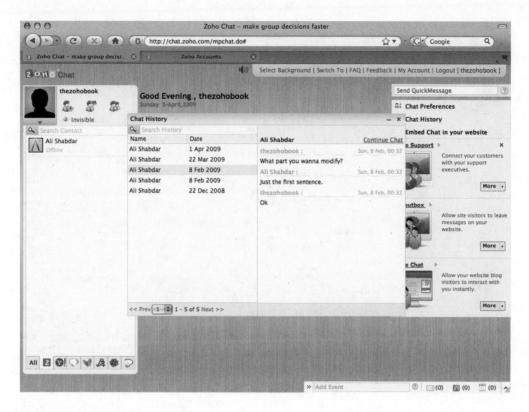

Figure 6-29. `Chat History` window

Doing more with Chat

As I mentioned, Chat has some unique features that make it a competent business tool for entrepreneurs, small to medium businesses (SMBs), and even large businesses. Live support, shout boxes, and live chat are the most important tools allowing you to offer better customer support in your daily workflow.

Live support

With live chat, you can embed (include) a chat box for your site visitors to chat with a customer support or sales representative. This feature is quite useful when you need to have person-to-person communication with your clients or prospects in order to maximize your profits and to offer better service. Visitors can chat privately with a representative and solve their issues or be presented about the exciting services your company offers.

To create a Live Chat box, follow these steps:

1. Click `Live Support` in the right pane. The live support configuration dialog box opens (Figure 6-30).

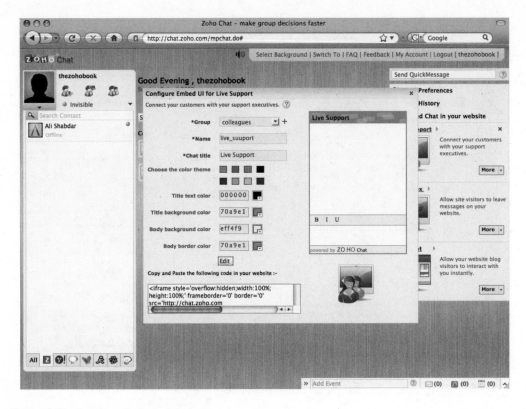

Figure 6-30. Creating a live support chat

2. Select a group of chat representatives for **Group**. Create one (the green + button) if there are no suitable groups. Each representative (group member) will pick up a visitor to chat with.

3. Fill in the **Name** and **Chat title** fields, set up different colors, and check the preview (right) to make sure it looks suitable.

4. Copy the generated code snippet, and paste in the web page you want the live support box to appear on.

Shout boxes and live chat

Creating shout boxes and live chats are similar processes too. But there are some differences in using them. A **shout box** is basically a public chatting platform for the visitors of your website. It is a good tool for having open discussions in support or educational sites.

Live chat, on the other hand, is almost the same as live support but without defining a group of representatives dealing with clients. Visitors will chat only with you as the session owner. It is suitable for small-scale customer support purposes.

It is possible to set up multiple chat boxes for different websites. You can always list and manage them by clicking **Chat Preferences** (right pane) and selecting **Embed Chat**. There you can create new boxes, extract the code snippet, and delete the boxes you no longer need (Figure 6-31).

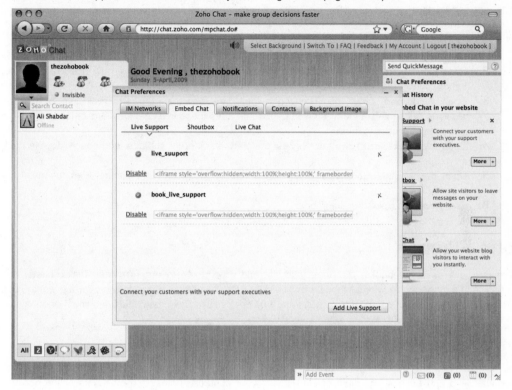

Figure 6-31. Managing available chat boxes

Events

Chat has built-in quick and easy event management. You can add events for a later time and set notification easily. All added events will be entered in Zoho Calendar (see Chapter 1), which is available for both personal and business use (see Chapter 9 for more information). Integration between Zoho applications is always an important factor in boosting your performance and productivity.

To add an event, follow these steps:

1. Type in the event, in a human-readable manner, such as **Important meeting on Monday at 9:00 am**, in the events bar (on the bottom right of the page). See more samples of how easily you can enter events by moving the mouse pointer over the question mark button next to the event text box.
2. Press Enter (on your keyboard) to add the event.
3. Set a reminder in the **Event Reminder** dialog box, and click **OK**.

The event will be added to the pending events (the calendar icon in the events bar) as well as to Zoho Calendar.

Chat preferences

One last thing you need to know is how to customize Chat:

1. Click **Chat Preferences** on the right pane.
2. Open the **IM Networks** tab. Review the added accounts, and add a new one (for example, Yahoo) by clicking **Add Account**.
3. Open the **Embed Chat** tab. Then open the **Live Chat** subtab, and click **Disable** for all sessions to deactivate them. All web pages that have these live chat sessions embedded will no longer have access to them.
4. Open the **Notifications** tab. Review the alerts in different subtabs, and enable/disable them as you prefer.
5. Open the **Background Image** tab. Then choose a background picture from the available images.
6. Click **Apply** to close the dialog box.

Zoho Planner

People have used notebooks, planners, journals, and other tools to organize their tasks, plans, and projects in a manageable way for thousands of years. With the computer age taking over the world, such tools were replaced with personal computers and PIM devices like Palm handhelds and smart phones.

> *To read more about PIM, visit*
> `http://en.wikipedia.org/wiki/Personal_information_management.`

Of course, with the Internet being available at your fingertips in recent years, planner software took another leap and became available online. Having your contacts, notes, and calendars online not only gives you the maximum information availability (meaning you have access to your information from anywhere at any time) but also allows you to easily share such information with people who are somehow involved in your personal or business life.

Zoho Planner is a cloud-based personal/business organizer application that offers you a few more features compared to conventional applications. Using Planner, you can manage and organize tasks and events online and share them with the world. In addition to that, it has a reminders section where you can put anything that you need to remember, such as birthdays, bill due dates, monthly payments, and so on.

Getting started with Planner

Open Planner by visiting `http://planner.zoho.com` or Zoho Personal. It has a simple and easy-to-use interface allowing you to quickly set up and organize your plans (Figure 6-32).

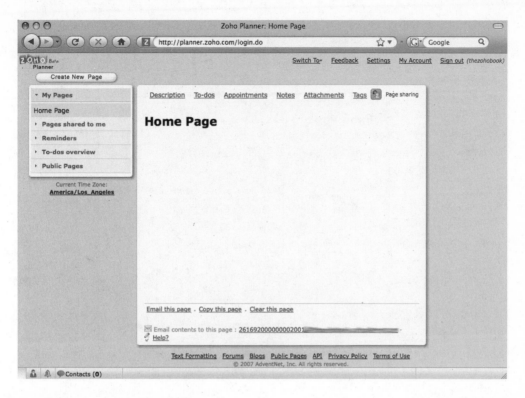

Figure 6-32. The user interface of Planner

On the left side you'll see a pane divided into different sections. The white area in the middle is your workspace.

Planner uses pages to divide different plans/events, meaning for every new event, you need to create a new page. You can add a description, to-do lists, appointments, and notes to your plans. It is also possible to attach files and tag the pages to organize them easier.

By default, Planner creates a page called `Home Page` that you can start using right away. However, we are going to start discovering Planner by creating a new page from scratch.

1. Click `Create New Page` on the top of the left pane.
2. Enter `May Tweetup` in `Name your new page`, and click `Create` (Figure 6-33).

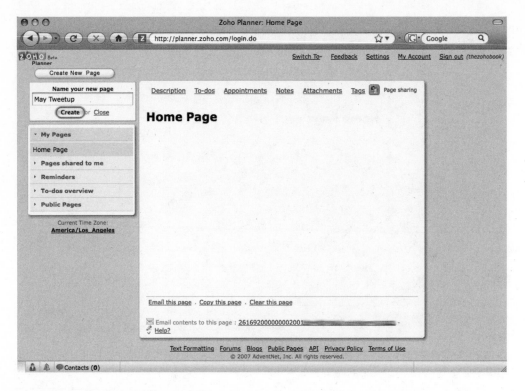

Figure 6-33. Creating a new Planner page

> *In case you are wondering, a **tweetup** is a casual meeting where people who follow each other on Twitter hang out. If you don't know what Twitter is (I wonder!), check www.twitter.com.*

3. Click the **Description** link on top of the page, and enter some details (Figure 6-34). Then click **Save Desc** to apply the changes.

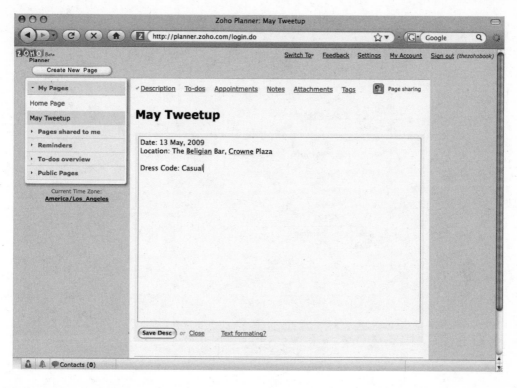

Figure 6-34. Adding a description

4. Click **To-dos** to add the tasks to be done for the event. Each task (to-do) needs to be added to a to-do list to keep related tasks grouped in different lists.

5. Click **Add list** to create a to-do list. Then enter a name such as **Finalize the bookings** for the list, and click **Add list** below it (Figure 6-35).

Figure 6-35. Creating a to-do list

6. Add a to-do item by filling in the `To-do description` field. Then set the `Due Date` setting, and select a reminder from `Remind Me` too (Figure 6-36).

Figure 6-36. Adding to-do items

7. Click **Add list item**. You can still continue by adding more to-do items for the list.
8. Add an appointment related to the event by clicking **Appointments**.
9. Fill in the fields, as shown in Figure 6-37. Then click **Add appointment** to register the appointment.

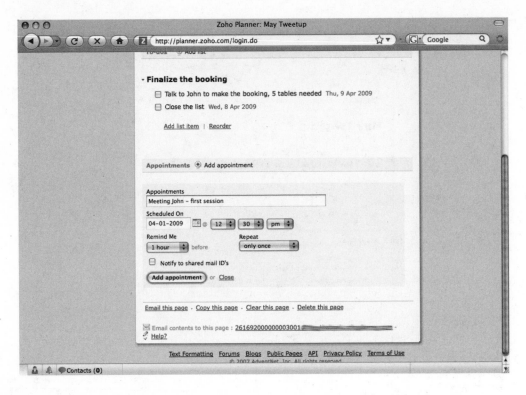

Figure 6-37. Inserting appointments

10. Add extra information by clicking **Notes**. Enter a title and body, and click **Add Note** to proceed (Figure 6-38). Creating a FAQ about the event is a good example of additional notes.

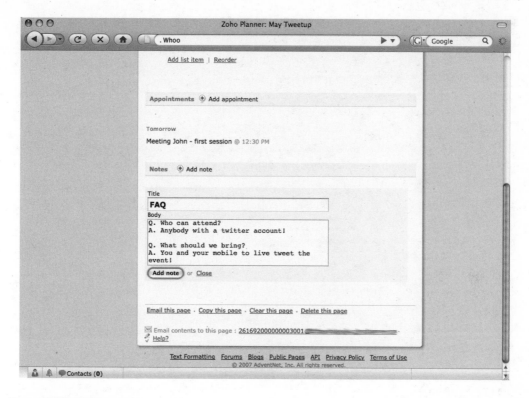

Figure 6-38. Adding a note

11. Upload a location map for the meet-up venue by clicking **Attachments**. It is possible to attach various files to a plan.

12. Click **Browse** to find a file on your computer, add a short description, and then click **Upload attachment** (Figure 6-39).

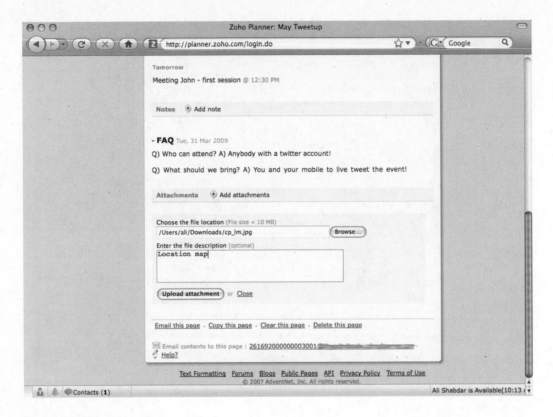

Figure 6-39. Attaching a file

13. Tag the plan to find it easier later by clicking **Tags** and entering tags separated by commas (Figure 6-40). Then click **Save Tags** to store them.

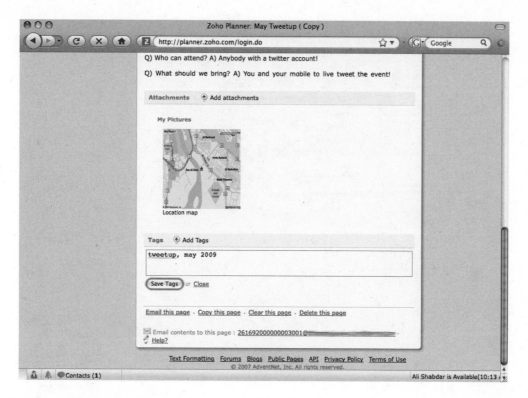

Figure 6-40. Adding tags to the plan

After this long walk-through, you can see a complete plan with different sections listed next to each other.

In the left pane, open **To-dos overview ▶ All my to-dos** to see the pending tasks and possibly the overdue ones, or open **Reminders** to see how their content is updated. Selecting each to-do will make it **Done**. Keep the status of to-dos up-to-date to maintain an accurate plan status.

Doing more with Planner

There are still three more things to discuss about Planner before we end this chapter: reminders, sharing, and settings. Then you can go ahead and plan your life in the cloud.

Reminders

By setting as many reminders as you want, you will never miss an important occasion. Whether it's your friend's birthday, monthly payment of your credit card, an important meeting, and so on, you can set up a reminder for it that notifies you once or recurs every day, month, year, and so on.

1. Click **Reminders ▶ My Reminders** on the left pane. The **Reminders** page appears.
2. Click **Add new reminder**, and fill in the reminders shown in Figure 6-41.

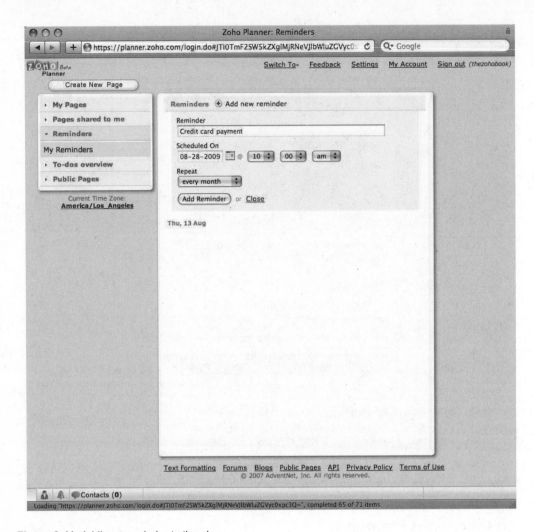

Figure 6-41. Adding a reminder to the plan

3. Click **Add Reminder** to store it.

Once the date and time are set in the reminder, you will receive an e-mail from Planner notifying you of the big day.

Sharing

You can keep pages (plans) for yourself or share them with others. Just like other Zoho applications, you can share content in Planner with a select group of invited people or with the world by making it public.

1. Open the `May Tweetup` page (created in the previous sections) from `My Pages` in the left pane.
2. Click the `Page sharing` button in the upper right of the page. Two sections appear: `Public Sharing` and `Private Sharing` (Figure 6-42).

Figure 6-42. Sharing options for the plan

3. To share the page with everybody, check `Share this page publicly`, and then click `Share`.

A small box will appear containing the link to your page. Cancel the share at any time by deselecting `Share this page publicly` and clicking `Save` again.

To share the page with specific people, you need to enter their e-mails in the `Read Only` or `Read/Write` boxes in the `Private Sharing` section. Clicking `Share` will dispatch an invitation message to the e-mails mentioned in the boxes. Then they will see your page listed under `Pages Shared to me` on the left pane.

> *Whenever people with whom you shared a page get online, you will see their status becoming available, and you can chat with them as well.*

Settings

There are not many settings in Planner, but it is worth a quick look.

1. Open the settings page by clicking **Settings** in the top menu bar (Figure 6-43).

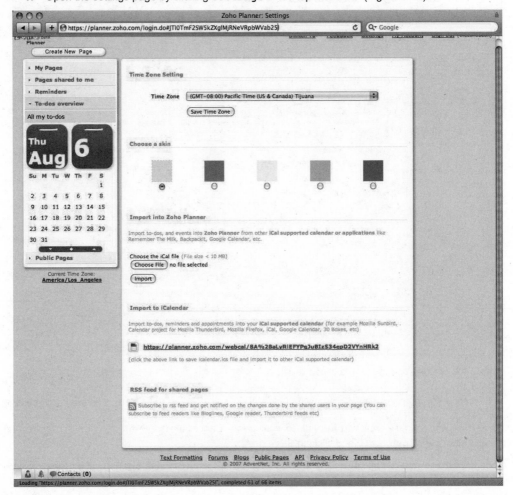

Figure 6-43. The settings page

2. Change your time zone if you intend to share events (pages) with people so they get a fair idea of your time.
3. Import other calendars with applications compatible with iCalendar standard, for example, Google Calendar, by clicking **Choose file**, selecting the exported `.ics` file, and clicking **Import**.

> *To learn about iCalendar format, visit Wikipedia at*
> `http://en.wikipedia.org/wiki/ICalendar.`

4. To import your plans into any iCalendar-compatible calendar tool, save the `.ics` file through the link available under **Import to iCalendar**, and then import it into the destination application.

5. Subscribe to the RSS feeds of a shared page by clicking the feed icon in order to be notified once there are any other shared users who have made changes to the page.

Getting help

Mail, Chat, and Planner are easy-to-use applications that might look familiar to most people. However, there are times that you need some help or need to report potential issues in the applications.

Make sure you visit Zoho forums at `http://forums.zoho.com/#Forum/zoho-planner`. There you can find forums for all applications including Mail, Chat, and Planner.

You can suggest new features you think would be nice to have in Zoho applications through the forums. Many features you see made available by Zoho were once in somebody's wish list.

Summary

Using e-mail, instant messaging, and organizer software is common sense for today's Internet user. There is also tough competition between different tools, and there is an endless list of related applications to choose from.

Although using and learning new tools for this purpose might look pointless, it is sometimes worth it to try new solutions and see what else they can offer over your current tools.

Zoho Mail is a real deal for personal and business e-mailing. Supporting all features of a modern e-mail application, it takes Internet-based e-mail to the next level by offering multiple account management, personalized accounts, offline access, and a built-in document viewer. E-mail management is also much easier using the rich collection of tools Mail offers, for example, folders, labels, tags, filter, and so on.

Zoho Chat adds a new perspective to the old playground of instant messaging by introducing business-friendly features, such as live support sessions. It also allows you to centralize all your instant messaging activities in one place and is a nifty event management tool.

Zoho Planner gives you a simple and easy-to-use platform to set up events and share them with others. Create rich plans with to-do lists, notes, and attachments as well as set up reminders for the important occasions of your life. The busier we are, the more we need planners and reminders to survive our days.

In the next chapter, you will see how to contribute to the cloud by publishing your wisdom using other Zoho tools.

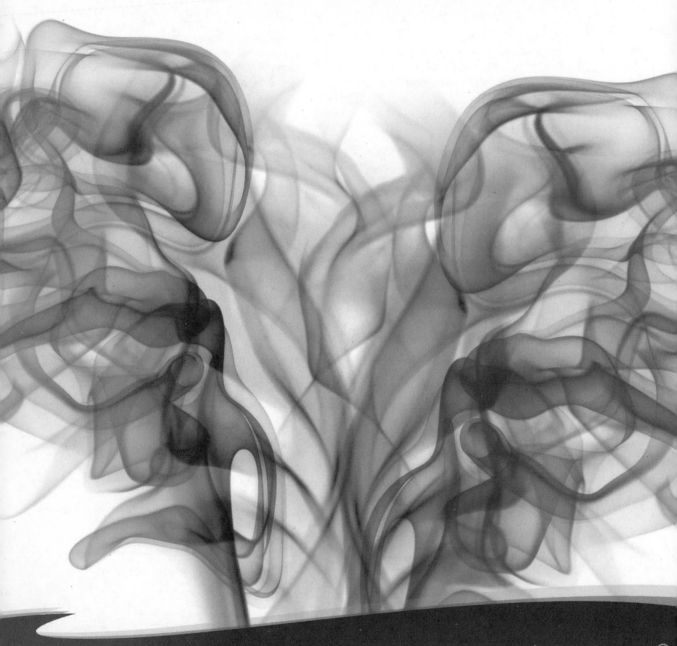

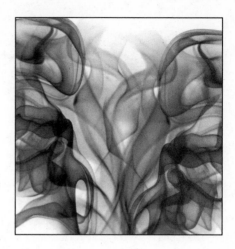

Chapter 7

Publish in the Cloud

When the World Wide Web started to spread around the world, there were only a (relatively) small group of elite computer-savvy individuals able to create web content. Although it was all ugly (but formatted!) text and occasional low-quality images, it was a hard and time-consuming job to develop for the Web.

Since then, we have seen exciting technologies making it easier for people to create web content. **Blogs** (short for weblogs), for example, provide a user-friendly interface for the rest of us to make web pages and contribute to the Internet as easy as making word-processing documents.

For content-rich websites, wikis are a better solution, allowing you to create and connect endless pieces of text, images, and other kinds of media. Simply put, a **wiki** is a website made of interlinked web pages that is usually used for community websites and massive textual content. The best example of a wiki is Wikipedia, which is the biggest community-maintained encyclopedia.

> To learn more about blogs, and wikis, visit Wikipedia at
> http://en.wikipedia.org/wiki/Blog and http://en.wikipedia.org/wiki/Wiki.

That is not all. Online note taking plays an important role in gathering information that is manageable and accessible from anywhere, especially useful for businesspeople, students, and scholars.

On the other hand, sharing documents with peers, instead of sending bulky attachments through e-mail, changes the way we communicate and stay in sync with the flow of information.

You might have already jumped on the web wagon, maintaining a blog or a wiki, or maybe you upload your video clips and images in the cloud using Flickr and YouTube. Or you might just think, "Why would I care?" Like it or not, the Web is part of your life, and you—as a citizen of the world—will probably want to contribute to it at some point.

In this chapter, you will see how Zoho harnesses the current technologies available for web authoring in new solutions that could be an enormous help to your online presence. Running wiki sites, creating online notebooks, and sharing documents online are three of the tasks today's Internet users do for personal and business purposes, and Zoho has the right tools for you to get started with all of them quickly and easily.

Zoho Notebook

There are many tools and platforms to help you contribute to the Web and create content that matters to you in your business and personal lives. Zoho Notebook provides you with a new platform. With Notebook, you can create web pages in the form of notebooks (or **books**) that exist on the Web and contain different types of information from different sources.

In other words, you can mash up various content into notebooks in order to create a new form of media. The result is a website in the format of a book consisting of other web objects.

For example, you can write a few pages about a tourism attraction mashed up with some select articles, an updated price list, a location map from Google, plus related video clips from YouTube all in a single notebook. Then publish it for your users (or yourself) to have access to multiple sources of information from one single portal.

Although Zoho itself refers to Notebook as an online note taker, I believe this is an underestimation for a potentially great tool that can be used in more useful ways.

You are about to see how Notebook can make your life easier, especially if you are an active contributor to the cloud.

Getting started

When you run Notebook directly from `http://notebook.zoho.com` or from within Zoho Personal, it opens a new book (`New Book 1`) for you to start immediately (Figure 7-1).

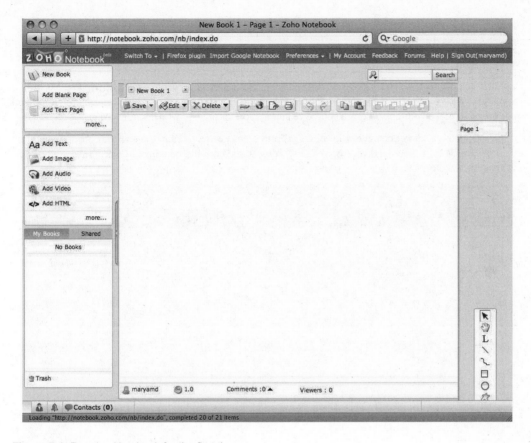

Figure 7-1. Running Notebook for the first time

Just like other Zoho applications, the UI is simple and easy to use. In the sidebar (on the left), there are four panes:

- The first pane carries only one button, **New Book**, that creates new books for you. Each book represents an online notebook.
- The next two panes contain different components to be added to the pages of the current book. You are about to use most of them in the upcoming walk-through.
- The fourth pane, **My Books**, lists all your books, and **Shared** shows the books you have shared with others. (There are no books listed here when you first run Notebook.)

Every book consists of pages, and each page opens in the workspace in the middle. You will place different components (or **containers**, since they contain different kinds of data) to pages in order to assemble your books. Each page has a tag on the right side showing its name (**Page 1** for the first page in a new book, as shown in Figure 7-1).

There is also a small toolbox on the right side that contains tools for placing text, lines, and shapes on the pages as necessary.

Now let's start creating a new book and learn how to use Notebook.

Suppose you want to create a book about a digital camcorder you recently bought (Kodak Zi6 in this example). You are going to put summaries from the vendor's site, a review, a few pictures, and other cool information to make your book a great source of information for anyone who intends to buy this camcorder.

1.   Double-click the book title **New Book 1**, and enter **Kodak Zi6** in the **Rename Book** dialog box (Figure 7-2). You need your book to be professional from the beginning. Click **Rename** when you are finished.

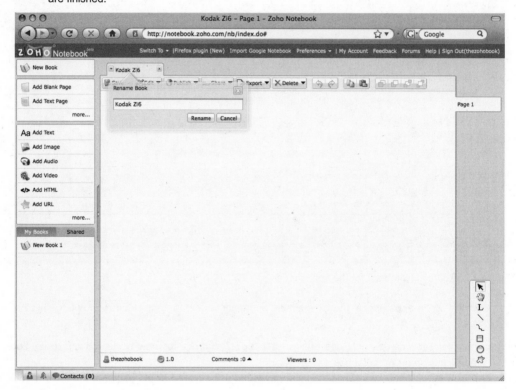

Figure 7-2. Renaming the book

2.   Insert a text box on the page by clicking **Add Text** (in the third pane).
3.   Copy and paste some of the introduction text about the device found at http://www.kodak.com/eknec/PageQuerier.jhtml?pq-path=9/13061/13063/13064&pq-locale=en_US. (This text is available for personal use only.)
4.   Format the text using the format toolbar on the top of the text box. Make it look like Figure 7-3.

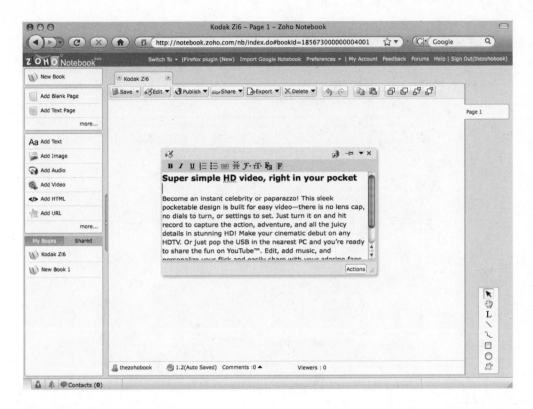

Figure 7-3. Adding text to a page

5. Once you're done editing, move the text box around the page to place it properly on the page. To resize the text box, use the designated handle on the bottom right of the box.

6. When you have made sure the size and position of the text box is final, **pin it** by clicking the pin icon on the upper right of the box, which means it can't be repositioned accidentally. You can unpin the container at any time.

7. On the top of the text box, above the formatting toolbar, click the `Edit title` globe icon (with the container selected). This is used to create a linked title that can be used either to link to more information on the article or, in our case, to link to the source site from which you took the original content.

8. Fill in the `Description` and `Link` fields for the title to be enabled. The link is the same as in step 3 (Figure 7-4).

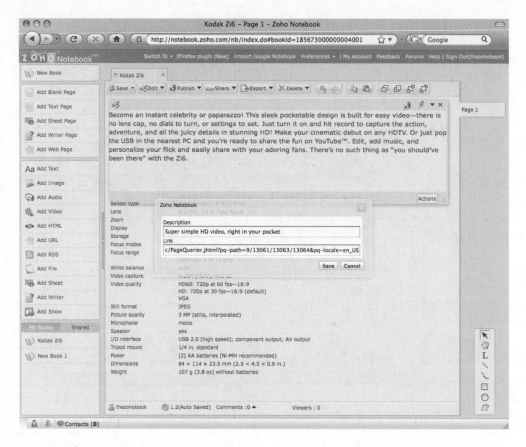

Figure 7-4. Editing the title of the intro text box

9. Click `Save` to proceed.

> *Clicking outside the box (anywhere on the page) will hide the surrounding box as well as all the editing tools on it. Your readers also won't see any of it anyway.*

10. Now add a second text box below the first one using the text at `http://www.kodak.com/eknec/PageQuerier.jhtml?pq-path=9/13061/13063/13065&pq-locale=en_US`.

Adding an image

Your book pages need more than just some formatted text with links. You can add as many images as you want to pages to make your point clearer:

1. To add some related pictures to the page, click `Add Image` in the sidebar. This opens the `Add Image` dialog box.

2. Choose the **From URL** tab, and enter this link: http://www.kodak.com/MEDIA/ProductCatalog/M7752_EKNO35874enZi6_FL-BF_black02_250x200.jpg (image courtesy of Eastman Kodak). Then click **Insert** to continue (Figure 7-5).

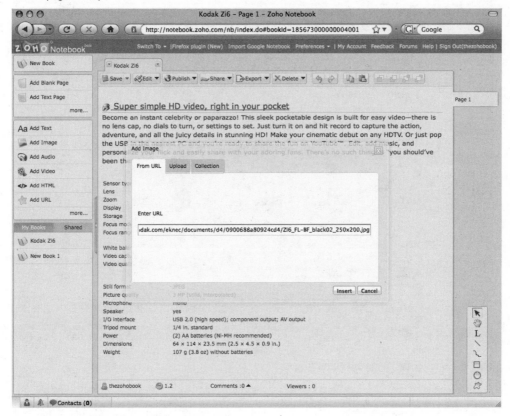

Figure 7-5. Inserting an image from the Internet

3. Deselect the image by clicking somewhere on the page to make the surrounding box containing the image disappear. Then check whether the position of the image on the page is satisfactory.

4. If the image is overlapping the second text box, causing a small portion of the text to become invisible, select it again, click **Menu** (the downward arrow on the upper right of the image container), and select **Send To Back** (Figure 7-6). This will make the text box at least one layer above the image container so you can see everything at once.

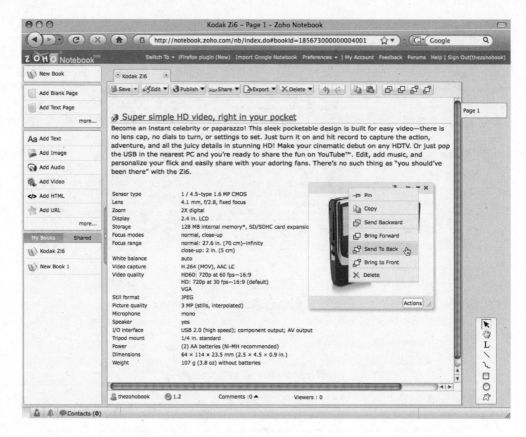

Figure 7-6. Sending the image box to back

> *Each object (for example, the text box or image) you add to a page is placed in a separate transparent layer. Look at it like putting pieces of transparent acetate on each other. Layers are virtual pieces that you put together (like a collage) to form a bigger, more complex piece, such as a notebook page. The objects on layers are opaque and might overlap each other, so you will need to rearrange and reposition them to get the optimal result you want.*

Adding new pages

Your notebook needs more pages to actually become a notebook. You can add multiple pages and group different subjects in each one. Every page has a title (on the right side of each page) that acts as a shortcut to access pages quickly.

You can choose from five different types of pages: blank, text, Sheet, Writer, and web pages.

- Blank pages are just empty pages that allow you to add any kind of content.

- Text pages are empty pages that can contain only text boxes.
- Sheet and Writer pages, on the other hand, can only contain embedded documents from their respective Zoho applications.
- Web pages allow you to embed live web pages into a notebook page.

You are going to see these pages in action in the upcoming walk-throughs:

1. Click **Add Text Page** in the sidebar to create a new text-only page.

   Each new text page already comes with a text box added by default. You can add more text boxes, but first you need to write some text in the first one. Then you can click the gray line appearing below the first text box (when you move the mouse pointer there) to add another text box.

2. Enter a portion of a review from CNET (`http://reviews.cnet.com/digital-camcorders/kodak-zi6-black/4505-6500_7-33141798.html?tag=mncol;lst`). Then change the text size and format similar to Figure 7-7. You can add as much text as you want, but don't bore your readers with lots of "blah blah."

   People tend to read less and look (or watch) more nowadays. So, if you want your book to remain engaging, make sure you avoid using long blocks of text, and also use images, shapes, and video generously. Writing an online novel, however, is a different story.

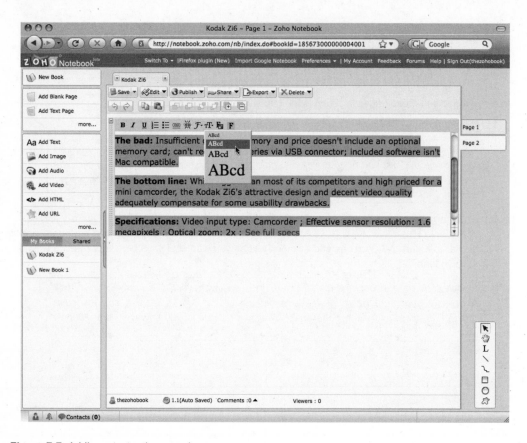

Figure 7-7. Adding a text-only second page

3. To make sure every page in your book has a meaningful title, rename them (you have two pages so far) by double-clicking each page name and renaming it, as shown in Figure 7-8. Then click **Rename** to apply the changes.

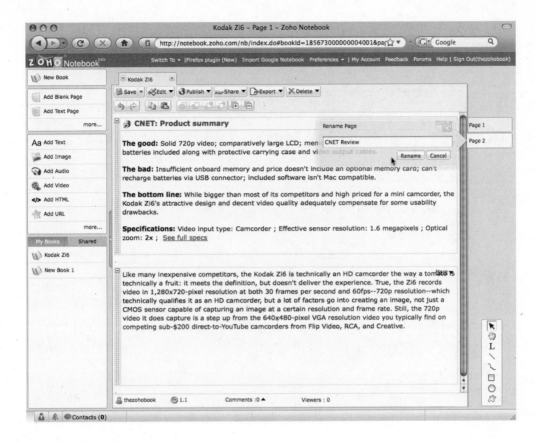

Figure 7-8. Renaming pages

Adding more objects

There are still many objects you can insert into the book pages, and you will now see some of them in action. RSS feeds, for example, are used to fetch the latest news on a subject related to the target page (where you place the feed). They give your book live data input like no other book.

1. First, create a news page by clicking **Add Blank Page**, and then rename it to **News**.
2. Click **Add RSS** in the sidebar. Click **more…** if the button is hidden (see Figure 7-9).

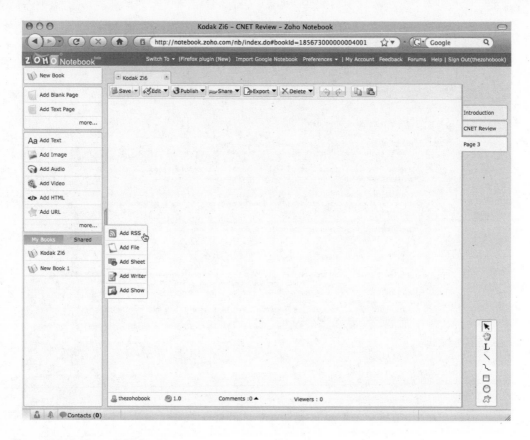

Figure 7-9. Adding a RSS feed

3. Enter the URL of the RSS feed you want to insert, such as
   `http://news.google.ae/news?um=1&ned=us&hl=en&q=%22kodak+zi6%22&output=rss`
   (see Figure 7-10).

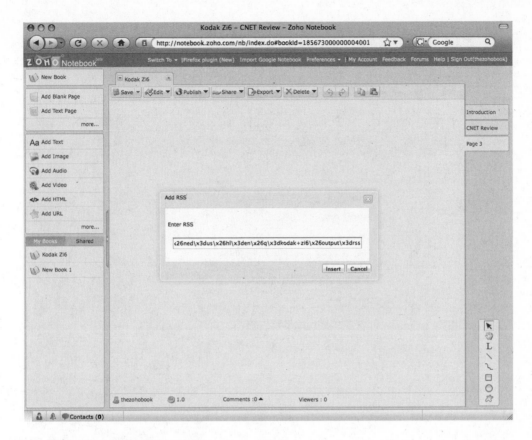

Figure 7-10. Entering the RSS feed URL

> *For this example, search for* Kodak Zi6 *in Google News, or just visit*
> *http://news.google.ae/news?um=1&ned=us&hl=en&q=%22kodak+zi6%22&output=rss.*
> *Then get the RSS feeds for the search results and place it in Notebook. In general, this*
> *is a useful technique to create custom-made news feeds.*

Since we are talking about a digital camcorder, readers will be excited to watch some sample videos to
see the device in action. You can easily embed online video into pages and make your book livelier. Let's
add a video and garnish it with some text and a shape, that is, another object you can add to the pages.

4. Create a new page, and call it `Sample Videos`. Then click `Add Video` on the left pane, and
    paste the embedded code of the video clip in the `Embed` tab (Figure 7-11). Click `Insert` to
    continue.

For this example, you can use the clips already uploaded on Viddler at *http://www.viddler.com/explore/alishabdar/videos/1/* and *http://www.viddler.com/explore/alishabdar/videos/2/*. To learn how to embed a Viddler video in web pages, visit *http://www.viddler.com/help/faq/*. For other video sites like Vimeo and YouTube, check their help pages.

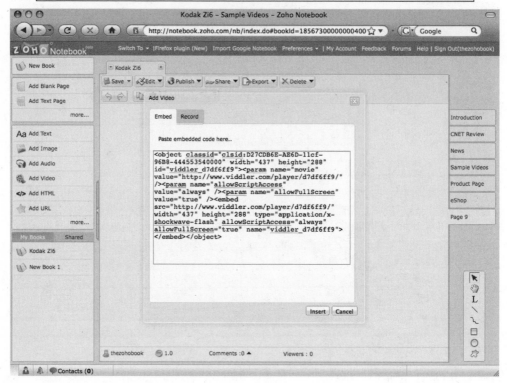

Figure 7-11. Embedding video in the page

5. Add some description text just like you see in Figure 7-12.
6. To drag more focus to the featured video, add an arrow by clicking the **Shapes** button on the toolbox (the bottom right of the Notebook window).
7. Change the color of the arrow shape by first selecting it using the **Select** tool (the first item in the toolbox) and then clicking **Fill Color** on the toolbar (Figure 7-12). Click **OK** after you picked a suitable color.

Figure 7-12. Finalizing the video page

It is also possible to embed a complete web page in the book. It can bring a lot of content quickly into the book.

8. Click **Add Web page** in the sidebar.
9. In the **Add Web Page** dialog box, enter the page URL (http://www.kodak.com/eknec/PageQuerier.jhtml?pq-path=9/13061/13063&pq-locale=en_US), and then click **Create** (Figure 7-13).

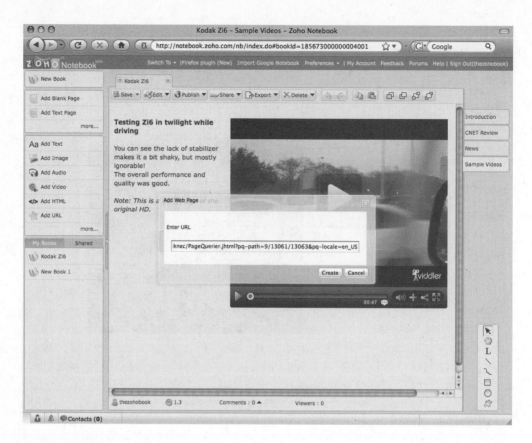

Figure 7-13. Adding a web page to the book

> **10.** Finally, rename the page to `Product Page`.

Notebook creates a new page and loads the web page in it (Figure 7-14). This is live content and will update as the original web page updates.

Figure 7-14. The embedded web page

To make the book even more exciting, let's add an online shop for the convinced reader to directly proceed with the purchase from within the book. For this purpose, I am going to place an HTML snippet from Amazon that takes the visitors to the online store to make the purchase.

> *You can apply for your own Amazon associates program and start making money online. Visit https://affiliate-program.amazon.com/ to learn more about this program.*

1. Create a new blank page, and rename it to **eShop**.
2. Get the generated code snippet from Amazon.com (the merchant). For this purpose, you should find products that match your camcorder, such as a tripod.
3. Click **Add HTML** on the sidebar, and paste the code snippet (Figure 7-15). Then click **Insert** to continue.

355

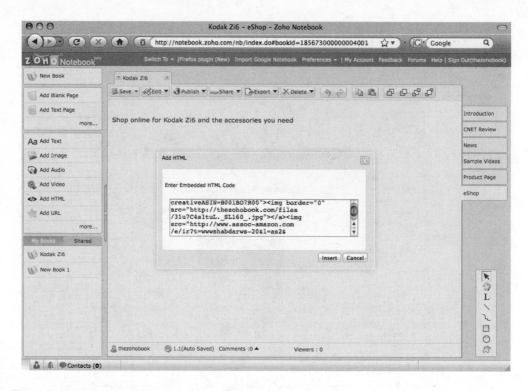

Figure 7-15. Embedding HTML code in the page

4. Add a few more products using the methods in steps 2 and 3.

5. Make the store more attractive by adding related descriptive text and shapes, similar to Figure 7-16.

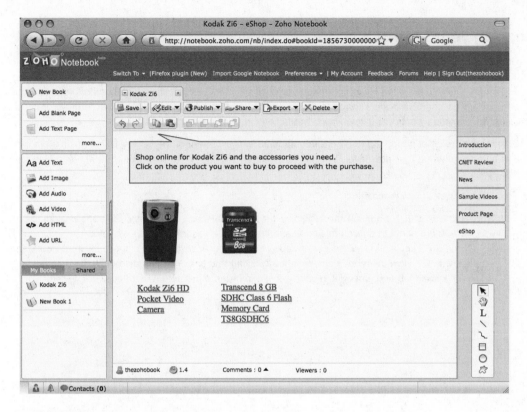

Figure 7-16. The online store, ready to go

> *Some HTML tags `<iframe>` and `<script>`, if embedded into a page, might not act as you expect them to act, as you saw in the previous walk-through.*

Congratulations—you just made you very first book online.

The book about a digital camcorder was just a simple example of what you can do with Notebook. You can go as far as your imagination lets you. The good thing about Notebook is that, unlike printed books and e-books, you are not just limited to text and images. You can add video and embedded content too. It gets even better when you add word-processing documents, spreadsheets, and presentations from other Zoho applications.

Creating sophisticated yearly reports, market research booklets, school essays, cookbooks, and so on, is an easy and rewarding job with Notebook.

Now you'll see how you can publish your masterpiece to the world.

Sharing your books

How useful would a book be if only the author could read it? To let the world read your books, you need to publish them. Then people can access the notebooks you have published, navigate through the pages, search for content, and even leave comments for each page. A useful feature Notebook offers is that you can publish (or share) a book, a page, or even an object (a text box, image container, and so on). This gives you maximum control and flexibility over the content people have access to.

Sharing, on the other hand, allows others to contribute to the content of the books. Using this feature, you can take coauthoring to a new level. You will learn about sharing content in a bit, but first let's start with publishing.

To publish a book, follow these steps:

1. Click **Publish ▶ Book** on the toolbar. The **Publish Book** dialog box will appear alerting you that you are about to publish this book and that it will be readable by everybody.

2. Click **Publish**. A link will be generated, which is the access point to the published book (see Figure 7-17). Now everybody can read it by visiting that link. You can also copy the code snippet in the **Embed** tab and embed it in your website in order to promote it to the website visitors.

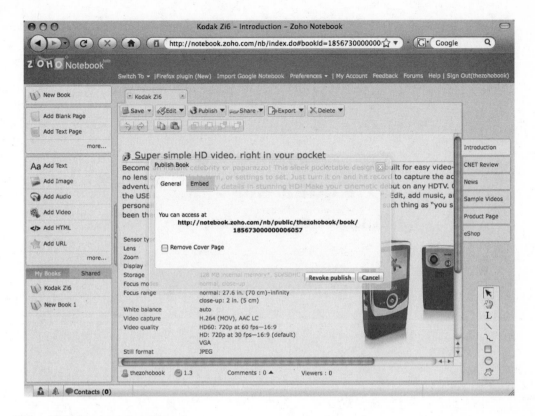

Figure 7-17. The book is published.

> Use **Revoke publish** at any time to make the book private again. The link will be
> disabled immediately.

3. Check out the link to see how the book looks in real world (Figure 7-18). Then return to Notebook
   and edit it if there are elements missing or misplaced.

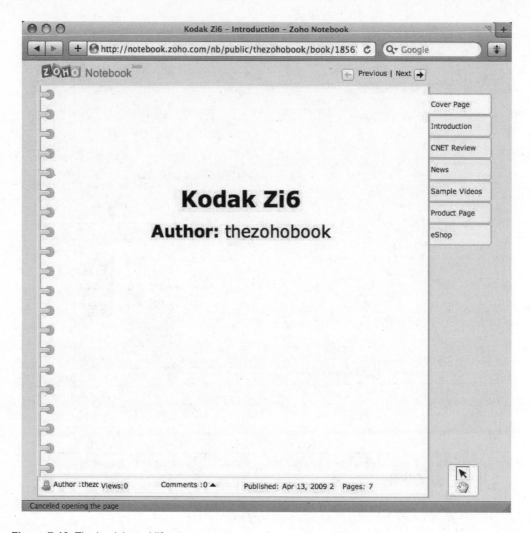

Figure 7-18. The book in real life

Note the number of views and comments below the pages. People can visit the link, read through the book, and leave their feedback. This is so much fun!

You can clearly see that it is possible to make great stuff with Notebook. Take a school teacher or a team of university professors, for example. They can author/coauthor educational textbooks with Notebook without going through the hassles of traditional publishing. Editing and updating content happens in real time, and authors can communicate with readers (students) via comments as well as other Zoho tools.

Speaking of coauthoring, let's see how you can share a book (or a single page or individual objects inside pages) with others so they can collaborate in the process.

To share a page, follow these steps:

1. Open the page, and select **Share ▸ Page** in the toolbar.
2. Enter the e-mail address (or Zoho ID) of the people you want to have access to the page, separated by comma.
3. Optionally give read or read/write access to the content, or add a custom message.
4. Click **Share** to send the invitation message to the contributors (Figure 7-19).

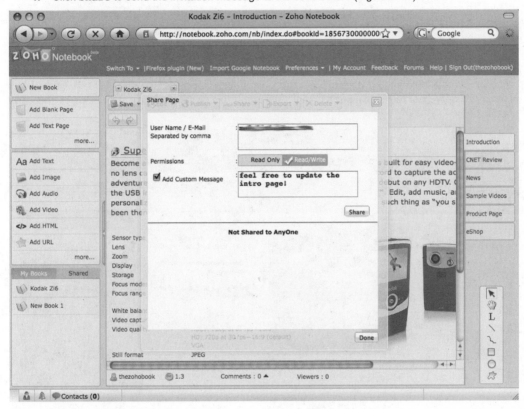

Figure 7-19. Sharing a single page

5. Click **Done** to close the dialog box.

> Having the ability to share different objects in a book allows you to set, for example, who can edit the introduction page and who will be able to change the first video clip in the sample videos page.

More Notebook

Although this chapter will not cover every single aspect of `Notebook`, there are still two more features worth discussing before we move on. First I'll cover the versioning facilities that help you keep track of the changes done to notebooks, and then I'll cover the Notebook browser plug-in that allows you to take notes while surfing the Web without interruption.

Tracking changes

Notebook offers you a quick way to keep track of the changes in your books. You can check the versioning information of every page and object in a book.

When you are editing a page, it shows a version number below the page (for example, 1.3). Clicking this number will open the versioning environment where you can compare different versions of the page (Figure 7-20).

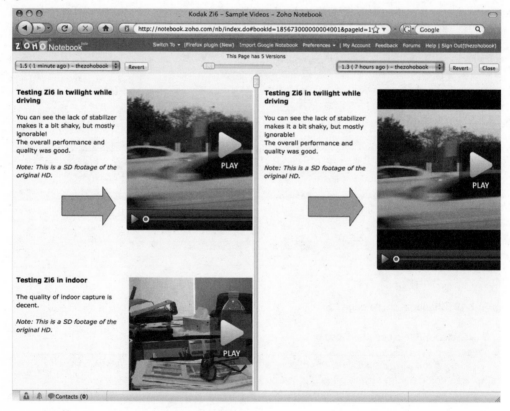

Figure 7-20. Version control in Notebook

To revert to an older version, click **Revert** next to the version drop-down list on the top of the screen.

Taking notes as you go

Another area where Notebook can come in handy is when you collect information while surfing the Web. You can clip pages or portions (selections) of the pages and add them to your books. This approach is similar to what Google Notebook used to offer (which may be discontinued by now).

To make this process easier, Zoho has released a Firefox add-on that allows you to add content to the books in Notebook. Internet Explorer and Safari are not yet supported (as of this writing), so you might find yet another reason to switch to Firefox!

To install the add-on, follow these steps:

1. http://notebook.zoho.com/nb/ext/index.html, or click the Firefox plug-in link at the top of the Notebook main screen. Then click the download link for the add-on (http://notebook.zoho.com/nb/ext/zoho_notebook_helper-1.0b6.xpi, as of August 2009).
2. Firefox might notify you (in a golden bar above the page) about preventing notebook.zoho.com from installing software on your browser. Click **Allow** to proceed.
3. In the installation dialog box (Figure 7-21), click **Install**. Firefox downloads and installs the add-on.

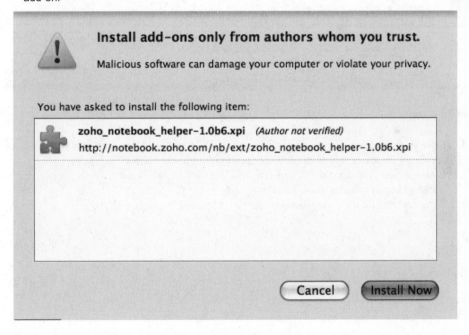

Figure 7-21. Installing the add-on

4. To complete the installation process, restart Firefox, because it will notify you in the `Add-ons` dialog box. Once restarted, it will notify you again that the add-on is successfully installed.

5. To use the add-on, click the Zoho Notebook button appearing on the status bar of Firefox (on the bottom right), and you will be asked to log in to Zoho (Figure 7-22) if you are not already not logged in.

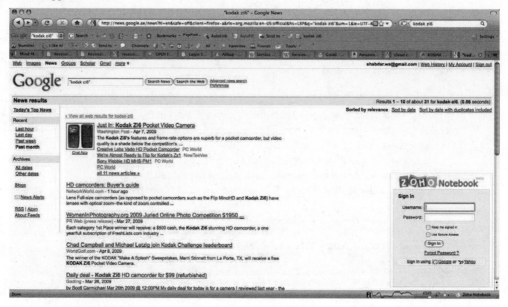

Figure 7-22. Logging in

6. Enter your Zoho credentials, and click `Sign In` to continue. After a successful login, a box will appear on the lower right of the window showing your current book.

7. Create a new book by clicking `Create New Notebook`, and create a new page in the current book by clicking `Create New Page`.

8. Enter the book (or the page) name, and click OK to continue (Figure 7-23).

Figure 7-23. Entering name for the new book

9. To take notes (in other words, add content to your books while surfing), select a portion of the desired text, right-click, and select `Add to Zoho Notebook` from the context menu. The text portion will be added to the destination book page with a title linked to the original post (Figure 7-24).

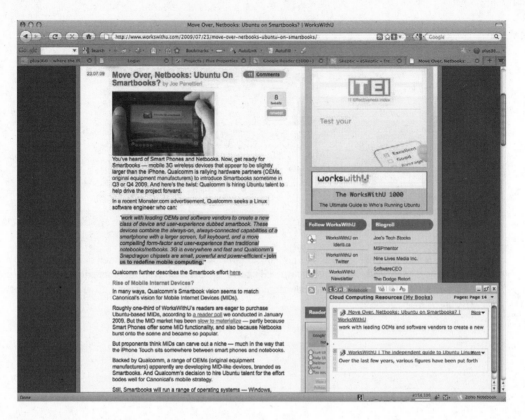

Figure 7-24. Selected text added to a book page

You can still do few more tasks using the Notebook add-on. For instance, if you added text to a book or a page by mistake, you can easily move it to another book or page. Simply click `More` (in front of the entry in the Notebook small window), and select `Move`. Then set the destination book and page for the text box, and click `move` (Figure 7-25).

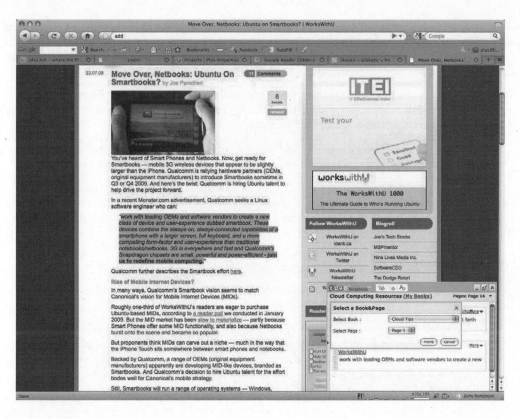

Figure 7-25. Moving a text

> Note that the Notebook add-on will not work if you have already opened Notebook in the same window or in a different tab. You need to close Notebook first for the plug-in to work properly.

Zoho Wiki

A wiki is a collection of web pages designed to enable anyone to contribute to or modify the content using a simplified markup language. You can set up a website using a wiki platform and start creating pages and adding content immediately with almost no prior technical knowledge needed. Then you can allow others (the public or a limited list of people) to contribute to creating and maintaining the web pages. Such efforts can result in content-rich websites that are the outcome of the collective knowledge and public wisdom.

Wikipedia (www.wikipedia.org) is a great example of such a website. It would be almost impossible for a single team or organization to build a website on the same scale of Wikipedia. It is the work of a team of millions of people and made possible with a simple wiki platform.

Well, there are many other uses for wikis other than creating gigantic sites. Because of the special structure and features wiki platforms provide, you can set them up for different purposes. A user's manual for your product, a community website for the university, a personal website, and more are all possible with just a wiki platform.

There are many different wiki platforms that you can choose from. Zoho Wiki is a new kid on the wiki block, but it offers unique features that make it a good choice for small to medium-sized business websites that focus on big chunks of information instead of pure eye candy.

> *If you want more information, the Wiki Matrix at http://www.wikimatrix.org/ is your one-stop destination for comparing different wiki platforms and checking out the features of each one.*

Don't worry if you are confused about all this or have no idea what a wiki platform can do for you. In this section, you are going to create a small company wiki while learning about nuts and bolts of Wiki. Then you can decide where and how you are going to use Wiki.

Getting started

To open Wiki, log on to http://wiki.zoho.com or find it in Zoho Personal. When you open Wiki for the first time, it will immediately ask you to set up a new wiki.

> *Zoho Wiki provides you with a platform where you can create multiple wiki sites. Zoho Wiki allows you to create up to two wikis for free with a total storage space of 50MB. This is quite enough for testing purposes and even a small amount of information, but as your information grows, your requirements grow too. In that case, you should apply for the paid services. You can check the different plans at http://wiki.zoho.com/Wiki-Pricing.html.*

As you can see in Figure 7-26, you should start with giving your new site a title in the `Title` section. The URL (web address) is already set to http://<YOUR_ACCOUNT_NAME>.wiki.zoho.com.

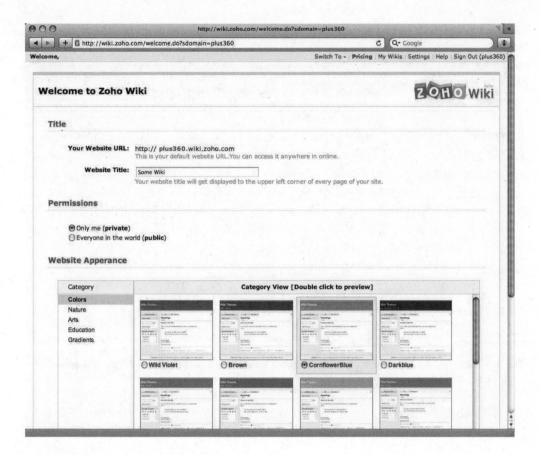

Figure 7-26. Running Wiki for the first time

Next, you should set the wiki to be private or public in the `Permissions` section. If you choose `Only me`, nobody except you can see the content of the wiki. This is good when you are going to use Wiki to create a website with private information such as classified data or internal company information.

On the other hand, if you chose `Everyone in the world`, it means that this wiki is accessible globally, making it suitable for publishing anything that basically is not private.

> *It is a good idea to start a wiki in private mode (default) while you are setting up the basic structure. Once ready for rollout, you can make it public.*

Finally, there is a collection of themes to choose from in the `Website Appearance` section. Once you selected how your wiki will look, click `Create` to proceed.

After you created your first wiki site, you will be redirected to the `My Wikis` page (Figure 7-27) where all your wikis (one for now) are listed. You can customize each wiki by clicking `Settings` or make any one of them the default wiki by clicking `Set as landing wiki`. This way you will be redirected to that particular site/page every time you log in.

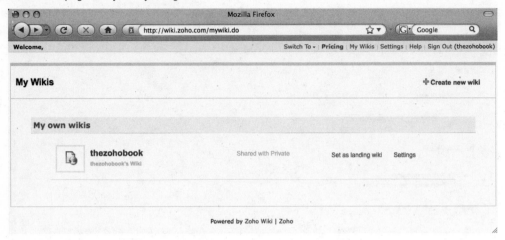

Figure 7-27. First wiki created

Let's get started—click the wiki title to open it for editing.

The first page you see when you open a wiki is the `Dashboard` page (Figure 7-28). This is where you control everything from editing pages to changing the settings.

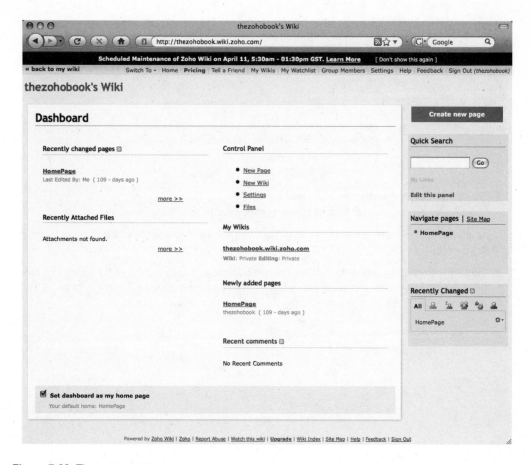

Figure 7-28. The `Dashboard` page

In the sidebar, there are quite a few options such as searching for specific content in the wiki (when it gets bigger), navigating through pages, and monitoring the changes.

> *Wikis are usually very active sites and get updated by more than one person. In fact, there might be hundreds or thousands of people maintaining one. However, in our example, you won't see such traffic.*

The workspace (the white area) is divided into different sections:

- **Recently changed pages**: Lists the latest pages you (or the collaborators) modified along with the modifier's name and the modification date
- **Control Panel**: Gives shortcuts to create new pages and wikis, configuring the current wiki, and listing the files uploaded to the current wiki
- **Recently attached files**: Lists the latest files added to the current wiki

- **My Wikis**: Lists all your wikis for a quick switch between them
- **Recent Comments**: Lists the feedback wiki readers left for you (and the collaborators) to check

You will use these sections more as your wiki grows.

Working with pages

A wiki is a collection of pages that are linked to each other back and forth. You should keep these points in mind while creating pages. A wiki should consist of pages that are the following:

- Easy to read and navigate
- Subjective
- Descriptive but short enough to follow easily
- Linked (as many as needed) to corresponding pages inside and outside the wiki

For now, let's start with modifying the home page. Then you will add more pages and insert real content to shape up your very first wiki.

1. Click the **HomePage** link in the sidebar (in the **Navigate Pages** section). The homepage opens in view mode, and you can see that it is filled with some sample introduction text (Figure 7-29).

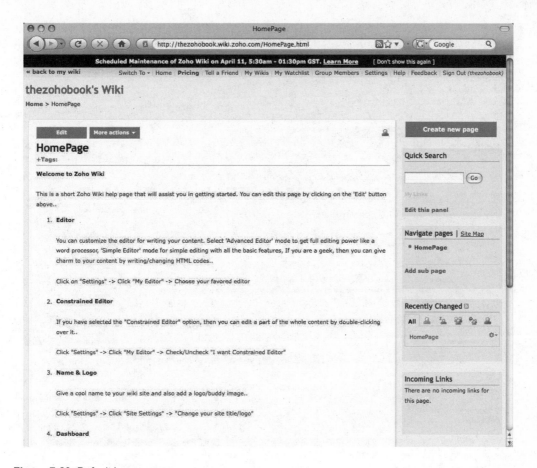

Figure 7-29. Default home page

2. Click **Edit** on the top of the page to modify the content. This opens the page in the editor where you will be able to insert formatted text, images, links, widgets, and other useful elements to the pages (Figure 7-30).

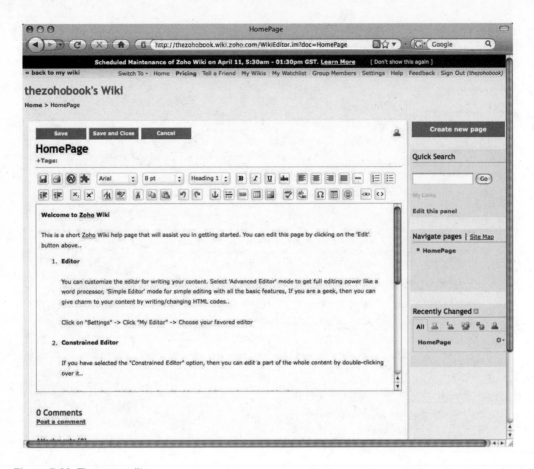

Figure 7-30. The page editor

3. Replace the existing text with the paragraphs you see in Figure 7-31. Feel free to format the text using the toolbar.

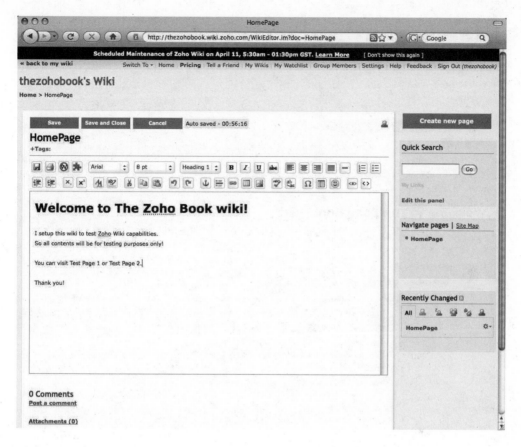

Figure 7-31. Editing the home page

4. Select `Test Page 1` in the text, and click the `Link` button on the toolbar.
5. Click the `New Wiki Page` tab in the `Insert/Modify Link` dialog box, and click `OK`.

> *As you probably noticed, it places* `Test Page 1` *automatically in the* `Page Name`, `Text`, *and* `Title` *fields (Figure 7-32). It will actually create a new page called* `Test Page 1`, *so you don't need to do it manually. This is a great technique when you link to a page you know doesn't exist yet.*

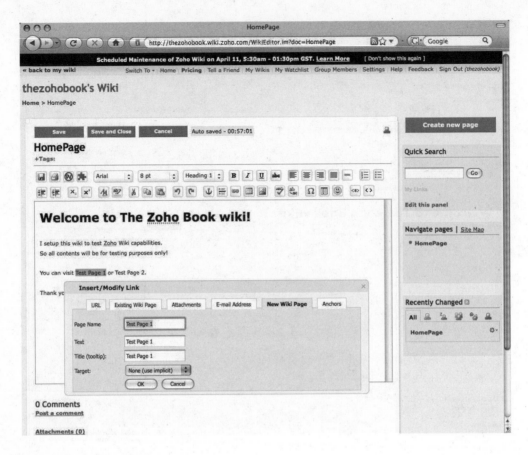

Figure 7-32. Adding link to a new page

6. Repeat step 5 for `Test Page 2` as well.
7. Select `Friends of ED` in the text, and click the `Link` button again.
8. Select the `URL` tab, and insert www.friendsofed.com in the `URL` box. `Text` and `Title` are filled in automatically.
9. Select `Target` as `New window`, and click `OK` (Figure 7-33).

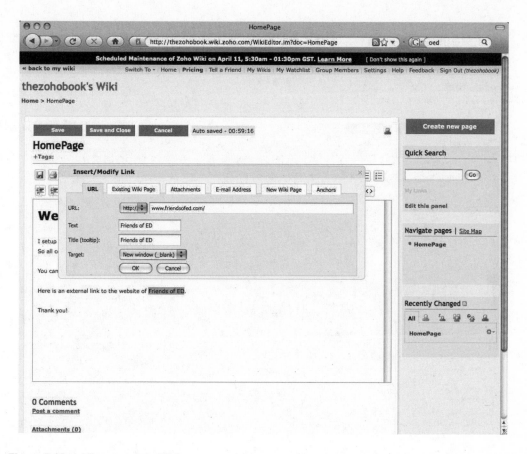

Figure 7-33. Adding an external link

> This is how you insert external links. They simply link to a page outside the wiki as opposed to page links that take you between the pages of the same wiki.

10. Click the **Test Page 1** link in the homepage. Wiki will automatically create a new page called **Test Page 1** and open it for editing (Figure 7-34).

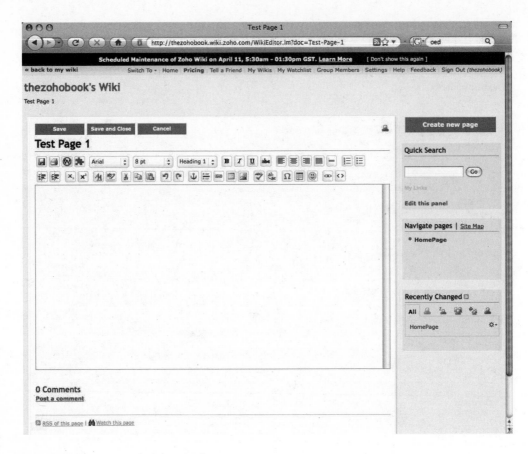

Figure 7-34. New page created on the fly

11. Write some dummy text in the page. You can take some paragraphs from www.lipsum.com.

Adding more to pages

Although text plays an essential role in wiki pages, other media such as images will result in more engaging and more sophisticated content. In this section, you'll begin with adding an image and then proceed with adding a widget to your wiki.

> *Using widgets, you can place external objects to your wiki pages, either from other Zoho applications (for example, Writer or Sheet) or from third-party services like YouTube. This helps you make wikis more content rich by allowing you to embed almost any embeddable online content in the pages.*

1. Click the **Image** button on the toolbar. Browse for a picture file in your computer. Wiki will start uploading it immediately, and once it's finished, you'll see a preview of it (Figure 7-35). Then set **Layout** and **Spacing** as you see in the figure, and click **Insert** to proceed.

Figure 7-35. Inserting an image

2. The result should look like Figure 7-36. Click **Save and Close** on the top of the page to save the changes and return to the dashboard.

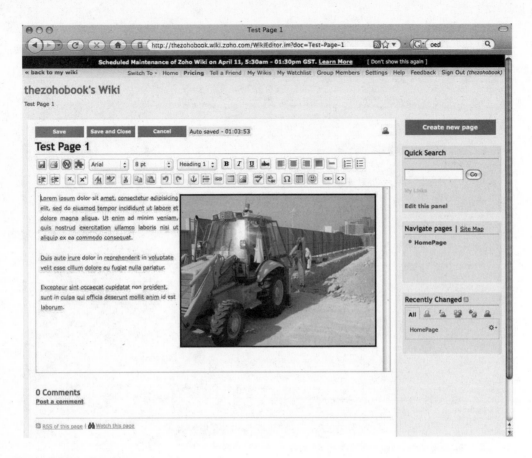

Figure 7-36. Inserted image

> *It is also possible to select a picture from the* `Uploaded Images` *tab (if there is any) or enter the address of the image file directly in the* `URL` *tab.*

3. Open the homepage in the view mode, and click `Test Page 2`. This will open a new (empty) page called `Test Page 2`.

4. Enter some dummy text, and then click `Widget` (the green puzzle icon) on the toolbar. There are many useful widgets to choose from.

5. Click `Zoho Writer` in the left pane, and select a document on the right side. Then click `Insert` to continue (Figure 7-37).

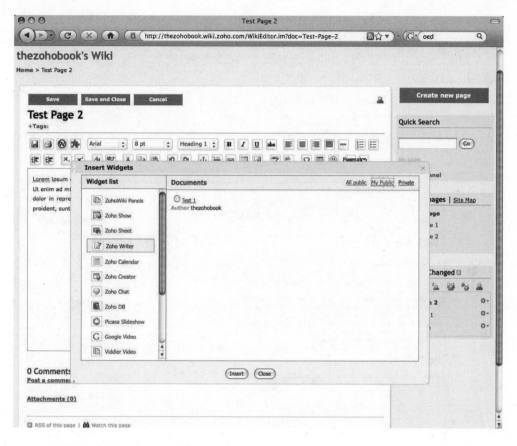

Figure 7-37. Inserting a Writer document

> Note that you can insert private or public documents (from Writer, Sheet, Show, and so on) by selecting the proper link in the upper right of the dialog box.

6. Click the `Save and Close` button. You can see the Writer document loads inside the page, demonstrating how mashing up different content in the same page works (Figure 7-37).

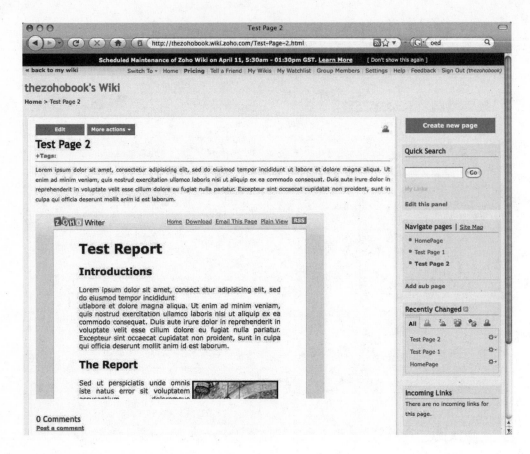

Figure 7-38. Writer document showing in the wiki page

Now you can open every page separately or navigate through them via the internal links you have made. For your reference, all pages (and subpages) are listed in the sidebar under `Navigate pages` as well.

You can create more pages and make links between them using the internal links. This is how a wiki works. It's many pages all logically interconnected to form a bigger collection that serves a common purpose.

Unleash your wikis

The general purpose of creating wikis is to share them with people. Wiki provides you with a platform where people can easily read through big chunks of content and also contribute and help maintain it.

For example, when you are working on a help website (such as an online user's guide or similar) for a product or a service, you can invite a group of people to help you write the pages. An engineer can contribute to the technical parts while a marketing expert can work on the introduction.

At this stage, your wiki is private, meaning only you can see it. You are going to see how to share it with a group of people or just make it public for everybody to enjoy the content.

Working in a group

One way of sharing a wiki is assigning its read/write permission to members of a group. You can create one group per wiki and then add members to it:

1. Click `Group Members` on the top menu bar.

2. In the `Group Members` dialog box (Figure 7-39), add the e-mail addresses (or the Zoho ID) of the people you want to add to the group.

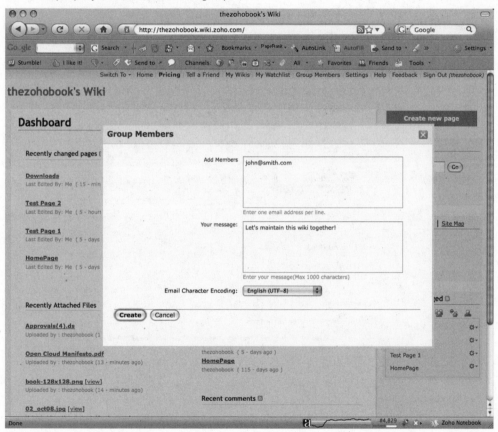

Figure 7-39. Inviting group members

3. Write a custom message for the invitees to know why they receive this invitation.

4. Click **Create** to send the invitations. You can see the list of invited people with **Pending** status. When the recipients click the link included in their invitation messages, the status will turn to **Subscribed,** meaning they are officially part of the group.

5. Close the dialog box.

6. Click **Settings** on the top menu bar, and navigate to the **Permissions** tab.

7. Change **Reading** and **Editing** permissions to **Group** (Figure 7-40). This means the group members can read all the pages (of the current wiki) and modify them too. But you are still the only person who can create pages, delete them, or leave comments because you just granted reading and editing permissions.

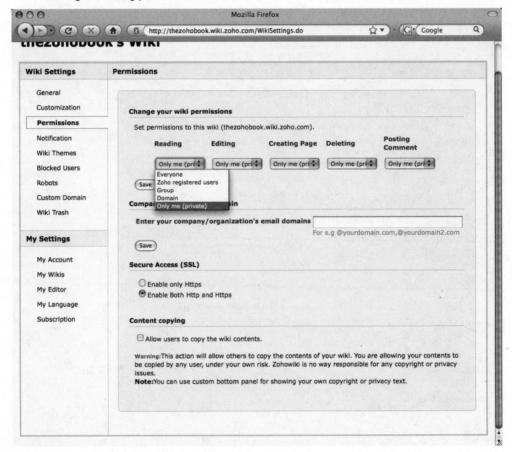

Figure 7-40. Changing the permissions

8. Click **Save** for the changes to apply.

> *Note that changing settings is applied only to the current wiki and not all other wikis you have in your account.*

You can test the recently assigned permissions by asking the members to log in and view the pages. Change the permissions at any time to give them more or less access level (such as `Editing` and `Posting Comments`).

Publishing wikis

After working on the basis of a wiki, you usually want it to be publicly accessible. You can let the world read the wiki, such as when you are publishing help wikis or community sites, or you can let the people maintain the wiki by giving them edit permission. However, you should be very careful with the level of permissions you give to people since they can accidentally (or deliberately) change or destroy information or put harmful content on your wiki.

> *Make sure you consult a lawyer to put a proper disclaimer and a privacy page in your wiki if you intend to open it for public access.*

The process of making a wiki (or selected pages) public for viewing is similar to sharing it with a group of people. You just need to set the `Reading` permission to `Everyone` in the `Permission` section of the `Settings` page. If you want to let people edit the content, it is risky to change the `Editing` permission to `Everyone`. It is a better idea to at least select `Zoho registered users` in order to minimize possible spamming or malicious acts from unknown sources.

Another method, which is very useful for business users, is when you need to share wikis within your organization only. This means only the people who work for your organization should have access to the data stored in the wiki. Usually people who work for the same company have an e-mail address that shares the domain name (for example, john@yourcompany.com and sue@yourcompany.com).

Therefore, all you need to do is set the permissions to `Domain`. This means only the users who are registered in Zoho using an e-mail address belonging to a particular domain (yourcompany.com) are allowed to have access to this wiki.

In Figure 7-41, note the domain name entered in `Company/Organization Domain`. Setting `Reading` permission to `Domain` tells Wiki that only the users who are logged in to Zoho with an e-mail address from this domain are allowed to have access. In this example, all people who belong to the domain name specified are allowed to view the wiki, but only members of the group can edit it. Other permissions, however, are still exclusive to you as the wiki owner.

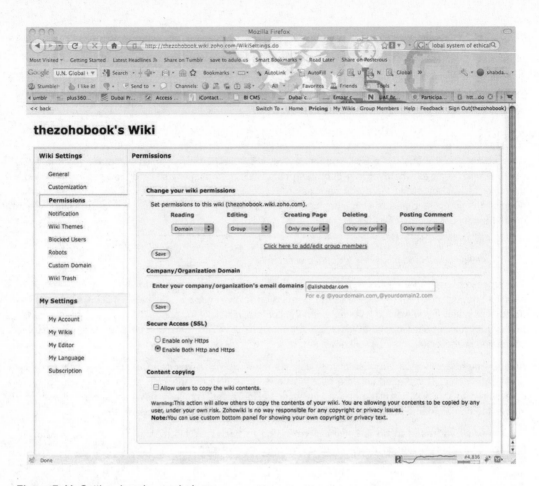

Figure 7-41. Setting domain permissions

On a smaller scale, Wiki allows you to apply different permissions to every page in order to create complex access levels. Click **More Options** on top of each page (in view mode), and select **Permissions**.

By default, it is set to the global wiki permissions, meaning it is as per the configurations in the **Settings** page. Instead, you may select **Set custom permissions for this page** and override the default settings for the current page only. For example, if you want the people from your organization to be able to leave comments on the **Downloads** page only, set **Posting Comments** to **Domain** (Figure 7-42), and then click **Save** to apply the changes.

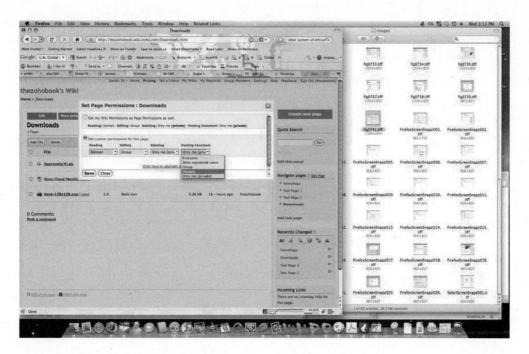

Figure 7-42. Setting permissions at the page level

Customizing Wiki

You have used **Settings** before to change the permissions and sharing behavior of your wiki. But there is more to change to make Wiki fit in your requirements. Let's go through a couple of the settings you might use the most. You can keep discovering the rest by yourself.

1. Click **Settings** in the top menu bar, and then navigate to the **Customization** tab where you can revamp the whole layout of the wiki by repositioning and removing panels and the page elements (Figure 7-43).

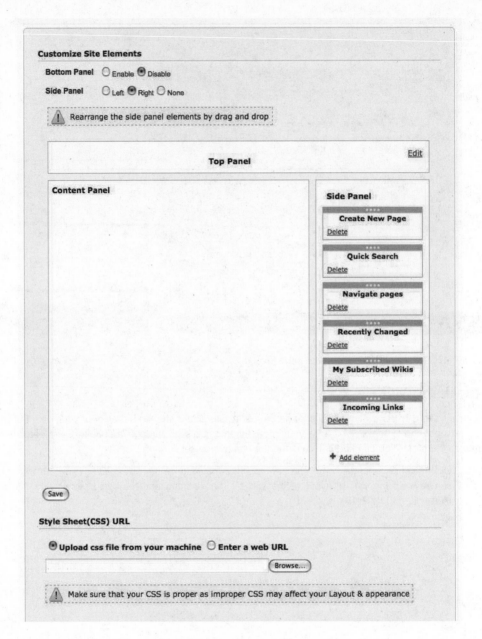

Figure 7-43. Customizing the layout

2. Check and modify the top panel by clicking **Edit** on the **Top Panel** placeholder to customize the title bar. Change your logo and wiki title as you want.

> *You can also upload (or just paste the address of) a custom Cascading Style Sheets (CSS) file in order to modify the look and feel of the wiki even more. But you should be very careful not to mess up the layout. If you are not familiar with CSS, http://reference.sitepoint.com/css is a good place to start.*

3. Click **Save** your changes before you navigate away from this tab.

4. Next, navigate to the **Subscription** tab to see the available quota for your account (Figure 7-44). You should keep an eye on this page because you don't want to run out of space when your wikis are thriving. For the free plan, you have 50MB of space and only two wikis to create. Moving to higher plans that offer more space and more wikis is always possible through upgrading to paid subscriptions; just click **Upgrade**.

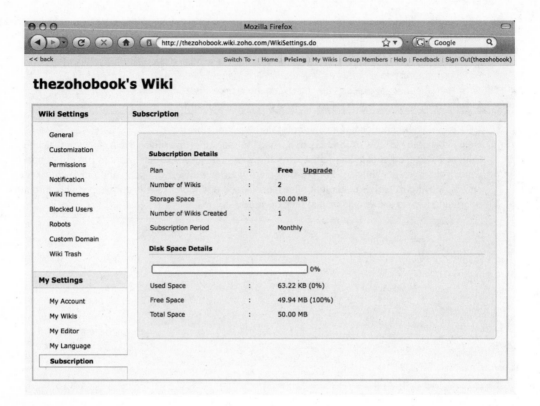

Figure 7-44. Checking the available quota

More Wiki

Before we finish with Wiki, I'll talk about three more topics in brief: creating new pages from scratch, monitoring the changes in different wikis or pages, and sending messages inside Wiki. After that, you can confidently continue working with your wiki sites knowing that you understand all the basics.

Creating pages from scratch

Previously in this chapter you saw how to create pages on the fly by adding internal links to new wiki pages. However, sometimes you need to create pages from scratch. For example, you can create a download page for the test wiki (that you made in this chapter) and put files for the wiki visitors to download. This page was not created through a link and needs be added from scratch.

1. Click `New Page` in the `Control Panel` in the dashboard.
2. In the `Create New Page` dialog box (Figure 7-45), enter `Download` in `Page Name`, and select `File cabinet` as `Page Type`. Then click `Create` to proceed.

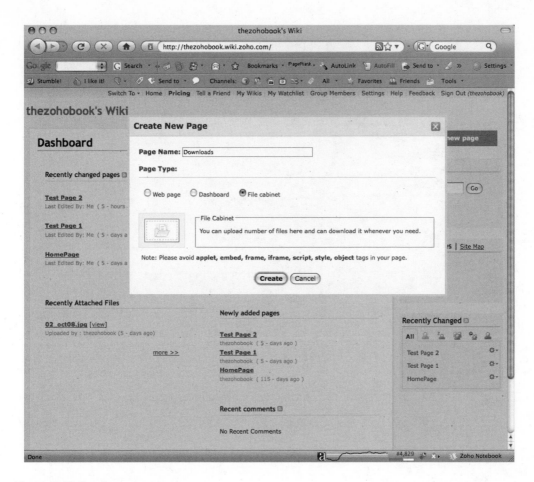

Figure 7-45. Creating a new page

*Wiki has three different page templates (**Web page**, **Dashboard**, and **File cabinet**), each one providing you with a different user interface (UI). Try them all to see what features they offer.*

3. Try uploading some files by clicking **Add File**. Browse for any file smaller than 50MB in size, and add a short but meaningful description (Figure 7-46). Then click **Upload File**.

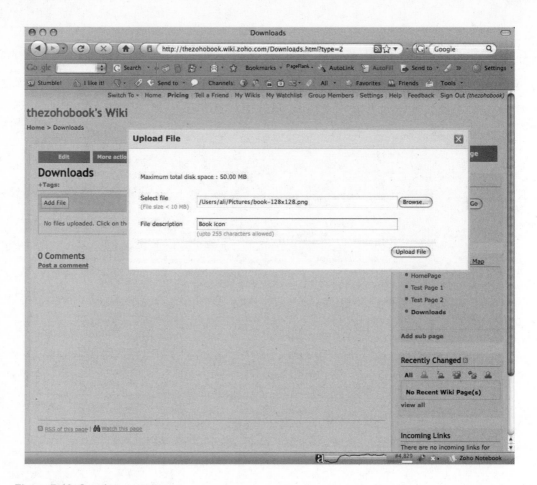

Figure 7-46. Creating a new page

> *Wiki accepts all file formats to be uploaded. Supported documents such as word-processing documents, spreadsheets, and presentations can be opened by Zoho applications on the fly, but other files are just downloadable.*

A nice feature of Wiki is that if you upload a newer version of a file that already exists in the file list, it replaces it with the newer version and adds to the version number, keeping the old versions accessible for you to retrieve if needed. You can click the version number of the file (see Figure 7-47) to see a list of older files available to be downloaded. This is great for your wiki community to keep track of the changes of the shared files.

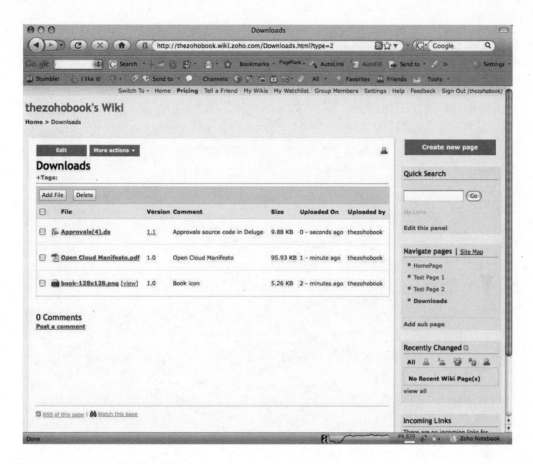

Figure 7-47. File list with all versions

Monitoring the changes

Below every page there is a tiny link, `Watch this page`. It adds the page to your watch list, meaning whenever the page is updated you will receive a notification e-mail. All people with read access to wikis or pages can add them in their watch list. This is useful for wiki owners, authors, and viewers to keep an eye on their favorite content.

You can manage your watched pages via `My Watchlist` accessible from the top menu bar. You may also deactivate or delete some or all of them as required (Figure 7-48).

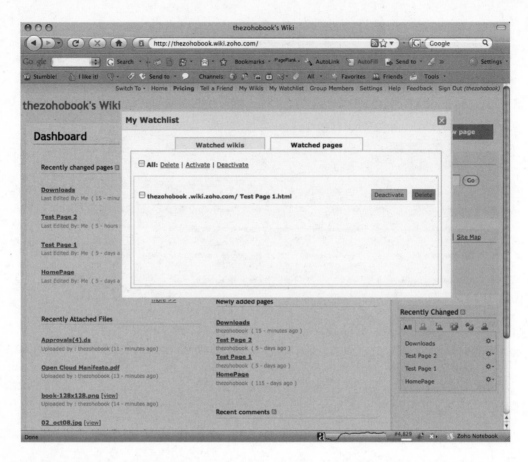

Figure 7-48. Managing your watch list

Sometimes you may need to watch an entire wiki. This is possible by clicking `Watch this wiki` at the bottom of the `Dashboard` page of a wiki. In a similar approach to the watched pages, all watched wikis will be listed in `My Watchlist` on the `Watched wikis` tab.

Communicating inside wikis

If you want to communicate with the authors who contribute to a wiki, a simple way is to just click their name next to each page. A mail window will open, allowing you to send a message to the author directly from within Wiki (Figure 7-49). Once again, this is accessible to all people who can see the pages.

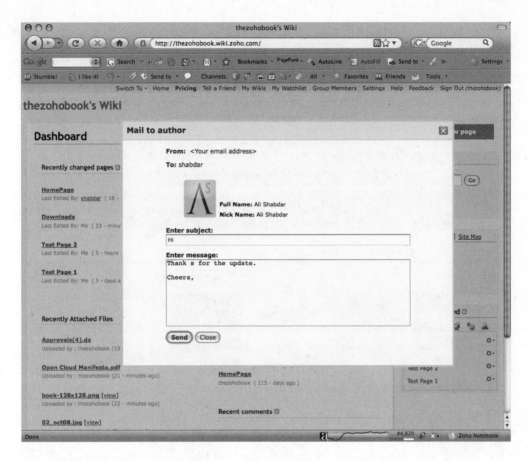

Figure 7-49. Sending messages to authors

Zoho Share

So far, you have learned how to create and share content with others using various SaaS applications provided by Zoho. These applications provide you with loads of feature, one of which is sharing files. Zoho also has a sharing-only application called Share that does nothing but manage your shared documents online.

You might ask, however, with all those applications being capable of sharing files and with Docs managing my documents online, do you need another application just for sharing files? The answer is yes, you might. For some users, sharing documents is the most important (and sometimes the only) feature they require, and Share will probably be their best choice. It is easy to use, focused on the task, and free. So, why not to use it? For example, a teacher can share a weekly exercise document on Share and ask all students to download it without even having a Zoho account. Or a seasonal public report about your company could be accessible for the public by using Share only.

Getting started

Share is very easy to use. It gives you the necessary tools to share documents with the world and manage them in few simple clicks. To tour Share, follow these steps:

1. Log on to `http://share.zoho.com` to open the homepage. The homepage lists the recently shared documents by the Zoho community as well as the featured items (Figure 7-50).

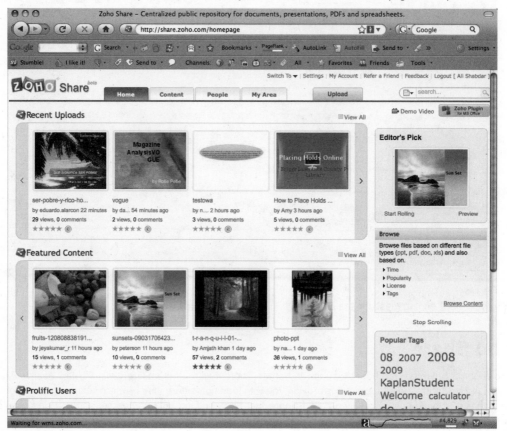

Figure 7-50. The homepage of Share

2. Check out other highlights like **Editor's Pick**, **Prolific Users**, and **Recent Users** that are shortcuts to view other people's (publicly) shared documents. Share allows you to view documents, check out the author pages, rate the documents, and add comments.

3. The `Content` tab focuses only on the files being shared with the community, categorized to **Presentations**, **PDF**, **Documents**, and **Spreadsheets**. Navigate through different categories, and open some files for viewing.

4. Finally, use the search box (at the upper right of the window) to find a file related to your search term. Enter `SaaS`,•for example, and press Enter (on your keyboard) to get a list of related files.

Sharing in action

The command center of Share is `My Area` (Figure 7-51). In the sidebar, you have your mini-profile placed on top followed by the links to your files, trashed files, the items you favor, your friends, messages, and settings. By default Share lists your public files categorized by file type. If you have made some files public before (using Writer, Sheet, Show, or Docs), they will be listed on the respective category tabs.

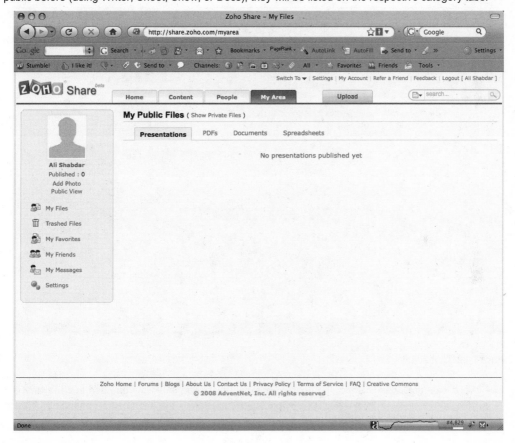

Figure 7-51. `My Area`

You can also upload files for sharing from within Share.

1. Click the yellow tab, **Upload**.
2. Browse for the file in your local machine. The file needs to be a supported type (**DOC**, **SXW**, **ODT**, **RTF**, **SXC**, **ODS**, **PDF**, **PPS**, **PPT**, **ODP**, **SXI**, **XLS**, or **CSV**) 10MB or less in size.
3. Click **Upload** to start the process (Figure 7-52). You can upload only one file at a time.

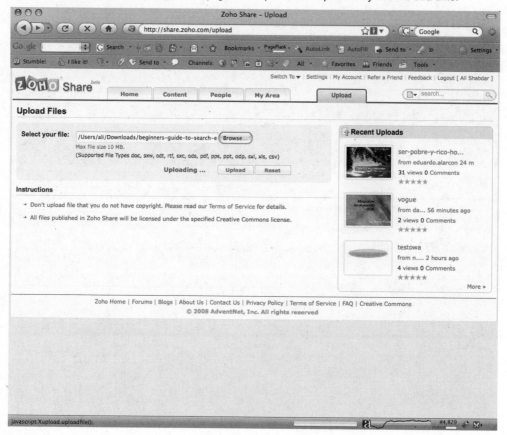

Figure 7-52. Uploading a file

4. Once the upload is finished, the publish window will appear, in which you need to certify that the file you are about to share with the public complies with the terms and conditions of Zoho (Figure 7-53). Click the check box if it does, and choose the right copyright license for the file.

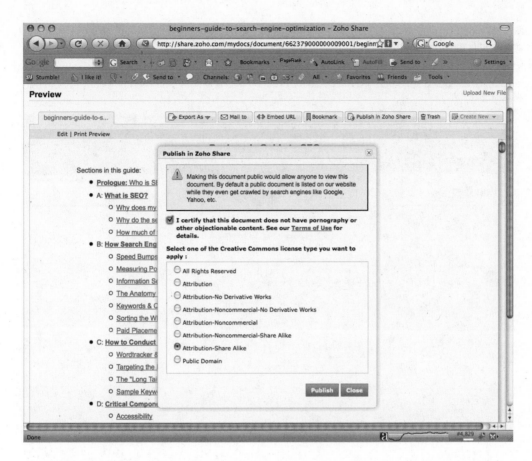

Figure 7-53. Finishing the publish process

> Documents shared on `Zoho Share` should be licensed under the Creative Commons. To learn about Creative Commons and the differences between the various licenses, visit http://creativecommons.org/.

5. Click `Publish` to continue.

Once the publishing is done, your file is public, and everybody will be able to view it. Viewers (including you) can perform the following tasks on the shared documents:

- Export them to various formats (`DOC`, `PDF`, `HTML`, `SXW`, `ODT`, `RTF`)
- Send them by e-mail to others
- Embed them in their web sites
- Publish them in different social bookmarking websites like `Yahoo`, `Reddit`, `Delicious`, and so on

Now if you check **My Area**, the uploaded file is listed under the right category. It shows the number of visits and comments, the published date, and the rating status.

As you can see in Figure 7-54, you can make the file private at any time by clicking **Remove Public** next to each file. By doing so, others will not be able to see the files anymore, and it will be removed from public listings.

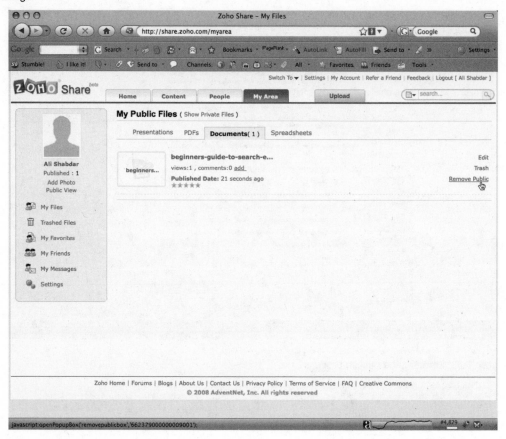

Figure 7-54. Listing published files

Clicking **Show Private Files** will list your private files that you either created in Zoho applications or uploaded to Docs (Figure 7-55). There is a link in front of every private document, **Make Public**, to share it with everybody immediately, only after passing through the publish page (as you saw in Figure 7-53).

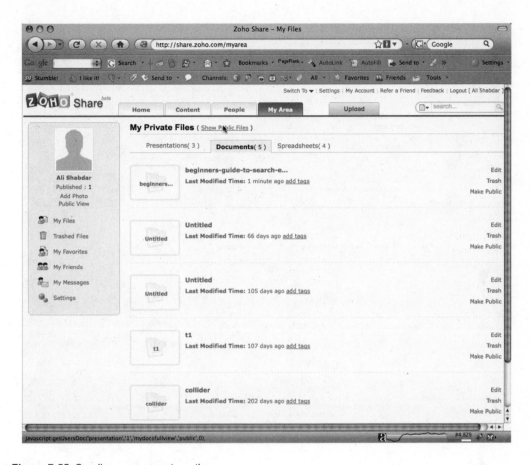

Figure 7-55. Sending messages to authors

Configuring Share

Before we finish this chapter, let's take a quick look at the `Settings` page in `My Area`. Although there are not many settings to change, it is always a good idea to check this section to make the application work the way you want.

1. Click `Settings` on the top menu bar. Alternatively, you can use `My Area ▸ Settings` too.
2. On the settings page (Figure 7-56), change your display name if needed. It could be your full name, nickname, and so on. Don't put your Zoho username (login ID) here, because it is a very bad idea from the point of security. Click `Save` to apply the changes.

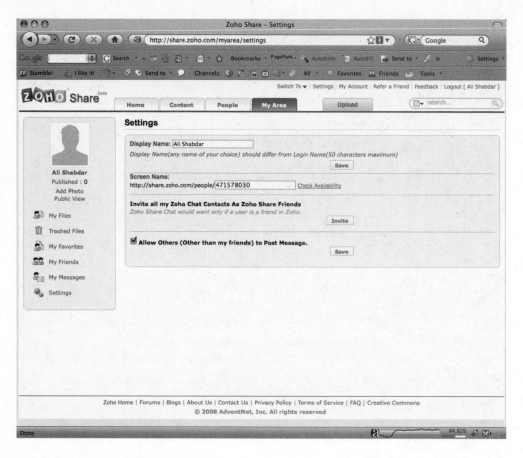

Figure 7-56. Sending messages to authors

3. Set a new screen name. By default, your screen name, which happens to be part of your profile address (URL), is just a random number. Change it to something meaningful, and click **Check Availability** to see whether this link is already taken.

> *Never use your Zoho username as the display name or screen name because it might help hackers and spammers guess your login information easier.*

4. To share files with your chat buddies and befriend them in Share as well, click **Invite**. After showing a list of your chat friends, Zoho sends the selected people an invitation message so they can come check out your shared files.

Getting help

If you have followed the walk-throughs of this chapter, you have to be pretty comfortable doing everyday tasks with Notebook, Wiki, and Share. However, the key to master all features is to practice and discover them yourself. Try all the features, and see what the outcome is. Don't forget to practice before you share your content because you don't want others to see messed-up pages.

Check the forums as the best place to get quick and (mostly) accurate answers. Visit `http://forums.zoho.com`, find the right forum for the application, search for the questions already answered, or click `New Topic` to start your own conversation.

> *Before asking a question, search for it; it has probably been asked and answered before.*

Summary

Creating new things in general is a big joy for humans. Creating wikis that serve a purpose—even small and limited—is fun and rewarding. Contributing to the Internet and creating content online for business or fun is no exception and can be even more interesting because you potentially have millions of people as your audience.

Notebook and Wiki are just the right tools to start creating for the Web and targeting potentially millions of people. They provide you with robust platforms so you can focus on enriching the content instead of learning coding or doing time-consuming administrative tasks.

Using Wiki, you can create the following:

- Simple help sites
- Complex wikis maintained by a large community
- Informative company websites
- And so on

Notebook is your best friend for becoming an author. There's no need for publishers and thousands of dollars spent on marketing campaigns. For example, you can use it for the following:

- Easy online publishing
- Taking notes
- Creating multimedia training material

Finally, Share allows you to reach your audience in a different way. You can publish your wisdom in a document, share the yearly market report with clients and stakeholders, and make the presentation files of your last seminar available for people to enjoy.

In the next chapter, I'll wrap up the first part of this book by discussing some of the other Zoho tools that can make your online life even easier.

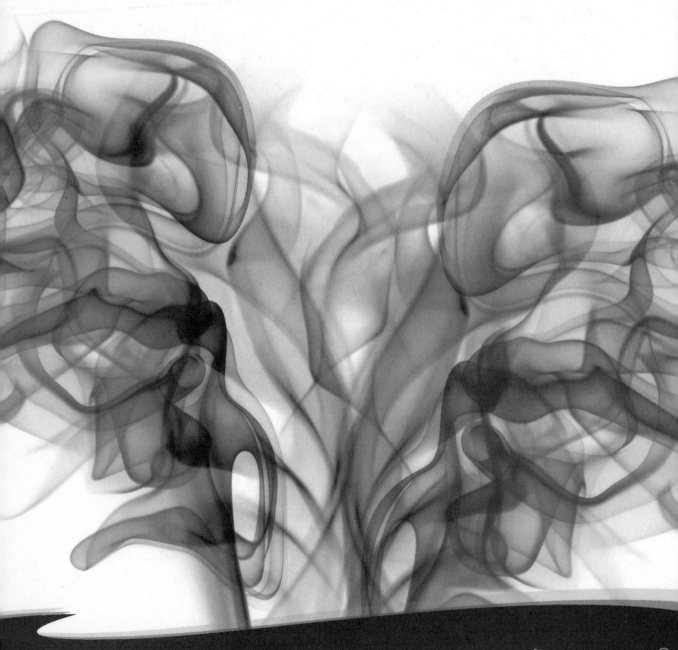

ZOHO ®
Work. Online

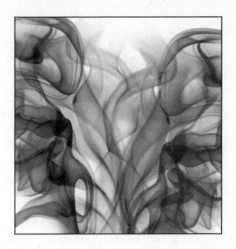

Chapter 8

Zoho Utility Applications

So far, you have learned about all the Zoho productivity applications such as Write and Sheet as well as others such as Notebook and Wiki. Zoho offers you tools for almost every aspect of your online life, and as you can guess, there are still few more that, despite being smaller than the ones you have already learned to use, can be really helpful in conjunction with other applications. Among these tools are gadgets, plug-ins, and utility applications. The utility applications are 24x7, Polls, Viewer, and Challenge, and they are not integrated with any other Zoho applications. They act as stand-alone tools for different purposes. You can find these utilities on the Zoho.com front page.

In this chapter, I will be focusing on gadgets and plug-ins; I'll leave the utility applications to you to discover and use according to your requirements.

Placing Zoho everywhere

Zoho **gadgets** are very useful widgets that allow you to place Zoho productivity tools almost everywhere. You can embed Docs, Mail, Calendar, Tasks, Contacts, and Planner gadgets in different websites to share content with the world.

- For example, suppose you want to share your task list with your Facebook friends so they know what you are working on.
- You can also list your public files on your iGoogle page so that every time you log into your Google homepage, you will be able to access your public documents such as presentations.

- Or, you might want to embed the Mail interface in your private content management system (CMS) so users won't need to check two different websites and can have direct access to their e-mails from within the CMS interface.

Gadgets give you the ultimate flexibility to mash up Zoho tools with other online applications in order to streamline the content sharing and improve productivity. The good news for Google users is that since Zoho supports Google logins (through OpenID, covered in Chapter 1), your iGoogle page can automatically show your Zoho gadgets and the respective content. This is because you logged in with a Google account in the first place.

Placing gadgets on the web pages is a simple task, and you don't need to know any programming. To place a gadget, first you need to open the Gadgets page at `http://gadgets.zoho.com`. As you can see in Figure 8-1, there are nine product gadgets as well as a utility gadget. The product gadgets will place a small window into your information that's stored in the respective Zoho application in one of four available destinations: `Web page`, `iGoogle`, `Orkut`, and `facebook`.

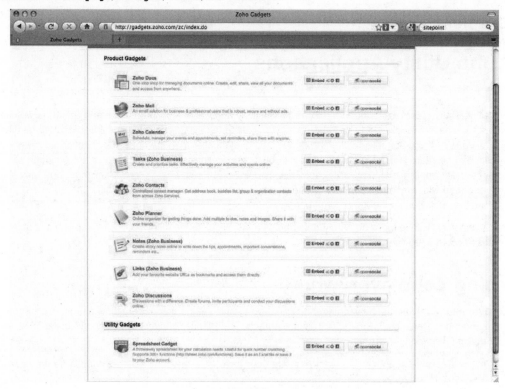

Figure 8-1. Available gadgets

Clicking the gadget name (such as `Zoho Docs`) will open a page where it shows a live demo of the gadget as well as the code snippet to be placed in your web page (Figure 8-2). All you need is to copy the HTML code and paste it into the web page where you want the gadget.

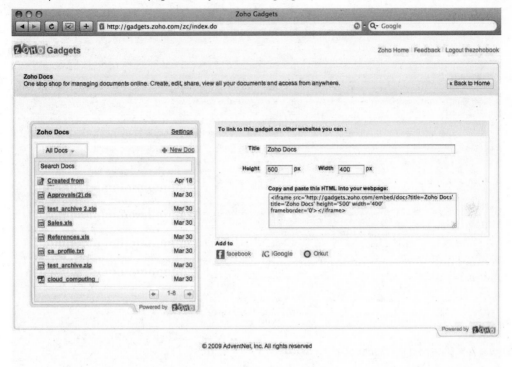

Figure 8-2. Getting the gadget code

You need to paste the code inside the HTML body of a web page or a blog post. Placing it as text will not have the outcome you want. Although you don't need to know HTML, you should understand the difference between the HTML code and the normal text to be able to use the code snippet properly.

To add a gadget to Facebook, iGoogle, or Orkut, you won't need to deal with any code. Simply click the **Embed** link for the gadget, and you will be redirected to another page where you can add it with just a few clicks.

The last way of adding gadgets is by generating an OpenSocial Extensible Markup Language (XML) file. When you click **OpenSocial ▶ Get XML** for any gadget on the home page (see Figure 8-1), a dialog box will appear containing the link to the XML file you need as well as a sample guide on how to add it to Gmail (Figure 8-3). For other websites/services, refer to the documentation provided by them.

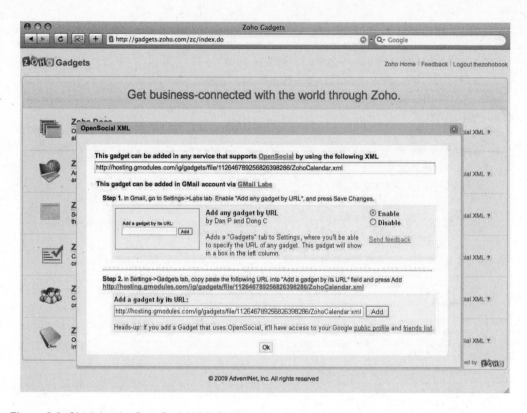

Figure 8-3. Obtaining the OpenSocial XML file link

> OpenSocial is a set of common application programming interfaces (APIs) for web-based social network applications, developed by Google, MySpace, and a number of other social networks. Visit Wikipedia at http://en.wikipedia.org/wiki/OpenSocial and Google Code at http://code.google.com/apis/opensocial/ to get more information.

Connecting to Microsoft Office

For Microsoft Office users, it can be hard to give up your favorite tool for other alternatives. Although pricy and bulky, Microsoft Office has had deep roots in the business world for many years. It is often hard to adopt a new tool once you are used to an older one, despite the pros and cons of moving to the cloud.

Zoho offers a totally different way of working in today's connected world, and it could be many people's only office application. Despite that, the people at Zoho understand that currently the majority of businesspeople use Microsoft Office on Windows machines. So, Zoho supports Microsoft Office out of the box using the Office plug-in for Windows.

This plug-in connects your Microsoft Office installation to your Zoho account, or rather, it connects Microsoft Office to the cloud. This means you can still use Microsoft Office (if you already have it installed on your computer), connected to Zoho in a way that you have your documents in the cloud as well. Microsoft Office and Zoho are in sync, so you can use either of them when available to work on your documents.

You can benefit from this plug-in in several ways:

- Using your existing investment (Office licenses purchased before)
- Leveraging the power of the cloud by connecting Microsoft Office to Zoho and having your documents available online
- Collaborating better using Zoho's concurrent editing features, which allow multiple users to work on a document at the same time

Before you install the plug-in, you should know that it works only on Microsoft Office 2003 (or later) installed on Windows machines.

To install and use the plug-in, follow these steps:

1. Download the executable file (zohoplugin.exe) from the Zoho website (http://www.zoho.com/zohoplugin/home.html).
2. Close all Office applications (Word, Excel, and so on).
3. Install the EXE file as you normally do in Windows, but if you need help installing it, refer to http://show.zoho.com/embed?USER=help&DOC=zohoplugin&SLIDE=1 or http://writer.zoho.com/public/help/zohoplugin/fullpage#InsZP.
4. Open Microsoft Word, and look for the newly placed add-on toolbar for Zoho (Figure 8-4) by which you can connect to your Zoho account. Microsoft Excel will also show the toolbar installed.

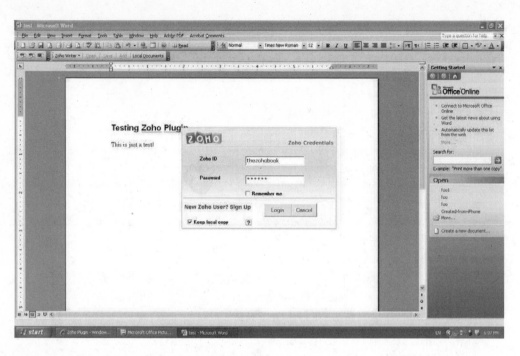

Figure 8-4. Zoho toolbar and the login window in Word

5. Click **Login** on the toolbar, and enter your Zoho credentials in the login box (Figure 8-4).
6. Check **Remember me** to avoid having to enter your Zoho ID and password every time. Check **Keep local copy** to make sure Zoho will retain a local copy of the documents you use between Zoho and Office.
7. Click **Login** to continue. If the login was successful, the other buttons on the Zoho toolbar will be enabled.
8. Type a line or two in a blank Word document, and click **Save** or **Add** on the Zoho toolbar. (Since this document is new, clicking **Add** and **Save** will have the same effect.) The plug-in will check the Zoho account and inform you that the document doesn't exist.
9. Click **Yes** to store the document in Zoho when you are asked to add the document.
10. Open Docs or Writer, and check that the recently created document is available in your account.
11. Now click **Open** (on the Zoho toolbar), and it will show you a list of your online documents (Figure 8-5). Select a document, and click **Open**. Wait a few seconds for Word to open the file.

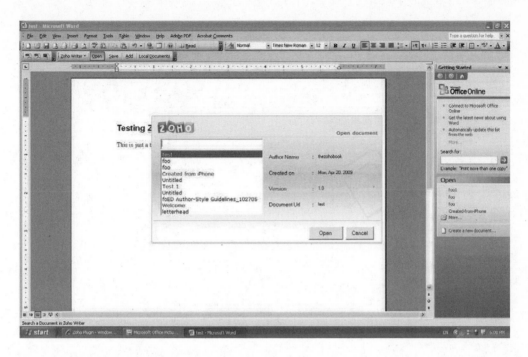

Figure 8-5. Opening files from Zoho

12. Edit and save the document locally in Word, and it will be saved online too.

> *Since the collaboration features are not working inside Word, you need to be careful not to destroy the updates done by others while editing a document in Word. You will be alerted if your copy is older than the remote copy anyway.*

The same procedure applies for Excel, and you can perform the walk-through to work with spreadsheets between Excel and Sheet as well. PowerPoint might be supported in the future, but as of this writing, the plug-in supports only Word and Excel.

When you log in, you can specify whether the Zoho plug-in should keep a local copy of the files you are working on. If you do this, you can find the files in a folder named after your Zoho account in your `My Documents` folder (Figure 8-6). It is important to know the location of this folder because when you work on online documents (stored in your online space on Zoho), they are not saved on your local computer unless you select the check box in step 5 of the previous walk-through. This is the location where they are going to be saved. So, you can check here if anything bad happened (however unlikely) to your document.

411

Figure 8-6. The locally saved documents

Zoho Office for SharePoint

Another exciting tool Zoho has released is Zoho Office for Microsoft SharePoint. This is basically an add-on you (as a SharePoint administrator) can install on your servers to make SharePoint Zoho enabled. This tool allows you to do the following:

- Collaborate in real-time using the concurrent editing features of Zoho
- Store data (documents) in-house on SharePoint servers, which is good news for IT managers and CIOs who are not comfortable storing files elsewhere
- Support more users and more platforms (using Zoho applications) for editing content residing on SharePoint servers
- Keep your current SharePoint infrastructure in use and extend it with Zoho
- Implement a low-cost solution with a pay-as-you-go scheme that avoids big investments in buying additional licenses

> *Microsoft Office SharePoint Server 2007 is an integrated suite of server capabilities that can help improve organizational effectiveness by providing comprehensive content management and enterprise search, accelerating shared business processes, and facilitating information sharing across boundaries for better business insight. You can learn more about SharePoint at http://sharepoint.microsoft.com/.*

Talking about how to install Zoho Office for SharePoint is an advanced topic suitable for SharePoint administrators. It is beyond the scope of this book, but I wanted to mention it because it is a really useful tool for the enterprise.

You can get more information on installing and using this add-on at `http://www.zoho.com/sharepoint/`. Make sure you watch the product tour at `http://www.zoho.com/sharepoint/tour.html` to get an overall look at it.

Browser plug-ins

Sometimes while browsing the Internet you click links to download certain files, such as Word documents or CSV files, for viewing on your local computer. Zoho offers a nifty browser plug-in for you to open different kinds of documents directly in Writer, Sheet, or Show without downloading them. This plug-in supports DOC, RTF, SXW, ODT, XLS, SXC, CSV, PPT, PPS, and SXI files.

This plug-in is a real time-saver since you don't need to download the files first and then open them in applications like Word or Excel. It opens documents online, ready to view or edit. You can also save them on the spot in your Zoho online space for later reference.

This plug-in is currently available for Firefox and Internet Explorer (IE). Safari and other browsers aren't supported yet, but the good news is that because Firefox is supported, you can use the plug-in on Windows, Mac OS, and Linux.

The Firefox plug-in

The Firefox plug-in is called Zoho QuickRead, and you need to install it just like you do any other Firefox add-on:

1. Visit `https://addons.mozilla.org/en-US/firefox/addon/3328`, or search for the plug-in in the **Add-ons** dialog box after selecting **Tools ▶ Add-ons ▶ Get Add-ons** in Firefox.
2. Install the add-on, and restart the browser to activate the plug-in.
3. Once installed, open Google, and search for *report filetype:doc*. A list of DOC files will be returned.
4. Try the plug-in by right-clicking the first link that points to a DOC file and selecting **Open with Zoho Writer**. The document opens in Writer ready to be viewed, edited, or saved (Figure 8-7). For other file formats, the plug-in will automatically open the suitable application.

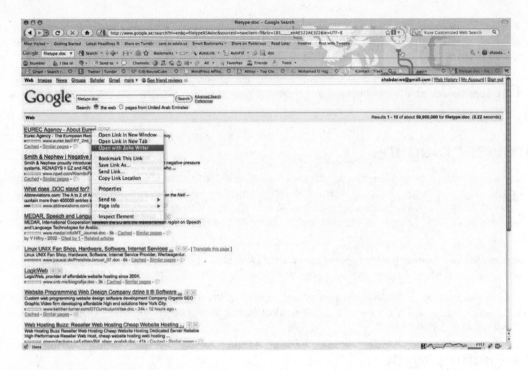

Figure 8-7. Zoho QuickRead in action

This plug-in (and others too) might not be compatible with the latest installation of your browser. It usually takes some time for a plug-in to be updated after a new version of a browser is released.

The IE plug-in

Since Internet Explorer doesn't have a built-in add-on installation facility like Firefox, you need to download the plug-in setup application in order to install the tool:

1. Download the executable file (zohoquickread.exe) from the Zoho homepage or directly from http://www.zoho.com/downloads/zohoquickread.exe.

2. After downloading the file, you can run it. Read the short introduction about the application, and then click **Install** to proceed (Figure 8-8).

Figure 8-8. Installing Zoho QuickRead for Internet Explorer

> *To install applications in Windows, you might need administrator credentials. Contact your IT department if you are trying to install the plug-in on your workstation.*

3. Restart Internet Explorer to finish the installation.

To use the plug-in, similar to what you have done in Firefox, right-click the document links to open them in the respective Zoho applications (Figure 8-9).

415

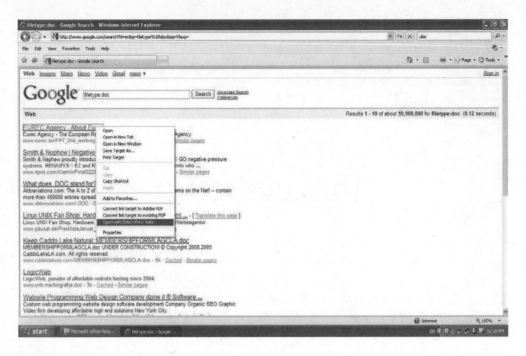

Figure 8-9. The IE plug-in in action

In Figure 8-10, you can see a document opened in Writer using the plug-in. No download, no upload. The document opened with a single click.

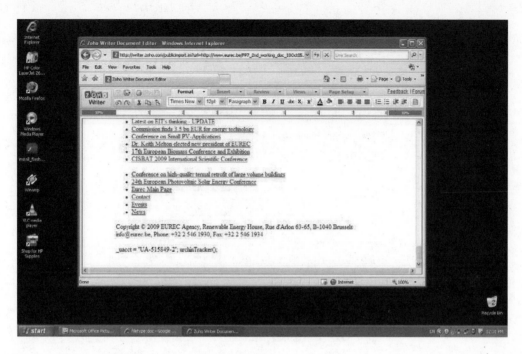

Figure 8-10. Writer opens a document from the Internet.

Zoho on the go

There is no doubt that we are witnessing a revolution in the mobile Internet thanks to the fast connections of 3G and powerful Internet-enabled devices. With all of them wanting to grab a bigger share in the business and personal consumer market, companies like Zoho can't ignore that a successful suite of applications should work on mobile devices too.

Zoho pretty much supports all major mobile platforms: iPhone, Android, Blackberry, Windows Mobile, and Nokia S60 (like the E series). Zoho calls this functionality Zoho Mobile, and in this section I'll discuss the iPhone interface of Zoho. Using other platforms is a similar experience, and you can easily apply what you learn here elsewhere.

Zoho Mobile gives you access to Mail, Calendar, Writer, Sheet, Show, and Creator. This means you have almost all your documents and other information available in your pocket.

> *You can also open your database applications created in Zoho Creator, which will be discussed in detail later in this book.*

Now, let's see how it works:

1. On your iPhone, open Safari, and log on to `http://mobile.zoho.com`. Enter your Zoho credentials, and click `Login` (Figure 8-11).

417

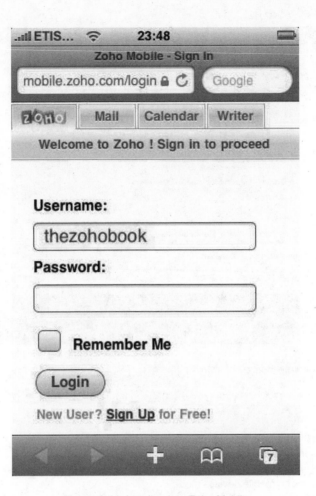

Figure 8-11. Logging into Zoho Mobile

> *It is a good idea to bookmark the Zoho Mobile page so it is accessible with a minimum of effort. It is even better to create a shortcut icon on the home screen of your iPhone. Simply click the + icon at the bottom of the page, and select either* **Add Bookmark** *or* **Add to Home Screen**.

2. On the homepage (Figure 8-12), check today's events, e-mail messages, and the recent documents listed to have quick access to the important information immediately.

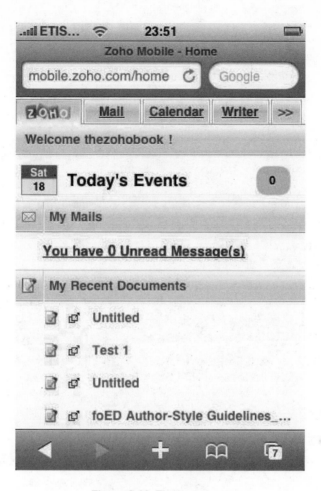

Figure 8-12. The homepage

> *On the top of the page, you can select between different applications by selecting the corresponding tabs. Tap >> on the top right for more applications.*

3. Check your e-mails by tapping the `Mail` tab. Then compose a new message by tapping `Compose` (Figure 8-13). Note that this is the same Mail application you saw in Chapter 6, only on a smaller scale.

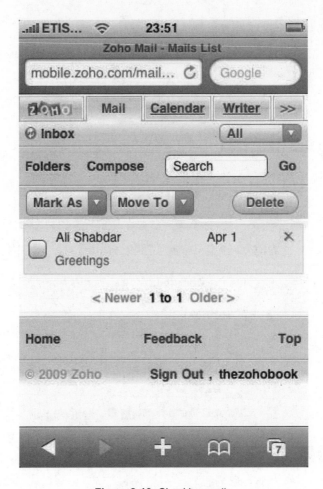

Figure 8-13. Checking mails

4. Open the `Writer` tab, and see that all your word-processing documents are listed (Figure 8-14). You can create new documents by tapping `Create New`.

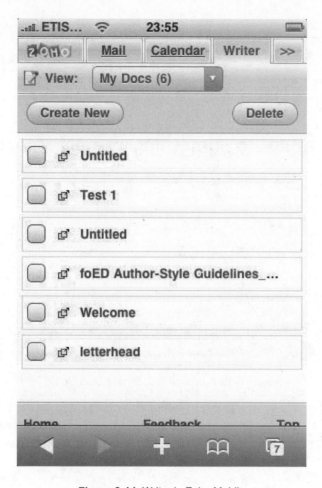

Figure 8-14. Writer in Zoho Mobile

Creating new documents is very limited in Zoho Mobile. You can enter only simple text, without any formatting available. Still, this is useful for quick note taking. Later, in Writer, you or other collaborators can add formatting to the document.

5. Open a document from the list for viewing, and see how it looks like on your mobile device (Figure 8-15).

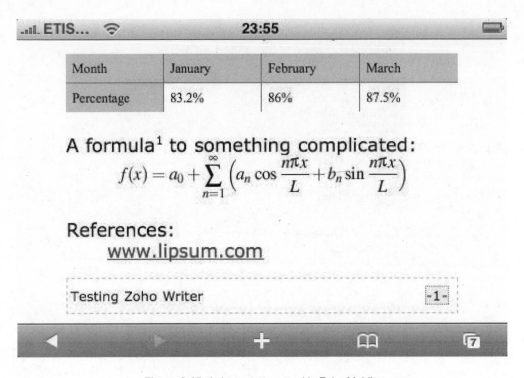

Figure 8-15. A document opened in Zoho Mobile

Another limitation Writer has in Zoho Mobile is that you can't reopen a saved document that you created on your mobile phone if you closed it after saving. So, if for any reason you closed that specific document, you need to create a new one and continue working there. Later, while logged in to Writer (not the mobile edition), you can merge documents that were pieced apart.

In Figure 8-16, you see Zoho Mobile warning you about this very matter.

Figure 8-16. Warning the user

Working with spreadsheets in Zoho Mobile is also simple. You can open spreadsheets for viewing by tapping the **Sheet** tab. The tab will list the available documents (Figure 8-17).

423

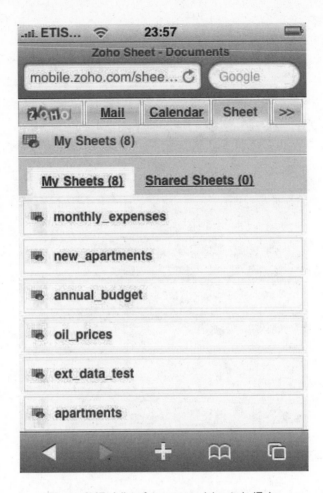

Figure 8-17. A list of your spreadsheets in iZoho

Suppose you need to have access to the latest sales information (similar to Figure 8-18) while you are in a meeting with a client. You can easily open the inventory list or the client information data stored in a spreadsheet that is being updated in real time (you saw how to connect spreadsheets to external data sources in Chapter 3) and surprise your client with the latest information available in your pocket. In such cases, Zoho Mobile is a great companion that works seamlessly with the Zoho suite to keep you prepared all the time.

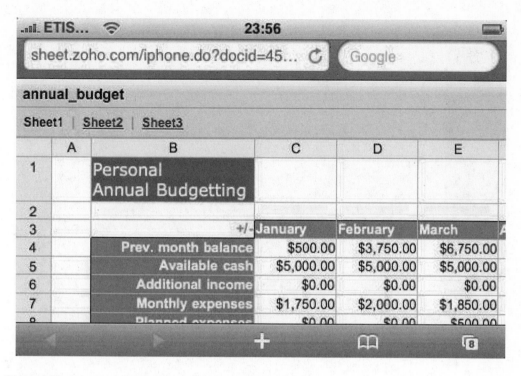

Figure 8-18. Opening a functional version of a spreadsheet

Finally, presentations created in Show or uploaded to Zoho can be opened in the Zoho Mobile by tapping the `Show` tab (tap >> if it is invisible) and opening them from the list of available presentations (Figure 8-19).

You can connect your iPhone to a big screen (via available A/V cables) and run a mobile presentation from anywhere at any time. Imagine when you impress your professor with a nice presentation by just connecting your mobile device to the LCD screen of your class. You'll also impress the other students, too, I bet!

Figure 8-19. Running a slide show on iPhone in Show

Developing Zoho

Although Zoho provides you with a great collection of applications, there are times when you need more functionality. Embedding Zoho documents in different websites or bringing external content such as video into Zoho applications can create mashups that extend the applications, but more complex solutions will not be possible that way.

The Zoho application programming interface (API) provides you with programming tools that allow you to interact with Zoho applications at an advanced level. By creating applications that communicate with Zoho in the background, you can leverage the power of Zoho tools in your applications. This will save you a tremendous amount of time and money while adding great features to your applications. You will be developing the features of Zoho applications by adding them to another platform that offers more features.

As you might have guessed, you need prior knowledge in programming and particularly web development to use the Zoho API. Fear not, you are not going to see such horrifying scenes in here. Although programming, especially web development, is so much fun, I won't discuss any of it in here. Actually, I'm not going to even talk about the API any further.

The reason I'm mentioning the API in this chapter is to make sure you know about the availability of this important feature. You can discover it yourself, create amazing tools, or hire somebody to do it for you.

> *A good example of how you can benefit from the Zoho API is how Box.net uses the Zoho productivity suite to preview the documents stored on its servers as an added value to their clients (Read http://blogs.zoho.com/general/boxnet-integrates-zoho for more information.) You may want to do something similar for your organization.*

Visit http://api.wiki.zoho.com/ to get started with developing with Zoho API. You never know, it could make you famous—and somewhat rich.

Summary

In this chapter, I discussed some of smaller Zoho tools that can make your life easier. You can create useful mashups using gadgets and amaze yourself with its simplicity and flexibility. Installing the Microsoft Office integration plug-in and the browser add-ons will help you work even more efficiently.

With everyone going mobile and people becoming more connected, the mobile interface of Zoho provides you with a powerful platform to stay connected to your valuable information everywhere, because it's available in your pocket.

You are now officially an intermediate Zoho user who can easily work in the cloud. Starting from the next chapter I will focus on the advanced business applications available in Zoho.

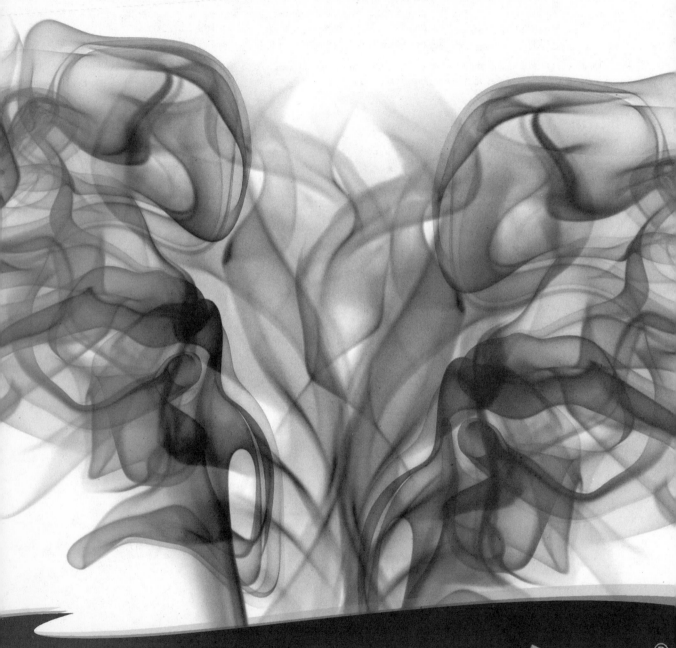

ZOHO®

Work. Online

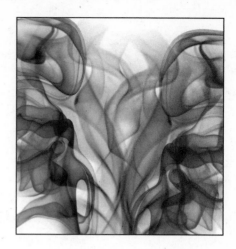

Chapter 9

The Plaza

You might remember from Chapter 1 that Zoho Personal provides you with an environment in which you can work with your favorite Zoho applications from within a single portal. Everything is available just one click away, and you can customize the environment as you like. Zoho Business is a very similar tool but more focused on the business tools. It is in fact the one-stop destination for the online applications used in your organization.

Using Zoho Business, you can create your domain and host your e-mails on Zoho without needing another service. Teamwork and collaboration services are ready out of the box, and it is free for up to 10 users. Setting up your online office with almost no boundaries is an easy job with Business. So, let's see what Zoho Business is capable of and how you can set it up to meet your business needs.

Getting started

Visit http://business.zoho.com (or find it on the Zoho homepage), enter your Zoho credentials in the `Sign In` form, and then log into Business by clicking `Sign In`. You can use the same account you used for the personal productivity tools, but it is recommended that you create a separate account for your business needs. It is important to know that this account is the super administrator of the future portal of your organization. The best solution may be to create a dedicated account for your organization (such as using your company name) to keep it separate from your personal account.

> If you forgot how to set up an account in Zoho, refer to "Getting started" in Chapter 1.

Once you are logged in, by having a quick look around, you can see how familiar the environment is. It's almost identical to Zoho Personal, so it's effortless to start using Business immediately. First let's do the essential configurations:

1. When you open Business, a dialog box will remind you about the tasks you should do first (Figure 9-1). Although are going to perform those tasks in while, you can still read the information given in this dialog box. Then select **Do not show at startup** to close the dialog box.

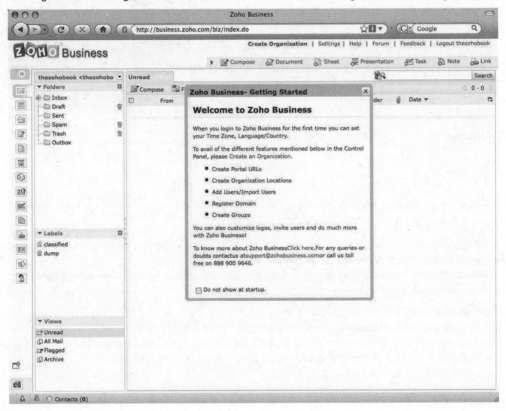

Figure 9-1. Zoho Business default homepage

2. Click **Create Organization** in the top menu bar. This redirects you to another page. Because it is your business portal, you need to tell Business a little bit about your organization.

3. In the **Organization Name** text box, enter your company name (Figure 9-2). You can enter anything that represents you such as your brand, your organization, or even your name. After all, in the age of social media, your name could be your brand.

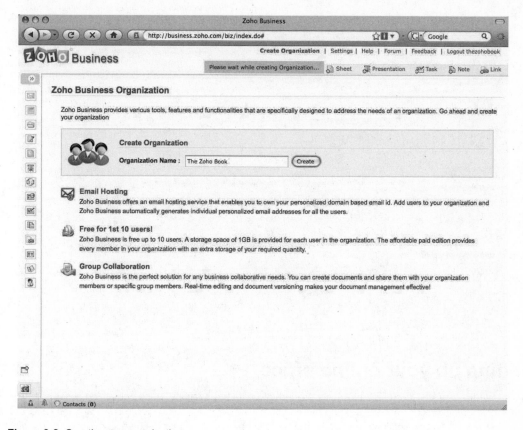

Figure 9-2. Creating an organization

4. Click **Create** to continue.

Now that you have created the organization, the **Control Panel** will open, through which you can configure Business to meet your requirements (Figure 9-3). The setup process is very important, and in fact the entire next section is about this subject, so don't skip it.

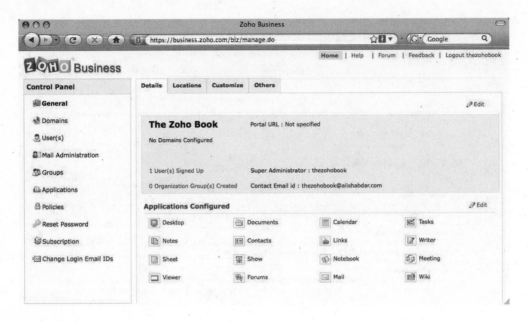

Figure 9-3. The `Control Panel`

Setting up your online office

As you just saw, the `Control Panel` is divided into different sections, each containing a set of similar settings. Some sections are divided into more subsections using tabs. As you proceed with the `Control Panel` in the following sections, you will learn how to set proper values for each section.

General settings

You configure some basic features and settings in the `General` section. When you open the `Control Panel`, it opens the `Details` tab in the `General` section. You can see that there are no domains or portal URLs configured yet. This is where you'll begin the configuration:

1. Click **Edit** in the upper right of the `Details` tab. The `Enter Details` dialog box opens.
2. Enter a name for **Portal URL**. This is the address people in your organization will use to log on to Business, so be precise and choose an appropriate name. Your company name (in lowercase letters) is a good example (see Figure 9-4).

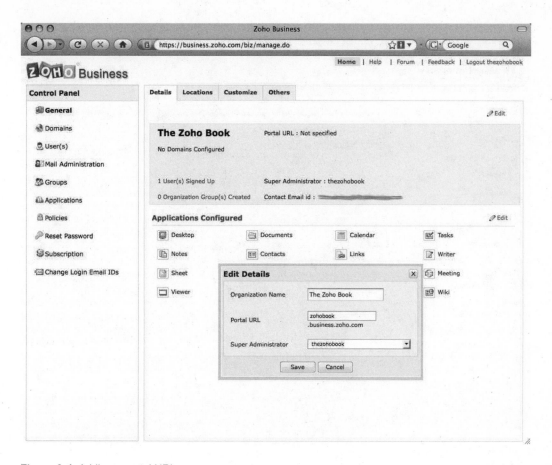

Figure 9-4. Adding a portal URL

3. Leave the other fields as is, and click `Save`. If the portal URL is not already taken, the dialog box will close successfully. If not, you'll need to try your luck with other names.

4. On the `Locations` tab, click `Add location`. You define locations to tell the users (your employees/partners) where your organization is located—either where offices are or where employees are. For instance, your headquarters could be in New York with teams/offices in Rio, Paris, and other cities.

5. Add all your locations by entering your city in `Location Name`, setting the `Time Zone` field, and specifying the address of those locations (Figure 9-5). Click `Add` for every location.

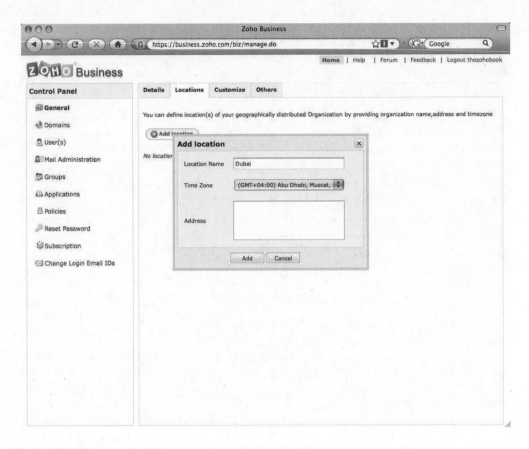

Figure 9-5. Adding new locations

6. Open the `Customize` tab, and replace the default Zoho logo with your own logo. Select `Custom Logo`, and browse for a logo image in your local machine. Then click `Save`, and wait a few seconds for the image to be uploaded (Figure 9-6). Finally, refresh the page to see your own logo on the header of the page.

> *Using a 150x40-pixel image for the logo is recommended. Otherwise, you will see the logo either stretched or zoomed out. Upload a 72 dpi JPEG, GIF, or PNG image with a white or transparent for better results background (JPEG can't have transparent background).*

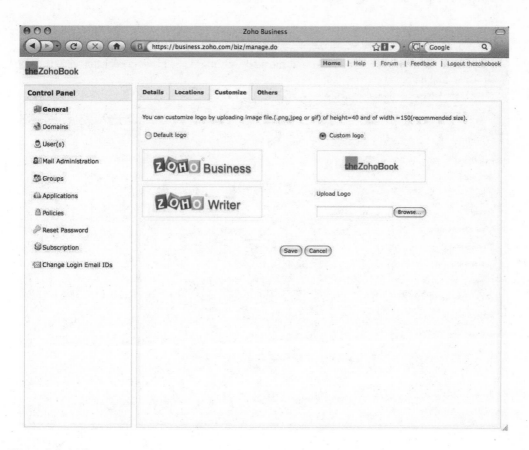

Figure 9-6. Adding a custom logo

Domain settings

The ideal setup of Business is for it to be the real portal to your online office (or back office). Some of the features that enable Business to become the ultimate online office need at least a domain name to be configured. Without getting into technicalities, a **domain name** is an Internet name, such as yourcompany.com, that usually hosts your website.

Business allows you to set a domain name to your online office portal by using the existing domain you purchased from a third-party provider such as GoDaddy.com or by creating a new one on the fly from within the `Control Panel`. You can do the latter by selecting `Control Panel` ▶ `Domains` ▶ `Register Domain`. If you are having trouble with the whole domain name concept, you need to either read the documentation offered by your third-party domain provider or get a consultation from a network/web specialist.

1. Click the `Domains` section in the `Control Panel`.

2. If you already have a domain name that you purchased from a registrar like GoDaddy.com, click **Add Domain**, and enter the domain name (Figure 9-7). Click **Add** to continue. Otherwise, you need to click **Register Domain** and proceed with the domain name registration, but I won't cover that here.

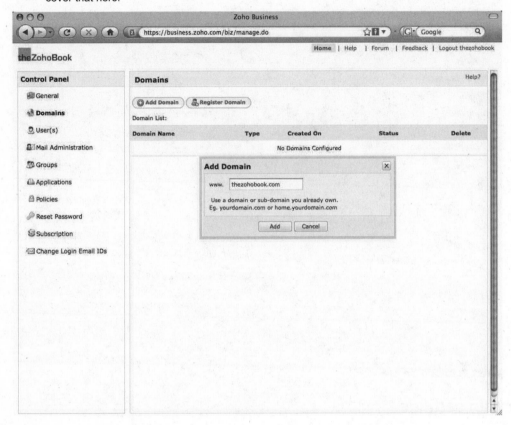

Figure 9-7. Adding a domain name

3. Once you have added your domain, you need to validate it to confirm that you are the owner of that domain. Click the **Validate** link to the right of the domain name. In the **Validate Domain** dialog box (Figure 9-8), select **HTML File Method**. See my notes after the walk-through about why you selected HTML.

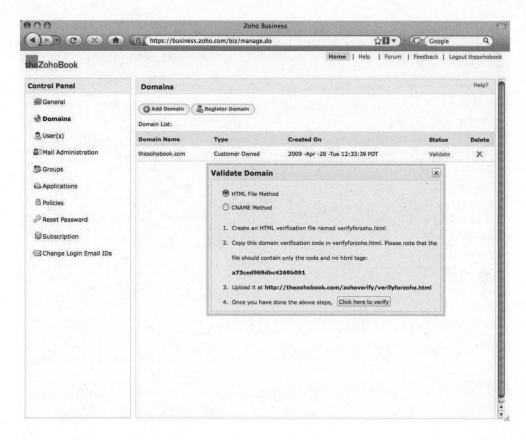

Figure 9-8. Validating a domain name

4. On your computer, using any available editor (TextEdit, Notepad, and so on), create an empty file, and paste in the code you see in the dialog box (Figure 9-8). Then save it as `verifyforzoho.html`. It must be saved in plain-text (ASCII) format.

5. Using an FTP utility (CyberDuck, FileZilla, and so on), log into your host, and create a new folder in the root directory called `zohoverify`. Then upload the HTML file you just created to that folder.

6. Now click `Click here to verify`. This will check for the file on your host and will conclude that it must be your domain since you can perform those operations on it.

> *If for any reason the validation process doesn't work, delete the domain, and start over again.*

7. If the validation was successful, you will be asked to host your e-mails with Zoho. In the `Mail hosting` dialog box, enter an e-mail ID to set it as the default e-mail address you want to define for this domain name (Figure 9-9). `info` or `admin` is a good first choice. Then click `Add` to create the e-mail address.

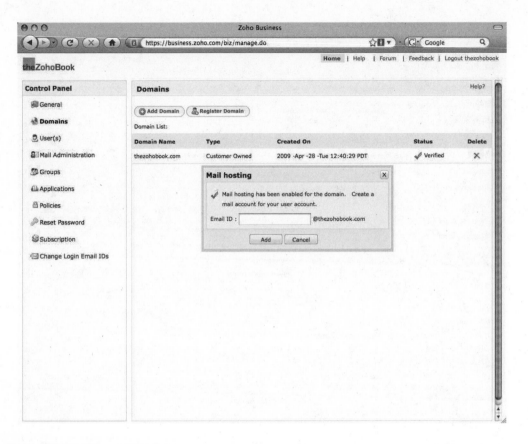

Figure 9-9. Hosting e-mails in Zoho

In many cases, especially when you start from scratch (meaning no website or e-mail addresses defined for this domain yet), it is a great idea to host your e-mails on Zoho, simply because you won't need to configure e-mails separately through a third-party web host, and you will be able to use Zoho Mail (covered in Chapter 6) as the e-mail client. This means your e-mails are seamlessly connected to your work environment as well as to the various Zoho applications.

Regarding the domain name verification, as you saw in the previous walk-through, before you can use the domain name, you need to validate it so Business can make sure you are the genuine owner of that domain. There are two ways to do this: by using an HTML file or by changing the CNAME settings of the domain.

Using each one of these methods is a personal choice. The HTML file method is a bit easier to set up if you already have write access to your web host and have a hosting plan. On the other hand, if you are comfortable with tweaking the domain information in a lower level or you don't have a hosting plan for your domain, you can use the CNAME method. In either case, you might still need the help of an IT consultant.

User settings

Your organization will definitely have more than one user. Every employee needs to have a username and password to enter the online office to be able to work and collaborate with others. There are basically two ways to add users. If you have five (or fewer) users, you can add them one by one. For each user, you can either define a new user using the domain you defined before, such as username@yourcompany.com, or just send an invitation to their existing e-mail addresses.

Open the `User(s)` section in the `Control Panel`, and start adding new users. You can add users one by one by clicking `Add User`. Enter an e-mail ID as well as a password for every user, and click `OK` to add the user.

When it doesn't make sense to add them one by one, you can import a file containing the users' information in order to add multiple users in one batch. For this purpose, click `Import User` on the `Users` page, and upload a CSV file containing only the username (will be used for the e-mail ID) and password of all users. Select the corresponding domain, and click `OK` to create the users accounts in one batch (Figure 9-10).

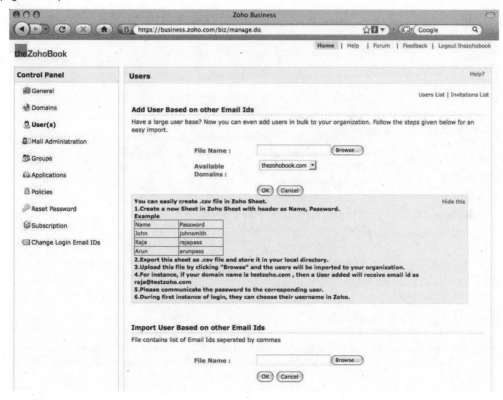

Figure 9-10. Importing users

Mail settings

It is possible to host your e-mails on Zoho. Your users' and employees' e-mails (for example, user1@yourcompany.com) and the e-mail account itself (including the `Inbox`, messages, and so on) will be kept on the Zoho servers. Then you won't need additional hosting plan for your e-mails. If you want to host your e-mails on Zoho, you need to modify the MX entries on your domain registrar point, so you should be familiar with that. Reading the documentation of your registrar is a good place to start learning about MX fields.

To host your e-mails on Zoho, follow these steps:

1. In the `Mail Administration` section, click `Email Domains`.
2. As you can see in Figure 9-11, change the MX records of your domain name (through the registrar or the web host) to Zoho's.

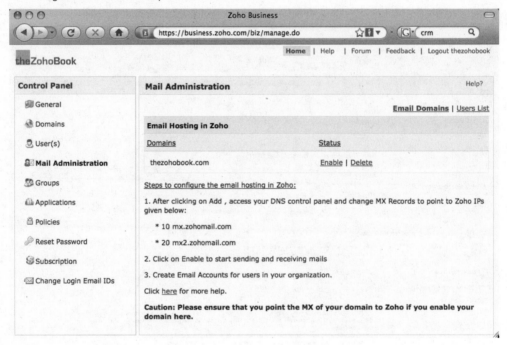

Figure 9-11. Finalizing the mail hosting

3. Click `Enable` in front of the respective domain name for the e-mail hosting to be activated. Now all e-mails sent to your domain will be routed correctly to the corresponding addresses.

Groups settings

Groups in Zoho Business have more importance than in Zoho Personal. By creating organizational groups, you actually resemble the structure of your organization. You can assign a group to each department (such as sales) or simply add the people working together in the same group.

1. Click `Groups` in the `Control Panel`, and then click `Create Group` in the `Organization Groups` area.
2. Enter a name for the group, such as `Sales` (Figure 9-12).

Figure 9-12. Creating an organizational group

3. It is a good idea to change the group logo, so click `Choose` below the logo image, and choose from the available logos.
4. Add a short description about the group, and then click `Create` to add the group.
5. The group you just created is empty, so you need to add people to it. With the group open for editing, open the `Group Members` tab, and click `Add Member`.
6. Add members from the available users, and click `OK` to proceed (Figure 9-13).

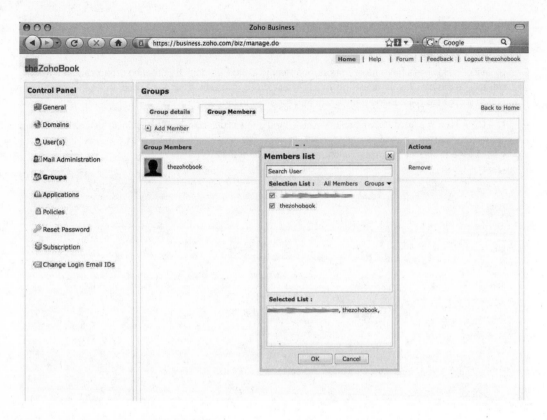

Figure 9-13. Adding members to the group

> *You can add as many as people as you want to each group. It is possible to choose people from other groups to be added to the new groups too. For example, people in the* Accountants *group can also be members of* Finance_dept.

Application settings

When you open Zoho Business, there is a sidebar (on the left side of the screen) that includes shortcuts to various (but not all) Zoho business applications. To centralize Business as the main portal of your organization, you can add more applications to this list, either from other Zoho applications or from other third-party web applications.

1. In the **Applications** section in the **Control Panel**, under **Zoho Applications**, click **Add Apps**.
2. Enter the application title as well as the corresponding URL (for example, http://crm.zoho.com; **CRM** will be covered later).
3. Choose an icon, and click **OK** to add the application.

4. Similarly, for the third-party applications (for example, a CMS application that your organization is already using), click **Organization Applications**, and click **Add Apps** (Figure 9-14). Fill in the fields, and click OK.

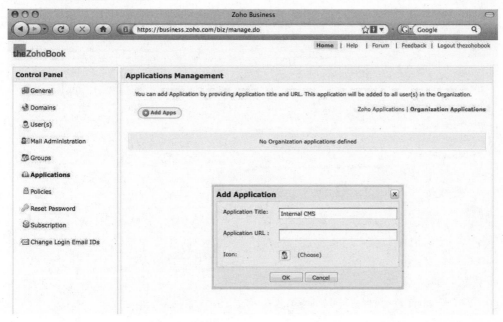

Figure 9-14. Adding applications to Business

> *Adding applications to Zoho Business has no effect on the normal behavior of the application, and it doesn't add functionality to the platform (such as interoperability between different applications). It is only to provide you with shortcuts from within a single environment.*

Policy settings

Organizational policies, which are another very important feature, also need to be configured. They allow you to limit the available functionalities for different levels of users. Business offers four different access levels: **Super Administrator**, **Administrator**, **All Members**, and **None**. These are just indicators and could have different meanings for different organizations,

To use the policies, you need to change each one according to your organizational preferences in the **Organization Policies** area in the **Policies** section. For example, as per Figure 9-15, only the super administrator is allowed to create organization groups. Or, everybody can export or publish documents since it is assigned to **All Members** (that include administrator and super administrator too).

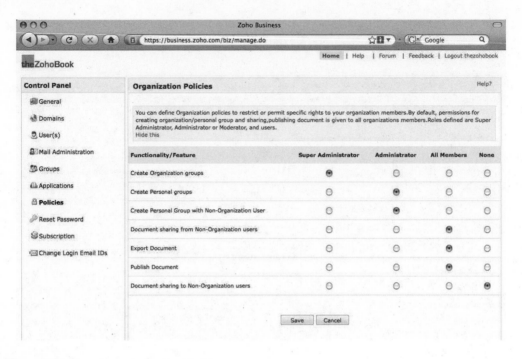

Figure 9-15. Changing organizational policies

When you're done, don't forget to click `Save` for the changes to take place.

Other settings

By performing the actions in the preceding section, you are done configuring Business if you want. But just so I cover everything, let's see what the last three sections are for.

For security reasons, it is recommended that you change your password every now and then. Business allows you (as an administrator) to change the password of each and every user who has login access to it. This is useful in many cases and gives you more control over security. For example, if a user account has been compromised for any reason, you can immediately reset that user's password via the `Control Panel`.

To change a password, follow these steps:

1. Open the `Reset Password` section.
2. Select a user by clicking the + button next to `Username` and selecting a user from the list.
3. Enter the new password and the confirmation, and then click `Change Password` to proceed.

Business offers a package for ten users by default, free of charge. You can, however, add more users by upgrading to a paid service:

1. Open the `Subscriptions` tab, and click `Upgrade`.

2. In the upgrade form, enter the number of users you want to add to your subscription, and choose the subscription period.
3. Click `Continue` to proceed.

Finally, you can change the e-mail addresses of the people who can log in to **Business**:

1. Open `Change Login Email IDs` in the `Control Panel`.
2. Select a user by clicking the + button and choosing one from the list (Figure 9-16). Click `OK` to close the dialog box.

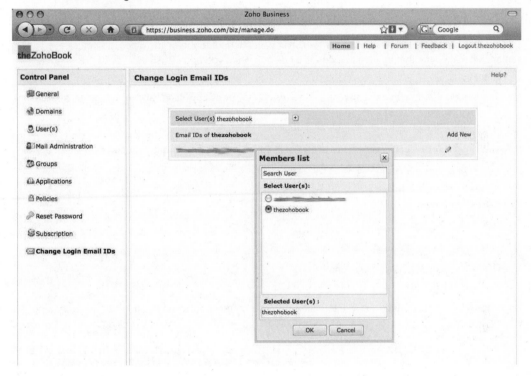

Figure 9-16. Changing the login e-mail IDs

3. Back in the form, click the pencil icon (`Edit Email`), and update the e-mail ID of the user. Enter the current password, and click `Save` to store the changes.

Using Business

Now it's time to see Zoho Business in action. Just like in Zoho Personal, you can start working normally using Writer, Sheet, Show, and other applications. The big difference however, is when you are using Mail for your organization's e-mails or when you work in organizational groups. The desktop, too, has few more sections keeping different parts of your online office only one click away.

The desktop

The desktop opens the `Dashboard` page, which is your shortcut to the online office, so before everything, you should make sure that the desktop opens by default when you open Business:

1. Click `Settings` on the top menu bar.
2. Select the `Applications` tab, and drag the `Desktop` icon above all other applications (before `Mail`).
3. Refresh the page to see it open by default.

By default, the `Dashboard` contains the latest list of your most important data grouped in different boxes:

- E-mail messages (Mail)
- Events (Calendar)
- To-dos (Tasks)
- Documents (Docs)
- Notes (Notes)
- Contacts (Contacts)
- Internal discussions (Discussions)
- Web links (Links)

Each box allows you to have basic interaction with the corresponding application, including viewing the latest items and adding new content. You can add or remove different boxes by clicking `Manage Content` (on the upper right of the `Dashboard`).

> *Zoho Discussions is a private online discussion board for you and your peers. I won't cover this tool, but you can use it in Business or directly at* `http://discussions.zoho.com.`

Business groups

To see how groups differ in Business than in Zoho Personal, follow these steps:

1. Open Docs by clicking the `Documents` tab in Business.
2. Click Share (in Docs) on the toolbar.
3. Select `Group Share` in the `Share Document` dialog box (Figure 9-17).

Figure 9-17. Sharing content within organizational groups

4. Select an organizational group, such as `Sales`. Then select the proper read/write permission.
5. Click `Submit` to share the document with the targeted group.

Now the members of that specific group will see the document listed under the `Shared to Me` section in Sheet and Docs as well as in the `Docs` box in the `Dashboard`.

Another feature of organizational groups is the common working environment in which members of each group can easily assign (or to be assigned to) tasks and share notes, links, contacts, and documents, isolated from people who are in the company but who aren't members of those specific groups. To test the common area, follow these steps:

1. Under `Apps` (in the sidebar), open `Groups` (bottom). This opens the `Groups` page and hides the links to the applications.
2. Under `Groups`, select a business group (such as `Sales`). You can see the desktop opens the links to group-wide shared material as well as a list of members indicating online people. Docs,

Tasks, Notes, Links, and Contacts all have their own tabs in which you can fully interact with the applications.

3. Add a new task, and assign it to different members (Figure 9-18).

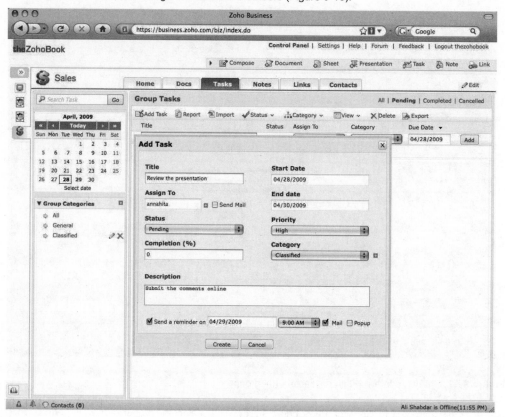

Figure 9-18. Assigning tasks to the group members

4. Create a note (from your brainstorming sessions, for example) or share work-related bookmarks through `Links` for the group members to use.

5. Share the business contacts within the group. For example, you can keep a list of the customers here for the sales department while keeping it separate from the suppliers list shared to the `BackOffice` group.

The user view

It is important to know that other users (for example, employees) interact a bit differently with the portal. There are places that they have no (or limited) access to, simply because they are not allowed by the super administrator (you). When you as the super administrator add new users or invite them to join the organization, you just set an e-mail address and a password. This is enough for the first log in.

All users need to visit the portal address (that you set earlier in the `Control Panel`) and log in with their credentials (Figure 9-19).

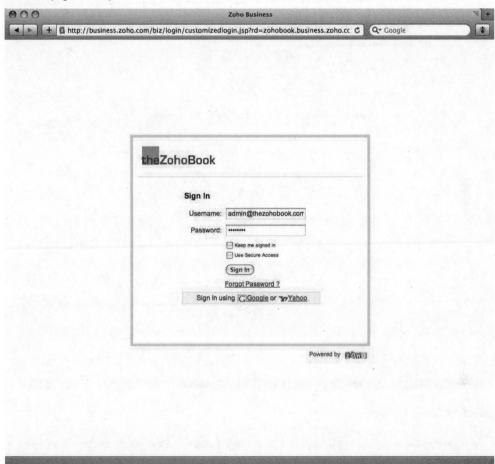

Figure 9-19. Logging into the organization portal

The first time they log in, they will be asked to enter a username and a new password for security reasons. They also need to agree with the terms of service and the privacy policy of Zoho (not your company). Clicking `Update` will take them to the homepage where the real work starts (Figure 9-20).

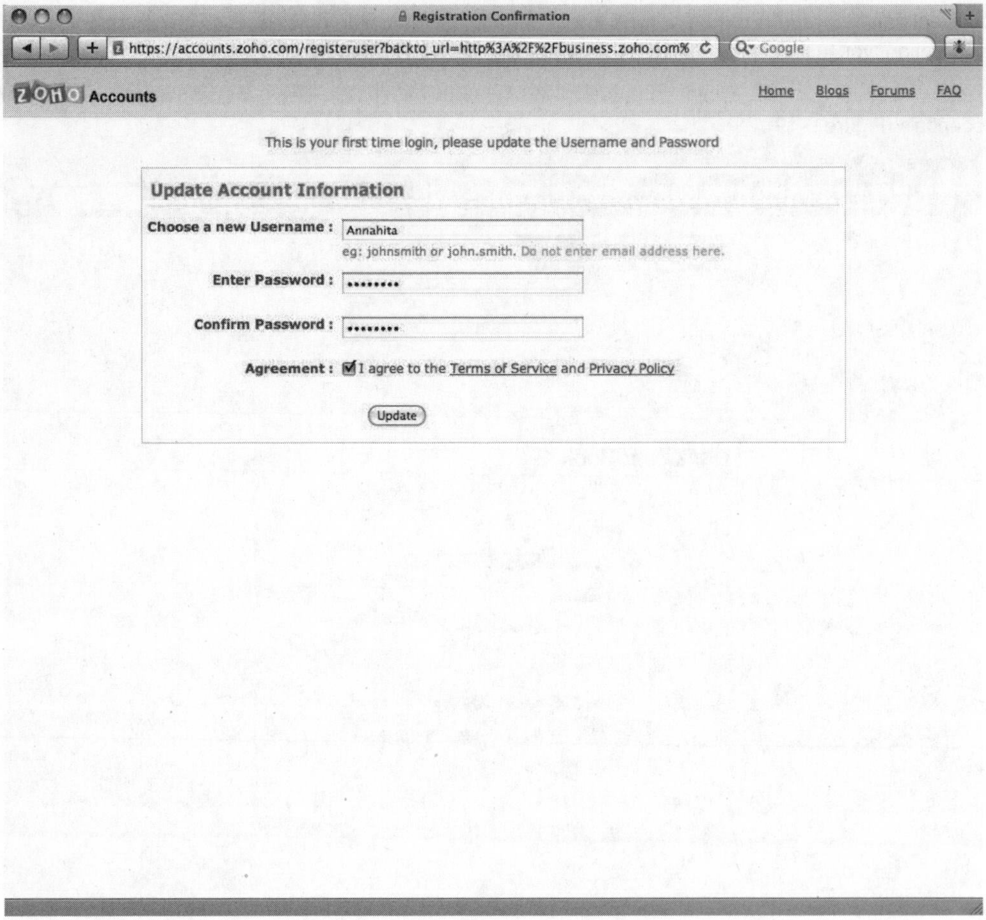

Figure 9-20. Users' first login

On the homepage, shared content is available at a user's fingertips. Documents, tasks, notes, links, and contacts are listed in groups for instant access. On the left side, online team members are listed, and one click will pop up a chat window ready for a live business talk (Figure 9-21).

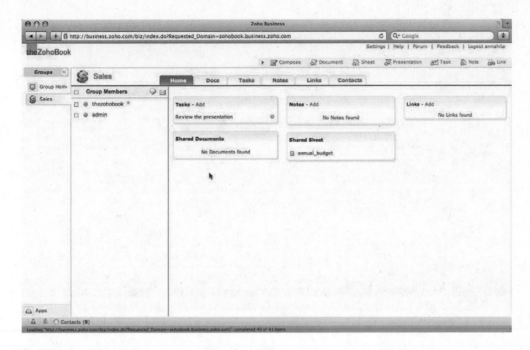

Figure 9-21. Group homepage

Opening the `Docs` tab will list all shared documents ready to be viewed or edited based on the user's permission (Figure 9-22).

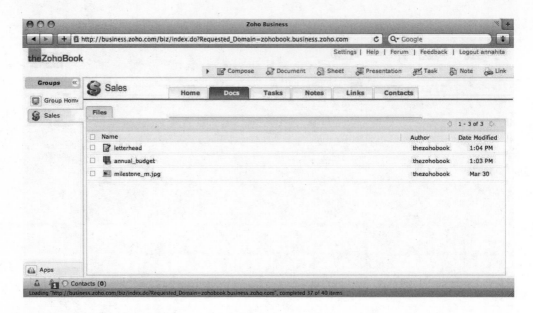

Figure 9-22. Group documents

Users can access the group documents from within the productivity applications (for example, Writer); they just need to go to the **Shared Docs** pane, open the **View** drop-down list, and select **Organizational Groups** (Figure 9-23).

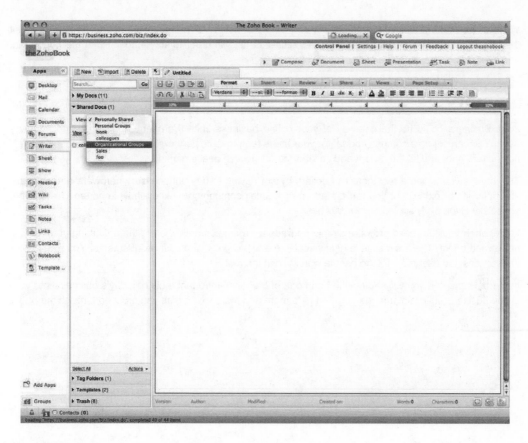

Figure 9-23. Opening group documents from within Writer, Sheet, or Show

Working with other tabs is almost identical to what your saw in Zoho Personal and doesn't need further explanation.

The bottom line is with the least resources spent (financial, human, and time), you can set up a fully functional online office that brings all your employees under one virtual roof, providing them with a highly scalable and productive environment.

Getting help

After reading the instructions in this chapter, if you still need help in setting up the environment (especially configuring domains and mail hosting), make sure you get proper expert support. It is crucial to configure your online office carefully and according to your business requirements from the very beginning.

You can also take a look at the official support pages at `http://zb.wiki.zoho.com/`. Don't forget to visit the related forum at `http://forums.zoho.com/Zoho-Business` in order to stay in touch with the Zoho team and benefit from the expertise of the community.

Summary

Zoho Business could be the gateway of your online business suite if properly configured and regularly used. You can set up a company portal for your users (employees, partners, and so on), have their e-mails hosted on Zoho, and let them work and collaborate online with peace of mind.

This means you saved a few thousand dollars by not having to buy unnecessary hardware and software and doing it the old way. If you run a start-up or a small company, you know how important this can be, especially at the early stages of your business.

Later, when your business grows, a simple upgrade for a small monthly fee is the only thing you need to be worried about. The Zoho suite is highly scalable and will grow with your requirements. You just pay for the services you use and let Zoho people worry about the rest.

In the next chapter, you will see how to bring one of the most important tools of today's business into your online business suite. So, turn the page—it gets more and more exciting as you proceed through the book.

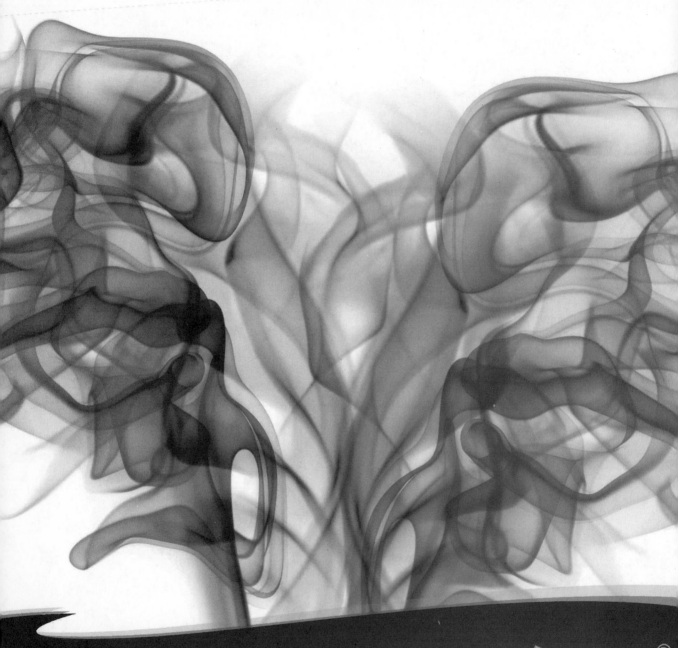

ZOHO ®

Work. Online

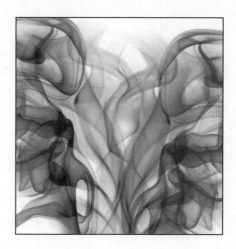

Chapter 10

Manage Your Business

Regardless of the nature of your business, you probably go through the same business cycle as other businesses to generate profit. As shown here, a typical business process starts with marketing, continues with sales, and ends up with support. It is a cycle in which customers are kept happy with the overall experience and that will start over with each new marketing campaign. You need to first market your business, then gather leads and turn them into potential buyers, and finally finish the deal successfully. However, closing a successful deal is not the last step, because you need to retain your customers and keep them loyal. The last thing you want to do is lose a good client to the competition.

Illustration 10-1. A simple business cycle

Interestingly enough, if you are a piano teacher, a food producing company, or a car dealer, you need to pass through every stage of this circle to guarantee a successful market presence. And to pass through every stage of the business cycle successfully, you need to employ reliable tools to track and organize your contact information for current and prospective customers. This chapter will introduce you to one of the most essential tools for this purpose.

CRM in a nutshell

In short, **customer relationship management** (CRM) consists of the processes a company uses to track and organize its contact information for its current and prospective customers.

That said, CRM goes beyond just tracking and organizing customers. Implementing CRM solutions helps businesses learn more about their target markets and helps them offer the products and services that their clients want.

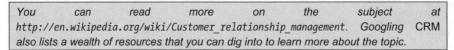

> You can read more on the subject at
> http://en.wikipedia.org/wiki/Customer_relationship_management. Googling CRM
> also lists a wealth of resources that you can dig into to learn more about the topic.

Apart from it being a way of working, CRM often refers to the software used in these processes. Such software plays a vital role in the business cycle of organizations of any size—from small office/home office (SOHO) to large enterprises—to help organize and monitor the entire sales process.

> SOHO usually refers to very small businesses, with one to five people.

Why CRM?

There are many benefits to implementing a CRM solution for your organization. Although I can't cover all aspects of CRM in this one chapter, here are some of the most important benefits you can get from using a suitable system for your business:

- Reduced costs and increased return on investment (ROI)
- Better customer service
- Increased customer satisfaction
- Increased customer loyalty
- Increased new business
- Easier data sharing and decision making
- More accurate forecasts
- Automated business workflows
- Agile business growth
- More control over business processes

All of these benefits are tightly dependent on each other. CRM is not magic, and purchasing the best software available in the market will not guarantee you that you will become a millionaire overnight, but it provides you with a vast array of necessary tools to become one.

SaaS and CRM

Traditionally, companies purchased CRM software that was installed on their local data centers and distributed over the network to users in a client-server model. Such implementations, however, were usually more expensive than what small to medium businesses could afford.

With the emergence of SaaS, CRM software became much more available to businesses of all kinds. It is in fact one of the most popular applications in the SaaS arena. Many companies have created amazing CRM software and made it available in a pay-per-usage model. It is a competitive market, which provides consumers with plenty of choices to fit in their business model.

Add all the benefits of CRM to the advantages of running it in the cloud, and it is a no-brainer:

- You'll benefit from the highly available (access anywhere) and expandable model of SaaS.
- You'll minimize the investment risk by paying for only the services you use.
- You'll avoid implementing an excessive hardware infrastructure.
- You won't have to worry about upgrades and patches, because they are the responsibility of the provider.
- You'll gain more security by leveraging the facilities provided by the SaaS vendors.
- You'll get on-demand support.

Zoho CRM

You can surf the Internet and ask SaaS providers' representatives for presentations and demos so you can compare and choose the solution you think is suitable for your business, but our focus here is Zoho CRM, which is a fantastic choice for many reasons:

- It is a cloud-based CRM solution, available anywhere/anytime.
- It is powerful enough for many businesses, including small to medium enterprises.
- It is easy to use and set up, and it features a user-friendly and responsive UI.
- It is moderately priced, making it affordable for almost anybody to use, and amazingly enough, it is free for entrepreneurs and small businesses with three or fewer users.
- It integrates seamlessly with some of the Zoho tools you already use, such as Mail.

> Check the pricing page at *http://www.zoho.com/crm/zohocrm-pricing.html* to compare it to other CRM solutions.

In this chapter, you will take a look at the main features of Zoho CRM to get yourself started with the platform. It is then up to you how much further you want to go with it.

Getting started

CRM is a full-fledged customer relationship management system with lots of features for a typical small to medium enterprise. It is obvious that a single chapter can't cover even half of its capabilities. For this reason, I'll walk you through a scenario in which you will set up CRM for a small (imaginary) company and use its main features to run the business.

Later, when you want to set it up for your company (of any size), you can apply your knowledge and extend it based on your business requirements.

To start using CRM right away, follow these steps:

1. Visit `http://crm.zoho.com`, and log in with your Zoho credentials.

2. If this is your first time being on the home page of CRM, select **Create a CRM account**. Then select **FREE Edition** (Figure 10-1).

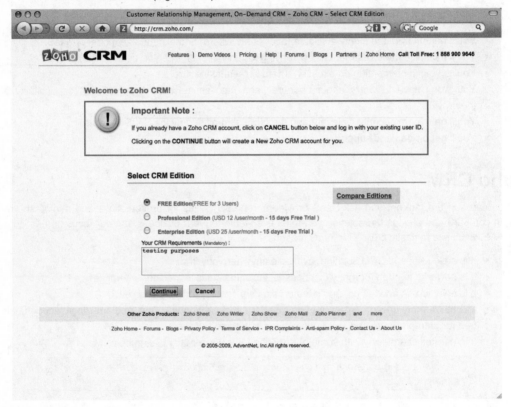

Figure 10-1. Creating a CRM account

3. Click **Continue** to log into CRM.

> *Even if you are planning to use a paid subscription, it is a good idea to first start with the free edition just to evaluate CRM for your requirements. Then you can easily upgrade to any paid plan without losing your data. This elasticity is a feature of SaaS applications. You pay as you go.*

The free account features the essential services (check the pricing page for a detailed list) plus 100MB of free space. This is quite enough for start-ups and small businesses, but you might want to order more space or upgrade to a paid plan depending on your business requirements.

The environment

Once logged into CRM, you can see that with so many tabs and sections positioned next to each other, it means serious business (Figure 10-2). You haven't entered any information yet, so all the sections are pretty empty. This somewhat intimidating UI is actually quite easy to use.

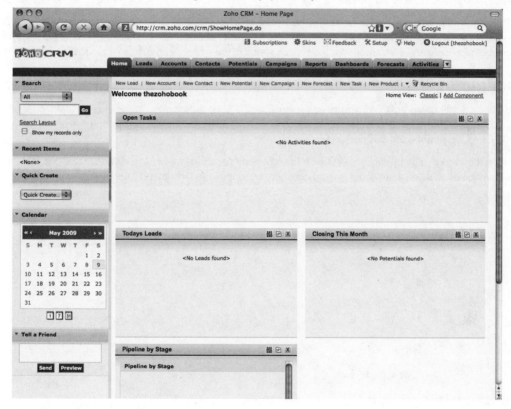

Figure 10-2. The initial CRM environment

On the top of the screen, you can see a menu bar containing shortcuts to different places:

- **Subscriptions**: Redirects you to the subscriptions page where you can upgrade your membership to various paid versions or ask for more features
- **Skins**: Opens a small window, containing six UI themes to choose from
- **Feedback**: Allows you to send a quick message to the Zoho support team

- **Setup**: Opens the setup page where you can configure CRM to act as you want
- **Help**: Provides you with enormous help on how to use CRM in different scenarios
- **Logout**: Logs you out of CRM securely

Below the menu bar are the tabs dividing the major tools and features of the application into different groups. You'll see all of them in action in this chapter.

In the sidebar (on the left side of the screen), you can see a number of frequently used features available at your fingertips. Among other things, you can search, check the recent items you have been working on, and quickly perform essential tasks.

The rest of the screen is your working area containing tools and features for different modules of the system categorized by more than ten tabs (**Home**, **Leads**, **Accounts**, and so on). The **Home** tab, for example, contains different reports for the current status of the system and acts as a monitoring room.

Configuring the basics

Before actually doing anything, you need to configure CRM based on your requirements. Make sure you go through all the steps of this section to become more comfortable with setting up the system when you are using it in a real-world business environment.

Open the **Setup** page by clicking **Setup** on the top menu bar. You can see the numerous options that can be configured, but you just need a few changes for the scope of this chapter (Figure 10-3).

Figure 10-3. The Setup page

> *Some options are not active for the free edition (such as **Role Management**). Having these options enabled might be crucial to your business in real life. Consider upgrading once you have determined that CRM is the right tool for you.*

Configuring the account information

All CRM users (including you) need to have their account information entered correctly in the system by a super administrator (that's you). General information such as your name, address, and locale needs to be updated for every user so that it can be used in other modules. This is, however, not the same as your Zoho account information and is visible only inside CRM.

1. In the General box, under Personal Settings, click Account Information.
2. Click Edit below the form to make the form editable (Figure 10-4). Then make the necessary changes for your account, and click Save once you are done.

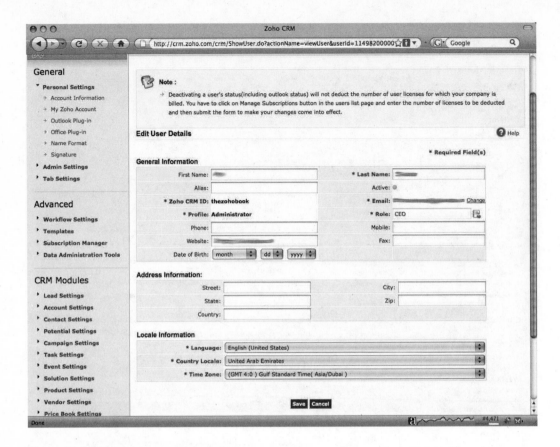

Figure 10-4. Setting the general information

Configuring the signature

Sending and receiving e-mails plays an important role in customer relationship. Apart from regular messages, you probably send quotes, invoices, and so on, to your clients and receive their replies accordingly. This will be discussed in detail in the upcoming sections, but before that, you need to set up a professional signature to appear below your messages.

You can create a simple signature (for example, one containing your company information only) or an active one containing merge fields in order to place values from the data stored in CRM. Merge fields are placeholders formatted especially for CRM to understand that it should replace a merge field with its corresponding value extracted from the system.

As you saw in the preceding section, you set up the account information including **First Name** and **Last Name**. These fields are unique for every user and are stored in each account. Now, to tell CRM to automatically set your e-mail signature to contain your first name and last name, you need to place two merge fields, ${User.First Name} and ${User.Last Name}, in the body of the signature.

So instead of putting this:

`Sincerely,`

`Ali Shabdar`

in the signature, I'd put the following:

`Sincerely,`

`${User.First Name} ${User.Last Name}`

CRM will replace the merge fields with the data it has stored. Similarly, you can add your company name, address information, and so on. This way, when, for example, you change your address in the account information, your signature will always show the latest address because it is actively extracted from the data stored in the system.

1. Click **Signature** (under **Personal Settings**) to edit the signature (Figure 10-5).

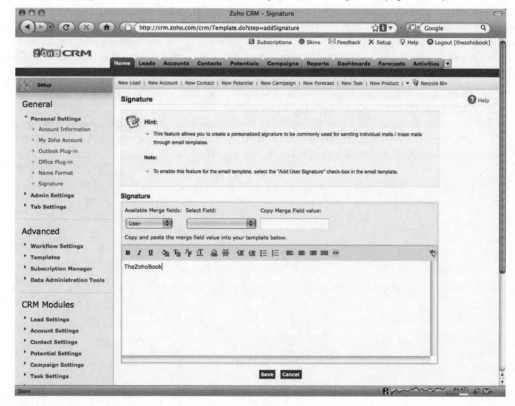

Figure 10-5. Configuring the e-mail signature

2. Make sure **User** is selected for **Available Merge fields**.

3. Select **First Name** for **Select Field**, and copy the value **${User.First Name}** next to it. Then paste it in the signature body.

4. Repeat step 3 for **Last Name** and **Mobile**, and make sure the final signature looks like the one in Figure 10-5.

5. Click **Save** to store the signature.

Configuring the users

CRM is a multiuser system, and almost everybody involved in the business process should have an account in the system. You can define as many users as your subscription allows and assign positions and permissions to them.

CRM supports role-based security in which you give users different access levels to the various modules. This helps you simulate the real-life hierarchy of your organization, so everybody has access only to the information they are allowed to access.

The free edition of CRM supports only three users (including you) and limits the role-based security, meaning you can't define more than two available roles, **CEO** and **Manager**. Note that roles are symbolic and actually help you distinguish people's position in the system. Profiles are separate from roles and give you full power to control the permissions for every user. Yet again, you have only two profiles in the free edition: **Administrator** and **Standard**.

6. Under **Admin Settings**, click **Users**. The only user listed is you automatically assigned as a **CEO** (the role) and an **Administrator** (the profile).

7. Click **Add User**, and fill in the form (Figure 10-6). Make sure you fill in the **Company Name** field and other mandatory fields (which appear in red with an asterisk) correctly. **Zoho CRM ID** must be a valid non-Zoho e-mail address (that is, not @zoho.com).

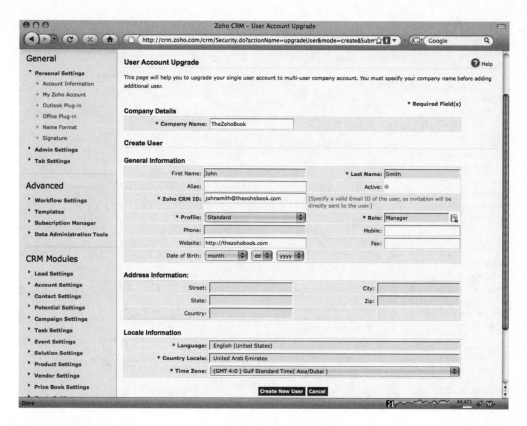

Figure 10-6. Adding users

8. Click **Create New User** to finish the process.

Backing up your data

Before you start using CRM, let me answer a question you might be asking, "How can I back up my data?" Well, this is a great question, and the answer to it is pretty straightforward. You can download a backup for every module of CRM separately.

1. Select **Setup ▶ Advanced ▶ Import Tools ▶ Export Data**.
2. Select the module you want to back up, and click **Export** (Figure 10-7).

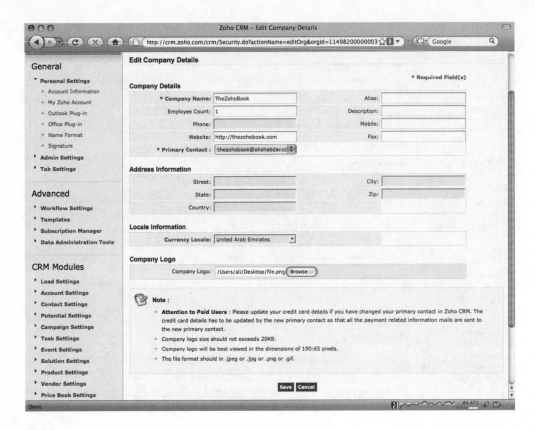

Figure 10-7. Exporting data

3. Store the downloaded CSV file in a safe place.

Although Zoho promises to take excellent care of your data, you should do this regularly in order to avoid any data loss as a result of human error or possible alien invasion.

There is also a (paid) way to get a full backup of the entire CRM data. You can get more information about it at http://zohocrm.wiki.zoho.com/Export-CRM-Data.html#Request_CRM_Data_Backup_(Export_all_data).

Using Zoho CRM for marketing

As you saw in the introduction to this chapter, a typical business cycle involves marketing, sales, and support. Each one of these stages might be assigned to a person, a team of people, or an entire department, based on the organization size. Here we start with the first stage, marketing.

Proper marketing is one of the most important factors of staying in business, which makes the marketers and the marketing department vital to a company. Marketers strive to attract new customers and retain them as well by understanding their needs. Then the company can offer them those products or services.

Every lead that a company collects, directly or indirectly, is the result of a marketing activity. Loyal customers also wouldn't stay with you if the marketers couldn't understand their needs.

> *If you are interested in learning more about marketing, there are many books, articles, podcasts, videos, and so on, that you can enjoy.*

CRM provides you with the necessary tools to run successful campaigns, manage leads, and perform other marketing operations.

Managing campaigns

A typical marketing department is always busy with some kind of campaign. Events, printed and online advertisements, exhibitions, promotional activities, and so on, are all parts of the marketing campaigns that companies run regularly.

You need to start these marketing activities by categorizing them into different campaigns and then assigning the necessary resources (time, people, money, and so on) and tasks to each campaign while monitoring them during their life cycles.

Here you can create your first campaign that will deal with a radio advertisement:

1. To add a new campaign, click `New Campaign` on the menu bar (below any tab title). There is also a button on the `Campaigns` tab (Figure 10-8).

469

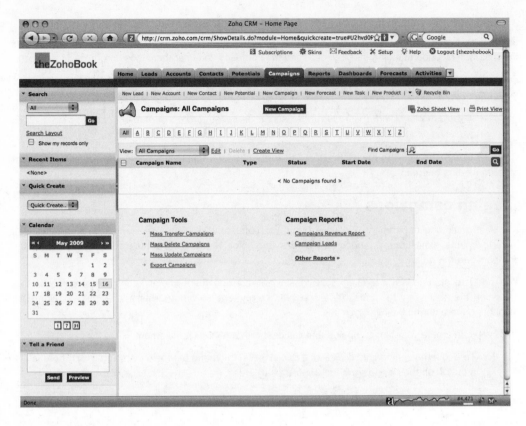

Figure 10-8. The `Campaigns` tab

2. Enter the campaign name (mandatory) as well as the other information (Figure 10-9). Set **Type**, **Status**, **Start Date**, and **End Date** because they are important values that help you monitor the campaign better.

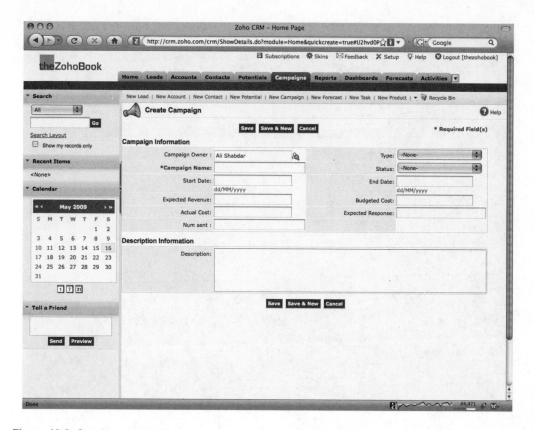

Figure 10-9. Creating a campaign

3. By default, the newly created campaign gets assigned to you (the current user), but you can assign it to other colleagues too. Just click the magnifier icon (**Owner Name Lookup**) right next to **Campaign Owner**, and select (or search for) the person you want to be the campaign owner (Figure 10-10). Then click **OK** to proceed.

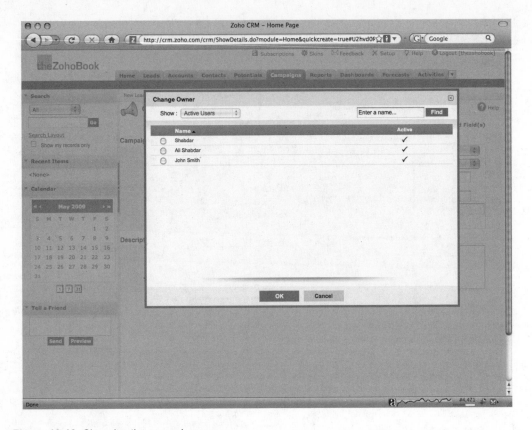

Figure 10-10. Changing the campaign owner

4. Finally, click `Save` in the `Create Campaign` form, but if you wanted to add more campaigns, you should click `Save & New`.

After saving the campaign, you will be redirected to the `Campaign Details` page, where you can fully manage the campaign (Figure 10-11).

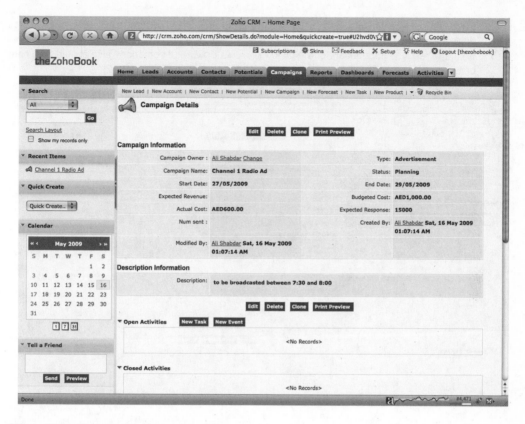

Figure 10-11. The `Campaign Details` page

Adding campaign dependencies

While running a campaign, you'll often set up events, define tasks and assign them to the concerned people, collect and generated related documents, and maintain related contacts and accounts. These are the **dependencies** of a campaign, and you can easily define and assign them to their campaigns in CRM.

Generally, you can add these dependencies to a campaign:

- Tasks, such as preparing marketing material
- Events, such as meetings with a client
- Attachments, such as copies of the advertisement artwork
- Contacts, such as suppliers

Start with adding a task:

1. Open the `Campaigns` tab, find the campaign you created in the previous section, and then click it to open the campaign details.

2. Below the campaign details, find the section **Open Activities**, and click **New Task** (scroll down if it's not visible).

3. Enter the required information for the task. Fill in **Task Owner** if somebody else should take care of it, and make sure you enter something for the **Subject** field (Figure 10-12).

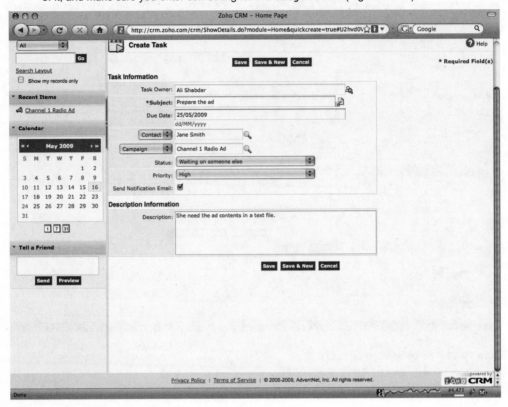

Figure 10-12. Adding a task to the campaign

4. Click **Save** to add the task.

You just saw in the task form that you could add a contact to the task (which we didn't). Contacts are usually people such as a salesperson who you work with. It is recommended that you assign every contact to an account. Accounts are basically entities (companies and so on) that you have a business relationship with. They could be your suppliers, business partners, or outsourcing companies. Basically, a contact is the person who is your connection point to a specific account.

To create an account, open the **Accounts** tab, and click **New Account**. Then fill in the **Account Information** form, and finally click **Save** to add the account.

Similarly, to create a contact, open the **Contacts** tab, and click **New Contact**. Then fill in the form, and select a proper account name from the accounts you have created (this is optional). Finish the process by clicking **Save**.

You can also create a contact while adding other objects, such as tasks, on the fly. For example, when you create a new task, follow these steps:

1. In the **Task Information** form (Figure 10-12), click the magnifier icon next to **Contact**.
2. Click **New Contact** in the **Contact Name Lookup** form.
3. In the **Quick Create** form, fill in at least the **Last Name** field of the person. Then select an account if applicable (Figure 10-13).

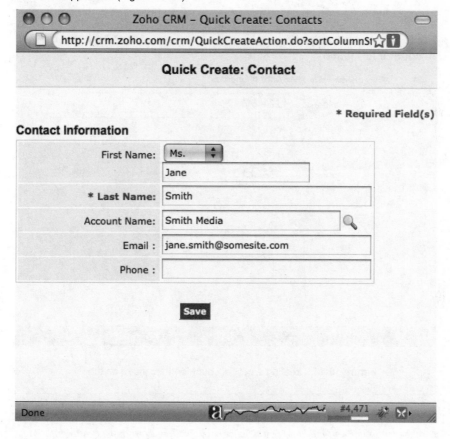

Figure 10-13. Creating a new contact while adding a new task

4. Click **Save** to store the contact, and go back to the **Contact Lookup** form.
5. Click the new contact's name to select it. It will automatically close the window and place the contact in the task form.

A similar approach applies to accounts. To assign an account to a new contact (or to do it when you are adding a task), either type the name of the account or look up an existing one by clicking the magnifier icon. You can always create a new account on the fly as well. Click `New Account` in the lookup form, then fill in the form, and finally proceed by clicking `Save` (Figure 10-14). Click the newly created account to select it, and close the lookup window.

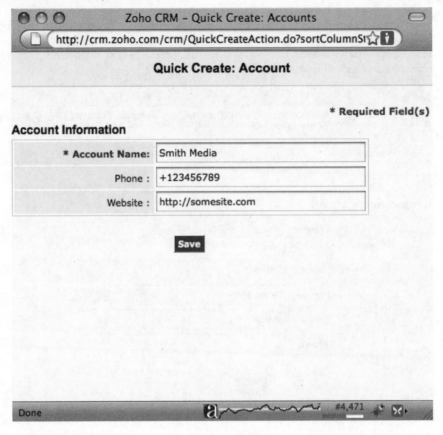

Figure 10-14. Creating a new account for the contact on the fly

> *Creating contacts, accounts, and other objects on the fly is easy and fun, but it might be a better idea to create them through their respective tabs before using them in campaigns and other modules. You usually know who you are dealing with in the daily business, so it is recommended that you sit and enter all of the contacts first and then move forward with the other tasks.*

Managing leads

Leads are the fruit of the marketing campaigns. A sales lead is a person or business entity interested in your products (or services) generated during a marketing activity and passed on to the relevant personnel to work with. Every lead is a prospect and could become a potential customer, so it is important to manage them properly, or the allocated marketing budget goes down the drain.

You need to know who exactly the leads are, how they came to know about your product (or service), and how serious each one of them is throughout the sales process. If you register and track every single deal and filter the good leads from the useless ones, you can help the salespeople in your organization big time.

Adding a new lead

You can add new leads to CRM by creating them one by one or by importing them in bulk. To add them one by one, follow these steps:

1. Click **New Lead** on the main menu bar or on the **Leads** tab. You can also click **New** in the **Leads** section of a campaign.
2. Fill in **Lead Owner**, and make sure you fill in **Company Name** and **Last Name** for the new lead (Figure 10-15). If you created the lead from a campaign (on the **Campaign Details** page), these are already set. Otherwise, you should select the campaign to which this lead belongs.

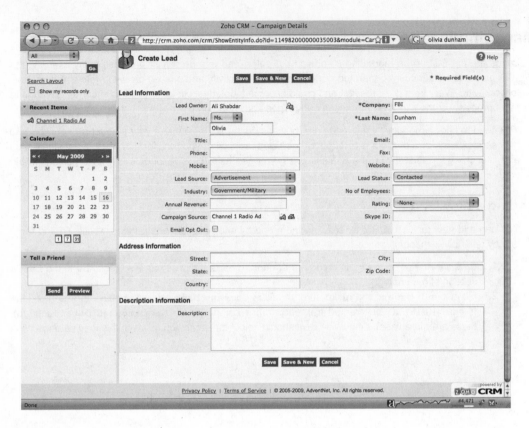

Figure 10-15. Creating a new lead

> *The more accurate information you enter, the better the quality of the information will be, so enter as much information as you can for every business object (such as leads).*

3. Click **Save** to store the lead.

Adding lead dependencies

Once the lead is created, you will be taken to the **Leads** page where all leads are listed. By default CRM lists the open lists including the newly created ones.

During the business process (marketing, sales, and so on), you perform activities to convert a raw lead to a potential lead and eventually to a successful sale. This process requires you as the lead owner to do various activities for the lead. These activities are grouped as tasks and events. By storing every single step you take, not only do you document the whole process for others or for your later use, but you also make sure that everything is happening according to the workflow of your organization.

1. Open the **Leads** tab, and click the third icon before a lead for a context menu to open (Figure 10-16).

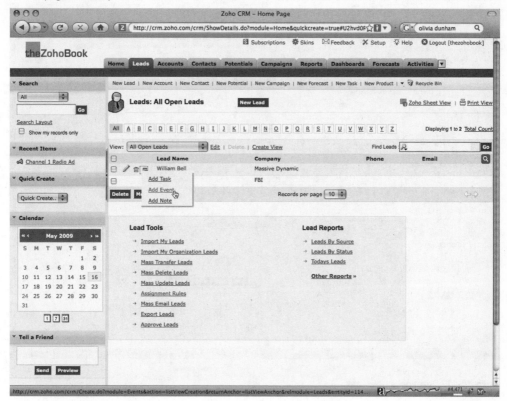

Figure 10-16. Leads list

2. Click **Add Task** to create a task about sending a message to the lead. Alternatively, you can add tasks and other dependencies on the **Lead Details** page.

3. Enter the subject, or select it from the predefined list of subjects (**Call**, **Email**, **Meeting**, **Product Demo**, **Send Message**). Note that the lead is already selected. Set the other fields as well, and click **Save** to assign it to the current lead (Figure 10-17).

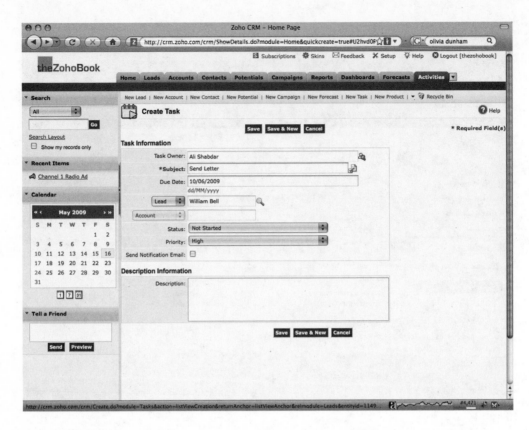

Figure 10-17. Creating a new task

> *You can change the* Subject *list and pretty much every list in CRM on the* Settings *page. Using lists instead of entering texts manually enhances productivity, minimizes human error, and creates a standard set of defined words throughout the system.*

4. Similarly, create a new event about a meeting you need to have with the lead. This time, click **Add Event**, fill in the mandatory **Subject**, **Start DateTime**, and **End DateTime**, and proceed with the rest of the form (Figure 10-18).

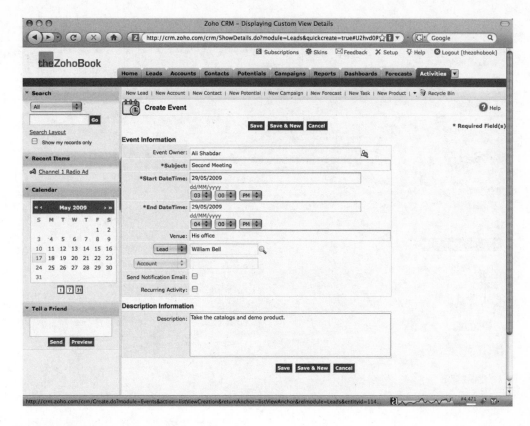

Figure 10-18. Creating a new event

5. Click **Save** when you are done.

6. To finish this section, add a note to the lead by clicking **Add Note**. Notes are not actually activities but are rather useful if you want to store additional information about the lead in separate pieces.

7. **Title** is mandatory, but you most probably need to fill in **Note Content** too (Figure 10-19). Then click **Save** to store it.

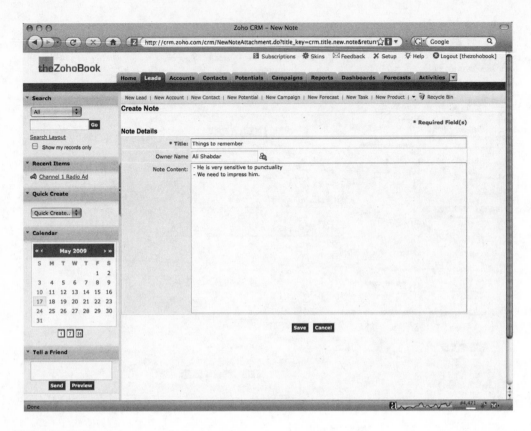

Figure 10-19. Creating a new note

Modifying leads

Editing leads is as easy as clicking the **Edit** button for every one of them:

1. On the **Leads** page, click the pencil icon (the first icon before every lead) for the lead you want to modify.

2. In the **Edit Lead** form, make the amendments. **Status** is one of the fields you need to update as the lead's status changes.

3. Click **Save** when you are done.

There are also times when you'll need to modify many leads in one batch. For example, you might want to update the web site of a group of leads:

1. Open the **Leads** tab, and click **Mass Update** at the bottom of the leads list. The next screen helps you tell CRM which leads should be included in the mass update. For example, if you want to update a field for all leads coming from a certain company, select **Company** in the drop-down

list, select **is** in the comparison list, and then enter the company name (Figure 10-20).

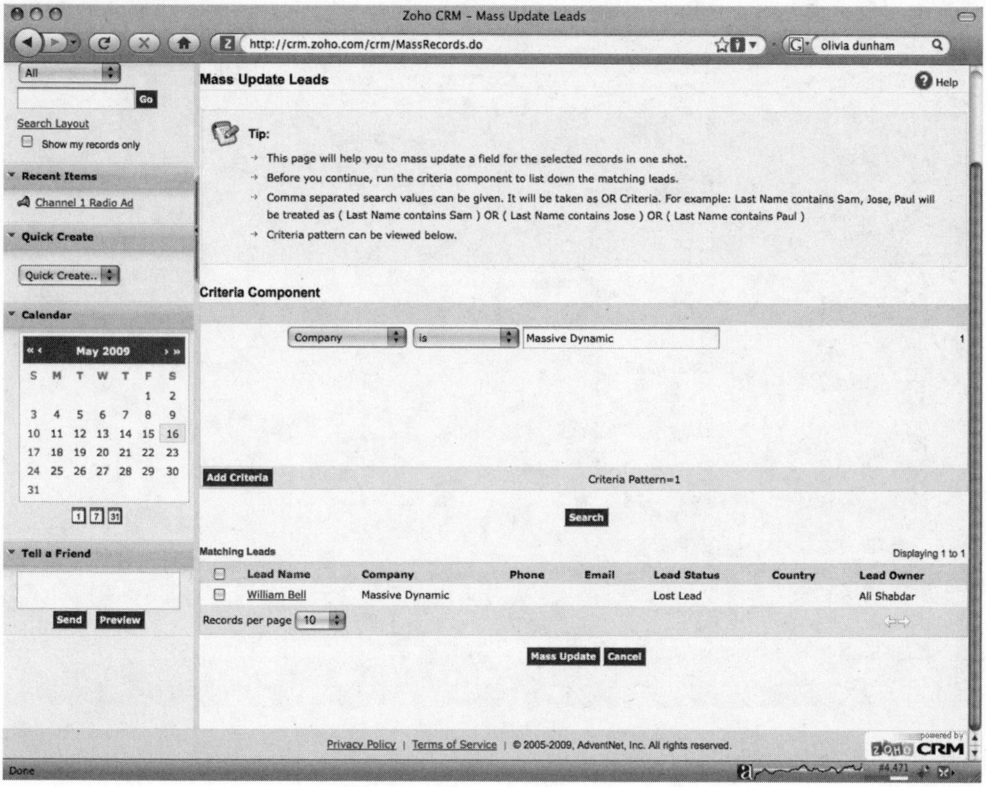

Figure 10-20. Mass updating the leads

> You can add as many criteria as you want by clicking **Add Criteria**.

2. Click **Search** to find all the matching records.
3. Once you were happy with the search results, select the entire list (or a portion of it), and click **Mass Update**. The screen will be grayed out, and the leads field list will appear. Choose the field (data column) you want to update (Figure 10-21).

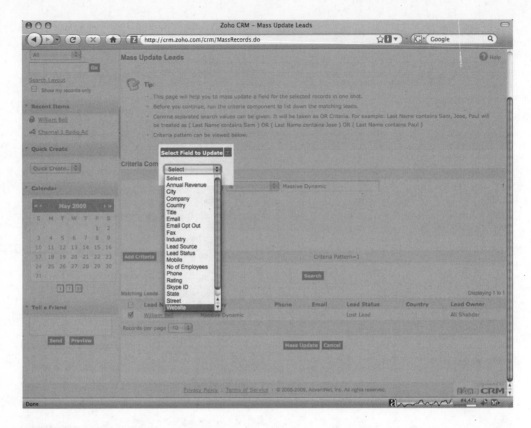

Figure 10-21. Selecting a field for mass update

4. In the next window, enter the new value for the selected field (Figure 10-22). Then click **Save** to apply the changes. All selected records will be updated with the new value in one batch.

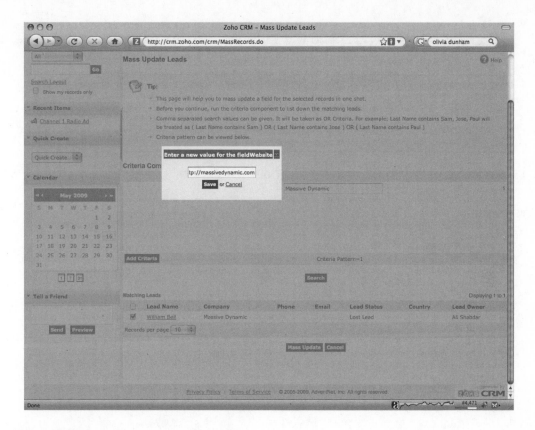

Figure 10-22. Setting the new value for the field

Transferring leads

Another useful feature of the leads module is the ability to transfer multiple leads to another **CRM** user. Such cases are common in companies where a new person takes over a bunch of leads in busy times or different stages of a deal.

Similar to doing a mass update, click **Mass Transfer**, and enter the criteria in order to list the leads you would like to transfer to another user (Figure 10-23). The difference is that you need to first create the transfer route by setting the **Transfer from** and **Transfer to** fields, so CRM knows who the current owner and the new owner are.

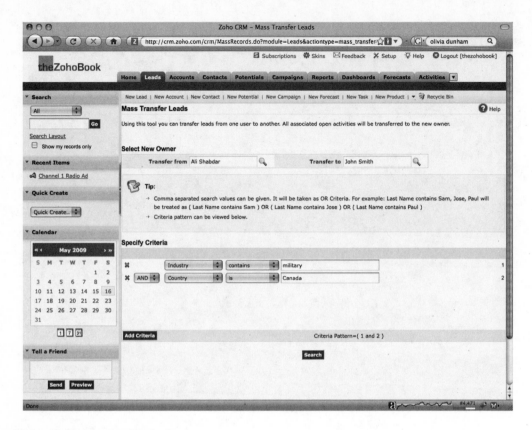

Figure 10-23. Mass transferring leads

Once the list is loaded, select the transferable leads, and click **Transfer** to finish the task (Figure 10-24).

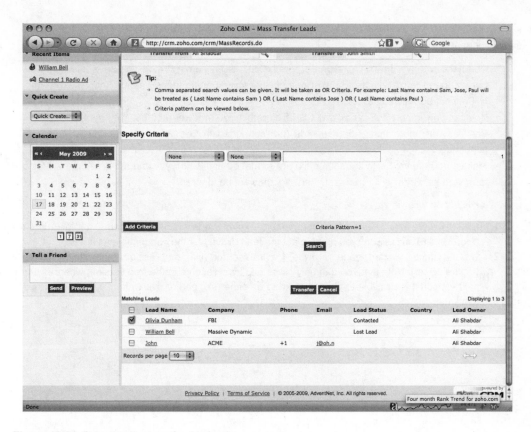

Figure 10-24. Selecting the transferable leads

Importing leads

It often happens that you need to import leads to CRM from an external source. Suppose your company was attending an exhibition overseas and your salespeople were able to collect a pile of business cards. After the information has been digitized (transferring it from paper to computer, that is) and filtered, you end up with a spreadsheet shared with you through Zoho Sheet, or perhaps you received it in a CSV file by e-mail. The bottom line is that you need to import these leads into CRM in order to assign them to the concerned people to start working on them.

> *A CSV file is a plain-text file with a custom structure. Information is organized in rows (records), and each row consists of values (fields/columns) separated by commas. The first row usually contains the field names, and the actual data starts from the second line. CSV is perhaps the safest and most platform-independent file format for importing and exporting tabular data of any size. To see how it looks like, simply export a spreadsheet document to CSV format and then open it in a text editor like TextMate, Vim, or Notepad.*

Before importing leads, make sure you read the instruction displayed in the import page. Here are the most important points:

- You need to have the **Data Import** permission. As an administrator, you have this permission, but you need to make sure the user responsible for importing leads has it. Otherwise, the import link will not be visible at all.
- You can only import XLS, VCS, and CSV files with 1,500 or fewer records.
- For files with more than 1,500 records (not supported in free version), only the CSV format is supported.
- Make sure date values in the source file are formatted as MM/dd/yyyy and the date-time values are formatted as MM/dd/yy hh:mm:ss. Otherwise, they will be ignored.

Import the leads as follows:

1. Click **Import My Leads** for your personal leads (registers in your name) or **Import My Organization Leads** (you need to set the lead owner) for the company-level leads.
2. On the import wizard page, browse for the source file, and assign other fields carefully (Figure 10-25). Note that you can only clone duplicate records in the free version, whereas in the paid version it is possible to choose them to be either skipped or overwritten. Then click **Next** to continue.

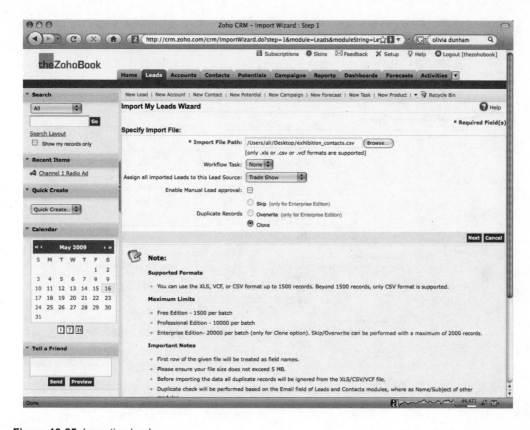

Figure 10-25. Importing leads

3. If the source file is formatted correctly, you can see in the next page that the `Lead Information` section is set correctly. CRM maps the fields in the source file to the default fields in the leads database for the import to be performed correctly.

4. Check the mapping carefully to avoid any bad imports, and set them manually if the fields are not correctly mapped (Figure 10-26).

Figure 10-26. Setting up the import

5. Enter the fields in the **Address** and **Description Information** sections if needed, and click **Next** to proceed.

6. In the **Confirm Mapping** page, go through the summary, and if everything is OK, click **Import**. Otherwise, click **Previous** if you needed to refine the import process.

> *If you were not happy with the results of the import, you can check* **Import History** *and roll back the whole process (Figure 10-27).*

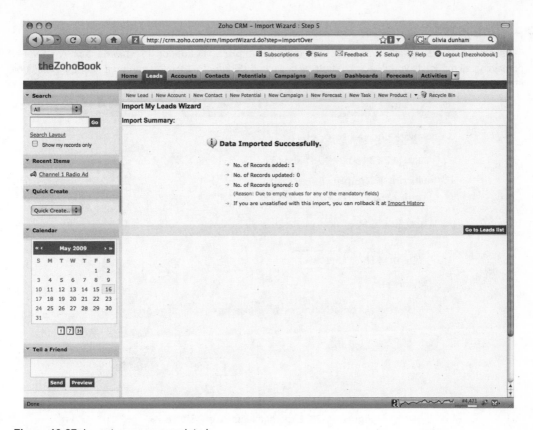

Figure 10-27. Import process completed

Exporting leads

To export the leads at any time, you can just click **Export Leads** on the **Leads** tab. A CSV file containing all the leads you deal with starts to download (Figure 10-28). You can then filter the results or import them directly into other applications.

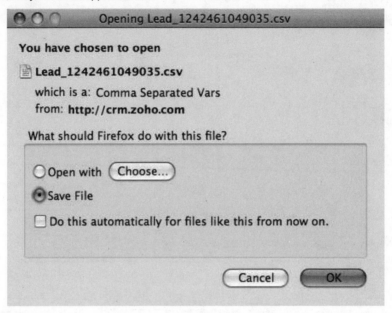

Figure 10-28. Exporting leads to a CSV file

Reporting leads

There is no doubt that you will need to generate reports based on the data stored in the different modules for various reasons. One of the areas to create reports is leads.

There are two ways to get reports on leads: through the **Leads** tab (on the **Leads** tab, click **Today's Leads**) or the **Reports** tab (click **Reports ▶ Lead Reports ▶ Today's Leads**), as shown in Figure 10-29.

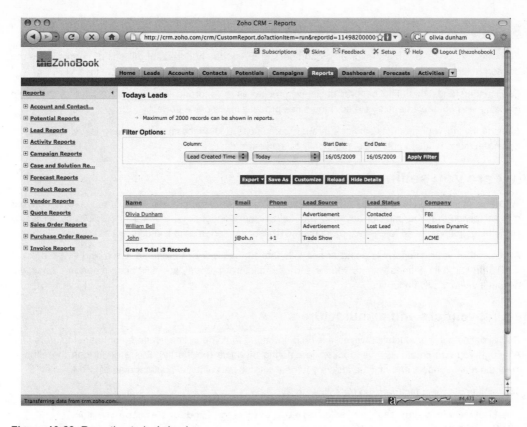

Figure 10-29. Reporting today's leads

On the report page, you have the option to export the report in XLS, CSV, and PDF formats. It is also possible to refine the report by changing the values in the **Filter Options** box right above the report. Try different values, and see the results by yourself.

You can also save a refined report as a new one to make it available for everybody.

Sending bulk e-mails to leads

Mass Email Leads (which is not functional in the free version of CRM) is quite useful when you want to send a message to all your leads (or a selected group of them) in conjunction with other marketing activities.

This could be another reason for upgrading to a paid plan, if you think you need this feature. Otherwise, you can use a third-party service like iContact (http://www.icontact.com) or Aweber (http://www.aweber.com) that provides you with mass e-mail facilities in addition to other tools and services. Using a third-party service is, however, less convenient than having a mass mailer inside CRM, because you need to first export the contacts from CRM and import it into such applications.

Using Zoho CRM for sales

The whole theory of business revolves around selling. Every day hundreds of millions of people leave the comfort of their houses to go out and sell something, such as a product, a service, or an idea.

CRM understands this. The general business process is a recurring loop in which sales is the main objective and other elements make sure the sales process takes place perfectly.

After marketing your products/services through campaigns and successfully collecting leads, it is time to transform those leads to potentials and ideally to active clients.

What are you selling?

Whatever position you hold in the business chain, you have something to sell. It could be a product of your own, a service that you offer, or anything you sell to other vendors and manufacturers. Obviously, to sell something, first you need to define it properly in CRM so you can refer to it in different activities.

Anything that your company is going to sell falls into the category of products. Each and every product should be carefully defined with its vendor and manufacturer properly set. CRM can manage a basic yet decent inventory system for you.

Creating vendors and manufacturers

Before defining the products, however, it is recommended that you define vendors and manufacturers first. Although you can create new vendors while creating products (on the fly), it is a good idea to define at least the main vendors and manufacturers you deal with as part of initial configuration of CRM.

To manage the manufacturers, do the following:

1. Open the `Setup` page, and select `Fields List` in the `Product Settings` section.
2. In the list, click `Edit` in front of the `Manufacturer` link. In the `Edit Pick List` area, a list of current manufacturers opens (Figure 10-30). You can easily remove items by clicking the trash can for each manufacturer.

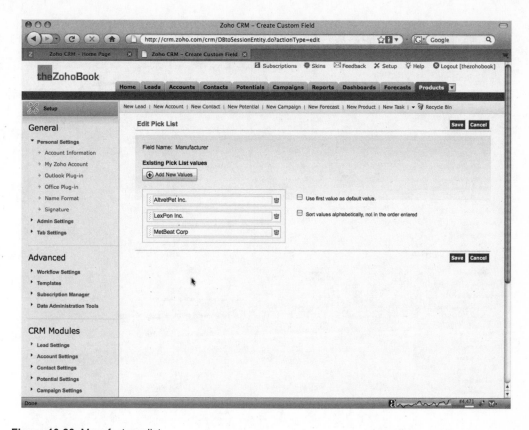

Figure 10-30. Manufacturer list

3. Click **Add New Values** to create new manufacturers. Enter the names of the manufacturers in the text box, and press the Enter key for each one (one manufacturer per line).

4. Click **Add** when you are done with the list, and then click **Save** to store the changes (Figure 10-31).

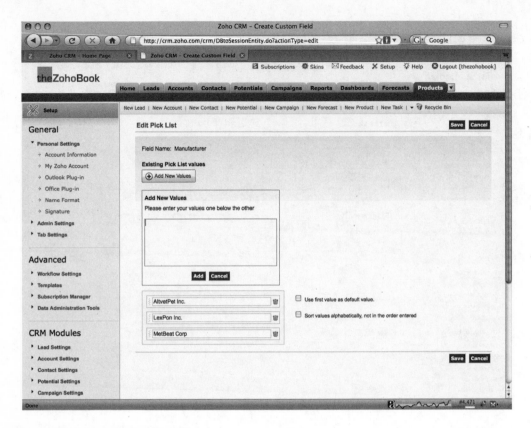

Figure 10-31. Adding new manufacturers

Now follow these steps to add a vendor:

1. Open the **Vendors** tab, and click **Add Vendor**.

2. **Vendor Name** is the only mandatory field, but you should provide at least some contact information as well (Figure 10-32). You can change the **Vendor Owner** field to the person who is dealing with this particular vendor and potentially earns commission from sales for this vendor's products.

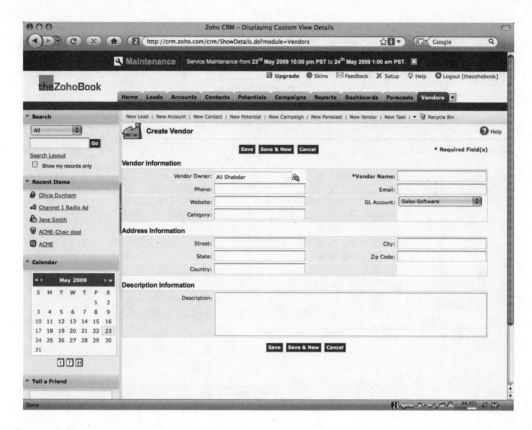

Figure 10-32. Add new vendors

> The **GL Account** (the general ledger account) drop-down list is also customizable through the **Setup** page.

3. Click **Save** to store the vendor information.

Creating products

Now that you created the manufacturers and vendors you regularly work with, it is time to create the products your company offers.

1. Click **New Product** on the main menu bar or on the **Products** page itself.

2. In the **Create Product** form, fill in **Product Name**. The more information you enter, the more manageable your inventory becomes (Figure 10-33).

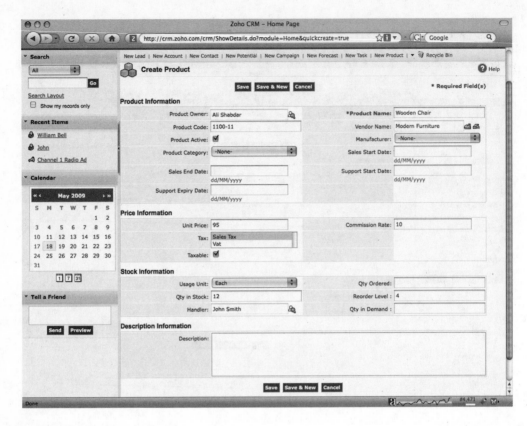

Figure 10-33. Adding a new product

3. Change the `Product Owner` field by clicking the magnifier next to its text box (Figure 10-34). Select a new owner, and click `OK` to proceed.

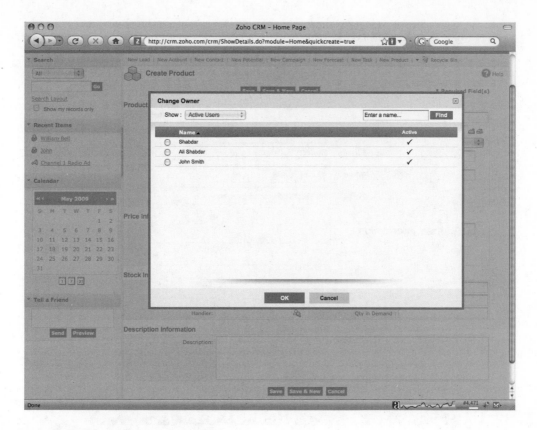

Figure 10-34. Changing the product owner

> *Setting the product owner is important when you have a person assigned to deal with particular products or the products from a specific vendor/manufacturer. This person is not necessarily the one who enters the information.*

4. To select a vendor, click the **Vendor Name Lookup** button next to the **Vendor Name** text box, and click the respective vendor.

5. Although you already created a number of vendors, there might be cases that you just need to create one on the fly. Just click the **New Vendor** button, and click **Save** to save the vendor once you are finished creating it (Figure 10-35).

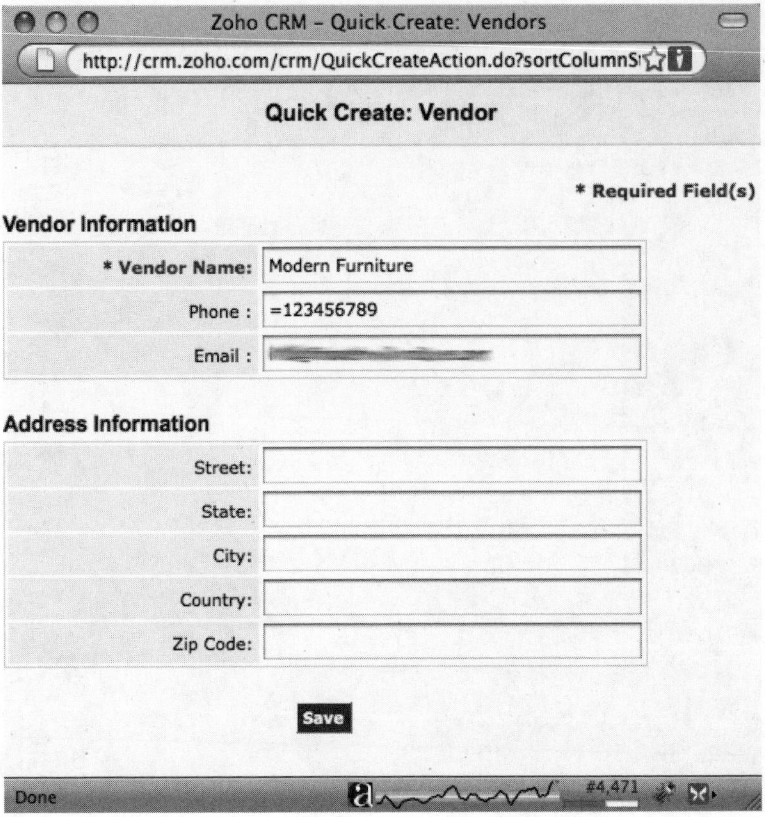

Figure 10-35. Creating a vendor on the fly

6. Click the vendor you just created from the lookup list in order to load it in the product form.

7. In the `Price Information` section, fill in `Unit Price` because it is required for other tasks such as issuing quotes and sales orders. Enter the tax information too if it is applicable.

8. Fill in the `Stock Information` section according to Figure 10-33. This section contains important fields used in automated calculations and the inventory management. For example, if the current stock of a product becomes lower than the reorder level, it will alert the product owner with an e-mail message reporting the situation.

9. Once you enter the product information properly, click `Save` to create the product and get back to the products list. Clicking `Save & New`, however, stores the current one and opens a new form to create another product.

Managing the inventory

CRM offers fairly basic inventory management facilities by maintaining the in-stock quantity of the products, minimum reorder level, and other fields you set when creating a product. It also allows you to issue purchase orders (POs) to update the stock.

Although you can't expect CRM to perform like a full-fledged inventory management system (because it is not), it will suffice for the requirements of many smaller companies.

> *Your company (or yourself as an entrepreneur) might not sell physical products. Let's say you just offer services like ballet training. Then your product is actually your service, and you might not need an inventory management system. But still, all sales and marketing modules are usable in your business model.*

When you add new products to CRM, it is highly recommended that you enter the stock information. This is essential to keep track of your inventory and update it by issuing purchase orders.

You can create POs from scratch by opening the `Purchase Orders` tab and clicking `New Purchase Order`. It is also possible to create them based on the required products in the inventory that the stock is below the reorder level.

1. Open the `Products` tab. Click `Generate PO` for the products below the `Reorder` level in the `Products Tools` section at the bottom of page.

2. On the next page, select the vendor you want to reorder goods from, and select the item(s) to be ordered. Then click `Generate Purchase Order`.

> *If there is no item needed, you will see the message* `No Vendor found with Products below Reorder level`.

3. In the `Create Purchase Order` form (Figure 10-36), enter the subject. `Vendor Name` is already selected for you from the previous screen.

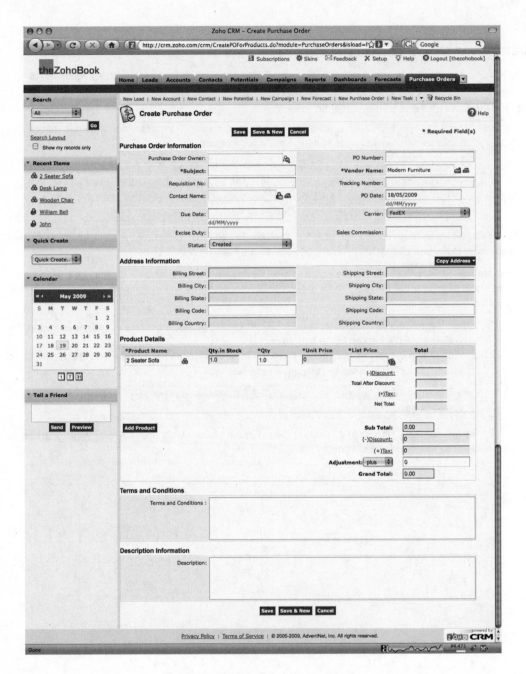

Figure 10-36. Creating a purchase order

4. Enter other fields carefully because this information will be visible in the printed (or exported) copy of the PO that you will send to the vendor.

5. The list of products you selected in the previous page is displayed in the **Product Detail** section. Enter the quantity in **Qty** for each item as well as the other numeric values. Note the price in **List Price**, and read the next walk-through about it.

6. Enter something for **Terms and Conditions** and **Description** if applicable, and click **Save** to create the PO.

The real price of a product is stored in **Unit Price**, but sometimes you need to have a secondary price that might vary for different clients or circumstances. Simply put, you should be able to sell the same product for different prices at the same time.

You can do this by creating **price books** and assigning products to them. Each price book offers a different set of prices, and each product can be assigned to multiple books.

When you create POs, sales orders (SOs), quotes, and invoices, you can use price books to set a different list price than the unit price of a product.

You can create a price book while adding a product to a list on the fly, but it won't be very useful because you can't set the values in there.

Here is the best way to do it:

1. Open the **Price Books** tab, and then click **New Price Book**.
2. Fill in **Price Book Name** as well as the other fields.
3. **Pricing Model** has three options: **None**, **Flat**, and **Differential**. These options basically calculate the amount of discount for bulk deals. **None** stands for no discount, but for **Flat** and **Differential**, you will see a series of ranges appearing in the **Product Details** section. Set the percentage of the discount if the order quantity falls in any of the given ranges. See Figure 10-37 for reference.

For example, if the quantity is 350 (eligible for up to 7.5 percent discount) and the unit price is $10, for a **Flat** model a value of $262.5 (7.5 percent) will be calculated as the discount. But if for the same case the **Differential** model were chosen, 50 of the 350 units would fall in 0 percent discount range, 50 would fall in the 5 percent range, and 250 would fall in the 7.5 percent range. The result in this case would be $25 + $187.5 = $212.5 of discount.

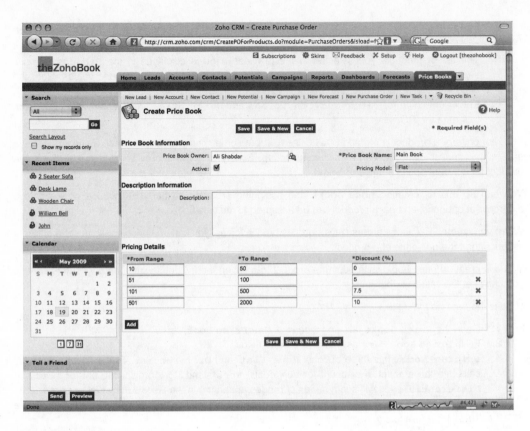

Figure 10-37. Creating a price book

4. Click **Save** to create the price book. Then in the list, open the recently created book.
5. Scroll down to see the **Products** section. This is where you assign products to this book so they follow the pricing rules you defined in this book (Figure 10-38).

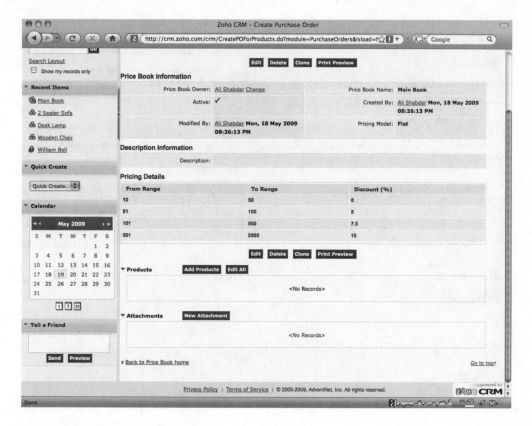

Figure 10-38. The price book information

6. Click **Add Products** to proceed.

7. Select the products you want to assign to the price book, and set **List Price** for every one of them.

8. Click **Add to Products** to finalize the task (Figure 10-39).

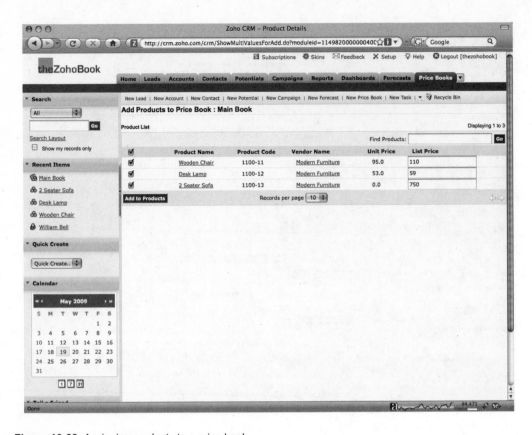

Figure 10-39. Assigning products to a price book

Define as many price books as you need to have them in handy for POs and other forms.

Catching the opportunities

After collecting the leads and filtering them down to the most valuable ones, it is time to convert them to potentials. This process is one of the most important steps toward successful sales. You will identify the status of the potentials to see whether they are viable sales candidates or you are losing them to the competition (or losing them because of other reasons). This process not only plays a crucial role in the business but also helps you make better marketing decisions in the future.

Creating potentials is done either by converting eligible leads into potentials or by creating new potentials from scratch. In this walk-through, you'll convert an existing lead that you think could be a sales opportunity in the later stages. Creating potentials from scratch is a similar process and is done through the `New Potential` button on the `Potentials` tab.

As you saw in the earlier sections, in order to have a full view of your business objects (that is, leads, products, and so on) and to understand the interconnections between such objects, you should gradually link the objects to each other in a sensible way.

You saw how to assign tasks and events to the leads. In a similar approach, you should be able to assign the products to a lead so that during the process you (or your colleagues) will know the full spectrum of the developing business relationship between your organization and the (potential) client.

To assign products to a lead, open **Lead Details** (on the **Leads** tab), and scroll down to the **Products** section. Then click **Add Products**, and on the next page, select the product(s). Then click **Add to Lead** to finish the job (Figure 10-40).

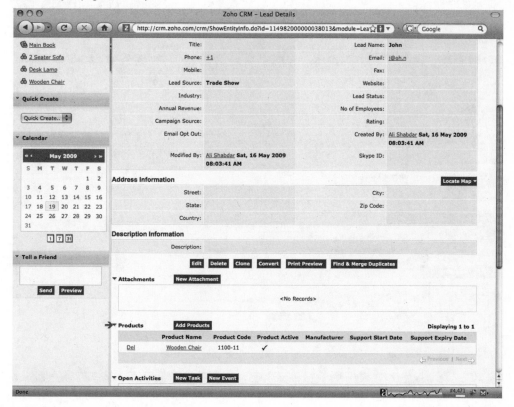

Figure 10-40. Assigning products to a lead

You should consider these points about potentials:

▪ A lead is upgradeable (convertible) to a potential when it is proven that there might be a chance, even the slightest, for a successful deal.

- You can track the life span of a client through the **Potentials** tab. From the moment a client enters the system as a lead until the time you win (or lose) it, every step taken can be registered. You can even enter the competitors who could steal them from you.
- To make the business workflow more sensible and manageable, you should assign products, quotes, sales orders, and even customer service case reports to the potentials at different stages of the business.

Now open a lead that you think should be upgraded to a potential, and click the **Convert** button to start the conversion process (Figure 10-41).

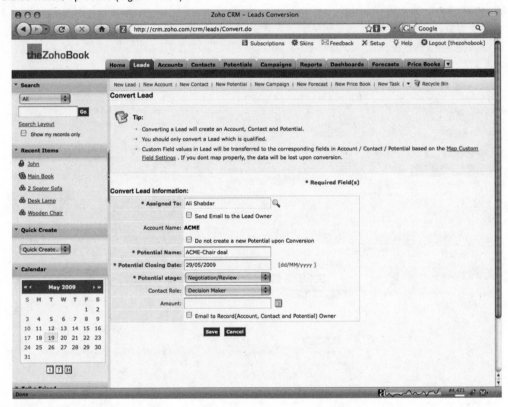

Figure 10-41. Converting a lead

Converting a lead to a potential will create three new objects:

- A new account
- A new contact for the account
- A new contact for the potential

If you are interested in seeing how CRM maps different fields of a lead to create these objects, read its conversion mapping guide at http://zohocrm.wiki.zoho.com/Working-with-Leads.html#Convert_Leads_to_Other_Sales_Records.

> To change the way CRM maps the fields, you need to click the **Map Custom Fields Settings** link on the conversion page (Figure 10-42).

Figure 10-42. Mapping custom fields

After filling in the fields, click **Save** to complete the process. Now check the potentials list on the **Potentials** tab to check the newly created record. Open the potential, and scroll down to see the business objects can be assigned to a potential: **Competitors**, **Attachments**, **Notes**, **Tasks**, **Products**, **Quotes**, **Sales Orders**, **Contact Roles**, **Emails**, and **Cases**. This is a full-spectrum view of your business (Figure 10-43).

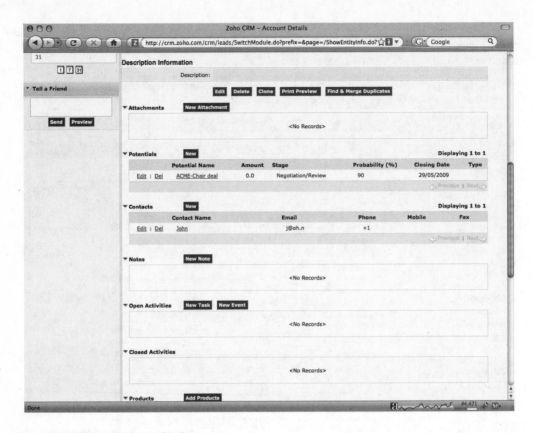

Figure 10-43. Potential dependencies

Editing potentials is easy. You can either click **Edit** to open all fields ready to be modified or hover the mouse pointer in front of different fields for an **Edit** link to appear and then modify only the field you want. You'll learn how to create other business objects and assign (connect) them to the corresponding potentials in the upcoming sections.

To create a competitor, you need to do it on the potential's details page. Click **New** in the **Competitors** section, and enter the name of the company you think might win this particular potential. Fill in **Strengths** and **Weaknesses** of the competitor for the record as well. Click **Save** to add the competitor (Figure 10-44).

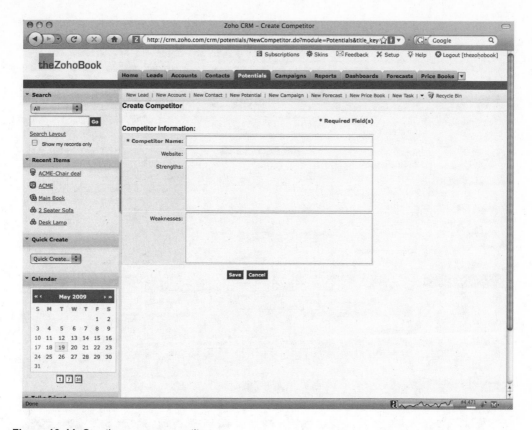

Figure 10-44. Creating a new competitor

Adding competitors and assigning them to potentials will not actually affect any workflow but helps the relevant people in your organization get instant access to the characteristics of competitors.

Turning opportunities into sales

Once you have made contact with the potentials and convinced them that your product is the one they are looking for, it is time to send them price quotes. Current clients also expect to receive quotes for new orders.

Once the quotes are initially approved, sales orders will be issued. After that, the products will be shipped, and the money will be in your account after invoicing the client.

Creating Quotes

Just like other modules, there are three ways to create quotes: from a potential's page, from the menu bar, and directly on the `Quotes` tab. The first option is preferable because it makes an automatic connection between the quote and the potential.

1. In the **Create Quote** form, enter all the mandatory fields (Figure 10-45).

Figure 10-45. Creating a quote

2. For the products, click the lookup icon to select from the available products or create them on the fly. Note that once you enter the quantity (**Qty**) and choose the price book, it will update the total price of the item as well as the grand total automatically.

3. Include any extra discount and tax calculations by clicking the **Discount** and **Tax** links. You can choose between a fixed amount and a percentage amount.

4. Fill in **Terms and Conditions** as well as the **Description Information** if there is any, and then click **Save** to create the quote.

Printing quotes

After creating quotes, you need to send them to the client (or the potential). Do this by exporting the quote to a PDF file so you can then print it on paper or e-mail it directly to the customer.

Before that, you may want to click **Print Preview** to see how the printed quote will look like. Choose a template (**Quote Template** is the only choice if you haven't created more templates yet), and then click **Preview** (Figure 10-46).

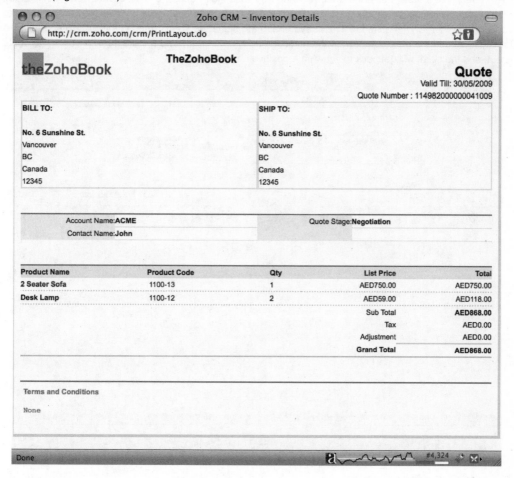

Figure 10-46. Previewing a quote

To actually export the quote, click **Export to PDF** on the **Quote Details** page.

> CRM allows you to create new templates or edit the existing ones for quotes, sales orders, and other forms. It is accessible through **Setup ▶ Templates ▶ Inventory Templates**. Check out http://zohocrm.wiki.zoho.com/Managing-Inventory-Templates.html to learn how to create templates in detail.

Sending quotes

CRM offers integration with Zoho Mail, allowing you to e-mail quotes to your clients from within CRM. Simply click **Send Mail** on the **Quote Details** page, which opens an empty message with the quote converted to PDF and attached to it. You even have the signature you created in the **Setup** page placed for you. Just add the recipient(s), write the message body, and click **Send** (Figure 10-47). *Voila!* The quote is out, and the client will get back to you with a positive answer.

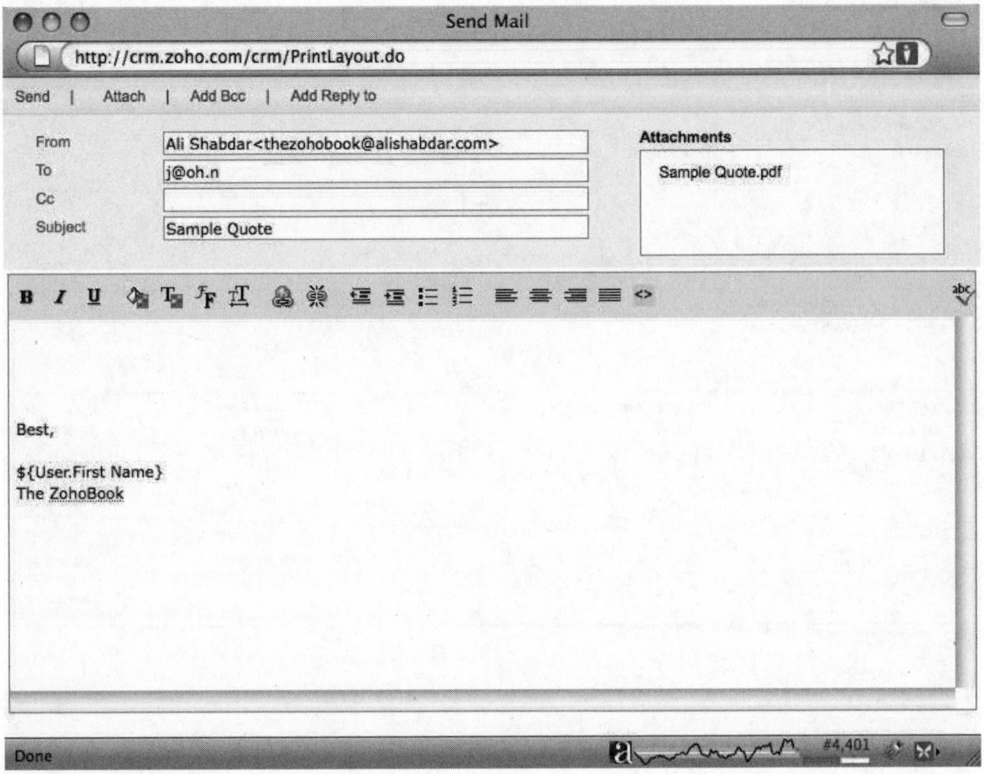

Figure 10-47. E-mailing quotes

> It is worth mentioning that Zoho recently released an add-on for CRM that adds an **Email** tab to the system, allowing you to manage your e-mails (Zoho, Gmail, and so on) in CRM. It is a paid add-on, so I won't discuss it here, but you can get more information about it from *http://www.zoho.com/crm/crm-email.html*.

Creating sales orders

You'll often send multiple quotes until the client finally accepts. This could be because of giving extra discounts or changes in the terms and conditions of the quote. This means you might need to edit the quote a few times by opening the quote details page and clicking **Edit** to modify the necessary fields.

Once the customer accepts a quote, it is time to issue a sales order to almost finalize the deal. Creating sales orders is almost identical to creating quotes. You can create them by converting quotes to SOs or directly through the main menu bar or the **Sales Orders** tab.

After you have created the SOs, you'll see they look suspiciously like quotes. You can assign business objects to SOs similarly to get a full view of the business process.

You can send SOs to clients by exporting them to PDF for print or by e-mailing them directly from within the **Sales Order Details** page (Figure 10-48).

Figure 10-48. `Sales Order Details` page

Creating invoices

One last step in the sales paperwork process could be issuing the invoices for the clients to pay for the products or services sold.

Yet again, you can create new invoices through the three familiar links. When you open a SO, the only option the `Convert` button gives you is `Invoice`, meaning it is the last stop for the journey of the quote. This will automatically generate an invoice that you can print, send, or edit on the `Invoices` tab. Figure 10-49 shows an invoice generated from a quote.

Figure 10-49. Invoice details

From quotes to sales orders to invoices, you saw how easy managing the standard sales paperwork in CRM is. With different objects connected to each other (for example, an invoice connected to a number of products, an account, a sales order, and so on), CRM gives you a 360-degree view of your business, traceable from all angles.

Forecasting your business

Now let's see how CRM can help you get a glimpse of the future. Generally, if you can forecast the volume of sales in the upcoming quarters (or months) and apply it to your sales plan, you will be able to better manage your resources in a way that helps you boost your sales and minimize possible bottlenecks.

CRM provides you with the basic tools for forecasting your business quarterly by allocating quotas and lower and upper committed amounts per quarter. Throughout time it will show you how well your organization is doing against the forecasted numbers.

Here is how you create a new forecast:

1. Click **New Forecast** on the main menu bar or on the **Forecasts** tab.
2. Set the **Year** and **Quarter** you want to forecast, and then click **Next** (Figure 10-50).

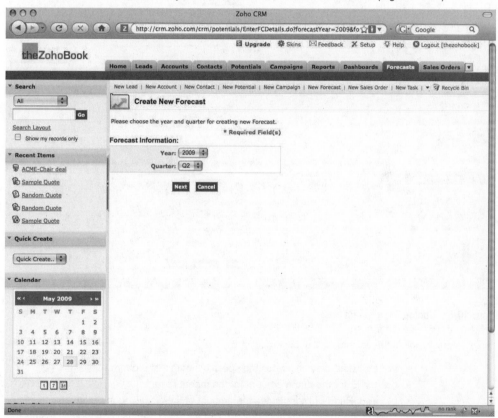

Figure 10-50. Creating a new forecast

> *It is possible to create only one forecast for the same period of time. For example, if you have already created a forecast for* `Q4, 2010` *and it won't fit your requirements, you need to edit the current one to carry the new values.*

3. On the next screen, **Forecast Edit**, enter the required values for all three months of the quarter (Figure 10-51).

Figure 10-51. Editing the forecast data

A quick look at the columns will show the following:

- **Month**: Read-only; indicates the specific month in the quarter.
- **Quota**: Enter the quota amount for the month here.
- **Closed**: Read-only; indicates the amount of the closed, won potentials.
- **Commit Amount**: Enter the total amount a salesperson is confident of closing.
- **Best Case Amount**: Enter the amount a salesperson might be closing.
- **Pipeline**: Read-only; indicates the current amount in the sales pipeline.

4. Below the list, you can see all the sales activities for every month in which you can categorize them to different forecast categories: **Pipeline**, **Omitted**, **Best Case**, and **Commit**. Click **Save** to store the forecast information.

> You can also click **Compute** to update the values in **Probability** and **Expected Revenue**.

Sales forecasting is an important and somewhat complex aspect of business. You may want to read more about this subject before using it in practice.

Using Zoho CRM for support

A considerable part of the relationship management between the provider (your company) and the customer promised by CRM applications involves supporting the customers. Customers often have questions about the products and services you provide. Sometimes they face difficulties using the products or find defects or missing parts. Registering such cases and tracking the steps you took toward solving such issues helps organizations keep customers happy and loyal, while saving a lot of time and money avoiding the old mistakes.

The business cycle does not end with a successful sale. In fact, a healthy amount of money and effort needs to be spent on after-sales service. Tracking customers' issues (cases) and managing them in the right way plays an essential role in the CRM process. Zoho CRM offers a simple yet useful case-handling and solution management system to tackle the issues related to the customer service department.

Managing cases

When a customer raises an issue, you or the concerned personnel in the customer service department need to file a **case** describing the situation in detail.

> As the admin of the system, you will need to grant read/write permission for both the **Cases** and **Solutions** modules (tabs) to the customer service personnel.

You can create cases from scratch or import them in bulk into the system. It is also possible to create them through web-to-case online forms (in which the data comes from embedded case submission forms) or through Microsoft Outlook. The latter two are exclusive to enterprise members.

To create a case from scratch, follow these steps:

Click **New Case** on the main menu bar or on the **Cases** tab.

1. In the **Create Case** form, enter enough data to describe exactly what the issue is about (Figure 10-52). **Case Origin**, **Status**, and **Subject** are mandatory fields, but filling in other fields will help you understand the situation better and diagnose it faster in the future.

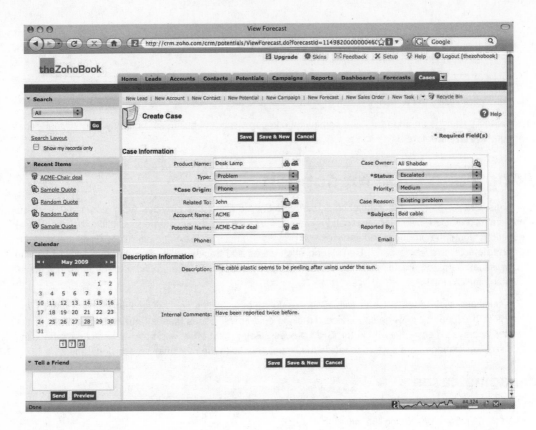

Figure 10-52. Creating a case

2. Click **Save** to store the case information.

Later you can just open the case and edit **Solution Information** to store any solutions found for the issue. This will be a great reference for the future when something similar happens to other customers. You can also assign tasks, events, and attachments to the case in order to register all necessary steps taken toward solving the issue (Figure 10-53).

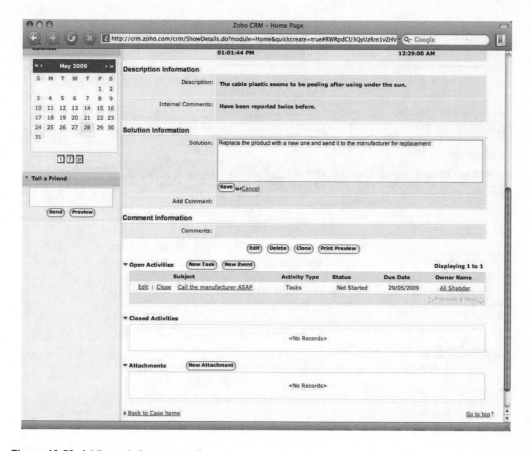

Figure 10-53. Adding solutions to a task

Managing solutions

CRM features a `Solution Management` module (tab) that acts like a knowledge-base system. In other words, every solution you define in the system is actually a **scenario** in which a question (the issue) about a product is asked and an answer (the solution) is given. As the solutions database grows, it gets more powerful because it holds all the possible issues a customer can face using the product/service of your company.

Solutions module can play an important role in customer service because they provide the customers with the quickest and best answers to their questions.

> *Cases should not be mistaken for solutions since they are tickets assigned to the issues raised by the customers. Cases need to be distributed to the concerned people and solved as quickly as possible. Solutions, on the other hand, are the reference database of the customer service department.*

To create a new solution, follow these steps:

1. Click New Solution on either the main menu bar or the Solutions tab. You can also import solutions from an external file.
2. When you create solutions from scratch, fill in the Solution Title, Question, and Answer fields. Try to enter clear, brief questions and answers (Figure 10-54).

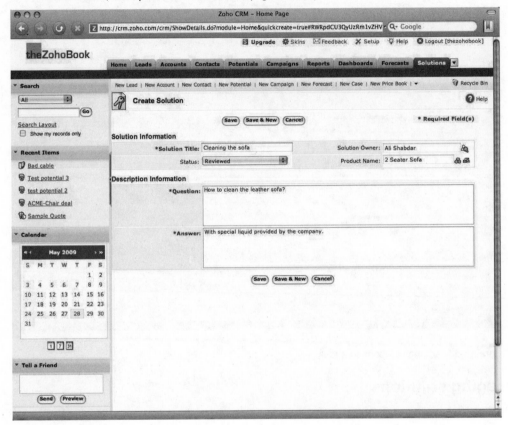

Figure 10-54. Creating a solution

3. Fill in **Product Name** so you (and other staff) will know what the available solutions are for a specific product.
4. Click **Save** to store the solution in the system.

More CRM

There are still many features of CRM that I didn't cover in this chapter. They either fall into the advanced topics or are not included in the free edition.

However, before I wrap this chapter up, I'll briefly talk about the **Reports** tab, the **Dashboards** tabs, and the **Home** page. The reason I saved them for the end of the chapter is simply that you have now entered enough data in the system that you can see these modules in action.

Reports

One of the main reasons you store data in a system is to be able to generate various reports based on the information. CRM provides you with a set of ready reports for all modules as well as powerful report-creating tools for you to make new reports.

All modules in CRM (leads, campaigns, and so on) feature a **Reports** section in their tabs. For example, if you open the **Quotes** tab and select the **Quotes by Accounts** report below the quotes list, a relevant report will open in which you can view, sort, and filter the results (Figure 10-55).

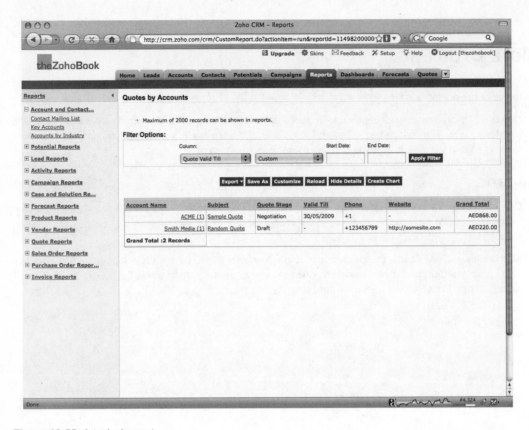

Figure 10-55. A typical report

You can also customize the report or save it as a new report for later use. It is possible to export the report to CSV, XLS, and PDF documents in order to send it to others or import it into other applications (such as third-party accounting software).

Charts are very powerful tools for showcasing numerical data in a pleasant and more understandable way. You can create different types of charts for all the reports in CRM:

1. Open any report, and then click Create Chart on the Reports tab.
2. On the next screen, select a chart type, and set the axis accordingly (Figure 10-56).

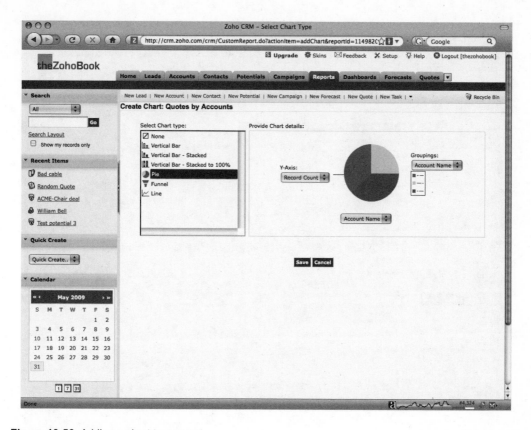

Figure 10-56. Adding a chart to a report

3. Click **Save** to continue. You will be redirected to the report page where the chart is placed on top of the report.

> *Charts will not be included in the exported report, so you will need to regenerate them in the application in which you import the reports.*

In general, the **Reports** tab is your reporting command center. All reports, including the ones created by you, are listed and categorized by module. You can create new reports and edit and customize them (Figure 10-57).

Figure 10-57. The `Reports` tab

A nice feature in the `Reports` module is the ability to create report folders. These folders allow you to organize different reports as per your business requirements and optionally limit the access to them. For instance, a folder called `Auditors` can contain only the reports concerning the auditors with exclusive access given to them so others can't see the reports in that specific folder.

`Report Scheduler`, on the other hand, offers a great tool to generate automatic reports and send them to a list of recipients by e-mail at certain intervals. All you need to do is select the report, the interval, and the recipients. The report will be generated based on the latest data available in the system and will be sent to the recipients automatically. As an example, you can set up a monthly sales report to be sent to your boss and not worry about her nagging you about delays when compiling it manually.

Dashboards

To put it simple, the `Dashboards` tab visualizes everything happening in CRM for you. Via charts and funnels, you can see comparisons, patterns, and trends in all stages of your business in real time. Check what marketing campaign gave you a better feedback, which products are selling better, and so on, by just having a quick look at the visuals.

Dashboards is divided into different sections (components) that represent different data channels (Figure 10-58). The charts (including the funnels) are Adobe Flash objects displaying the data dynamically. As a manager or a supervisor, you can keep this page open all the time to see what is happening in your organization/department.

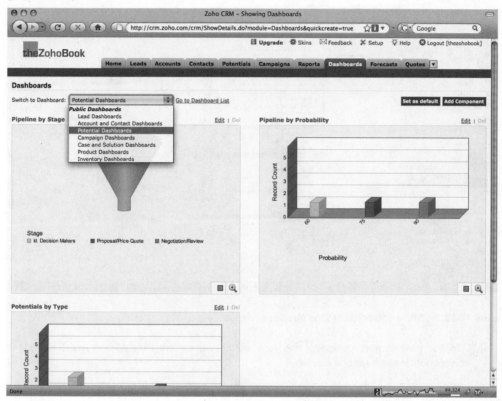

Figure 10-58. A typical **Dashboards** tab

You can add more components to the **Dashboards** tab based on your requirements:

1. Open the Dashboards tab, and click Add Component.
2. In the Add Component form, choose between a chart or a table for Component Type.
3. Enter something in Component Name, and then select which Source Report item you want to use to get the information from (Figure 10-59). Click **Next** to proceed.

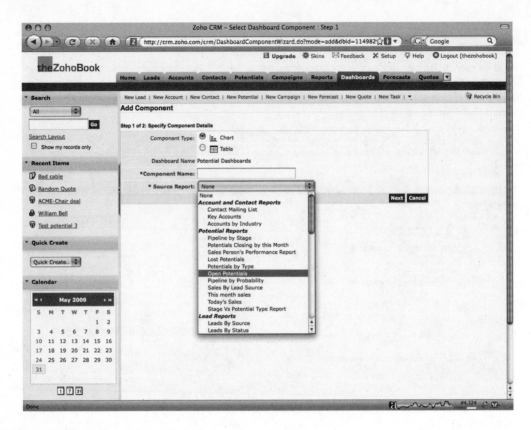

Figure 10-59. Adding a component to the **Dashboards** tab

4. On the next screen, customize the look of the component, and click **Finish** to add the component to the **Dashboards** tab.

You can rearrange the **Dashboards** tab by dragging and dropping components. Once you find your ideal setup, you can rely on it to be your main monitoring portal of CRM.

Home

The **Home** tab is the first page to open when you log in to CRM. It contains components of the different modules, showing the latest data records for each one (Figure 10-60).

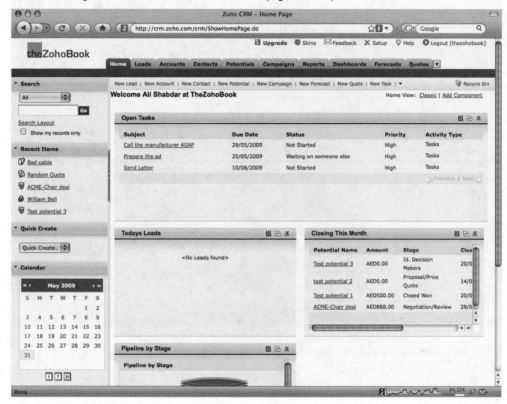

Figure 10-60. The **Home** tab

Unlike the **Dashboards** tab that shows you comparative reports and the different trends, **Home** provides you with shortcuts to different objects such as open leads, recently issued quotes, potentials, and so on.

It is possible to customize the **Home** tab by clicking **Add Component** and putting new views to the system right at your fingertips. Just select which module you want to add, and after a quick configuration, the component will be added to the page. It is then possible to drag and drop components to reach the optimum interface (Figure 10-61).

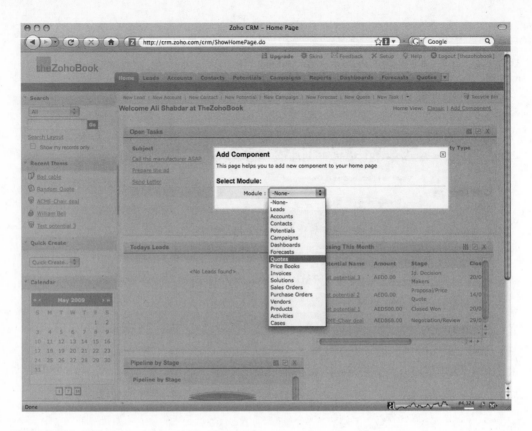

Figure 10-61. Adding a component to the home page

Getting help

If, based on this quick-start chapter, you have found Zoho CRM useful for your business, you can get more help through the official documentation, which is pretty extensive. You can open the help page by clicking **Help** on the top of the screen or by visiting http://zohocrm.wiki.zoho.com/ directly.

Asking your question in the dedicated forum page in the Zoho forums is another way to get answers quickly. Visit http://forums.zoho.com/Zoho-CRM, check what other people are saying, and ask your questions. Search for your question first. It was probably asked by somebody else before you, so you might get the answer quicker that way.

Last but not least, if you are new to customer relationship management, there are numerous books and articles around. Check out Amazon (http://www.amazon.com) for some recommendations, or consult a CRM expert.

Zoho also offers a basic crash course in CRM at `http://www.zoho.com/crm/new-to-crm.html` that might come in handy. The more you learn about customer relationship management techniques, the more effectively you can use Zoho CRM.

Summary

CRM is the first business-only application of the Zoho suite covered in this book, and in this chapter you got a good idea of what Zoho CRM is and what it can do for your business.

It can easily manage the business processes in the marketing, sales, and support departments. Although it might not be the answer to everything, it can definitely perform well under real and difficult situations.

With CRM, you will be always supported by timely updates and on-demand help from Zoho Corp. It is a perfect example of a successful SaaS application.

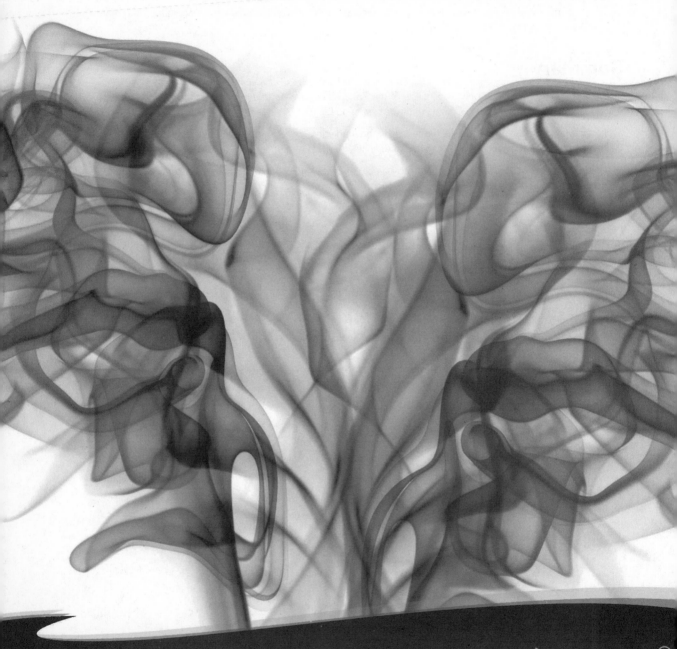

ZOHO®

Work. Online

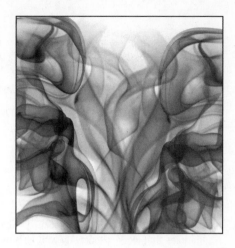

Chapter 11

Manage Your People

As your organization grows, the number of employees you have will grow too. It is easy to manage a few people's administrative tasks, but the more people you hire, the more you'll need to implement a human resource (HR) management system.

Using such a system is important not only for the current staff of the company, but it also plays a vital role in extending the workforce in a healthy and manageable manner. Implementing HR management solutions can help you minimize the administrative workload as well as give you better tools when you recruit new people.

For smaller organizations with 50 people or less, hiring an HR professional or even outsourcing the HR tasks will suffice. For a bigger firm, however, you'll often need to form an HR department consisting of HR managers and officers to control the entire HR process.

In general, the following tasks fall into the category of HR:

- Managing the job openings
- Finding the best job candidates
- Recruiting new employees
- Providing training facilities for the employees (which could be part of HR development in bigger organizations)
- Managing the employees' benefits, compensations, policies, and so on
- Staying in sync with the accounts department regarding payments

It is obvious that different organizations have different scopes of work, but this list is common ground for most HR departments.

> To get started with the concepts related to human resources, check out Wikipedia at *http://en.wikipedia.org/wiki/Human_resources*, About.com at *http://humanresources.about.com*, and the Free Management Library at *http://managementhelp.org/hr_mgmnt/hr_mgmnt.htm#anchor538960*.

In this chapter, you'll get started with Zoho People, a powerful cloud-based human resource information system (HRIS) that provides you with a powerful platform to address most (if not all) of your requirements in the HR department.

Zoho People

As a member of the Zoho business suite, Zoho People is a capable HRIS that provides businesses with a rich yet compact solution to tackle their day-to-day HR issues. It is also a great tool for recruitment agencies that work extensively with HR, offering them an online system to manage their businesses on a highly available and expandable platform.

People comes in different packages (subscriptions) for various businesses; the essential difference is the size of the organization it can manage. Supporting organizations of 10 to 1,000 employees, People is able to host small to medium businesses (SMBs) comfortably.

> To learn more about the current definition of SMB, visit *http://en.wikipedia.org/wiki/Small_and_medium_enterprises*.

People offers a set of tools to help companies more easily manage their HR departments by eliminating the unneeded paperwork. It does the paperwork for you so you can focus on how to manage your people better.

In general, People features the following:

- A complete HRIS containing interactive employee management tools, business workflows, and customizable HR-related forms
- A full-fledged recruitment management system
- A staffing solution based on the previously mentioned systems

In this chapter, you'll find out what People can do for you and if it can play a role in your organization.

> *Before we continue, let me mention that discussing the science of HR is an advanced topic and beyond the scope of this book. The aim is to just get you started with People to see whether it is the right tool for you. Then (with enough knowledge in HR itself), you can set up your organization in People to start using the tool for real.*

In this chapter, you'll use the free subscription, which is limited to 10 employees (including yourself). It is recommended that you start with a free account; then, after you have made sure People is the HR solution for your company, you can upgrade to any paid plan at any time.

Although many smaller companies with 10 or fewer employees can still benefit from the features of People for free, the fact that People is software as a service (SaaS) allows you to pay as you go. This means that you pay only for the number of users (licenses) you need at the moment based on the available packages—10, 25, or 50 users.

Getting started

The gateway to access People is `http://people.zoho.com`. You can also set up Zoho Business to contain a shortcut to People for easier access. Log in with your Zoho account, and click the `Close` button for the alert box that appears in order to move to the next section. I'll go through the basic features here, so there's no need to take the video tour at this point.

Configuring People

When you first start People, it opens the `Getting Started` tab for you to quickly configure the system. The next time you log in, it will automatically open the dashboard, which is the command center of People.

Before you start using People, you have to configure some settings. Ignore the `Getting Started` tab, and click `Settings` on the top menu bar so you can make some changes.

> *Before you start configuring People, you should know that you might see some terms and features you are not familiar with. Just read on, and you will learn more about different features as you go.*

Once the `Settings` page is opened (Figure 11-1), you can see different options divided into sections with shortcuts made accessible in the sidebar.

Figure 11-1. Modifying the security settings

Configuring security settings

People follows a role-based security model, meaning each user has a role (such as `Manager`) in the system and is allowed to do only the tasks permitted in the boundaries of that specific role.

Roles are managed in the `Security` section of the `Settings` page. This page opens by default and contains the available roles listed and ready to be customized. There are four predefined roles in the system: `Admin`, `Director`, `Manager`, and `Team manager`. Apart from the admin role, which has all privileges and can't be edited, you can modify the permissions of other roles to match your requirements. You can grant or deny each role's access to almost every tiny piece of the system, which emphasizes the importance of security and access control for People.

> Before editing any permissions, note that there is no *OK* or *Submit* button, and the settings take effect immediately as you change them. This might affect other users who are logged in at the moment, so you need to be extra careful while changing the security settings.

To review the permission settings, click `Edit security` for the `Director` role. The permissions are divided into four tabs:

- **`Form permission`**: There are many forms, such as exit forms used when someone leaves a company, that are used in different stages of HR workflows. You can set `View`, `Edit`, and `Delete` permissions for each available form in the system for the corresponding role, such as `Director`, here (see Figure 11-2).

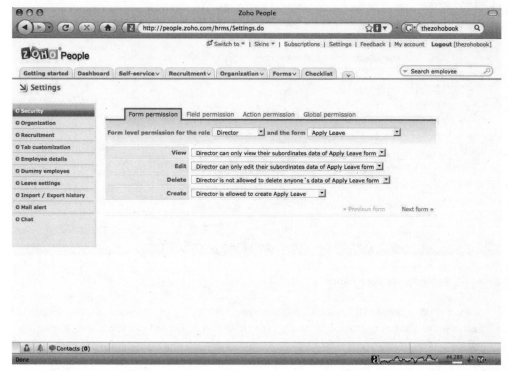

Figure 11-2. Form permissions

- **`Field permission`**: Every form consists of data fields that store pieces of information about a form added to the system. `EmployeeID` and `Housing Allowance` are examples of fields belonging to the `Benefit` form. You may set whether a role can have only view access or view and edit access to each field throughout a specific form (Figure 11-3). For example, you can set whether a `Director` can view all fields in the `Benefit` form but can only edit the fields related to allowance.

Figure 11-3. Applying field permissions

- **Action permission**: Each form has a set of actions that can be limited for specific roles. These actions are **Import**, **Export**, **Mail alert**, **Form Customization**, and **Embed form** (Figure 11-4). You may enable or disable each action of every form for a particular role. For example, a **Director** can import an asset form but not export data from it.

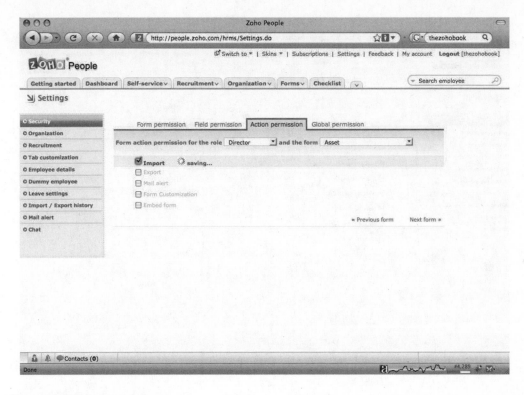

Figure 11-4. Action permissions

- **Global Permission**: As the title implies, the **Global Permission** tab contains the permissions a role has or doesn't have system-wide, meaning these permissions are not specific to a form or a field but to the entire system. For example, a **Director** can see the information of the department (**Department Data**) but not the **Dummy employee** (Figure 11-5).

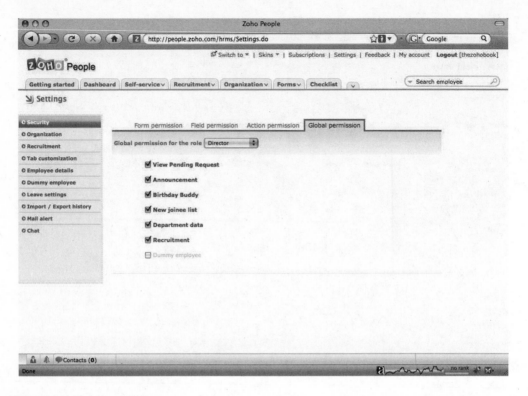

Figure 11-5. Global permissions

As I mentioned, you can create new roles and later assign them to the different employees. Creating new roles is basically done by cloning an existing role and then updating the permissions according to the requirements of the new role.

> It is a good idea to first modify one of the existing roles (**Team member** is a good candidate) according to the general policy of the company. Then, when you clone new roles, it will be quicker to modify them for that specific role.

1. In the **Security** section, click **Create Role**. The **New role** dialog box opens.
2. Enter a name in **New role name**, and then select which existing role it should be cloned from (Figure 11-6).

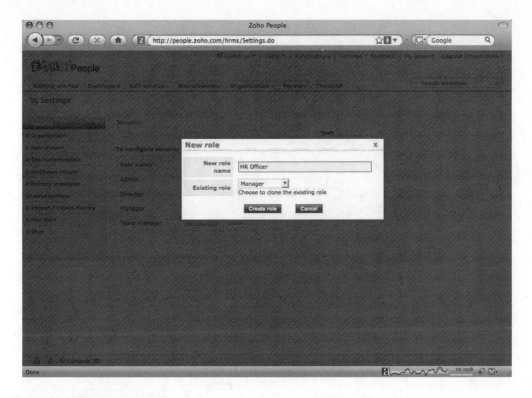

Figure 11-6. Creating a new role

> 3. Click **Create Role**.

After you have created the role, review and possibly edit the permissions as per your requirements.

Configuring organization setting

In this section, you should enter the basic information about your organization. This information appears in different parts of the system, such as on printed documents, so it is important to enter it carefully.

> 1. On the **Settings** page, click **Organization** in the sidebar. The **Organization settings** page opens (Figure 11-7).

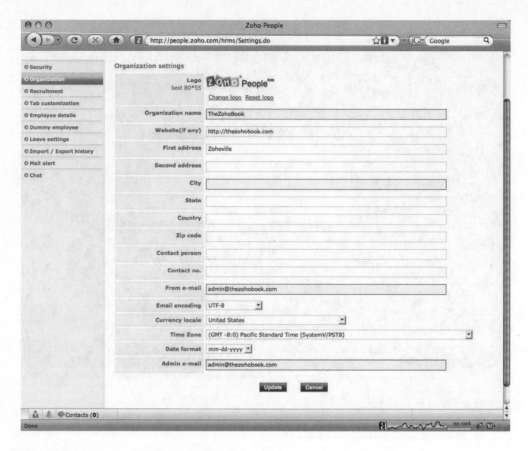

Figure 11-7. `Organization settings` page

2. Fill in `Organization name`, `Website`, and the relevant text boxes for the company address.
3. Enter a new `From e-mail`, because this will be the e-mail address that is visible (to the sender) in all outgoing messages.
4. Fill in the `Currency Locale`, `Time Zone`, and `Date format` fields properly.
5. Fill in the `Admin e-mail` field. All administrative messages to users will be sent from this address.
6. Click `Update` to apply the changes.

Configuring the tabs

You might want to change the user interface (UI) by adding or removing different tabs or by reordering them. You can also enable/disable different sections of each tab. Removing tabs (or the underlying sections) will just make them invisible and is good when you don't need certain features in your business model. Showing only what you need is a good practice and eliminates confusion as well as security issues.

To add/remove tabs and sections, follow these steps:

7. Open **Tab customization** on the **Settings** page (Figure 11-8).

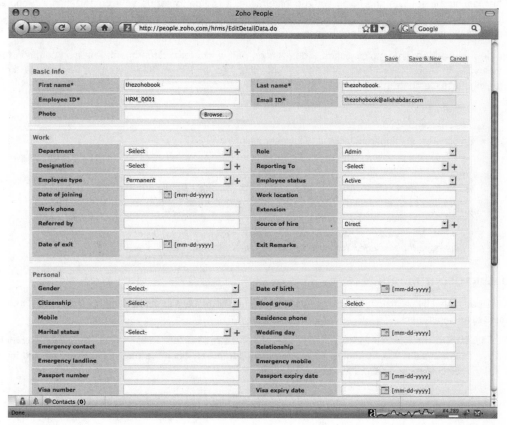

Figure 11-8. Customizing the tabs

8. To make a tab visible, select it in the **Unselected tabs** list, and click **Add selected items** (the first blue arrow).
9. To remove a tab (making it invisible), select it in **Selected tabs** list, and click **Remove selected items** (the second blue arrow).
10. Click **Save** for the changes to take place.
11. To reorder tabs, drag and drop them up and down in the list below the form.
12. Click **Enabled** for each section (on the respective tab) to disable it. Clicking **Disabled** will make them visible again.

Implementing the current organization

After touring the settings and doing some configuration, it is time to set up your organization in People. You can do this by implementing the organizational hierarchy of your company inside People by defining departments, designations, and employees.

In the real world, every employee has a designation and works for a department. It is also common for employees to report to a higher-ranking staff member. To implement this hierarchy, you should start creating these elements in People:

- Departments
- Designations
- Employees, starting from highest to lowest ranking

> It is important not to mistake designations with roles. **Designations** are the official positions each employee holds in the company, but **roles** define the permissions these employees have throughout the system. For instance, you can have two employees, **Sales Manager** and **Marketing Manager**, who hold two different designations, but both have the **Manager** role with the same set of permissions.

Creating departments

Let's get started by creating the departments first and then continue with other elements. Here you'll create the **Sales** department:

1. Move the mouse pointer over the **Organization** tab, and select **Organization ▶ Department ▶ Add** (Figure 11-9). You can alternatively open the **Organization** tab and then select **Related Links ▶ Add department**.

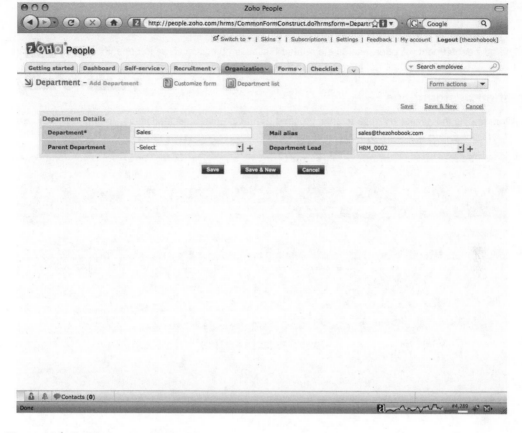

Figure 11-9. Creating a new department

2. Enter `Sales` for `Department`.
3. Enter sales@yourcompany.com in `Mail alias`. This will appear in the e-mail messages sent from this department.
4. Leave `Parent Department` because there is none at this point. You should use it when applicable.
5. Select your account, identified as `HRM_0001`, in `Department Lead`. This should point to the real department lead, in other words, the head of the sales department.

> *You can add a new department lead by clicking the + button next to it. This opens a window allowing you to create a new employee on the fly and then assigns it automatically as the department leads.*

6. Click `Save` to create the department.

> *Clicking Save & New instead of Save creates the department and then refreshes the form for you to enter a new department immediately.*

The new department will open with all the related business objects such as job openings, employees, and so on. Ignore this page until you learn more about other elements later in this chapter.

Creating designations

After creating the necessary departments, proceed with adding the designations, such as **Sale Manager**, **HR Officer**, **Junior Accountant**, and so on.

1. Select **Organization ▶ Designation ▶ Add**. The **Add Designation** form opens (Figure 11-10).

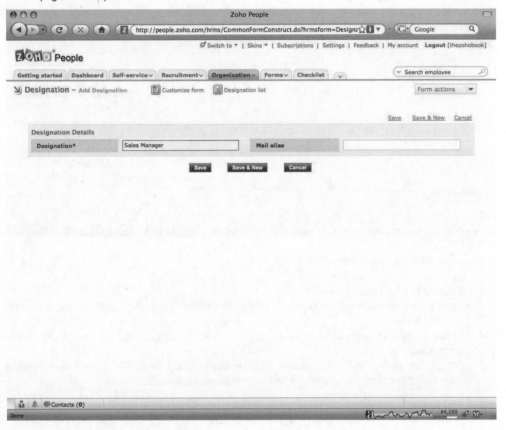

Figure 11-10. Creating a new designation

2. Enter **Sales Manager** as **Designation**.

3. Click **Save** to add the designation. You can click **Save & New** to add more designations right away.

Creating employees

The last step in creating the organizational chart of a company is creating the employees. Each employee has a designation, works for a specific department, and reports to a supervisor or manager.

To add employees, follow these steps:

1. Select **Organization ▸ Employee ▸ Add**. The **Add Employee** form loads (Figure 11-11).

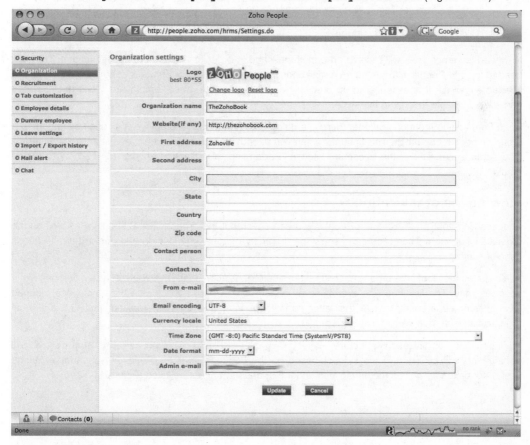

Figure 11-11. Adding a new employee

2. Fill in **First Name**, **Last Name**, **Employee ID**, and **Email ID**. People adds a default code in the **Employee ID** field (incremental, starting from **HRM_0001**), but you can come up with any coding system that suits you.

3. Click **Browse** to upload an employee photo.

4. Under the **Work** section, set **Marketing** for **Department**, and set **Sales Manager** for **Designation**.

5. Set **Manager** for **Role**. This sets the permissions based on the role-based security rules defined (see "Configuring security settings" earlier in this chapter).

6. Set **HRM_0001** for **Reporting To**. Then proceed with filling in the other fields, as shown in Figure 11-11.

> *Note that it is possible to add new items to all fields with a green plus icon next to them. Simply click the icon, and proceed with creating a new item. It will be then added to the list to be selected, such as a new department.*

7. Click **Save** once you are done.

Newly added employees will receive an e-mail message in order to activate their subscriptions. They will need to log into People with the same e-mail address of the invitation or create a Zoho account using that specific e-mail ID. It is essential to do precisely as instructed; otherwise, employees won't get activated and will not be able to log into the system.

Apart from adding them one by one, there is a quick way of entering all employees at once by importing a group of them in one batch. This is useful when you already have a list of employees stored in a database or a spreadsheet. Check the upcoming section "Performing miscellaneous tasks" to see how to import employees.

Reviewing the organization

After creating your organization in People, you can check out the organizational structure as well as the organizational chart. There you can review the hierarchy of your organization and perform modifications once needed.

As similar as they look, the organization structure and organization chart give you a different perspective of your company. The first one lists everything by department, allowing you to see the employees grouped into different departments, while the latter sorts them in a tree by their ranking, just like a normal organizational chart. It's less fancy, though.

To open the organization structure, select **Organization ▸ Organization Structure**. All departments will be listed in the sidebar based on the defined hierarchy. For every department, some basic information as well as the employees under that department will be listed (Figure 11-12).

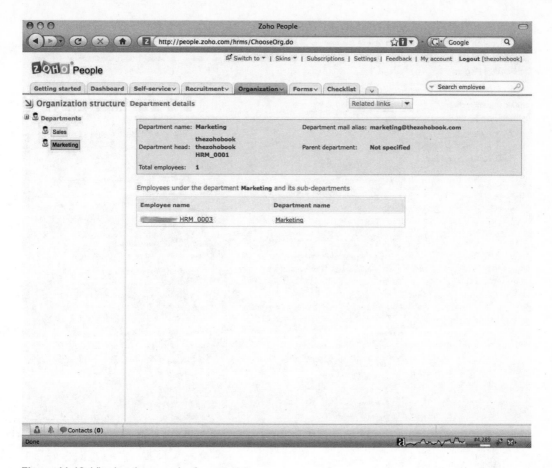

Figure 11-12. Viewing the organization structure

Clicking the name of a listed employee will open a details page where you can view and edit the employee information.

If you want to reorder departments or move one department under another, you can simply drag and drop departments in the sidebar.

Similarly, selecting `Organization ▶ Organization Chart` will open the organizational chart where employees are listed in a hierarchical order. Clicking an employee will open a details page where you can view and edit various information fields.

To reorder an employee in the chart, you can simply drag and drop it under the suitable node (Figure 11-13).

Figure 11-13. The organization chart

Managing human resources

People includes various modules needed to manage human resources. Our focus here is on the following four modules:

- **Employee** portal: Manages the employees' database and the related information
- **Self-service** tab: Provides employees with an interface to perform basic HR tasks themselves
- Organization chart: Gives a tree view of the structure of your organization, which we covered earlier (see "Reviewing the organization")
- **Checklist**: Designs and enforces the business processes and custom workflows

All these modules, combined with other features (such as role-based security), make otherwise time-consuming administrative tasks much easier, allowing the HR personnel to focus more on the personnel than the paperwork. After learning the basic features of the HRIS here, you will be able to put these modules in practice in a way that addresses the issues of your own organization.

Using the Employee portal

You have already used some of the features of the `Employee` portal. You added new employees and listed the current employees for viewing and editing, but the `Employee` portal has more to offer.

As you can see in Figure 11-14, all tools in the portal are accessible in the `Employee` page (`Organization ▶ Employee`).

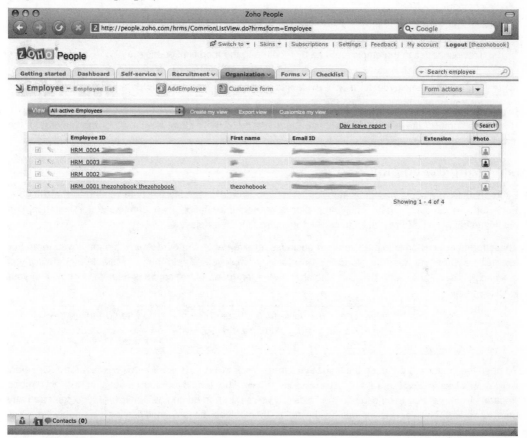

Figure 11-14. A list of employees

Using the `Employee` portal, you can do the following:

- List, view, and search for employees
- Add new employees by clicking the `AddEmployee` button on the top of the list or by selecting `Form actions ▶ Add`
- Manage the current employee database
- Manage the dummy users, which are special type of employee you will learn about later in this chapter
- Customize the employee form to make sure the data collected for employees matches your company policies
- Configure mail alerts to help you monitor the slightest movement in the system, such as informing you by e-mail whenever a new employee is added
- Track changes in the employee data by monitoring the modification history
- Import and export data from and to various formats
- Embed the employee form in a web site in order to interact with data in a private or public environment without exposing the whole system

I'll discuss some of the previously mentioned features that I think might be useful for the majority of the users in the upcoming sections. You can then dig into the help pages (see "Getting help") to find your way.

Customizing the employee form

Every module in People has dedicated forms for you to add or modify the data related to that module. Each form resembles a data entity that stores related information in a database. For instance, the employee entity has a form that contains all data stored for an employee.

These forms are customizable as per your business requirements, but our focus is the employee form. For example, if you never keep the `Wedding Day` for any employee (a field that is available by default), you can simply disable that field. You can also change the language of the captions (labels) to show it in your local language.

> *Customizable forms are one of the powerful features of People. They often eliminate the need to bring third-party software developers in or buy other applications, especially when all you need is just few tweaks in the data model.*

To open the customize page, on the `Employee` page, click `Form actions ▶ Customize` form. Or select `Organization ▶ Employee ▶ ~ Customize Form`. The employee form opens in the edit mode (Figure 11-15). Although you can see the fields (as you saw when adding an employee), you can't add any data to fields. This place is for editing the fields themselves, so any modification you apply here will somehow affect the way the employee forms works. Simply put, be careful.

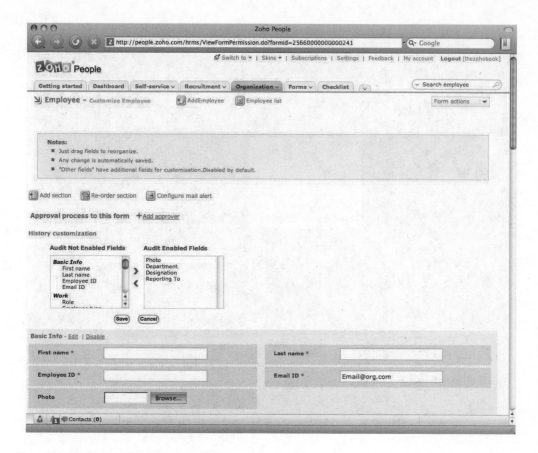

Figure 11-15. Customizing the employee form

There are three buttons below the `Notes` yellow box:

- `Add section`: Creates new section in the pages
- `Re-order section`: Brings different sections up and down
- `Configure mail alert`: Adds and modifies e-mail alerts for activity monitoring

For instance, suppose you want the `Work experience` section in the form to be placed between `Work` and `Other fields`. Follow these steps:

1. Click `Re-order section` to open its dialog box (Figure 11-16).

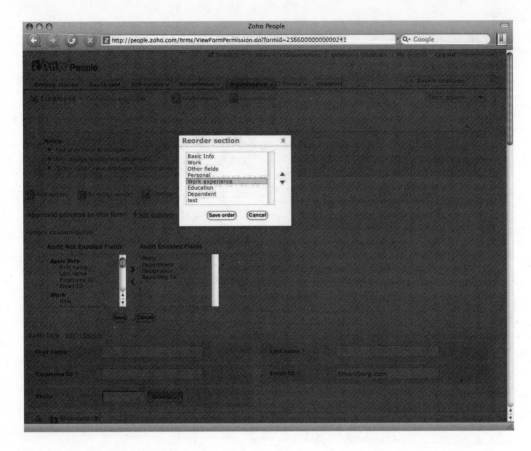

Figure 11-16. Reordering the sections

2. Select `Work experience`, and then click `Move up` (the blue arrow heading up) until the section reaches the right position in the list.
3. Click `Save` to apply the changes.

Below these buttons there is a link, **Add approver**, by which you can specify who will approve this form. This means every time a new employee is added or an existing one gets modified, it should be first approved by the approver before the changes shown in the system.

1. Click **Add approver**. The form will scroll down to the bottom, `Configure Approval Process`.
2. Choose a ranking by selecting `Any Admin`, `Reporting Manager of the Employee`, or `Allow the Employee to choose any employee as approver` (Figure 11-17).

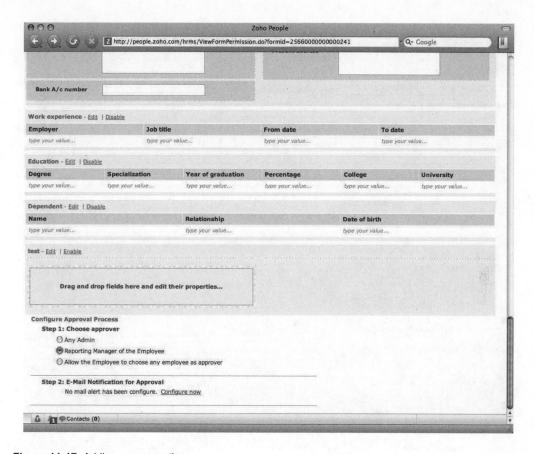

Figure 11-17. Adding a new section

3. Scroll back to top of the form, and check that the approver is added.

The next section is `History customization`. You will specify here which fields of the employee form should be audited during any modification process. This means every time an authorized user, such as the HR officer, edits the information of an employee, the old value of auditable fields will be stored in the history in order to track the changes over time. You can later access the history and check who changed what data in the employee database and when they changed it.

All the fields listed under `Audit Enabled fields` will be audited on every modification, so you should add important fields whose audit is important to this list.

1. In the `Audit Not Enabled Fields` list, select the field(s) you want to be audited.
2. Click `Add selected items` (the first blue arrow) to add the fields to `Audit Enabled Fields` (Figure 11-18).

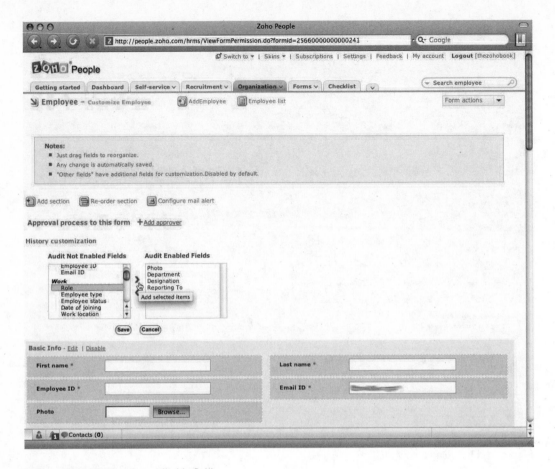

Figure 11-18. Editing the auditable fields

3. Click **Save** to apply the changes.

The last step in editing the employee form is to modify the fields themselves. You can do the following:

- Move fields inside or between different sections by dragging and dropping
- Edit the features and behavior of the fields including the following:

  - Field label (caption)
  - Validation methods (see below for more on validation)
  - Field length in characters (how many characters it can accept)
  - Editing the field description

- Enable or disable fields to make the visible or invisible

To edit a field, follow these steps:

1. In the `Customize employee` page, under `Basic Info`, find `Email ID`. Then move the mouse pointer over it so it gets highlighted and a context menu appears (Figure 11-19), and click `Edit this Field`.

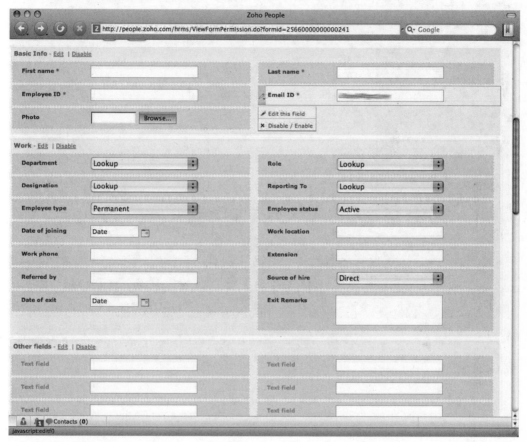

Figure 11-19. Editing a field

2. In the `Editing Email ID` dialog box (Figure 11-20), change the `Label Name` field to `E-mail Address`.

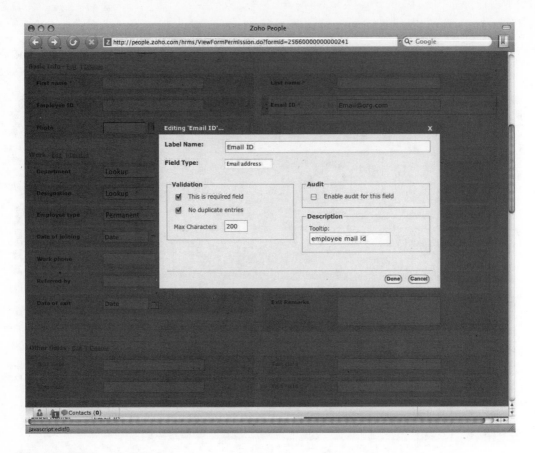

Figure 11-20. The edit dialog box

3. Select **This is required field**. This particular field becomes mandatory for a new employee to be added to the system. If the user leaves e-mail empty in the form and tries to save the form, People will show an error message indicating the problem.

4. Select **No duplicate entries**. This will make sure that each e-mail address—which is a globally unique address—can be entered only once in the system, meaning no two employees can have the same e-mail address. If you try to enter duplicate values, you will receive an error message.

5. Click **Done** to close the dialog box.

Validation, as you saw in steps 3 and 4 of the walk-through, is in fact an effective way of controlling the user input to make sure the data entered in the system is as clean as possible. People offers powerful form validation. For example, for an e-mail type field, you can't enter nonvalid e-mail values, such as a number, or it will show you an error message asking you to fix it.

When you say the e-mail field is required and there should be no duplicate entries, the value entered for each employee will be checked against these constraints. If it passes the test (along with other validations throughout the form), then the form will be submitted, adding new or updating the existing employee in the system.

You can see different methods of validation in other applications, such as when you fill out a sign-up form on a web site or when you enter billing information while shopping online. Validation minimizes the data entry mistakes.

Changing e-mail alerts

A good way to monitor the activities happening in the system is to generate e-mail alerts sent to the concerned personnel when certain data gets updated in the system. This feature is disabled by default and needs to be activated. Then you can start configuring the alerts for different forms.

To customize an e-mail alert, follow these steps:

1. Open the `Settings` page by clicking `Settings` on the top menu bar.
2. Open `Mail alert`, and select `Enabled`. This will show a success message, meaning the e-mail alerts are now enabled (Figure 11-21).

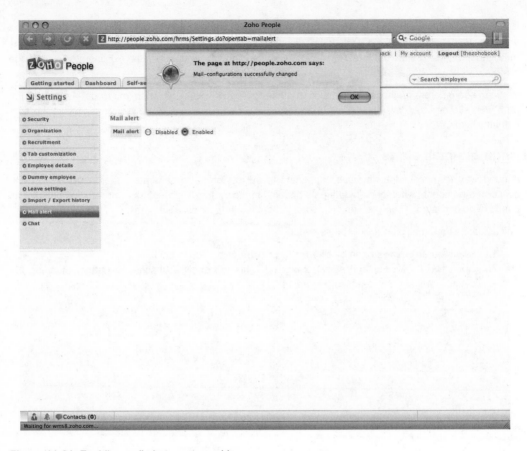

Figure 11-21. Enabling mail alerts system-wide

3. Select **Organization ▸ Employee ▸ ~ Customize Form** to customize the e-mail alerts for the employee form.
4. Click **Configure mail alert**. You can also select **Organization ▸ Employee ▸ Mail alerts**.

On the **E-mail Notifications** page, all possible actions applicable to the form are listed:

- Creating new employee
- Editing existing employee
- Deleting employee
- Approving employee
- Rejecting employee

E-mail alerts should be added for each action. For example, if you add an alert under **Create** actions, it will be sent when a new employee is created.

For each action, there are templates. **Templates** are predefined structures that, when People composes e-mail messages, are used as the basis of the message body. You can create new templates for different actions. For example, the `Alert to All` template (which exists by default) contains the structure of the alerts sent by the system when a new employee is created.

To get more familiar with these templates, let's create one for when an employee is removed from the system. People will compose (based on the custom template) and send an alert to certain people informing them about the recent event.

One of the strengths of the templates is that you can merge active content by using tags in the message body of a template. Suppose in your e-mail that you want to mention the name of the employee who has just been removed (because that's why the recipient received this e-mail). Since this is an automatic process and you (or other users) don't compose the message manually, you need a way to tell People to place the right name in the message body. That's where tags come in handy.

A **tag** is basically a field name that is specially formatted (surrounded by special characters) to be added in the body text so the system understands that it should replace the tag with the extracted value. Tags in People are created with a ${} surrounding the field name, so if you want to place the first name of an employee, it will be ${First name}. Similarly, you can place ${Last name}, ${Department}, and so on.

> Note that tags are case sensitive and must be entered correctly. *${Firstname}*, which is missing a space between *First* and *name*, is not a correct tag in People and will result in badly formatted e-mails.

1. Click `Add action for delete`. The `Add Action` dialog box appears (Figure 11-22).

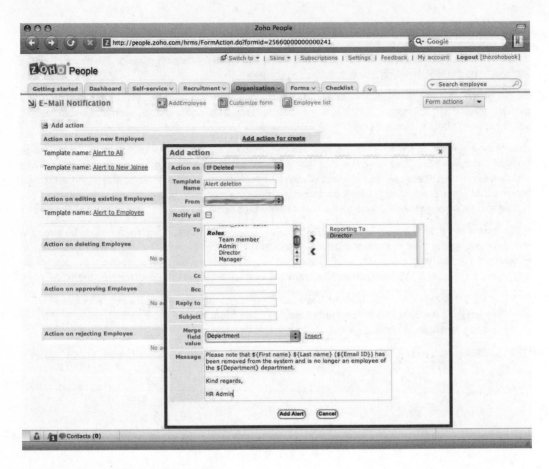

Figure 11-22. Creating a new e-mail alert

2. Set **Action on** to **If Deleted**.
3. Enter **Alert deletion** in the **Template Name** box.
4. Specify the recipients in **To** by adding them from the list box in the left to the one in the right side. Recipients are usually concerned managers or higher-ranking supervisors.
5. Enter a short but descriptive subject.
6. Type in the message, as in Figure 11-22, and note the tags inside the message body. You can either type the tags or select them **from Merge field value** and then click **Insert** to place them at the cursor. This list is a good reference and helps you enter the tags correctly.
7. Click **Add Alert** to create the template.

Once created, the template will be listed below the respective section. Newly added templates are enabled by default, meaning the e-mail alert will be generated and sent for the action it belongs to. You can, however, click **Enabled** and disable it. It will turn to **Disabled**.

Exporting employees

Although you will work with the employee information inside People and rarely need another application, sometimes it is useful to export the employee data to an external file. One of these occasions is when you want to generate custom reports other than what People offers. You can export the entire employees database to XLS, CSV, or TSV files. It is also possible to export it directly to a spreadsheet in Zoho Sheet.

1. Select **Organization ▸ Employee ▸ Export data**.
2. In the corresponding dialog box (Figure 11-23), select the intended format for the exported information.

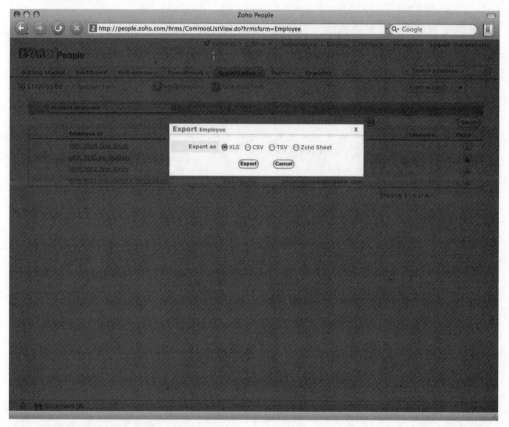

Figure 11-23. Exporting the employees database

3. Click **Export** to proceed.

Exporting data is a sensitive action and can compromise the data's security, so you need to be extra cautious and assign proper permissions in the role-based security settings. It should be limited to the authorized personnel only.

Importing employees

Suppose there is a list of employees stored in another application and you want to save time importing everyone on the list at once without going through the hassle of entering the records one by one. The good news is that you can add multiple employees through importing.

> *Note that you can import employees as many as your quota allows. This means that if you have six licenses left in your account, you can import only six employees, or you need to upgrade before import.*

1. Select **Organization ▶ Employee ▶ Import data** (Figure 11-24).

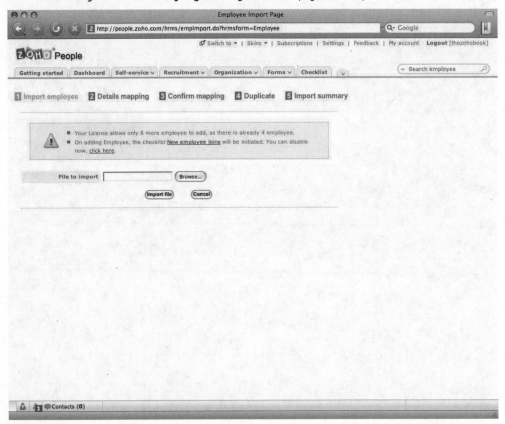

Figure 11-24. Importing employees from an external file

2. Click **Browse**, and select the file containing the list of the employees.
3. Click **Import file** to start the procedure.
4. In the **Details mapping** area, map the fields for People to know where to look for the data in the source file. Then click **Next** to proceed.

5. If there some fields in the employee form that were not mapped for any reason, you will receive a message saying that those fields won't be imported. Click **Import** to proceed, or click **Previous** to go back and fix the issue.

6. Once the imported data tested for duplicate entries, it will list the duplicate employees who already exist in the system. Select **Skip** or **Overwrite** for each entry. You can also select **Skip All** if you want to skip all duplicates or **Overwrite All** if you want to overwrite them all.

7. Click **Update**. This will finish the import and take you to the **Import summary** page.

8. Check the import summary for the added, updated, and skipped records. Click **view import history** to list a history of all imported (and exported) tasks, or click **View Organization chart** to check the lasted changes.

Embedding employee form in a web site

Sometimes you'll need to put the employee form on the Internet (or an intranet) in order to give public (or limited) access to the information without exposing the other parts of the system. All you need to do is embed the form in a web page that has public or private access.

Embedding a form can also be used to extend a third-party application where you can mix different forms in a web site to achieve a different business target. For example, you can embed an employee form in a payroll application for easier data access.

To embed a form, follow these steps:

1. Select **Organization ▸ Employee ▸ Embed in website**.

2. In the embed dialog box, click the little arrow (in the same row as **Customize Look**) to show the customization tools (Figure 11-25). You can change the look and feel of the embed form here.

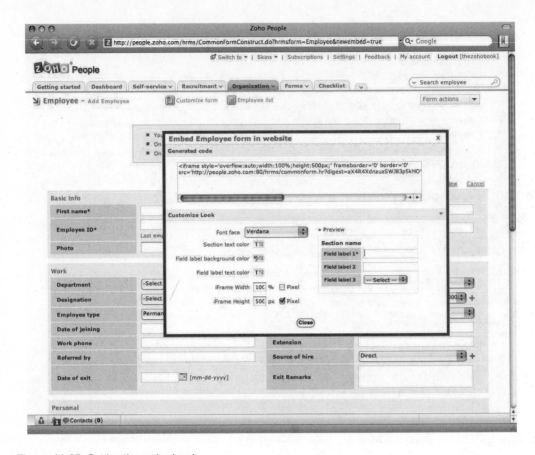

Figure 11-25. Getting the embed code

3. Change the values to match the web page in which the form will be embedded.
4. Copy the code snippet in the `Generated code` box, and paste it in the source code of the target web page.

> *If you are not familiar with HTML and web development, you should consult an expert before doing anything.*

Managing dummy users

The last topic I'll discuss in the `Employee` portal is the **dummy user**. Dummy users represent the temporary employees (those who are contract based) who don't need to log into the system but should be stored in the system for HR reasons. This saves you money (in your Zoho subscription) since Zoho charges only for the users with login permission.

> *Dummy employees don't receive any e-mails from the system, so you will need to send important messages to them manually, such as by using Zoho Mail.*

To add a dummy user, follow these steps:

1. Select `Organization ▸ Employee ▸ Add dummy user`.
2. In the `Add dummy user` dialog box, fill in `First Name` and `Last Name` fields (Figure 11-26).

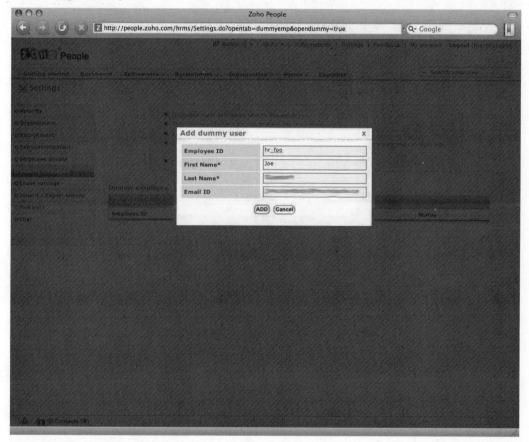

Figure 11-26. Adding a dummy user

3. Click `ADD` to proceed.

The new dummy user will be listed in the `Dummy employee` section in the `Settings` page, not the employees list.

Whenever you need to make a temporary employee (dummy user) permanent, you should use the migrate tool. This tool turns the dummy user into a normal user without losing any data related to that user.

1. Open the **Settings** page, and select the **Dummy employee** section.
2. Find the employee you want to make permanent, and click **Migrate** (in front of its listing).
3. In the **Migrate employee** dialog box, check the employee information, and make the necessary modifications (Figure 11-27).

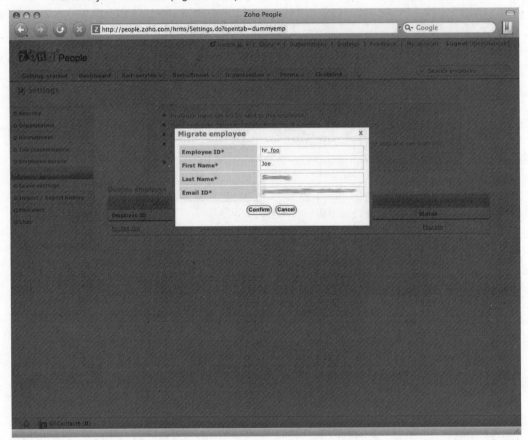

Figure 11-27. Migrating a dummy user

4. Click **Confirm** once you are done.

An invitation e-mail will be sent to the migrated user for joining the system. After a migrated user joins People successfully, Zoho will issue a new license, deducting it from the available ones in your subscription.

Managing the Checklist

HR management involves many tasks, and the people involved often need a task manager to make sure they don't miss a step. People has a handy module, `Checklist`, that automatically generates the list of actions needed for each procedure and adds them to a task list. It also helps you define the various business workflows in the system.

For task management, `Checklist` knows (based on the workflows defined) what tasks must be done for each action (for example, adding a new employee) and who is responsible for such tasks. Then it adds the corresponding task to the concerned personnel's `My tasks` section (Figure 11-28). Users can use `My tasks` as a reference in daily business.

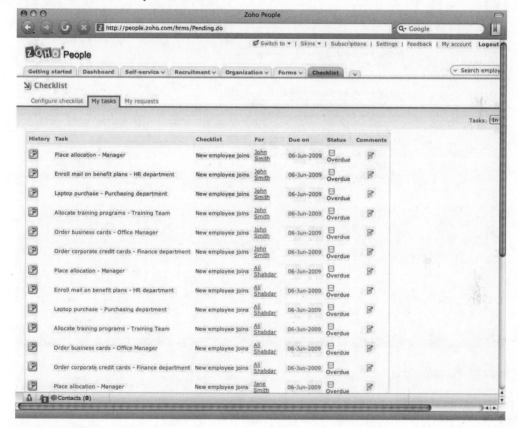

Figure 11-28. `My tasks` in the `Checklist` tab

Configuring checklists

The real power of the `Checklist` module is when you define the business workflows enforced by the HR department. It allows you to define every single step that needs to be taken for actions such as joining new employees, issuing a leave form, and so on, along with the people involved in the different stages of the process.

Open the `Checklist` tab and then the `Configure checklist` subtab. By default, the only available checklist is `New employee joins`. It defines the steps to be taken once for a new employee to be added to the system. Click the checklist to open it (Figure 11-29).

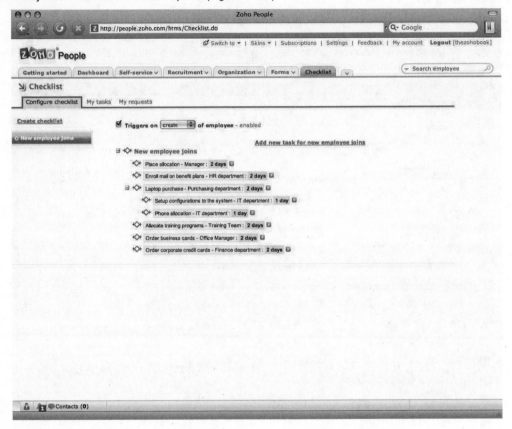

Figure 11-29. Configuring the checklists

`Triggers on` indicates when this checklist will trigger and could be set to `create`, `edit`, `approval`, and `rejection`, which are all different stages of hiring a new employee.

You can change the order of checklist items by dragging and dropping them up and down in the list. The item list is a hierarchical tree that itself defines the logic of how different checklist items are related to each other.

Clicking each item will open the modification dialog box in which you can edit that item.

Creating new checklist items

Apart from editing the existing checklist items, you can add new items. For example, to include an extra step for a new employee, you can add an item informing the IT department to create an e-mail account for the newly joined person:

1. Click **Add new task for <CHECKLIST>** (where **<CHECKLIST>** is the name of the checklist, such as **employee joins**).

2. In the **Add checklist** dialog box, enter **New Email address** in **Item label**. Then add a brief description (Figure 11-30).

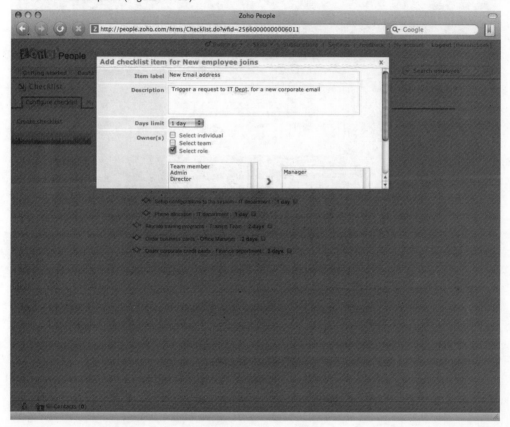

Figure 11-30. Adding a new task to a checklist

3. Select **Select role** as the owner, and add **Manager** to the list on the right side. This will set any user with the **Manager** role as the owner of this item. It could be any suitable role, though.

4. Click the **Add checklist** item to finish.

The new item will be added to the items tree, and you can arrange its position by dragging and dropping.

Creating checklists

After enhancing the available checklist, you might ask, "What if I wanted a new checklist?" The answer is you can create as many checklists as you want. To create a new checklist from scratch, follow these steps:

1. On the `Configure checklist` subtab, click `Create Checklist` (Figure 11-31).

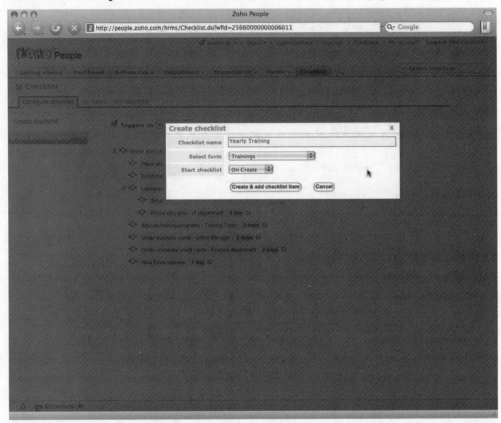

Figure 11-31. Creating a new checklist

2. Enter a name in `Checklist name`.
3. Select the target form for which the checklist is defined.
4. Select the action triggering the checklist in `Start checklist`.
5. Click `Create and add checklist item` to proceed.
6. Add necessary items to the checklist as you saw in the previous section.

Working with HR tasks

The last tab in the **Checklist** module is **My requests**, which contains the list of the tasks (in workflows) concerning the current user. These tasks were generated as a result of triggering different checklists throughout the system whenever a relevant action, such as approving a leave form, has occurred (Figure 11-32).

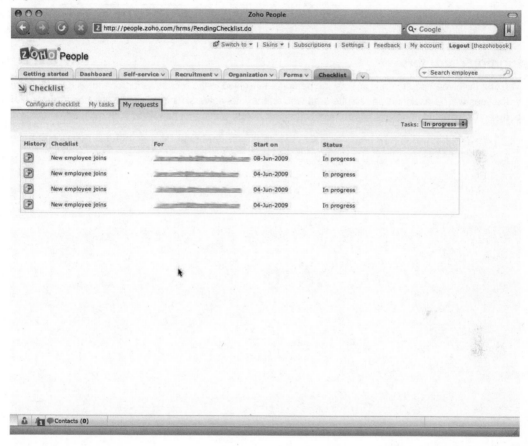

Figure 11-32. My requests

Clicking the **History** button of each item will open the respective checklist with all tasks listed for you to trace the process. Use **Checklist** extensively in order to manage the workflows and implement an effective task management system.

Recruiting people

Recruiting new people is an important part of the HR management workflow. From the moment a job opening is posted until the time a new employee is hired, many steps must be taken carefully. As you might have expected, People provides you with the necessary tools needed for the job, allowing you to easily manage and monitor the whole process.

> *For a quick overview of the recruitment procedures in People, check* `http://people.zoho.com/hrms/images/recruitment_flow.gif`.

Assigning recruiters

The first thing you need to do is specify the personnel involved in the recruitment procedures. One or more employees will be assigned as recruiters as well as the interviewers. They could be the same people for both recruitment and interview, or you might choose different personnel based on your company structure.

1. Open the **Settings** page (click **Settings** on the top menu bar to open this page), and open the **Recruitment** section (Figure 11-33).

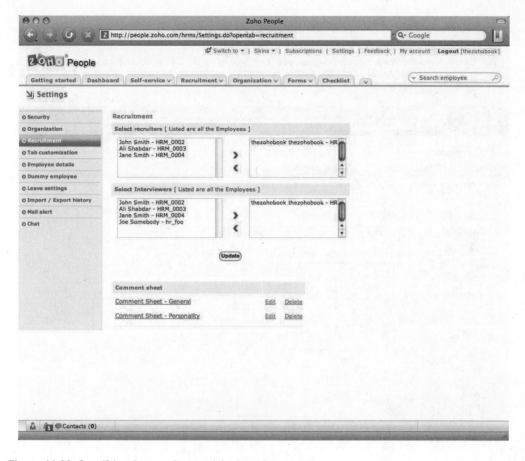

Figure 11-33. Specifying the recruiters and the interviewers

2. Assign the recruiter(s) by selecting them in the list under **Select recruiters** and clicking **Move selected items to right**.
3. Similarly, select the interviewer(s) under **Select Interviewers**.
4. Click **Update**.

Posting job openings

The next step is to post the job openings. This could be done directly from within the system or through an embedded form in a web site.

> *Posting jobs in an embedded form is especially suitable for the recruitment agencies, allowing various companies (clients) to post openings.*

To post an opening directly, follow these steps:

1. Select **Recruitment ▸ Job opening ▸ Add**.
2. Enter the necessary information, as you see in Figure 11-34. **Posting title** and **Hiring Manager** are the only mandatory fields, but you should enter enough information to make the posting valuable.

Figure 11-34. Posting a job

3. Click **Save** to submit the posting.

The new opening will be listed under **Recruitment ▸ Job openings ▸ List**. The status of the new opening is **Waiting for approval** (Figure 11-35), meaning it should be first approved by the relevant person in order to be visible in the system. You (as a concerned person) will see a list of pending jobs on the **Dashboard** tab.

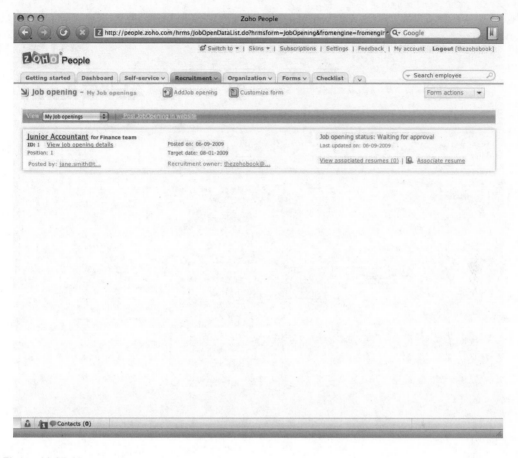

Figure 11-35. New opening

Adding résumés

Another essential task in the recruitment process is to deal with résumés (or CVs). You can add them to the system directly or through a résumé submission form embedded in a web page.

To add a résumé directly in the system, follow these steps:

1. Click **Recruitment ▶ Resume ▶ Add**. The **Add Resume** page opens (Figure 11-36).

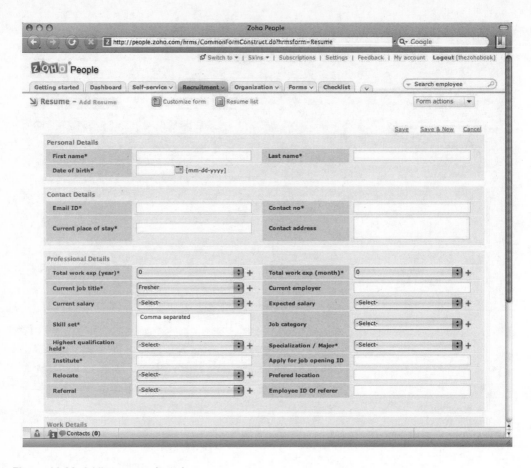

Figure 11-36. Adding a new résumé

2. Enter the detailed candidate information in the form, making sure you fill in all the mandatory fields (those with an asterisk and in red). You can also upload a CV document to be attached to the résumé entry for later reference.

3. Click `Save` to create the résumé.

Once a résumé is added, it will be listed in the `Resume Pool` listing (`Recruitment` ▶ `Resume` ▶ `List`), where all the posted résumés are stored.

Working on résumés

Now let's return to the job openings. Select `Recruitment` ▶ `Job openings` ▶ `List`, and click the title of the job opening you just posted in the preceding section. As you can see in Figure 11-37, this is where you can manage the opening.

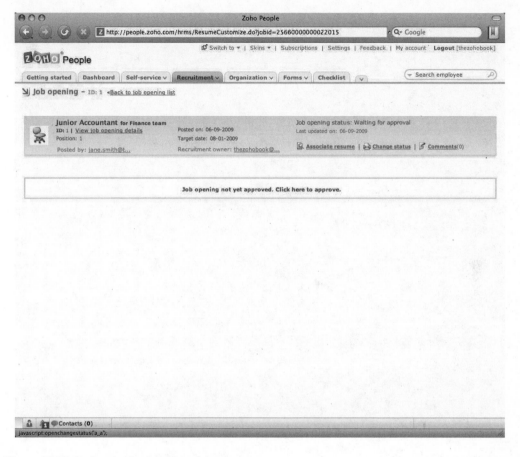

Figure 11-37. Performing basic task on job openings

Suppose you are the person in charge of approving (or disapproving) the job openings. Once you open a pending job opening (check the dashboard), you will either approve or disapprove it after reviewing, so everybody knows it is a genuine posting.

You may also attach résumés to a job opening by clicking **Associate resume**. A single opening can have multiple résumés for the perfect candidate to be selected from in the later steps.

It is also very important for you and other colleagues at the HR department to know at what state a certain job opening is. Click **Change status**, select the latest status such as **Approved** from the list, and then click **OK** (Figure 11-38).

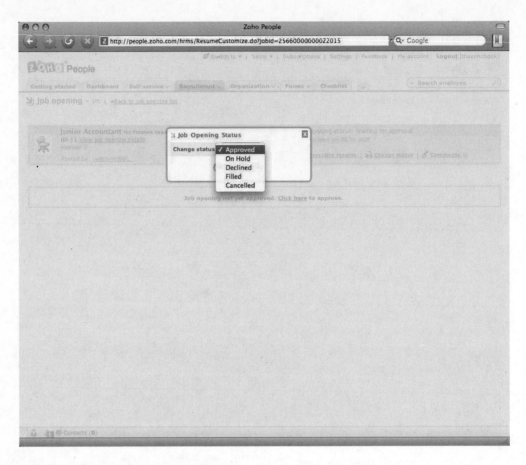

Figure 11-38. Changing the status for an opening

As mentioned, to associate candidates with a job opening, you should assign their résumés to it. Click `Associate resumes` for the opening, and then select the desired item(s) from the list of available résumés. Click `Associate directly` to immediately assign the selected item(s) to the opening.

Hiring people

After assigning résumés, you can start the hiring process. Once an opening is approved with a résumé associated, there will be five tabs opening below it: `All`, `Shortlist`, `Interview`, `Offer`, and `Hire` (Figure 11-39).

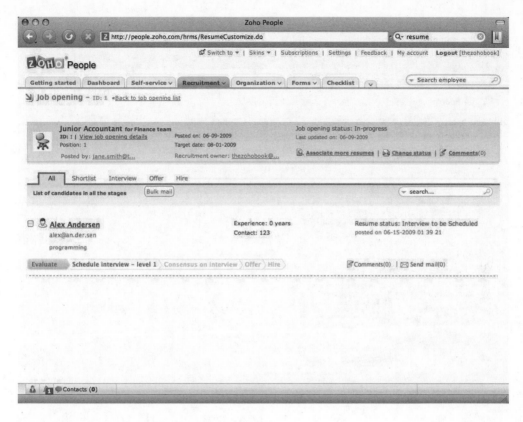

Figure 11-39. Listing the candidates for a job opening

Let's focus on the `All` tab in here, which has the button you need to start the hiring process: `Evaluate`. By clicking `Evaluate`, you will take the opening forward throughout the different stages of the hiring process. A typical hiring process involves passing through all the steps mentioned in the tab: `Evaluate`, `Schedule interview - level 1`, `Consensus Interview`, `Offer`, and `Hire`.

> Try all the steps of the hiring process carefully to see it in action.

Accepting online job postings

Apart from adding job openings and résumés through the résumé form, it is common to allow candidates to post their résumés online (such as in the careers section of your company web site). To create an interface available to the candidates easily that is connected directly to the HRIS, People provides you with the ability to embed the job openings in your web site.

1. Click `Recruitment ▸ Job opening ▸ Post in website`. You can see all job openings are listed.

2. Click **Create Job Opening in Website**. This will open a form in which you can customize the settings of the posting (Figure 11-40).

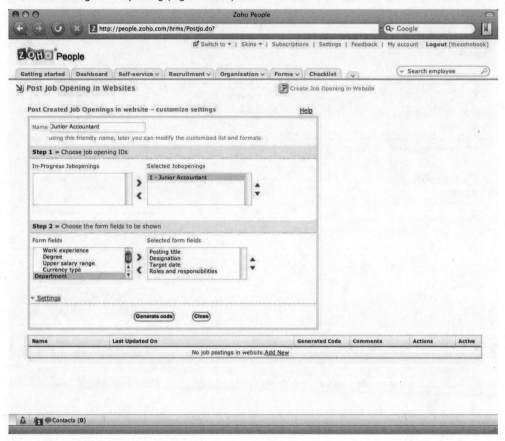

Figure 11-40. Creating an online job posting form

3. Enter a meaningful name in **Name**.
4. Under **Step 1**, select an entry (or more) from the **In-progress Job-openings**, and click **Add selected items** (the first blue array).
5. Under **Step 2**, select the fields you want to be shown in the web site from **Form fields**, and then click **Add selected items**.
6. Click **Generate Code** to get the HTML code snippet (Figure 11-41).

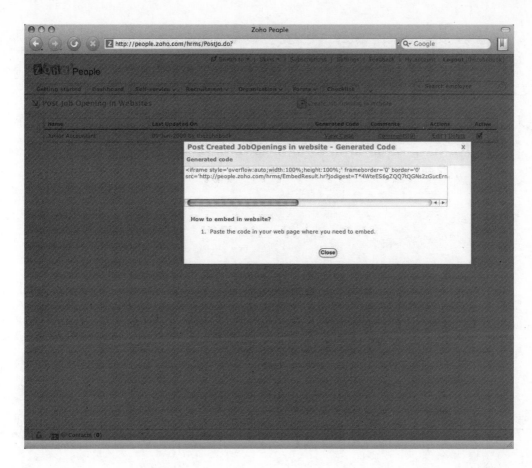

Figure 11-41. The generated HTML code

7. Copy the code and paste it in the body (source) of the target web page.

Figure 11-42 shows a sample web page containing the job posting. It is created with the code generated in the last walk-through.

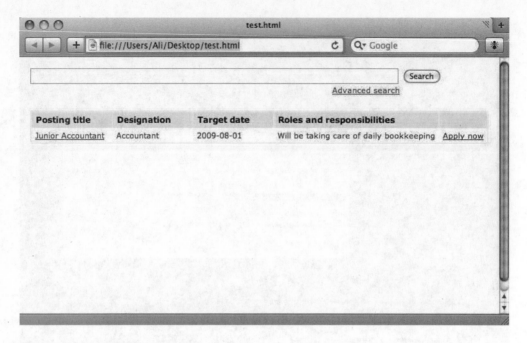

Figure 11-42. A sample job posting page

Once a candidate lists the openings in the career page of your web site and finds an interesting opening, clicking the title will open the online résumé submission form (Figure 11-43). Résumés submitted through this form will directly go to the résumé pool, so the concerned people can approve or disapprove them accordingly. You can also find them attached to the corresponding job opening, making it easier to follow up with the incoming information.

http://people.zoho.com/hrms/commonform.hr?digest=ySUs*6td*dz4dN8Yq5V8A.p3GjtwgsEc&T=757575&lay=FFFFFF&ti...

Personal Details

First name*		Last name*	
Date of birth*	[mm-dd-yyyy]		

Contact Details

Email ID*		Contact no*	
Current place of stay*		Contact address	

Professional Details

Total work exp (year)*	0	Total work exp (month)*	0
Current job title*	Fresher	Current employer	
Current salary	-Select-	Expected salary	-Select-
Skill set*	Comma separated	Job category	-Select-
Highest qualification held*	-Select-	Specialization / Major*	-Select-
Institute*		Apply for job opening ID	1
Relocate	-Select-	Prefered location	
Referral	-Select-	Employee ID Of referer	

Work Details

Employer	Job title	From date	To date
type your value	type your value		

Add more

Educational Details

Degree	Specialization	Year of graduation	Percentage	College	University
type your value	type your value	type your value	type your value	type your value	type your value

Add more

Upload Resume

Attach resume	Choose File no file selected	Additional Info	Max 250 characters

Save

Figure 11-43. The online résumé submission form

585

More Zoho People

Now that I've discussed the basics of People, I'll continue with few more topics that are definitely worth talking about. The `Self-service` tab is where the employees can serve themselves using various tools available for them and thus skip bugging the HR department for every small task.

The staffing subsystem is made of other modules to help the recruiting agencies and gets to be mentioned in this chapter, because it could be interesting for many companies.

Self-service

All employees (if given enough permissions) can open the `Self-service` tab and perform basic tasks by themselves to save time for the HR department. From updating personal information to filling various forms, all can be done in few simple steps from within the system.

Accessing the employee profile

Employees can view and update their own profiles according to the role-based security permissions.

1. Open the `Self-service` tab, and click **My Profile** in the sidebar. Your own profile opens (Figure 11-44).

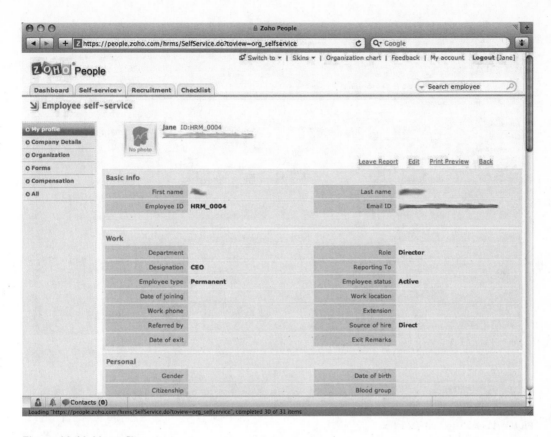

Figure 11-44. My profile

2. Click **Leave Report** to open a dialog box with the full details of your vacation.
3. Click **Edit** to modify the information in your profile. This might not be available for all employees.

Submitting general forms

Other HR tasks can be done in the **Self-service** module too. Filling and submitting various forms is one of the time-consuming (and often confusing) tasks employees and the HR department deal with on a daily basis.

Using the **Forms** page, you have access to all HR forms needed for a typical organization. Forms for leave, training, travel expenses, and so on, are all accessible here, and you can submit them without even walking over to the HR department.

Open the **Self-service** tab, and click **Forms**. A list of common HR forms will appear (Figure-45).

Figure 11-45. The forms section

4. Click **Add** in the **Apply Leave** section.
5. Fill in the leave form, and click **Save** to submit it to the HR department (Figure 11-46). Somebody from the HR department will (I hope!) get back to you after receiving your request.

Figure 11-46. Applying for a leave

Another point about forms is that just like the employee form (as you saw in the **Employee** portal), all other forms in People feature the following tools:

- Customization of form elements and behavior
- Mail alerts for different actions of the form
- Security settings
- Import and export data
- Embedding in the web sites

Simply move the mouse pointer on the **Forms** tab, and select the destination from each form, such as **Forms ▶ Holiday ▶ Customize form**.

Submitting compensation forms

Another area quite useful for the HR department is the **Compensation** page. This page contains links to manage the **Performance Appraisal**, **Asset**, **Benefit**, and **Salary** forms. It is actually very similar to the **Forms** module but contains a different set of information focused on financial data. You may add data, list the data added, and customize these forms as you normally do in other forms.

Open the **Self-service** tab, and click **Compensation** to open the compensation page (Figure 11-47). Note that access to commands such as **Add** is subject to the permissions granted to the current user in the role-based security and should not be available for all users.

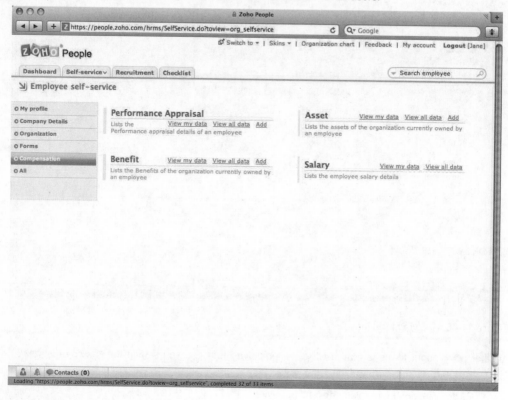

Figure 11-47. The **Compensation** page

Using People for recruitment agencies

Staffing companies and recruiting agencies are two other types of businesses that can harness the power of People. Considering the nature of such businesses that deal with candidates, résumés, interviews, and so on, People can be a one-stop out-of-the-box solution. It can play an important role in the daily workflow of such organizations featuring a rich set of features in conjunction with other Zoho applications such as CRM. As you know, it is a highly available (cloud-based), elastic (expandable based on your needs), and economic solution (pay as you go).

I won't discuss the staffing facilities of People in here. Just know that using the staffing facilities, you can manage the following:

- Clients
- Job openings
- Résumés
- Online forms
- Interviews
- Offers and hires

Additional features such as customizable forms, role-based security, and workflow checklists will make you almost independent, barely needing another application to run your staffing business.

Getting help

For the HR newbie, there are endless online and printed resources to learn about HR management. Just search the Internet for *HR* to see how many results you will get.

If you already are an HR professional, you will find your way easily after reading this chapter, but if you still need more information about People, you can always check the help pages at the following locations:

- **Employee** portal at http://www.zoho.com/people/hris.html
- **Self-service** module at http://www.zoho.com/people/employee-self-service.html
- Recruitment management modules at http://www.zoho.com/people/applicant-tracking-system.html

> *You need to log out to see the help links on http://people.zoho.com. There is no dedicated help page for People.*

Zoho forums at http://forums.zoho.com/Zoho-People and Zoho blogs at http://blogs.zoho.com/category/people have valuable information helping you with day-to-day tips and tricks.

Finally, practice is the key to become savvy in People. Test all modules, especially the ones you will use in your organization. You can do this on your personal account and move to prime time when you feel confident.

Summary

People is a powerful HRIS suite that offers a collection of rich features for businesses of all kind, which at some point deal with the human resources. Of course, entrepreneurs, small office/home office (SOHOs), and small to medium businesses (SMBs) might not find it as exciting because of the lower number of employees they manage. But any business of ten or more people can use People to make HRM a pleasant and painless job.

You saw how to run an HRIS with managing the employee database, customizing the related forms, and doing more employee-oriented tasks in the **Employee** portal. The **Checklist** defines and enforces business workflows, while the recruitment, being another vital part of the HRIS, takes care of recruiting new human resource.

The **Self-service** tab gives access to employees to perform some of the basic HR tasks themselves saving time for themselves and the HR department.

With different modules covering almost all aspects of the HR management, People does a good job for what it is made for. You can use it as it is or customize it according to your business needs and expand it at any time by upgrading to a better plan.

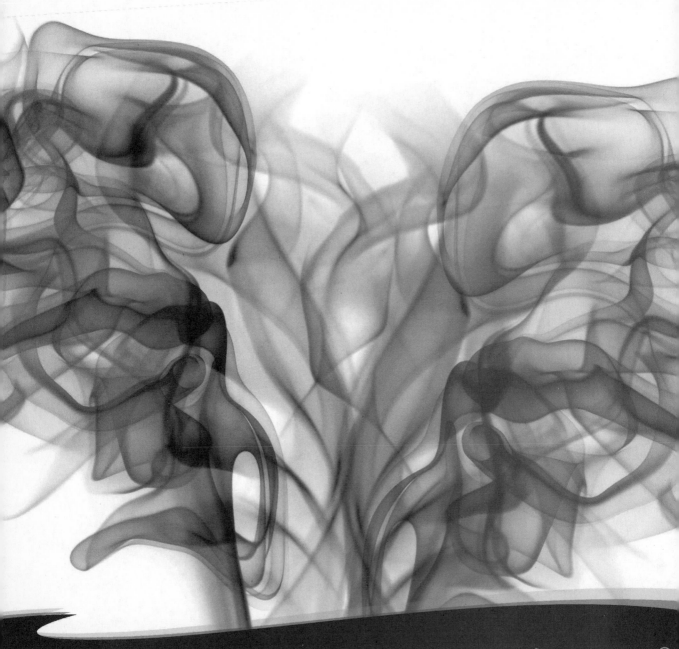

ZOHO®

Work. Online

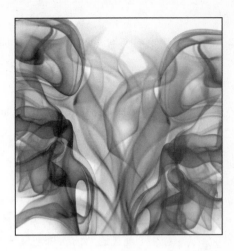

Chapter 12

Manage Your Invoices

The Merriam-Webster dictionary defines *invoice* as "an itemized list of goods shipped usually specifying the price and the terms of sale." When companies sell products or services to their clients, the final piece of paperwork they send to the customer is the invoice. It lists all the items sold, along with the unit price, total price, grand total, discount and tax information, and so on. Addressed to the customer, it also contains the terms and conditions of payment.

I am sure you have dealt with invoices at least a few times in your life, as a seller or a buyer. Although most invoices contain basically the same types of information, different companies create various formats for their invoices.

Many software packages are available with invoice management features. Customer relationship management (CRM) systems, accounting packages, and inventory systems all include some sort of invoicing facility. There are also many applications, often web-based, that are specifically for creating, sending, and tracking invoices. Such applications are quite suitable for SMBs or entrepreneurs who actually don't need the heavyweight packages like CRM solutions. They just need to create and send professional-looking invoices to their clients in order to get paid on time. Or they might need to implement a dedicated invoicing solution when the current software doesn't offer invoicing features.

In this chapter, you'll meet Zoho Invoice, the cloud-based invoicing solution from Zoho. Invoice, with its powerful features and easy-to-use UI, is a perfect choice for an invoicing application. It runs in the cloud and easily interacts with other applications such as Zoho CRM, Excel, and so on.

Invoice is suitable for freelancers, businesses of all sizes, and service providers. Using Invoice, you can do the following:

- Issue quotes and estimates
- Accept online payments
- Generate live reports and monitor the system in real time
- Work with multiple currencies
- Use and create customized estimates and invoice templates
- Back up your data and keep it secure online

If you issue five or fewer invoices per month, you can start using Invoice for free right away. As your requirements grow, you can upgrade to a paid subscription.

> *Check out the pricing page at http://zoho.com/invoice/invoice_subscription_pricing.html for more information.*

Getting started

Invoice is quite easy to use. All you need to do is perform a quick configuration, and you can start using it right away. To open Invoice, log on to http://invoice.zoho.com. It is also accessible from within Zoho Business. The sign-in page appears, where you can sign in with your Zoho account (Figure 12-1).

Figure 12-1. Invoice login page

After you have logged in, since it is your first time using Invoice, you must fill in some basic data on the `Quick Setup` page (Figure 12-2).

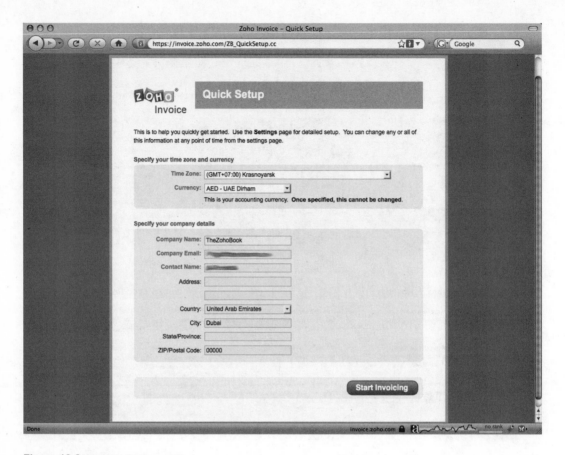

Figure 12-2. `Quick Setup` page

1. Set your local time zone in `Time Zone` as well as the default currency in `Currency`.
2. Enter relevant information in `Company Name`, `Company Email`, and `Contact Name`. The other fields are optional, but it is good practice to enter the address too, because you are going to use this information later.
3. Click `Start Invoicing` to proceed.
4. On the next page, `Welcome to Zoho Invoice`, select `Don't show at startup` to permanently skip this page in the future.

> *The next time you log in, you will be automatically redirected to the* `Home` *tab, which you'll take a closer look at later in this chapter.*

Configuring Invoice

Before you start creating invoices, it is important to perform some basic setup (beyond the quick setup you just did) to make sure everything works the way it should.

Configuring the company profile

First, let's make sure your profile is complete. This information will show up on quotes and invoices and therefore needs to be entered carefully. You entered the basics on the **Quick Setup** page, but there is still a bit more information needed.

1. Click **Settings** on the link bar (on the top of the page). The **Company Profile** page opens (Figure 12-3).

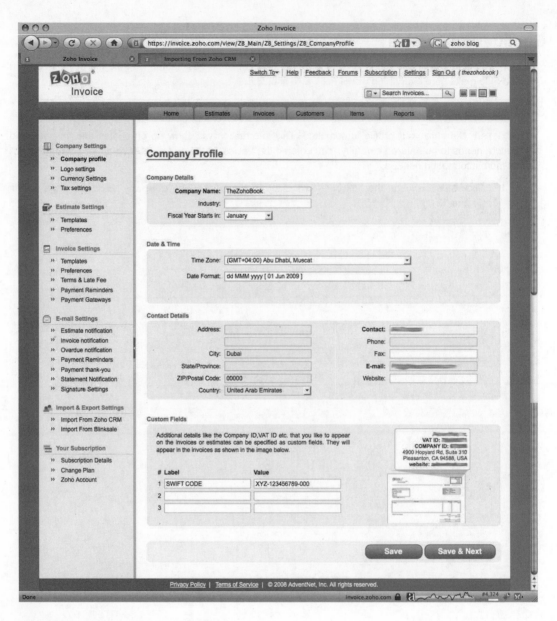

Figure 12-3. Setting up the company profile

2. Check out the information, and enter the relevant data.
3. Use the `Custom Fields` section if you need to have more information appear on estimates and invoices. A bank code printed at the bottom of invoices could be a custom field entered in here.

4. Click `Save & Next` to store the changes and move to the next setting page, `Logo Settings`.

Configuring logos

Most companies and entrepreneurs have a logo that represents their business. It is the first visual contact your clients might have with you, and it represents your passion and profession. In Invoice, you can upload two logos: a system logo and an invoice logo. The system logo will display on top of all the pages of Invoice, while the invoice logo will be placed on actual quotes and invoices.

The recommended specifications for the system logo are 140×60 pixels with 72 dpi, making it suitable for on-screen display. The invoice logo, however, can be up to 580×250 pixels with 300 dpi so it will print nicely on paper.

To add a logo, follow these steps:

1. In `Logo settings` (accessible in the sidebar), for both `System Logo` and `Invoice Logo`, click `Change` and then click `Choose File` to browse for a logo image (Figure 12-4).

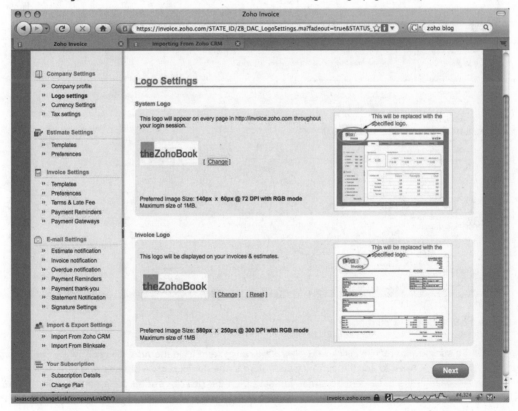

Figure 12-4. Setting the logos

2. Click **Next** to go the next page, **Currency Settings**.

Configuring currencies

Working with different currencies is one of the strengths of Invoice, especially when you work with multinational companies. You can add as many currencies as you want to work with:

3. On the **Currency Settings** page (accessible in the sidebar), specify any additional currencies you will work with (Figure 12-5).

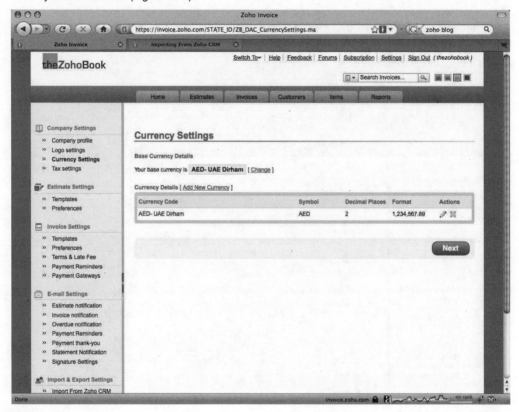

Figure 12-5. Adding new currencies

4. To add new currencies, click **Add New Currency**, and fill in the **Add Currency Details** form. Then click **Save** to add the currency and return to the **Currency Settings** page.

5. To change the base currency (that you set up on the **Quick Setup** page earlier), click **Change**. Then select the new base currency on the **Change Base Currency** page, click **Save** to store the changes, and return to **Currency Settings** page.

6. When you are done adding currencies, click **Next** to move to the next page, **Tax Settings**.

Configuring tax information

Many businesses have to pay taxes and deal the paperwork related to tax information. You can add tax information in order to use it in your calculations:

1. On the `Tax Settings` page, enter the tax information (Figure 12-6). Fill in `TaxID` and `Percentage` for every entry, and then select `Apply On`. To add more tax options, click `Add New Tax`.

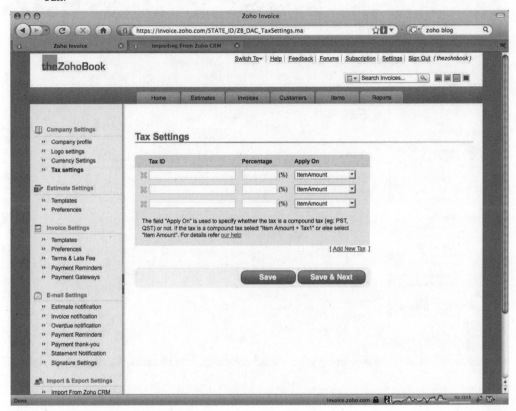

Figure 12-6. Entering tax information

2. Click `Save` to apply the changes.

Configuring online payments

One of the nice features of Invoice is the ability to accept online payments through different gateways. If you are going to work with PayPal, Google, or Authorize.net, you can configure Invoice to accept payments coming from these sites. Then, whenever you invoice customers and they pay through the services you configured, the customer balance will be updated automatically.

To get more information about these three gateways, check their respective websites. To register your account, follow these steps:

1. On the **Settings** page, click **Payment Gateways** in the sidebar. The **Payment Service Providers** page opens (Figure 12-7).

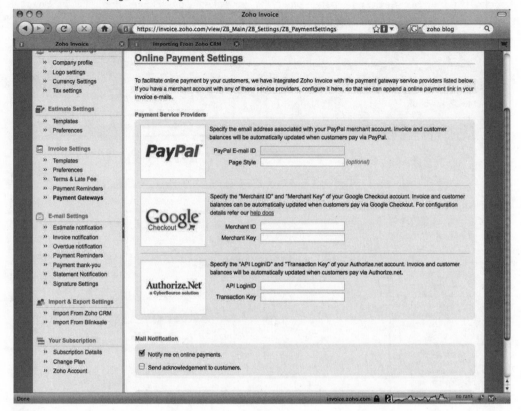

Figure 12-7. Configuring the payment gateways

2. Enter your merchant account information (see the on-screen instructions) for the respective gateway(s).
3. Select **Notify me on online payments**, and then click **Save** to register the accounts.

Although the basic configuration is done, you may want to take a look at the other options depending on your requirements.

Using Invoice

As I mentioned earlier, Invoice is capable of managing your products, customers, and estimates, in addition to taking care of your invoices. Although limited in product and customer management, these modules will do the trick for many companies.

Bigger organizations too that maintain their inventory in full-fledged packages can use Invoice by importing data from such applications.

Managing the items

Items are basically the products (or the services) you sell. You should maintain a basic list of the sellable items in order to use them in the estimates and invoices.

Items are maintained and managed on the `Items` tab. Obviously, when you first open this tab, it will show a message indicating there are no items in the system. You can add items one by one or import them in bulk from another application.

On the sidebar (on the left of the `Items` tab), you can add a new item by clicking `New Item`. It is also possible to view a list of active (click `Active Items`) and inactive (click `Inactive Items`) items. All newly added items are active unless you explicitly deactivate the ones you no longer use (or sell). I'll cover this in a bit.

Importing Items

To import items in bulk, first you need to export them from the source application (such as any inventory management package). The supported formats are comma-separated value (CSV) and tab-separated value (TSV). It also allows you to easily import CSV files that were exported from Zoho CRM.

Before you start importing, you need to make sure the exported file has the following data columns, meaning it should have this information, in every row, ordered and separated by comma.

- `Item Name`: The name of the product, such as `Skimmed Milk`.
- `Description`: Some details about the item, such as `ultra-high temperature (UHT)`.
- `Rate`: Unit price, such as `$3`. There is no field to store the unit (such as `gallon`), so you might need to work around this in `Description`.
- `Tax1 Name`: First tax option, if applicable.
- `Tax1 Percentage`: The amount of first tax option.
- `Tax1 Type`: First tax type, if applicable.
- `Tax2 Name`: Second tax option, if applicable.
- `Tax2 Percentage`: The amount of second tax option.
- `Tax2 Type`: Second tax type, if applicable.

Actually, you don't need to fill in every field. Apart from `Item Code` and `Rate`, which are mandatory, Invoice will ignore the empty fields. To get a better idea about the structure of the importable files, check the sample file at http://invoice.zoho.com/zohobooks/common/import/sample_items.csv. You can even use this file to test how the importing process works.

To import multiple items stored in a CSV file, follow these steps:

1. On the **Items** tab, click **Import Items** (in the upper right).
2. Click the **CSV** button on the **Import Items** page (Figure 12-8), and then browse for the file on your computer.

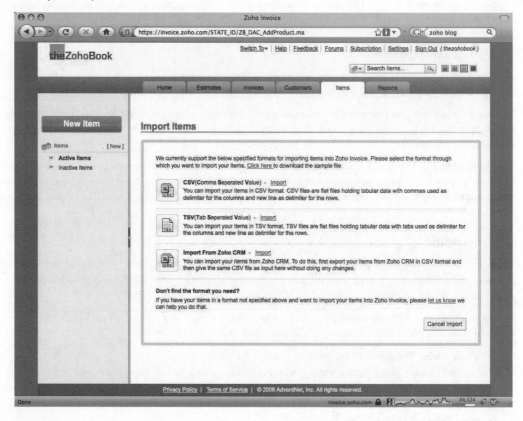

Figure 12-8. Importing items in bulk

This will automatically start importing the items and finish the operation with a successful import announcement. You will immediately be redirected to the **Active Items** where the newly imported items are listed.

> *When you export from Zoho CRM, you don't need to worry about the file structure. Simply browse for the exported products file, and Invoice will do the rest.*

Adding items one by one

Whenever you have new products or services to offer, you need to add them to the items as well. So, instead of bulk entry, you are going to add them one by one.

To add a single item to Invoice, follow these steps:

1. On the `Items` tab, click the big `New Item` button in the sidebar.
2. In the `Add New Item` form, enter at least the mandatory fields, which are the ones with the bold labels (Figure 12-9).

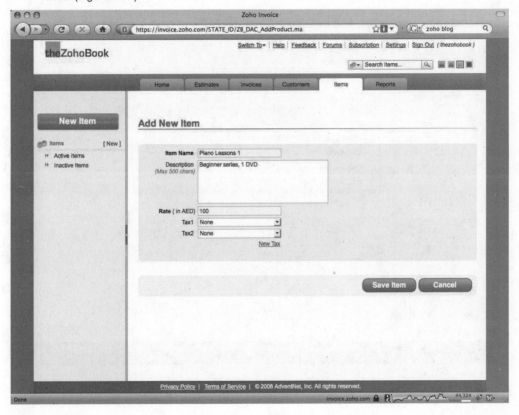

Figure 12-9. Adding an item

3. Click `Save Item` to add the item.

Performing basic tasks on items

After you have entered the items (whether by importing them or by adding them one by one), you can see them listed on the `Active Items` page because every new item is active by default. Basic item management is possible in these lists (Figure 12-10).

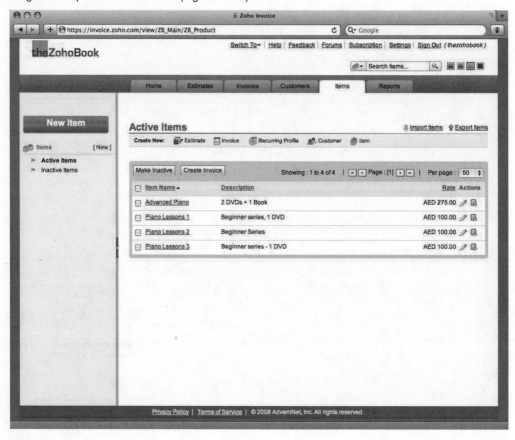

Figure 12-10. Viewing the items

To edit an item on either of active items or inactive items lists, follow these steps:

1. Click the item name to open the item details page. This is equivalent to clicking the `Edit this item` button (the pencil icon).
2. Make the modifications, and click `Save` Item to apply the changes.

There are two ways to remove the items. First, you can deactivate them so they won't show in the `Active Items` list, but they will still accessible through the inactive list in case you wanted to bring them back to use later. Second, you can remove them permanently from the system.

- To deactivate items, in the `Active Items` list, select the items by checking them in the list, and then click `Make Inactive`.
- To remove the items permanently, simply select the items, and click `Delete`. You can remove items from both active and inactive items permanently.

Managing customers

Every invoice needs a recipient, and that recipient is your customer. Just like with the items, you can import a list of your existing customers from another application. There are also special facilities to import customers from Zoho CRM and Blinksale, which you can easily find out by yourself.

> *Blinksale is a third-party online invoicing service similar to Invoice. Check out http://www.blinksale.com/ to get more information about it.*

Importing customers

Similar to what you saw with items, there is an easy way to import multiple customers in one batch, but first you need to have a list of customers exported into a CSV or TSV file. But if you don't have a list to import, you can download and use the sample customer list at http://invoice.zoho.com/zohobooks/common/import/sample_customers.csv, courtesy of Zoho.

1. On the `Customers` tab, click `Import Customers`.
2. Click the CSV button, and browse for the CSV file containing the customers on your computer. This will start the import.

Once finished, you will be redirected to the `Active Customers` list in which the newly imported customers are listed.

Adding customers one by one

As your business grows, you will no doubt attract more and more customers. To create a new customer from scratch, follow these steps:

1. Open the `Customers` tab, and click `New Customer` on the sidebar. You can also click `Customer` on the toolbar. The `Add New Customer` form opens (Figure 12-11).

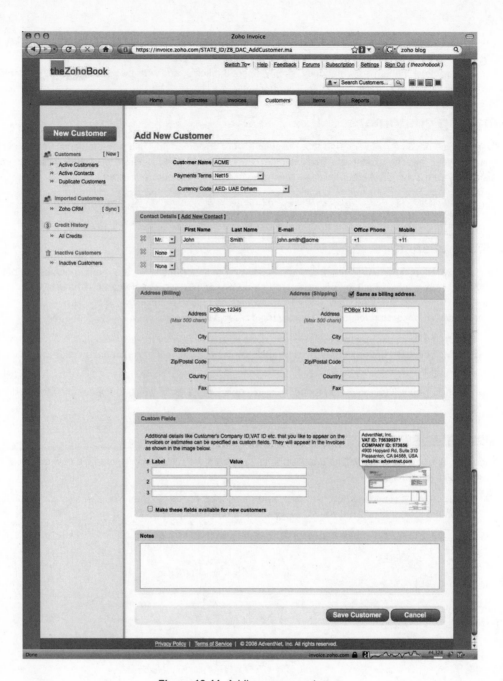

Figure 12-11. Adding a new customer

2. Fill in **Customer Name**. This is often the name of the company that is your customer, not a person's name.
3. Under **Contact Details**, enter the details of each contact in the customer organization.
4. Proceed with filling other fields as per your preference.
5. Click **Save Customer** to finish the process.

> *This information will appear on all documents you generate (estimates, invoices, and statements).*

Note that you can add new currencies for the customer on the fly by selecting **Add New Currency** in the **Currency Code** drop-down list. This will open a window allowing you to add a new currency to the system and assign it to the customer.

Performing basic tasks on customers

Once you add a new customer, you will be redirected to the active **Customers Details** page.

On the details page, you can see full details of the customers, such as their basic information plus the related invoice details (Figure 12-12). You can perform all customer-related activities here, which you will learn about in the following sections.

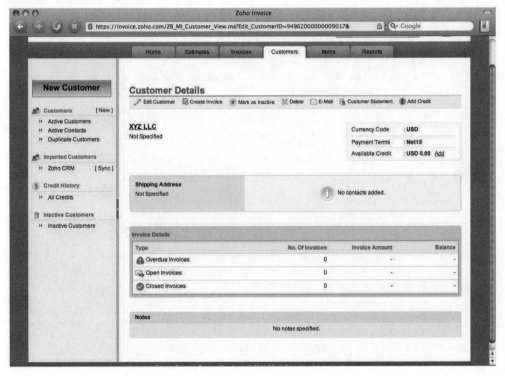

Figure 12-12. Active customers list

611

Back in the `Customers` list (click the `Customers` tab to get there), you can edit the customer information at any time by clicking `Edit Customer` on the details page or by clicking the `Edit this customer` button (the pencil icon) in the customers list.

You can make customers inactive by selecting them and clicking the `Make Inactive` button above the customers list.

Managing the estimates

When you do business with your customers (or potentials), you send estimates (quotes) before the deal actually goes through. You might even need to send multiple estimates for the same deal to better match the offer of both parties.

Once both you and the client have approved the price and the terms and conditions mentioned in the estimate and you have delivered the product or service, you will send an invoice to the customer. In multiphase projects, it is common to invoice the customer based on every phase completed, in which case you'll end up with multiple invoices for a single project. It is then that the customer can make the payments against invoice(s) received. What a glorious moment when you (finally) get paid!

Creating estimates

You can create new estimates by importing them from other applications as well as creating them one by one. I'll leave the import part to you to discover since it is similar to what you have done with items and customers, but let's take a quick look at creating them one at a time:

1. Open the `Estimates` tab, and click `New Estimate`. The `Add New Estimate` form opens (Figure 12-13).

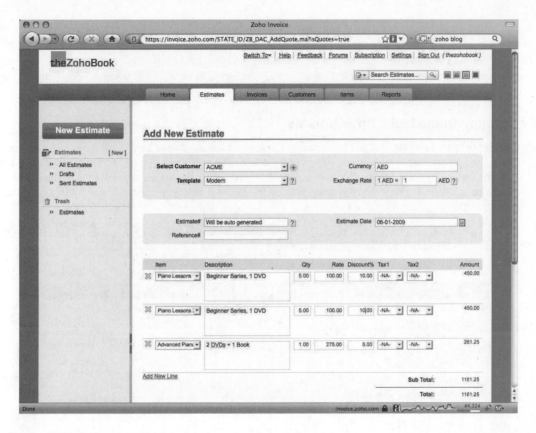

Figure 12-13. Adding an estimate

2. In the **Select Customer** drop-down, select to which customer this estimate is addressed, or add a new customer on the fly by clicking the green + button next to it.

3. Set the **Estimate Date** option (set to today by default) if needed.

4. Add the products from the **Items** drop-down list, and set the **Qty** (quantity) for each one. **Description** and **Rate** will be taken automatically from the item's data.

5. Enter the **Discount** percentage, and select the **Tax** options if applicable. The total amount will be updated as you enter these values.

6. Finish the estimate by filling in the optional **Customer Notes** and **Terms and Conditions** fields.

7. Click **Save** to store the estimate or **Send** to save the estimate and send it to the customer's e-mail address immediately.

There are two points worth mentioning here:

- **Estimate#** is a unique code created automatically for every new estimate. You won't need to worry about it.

- **Invoice** allows you to use and create custom templates for estimates and invoices in order to change the format and design of them when sent or printed. In the walk-through, we skipped the **Template** field, which is set to the **Classic** template by default. You could, however, choose another template from the list. Get more information on this at http://invoice.wiki.zoho.com/Estimate-template.html #Custom-templates.

Performing basic tasks on estimates

After creating an estimate, you will be redirected to the **Estimate Details** page (Figure 12-14). There, through the commands in the toolbar, you can edit, delete, and send the estimate. You can also export it to PDF for printing in case you want to e-mail it to the client. Clicking **Print** will have the same effect of downloading a PDF file for you to open and print on the paper in case you needed to send it by fax or snail mail.

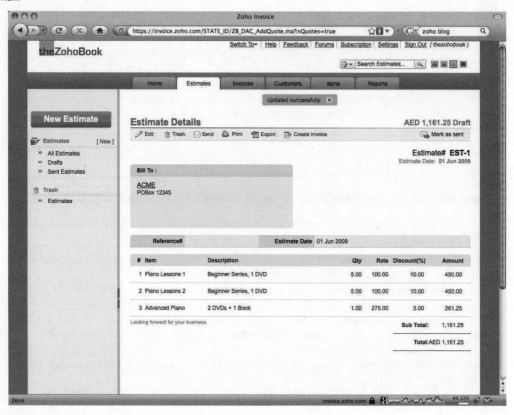

Figure 12-14. Estimate details

Looking at the sidebar (left), there are three options for estimate lists:

- If you just saved the estimate, it will show in the **Drafts**
- But if you sent it directly, you can find it in the **Sent Estimates**.
- To see the entire list, click **All Estimates**.

To send an estimate to clients at any time, follow these steps:

1. On the **Estimate Details** page, click **Send** on the toolbar. This is similar to when you directly send the estimate while creating it.
2. On the **Send Estimate** page (Figure 12-15), fill in the recipient's e-mail address in **To**.

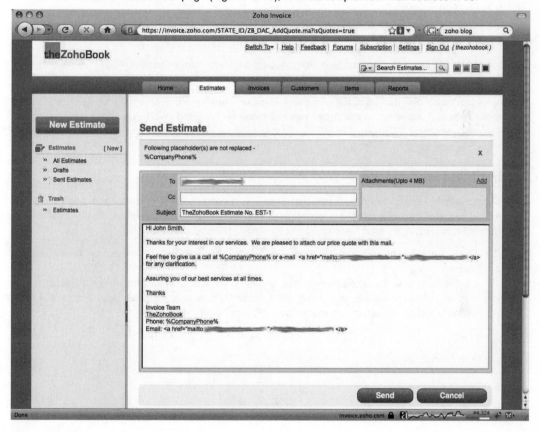

Figure 12-15. Sending estimates by e-mail

3. Fine-tune the subject and the message body that is being generated by Invoice.
4. Click **Send** to dispatch the message.

While fine-tuning the message body (step 3), you should know that Invoice extracts some information from the customers list while generating the message, such as the contact's first name and last name, and places them in the body. That's how you see in Figure 12-15 that `John Smith` is entered in the first line of the message.

This feature saves you time and helps you avoid human error, but if you didn't enter this information completely (while adding the customer), Invoice wouldn't be able to place the right information in the message. So, it places a placeholder such as `%CompanyPhone%` if the company phone of the customer is missing in the system, similar to Figure 12-15. Then it warns you on top of the message form to take care of these placeholders by manually entering the proper data. In other words, don't send the message before fixing the missing information.

Managing the invoices

Issuing invoices is usually the last stage in which you let the customers know how much they need to pay for your products/services.

Every invoice has a due date, and the client should make the payment by this date for you to successfully close the invoice. If, however, the payment was not made on time, the invoice becomes overdue, and you need to send reminders (by any means) to the client to fulfill the payment. An invoice is not closed until there is no overdue balance.

Creating invoices

There are multiple ways to create new invoices. A quick and good way is to convert estimates to invoices. It is a logical business transition to have successful estimates ending up being invoices, and this will save you time and effort because you don't have to the invoice details twice.

1. Open the estimate you want to convert to an invoice, and then click **Create Invoice** on the toolbar.
2. On the **Add New Invoice** page (which opens on the **Estimates** tab), check the fields to make sure everything is correct, and make the necessary changes if there are any. The form is loaded with information extracted from the estimate (Figure 12-16).

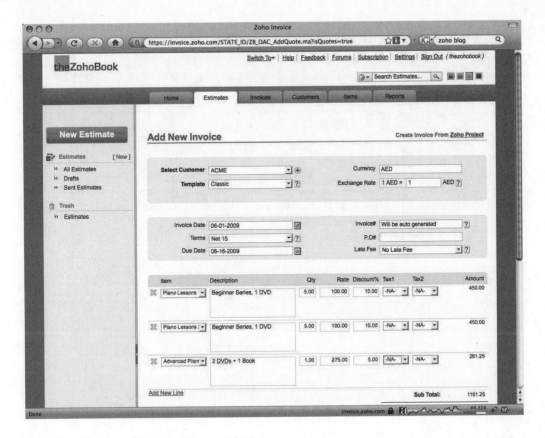

Figure 12-16. Creating an invoice from an estimate

3. Click **Save** to store the invoice as a draft or **Send** to save it and send it to the customer by e-mail.

Adding payments to invoices

If you sent the invoice to the client (by clicking **Send**), the status of the invoice will be set to **Open**, meaning it is ready to receive payments by the invoice due date. Later, if you check the details of an open invoice, you can see the section **Payments Received** that lists all payments made against that invoice (Figure 12-17). The payments made through online gateways (that you configured earlier in the chapter) will automatically show up here as well.

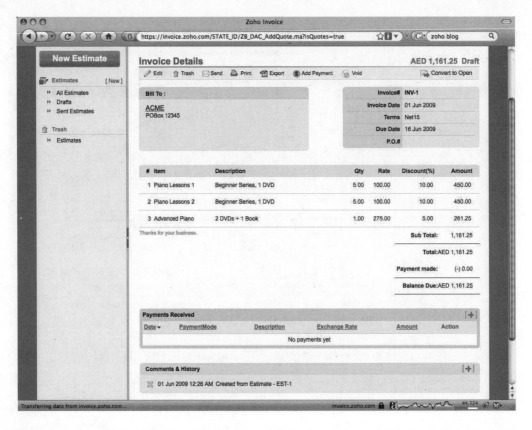

Figure 12-17. Received payments for each invoice

It is also possible to add payments to the invoices manually when you receive offline payments via cash, check, and so on.

1. On the Invoices tab, open the invoice, and click **Add Payment** on the toolbar on the **Invoice Details** page.

2. In the **Add Payment** page, fill in the **Received Date** and **Amount** (Figure 12-18).

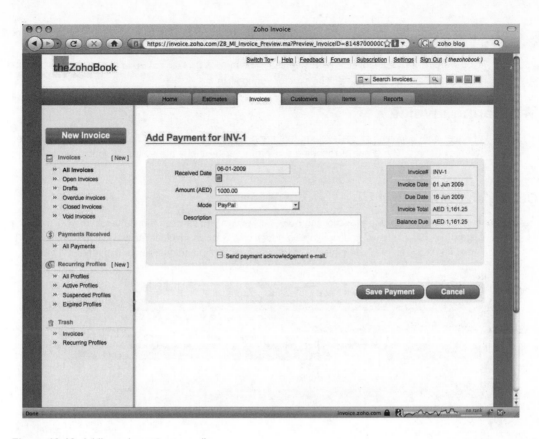

Figure 12-18. Adding payments manually

3.   Select the payment type in `Mode`, such as `Cash` or `Check`.
4.   Check `Send payment acknowledgement e-mail` if you want the payee to be notified with a message that you have received the amount.
5.   Click `Save Payment`.

More on invoices

The following are important details about invoices:

- You can receive payments in pieces. Every time a payment is being added to an invoice, it will deduct from the balance, and the result will show in the reports.
- Invoices with overdue payments, meaning their balance didn't reach zero by the due date (set in the invoice creation process), will be listed in the `Overdue Invoices` list. This list is accessible through the sidebar in the `Invoices` tab.

- You can import invoices from other applications using CSV and TSV files. Blinksale users can import their invoices directly by registering their Blinksale account with Invoice.
- If you want to create an invoice from scratch, you can click **New Invoice** in the **Invoices** tab or on the toolbar. This will open a blank invoice for you to fill in.

Monitoring Invoice

Once you have many invoices in the system, it is important to check what is happening in your business. Invoice will provide you with a set of reporting tools in order to check the status of your payments in real time.

Getting an overall view

The handiest view is the **Home** page (click the **Home** tab) where you can see the status of your payments at a glance (Figure 12-19). It shows you the total amount of the open invoices as well as the history of the overdue amounts. You can also see a history of the sales, receipts, and due amounts sorted in a table at the bottom.

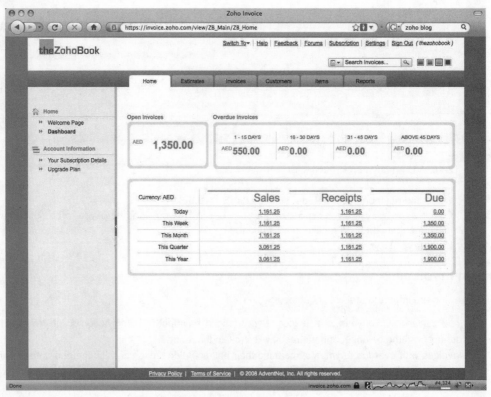

Figure 12-19. The **Home** page

Click any amount to list the corresponding invoices for you to take further action. For instance, if you want list the invoices that have due dates for this month, find the amount under the **Due** column and the **This Month** row.

Monitoring customers

To check out the status of the invoices related to a specific customer, open the **Customer Details** page, and review the **Invoice Details** section (Figure 12-20).

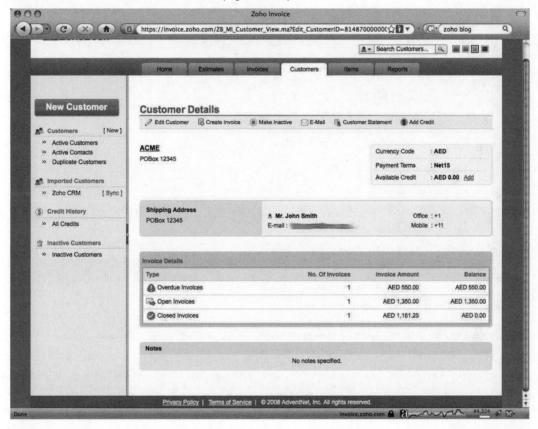

Figure 12-20. Checking the customer details

For example, if you want to remind a customer about an overdue payment, this is the place to check. You can see how much a customer owes you by checking the amount of the **Overdue Invoices**. Then send an e-mail directly (click **E-mail** on the toolbar) and ask them to take action.

To get a full history of a client, click **Customer Statement**. This will show you a complete list of the invoices as well as the transactions related to that client for a specific period of time (Figure 12-21).

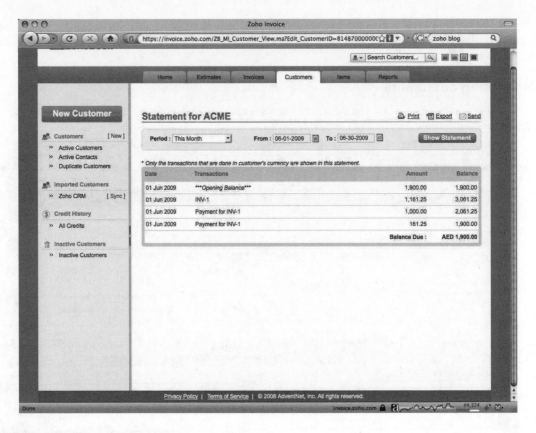

Figure 12-21. The customer statement

To send the statement to the client or to third parties, such as your accountant, you can export this list as a PDF (click **Export**) or send it directly by e-mail (click **Send**).

All these reports will help you monitor the cash flow in your business. They can also be a great help when you are auditing your income or submitting documents to the IRS or other tax office. It will also register your monthly income, balance, and so on, which will be a useful reference for future plans.

Getting help

Invoice is one of the easiest-to-use business applications of the Zoho suite. After reading this chapter, you may not need any help, but to make sure all your questions are answered, you can always check the official help at http://invoice.wiki.zoho.com/ or the forums at http://forums.zohoinvoice.com/.

There are also useful tips and news related to Invoice in the official blog at http://blogs.zoho.com/category/invoice.

Summary

No matter what type of business you are running, dealing with quotes and invoices is inevitable. Zoho Invoice provides you with nifty and powerful tools to take care of these precious documents. It stores and manages the essential elements—products and services, customers, estimates, and invoices—while also creating a logical connection between these elements.

The ability of importing and exporting data gives extra power to Invoice, allowing you to connect it to other business applications seamlessly. Accepting online payments will save you a lot of time and effort, especially if you run an online business. The accountants and auditors too will be happy to get their hands on professionally prepared reports.

If Zoho CRM is overkill for your requirements, Invoice could be a great alternative. You can use it along with other Zoho applications such as Sheet, Creator, and Reports in order to manage your business funds.

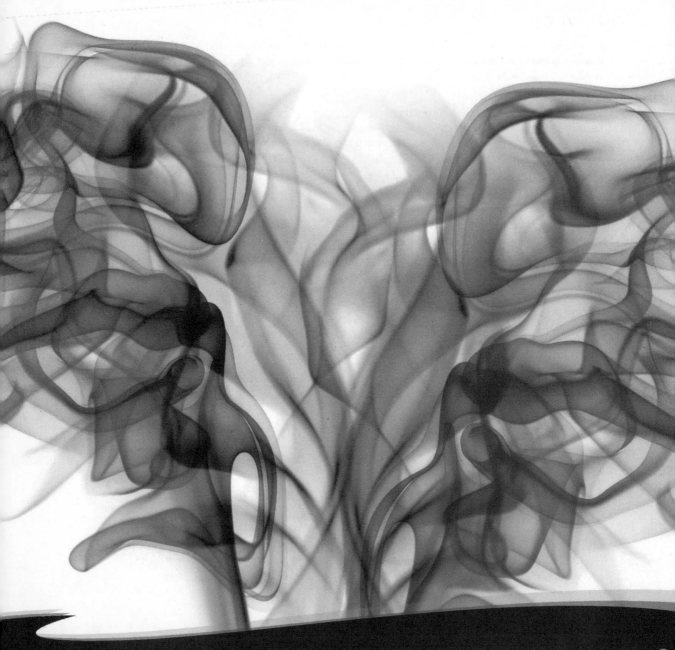

ZOHO®

Work. Online

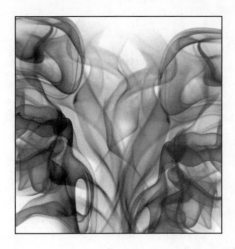

Chapter 13

Manage Your Projects

According to Wikipedia, **project management** is the discipline of planning, organizing, and managing resources to bring about the successful completion of specific project goals and objectives.

> Check out http://en.wikipedia.org/wiki/Project_management to get more information on project management, its history, its approaches, and so on.

A **project**, in general, defines the scope of actions to be done in a specific period of time and within a defined budget in order to achieve a goal or a set of goals. A team of people is usually involved in the process, working on the project from the day the idea of a goal sparks until the day the big outcome debuts.

People employ methodologies and tools to help manage projects. In fact, many people study special skills to become experts in project management. Business and engineering schools include related courses in their curriculum, for example, and there are even certifications, like Project Management Professional (PMP) offered by the Project Management Institute (PMI; http:///www.pmi.org/), to guarantee the certificate holder is an expert in project management techniques.

All said, there should be no doubt that project management is a very important subject in today's business world. You can check Capterra (http://www.capterra.com/project-management-software) for a long list of project management tools, but our focus in this chapter is Zoho Projects, a medium-sized cloud-based project management application that not only does the job well but also brings a few innovations to this area.

Zoho Projects

Zoho Projects is a simple yet powerful application for managing small to medium-sized projects. It provides organizations with what they need to run successful projects.

Apart from the essentials of a project management tool, Projects offers built-in collaboration and documentation facilities in a highly available and scalable form. With this new approach, Projects wraps the working experience in a rather familiar social networking environment that can boost the team's productivity and collaboration power.

Projects is easy to configure and use; it gets you started almost immediately and allows you to stay focused on the project rather than the learning curve. Projects features different modules and interacts with some of other Zoho applications to maximize performance and make your life in the cloud easier. You can interact with Writer, Sheet, Show, and Invoice in order to prepare and connect various documents.

Communication and collaboration are at their best in Projects, because it has a chat function, forums, a wiki, and a content-rich homepage. It addresses a crucial issue in project management, communication, quite well.

Projects is available in a free version, in which you can manage a single project for free. I have to admit that you'll probably rarely find any company with only one project, but for small entities, it might still be a good starter kit. The free version is what I'll showcase in most cases in this chapter.

The free plan has a few limitations (storage space, secure connection, and so on) compared to the paid versions. You can opt for as many features your organization needs by purchasing one of the various monthly plans. To get more information about subscriptions, check out `http://www.zoho.com/projects/zohoprojects-pricing.html`.

> *Before you upgrade to the paid plan, I recommend you finish this chapter to get a fair idea of the capabilities of Projects. You may even want to run a real project and then decide about upgrading. Remember, you are by no means limited to your current subscription, paid or free, and can change to any available plan at any time.*

Getting started

To run Projects, log on to `http://projects.zoho.com`. You can open it from within Zoho Business too.

The first time you log in, Projects will ask you to create a portal URL. This is the URL your team members (or other people who are authorized to log in) will use to get access to the projects. Enter the portal URL of your company, and click `Create New Portal` to proceed, as shown in Figure 13-1.

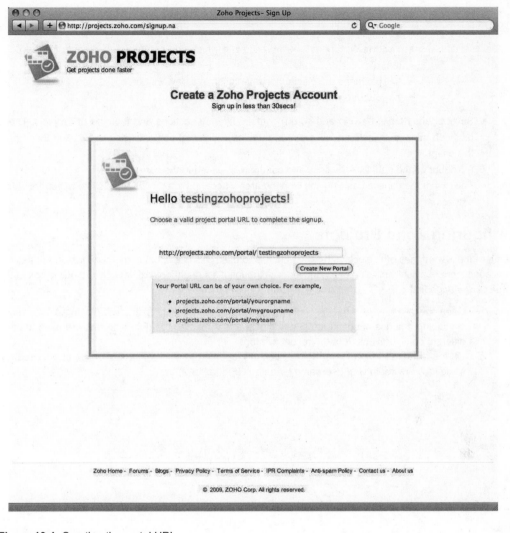

Figure 13-1. Creating the portal URL

After the portal is created, you will be redirected to the URL you just created. There you can see the **Home** tab asking you to create a new project, but we'll skip this for now and review the user interface first:

- There is a link bar on the top of the page containing some essential shortcuts to the places that are accessible system-wide:

  - **What's New?**: Opens a page in which you can read about the new features of the current version of Projects

- **My Home**: Opens the **Home** tab that is the command center of Projects
- **Settings**: Opens the **Settings** page where you can configure the application
- **Feedback**: Opens a new window in which you can leave comments for the Zoho team
- **Help**: Opens the official documentation in a new window
- **Logout**: Logs you out of Projects

- Several tabs (**Home**, **Users**, and so on) contain different sections and features of Projects. These tabs can change or increase/decrease in number in different contexts, as you will see throughout this chapter.
- A sidebar on the right lists the links and commands related to the current page.
- The rest of the page is basically the working area where you interact with the system, your projects, and so on.

Configuring Zoho Projects

One of the advantages of Projects is how simple it is to use. This is evident in the configuration phase too because there is actually nothing much to tweak. Although it's straightforward, let's take a quick look at the **Settings** page first:

1. Open the **Settings** page (at the top right of the screen). It is divided into three tabs, each containing a series of configurable items plus a few links on the right side that are used to open different configurations from the respective tabs.
2. On the **General Settings** tab (the default), update the values in **Full Name** and **Nickname** since they are set to your username by default (Figure 13-2).

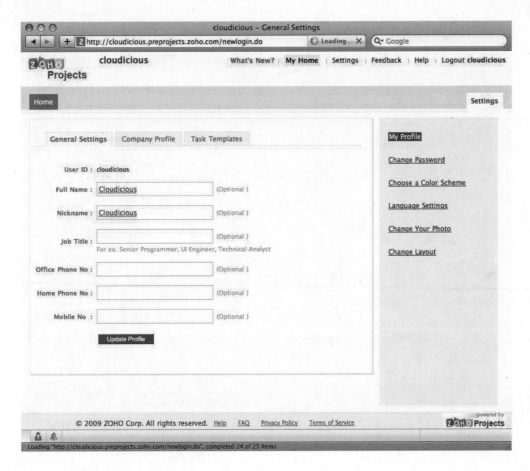

Figure 13-2. Updating the basic settings

You can also upload your avatar (click **Upload Photo**) to show your photo to colleagues throughout the system. Click **Update Profile** when you're done.

3. On the **Company Profile** tab, enter the company information including **Company Name**, **Web Address** (as in http://www.yourcompany.com), and **TimeZone** (Figure 13-3).

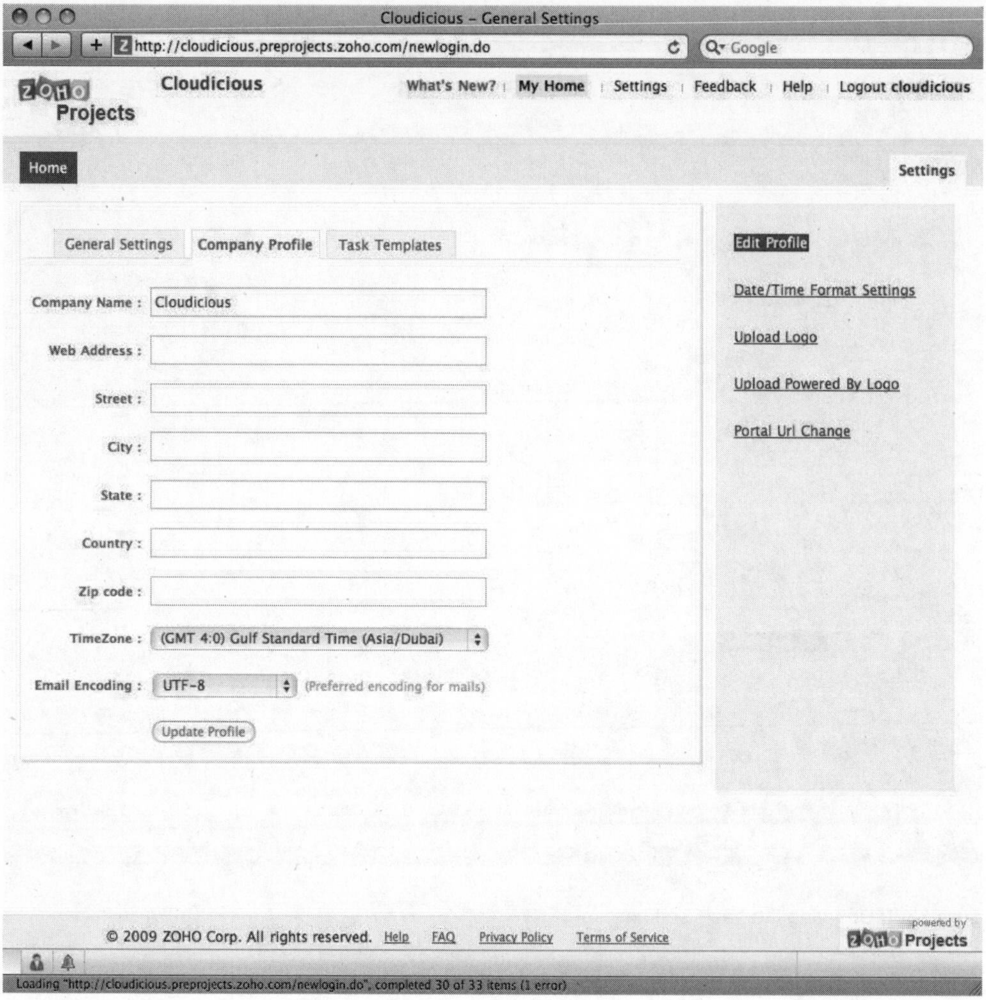

Figure 13-3. Updating the company profile

You can also change your company logo (click **Upload Logo**) and the portal URL (click **Portal URL Change**), which is the address you created earlier (shown in Figure 13-1). Note that if you do so, you need to inform your team members about the updated URL. Again, click **Update Profile** when you're done.

Adding new users

By adding new users, you specify the people who will be involved in your projects. These are your colleagues and third-party contractors who will be working on the project with you.

To add a new user to Projects, follow these steps:

1. Open the **Home** page by clicking **My Home** on the link bar at the top of the screen. Then click the **Add User** link in the sidebar on the right.

2. On the **Add New User** page, enter the user's e-mail address and the user's role (such as manager, employee, or contractor). The role is for your reference only and helps you distinguish the people involved in your project (Figure 13-4).

Figure 13-4. Adding a new user

3. Click the `Add User` button to proceed.

Users are globally accessible, meaning you can assign them to different projects. It is possible for a user to be involved in multiple projects. Later you will see how to assign users to projects.

Adding new clients

Clients are essentially the companies you work with. If you are working on a project for a client, you should define them in the system so you can assign them to the corresponding projects. To do so, follow these steps:

4. Open the `All Users` tab, and then click the `Company Clients` subtab. Then click `Add Client`.
5. On the `Add Client` page, enter the client's company in `Client Company Name`.
6. Click `More` (below the project list) to show more fields for the client (Figure 13-5). Then fill in at least the `Web Address` field. It's not mandatory, but it is a good practice to enter the complete information of your clients.
7. Click the `Add Client` button to store the information in the system.

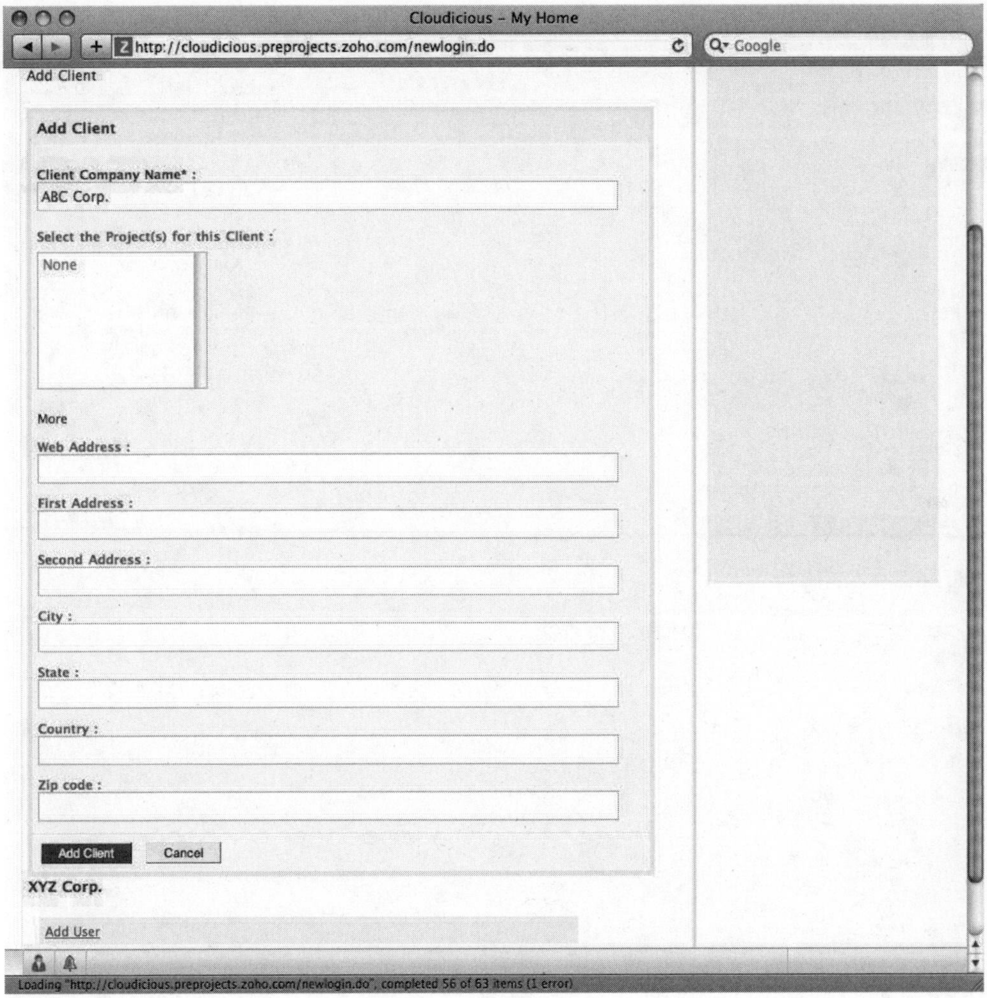

Figure 13-5. Adding a new client

For every client you can add a contact (or more), which is basically an e-mail address. This contact represents the person who is in direct contact with your company.

To add a contact to an existing client, follow these steps:

1. On the **All Users** tab, open the **Company Clients** subtab.
2. Under the name of the client, click **Add User**, and enter the contact's e-mail address in **User Email** (Figure 13-6).

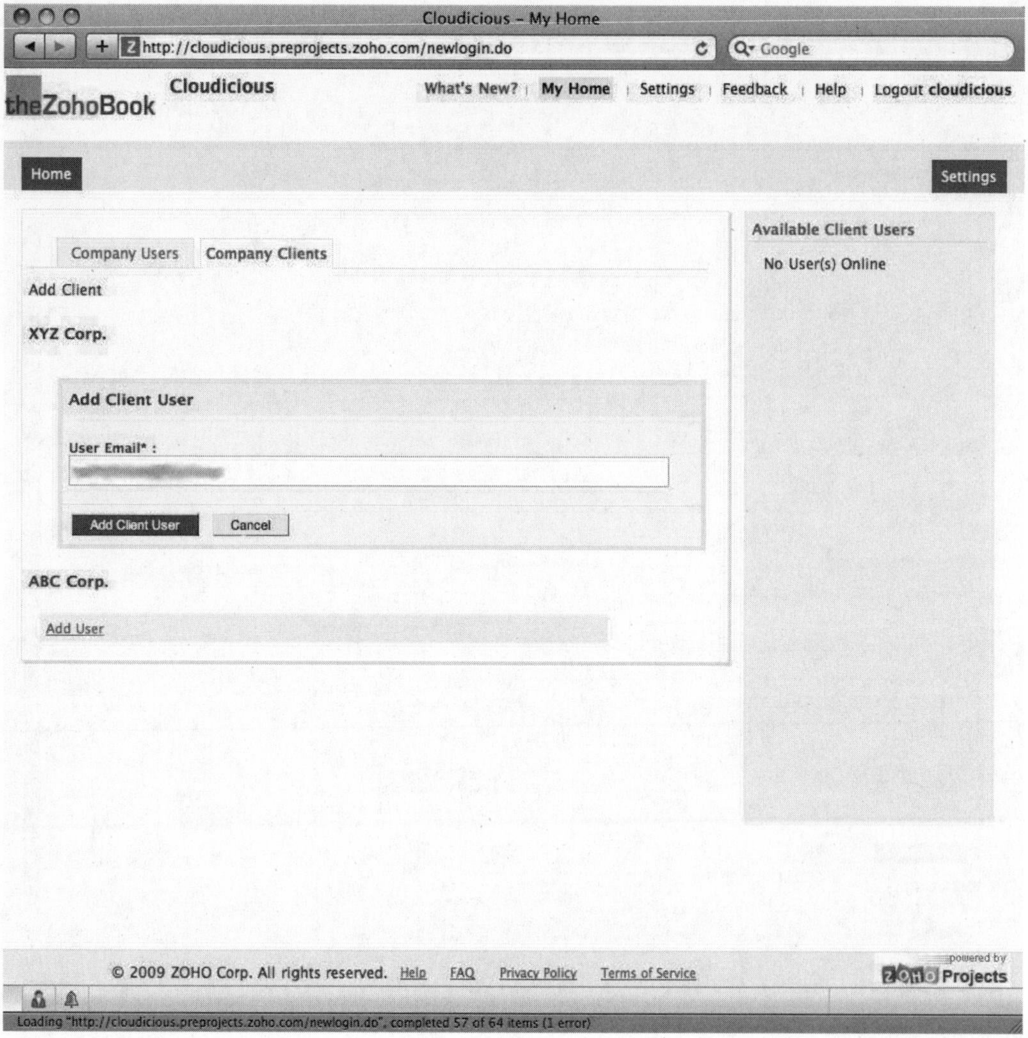

Figure 13-6. Adding a client contact

3. Click the **Add Client User** button to assign the contact to the stored client.

Using Zoho Projects

Every project has different but interconnected parts. Although I won't go any deeper about the concepts of project management, it is important to know the elements of a project plan:

- When you define a project in Projects, you create a **plan** so you can start and finish that project successfully within the defined constraints, such as time.
- During the life span of a project, **milestones** identify the time the project reaches major points such as finishing a phase or releasing a deliverable.
- Each milestone contains **tasks** that need to be done in a certain order or in parallel during a defined period of time. These tasks should be grouped in **task lists** for easier management.
- One of the **events** happening during a project is a meeting with the stakeholders, be it colleagues, contractors, or clients. Meetings need to be scheduled and mentioned in the plan.
- Meetings and other project objects often have **documents** to be attached with further handy information. Letters, spreadsheets, and so on, need to be created or uploaded to be part of the plan.

In addition, maintaining steady communication between the stakeholders is important throughout the project, and Projects offers a set of helpful tools for this purpose.

Creating your first project

In this walk-through, you'll create a simple project about redesigning an office. It could be a plan for redesigning your office or your client's office.

To create your first project, follow these steps:

1. Open the `Home` page by clicking `Home`. Since there are no projects defined yet, there is a form waiting for you to add your very first project.
2. Enter Redesigning the office in **Project Name**.
3. Click `Click here` to add a client and users for the project. Then select an item in the **Client Company** list as well as a user or two in the **Users** list (Figure 13-7).

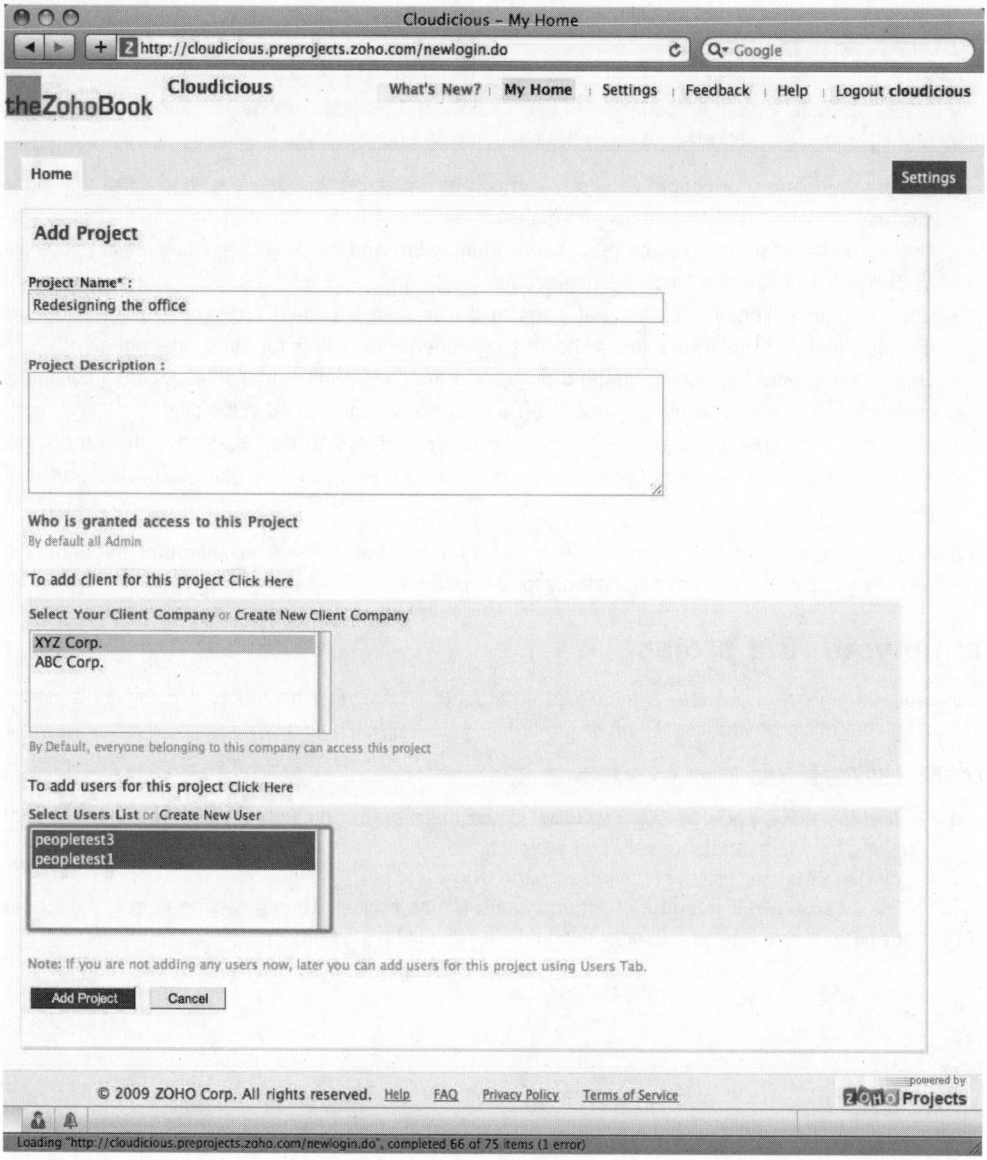

Figure 13-7. Creating a new project

4. Click **Add Project** to create an empty project.

Navigating the UI

Once the project is created, you will be redirected to the **Dashboard**. This is probably a familiar UI because it resembles well-known social networking sites like Facebook. You'll notice that additional elements now appear in the UI. This is because you are inside a project (the one you just created), so additional tabs and other elements provide the project-specific features.

You can see your picture (if you uploaded an avatar during the setup phase) followed by the other peers involved in the project. The latest activities are listed in here. Basically, anything you do in the project will update the activities list. It is also possible to update your status manually by entering text in the status text box (Figure 13-8). Just type your status, such as `working on the blueprints`, in the text box below your username that has `What am I working on right now..?` in it.

Figure 13-8. The project `Dashboard`

Projects does a great job of merging some social networking behaviors into the old-school project management environment, helping you stay more in sync with other peers while having fun working.

Whereas `Dashboard` acts as the command center of the current project, `Home` (which you can reach by clicking `My Home`) plays the role of the command center for the entire application, featuring all projects available to you in the system. These pages fundamentally serve same purpose but from a different perspective.

Managing milestones and tasks

Setting milestones in Projects helps you divide the process into more manageable pieces. Usually when a milestone is reached, a major phase of the project is finished. Tasks, on the other hand, are the smaller pieces of work done by a project member for every milestone.

Creating milestones

To create a new milestone, follow these steps:

1. Open the `Tasks & Milestones` tab, and click `Get started by creating your first milestone` (which shows only the first time, when no milestone is defined yet).
2. Enter the milestone information you see in Figure 13-9. The title is mandatory, but you can skip the rest (although it is recommended that you set a start date and an end date as well).

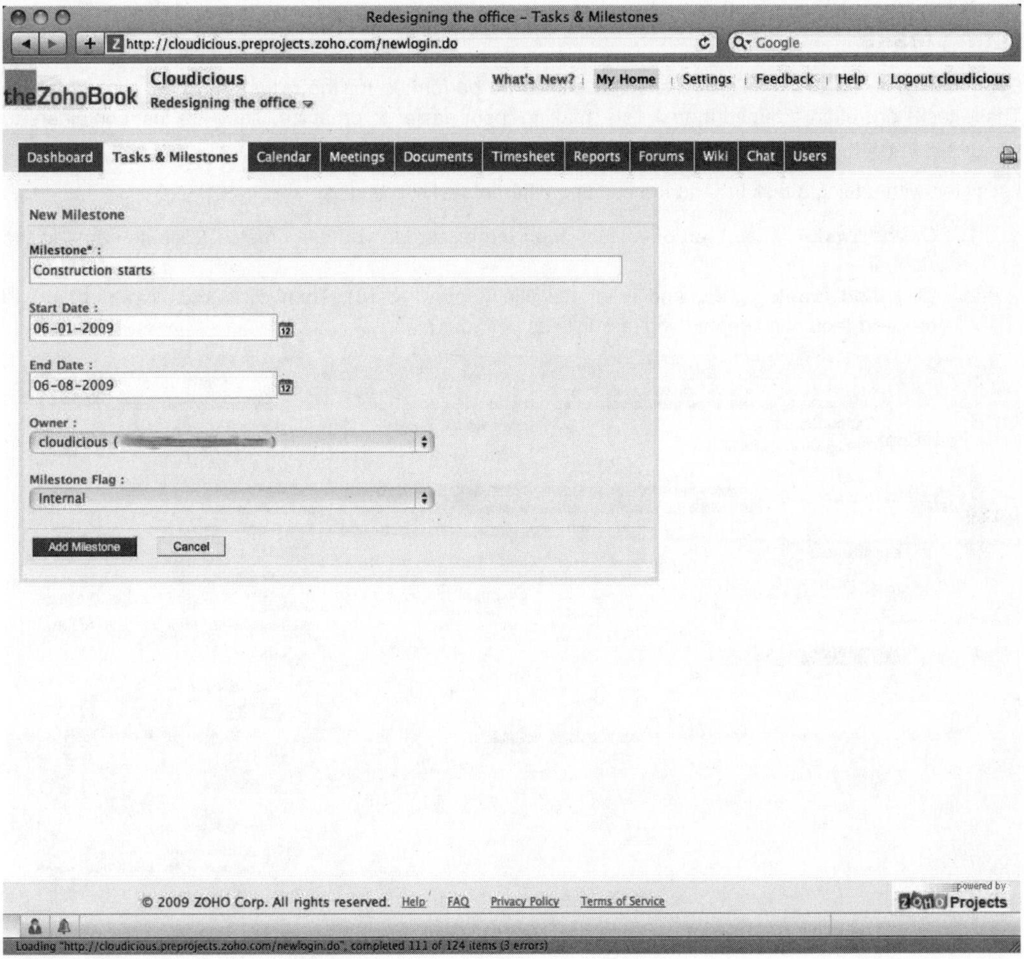

Figure 13-9. Adding a new milestone

3. Click **Add Milestone** to proceed.

The milestone will appear on the sidebar under **Upcoming Milestones**. Overdue milestones are listed separately in the sidebar. Selecting a milestone will make it complete, and it will be listed under **Completed Millstones**.

Creating tasks

Every milestone contains multiple tasks that should be performed for the milestone to be accomplished. These tasks are often grouped in task lists, making them easier to organize. They are just containers to categorize tasks.

Let's start with adding a task list and then adding different tasks to that list:

1. On the **Tasks & Milestones** tab, open the milestone you just created (click its name in the sidebar).

2. Click **Add Task List**, and enter the title (Figure 13-10). Then click **Add Task List** to proceed. You can keep adding task lists as per your plan.

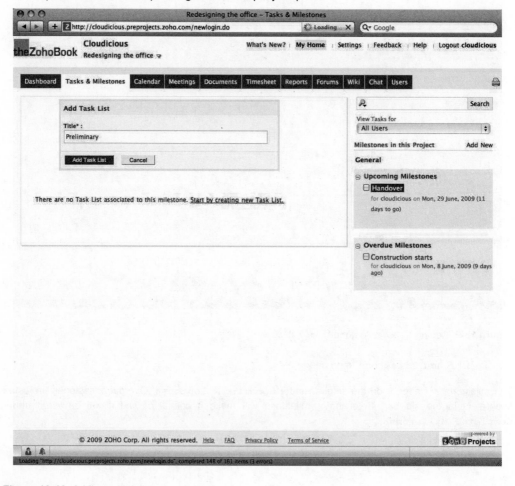

Figure 13-10. Adding a task list

3. Click **Add Task**. This opens the **Add Task** form.

4. Enter the task in the **Task** text box. You can be as descriptive as you like here. Note that the task list is already selected in the **Task List** area.

5. Select the owners of the task in the **Owner** list. **Owners** are the people who will do the task.

6. Click **Show Advanced Options** for more fields to show up (Figure 13-11). Then set a start date and an end date for the task.

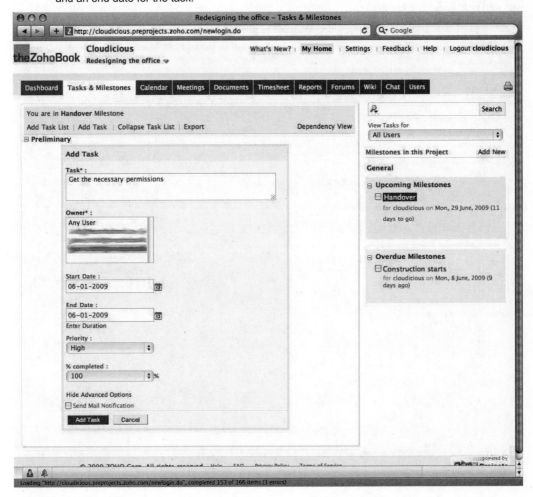

Figure 13-11. Adding a new task

7. Check **Send Mail Notification** to send a message to task owners to know about it.

8. Click **Add Task** to store it in the system. Repeat this step for every additional task.

After adding different task lists and tasks for each milestone, you can review them. Your project has a hierarchical structure: milestones contain the task list, and the task lists contain the tasks. As a project progresses, you have to open the respective tasks and mark them as done or update their progress status. This is very important because it means you can track the project in the system, which is essential for reporting.

For instance, in Figure 13-12, you can see a task list (`Preliminary`) with the corresponding tasks listed, with one task already completed.

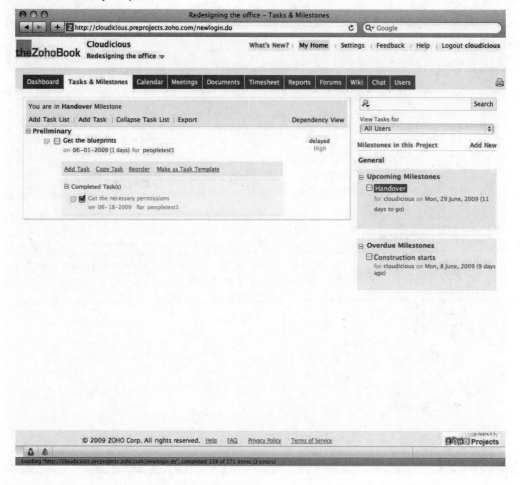

Figure 13-12. A typical view of the tasks and milestones

Here are the actions to perform on tasks while working on a project:

- To update the progress of a task:

  1. Open the corresponding milestone, and find the task under the containing task list.
  2. Move the mouse pointer on it, and click the **Edit Task** button (pencil).
  3. Select a new value for the **% completed** list, such as **60**.
  4. Click **Update Task** to apply the changes

- To mark a task as completed, simply select it, and it will be listed under **Completed Tasks** in the task list.

Scheduling meetings

As discussed earlier, meetings are essential during a project, and they need to be scheduled ahead of time. But you have to keep in mind that it is not possible to schedule a meeting for the past, even if you are doing this only to keep a log of the past meetings in the system.

To schedule a meeting, follow these steps:

1. Open the **Meetings** tab, and click **Get started by scheduling your first meeting** (which displays only the first time).
2. Enter the meeting details similar to Figure 13-13.

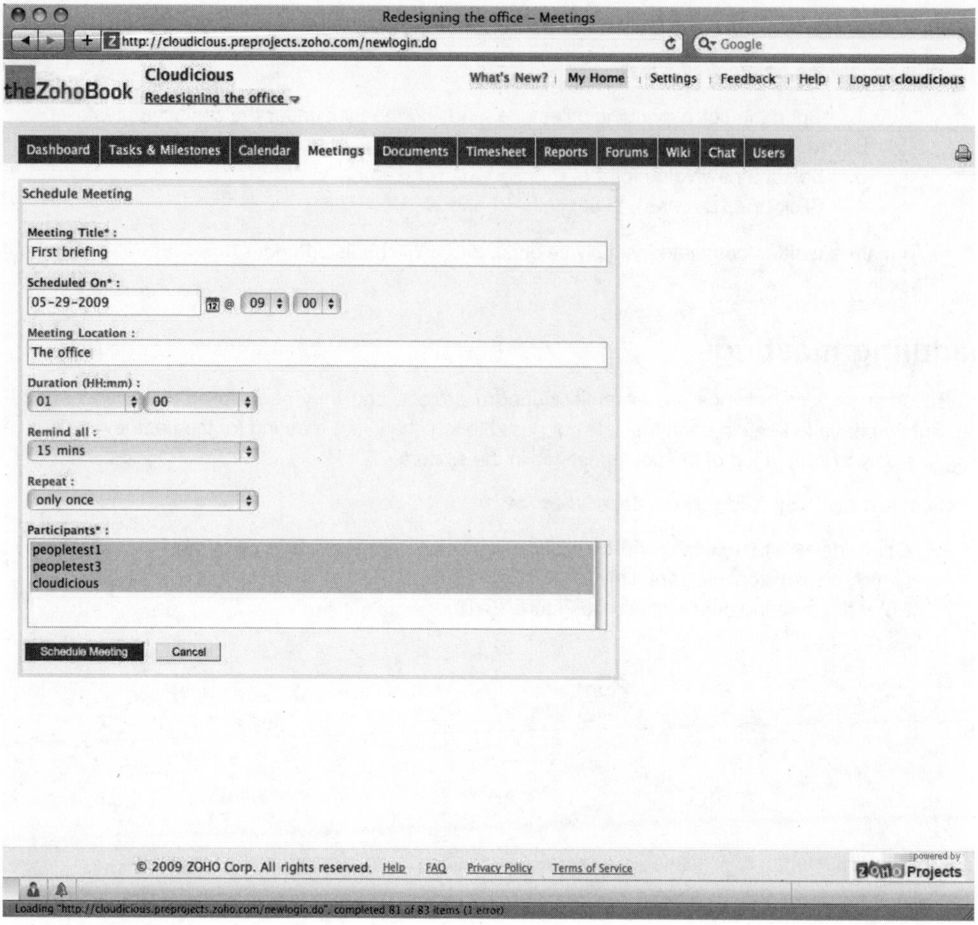

Figure 13-13. Scheduling a meeting

3. Click `Schedule Meeting` to register it in the system.

> You can hold/attend meetings using Zoho Meeting. For example, leave the meeting key
> in the `Meeting Location` field so everybody knows where to go. Refer to Chapter 14
> to learn about this powerful tool.

Once a meeting is scheduled, it will be listed on the `Meetings` tab under `Upcoming Meetings`. You can
add notes, edit the meeting information, or associate documents (to be discussed in a bit) to a meeting
here.

Figure 13-14 shows a note being added to a meeting (by clicking `Add Notes`). To quickly schedule new
meetings, you can fill in the form on the sidebar and click `Schedule Meeting`.

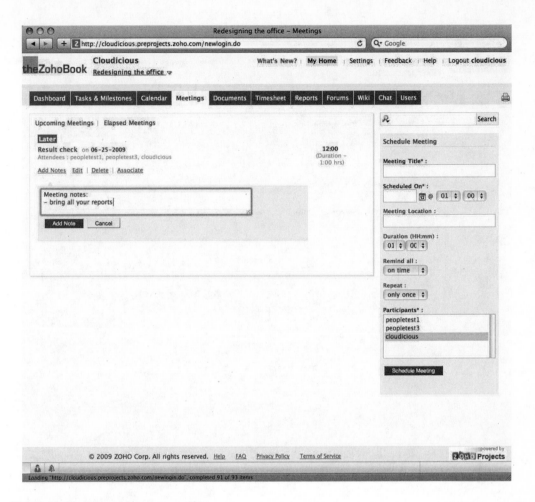

Figure 13-14. Adding notes to a meeting

Using the calendar

Calendar acts as a center point to quickly find (and also create) the events and other objects such as tasks in a monthly view. Opening the `Calendar` tab will show you the tasks, milestones, and meetings listed based on their dates of occurrence. You can navigate through months and filter the view to see only tasks, milestones, or meetings (Figure 13-15).

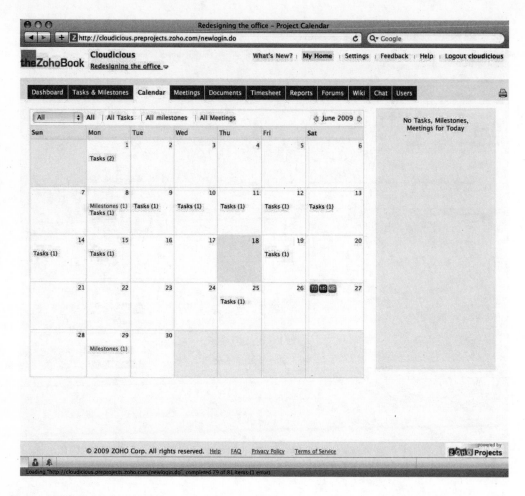

Figure 13-15. Using the calendar

Moving the mouse pointer over a day in the calendar will show three icons: **TD** (task), **MS** (milestone), and **ME** (meeting). Clicking these items allow you to quickly create one of the items. When you click, a form will open in the sidebar for quick data entry.

Managing documents

It is quite normal to maintain information about different types of documents while working on a project. You might need letters, price lists, or presentations that related to the project to be accessible to the team. Projects allows you to upload documents and share them with your peers. The good news is that you can upload them from your local machine or from your online documents in Zoho Docs.

After that, you (and other peers) can open them online using Writer, Sheet, and Show. This document management system works seamlessly with your project management tool without you needing any external tool. (Please note that this feature is not available in the free version of Projects.)

1. Open the **Documents** tab, and click **Get started by uploading your first document** (which shows the first time only).

2. Click **Choose File** to upload a local document or **Browse using Zoho Docs** to pick one from your online library.

3. Set the target folder in **Select Folder**, and then click **Upload File** (Figure 13-16).

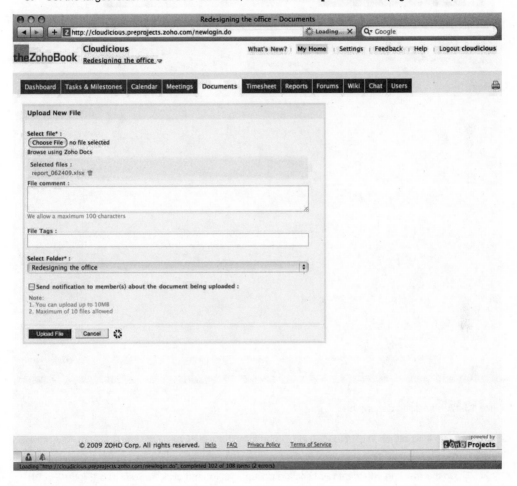

Figure 13-16. Uploading files

The uploaded documents are listed on the **Documents** tab. To organize the documents, you can create a new folder by clicking **Add Folder** (Figure 13-17). On the other hand, you may create documents directly using the links **New Document**, **New Spreadsheet**, and **New Presentation**. This will open the respective Zoho tool for you to create a document without needing any third-party tool such as Microsoft Office.

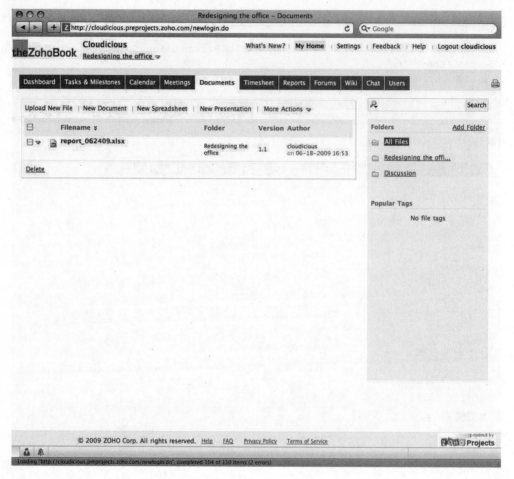

Figure 13-17. Managing documents

It is also possible to attach the uploaded documents to the meetings. For example, you can associate meeting notes, statistics reports, or some presentation notes with a meeting:

1. Open the meeting you want to associate documents to, and click **Associate** (Figure 13-18).

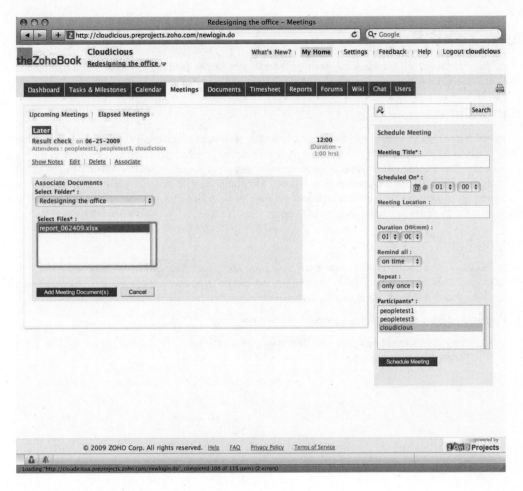

Figure 13-18. Assigning documents to the meetings

2. Select the containing folder and then the documents.
3. Click **Add Meeting Document(s)** to finish the job.

More Zoho Projects

Now that I've discussed the essential modules, I'll talk about other features of Projects that can help you bill your clients, generate nice reports, and communicate better in your team.

Billing clients

Projects allows you to register the hours you (and your team) put on different tasks so you can bill your clients based on such data and pay the third-party contractors accordingly. This makes it easy to track the work done. The `Timesheet` module is responsible for this job. It registers the time spent by each user on a certain task and indicates whether it is billable. More important, it integrates with Zoho Invoice (see Chapter 12) to help you prepare professional invoices to be sent to your clients. (Please note that this feature is not available in the free version of Projects.)

Logging hours

The first thing you need to do is log how many hours you and your colleagues have spent on specific tasks in a project. Then you will be able to actually bill the clients by showing them the time allocated to the project in general and the tasks in detail.

To log work hours in the `Timesheet` module, follow these steps:

1. Open the `Timesheet` tab. A calendar opens showing the various tasks in the project (Figure 13-19).

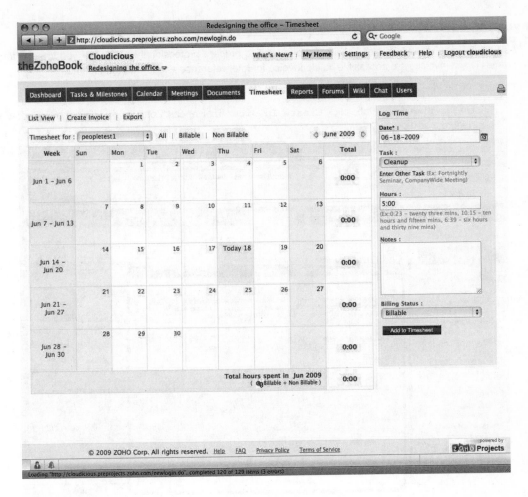

Figure 13-19. Filling the sheet

2. In the calendar (or through the sidebar), select a date, and choose a task belonging to that day from the **Task** list.
3. Enter the time spent on the task in **Hours**, and then set the billing status (**Billable** or **Non Billable**) in **Billing Status**.
4. Click **Add to Timesheet** to log the work.

After adding each log, the total of hours spent on various tasks on a specific day will be displayed on the calendar, linkable to a details page.

To get a quick report on how many hours every user spends doing different tasks, click **Export** on the top of the timesheet.

Invoicing clients

As I said, Timesheet works closely with Zoho Invoice to prepare professional invoices for you to send to clients. These invoices are accessible inside Invoice for later reference and further management.

To generate an invoice for the (logged) billable tasks, follow these steps:

1. On the `Timesheet` tab, click `Create Invoice`. This opens Zoho Invoice in a new window (Figure 13-20).

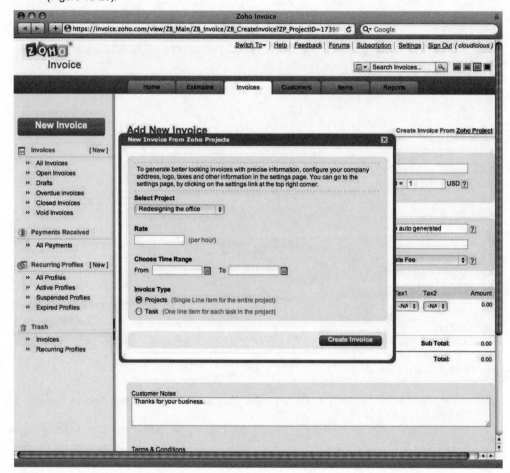

Figure 13-20. Issuing an invoice through Zoho Invoice

2. Enter the rate for every hour in `Rate`.
3. Set a time range by setting dates in `From` and `To`. This will tell Invoice to add the logged tasks performed during this period of time.

4. Select `Task` to list each task separately and invoice each item.
5. Click `Create Invoice` to proceed.
6. In Invoice, review the generated invoice, and follow the on-screen instructions to finalize the invoice.

Reporting projects

What would a project management application be without reports and especially Gantt charts? Projects offers a decent reporting module that is very easy to use and provides you with several types of reports.

> **_Gantt charts_** _are bar charts in which each bar indicates the progress of a specific task in a project. You can get more information about them at http://en.wikipedia.org/wiki/Gantt_chart._

Printing reports is as easy as clicking the printer icon (on the top right of the **Reports** tab). This will open the standard print dialog box, and you can change the settings (page size, orientation, and so on) before printing.

To access reports, open the **Reports** tab, and select between various reports and statistics from the sidebar. You can see the following:

- A Gantt chart for the open tasks in Figure 13-21
- A Gantt chart for closed milestones in Figure 13-22
- A list view of the open tasks in Figure 13-23
- A user task summary report in Figure 13-24

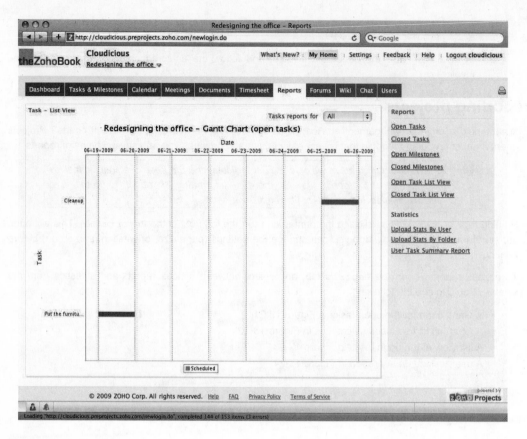

Figure 13-21. Gantt chart

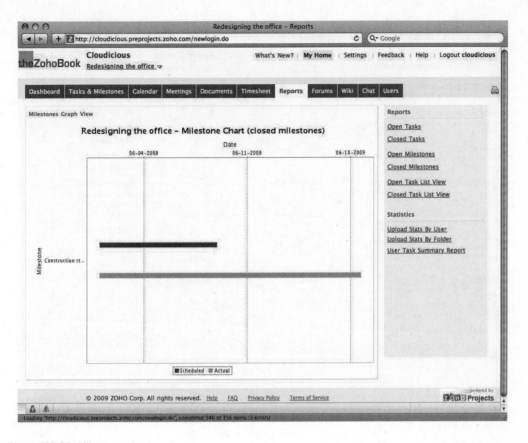

Figure 13-22. Milestone chart

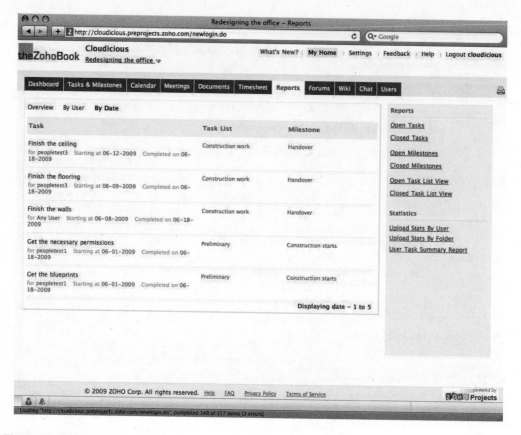

Figure 13-23. Task list

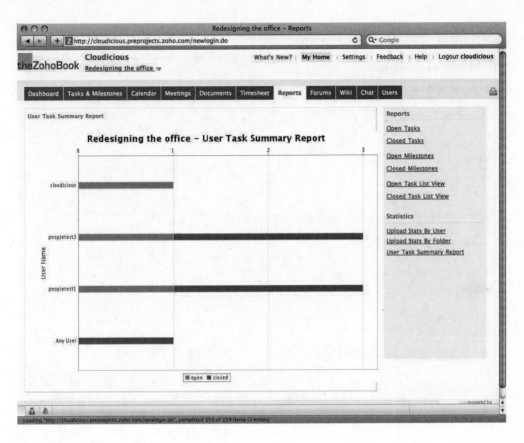

Figure 13-24. User task summary

Communicating with peers

As mentioned a few times in the previous sections, Projects offers you a set of communication tools to help you stay in sync with peers and document the project life cycle as you go. Not many (if any) project management tools provide such a rich set of built-in collaboration tools. You can use the forum, wiki, chat, and homepage to communicate uninterruptedly with all people involved in your project.

Using the forum

The `Forums` module provides you and other team members with an easy-to-use platform in which you can start discussions around the current project and post replies to share the information with the team.

The first time you open forums, you need to click `Get started by posting your first forum post`. Enter something for `Title` and `Content` regarding the discussion. Then click `Submit` to start the discussion thread (Figure 13-25).

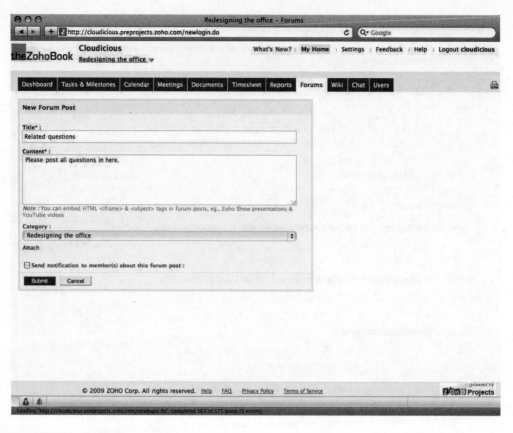

Figure 13-25. Creating a forum thread

Users can check the forums and participate in the discussions by posting replies to a thread (Figure 13-26). It is possible to attach documents and set specific users to be notified about a reply. You will soon have a plethora of valuable information documented in the system for current and future projects.

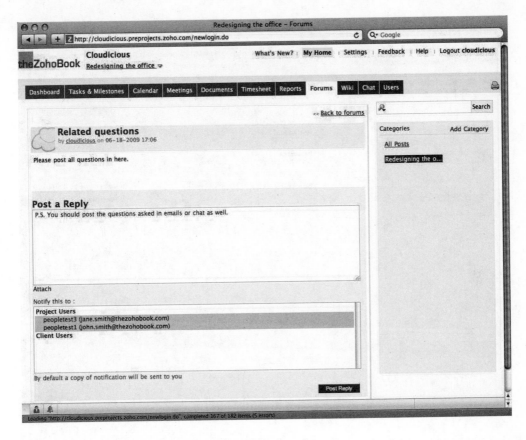

Figure 13-26. Posting a reply to a thread and notifying the users

You can create additional categories (only one by default) by clicking **Add Category** in the sidebar. It is also possible to search in the post for specific terms. Just enter the search phrase in the search box on top of the sidebar, and press **Enter** on the keyboard.

Using the wiki

You learned about Zoho Wiki in Chapter 7. Projects features a limited version of Wiki for every project, which allows you to document almost anything concerning the project (Figure 13-27).

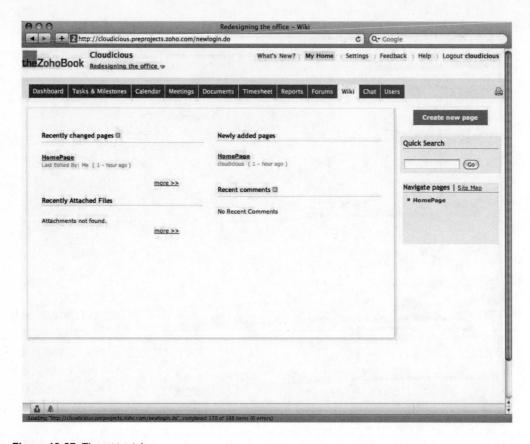

Figure 13-27. The `Wiki` tab

Although a wiki is not really a communication tool, it helps you share information and collaborate. Open the `Wiki` tab, and you will see the familiar face of Zoho Wiki. You can add pages, attach files, and comment on different content.

> *Refresh your memory by taking a quick look at Chapter 7 if you have trouble using the* `Wiki` *module.*

Using the chat

It is useful to have a chat feature available to brainstorm and discuss with other team members while working on a project.

Open the `Chat` tab to start chatting with other online peers right away. You can start new topics, add new participants, and send files while chatting (Figure 13-28).

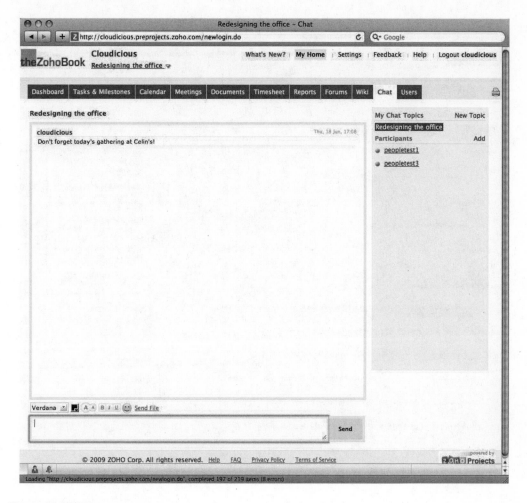

Figure 13-28. The `Chat` module

Using the `Chat` module, it doesn't matter where the users are. With seamless communication, it can feel like everybody is working in the same room.

Back home

It might sound strange to talk about the `Home` page at the end of this chapter, but if I had discussed it at the beginning, it would look like an empty and pointless page. Now that you have created a project and entered information in the system, you can open the `Home` tab by clicking `My Home` at the top right and check out the somewhat crowded command center (Figure 13-29).

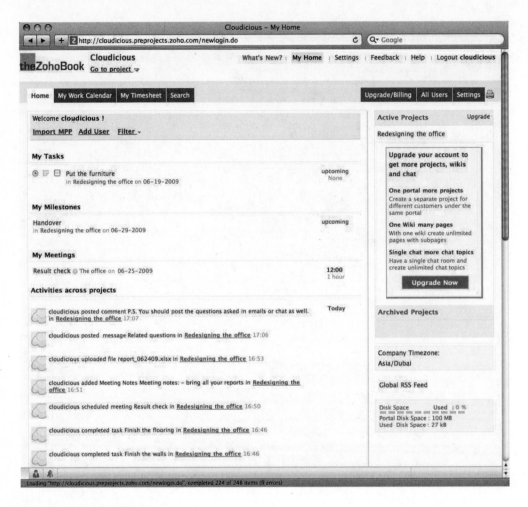

Figure 13-29. The Home page

On the Home page, you can do the following:

- Check your pending tasks and milestones
- Check your upcoming meetings
- Monitor the system-wide activities, related to all projects (based on your access level)
- Quickly access to your work calendar and timesheet

You can also subscribe to the global RSS feed that contains the latest activities, which are basically short messages about who is doing what in the system. This helps you monitor the activities using any standard feed reader (Google Reader, and so on) on your computer or your mobile device.

A tiny bar below the RSS link will show you the used disk space so that you can upgrade before your account exceeds the quota. Any kind of information you add (documents, wiki, tasks, and so on) uses some of the available disk space, so you need to keep an eye on this section.

Click **Filter** on the menu bar to open a box in which you can filter the output of the activities list (Figure 13-30). This makes it easier to monitor a specific user, certain project, and so on. Click Go to apply the filter. To show all activities again, select **All**, **All**, and **Any user** (in the given order) in the drop-down lists.

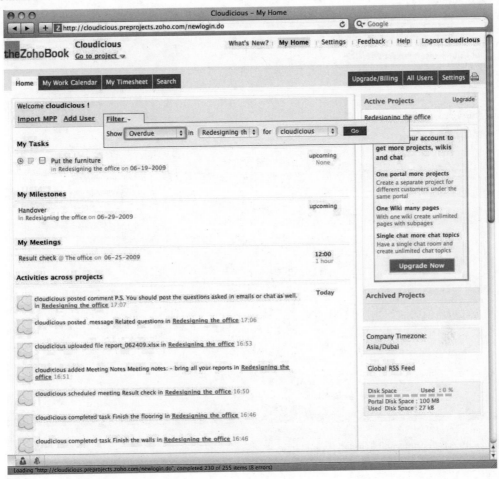

Figure 13-30. Filtering the output

Finally, you can import Microsoft Project files into Projects. This makes the migration process much quicker, in case you want to manage your projects in the cloud.

1. On the **Home** tab, click **Import MPP** in the menu bar.
2. Click **Choose File**, and browse for the Microsoft Project file in your computer.
3. Select the destination project in **Select Project Name**, and then click the **Import MPP** button (Figure 13-31).

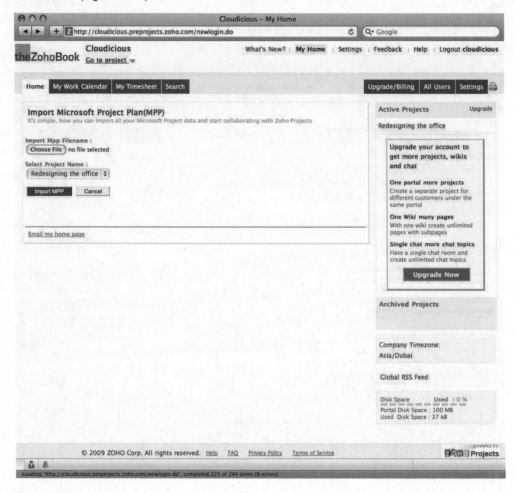

Figure 13-31. Importing a Microsoft Project plan

Getting help

These links can be useful if you need more information about project management:

- `http://www.nickjenkins.net/prose/projectPrimer.pdf`
- `http://www.suite101.com/course.cfm/17517/lessons`
- `http://www.ccpace.com/resources/documents/agileprojectmanagement.pdf`

Zoho also provides completely updated documentation for the latest version of Projects. It is available from `http://www.zoho.com/projects/help/`. Checking related threads in the forums at `http://forums.zoho.com` will be a great help too.

Summary

Many businesses use project management tools in order to control the progress of their projects and the resources involved. Zoho Projects is a solution that stands out well in the crowd. Featuring an innovative approach, it adds social networking features to the basic tools, which makes it a perfect candidate for managing small to medium-sized projects.

It is very easy to use and can be set up for a production environment in a matter of minutes. It interacts well with the user, thanks to its engaging UI, and provides the latest information in an uncluttered environment.

Projects is well connected to some of other Zoho tools, such as the productivity suite and Invoice, adding even more value to the package. For additional interoperability, its import and export features come in handy.

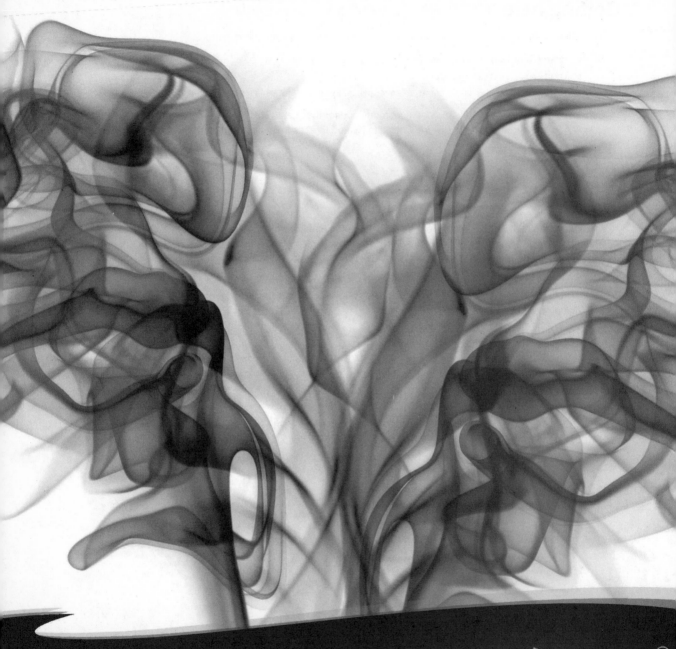

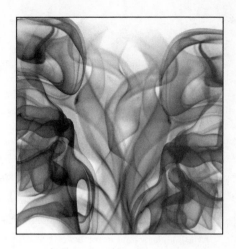

Chapter 14

Take Control of Your Meetings

In a world where everybody has access to the Internet (mostly through a fast connection), walking to business meetings is overrated—let alone traveling business-class thousands of miles and wasting time, money, and the environment—just to attend a meeting.

> *You might be thinking that not everybody has an Internet connection. Well, I'm assuming everybody who goes to business meetings has some sort of access to the Internet.*

Holding and attending online meetings is convenient, is cheap, is eco-friendly, and makes sense most of the time. I can hear the skeptics now, but people said similar things when the telephone was not very popular and shouting over a weird handset was awkwardly suspicious.

The benefits of face-to-face meetings are obvious, but in many cases preferring them over online meetings is like saying "Instead of giving my clients a call, I'll just drop by their office." Face-to-face meetings might be more effective at times, but it can waste a great deal of time and money getting there, especially if you work with people around the world.

In this chapter, you'll evaluate one of the cloud-based applications, Zoho Meeting, that allows you to run online meetings and more.

Zoho Meeting

Zoho Meeting is a powerful tool for running business meetings, presentations, and remote assistance. You can virtually skip many face-to-face meetings by leveraging the features of Meeting in your business.

Using Meeting, you can do the following:

- Run meetings and web conferences with an unlimited number of participants (and run free one-to-one meetings)
- Participate in multiple meetings simultaneously
- Ensure a secure session via Secure Sockets Layer (SSL) connections
- Share desktops for demonstration and presentation purposes
- Run customer service sessions with desktop sharing and remote assistance facilities
- Run presentations with multiple presenters anywhere/anytime
- Embed meeting sessions in websites, allowing visitors to interact with your products

> *Meeting supports voice conferencing facilities if you live in the United States or Europe. It also supports SkypeOut, an outgoing call service from Skype (http://www.skype.com).*

With Meeting, time and location are no longer barriers to your communications. You can sit in your living room in New York and participate in a presentation session happening live in your branch office in London. The presenter can share her desktop with other participants to show everybody an analysis chart about the last season's sales. You can then take over the meeting (still in your living room) to explain your specialty.

In another scenario, if your customers call your customer service department asking for troubleshooting help, your support team can start a remote assistance session, taking control of the customer's machine while trying to solve the issue remotely.

All said, let's tour Meeting to see how it can help you in your business.

Getting started

To open Meeting, log on to http://meeting.zoho.com. It is accessible from within Zoho Business too. After logging in, you will be redirected to the Meeting home page where a simple UI welcomes you.

You can see the essence of Meeting summarized in two buttons: **Create Meeting** and **Remote Assistance** (Figure 14-1). These are the destinations you will go to most of the time.

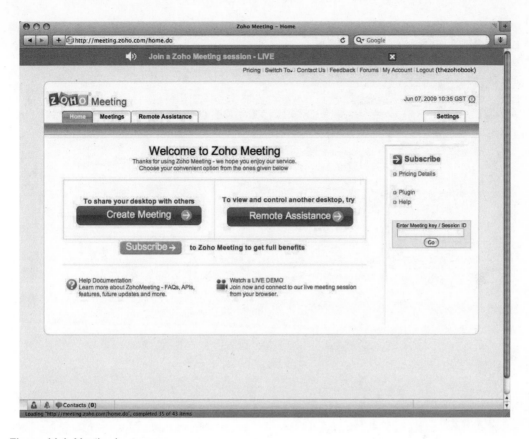

Figure 14-1. Meeting home page

Using Meeting

Using Meeting is all about creating meetings. Remote support is just a meeting session with a few more features, which you will learn about later in this chapter.

Creating a meeting

To set up a new meeting session in which you are going to be a presenter (the one holding the meeting), follow these steps:

1. Click **Create Meeting** in the home page.
2. In the **Create Meeting** form, enter the meeting information (Figure 14-2).

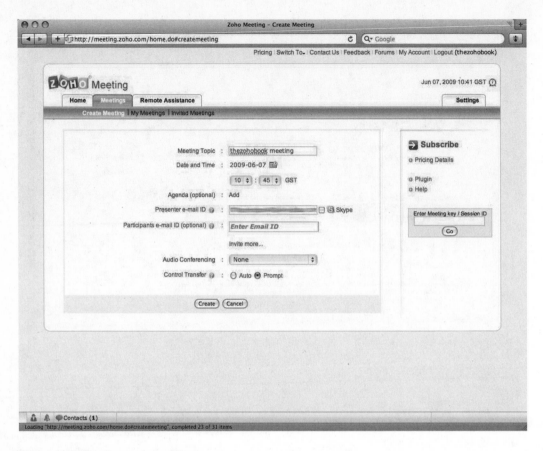

Figure 14-2. Creating a new meeting

a. Set a topic and a date when the meeting takes place.

b. Click **Add** next to the **Agenda** heading to enter a few lines about the subjects that will be covered in the meeting.

c. Leave the **Presenter e-mail ID** (it will be your default address, but you can select Skype and enter a valid Skype ID to make voice chat available).

d. Select Zoho Audio in **Audio Conferencing**.

e. Leave **Control Transfer** to be set to Prompt for participants to ask every time they want to take control. In other words, this sets how you (as the presenter) want other participants to take control of the meeting.

Click **Create** to proceed. On the next page, a summary will show you the meeting details. Although the meeting is created, it is not yet active.

3. Click **Start** to begin the meeting (Figure 14-3).

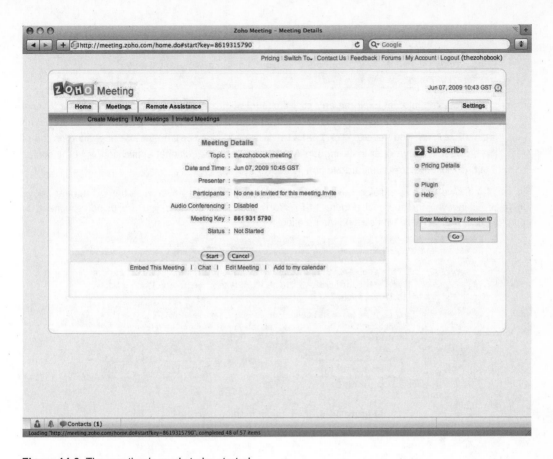

Figure 14-3. The meeting is ready to be started.

Note the **Meeting Key** field. It is the key that people (anybody who is not invited initially) can use to join the meeting.

There is a useful link below the meeting details: **Add to my calendar**. This adds the meeting date and time to Microsoft Outlook, Yahoo Calendar, or Google Calendar.

An important point is that Meeting will open a secondary window that holds a tool in charge of running the meeting for you. This tool will be installed automatically for you. Although you are probably not interested in what happens in the background, you should know that for security reasons this application needs your permission to start.

- If you are using Firefox or Safari, a Java applet (the tool) will be installed. A **Java applet** is a special kind of program that downloads and runs on your computer when certain functionalities are not possible via the conventional browser capabilities. Although Java is designed to minimize security threats, you need to know the source of an applet before trusting it.

> *You need to have Java runtime environment (JRE) in order to run Java applets. Most modern operating systems ship with some kind of JRE, but if the browser warns you that you don't have one, you must install one after downloading it from http://www.java.com/en/download.*

- If you are using Internet Explorer, an ActiveX control will install. ActiveX controls are similar to Java applets in functionality but run only on Internet Explorer (Windows only). So, if you are using Internet Explorer, you need to click `Install ActiveX Control` on the bar appearing on top of the browser window. After installing the ActiveX control, an additional application will be installed that has more features compared to non-Windows users.

Figure 14-4 shows a warning dialog box in Safari. In Internet Explorer, however, a bar will appear above the page asking you for approval (Figure 14-5). No matter what browser you are using, you need to approve (trust) it to proceed with starting the meeting.

Figure 14-4. Java applet running warning

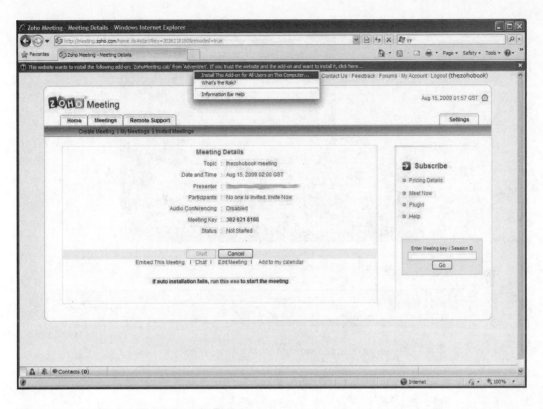

Figure 14-5. The warning bar in Internet Explorer

Once you have trusted the applet/ActiveX control, you will see the meeting bar appearing on the bottom of your screen as well as the **Meeting** window. As you can see, the appearance of the meeting bar is a bit different for Windows users (Figure 14-6) and non-Windows users (Figure 14-7). Don't close any of these windows while the meeting is running.

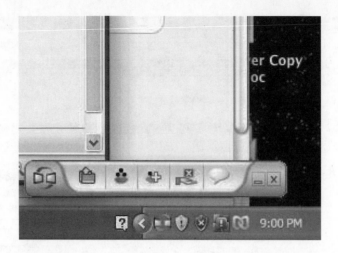

Figure 14-6. The meeting toolbar for Windows users

Figure 14-7. The meeting toolbar for non-Windows users

The secondary window holding the applet control will look like Figure 14-8. Windows users won't see this.

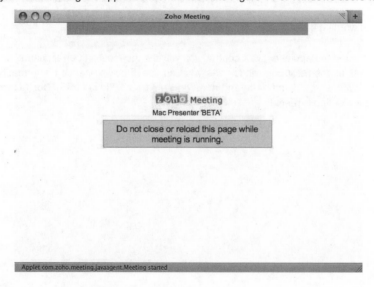

Figure 14-8. The applet page for non-Windows users

The meeting session has started, and the participants can see your screen. You can now open documents and presentations to share with them while having text and voice conversations.

Now let's see the other side of the story.

Participating in a meeting

Suppose you are a participant who wants to join a meeting session. There are two scenarios:

- First you receive an e-mail invitation containing a link to the meeting page. Just click `Join Session`, and you are in.
- If you are not invited by e-mail, you need the meeting key to join the session. Here is what you need to do:
    1. Obtain the meeting key.
    2. Visit the home page of Meeting (`http://meeting.zoho.com`).
    3. Click `Join Meeting Session` to proceed.
    4. On the next page, fill in the `Name` and `Email`. Then enter the meeting key in `Meeting Key/Session ID`.
    5. Click `Join Session` to take you there.

A dialog box will appear asking you whether you want the Java viewer or Flash viewer (Figure 14-9). Windows users will have an extra option, an ActiveX viewer. Choose the Java or ActiveX viewer because with them, you can participate actively, meaning you can take over the presentation by asking for control. With the Flash version, you can only be an audience member.

Choose your viewer, and click `Join` again to start the session. You might see the certificate confirmation dialog box again asking you to trust the Java applet. Click `Trust` to proceed.

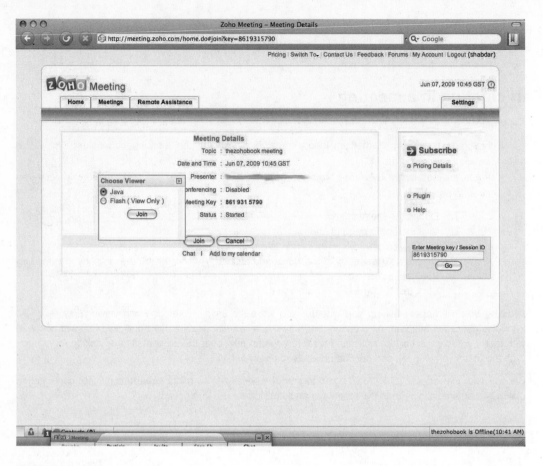

Figure 14-9. Joining a meeting

Depending on your connection speed (and the presenter's too), it will take a few seconds until you see the presenter's screen on your computer. You can see what the presenter is doing in decent resolution and color. As you can see by comparing the two screens (the viewer's screen in Figure 14-10 and the presenter's screen in Figure 14-11), the user experience is very good, and you can see everything as it happens, although at a slower pace.

Figure 14-10. The desktop sharing window

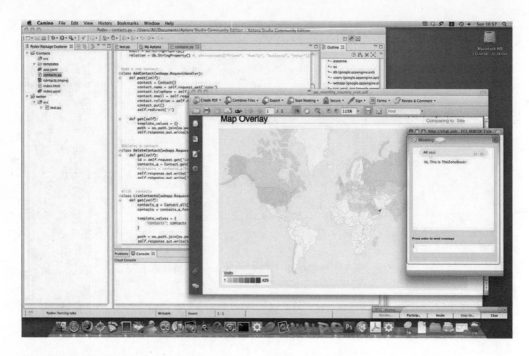

Figure 14-11. The original desktop (refer to Figure 14-10)

> *I am running both parties on the same computer, which is why they have similar screens. In a real-life scenario, it will definitely look different.*

Running a support session

One of the great features Meeting offers you is the ability to hold support sessions through remote assistance. This is especially useful if you are running an IT-related business or have an IT department taking care of many workstations in different locations.

Suppose a client of yours is having trouble using a software package you sold them. Instead of requiring the client to make frequent field trips, wasting time and money, your support team can simply log on to the clients' workstations and solve the issue remotely.

In a similar case, you can do remote support for your own organization where you have hundreds (or thousands) of employees struggling with trivial issues such as running a specific program, printing, backing up data, and so on, every day. This will save you time and money.

> *As of this writing, Meeting works better (on the host part) on Windows machines. Linux and Mac OS support are in beta phase, meaning they will have the full support soon.*

There are two ways to perform a remote support session:

- While having a normal meeting by asking for control permission. This is when the peer who wants to perform the support tasks wants to control the host machine. This is done by clicking the **Request Remote Control** button on the viewer toolbar (an orange and white icon with a green arrow on it).
- By running a dedicated remote support session, which you'll learn about next.

To perform remote support while in a normal meeting, follow these steps:

1. Click **Request Remote Control** in the viewer toolbar (Figure 14-12).

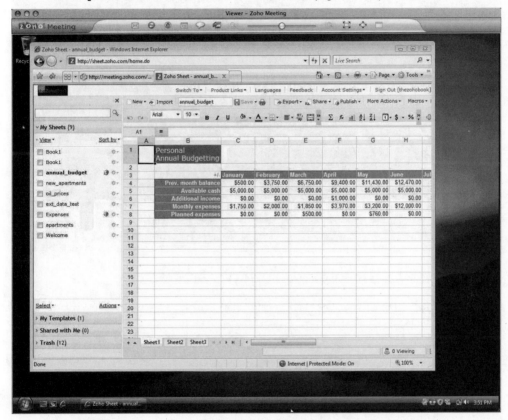

Figure 14-12. The **Request Remote Control** button on the viewer toolbar, sixth from the left

2. As the host (presenter) asking for the support session, click **Yes** for the confirmation dialog box asking for permission to allow you to perform the task (Figure 14-13).

Figure 14-13. Remote control confirmation appearing on the host machine.

3. Click OK in the dialog box announcing that you have a successful control transfer (Figure 14-14).

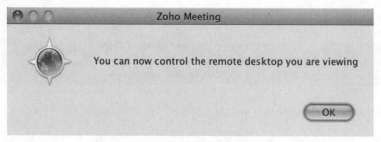

Figure 14-14. The remote connection allowed

In Figure 14-15 you can see a meeting view with granted control displaying the desktop of a Windows Vista machine. It is now possible to run different applications and perform troubleshooting remotely on the host.

Figure 14-15. Controlling the remote computer

The second way of running a remote session is to directly create a `Remote Support` meeting at the beginning. This should be done by the support professional.

To run a remote support session, follow these steps:

1. On the `Home` tab in Meeting, click `Remote Support`.
2. On the next page under `Start Session`, enter the e-mail address of the customer (needing assistance), and then click `Start` (Figure 14-16).

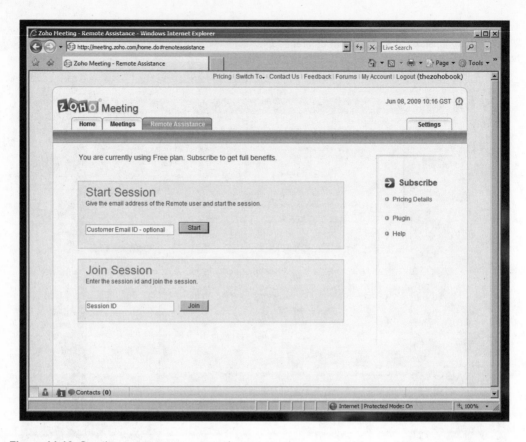

Figure 14-16. Creating a remote support session

Once the session is started, the customer will receive a message with a link to the meeting. Additional people can join using the meeting key provided.

After the other party joins the session (through e-mail or directly using the meeting key), she will see the viewer window opening along with the `Meeting Details` and `Chat` windows. Just like in Figure 14-15, this will display the host machine ready to be controlled remotely. But if the host is still not connected (or temporarily disconnected), a blue screen with the message `Waiting for the Presenter`... will be displayed (Figure 14-17).

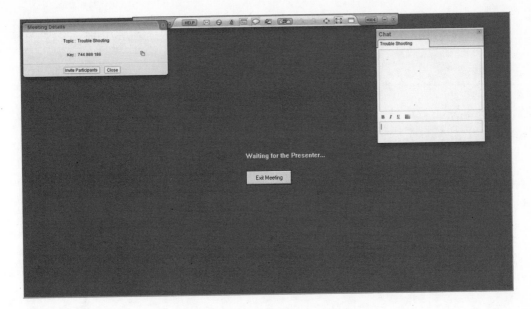

Figure 14-17. Waiting for the presenter

Managing meetings

After running multiple meetings and remote assistance sessions, you will be happy to know that Meeting keeps the sessions you have created, in case you need to run them again. The `Meetings` tab holds a few more features by which you will be able to manage your meetings.

It has three subtabs (or pages):

- `Create Meeting`: Creates a new meeting. You saw this in the previous sections.
- `My Meetings`: Lists all the meetings you have ever created along with some tools to manage them.
- `Invited Meetings`: Lists the meetings you are invited to.

Taking a closer look at `My Meetings` (Figure 14-18) will show you the following tasks that could be done through this page.

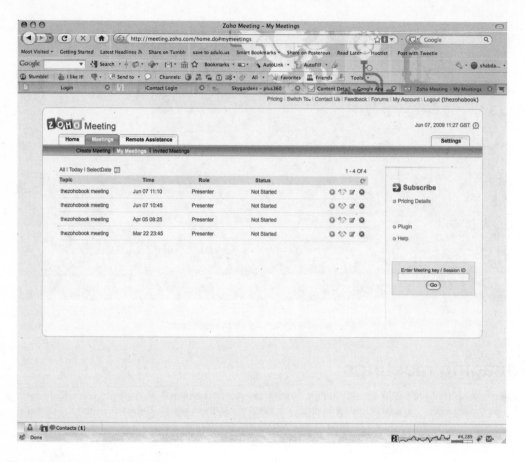

Figure 14-18. Managing the meetings

- Clicking each topic (under `Topic`) will open the meeting details.
- `Time` shows when the meeting was created.
- `Role` indicates your role, such as presenter, in that specific session.
- Status could be either `Started` or `Not Started`, showing whether that session is running.
- The green icon, `Start Meeting`, will start the session immediately. Then it will turn red, `Stop meeting`, and clicking it again will stop the session.
- The shake-hand icon, if enabled (when a meeting is started), allows you to join that specific meeting.
- The next icon is `Edit Meeting`, allowing you to modify the meeting.
- The last icon, `Delete meeting`, removes the meeting permanently.

Suppose you have weekly board meetings that happen every Thursday at 10 a.m. Once you create the session in Meeting for the first time, you can rerun it every Thursday instead of creating it again. Since the participants already have the meeting key, there is no need for sending invitations every week. They just have to log onto Meeting and join the session by entering the meeting key.

Configuring Meeting

The last tab to be discussed is the **Settings** tab (Figure 14-19), where you can perform some basic configuration. There's not much to be configured, but you should still review this page.

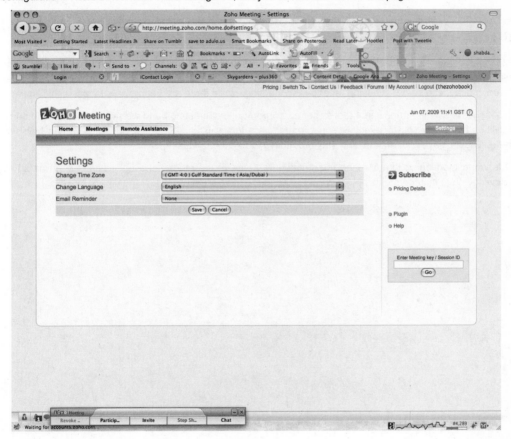

Figure 14-19. Basic setup

3. On the **Settings** tab, set the time zone to your local time.
   Set an e-mail reminder to help you remember the upcoming meetings, such as 30 minutes before.
4. Click **Save** for the changes to apply.

Getting help

Meeting is very easy to use, even though it offers you some very powerful tools. Since I covered most of its features in this chapter, you can get started with it right away. If you get stuck at some point, you can always check the official documentation at `http://meeting.zoho.com/home.do#help`.

You can also always check the forums to find answers to your questions (`http://forums.zoho.com/#Forum/zoho-meeting`).

Summary

Meetings are as old as history itself, and surprisingly enough, there hasn't been much improvement in the way we have held meetings throughout the centuries—until the cloud, that is. We waste a lot of resources (time, money, and so on) in having face-to-face meetings while there are better ways to tackle this issue.

Meeting is a simple yet powerful tool to set up corporate-level meetings and web conferences. It features facilities that allow you to remotely control computers for assistance or other purposes. It can help you reduce costs, save a lot of time, and stay productive in day-to-day business.

It is worth mentioning that Meeting integrates with some of the other Zoho applications such as CRM, allowing you to incorporate its power in customer support into Meeting.

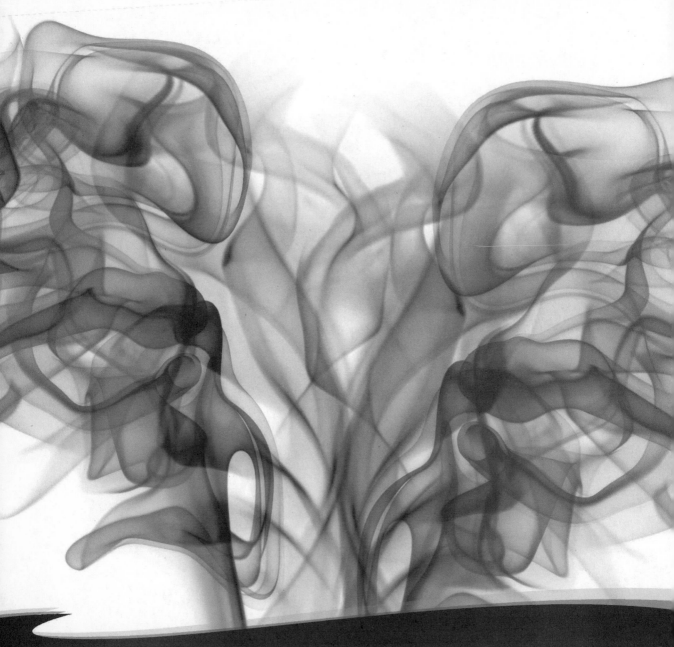

ZOHO®
Work. Online

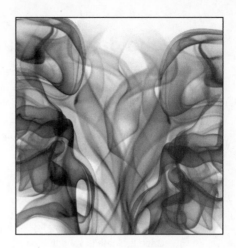

Chapter 15

Data Is Everything

Us humans, being the most intelligent beings on Earth, can process huge amounts of information. Whether it's in the form of text or visuals, there have been endless pieces of information stored on stone, animal skin, and paper throughout the thousands of years of human civilization. From the Cyrus cylinder (http://en.wikipedia.org/wiki/Cyrus_cylinder) to *On the Origin of Species* (http://en.wikipedia.org/wiki/Origin_of_species), valuable information had been processed, written, and kept safe for us to refer to and reuse.

Living in the Internet age, we have come a long way in how we store information (data), preserve it, and present it to the world. I won't bore you with the details of how data is stored in computers, but I would like to emphasize that almost any kind of data you access is stored in some kind of database.

In this chapter, you'll take a quick look at what databases are. Then you will learn how to create database and business intelligence (BI) applications using cloud-based tools to solve complex problems. The chapter's focus will be on Zoho Creator and Zoho Reports, two powerful applications that can satisfy your data management, analysis, and report-generating requirements. You will also get a glimpse of cloud-based database application development using Google AppEngine and Zoho CloudSQL.

To get the most of this chapter, you don't need to have prior knowledge of data structures or database design. Just bring your general ability of using computers. Being familiar with spreadsheets is also beneficial.

Before you continue, I'll mention that in other chapters of the book, you were an end user only. In this chapter, however, you have two roles: user and developer. In your first role, you will use Zoho Creator and Zoho Reports as a developer creating new tools that others (your clients, colleagues, and so on) will use, and that, my friends, is pretty exciting.

Why Zoho data applications matter

There are many database platforms (for example, Microsoft Access, MySQL, and SQLite) that store and manage big volumes of data. They are also used extensively in online applications, such as in yellow pages, CMSs, blogs, and e-commerce sites.

When you as an end user run any application that somehow deals with data, either on your computer or on the Internet, a lot is going on in the background, apart from the shiny user interface (UI) that you interact with.

For example, in an address book application, a simple task such as adding a new contact involves many steps. To put it simply, for a new contact to be added, the application must take these steps:

1. Collect the contact information (name, telephone number, and so on) through the UI.
2. Validate the information. For example, is the telephone number correct?
3. Once the data is validated, store it in the database.

Although I've simplified this a bit, it shows that a typical task involves three layers:

- *Presentation layer*: Where user interaction happens through the UI, such as in forms and reports
- *Logic layer*: Where the evaluations, calculations, and decisions are applied
- *Data layer*: Where the real data is stored

Implementing such processes can be cumbersome and time-consuming. Imagine a small address book application that could have dozens of such processes under the hood, which leads to thousands of lines of code and sleepless nights of debugging. That's why software developers drink a lot of coffee! Each one of these layers often needs a separate tool for design and development, so developers deal with at least two to three different tools to make software.

There are, however, solutions to make the process a little easier. Microsoft Access (for Windows) and FileMaker Pro (for Windows or Mac) are two popular software applications that provide users with everything in one package. You can create all three layers of a database application with one package. Input forms, reports and analysis, validations and calculations, and the data itself are all stored in one single package.

Such luxury was never possible online, meaning you needed to do everything separately and often manually. But with the emergence of SaaS, some companies started to offer better ways of creating online data-driven applications. In my opinion, Zoho took even a bigger step compared to other providers. Zoho Creator and Zoho Reports are two amazing applications that provide you with powerful application creation and BI tools. All these tools are cloud-based and benefit from the special characteristics of SaaS applications.

The reason it is so important to understand the value of these two applications is that creating online database-driven applications and providing cloud-based reporting and BI solutions are two of greatest challenges of the IT industry. Both Creator and Reports address many real-life issues.

> *Zoho Creator was the starting point for me to use the Zoho suite. When I made a small database application in a single day that could tackle one of the main bottlenecks we were suffering in my former company (back in 2007), I fell in love with SaaS and Zoho in particular. It is rather flattering to say that the company still uses my tiny application in parallel with an enterprise-level CRM. You don't need a Ferrari for a street race when a Golf GTI will do.*

Getting started with Creator

Before you get your hands on Creator and create jaw-dropping applications, let me tell you why you should be very excited about it.

So far in this book you have used various applications to solve your day-to-day problems. SaaS applications like Zoho Writer, Wiki, and CRM all offer plenty of features to work in the cloud.

Creator, on the other hand, is more of a PaaS service. To refresh your memory, PaaS stands for "platform as a service" and provides you with the means of creating applications that work in the cloud.

Imagine you want to run your real estate business online. Well, you have the productivity tools to create and manage your documents. You also have Invoice, CRM, and so on, to take care of your clients and other paperwork. But what if you want to manage the listings you sell or rent?

You could purchase or order a third-party software package that works online and connects to your website and CRM as well, but we are talking about a few thousand dollars of investment here.

Another solution is to develop your own software. I know, you are no software developer, and that is exactly why you are reading this chapter. Using Creator, you can create scalable database applications easily even if you are not database savvy.

> *There is also the option of hiring somebody to create the application in Creator for you. Even if you pay someone to create a database for you in Creator, it will be cheaper and faster to deliver because of Creator's unique features.*

Creator provides you with all the necessary tools for making capable database applications for personal and business use, hosted and managed by Zoho (which is a SaaS, remember?) for a low monthly cost (apart from the available free edition). It takes a few clicks and drags and drops for an application to get up and running.

If you know Microsoft Access and know how easy it is to create and run powerful database applications, it is probably true to say that Creator is Access for the cloud, although I believe it has even more potential.

Hoping you are already excited, let's get to work right away. If you have no idea what a database is and you have never created an application before, keep reading the next section; otherwise, you can skip it and proceed with "The Creator way."

> *If you're an absolute beginner, read all sections carefully, and practice by trying different options. Go through each subject more than once if needed until you understand the process, and use the resources introduced in "Getting help." Have patience and practice.*

Thinking database

Simply put, a **database** is a collection of information structured in a human-understandable manner. Although for thousands of years data was stored in mediums like paper, now data resides on and is managed by computers. Computers keep information safer, store it more efficiently, and provide us with much faster access to unimaginable amounts of data. It is incomparable to the pen and paper system.

You can store the entire book collection of the Library of Congress (http://www.loc.gov/) in a single database on a single computer and navigate through every single page of it in a matter of seconds.

The important point is that for computers, man-made structures have no meaning. They store data in their own way, which I will not discuss, but you need to learn about the basics of these structures so you can store your data properly.

What is a table?

In general, databases consist of one or more tables. A **table** is an entity in which the data is stored in a tabular structure, or at least we imagine it to be in a tabular structure in order to understand it better.

Take a grocery list or a client list, for example. They both structure information in tables with columns specifying different types of information, and rows of data follow next to each other. Generally, the columns are called **fields**, and the rows are called **records**.

Say I wanted to create an application to keep a record of my grocery shopping over time. I would need a table that stores the information in a format similar to Table 15-1.

Table 15-1. A Typical Grocery List

Date	No.	Item	Quantity	Unit
03.20.09	1	Milk	1	Gallon
03.20.09	2	Bread	2	Loaves
03.20.09	3	Eggs	1	Dozen
03.20.09	4	Pasta	3	Packs
03.20.09	5	Cereal	1	Packs

In this table, each row (record) of data has five columns (fields) storing all the information I need to store in the database. Each data value, for example, `Pasta`, resides on a certain row (**4**) and under a certain column (`Item`). So, it is easy to find a value if you know its row and column.

Later I can analyze the stored data by extracting certain portions of it and performing calculations on the information. For example, I might be interested to know how often I buy milk or what the average monthly spending is during the summer.

What are data types?

One important point you need to remember while creating databases (and tables in particular) is that computers store values in a way that they can differentiate their types. This means every data value stored in a table has a certain type.

For example, in Table 15-1, `Date` is a Date type, `No.` is a Number type, `Item` is a Text type, `Quantity` is a Number type, and `Unit` is a Text type.

The reason there are different data types is to make it easier for computers to perform calculations specific to those particular data types. For instance, the addition (+) calculation has a different effect depending on the data type:

- For a Number type: `1 + 1 = 2`
- For a Date value: `May 31, 2009 + 1 = June 1, 2009` (1 is a single day)
- For a Text type: "`John`" + "`Smith`" = "`John Smith`"

Why all the hassle? If you take a closer look at the previous example, you will see that for us humans it is rather easy and instantaneous to differentiate the data types while calculating. You know by heart how to add two numbers in a different way than adding two words, but computers, believe it or not, are very dumb. You need to sketch every single step of the road for them so they can do a job properly. But once they have done it properly once, it will be flawless and super-fast afterward.

By setting data types for each column in a table, you tell the database application how to treat the data. So, when you want it to calculate the total number of the items purchased in Table 15.1, the application will instantly know that `Item` is a Number type and the calculation on this column should a mathematical addition. The proper answer in this case is 8, but can you guess what the answer would be if you set `Item` as a Text type? It would be `12131` because the computer would have performed a textual addition, that is, **concatenation**.

Don't worry if this is still confusing. Once you practice with the examples in this chapter, you will feel more comfortable setting proper types for data columns.

What is a view?

It would be quite useless if applications allowed you to only store the information without the ability to view it. Since we store data to extract it later, we need ways to interact with data.

A database application usually has features for viewing, filtering, and searching for stored data. The results are extracted from the data by **querying**, which is basically asking the database to show a portion of the data based on the criteria you set in the body of a query.

For instance, in the grocery list application, I should be able to perform queries to get the following:

- The total spending each month throughout the year
- A list of purchased items in the last month sorted by item name
- The purchase trends in my household based on products and volume in a specific period of time

It is common to store a query (as a permanent part of the application) in order to make it accessible multiple times. A stored query is called a **view**. In other words, a query is like an oral request over the phone, and a view is more like a written request letter, accessible for the future reference. Views run a query in the background and show you the result as if you were looking at the data in the table. The result is often filtered and sorted, and it has calculated values.

Another common feature of a database application is the ability to generate reports. **Reports** are technically views that are formatted in different ways. A purchase trend report, for example, extracts the data from the grocery table using a specific view and formats the information in pages for you to print it professionally. Such reports usually come with custom headers and footers containing extra information such as a logo or contact information.

Visualizing a database

You can see a typical database application here. Tables, views, and reports are stored in the database (the yellow cylinder). The application layer (the blue bar) acts as a bridge between the users (the smiley faces) and the database. Different databases have different structures, so this diagram is a generic model.

Now that you have a glimpse of what a database is and how the data and what other objects (tables, views, and so on) are stored in it, you are ready to create your first application in Creator.

> It is hard to explain the concepts of data structure and database design in just a few pages, so you should refer to the related sources if you are interested in serious database development.

The Creator way

If you have already worked with databases before (such as MySQL or Oracle), you will notice that Creator offers a different approach. In traditional database servers, you create and manage the database separately and then develop an application that leverages the database.

In Creator, however, you as the developer focus on the application creation, and Creator will create the underlying database for you. It might seem weird at the beginning, but you will be amazed with the outcome. For example, in our grocery list application, instead of starting from the data layer that includes the database, tables, and views, you first create the forms that collect data from the user, and Creator will do the rest for you.

Forms are responsible for getting the information from the user, validating it, and storing it in the database. Most of the logic of the application happens in the forms, and that's why forms are essential to Creator. Once you have finished creating the forms, the application is pretty much finished and is ready to run. You are going to see how this works in the upcoming sections.

Using Creator

To open Creator, log on to `http://creator.zoho.com`. A chart will ask you to choose your membership plan. For now, choose the **Free** plan because it is quite enough for the purpose of this chapter (Figure 15-1). Later, you can easily upgrade your subscription to any of the available plans with one click.

Figure 15-1. The available subscriptions

Creating an application from a template

Once you have selected the plan, Creator will take you to a screen in which you will start creating your first application (Figure 15-2). You'll create a simple contact application based on the predefined templates available in Creator.

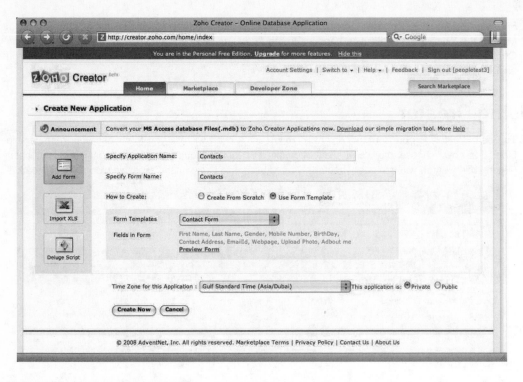

Figure 15-2. Creating a new application

When creating a new application, you have three options:

- Build it from scratch, with or without the help of existing templates
- Import a spreadsheet, and **Creator** will build the application based on the structure of the spreadsheet
- Write (or import) a Deluge script to build your application

> *Deluge is a powerful yet simple scripting language specifically designed for Zoho Creator. It will help you extend your applications greatly, but you can still create business-ready applications without knowing any coding. Because it's an advanced topic, I will not cover it in this book.*

To create a new application, follow these steps:

1. Select **Add Form** (if it is not selected) in the sidebar.
2. Enter **Contacts** for the application name and for the form name. Then select **Use Form Template**, and choose **Contact Form** from the **Form Templates** drop-down list.
3. Set the time zone for the application, and leave the **Private** status selected.
4. Click **Create Now** to proceed.

A new application will be created containing a single form: `Contacts`. Let me remind you that Creator will take care of the underlying table based on the form you have just created. All you need to do is to create the perfect form, and Creator will rebuild the table (in the background) automatically.

> Some good news for Microsoft Access users is that Creator allows you to import an Access database using a migration tool. This will save you a lot of time and effort compared to building everything from scratch.

Customizing the form components

Once the application is created, it will open the design environment (edit mode) where you can modify the current forms and add new ones as well. The `Contacts` form will be opened by default because it is the only form available (Figure 15-3).

Figure 15-3. The `Contacts` form in edit mode

The design environment is divided into five tabs. The `Forms` tab contains the tools available to design various forms with different options.

You can add different components to the form from the sidebar (on the left). Each component represents a data field (columns in a table) that can be used in the form. We'll just stick to the fields added by the template, but I'll explain the process a little more.

Suppose you need the `Contacts` form to have the first name and last name fields so that when the user runs the application, she can enter these values and store them in the database.

Since the first name and last name are just text values, such as John and Smith, you only need to drag a **Single Line** field from the sidebar and drop it on the form. Using **Single Line** components will tell Creator that these fields should accept alphanumerical values.

> *Because we used a template to create the* **Contacts** *form, Creator created the whole form automatically. However, when you want to create forms from scratch, you need to drag fields to the form manually.*

The reason many components are available is to provide you with the necessary tools to build professional applications. For example, although you can enter numerical values in a **Single Line** field, you should be using a **Number** component for the numerical fields in order to only accept numerical values (for example, age). Creator will check the entered value based on its field type in order to guarantee a clean data entry. This means if at runtime you enter **foo** (which happens to be a text value) in a **Number** field that asks for age, **Creator** will show an error message indicating that you need to enter a valid number for age.

> *Users with programming and database background will appreciate the great value of the out-of-the-box validation facilities.*

Let's get back to the form. After you have dropped the necessary fields on the form, you should start customizing them.

To customize the components added to the form, follow these steps:

1. Hover the mouse pointer on the **First Name** field until you see a (beige) rectangle.
2. Move the pointer on the pencil icon (on the left side), and a context menu will appear (Figure 15-4).

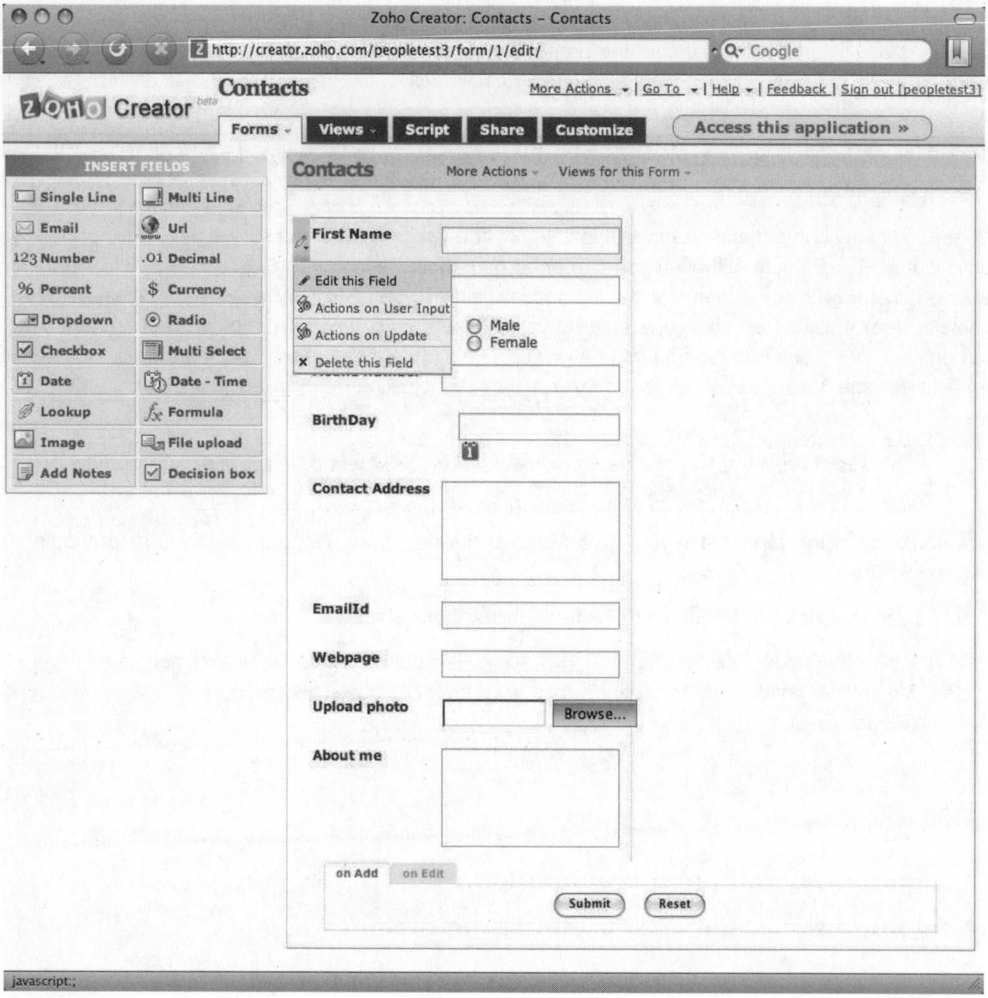

Figure 15-4. The field context menu

3. Click **Edit this Field** to proceed.

In the **Editing** dialog box, specifications of the selected field are ready to be modified. You might see different settings and values based on the field type. For the **First Name** component, which is a **Single Line**, you can set the options shown in Figure 15-5.

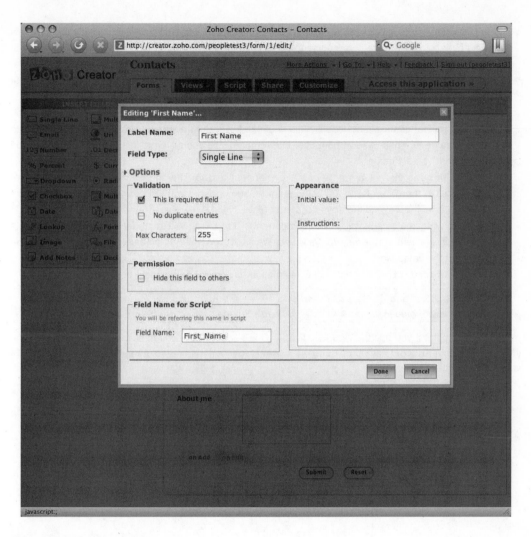

Figure 15-5. Updating a field

- **Label Name** is a caption to the component and gives a short yet descriptive idea about what the user should put in this field. You can put anything here, but make it short and descriptive.
- **Field Type** is actually the component type and is set to **Single Line** (for the first name). You might change this to a similar type, but leave this at this stage.
- If you check **This is required field**, whenever a user tries to add a new contact, **Creator** will check whether she entered this particular field; otherwise, it will display an error requesting the user to enter the field. Enable this validation parameter whenever you don't want users to miss entering a value for a specific field.

- If you select **No duplicate entries**, Creator will check whether the value a user enters for this field already exists in the corresponding table. If yes, it will generate an error asking for a different value. SSN and e-mail addresses are some of the fields that should be unique throughout the table. You can't have two people (two data records) with the same SSN or e-mail address, because that would be like having the same person's information entered twice.
- Checking **Hide this field to others** under **Permission** will make the field invisible in the runtime so that users will not see it. This is useful for custom purposes such as when you want to pass a value to a database without user interference. You should leave this unchecked unless you know what you are doing.
- **Field Name** is the actual name of the component and is different from **Label Name**. Creator uses **Field Name** to refer to the component in the code, but you will not need it unless you want to write code. It is beyond the scope of this book.
- You can write in a default value for a component in **Initial Value** under **Appearance**. It writes a value in the field at runtime, so if the user wants to skip entering a value, the initial value will be stored in the database.
- Finally, **Instruction** will hold textual instruction on how the field should be used.

> **Label Name** and the **Validation** section are the parts you will frequently use, and the rest will come in handy in more advanced scenarios, which are not covered here.

In another example, if you edit the **Gender** field, you will see that the edit form is a bit different because its type is **Radio Button** instead of **Single Line**. Radio buttons help users select from a given list of values for a field.

Let's add a new choice for **Gender**:

1. With the **Editing** dialog box open, click the **Add a Choice** button (the green +), as you see in Figure 15-6.

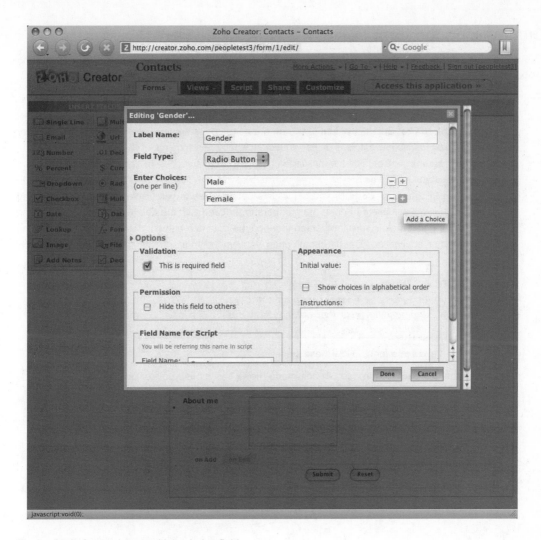

Figure 15-6. Customizing multiple-choice fields

2. Enter a new value (for example, **NA**).
3. Select **This is required Value** to make sure users enter this value.
4. Click **Done** when you finished editing.

> *Try editing other fields to understand the differences between them. This will help you customize the application and learn to choose the right fields for different purposes when you create forms from scratch.*

Customizing the form

Apart from the fields, you can make some customizations on the forms too. You can change the following parameters for every form:

- **Form Name**: Sets the label (caption) of the form, which will be displayed on top of the form at runtime.
- **Form Link Name**: Sets the actual form name as Creator refers to it internally. This is useful for coding purposes, so leave it as is unless you know what you are doing.
- **Success Message**: Contains the message displayed when a successful data record is added.
- **Label Width**: Leave it as is.
- **Need Verification Code**: If you select this option, Creator will display an image containing numbers and will ask users to enter the numbers to proceed with the data entry. It is usually called *CAPTCHA*, and it makes sure the person entering the data is a human, not a software robot trying to spam your application. This is useful when you embed forms in web pages that are publicly available.

> *A CAPTCHA (which stands for Completely Automated Public Turing Test To Tell Computers and Humans Apart)) is a program that protects web sites against bots by generating and grading tests that humans can pass but current computer programs cannot. Check out http://www.captcha.net/ for more information.*

To customize the **Contacts** form, follow these steps:

1. With the **Contacts** form open in edit mode, hover the mouse pointer over **More Actions** on top of the form, and then click **Form Properties** (Figure 15-7).

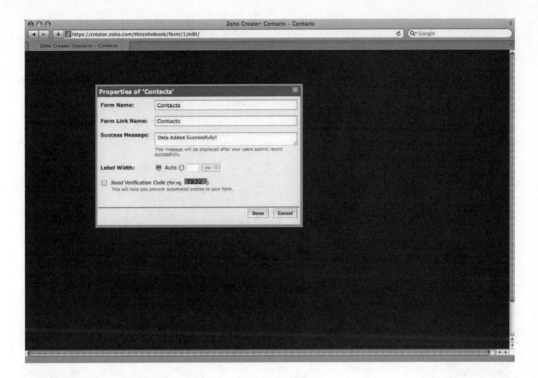

Figure 15-7. Customizing the form

    2. Change the `Form Name` to `Add new contact`.

    3. Click `Done` in order for the changes to take effect.

Setting notifications

You can notify certain people (for example, the administrator) when a new data record is added. This will keep the recipients alerted to the latest activities in order for them to take necessary action if needed.

To set up an e-mail notification, follow these steps:

    1. Click `More Actions ▶ Set Email Notification`. A dialog box will appear allowing you to enable e-mail notifications (Figure 15-8).

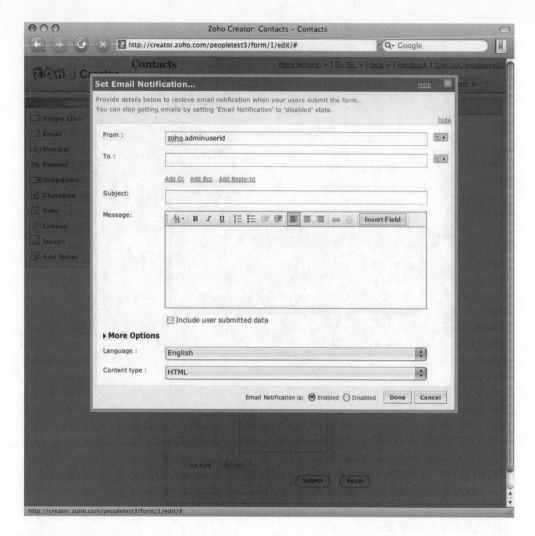

Figure 15-8. Setting up the notification e-mail

2. Type your message just as if you were composing an ordinary e-mail. The message should tell the recipient about the new data record added recently.
3. Select **Enabled** at the bottom of the dialog box, and click **Done**.

Running the application

So far, you have been in edit mode where you were creating and customizing the pieces for your applications. Now that you have a proper form designed, you can run the application and test it to see whether it is functioning as you expected. It is quite normal to switch back and forth between edit mode and run mode while creating an application to test and tweak every piece before rolling it out for others to use.

To run the application, click the big yellow button labeled **Access this application** (at the top right).

In run mode, all design elements vanish, and you can see the real face of the application as well as a sidebar containing the available forms and other objects. Run mode is how the users see the application and how they can interact with it. This interaction includes entering data through forms and querying through views. Since you are the developer (oh, yeah), you have access to both design and run modes.

The **Contacts** form opens by default since it is the only form available. In a multiform application, you can set which form will be the first to open.

Start testing the application by entering values in the fields. You can see that the fields you specified as mandatory in the design mode have a red asterisk in front of them indicating a required field (Figure 15-9).

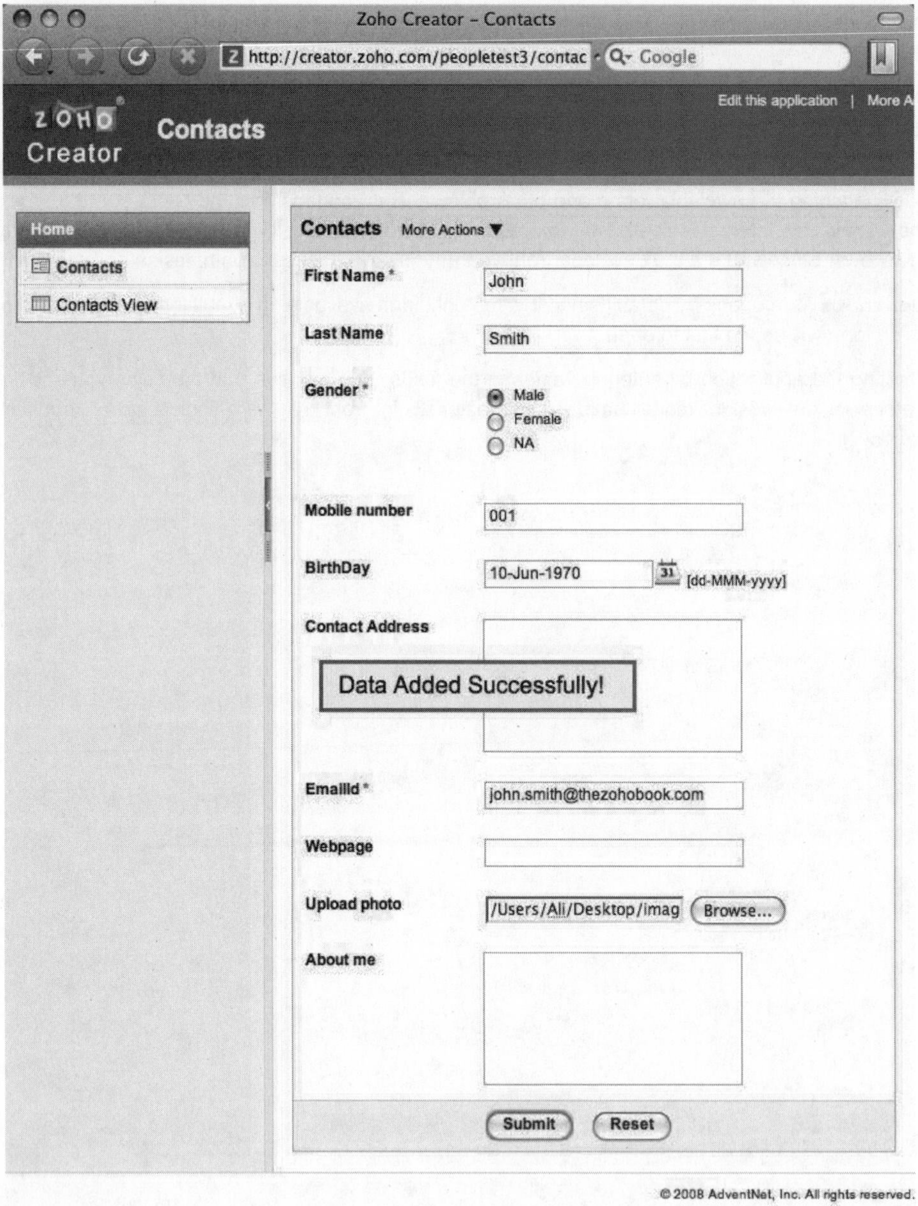

Figure 15-9. Entering data in the run mode

Note the difference between fields like `BirthDay` and `Emailid`; they accept different data types and use different components. `BirthDay`, for example, has a built-in calendar, and `Emailid` accepts only proper e-mail addresses. Using proper components helps design a better application with a more professional look and stronger data validation facilities.

Click `Submit` to add the data into the database. If successful, the success message will be displayed, and the form will be prepared for a new entry, meaning all fields will be cleared and the cursor will sit in the `First Name` field again.

Below the `Contacts` form link in the sidebar, you'll see the `Contacts View` link. Click this link to open the view shown in Figure 15-10. As you probably remember from the previous sections, views provide you with a formatted and customizable output of the stored data in the tables. Forms are used for data entry only, while views list the data in a nice format allowing you to filter the output and search for certain information. You'll use views extensively in your applications because a database application is about storing data once and accessing it multiple times in different ways.

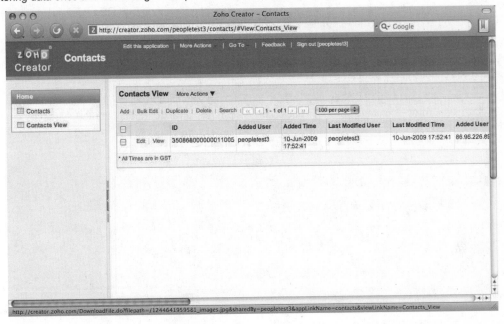

Figure 15-10. The `Contacts View` in action

Whenever you create a form, Creator will build a view too based on the data structure of the form. You can, however, disable this feature. `Contacts View` in this example was created automatically to save some time building it from scratch.

> *Experienced developers will be amazed about what Creator does automatically where in traditional web development you need to write hundreds of lines of code to just provide a fraction of this rich user experience.*

Views have paging controls that allow you to navigate through the data, when there are many rows in the table. You can also search for data and perform data entry. Most of these features are customizable, and you will see how to tweak some of them in the upcoming sections.

Customizing views

After creating and customizing the first form, `Contacts`, it is time to work on its view. Since Creator has already built a view based on that form, you just need to customize it. You can add as many views as you want based on various forms. It is also possible to create multiple views based on the same form and define different queries for each one.

If you are in run mode, click `Edit this application` on the top menu bar. Otherwise, just move the mouse pointer on the title of the `Views` tab, and click `Contacts View` in the context menu.

The design environment for the views is quite different from the forms. In the sidebar, you'll see various customization options listed. The working environment (the rest of the screen) will change according to the section you choose in the sidebar.

The first item is `Preview` in the `Display` section. It opens the view as it looks in run mode and allows you to drag and drop columns (fields) back and forth to arrange them in the desired order (Figure 15-11).

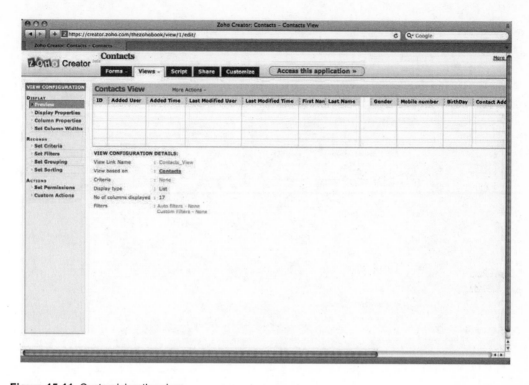

Figure 15-11. Customizing the view

Select `Display Properties` to change the view type. Each one of `List`, `Grid`, `Summary`, and `Calendar` will show the data in a different format (Figure 15-12). For example, if you are designing a view of a task list in a task manager application, the `Calendar` should be a good choice, but for this application we will stick to `List`.

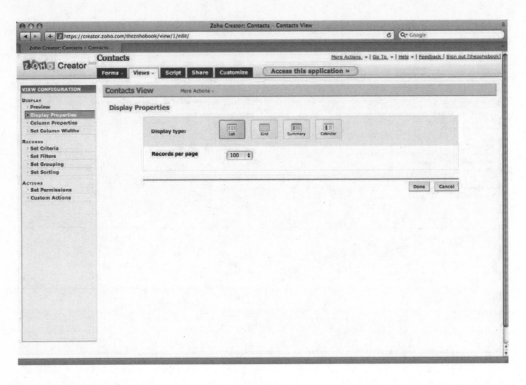

Figure 15-12. Setting the view type

You may also set `Records per page` (in the list). For this example list, `30` is a good option. Finally, click `Done` to apply the changes.

In the `Column Properties` section, you can set which fields you want to display in the view by selecting/deselecting `Show` for each field (Figure 15-13). Hiding fields is useful when you want only the needed information to be displayed in the view. For example, if you don't want people to see the telephone number of the contacts, you can hide it using `Show`. Although the data still resides in the table, it won't show for anybody in the runtime.

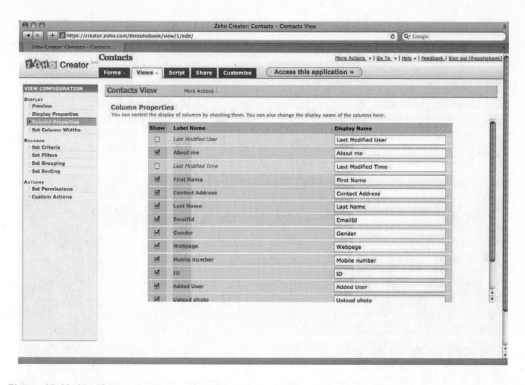

Figure 15-13. Modifying columns

You may also change the column labels (`Display Name`) if you don't like a title. You can even enter non-English labels.

There is still much more about views, but for this basic application, this much will do. I encourage you to go through the different sections, change some parameters, and see the results in action.

Sharing the application

After you finished creating an application and testing it thoroughly to make sure it works the way it should, you need to let others work with the application. After all, you are developing applications to be used by a group of people. Just like you use other people's or companies' applications (for example, Zoho CRM, Adobe Photoshop, Apple iTunes, and so on), you want others to use your applications too.

Creator offers various ways for an application to be published. The good news is that since applications like `Contacts` are SaaS applications, built on the Zoho Creator platform, you don't need to distribute or deploy them. This means there are no executables, setup disks, and installation hassles. You just need to publish your application to the users, and then it is ready to be used by them.

To give full or partial access to a group of users, you should share the application with every one of them. Just like you shared documents in the productivity applications (discussed earlier in the book), you can share an application by inviting people.

To share an application, follow these steps:

1. In design mode, open the `Share` tab, make sure the application name is selected in the sidebar, and then click **Share to Users**. If you are still in run mode, click **Edit this application** on the link bar at the top of the page.

2. In the `Share` dialog box, enter the e-mail addresses of the users, and set `Role` to `User` (Figure 15-14).

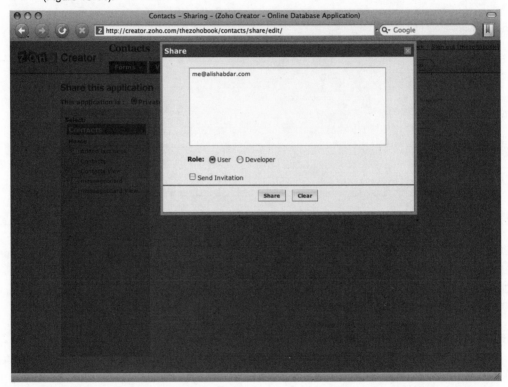

Figure 15-14. Sharing the application

3. Check **Send Invitation** if you want to send an invitation message, and click **Share** to proceed.

Controlling user permissions

All shared users have full access to all forms and views of the application. You should review these permissions and enforce the necessary policies on the **Share** tab (Figure 15-15). For example, if a user should only view the data (and not to add any), you need to remove that user's access to the forms because forms are used for entering data.

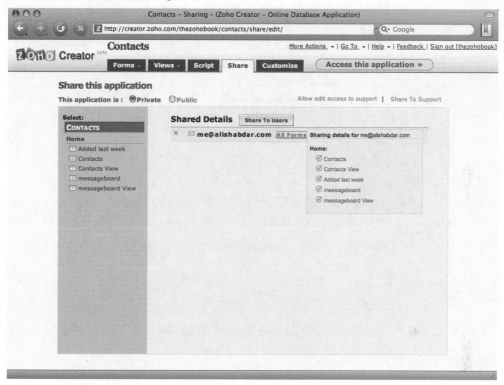

Figure 15-15. Checking the user permissions

> *Revisiting Figure 15-10, you can see that the **Add**, **Bulk Edit**, **Duplicate**, and **Delete** commands are enabled for the view. By default they are all disabled for users other than the application owner (you). This means forms are the only place shared users can add data. You may, however, give editing permissions in the views to certain users by selecting **Edit Record** in **Set Permissions** when designing a view.*

To remove a user's permissions for an object in the application, follow these steps:

1. In design mode, open the **Share** tab.
2. Select the object (for example, the **Contacts** form) in the sidebar. Shared details for the object will open.

3. Remove the users who shouldn't have access to the object, so when the user logs into the system, she won't see the unshared object in the sidebar at all (Figure 15-16).

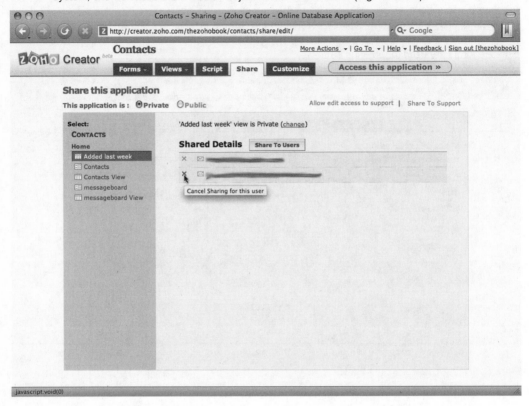

Figure 15-16. Limiting the users' access

Sometimes you might want to give full public access to certain objects. For example, if you added a message board to the application and you want everybody to be able to leave comments, you can simply select it and click **change** where it says `'messageboard' form is Private`.

When an object becomes public (Figure 15-17), not only can anybody who is logged in Creator with a standard Zoho account use that object, but also people who are not logged into Zoho can use it. This means everybody, and you should be very careful making a form or a view public. It can expose sensitive information and open doors for data entry from unknown sources. Also note that by making an object public, its old permissions will be deleted.

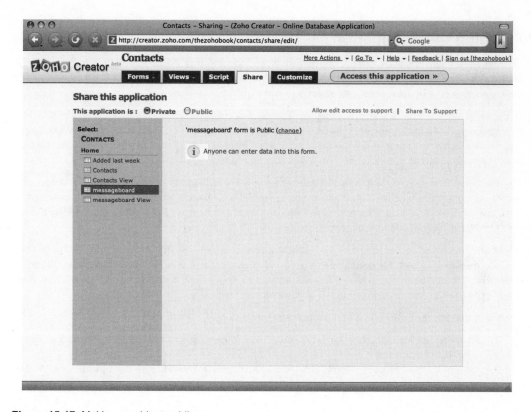

Figure 15-17. Making an object public

You can click **change** once more and make the object private again. Once again, be very careful with granting public access since it can expose sensitive information and open doors for data entry from unknown sources.

> *You can give the direct link to the application to the shared users, which is http://creator.zoho.com/YOU_USERNAME/YOUR_APPLICATION. So, for the Contacts application, it will be http://creator.zoho.com/thezohobook/contacts. This way, they won't need to find it in the shared applications tab in their Zoho homepages.*

Sharing applications and objects is very useful. It is one of the main channels by which users interact with the underlying data, but you need to be very careful what you share and how you share it.

There are, however, more ways to share the data stored in Creator, as you are about to see.

Publishing the application

Sharing applications involves using Zoho accounts and logging into Zoho. Although it is the preferred choice when you use the application in your organization or in your team, sometimes you'll want to merge the capabilities of your application with other tools and platforms.

Suppose you have created an inventory application for your company that maintains the business information such as products, availabilities, purchases, clients, and so on. And say you have a company website in which you want to make the price list of the available products accessible to the site visitors. It would be need to merge this information in a web page somehow.

The hard way is to extract data from the database manually by exporting it to a CSV file first and then entering it in the website. But Creator allows you to embed a view (or a form) in a web page, making data available almost everywhere. This not only saves time porting data from the database to the web site but also provides live information seamlessly to visitors.

In our small contacts application, you can publish a form or a view by embedding it in a web page. You can, for example, embed the `Contacts` form in the contacts page of your website, allowing visitors to enter their information in the system. You will end up having a wealth of information in your database ready to be used in analysis and reports. Everything is done almost automatically.

To embed the `Contacts` form in a web page, follow these steps:

1. Run the application (click `Access this application` in edit mode). Embedding is not available in edit mode.
2. On top of the `Contacts` form, click `More Actions ▶ Embed in your website`. A form containing the embed code will appear (Figure 15-18).

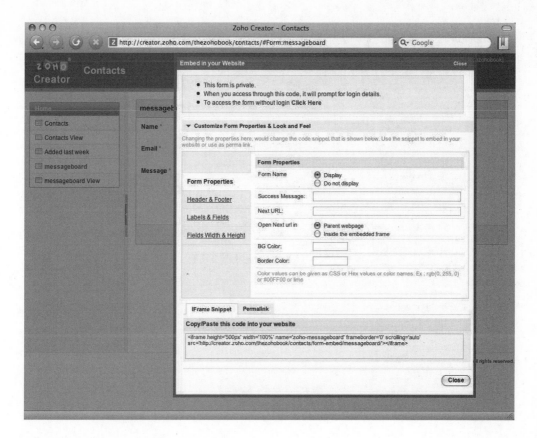

Figure 15-18. Embedding code for the object

3. Click `Customize Form Properties and Look and Feel` to show more options that change the appearance of the embeddable form in order to match the target web page, and then make the necessary changes by clicking the links on the left.

4. Copy the generated code, and paste it in the HTML code of the target page.

> *You need to know the basics of HTML in order to proceed with this step. Get a professional consultation if you like the idea of embedding but don't know anything about HTML.*

You can embed other forms and views with the same steps. In Figure 15-19 you can see the embed code placed inside the HTML code of the target web page. This is basically an `iframe` container linking back to the object. You can also change the dimensions of the container according to the design of the destination page.

Figure 15-19. Placing the code in an HTML file

Figure 15-20 shows the result of the sample form embedded in a web page.

Figure 15-20. The embedded form in action

With the embedding feature available, you can create complex websites to collect data and display various views and reports. Instead of going through all the hassles of scripting (with Python, PHP, Rails, and so on), debugging, and creating databases separately, you can easily use the ready-made tools and save a lot of time and money.

> *I won't argue with seasoned web developers about the unlimited power of scripting in Python, PHP, or Rails. The point here is that this is a fast, presentable way of working with data online.*

More Creator

Apart from the rich tools Creator offers for creating and publishing applications, there is more good news to come. You have the joy of creating your own applications in the first place, saving your organization considerable amounts of time and money that otherwise you would have to pay when buying expensive software and support licenses.

You can also create applications for profit too. Becoming a Creator developer is a part-time career you might want to consider.

Managing your precious data and extending Creator to the next level are also some of the subjects I'll cover in this section.

The control panel

Creator is a sophisticated platform that has many features. Surprisingly enough, this versatile platform doesn't need much configuration. But let's take a look at the **Home** page that acts as a command center where you can see your own applications, edit them, or run them directly, as well as access the applications shared to you (by other developers).

1. Click **GoTo** ▸ **Home** in the link bar, or just navigate to http://creator.zoho.com/home/index to open the **Home** page (Figure 15-21).

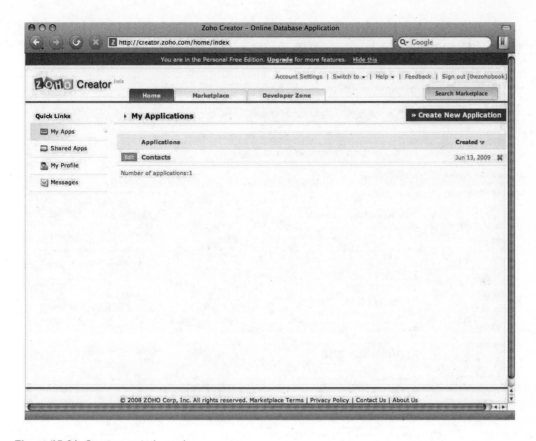

Figure 15-21. Creator control panel

2. Click `Account Settings` in the link bar to see a list of the users, your available quota, and the current subscription. You may add users or upgrade your subscription any time through this page.

3. To change your personal information, click `My Profile` in the sidebar. Then click `Edit Profile`, and fill the form. This profile is public, and other users will see it.

Buying and selling applications

You may want to make money by creating applications for others. After creating some for yourself and learning the ups and downs of the platform, you are ready to sell your masterpieces in the `Marketplace` where Zoho allows developers and clients to find each other. The `Marketplace` is still young, but it has great potential. Although not comparable in scope and popularity to Apple's App Store, its general approach is similar.

Basically, you (as a developer) post your application in the `Marketplace`, and clients searching for a similar solution find, try, and ideally buy your product. You can also find suitable solutions for your requirements that are already developed by others or hire developers to do a custom job for you.

To access the **Marketplace**, click **GoTo ▶ Marketplace** while you are in Creator, or simply log on to https://creator.zoho.com/marketplace (Figure 15-22).

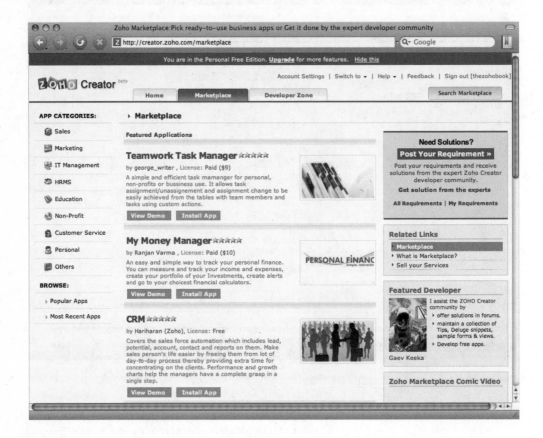

Figure 15-22. The **Marketplace**

Claiming your developer badge

Before you call yourself a Creator developer, you need to opt for a developer program. Open the **Developer Zone**, and become a registered developer with Zoho. It is recommended that you read the solution provider's paper at http://www.zoho.com/creator/marketplace/sell-your-services.html before signing up.

To access the developer zone, click **GoTo ▶ Developer Zone** while you are in Creator, or simply log on to https://creator.zoho.com/developer (Figure 15-23).

Figure 15-23. The `Developer Zone`

Managing applications

When you create simple documents, it is always recommended that you back up your files. With you becoming a database developer and creating exciting applications, it becomes rather essential to keep the different versions of your application in a safe place.

Behind the scenes, Creator stores every bit of the structure of the application in Deluge code. This means that your fancy application is actually pages of Deluge script, which is great since it makes it much easier to back up the applications that are just small-size script files.

To back up your application code, follow these steps:

4. Run the application. You can back up the application in edit mode.
5. Click `More Actions ▶ Save as Script` on the link bar. This will automatically generate a `.ds` file containing the full Deluge code of the application and download it for you.
6. Store the `.ds` file in a safe place.

You can open this file in any standard text editor and look at its structure (Figure 15-24). It is a good idea to back up your applications whenever a major update (to the design, not the data) is performed. This helps you keep different versions of your code. Later, if you lose or damage an application or you just want to install it on another account, you can simply import the Deluge code and create a new application identical to the old one.

Figure 15-24. A sample Deluge script

> *The data stored in the application won't get exported in the Deluge code, so if you deleted an application accidentally, even if you have the code backed up, the data won't be recovered. See the next section for more information about data backup.*

In case you are curious, you can duplicate an application into a new one through **More Actions ▸ Copy Application** in the link bar. Then you can safely play with the duplicate without harming the main application. It is also possible to do this by clicking **Duplicate** next to the application name in the **Home** page.

Managing the data

Forms are used to enter data in tables, one record at a time. But there are times when you need to add multiple records in one batch.

Suppose you have a contact list in Address Book or Outlook and want to add it all to the contacts database that you created earlier in this chapter.

Here is how to import many records into an application:

1. Export the data (a contact list in this example) to an XLS, CSV, or TSV file. CSV file is recommended over other formats.
2. Open the exported file in the respective editor, and copy all data to the clipboard.
3. Run the application and open the form (or the view) that should receive the imported data. In this case, it is the `Contacts` form.
4. Click `More Actions ▶ Import Data`.
5. In the `Import Data` dialog box, paste the copied information, and select the correct data in the `File Type` (Figure 15-25).

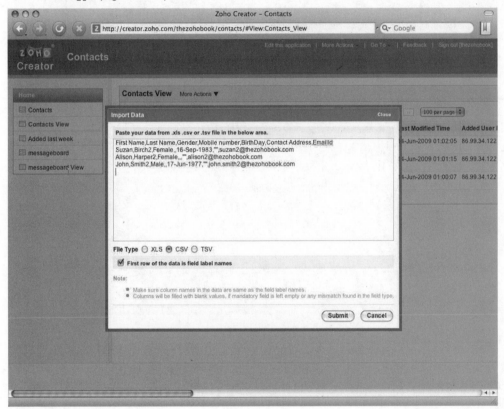

Figure 15-25. Importing data

6. Check `First row of the data is field label names` if necessary, and click `Submit`. Check the results by opening the respective view to see whether the data is imported properly.

On the other hand, you can export data from each table to various formats. Not only is it a good way of backing up data, it also provides you with a way of transmitting data to third parties.

To export data in supported formats, simply click **More Actions ▶ Export Data** in the runtime for each view. You can export data as spreadsheets, HTML documents, and PDF files (Figure 15-26).

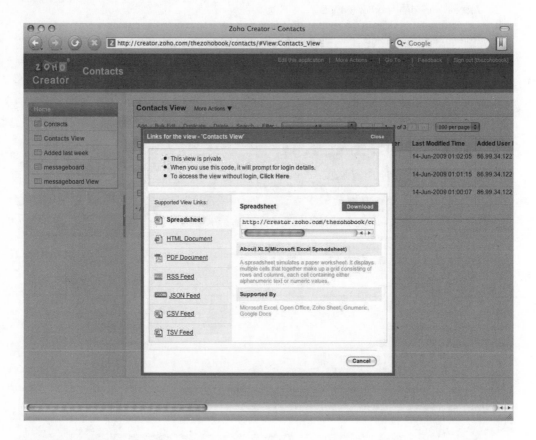

Figure 15-26. Exporting data

It is also possible to publish data using RSS, JavaScript Object Notation (JSON), CSV, and TSV feeds. Feeds will provide you with the data stream instead of just exported files, in other words, the third-party applications that are connected to the corresponding feeds and have persistent access to the live data.

> *Using feeds is suitable for experienced developers who intend to extend the application by connecting it to external tools.*

Unleashing the cloud

This section introduces advanced cloud-based web development. If you're not interested in advanced topics, you can move to the next section.

You've already seen that Creator provides you with a powerful platform to develop database applications in the cloud, but what if you can take it even further using one of the most advanced cloud platforms available in the market?

You might have heard of Google AppEngine, which offers a great platform for SaaS developers to create applications of all sizes and run them on the cloud. AppEngine provides them with the necessary hardware and software infrastructure, and the developers don't need to worry about anything but their own applications.

Although such advanced topics are beyond the scope of this book, I could not finish this section without saying a word about an amazing feature that Zoho offers for Creator. You can port your Creator applications to the AppEngine platform and extend them dramatically by employing the facilities that Google (one of the major cloud providers) offers.

To try this feature, open the application in edit mode, and then click **More Actions ▶ Deploy in Google AppEngine** on the link bar. Then you should follow the on-screen instructions to proceed with the task (Figure 15-27).

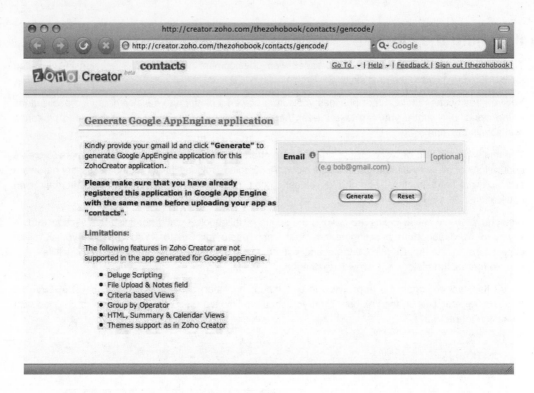

Figure 15-27. Publishing the application in the AppEngine

> *This is an advanced topic, and you should first learn both Creator and AppEngine basics before doing this.*

You can get more information on this subject from http://code.google.com/appengine/. A short demo is also available at http://www.viddler.com/explore/raju/videos/26/.

Getting started with Reports

Zoho Reports is an online reporting and BI tool that stores big chunks of data, performs sophisticated analysis, and generates sophisticated reports.

In short, Reports features the following:

- Flexible data import facilities compatible with the majority of file formats as well as direct push from other data sources such as Microsoft SQL Server, MySQL, Oracle, and so on
- Visual data analysis tools such as reports and charts
- Full-fledged SQL querying supporting well-known dialects, including Oracle, Microsoft SQL Server, IBM DB2, Sybase, MySQL, PostgreSQL, Informix, and ANSI SQL

- Sharing and collaboration data and analysis in real time
- Highly expandable by providing multiple data input channels as well as exporting data and BI information through flexible export, embeddable content, and a web API

With all these features, Reports is, unbelievably, free of charge. The table at `http://www.zoho.com/reports/Comparison-with-Spreadsheet-Reporting.html` compares Reports and Microsoft Excel from the point of view of reporting and BI features.

Unlike Creator, which is more focused on the application level and data collection mechanisms, Reports heavily invests in data management and data analysis features. The two applications can in fact be great partners, each one taking care of part of the business.

Simply put, you bring the chunks of data you have already collected into Reports. Then you clean it up, filter it, and start the analysis. After that, you can start generating sophisticated reports in different formats, including grouped listings, line charts, bar charts, Pivot charts and tables, and so on. The outcome could be exported, printed, embedded into other content, or ported to other platforms.

To start Reports, log on to `http://reports.zoho.com/`. Proceed with the next section to get yourself familiar while starting to work in Reports.

Creating a reporting database

Reports focuses on raw data and therefore provides you with the tools necessary to work with bulk information. Although it is possible to enter data one record at a time, I'm talking about entering thousands of data records here. Such data is usually collected in a third-party application, for example, Microsoft Access, MySQL, and so on, and just needs to be imported into Reports.

Similar to Creator, Reports keeps related data objects in separate databases. The difference in Reports is that you first need to create a database and then create tables and views for it.

> For your convenience, I have made the CSV file used in this walk-through available at `http://www.thezohobook.com/files/apartments.csv`. You can download it and use it, but you are also free to use your own data.

In this example you'll create a database directly by importing data:

1. Start **Reports** by opening `http://reports.zoho.com`.
2. On the homepage, you can see four options for creating a reporting database (Figure 15-28). Choose **Import .XLS, .CSV, .HTML** … to proceed.

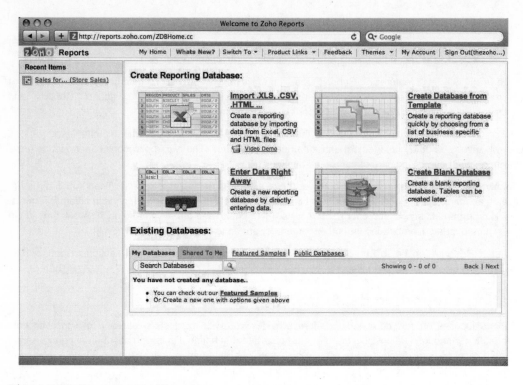

Figure 15-28. The start page of Reports

    3.   You'll see the database creation wizard, step 1 of 2 (Figure 15-29).

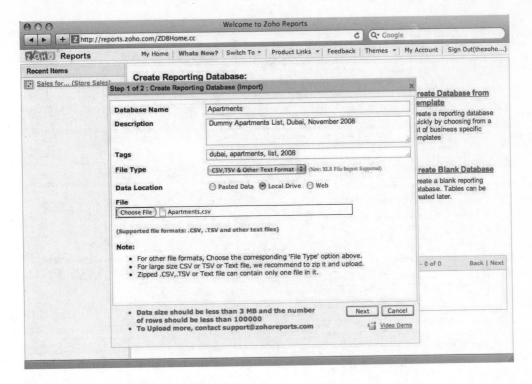

Figure 15-29. Creating a reporting database

a. Set `Database Name` to `Apartments`. Then enter `Dummy Apartments List` in `Description` and `dubai, apartments, list, 2008` in `Tags`.

b. Choose `CSV, TSV & Other Text Format` for `File Type` since the data you are about to import is in CSV format.

c. With the default of `Local Drive` selected for `Data Location`, browse for the file by clicking `Choose File`.

d. Click `Next` to proceed.

> *You might have noticed that you can choose `Web` for `Data Location` as well. A good practice in connecting Creator and Reports is to set the data location to a CSV feed link (Figure 15-26) and enjoy the best of both worlds.*

4. In step 2 of 2 of the wizard, enter `mainList` for the `Table Name`, and select `Yes` for `First Row Contains Column Names`. Make sure the field mappings and the data format are correct, and then click `Create` to finish the job (Figure 15-30).

> Reports can store different data types. `Date`, `Plain Text`, `Positive Number`, and others should be carefully selected for all data fields. It is important for proper data analysis in the later stages. For example, if you store currency values in a `Plain Text` field, normal currency calculations won't be applicable on the field since Reports will assume those values are just text, not real numbers representing money amounts.

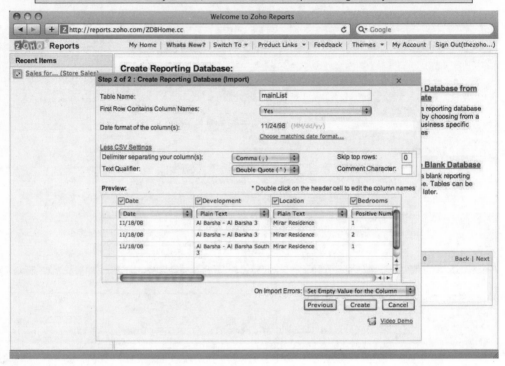

Figure 15-30. Mapping the data fields

5. Once the database and the table are created and data is successfully imported, Reports asks whether you want it to have an automatically generated collection of reports for the new database (Figure 15-31). Click **Yes** because you are going to use some of them in the upcoming steps.

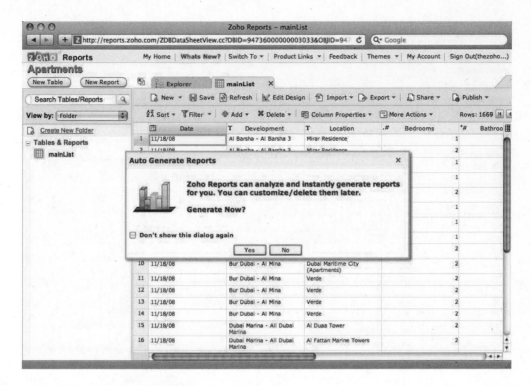

Figure 15-31. Generating autoreports

Using Reports

On the left side of the Reports screen, there is a sidebar containing the database objects. By letting Reports generate automatic reports, you will have a collection of usable lists and charts made based on the data structure of the database. Compare Figure 15-32 to Figure 15-31, and see how many items are added under `Auto Generated Reports`. Clicking each one will open it for viewing or editing.

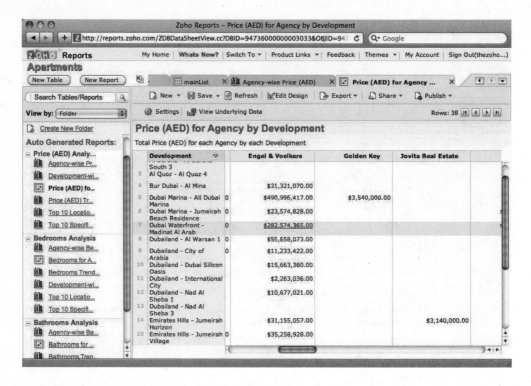

Figure 15-32. A sample autoreport

> *You can add more tables and reports at any time by clicking **New Table** and **New Report** on the top of the sidebar.*

Explore some of the items added by Reports by clicking them in the sidebar. **Agency-wise Price (AED)**, for example, shows a chart generated to visualize the cumulative value of the stock each agency offers (Figure 15-33). You notice that the elements are put wisely and not randomly, and minor modifications will make the report fit into your requirements.

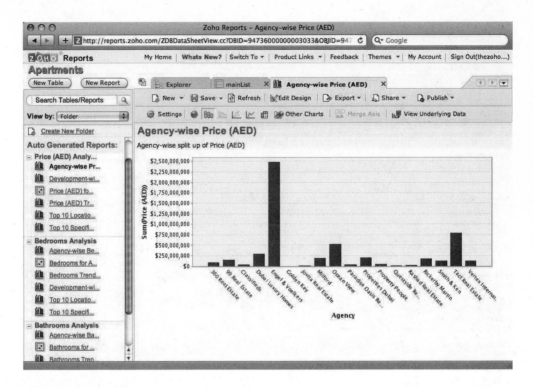

Figure 15-33. A sample autochart

Objects (such as tables and reports) open in a separate tab with a generic toolbar on top giving access to different actions such as creating new objects, saving and editing the current object, and so on. Each object might have custom toolbars added to the standard bar as well.

It is really useful to have Reports create such reports by analyzing the data in the table. This gives you some idea about creating your own objects and provides you with the basis you can customize to fit in your requirements.

Now let's try some of the tools and features.

Using filters

Filters are used to narrow down the output of a list when you are going through data. The filtered list can be saved and used as a view or simply exported to another application. A filter is basically a criterion that you set individually for each file involved in the filtration process.

For instance, in the apartments list, a simple filter can show only the two-bedroom apartments located in a certain location. So, the structure of the filter will involve `Bedrooms` and `Location` fields, and the criteria will be defined on these two fields.

To make it clearer, let's do it together:

1. Open the `mainList` table, and click `Filter ▶Create New Filter` on the toolbar. A series of drop-down lists and text boxes appear below every column title.

2. Set the drop-down list below the `Location` column to `Contains`, and enter `majara` in the text box below (Figure 15-34). This is how to define criteria for each field.

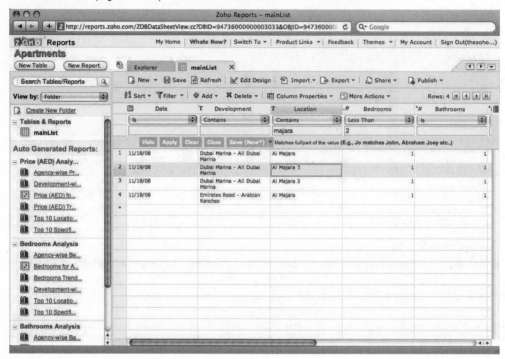

Figure 15-34. Creating a filter

3. Similarly, set `Bedroom` to be `Less Than 2`. It is pretty much like plain English because it says `show me the 2 bedroom apartments in majara`.

4. Click `Apply` for the list to be re-created based on the filter.

5. To save the filter, click `Save (New) ▶ Save Filter As …`

6. Enter `2 br flats in Majara` as the filter name in the `Save Filter` dialog box.

7. Click `Save` to store the filter for later use.

To disable a filter and list all rows back again, click `Clear` on the `Filter` bar.

Adding data manually

As I discussed, the main data input channel of Reports is through importing data. You saw how to import an external file, such as CSV. But sometimes you might want to add a few rows to a table manually without going through the import process.

To add data records one by one, follow these steps:

1. Open the `mainList` table, and then click `Add` ▶ `Add New` in the toolbar. An empty row will be added at the end of the table (Figure 15-35).

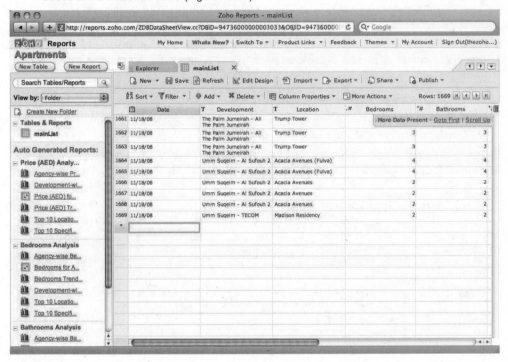

Figure 15-35. Adding new rows

2. Enter values for each column.
3. Click `Save` to apply the changes.

To delete rows from a table, select them, and then click `Delete` on the toolbar. Deleted rows will be removed from the screen immediately, but to actually delete them, you need to click `Save`. Then the rows will be removed permanently.

Adding formula fields

Suppose you have the unit price for each item in the table, and you want to calculate the commission amount. You could have an extra column called **commission** and put the calculated value for each row, but these are the problems with that approach:

- It is time-consuming.
- It stores extra data in the table, making it bigger.
- If the price of an item changes, you need to update the commission amount too.
- If the commission percentage changes, you need to change the entire commission values.

Well, you can create custom formula fields to avoid all these negative effects. Custom formula fields hold values calculated automatically based on other fields. For example, a commission field for the apartment database would contain 5 percent of the total price as the agency fees, so you can define a custom formula field to hold this value.

To add a custom formula field, follow these steps:

1. Open the **mainList** table, and then click **Add ▶ Custom Formula** ... in the toolbar. The **Add Custom Formula** dialog box appears (Figure 15-36).

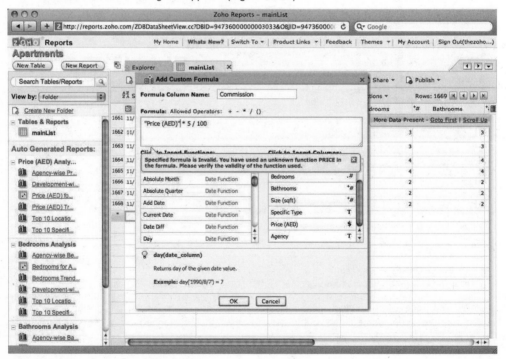

Figure 15-36. Adding a custom formula field

2.   Enter "`Price (AED)`" `5 / 100` in the formula box. You can use the available equations as well as referencing the available fields in the table.

3.   Click `OK` to proceed.

The reason I enclosed the field name, `Price (AED)`, in double quotes is that the name has spaces in it. If I write the formula without the double quotes, Reports will assume that `Price` and `(AED)` are separate fields. This will result in an error message, as you can see in Figure 15-36. For fields with one-word name, for example, `Location`, you can omit the double quote.

Once the formula column added, it will be displayed in the table like a normal column, although the values don't actually exist in the table and are just a result of on-the-fly calculations (Figure 15-37).

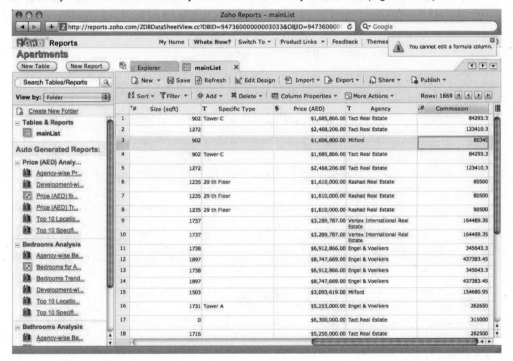

Figure 15-37. The custom field in action

Using formula fields addresses all four problems mentioned earlier: it is a very quick solution, there is no extra data stored in the table, and it is sensitive to value changes, meaning it updates automatically as the related values, or the formula itself, change.

Modifying the table structure

Columns (data fields) are the structuring pillars of a table forming its data model. Although it is usually not a good idea to modify the table structure frequently, sometimes it can't be avoided. For instance, during the import process in which new tables are being created, column types might sometimes be set wrongly, or an existing column might need to be removed.

Whatever the reason is, you can change the design of the tables in Reports. But it comes with its own issues. Here are some examples:

- If you remove a column, all data under that column will be deleted too.
- If you change the type of a column from (let's say) `Currency` to `Plain Text`, it will no longer be possible to perform monetary calculations on that column because it is no longer holding currency values. All data will be converted to `Plain Text`.
- Sometimes you might lose data during type conversion. For example, a `Decimal Number` can contain negative values, but if it is converted to `Positive Number`, it will lose its sign, so `-10` and `10` will be the same.

To make some changes in the design of a table, follow these steps:

1. Open the `mainList`, and then click `Edit Design` on the toolbar (Figure 15-38).

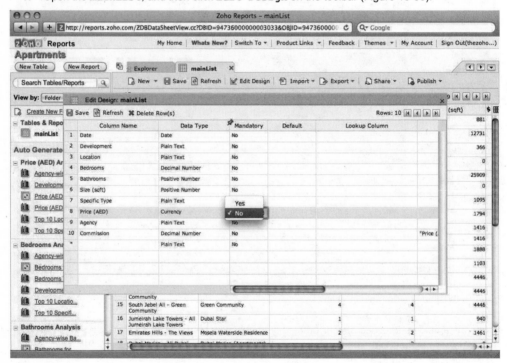

Figure 15-38. Modifying the table structure.

2. To change a field name, double-click `Date` under `Column Name`, and enter `Insertion Date`.

3. **For Price (AED)**, set **Mandatory** to **Yes**, so every data record will need to have a price in place.

4. Click **Save** for the changes to apply on the table.

Using the upload tool

You saw how to import data when you created your first database in the preceding sections, but there is still another way of bringing bulk data into Reports. Zoho has created an upload tool that gives you more facilities than the standard import tool you have used before.

The Zoho upload tool for Reports can do the following:

- Can send more than 100,000 rows and files bigger than 3MB, which surpasses the limits of the web interface (the way you did it before).
- Uploads data from CSV files stored in your computer automatically and imports them into Reports.
- Connects directly to databases in your local network, extracts the data, and uploads it automatically. Microsoft Access, MySQL, Microsoft SQL Server, and Oracle are supported as of this writing.
- Works well behind local firewalls.
- Can perform scheduled uploads for periodic data imports to keep the remote data residing in Reports up-to-date.

Using the upload tool is highly recommended if you work with big databases in a business environment. There are currently two versions of the application available for both Windows and Linux that you can download from http://reports.wiki.zoho.com/Upload-Tool.html.

> *Make sure you read the related documentation on the same page before using the upload tool.*

Sharing reports and collaborating

As you might expect with a Zoho application, Reports also provides a powerful set of sharing and collaboration tools. You can share database objects (for example, tables) with colleagues and peers in order to work on data and perform group analysis.

To share a table with others, follow these steps:

1. With the **mainList** table open, click **Share ▶ Share this View**. The share wizard opens (Figure 15-39).

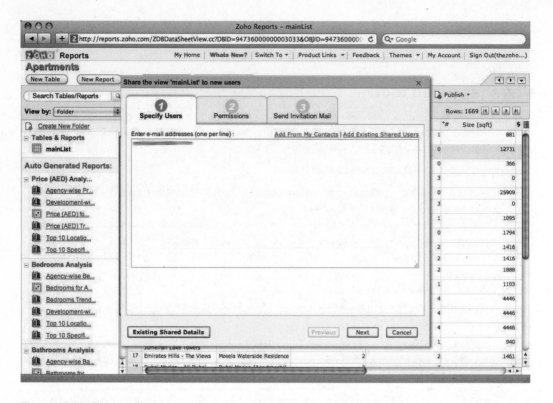

Figure 15-39. Sharing a table

2. In step 1, `Specify Users`, enter the e-mail address of the collaborators, one per each line. You can add people from your contacts as well.

3. Click `Next` to proceed.

4. In step 2, `Permissions`, specify how the invitees who will access the data. Check `Read Access` and `Export Data` under `Read Options` (Figure 15-40). This will share this table with third parties who only need to list data, such as your business partners.

Figure 15-40. Setting the share permissions

5. Click **Next** to continue.
6. In the last step, **Send Invitation Mail**, check **Send Invitation Mail** (Figure 15-41). It will enable an invitation message to be sent to collaborators, which you can customize it too.

Figure 15-41. Sending invitation e-mails to collaborators

7. Click `Share` to finish the task.

Once shared, collaborators can see the shared objects in the `Shared to Me` tab in their `Reports` homepage (accessible through `My Home` on the top menu bar) and interact with the content as much as their access level allows.

You can edit the share options at any time by clicking `Share ▶ Edit Existing Shared Details`. It is possible to edit the permissions for every collaborator or just remove them from the shared object (Figure 15-42).

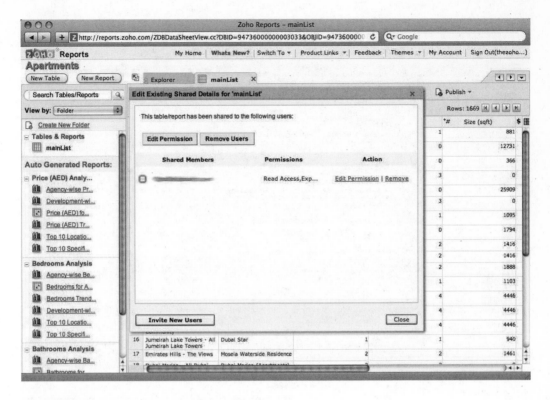

Figure 15-42. Editing current share permissions

Publishing reports

Sharing and collaboration tools are more suitable when you work in teams inside your organization or with your business partners. To let the world see your reports and business intelligence, you need to publish the data using the tools available in Reports. You can embed reports in websites, provide concerned people with links to the reports, or just make them public for everybody to see them.

Embedding reports in websites

Just like in Creator, it is possible to embed Reports objects in websites. By merging reports and charts into other web content, the power of delivering your message will be multiplied, especially because these reports are active. This means that unlike the inserted chart images or tabular data you usually see in other websites, the visitors of your website can click the charts and lists to interact with live data.

> *Check out the post at http://blogs.zoho.com/general/analyze-your-google-adwords-campaigns-with-zoho-reports about using Reports with Google AdWords to see embedded reports in action.*

To embed a view in a web page, follow these steps:

1. Click **Publish ▶ Embed in Website/Blog**... to open the embed dialog box (Figure 15-43).

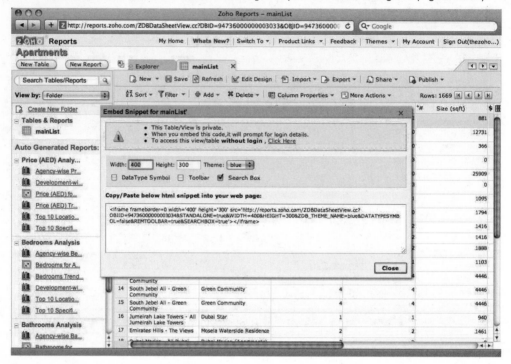

Figure 15-43. Getting the embed code of a table

2. By default, the embed container will need users to enter Zoho credentials to see the object. Click **Click Here** at the top of the dialog box to make it public for everybody to see.
3. Set the dimensions (**Width** and **Height**) and the look and feel of the embedded container.
4. Copy the code snippet, and paste it in the HTML code of the target web page.
5. Click **Close** to go back to the table.

Accessing data through links

By clicking **Publish ▶ URL for this view**..., you can publish a public link of an object (for example, a table) so people can just visit the link to access the data. Once again, it is possible to give public access to this links by making it accessible without logging in (Figure 15-44).

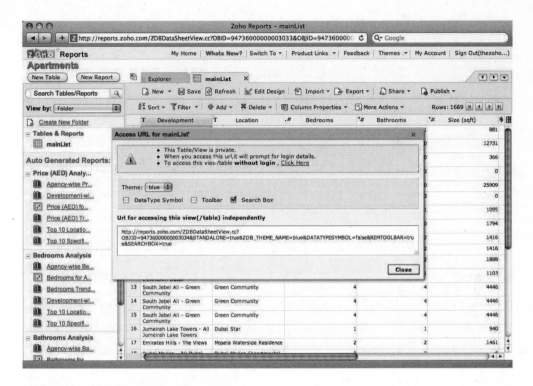

Figure 15-44. Getting the access URL of a table

You can see the result of a public link in the browser window. It is nicely formatted with navigation and search for more convenience (Figure 15-45).

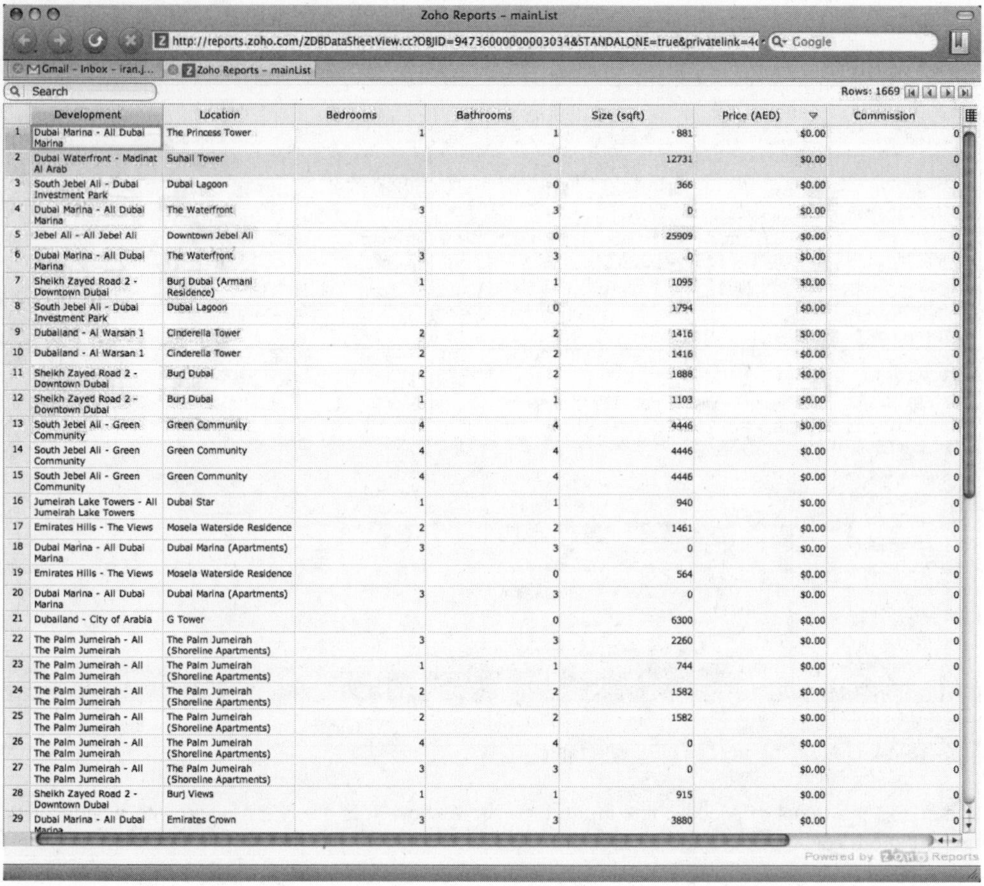

	Development	Location	Bedrooms	Bathrooms	Size (sqft)	Price (AED)	Commission
1	Dubai Marina - All Dubai Marina	The Princess Tower	1	1	881	$0.00	0
2	Dubai Waterfront - Madinat Al Arab	Suhail Tower		0	12731	$0.00	0
3	South Jebel Ali - Dubai Investment Park	Dubai Lagoon		0	366	$0.00	0
4	Dubai Marina - All Dubai Marina	The Waterfront	3	3	0	$0.00	0
5	Jebel Ali - All Jebel Ali	Downtown Jebel Ali		0	25909	$0.00	0
6	Dubai Marina - All Dubai Marina	The Waterfront	3	3	0	$0.00	0
7	Sheikh Zayed Road 2 - Downtown Dubai	Burj Dubai (Armani Residence)	1	1	1095	$0.00	0
8	South Jebel Ali - Dubai Investment Park	Dubai Lagoon		0	1794	$0.00	0
9	Dubailand - Al Warsan 1	Cinderella Tower	2	2	1416	$0.00	0
10	Dubailand - Al Warsan 1	Cinderella Tower	2	2	1416	$0.00	0
11	Sheikh Zayed Road 2 - Downtown Dubai	Burj Dubai	2	2	1888	$0.00	0
12	Sheikh Zayed Road 2 - Downtown Dubai	Burj Dubai	1	1	1103	$0.00	0
13	South Jebel Ali - Green Community	Green Community	4	4	4446	$0.00	0
14	South Jebel Ali - Green Community	Green Community	4	4	4446	$0.00	0
15	South Jebel Ali - Green Community	Green Community	4	4	4446	$0.00	0
16	Jumeirah Lake Towers - All Jumeirah Lake Towers	Dubai Star	1	1	940	$0.00	0
17	Emirates Hills - The Views	Mosela Waterside Residence	2	2	1461	$0.00	0
18	Dubai Marina - All Dubai Marina	Dubai Marina (Apartments)	3	3	0	$0.00	0
19	Emirates Hills - The Views	Mosela Waterside Residence		0	564	$0.00	0
20	Dubai Marina - All Dubai Marina	Dubai Marina (Apartments)	3	3	0	$0.00	0
21	Dubailand - City of Arabia	G Tower		0	6300	$0.00	0
22	The Palm Jumeirah - All The Palm Jumeirah	The Palm Jumeirah (Shoreline Apartments)	3	3	2260	$0.00	0
23	The Palm Jumeirah - All The Palm Jumeirah	The Palm Jumeirah (Shoreline Apartments)	1	1	744	$0.00	0
24	The Palm Jumeirah - All The Palm Jumeirah	The Palm Jumeirah (Shoreline Apartments)	2	2	1582	$0.00	0
25	The Palm Jumeirah - All The Palm Jumeirah	The Palm Jumeirah (Shoreline Apartments)	2	2	1582	$0.00	0
26	The Palm Jumeirah - All The Palm Jumeirah	The Palm Jumeirah (Shoreline Apartments)	4	4	0	$0.00	0
27	The Palm Jumeirah - All The Palm Jumeirah	The Palm Jumeirah (Shoreline Apartments)	3	3	0	$0.00	0
28	Sheikh Zayed Road 2 - Downtown Dubai	Burj Views	1	1	915	$0.00	0
29	Dubai Marina - All Dubai Marina	Emirates Crown	3	3	3880	$0.00	0

Figure 15-45. A formatted table accessible publicly through the link

> *In a traditional approach (coding it yourself), you would write hundreds of lines of code to just display this piece.*

Public links are temporary access portals that are useful for quick solutions like when your boss wants a report in five minutes (typical, right?). Sharing and embedding objects are more flexible and more controllable approaches for permanent solutions.

Making your BI data public

If your data concerns public interest (such as the trend of global warming for the last decade), you can make it public.

1. Click **Publish ▶ Public Setting for DB**....
2. Click **Show** **in** **Zoho** **Public** **Database** **Listing** (`http://reports.zoho.com/ZDBPublicDatabases.cc`) to publicize it (Figure 15-46).

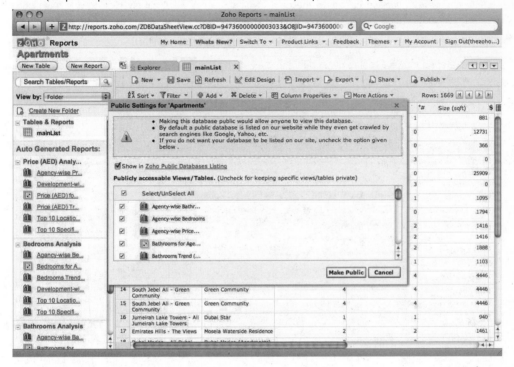

Figure 15-46. Making objects public

3. Select the object(s) you want to give public access to. Since all available objects in the database are selected by default, you have to actually deselect the items you want to stay private.
4. Click **Make Public** to finish the task.

More Reports

After learning about most of the tools you can use in Reports, it is time to focus more on the data analysis and reporting part. Charts and views are essential tools that provide sophisticated output for the data you maintain in Reports.

Let's start with charts to see how to present on-demand BI data at its best.

Working with charts

Charts are always the fun part of data analysis. With clear graphics, you can tell a boring story of numbers in a few exciting minutes. Reports provides you with a state-of-the-art collection of tools to create, manage, and share various charts.

To create charts from scratch based on the data of a table or a view, simply click `New ▶ New Chart View`. Reports treats charts as views, and they give a custom view of the data in the database.

To take a quick tour, let's look at a chart generated automatically by Reports.

1. In the apartments database, open the `Development-wise Price (AED)` chart from the sidebar.

2. Change the chart type by clicking `Line Chart` on the toolbar (Figure 15-47).You can switch between line, bar, pie, stacked, scatter, web, and table charts, although some might not be available based on the data model of the view.

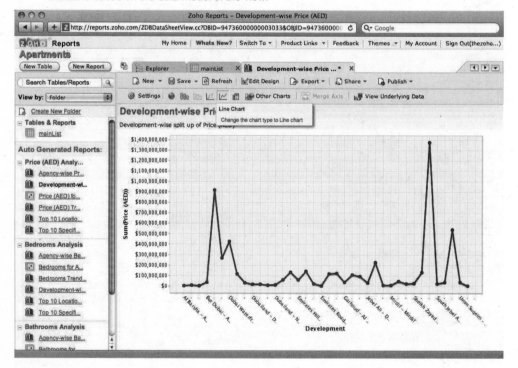

Figure 15-47. Changing the chart type

3. Click `View Underlying Data` to quickly list the data that builds the chart. You can filter the list, but it won't have any effect on the chart (Figure 15-48).

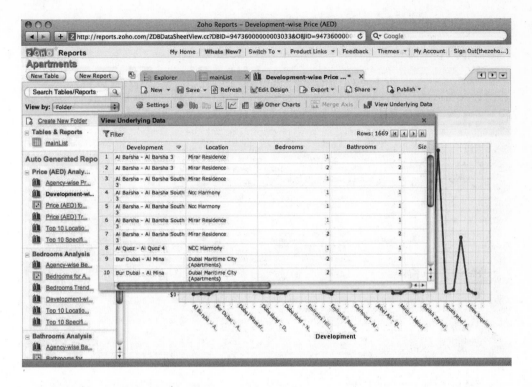

Figure 15-49. Viewing the underlying data

> *The best place underlying data comes in handy is when you embed a chart in a web page and clicking the chart brings up the underlying data.*

4. To customize the chart and try different options, duplicate the current chart to preserve the original one. Click **Save ▸ Save As**.

5. Give the duplicate chart a name, `Top 10 Locations by Price Average`, in the **Save As** dialog box. Then click **OK** to proceed (Figure 15-49).

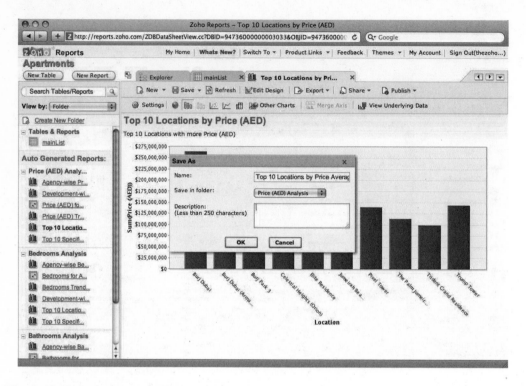

Figure 15-49. *Saving as a new chart*

6. With the duplicate chart open, click `Settings` in the toolbar.

7. In the `Settings` dialog box, change the chart `Title` to `Top 10 Locations by Price Average` (Figure 15-50).

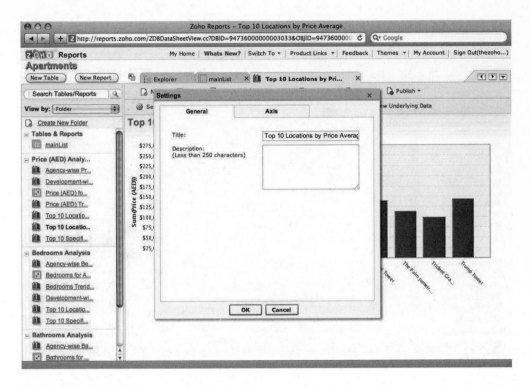

Figure 15-50. Changing the chart settings

8. On the `Axis` tab, enter `Price Average` for `Sum(Price(AED))`. Then click `OK` to apply the changes (Figure 15-51).

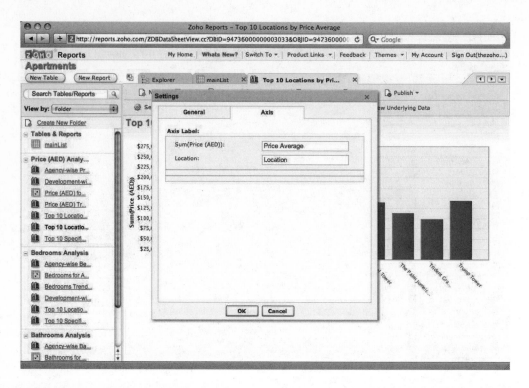

Figure 15-51. Modifying the axis labels

Editing charts structure

Now that you now the basics of charts, let's dig deeper and see how you can change the design of a chart. By *design*, I mean the underlying structure of the chart.

1. Click `Edit Design`, and start changing the structure of the chart.

   There are two horizontal tabs in design mode, `Graph` and `Filter`.

   The `Graph` tab contains the data to be represented in the chart axis. There is already a data field set to each axis. You can set how the values in the axis should be calculated.

   For example, if (according to Figure 15-52) you set `Sum` for `Price` in the `Y-axis` and `Location` in the `X-Axis`, the chart will show the summary of prices for every location in the table. Similarly, you can show the `Average` price of different locations.

   > *You can remove the fields in the axis and replace them with other fields (for example, `Size`) by dragging the field from the field list on the left side and dropping it in the axis box.*

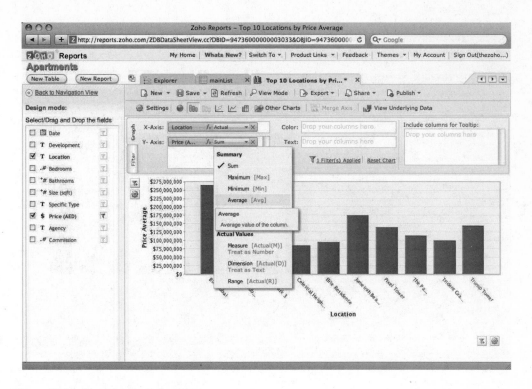

Figure 15-52. Changing the axis values

2. On the **Filter** tab, you can specify a limit by setting some criteria to specify what data should be extracted to generate the chart.

    For instance, you can drag **Price** to the **Filter** box and select **Top 10** (or more) in the range box. The result will be showing just the top ten items price-wise. You can mix various filters or define new ones to get more specific results (Figure 15-53).

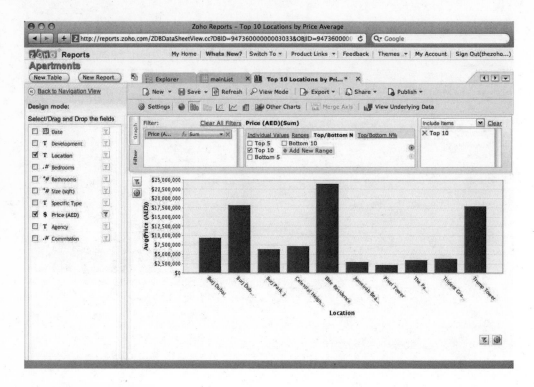

Figure 15-53. Applying filters

3. Colors are used to group the values based on a secondary field. If you drag a field and drop it in the `Color` box, the values will be grouped based on that field and make the chart more understandable.

In Figure 15-54, you can see that after adding `Development` to the color box, the chart is grouped by various housing developments. Indicated by different colors, you can distinguish different locations in the same developments at a glance.

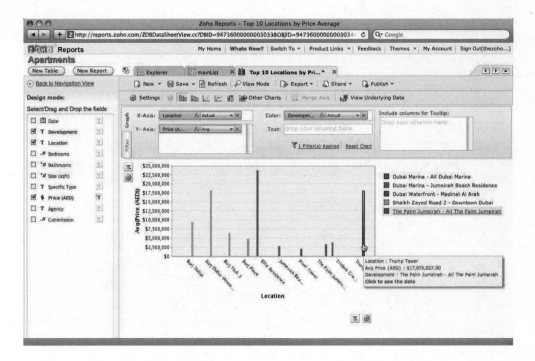

Figure 15-54. Using the color grouping

Practice charts more, and use different options to get different results. It is quite easy to create wonderful charts. It is even more fun when you embed charts in your web site to let the world to see your valuable data in an eye-catching way.

Creating views from scratch

Reports features four different types of views:

- *Tabular*: As the name implies, this provides you with a simple tabular layout of the data stored in a table.
- *Chart*: You saw charts in action in a preceding section.
- *Pivot*: This summarizes data in a grid (matrix) giving different angles of the data.
- *Summary*: This groups data and allows subtotals.

Tabular view is so simple to use that I leave it to you to discover; let's take a look at summary and pivot views.

Creating pivot views

To create a pivot view that shows the average price of the apartments in different locations based on the number of bedrooms, follow these steps:

1. Open the `mainList` table, and select `New ▶ New Pivot View` in the toolbar.
2. In design mode, drag `Bedrooms` from the sidebar, and drop it on the `Columns` list box (Figure 15-55).

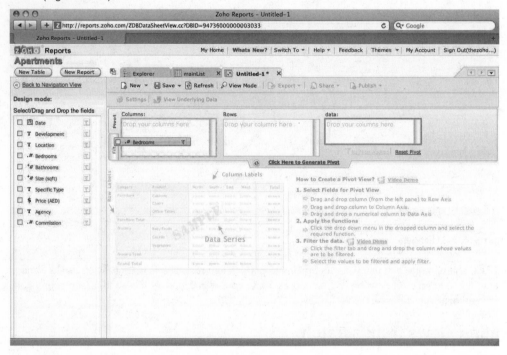

Figure 15-55. Adding fields to the pivot view

3. Similarly, drag and drop `Location` to `Rows` and `Price (AED)` to `data`.
4. In the `Columns` list box, click the little arrow next to `fx` in the `Bedrooms` field, and select `Actual(D)` from the drop-down list.
5. Click `Click Here to Generate Pivot` below the list boxes to see a preview of the pivot view. The result should look like Figure 15-56.

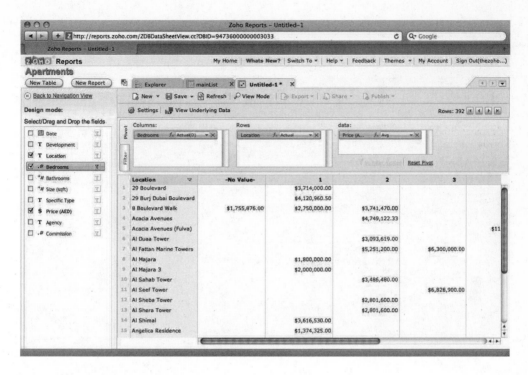

Figure 15-56. Previewing the pivot view

6. Click `Save` in the toolbar to store the view.
7. Enter `Average Price (Location and Bedroom)`, and select `New Folder` in the `Save in folder` drop-down.
8. A new dialog box will open asking you to enter a name for the new folder. Enter `test`, and click OK. Back in the `Save As` dialog box, click OK to proceed (Figure 15-57).

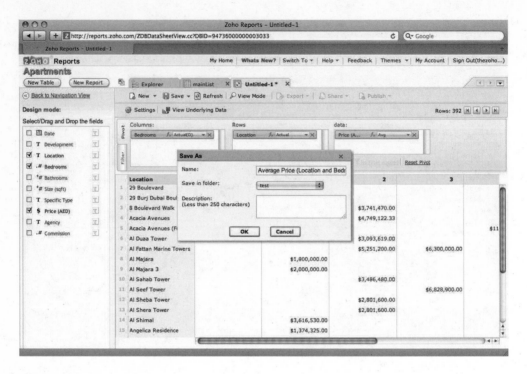

Figure 15-57. Saving the pivot view

9. Click **View Mode** in the toolbar to see the view in action (Figure 15-58).

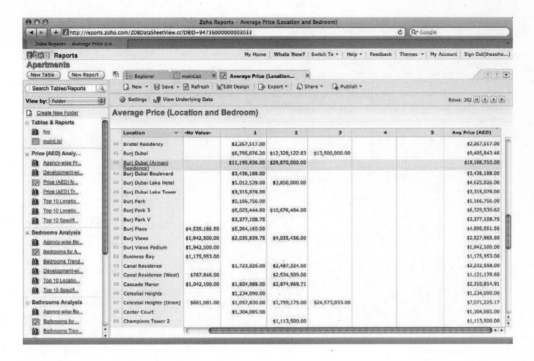

Figure 15-58. Viewing the pivot view

Pivot views, just like charts, can be embedded in web pages. Visitors can navigate through data and click the field you set as the row to see the underlying data.

Creating summary views

To create a summary view that lists the real estate agencies along with the total value and quantity of their availabilities, follow these steps:

1. Open the `mainList` table, and select **New ▶ New Summary View** in the toolbar.
2. In design mode, drag **Agency** from the field list in the sidebar, and drop it in the **Group by** list box.
3. Drag **Price (AED)**, and drop it in the **Summarize** list box twice. Then change the **fx** value for the first item to **Sum** and then **Count** for the second item (Figure 15-59).

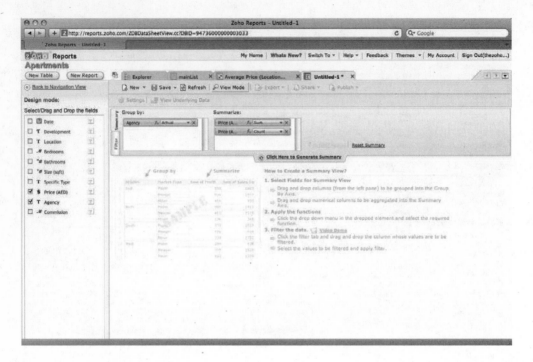

Figure 15-59. Creating a summary view

4.   Save the view as **Agencies Availabilities**, and then click **View Mode** to see the view in action (Figure 15-60).

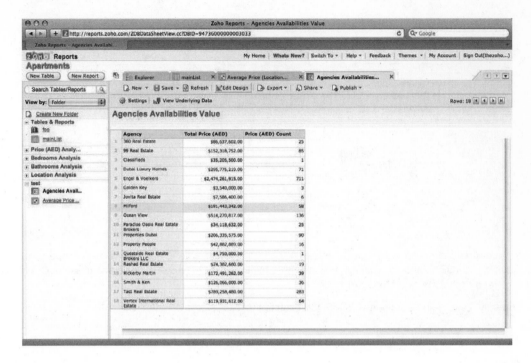

Figure 15-60. Viewing the summary view

CloudSQL

Zoho surprises its users with new tools every now and then; it has been launching major updates and new tools even while I was writing this book. One of the revolutionary tools launched in December 2008 was CloudSQL. This tool offers developers an interface where they can interact with data stored in Zoho business applications and connect it to external tools by using plain SQL. In other words, CloudSQL makes you think you are dealing with a normal database server (for example, SQL Server or Oracle). This is a big leap for developers who want to extend Zoho applications or just connect to business information in various tools.

> This is an advanced topic for experienced web and database developers. You can skip this section if you are not interested.

Zoho offers Java Database Connectivity (JDBC) and web application programming interface (API) drivers to make developers' lives even easier. Open DataBase Connectivity (ODBC) support is still in progress as of this writing. Figure 15-2 shows an overall model of how CloudSQL works. You can get more information from http://cloudsql.wiki.zoho.com/ to start you on your journey of unleashing the power of the Zoho platform.

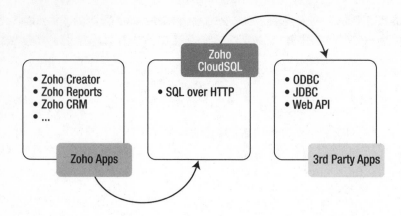

Zoho API

As introduced in Chapter 8, for most of its services, Zoho offers an extensive API to give developers more flexibility extending Zoho applications. It is also possible to extend the applications created on the Creator and Reports platforms with Zoho API.

Currently, Zoho Reports supports CloudSQL limited to the following:

- SQL `SELECT` statement
- Connecting through JDBC driver

More support has been promised by Zoho and is probably out by the time you're reading this book. To get more information and keep yourself updated with the latest developments, check the Zoho Reports CloudSQL documentation at `http://zohoreportsapi.wiki.zoho.com/Zoho-Reports-CloudSQL.html`.

> Check out `http://api.zoho.com` to learn about the Zoho API services.

Getting help

There is much to read about data structures and database design—but with Creator and Reports, you don't need to be database-savvy. A basic understanding of databases, tables, and views and some experience in using spreadsheet applications will be enough for you to create wonders.

You should, however, learn how to think like a developer in order to be able to create applications that work well and are usable by others. You need to be able to imagine the flow of work between database objects (forms, views, and reports) and understand the underlying relations among them. Try drawing lines on a piece of paper connecting the objects, actions, and behaviors of the applications you are planning to build. A good way is to look at other applications and learn how they work.

After getting yourself familiar with Zoho database applications by reading this chapter, you might need to refer to the online documentations:

- For Creator, `http://creator.wiki.zoho.com/` and `http://blogs.zoho.com/category/creator/` will help you find your way.
- You can read more about Reports at `http://reports.wiki.zoho.com/` and `http://blogs.zoho.com/category/reports/`.

Finally, don't forget to check out the forums at `http://forums.zoho.com/` if you have more questions.

Summary

Creator opens a new chapter in database application development, and Reports makes BI and complex reporting available to everyone. Providing robust and user-friendly PaaS with cost-effective plans, you can rely on Creator and Reports in your daily business. When using other tools like Google AppEngine and CloudSQL in conjunction with Creator and Reports, developing SaaS gets even more exciting.

You can focus more on the business logic than spending time coding thousands of lines of error-prone code just for trivial tasks. UI design, data analysis, and reporting in the cloud have never been easier.

In this chapter, you started with a quick overview of what databases are and continued with creating a simple application with Creator. Then you customized your application and worked with features such as sharing, importing and exporting, and web embedding.

Then you familiarized yourself with Zoho `Marketplace` so you can sell your database applications online.

With Reports, you learned about dealing with big chunks of data and storing and filtering them, and you took a brief look at analyzing information. Using views and charts, you can output your data in eye-catching yet professional ways and then share it with the world.

CloudSQL and the Zoho API give you even more options to extend the power of Creator and Reports and connect them to external applications and enterprise-level systems so you and your users can interact with critical data at a higher level.

What you learned in this chapter was just a glimpse of the power of Zoho database tools. Talking about them in more detail is impossible in such a small space, so I encourage you to learn more from the resources provided.

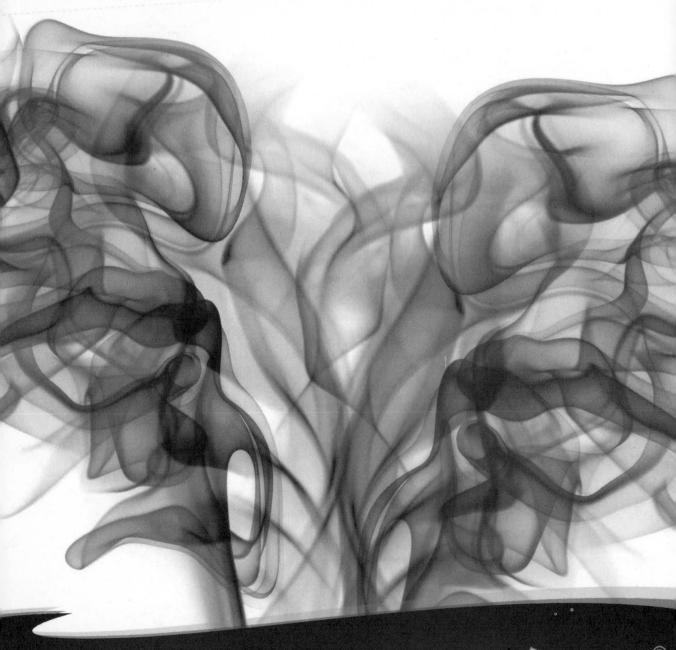

ZOHO®

Work. Online

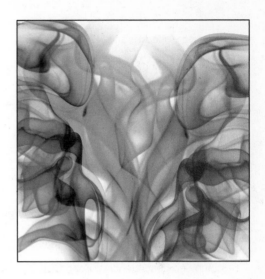

Index

A